VLADIMIR NABOKOV:
POETRY AND THE LYRIC VOICE

PAUL D. MORRIS

Vladimir Nabokov

Poetry and the Lyric Voice

UNIVERSITY OF TORONTO PRESS
Toronto Buffalo London

© University of Toronto Press Incorporated 2010
Toronto Buffalo London
www.utppublishing.com
Printed in Canada

ISBN 978-1-4426-4020-7 (cloth)

Printed on acid-free, 100% post-consumer recycled paper with vegetable-based inks.

Library and Archives Canada Cataloguing in Publication

Morris, Paul Duncan, 1961–
   Vladimir Nabokov: poetry and the lyric voice / Paul D. Morris.

   Includes bibliographical references and index.
   ISBN 978-1-4426-4020-7

   1. Nabokov, Vladimir Vladimirovich, 1899–1977 – Criticism and interpretation.
   I. Title.

   PG3476.N3Z75 2010   813'.54   C2009-904976-7

This book has been published with the help of a grant from the Canadian Federation for the Humanities and Social Sciences, through the Aid to Scholarly Publications Programme, using funds provided by the Social Sciences and Humanities Research Council of Canada.

University of Toronto Press acknowledges the financial assistance to its publishing program of the Canada Council for the Arts and the Ontario Arts Council.

University of Toronto Press acknowledges the financial support for its publishing activities of the Government of Canada through the Book Publishing Industry Development Program (BPIDP).

For Natascha … and Shirley … and now Sarah

Contents

Acknowledgments ix
Abbreviations: Primary Sources xi
Preface: Nabokov's Poetry: Seeing the Unseen xv

1 **Introduction: Locating Nabokov's Poetry** 3

2 **Reading Nabokov's Reception: Nabokov, Poetry, and the Critics** 32
   The Émigré Reading of Nabokov's Poetry 35
   Nabokov's English Poetry and the Critics 58
   Nabokov's Russian Poetry and the Academics 69
   Russian Literature and the Rediscovery of Nabokov's Poetry 82

3 **Nabokov's Lyric Voice: The Poetry of This World and Another** 90
   A Paradigmatic First Poem: Rereading 'The Rain Has Flown' 94
   Poetic Consciousness 98
   The Metaphysical Nabokov and the Otherworld 102
   Nabokov's Poetry: Five Themes 114
      I. Cosmic Synchronization 115
      II. Inspiration 119
      III. Love's Poetry 124
      IV. The Otherworld 136
      V. A Poet of the World – the Poetry of Trifles 163
   Four Poems 184
      i. 'The Swift' 184
      ii. 'Fame' 187
      iii. 'Restoration' 191
      iv. 'The Ballad of Longwood Glen' 195

4   **Staged Lyricism: The Play of Poetry and Dream-Logic in Nabokov's
    Drama**   202
       The Waltz Invention: The Lyric Consolation of Fantasy   225

5   **Nabokov and the Short Story: The Lyric Heights
    of a Small Alpine Form**   241
       Finding 'Perfection': Nabokov's Lyricism and the Short Story   263

6   **Lyricism and the Novel: Nabokov's Gift for Prose**   277
       The Gift: A Portrait of the Novelist as a Young Poet   284

7   **A Novel Snatched from the Sun: Nabokov's *Pale Fire***   318
       'Pale Fire' and the Poet's Pattern: Novelistic Text
          and Poetic Texture   329

Conclusion: In Place of an Ending   375

Notes   389
References   421
Index   435

Acknowledgments

This study of Nabokov's poetry and the nature of its place within his oeuvre has been a project of several years. Over the course of these several years, I have profited enormously from the encouragement and constructive criticism of numerous people. Happily for me, it is to individuals – rather than bureaucratic agencies or funding councils – that I owe my debt of gratitude for support during the preparation and writing of this book.

At the earliest stages of this project, Detlev Gohrbandt offered both practical and supportive advice regarding the writing of a *Habilitationsschrift*. Roger Charlton read several chapters in their draft stages and, perhaps more onerously, allowed me to test out still ill-formed ideas over numerous lunches. Arlette Warken kindly read an early version of the completed manuscript and offered her useful comments. Sergei Kozakov and Igor Volkov helped confirm my reading of Nabokov's Russian, for which I am grateful. The staff at the 'inter-library loans department' of the Saarländische Universitäts- und Landesbibliothek in Saarbrücken were unstinting in their efforts to help me locate various critical sources. The four central readers in my *Habilitationsverfahren* – Manfred Schmeling, Roland Marti, David Rampton, and Klaus Martens – offered comprehensive, detailed, and trenchant criticism of the manuscript upon its completion. Comments made by D. Barton Johnson were both encouraging and enlightening. Leona Toker also generously provided a forthright critique of the first chapters of the manuscript. The rigorous commentary and critique granted by these scholars allowed me to improve the manuscript greatly. I am grateful to each of them. Obviously, any conceptual, analytic, or stylistic weaknesses that remain are of my own doing.

It is Klaus Martens, however, whom I wish to single out for particular thanks. During the writing of this manuscript, Klaus Martens graciously acted as mentor, colleague, friend, and, not least, spur to greater achievement. Quite apart from acknowledging the debt of gratitude owed for his unwavering support of my research, I wish to express the feeling of privilege and pleasure I will always associate with my work with him and his team at the Universität des Saarlandes.

I would also like to thank all those at University of Toronto Press involved in the publication of this book; in particular, Ken Lewis, who undertook the meticulous copy-editing of the manuscript, and Richard Ratzlaff, who professionally and patiently guided me through the publication process. Publication of this book could not have taken place without a grant from the Canadian Federation for the Humanities and Social Sciences, for which I am also grateful.

Finally, I wish to acknowledge the myriad, often unspoken, forms of support provided by my wife, Natascha. She may think that her most significant help came via her prompt responses to my language queries – pleas for clarification urgently shouted from my study to her. In fact, she has given so much, much more. I can't thank her enough.

Abbreviations: Primary Sources

Ada   *Ada, or Ardor: A Family Chronicle*. 1969. New York: Vintage International, 1990.

AnL   *The Annotated Lolita*. Ed. with preface, introduction, and notes by Alfred Appel, Jr. 1970. Revised edition. New York: Vintage International, 1991.

BS   *Bend Sinister*. 1947. New York: Vintage International, 1990.

Def   *The Defense*. Trans. Michael Scammell in collaboration with the author. 1964. New York: Vintage International, 1990.

Des   *Despair*. 1966. New York: Vintage International, 1989.

EO   *Eugene Onegin: A Novel in Verse by Aleksandr Pushkin*. Trans. with commentary by Vladimir Nabokov. Bollingen Series 72. 4 vols. 1964. Revised edition. Princeton: Princeton University Press, 1975.

Eye   *The Eye*. Trans. Dmitri Nabokov in collaboration with the author. 1965. New York: Vintage International, 1990.

Gift   *The Gift*. Trans. Michael Scammell with the collaboration of the author. 1963. New York: Vintage International, 1991.

Glory   *Glory*. Trans. Dmitri Nabokov in collaboration with the author. 1971. New York: Vintage International, 1991.

IB   *Invitation to a Beheading*. Trans. Dmitri Nabokov in collaboration with the author. 1959. New York: Vintage International, 1989.

KQK   *King, Queen, Knave*. Trans. Dmitri Nabokov in collaboration with the author. 1968. New York: Vintage International, 1989.

LATH   *Look at the Harlequins!* 1974. New York: Vintage International, 1990.

Laugh   *Laughter in the Dark*. 1938. New York: Vintage International, 1989.

LDQ   *Lectures on 'Don Quixote.'* Ed. Fredson Bowers. New York:
       Harcourt Brace Jovanovich / Bruccoli Clark, 1983.
LL   *Lectures on Literature*. Ed. Fredson Bowers. London:
       Weidenfeld & Nicolson, 1980.
Lo   *Lolita*. 1955. New York: Vintage International, 1989.
LR   *Lectures on Russian Literature*. Ed. Fredson Bowers. New York:
       Harcourt Brace Jovanovich / Bruccoli Clark, 1981.
Mary   *Mary*. Trans. Michael Glenny in collaboration with the author.
       1970. New York: Vintage International, 1989.
NG   *Nikolai Gogol*. 1944. New York: New Directions, 1961.
NWL   *Dear Bunny, Dear Volodya: The Nabokov-Wilson Letters,
       1940–1971*. Revised and expanded edition. Edited and anno-
       tated, with an introductory essay, by Simon Karlinsky. Berkeley:
       University of California Press, 2001.
PF   *Pale Fire*. 1962. New York: Vintage International, 1989.
Pnin   *Pnin*. 1957. New York: Vintage International, 1989.
PP   *Poems and Problems*. New York: McGraw-Hill, 1970.
Pss   *Perepiska s sestroi*. Ed. Helene Sikorski. Ann Arbor: Ardis, 1985.
RLSK   *The Real Life of Sebastian Knight*. 1941. NewYork: Vintage
       International, 1992.
SL   *Selected Letters, 1940–1977*. Ed. Dmitri Nabokov and Matthew
       J. Bruccoli. New York: Harcourt Brace Jovanovich / Bruccoli
       Clark Layman, 1989.
SM   *Speak, Memory: An Autobiography Revisited*. 1967. New York:
       Vintage International, 1989.
SO   *Strong Opinions*. 1973. New York: Vintage International, 1990.
Song   *The Song of Igor's Campaign*. Trans. Vladimir Nabokov. 1960.
       New York: McGraw-Hill, 1975.
Ssoch *Sobranie sochinenii russkogo perioda v piati tomakh*. 5 vols.
       St Petersburg: Simpozium, 1999–2000.
Stikhi *Stikhi*. Ann Arbor: Ardis, 1979.
Stories *The Stories of Vladimir Nabokov*. 1995. New York: Vintage
       International, 1997.
TGM   *Tragediia Gospodina Morna* (*The Tragedy of Mister Morn*).
       1924. Reprinted in *Zvezda* 4 (1997): 9–98.
TRP   *Three Russian Poets: Selections from Pushkin, Lermontov and
       Tyutchev*. Trans. Vladimir Nabokov. Norfolk: New Directions,
       1944.
TT   *Transparent Things*. 1972. New York: Vintage International,
       1989.

USSR   *The Man from the U.S.S.R. and Other Plays.* Introductions and
translations by Dmitri Nabokov. San Diego: Harcourt Brace
Jovanovich / Bruccoli Clark, 1985.

WI   *The Waltz Invention.* Trans. Dmitri Nabokov. New York:
Phaedra, 1966.

Preface: Nabokov's Poetry: Seeing the Unseen

[Zinaida Gippius] at a session of the Literary Fund asked my father, its president, to tell me, please, that I would never, never be a writer.
— Vladimir Nabokov, *Speak, Memory*

Vladimir Nabokov's autobiography *Speak, Memory* culminates with the beguiling reconstruction of an event of apparent whimsy which encapsulates Nabokov's sensibility as individual and author. In the concluding passage, the Nabokov family is described walking toward the harbour and ocean-liner which would transport them from France to the United States and a new stage of exile. Nabokov recounts the joy he and his wife shared in anticipating the 'blissful shock' of discovery their infant son was soon to experience. The Nabokov parents knew, as their son still did not, that he was about to see something familiar and yet new. Out of a jumble of forms haphazardly placed on the child's visual horizon, an ocean-liner was poised to emerge – a ship never before seen in this dimension and now never to be washed from his consciousness, never to be unseen. Structurally, this scene prompts the return of his narrative to its beginnings through reversion to the theme of childhood consciousness which opened the book. Thematically, like the conclusions of so many of Nabokov's fictions, it portends the potential of a new beginning in another unforeseen realm. Furthermore, it illustrates the wonder of discovery which rewards the mind that is receptive to the trifle and whimsy of life. Consciousness is an integral, perhaps the central, theme of *Speak, Memory*. And here as a conclusion, Nabokov demonstrates the bounty visited upon the creative consciousness, the enchantment of aesthetic pleasure born of suddenly discovering that which was always present but which required a shift in perception finally to see:

... you and I saw something that we did not immediately point out to our child, so as to enjoy in full the blissful shock, the enchantment and glee he would experience on discovering ahead the ungenuinely gigantic, the unrealistically real prototype of the various toy vessels he had doddled about in his bath. There, in front of us, where a broken row of houses stood between us and the harbor, and where the eye encountered all sorts of stratagems, such as pale-blue and pink underwear cakewalking on a clothesline, or a lady's bicycle and a striped cat oddly sharing a rudimentary balcony of roofs and walls, a splendid ship's funnel, showing from behind the clothesline as something in a scrambled picture – Find What the Sailor has Hidden – that the finder cannot unsee once it has been seen. (*SM* 309–10)

Transferred from the realm of aesthetic experience of the environment to that of the criticism and reception of Nabokov's oeuvre, the same 'blissful shock' of discovery is afforded the student of Nabokov's writing upon shifting critical consciousness to perceive Nabokov's body of writing as that of a poet. Seen through the lens of poetry, the subtle tones of Nabokov's uniquely lyric sensibility are suddenly made apparent and revealed to have coloured and shaded Nabokov's writing in a manner which affected his entire oeuvre, changing it irrevocably for the reader. Once poetry, and the lyricism of Nabokov's artistic sensibility, is apprehended in the texture of his work, the contours of his writing seem to change. The horizon adopts a new shape and takes on a new dimension. In short, once seen, the fundamental importance of poetry in Nabokov's work cannot be unseen.

The intention of this study, *Vladimir Nabokov: Poetry and the Lyric Voice*, is to effect the shift in critical perception necessary to (re-)discover the place of poetry in Nabokov's oeuvre, to see what is still largely unseen in Nabokov's writing. In following this intention, I intend to make an initial contribution to renewed understanding of both Nabokov's verse and his lyric sensibility as author. The explicit goal of this study is thus a two-part one: first, to offer a comprehensive overview of Nabokov's poetry which simultaneously identifies the central traits of what I will propose as the lyric sensibility that permeated the rest of his astounding literary output; and second, to tender a reading of selections of Nabokov's drama, short fiction, and novels which illustrates the defining presence of poetry and Nabokov's lyric sensibility in his writing. My aim is not in the first instance to engage – as others have – in a discussion of the aesthetic merits or purported sources of influence of Nabokov's poetry. In a later chapter discussing the critical reception of Nabokov's poetry, this important topic will be addressed. Instead, individual poems will be assessed in the context of what I intend to propose as the internal system of poetics which characterizes his poetry and poetic oeuvre. Rather than focusing primarily on a critical evaluation of Nabokov's poetry, then, I will present a broader overview of Nabokov's poetry and its position within his work. This synoptic reading of Nabokov's extensive body of poetry will be proffered as a means of addressing a gaping lacuna in Nabokov criticism and also of realigning Procrustean assessments of his poetry while at the same time suggesting an innovative reading of Nabokov's entire oeuvre. In reading Nabokov's poetry, first independently and then as an integral component of his writing as a whole, I will suggest that his verse production was of central importance to his entire oeuvre and the key element necessary to a full understanding of the aesthetic, ethical, and metaphysical dimensions of his writing.

In demonstration of the centrality of poetry to Nabokov's body of work and as an extension beyond the examination of particular examples of verse, I wish as well to discuss the manner in which a cluster of poetic concepts and themes related to Nabokov's poetry crystallized out of his verse production to inform numerous facets of Nabokov's prose writing. I argue that even when not writing poetry, the lyric sensibility Nabokov developed in his verse pervades all of his writing; poetry is the wellspring from which Nabokov drew the stylistic and thematic specificity of his oeuvre. My argument concerning the place of poetry in Nabokov's writing extends, then, beyond analysis of his poetry in isolation to suggest the fundamental importance of a lyric sensibility which arose out of his writing as a poet and which may be seen imprinted in all of his writing. More bluntly expressed, my reading of Nabokov's Russian and English poetry rests on the simply stated, though far-reaching claim, that the formal and thematic specificity of Nabokov's writing as a whole is significantly determined by poetry. Rather than function as an ornament at the periphery of his oeuvre, poetry is central to Nabokov's poetics. It is the lyric foundation of Nabokov's oeuvre – in *every* genre he practised – which functions as the basis of his stylistic brilliance and which supports the thematic specificity of his art. In short, Nabokov's famed authorial voice owes its distinctive timbre to his lyric sensibility.

Astoundingly, Nabokov's verse has been accorded relatively limited attention in the by now ample tradition of Nabokov scholarship. One's surprise is provoked less by sentiments of academic injustice than of missed opportunity. At issue is the sober calculation that in Nabokov's poetry lies a rich vein of untapped scholarly material, regardless as to how one views the aesthetic quality of individual poems. Poetry, in its many dimensions, clearly seems a focal point in Nabokov's eminently literary life. It need only be recalled, for instance, that poetry was the sole genre practised by Nabokov throughout his career in both Russian and English, and was the genre which frequently served as the entry-point into his non-fictional writing as passionate critic and translator. Knowledge of his poetry would seem, at least potentially, an informative source of understanding regarding the shaping of his authorial voice. Stated differently, prior to the illustration of any particular argument regarding Nabokov's writing, reflection on his poetry would seem an exceptionally promising point of interpretive departure. The promise of critical reward is manifold. Awareness of Nabokov's verse offers itself as an excellent lever with which to gain critical purchase on a number of the intractable, broader-scaled issues which distinguish the scholarly treatment of Nabokov's oeuvre. A critical hypothesis foregrounding the role of poetry in Nabokov's writing, for instance, is excellently positioned to discuss the astounding persistence and distinctiveness of Nabokov's authorial voice across his entire career in works from various fictional and non-fictional genres. A critical ear attuned to Nabokov's poetry is party to otherwise hidden insights into the source of Nabokov's famed style. Likewise, identification of the characteristics uniting Nabokov's oeuvre across languages and literary traditions seems eased by concentration on his lyric voice; such a strategy serves as a substitute to the tendency to place primary emphasis on the corpus of his novels, which seems too easily divided into distinct Russian and American periods. The prickly question of Nabokov's problematic relation to a variety of modes and movements of twentieth-century literature – from Symbolism to Expressionism and, especially, Modernism to Postmodernism – is perhaps more fruitfully discussed with reference to the poetic sensibility and voice rather than individual novels. And finally, the contentious issue of the role of a metaphysical dimension in Nabokov's fiction is more easily broached from the perspective of his poetry. Nabokov's lyric sensibility and his poetry seem, at least hypothetically, key elements to a comprehensive understanding of his oeuvre.

Vladimir Nabokov: Poetry and the Lyric Voice was provoked by precisely such considerations and the desire to formulate a comprehensive response to them in an approach which acknowledged the stylistic and thematic coherence of Nabokov's writing across his entire career. The general initiative for the particular approach adopted here was also suggested by previous scholarship concerning the narrative and stylistic qualities of Nabokov's writing. Approximately twenty-five years ago, Pekka Tammi in his exceptional study *Problems of Nabokov's Poetics* observed the inclination in

Nabokov studies to an annotative form of analysis. In this mode, increasingly specific textual issues are localized in individual works and then subjected to close examination. Tammi himself proposed an alternative, more inclusive, synthesizing approach which would concentrate 'on the artistic system underlying the individual texts' which comprise Nabokov's multifarious oeuvre; important to this critical tack proposed by Tammi are not textual exceptions but the 'patterns of recurrence cutting through the entire bilingual writing career' (Tammi 1985, 14). In developing his synoptic approach to Nabokov's writing, Tammi also formulated an essential observation about the non-polyphonic quality of Nabokov's novels as one of the characteristics responsible for the stylistic uniformity of his writing: 'We may talk of a pronouncedly *anti-polyphonic* feature in the author's writing: *an overriding tendency to make explicit the presence of a creative consciousness behind every fictive construction*' (Tammi 1985, 100; emphasis in original). Tammi is referring to an oft noted quality of Nabokov's writing which will be discussed below in chapters 6 and 7, though the topic is of relevance here in the identification of a Nabokovian voice. The creative consciousness behind each of Nabokov's works is certainly a feature of the narrative specificity of his writing; it is, moreover, an issue with far-reaching stylistic ramifications. Nabokov's works are united by a creative consciousness visible in the narrative structure, but also identifiable according to the consistency of style and voice. A single, distinctive voice sounds through all of his works. The fixing in descriptive terms of the particular tenor of that voice is a topic as intriguing as it is elusive. Marina Naumann's observation that 'the greatest aesthetic impact of Nabokov's prose is *precisely* because of its poetic elements' (Naumann 1978, 72) provides an astute, albeit rare, suggestion that the relation between *voice* and *poetry* is worthy of investigation. I propose that the voice and sensibility orchestrating the staging of each of Nabokov's narrative modes and the casting of his characters is lyric. Proceeding out of acknowledgment of the omnipresence of Nabokov's creative consciousness – as identified by Tammi – and recognition of the fundamentally *poetic* quality of his writing – as formulated by Naumann – the present study seeks to demonstrate the role of poetry in shaping Nabokov's authorial voice. Tammi has identified a distinct authorial sensibility or consciousness; Naumann's comments single out a particular voice – the former is lyric, the latter poetic. Both find expression in Nabokov's poetry and the traces of his poetic writing found in the rest of his writing. In seven chapters of analysis, *Vladimir Nabokov: Poetry and the Lyric Voice* will thus both describe the defining features of the voice to arise out of Nabokov's poetry and demonstrate its pervasiveness throughout the generic breadth of his oeuvre.

The introductory chapter to this study is occupied with staking out general features of the institutional and literary-historical context(s) in which Nabokov's poetic and prose oeuvre(s) were produced and received. Of foremost interest is the attempt to signal the contradictory situation pertaining in a portion of Nabokov criticism. Nabokov, an author who wrote poetry throughout his career and who clearly considered himself a poet, has had his poetic writing relegated to a position of relative obscurity in an otherwise voluminous tradition of critical assessment. Nabokov's poetry has slipped from critical view. Here, it is suggested that a significant portion of the problem of recognition for Nabokov's verse production arises out of the exigencies of its appearance in two separate contexts, each with its own set of historical conditions and literary criteria of critical reception. Nabokov's poetry was first introduced to an extended readership in the inter-war period of his exile in the Russian émigré community of Western Europe. Nabokov's émigré poetry was subjected to a mixed, though predominantly critical, reception for reasons which I suggest were related as much to readerly misunderstanding as objective weakness. Nabokov's prose was also often harshly criticized, and outright misunderstood, before finding belated, at times begrudging, acceptance. In the émigré period of his career, Nabokov's poetry – unlike his prose – was never granted the same process of gradual acquaintanceship and normalization by his audience, a process which would certainly have led to greater understanding and balanced assessment, if not enthusiastic acceptance. Upon entering the Anglo-American literary tradition – primarily as a novelist – Nabokov's writing was subject to the critical reception of an institution which was undergoing changes of its own in the post-war period. Although Nabokov sought on several occasions to introduce his English-language audience to his English, but also Russian, poetry, his verse stumbled on the expectations of a readership anticipating the purportedly Postmodern wizardry of the author of *Lolita* and *Pale Fire*. Within the more enclosed institutional confines of Nabokov's studies, as well, Nabokov's writing was, and continues to be, received in a manner more amenable to the obvious strengths of his achievements in the novel form. Here, it is explicitly suggested that the more recent expressions of critical interest in the metaphysical dimension of Nabokov's writing demand fuller treatment of his poetry. Indeed, I claim that a fusion of the aesthetic, ethical, and metaphysical strains of criticism within Nabokov studies may best be effected through scholarly consideration which begins with his poetry. The second half of this study's introductory chapter turns from these contextual issues to attempt a delineation of the empirical scope of Nabokov's poetic oeuvre. Beginning with

Nabokov's first volume of poetry from 1916, *Стихи* (*Stikhi / Poems*), and concluding with his final, posthumous collection of 1979, likewise entitled *Стихи* (*Stikhi / Poems*), each of Nabokov's nine volumes of poetry is descriptively, if briefly, discussed. The intention here is not to descend into interpretive analysis of Nabokov's poetry – the project of a later chapter – but to provide an indication of its omnipresence in Nabokov's writing and to suggest the evolving, developmental trajectory of his poetic voice.

Chapter 2 provides a more detailed overview of the history of Nabokov's critical reception as a poet. Extending out of the more general comments from chapter 1 concerning the separate literary traditions in which Nabokov's verse was received, attention is directed to a comprehensive assessment of the central reviews and critical statements related to Nabokov's poetry in Russian, English, German, and French. As a means of securing a consistent critical perspective on the changing history of Nabokov's reception, analysis is divided into four separate stages. The first stage covers the European émigré period of Nabokov's poetic production, from the early 1920s until the appearance of Gleb Struve's influential retrospective assessment in *Russkaia literatura v izgnanii* (*Russian Literature in Exile*) in 1956. The second stage is devoted to the limited response to Nabokov's English poetry. The next stage reveals a change in format from reviews to scholarly assessment. This third stage is shown to have emerged from the publication of Nabokov's 1979 retrospective volume *Poems*. The fourth and final stage is tentatively identified as a continuation of the academic criticism of the third stage, though mixed with the increasing interest and appreciation of Russian readers currently 'discovering' a famous Russian writer whose poetry was previously inaccessible to them. Emerging from this review is a complex train of at times contradictory, at times repeated, criticisms of Nabokov's poetry. Early criticism of the supposed 'peacock-like' frivolity and banality of Nabokov's poetry is here demonstrated to have reappeared in various of the earliest émigré reviews. The not infrequent overlapping of criticisms – and even of phrasing in several of the reviews – suggests that previous assessments of Nabokov's poetry functioned as the catalyst for analysis rather than independent consideration. Curiously, for instance, the charge of banality first levelled during Nabokov's émigré years resurfaced in the English-language criticism of Nabokov's English poetry. Now, however, the accusation occurred in the post-war manifestation of 'light-weightedness,' a criticism seemingly appropriate for a writer deemed 'self-indulgent' in his presumed emphasis on style at the expense of meaning. Lightness of style was rashly equated with the absence of poetic heft. Both before and after the war, in the émigré community and in America, discussion of Nabokov's poetic voice was frequently reduced to identification of a bewildering – sometimes contradictory – array of purported influences. Thus, although the thrust of most criticism was negative, the conflicting reasons given for this assessment render the unquestioned acceptance of this received general opinion highly problematic. Still more problematic is the realization that Nabokov's poetry was more often categorized than analysed. Purported influence and speculation regarding Nabokov's aesthetic principles as derived from assertions regarding his prose all too often served as the basis for comment, rather than detailed engagement with Nabokov's poetry itself. Except for isolated exceptions, it was not until the third stage of criticism that Nabokov's poetry was granted the dispassionate, scholarly form of examination necessary to produce authoritative comment. Here, too, however, the absence of a comprehensive attempt to read Nabokov's poetry as a whole is still felt. *Vladimir Nabokov: Poetry and the Lyric Voice* is, belatedly, the first book-length discussion of Nabokov's poetry.

Chapter 3 forms the fulcrum of this discussion. This chapter proceeds as an attempt to subject Nabokov's corpus of poetic writing to an analysis which both presents that body of writing in a systematic, descriptive account and which offers an analytical, interpretive reading of the lyric sensibility and voice construed to underlie Nabokov's verse. It is this sensibility and voice which will be posited as the source and expression of the creative consciousness behind all of Nabokov's writing. In characterizing Nabokov's poetry, analysis advances out of the autobiographical account of his first, paradigmatic poem in chapter 11 of *Speak, Memory* to well-cited reference to numerous poems from across the breadth of his poetic oeuvre. As a means of doing justice to the intimidating volume of Nabokov's poetry while synthesizing it into an interpretive argument based on clear criteria, a group of five 'informing themes' has been proposed as representative of the main thematic arc of Nabokov's lyric voice. The themes of cosmic synchronization, inspiration, love, the 'otherworld' and wonder at the trifles of life are isolated as the central clusters of analysis. Treated in this order, the final two themes of the 'otherworld,' and 'wonder at the trifles of life' are particularly emphasized as evidence of a characteristically Nabokovian fascination with both this world, in its enchanting fullness of detail and empirical multiplicity, and with the intriguing metaphysical mystery of an intuited beyond. Chapter 3 concludes with a detailed reading of four of Nabokov's most impressive and still rarely discussed poems – two Russian and two English. The insights gained from an interpretive reading of Nabokov's entire poetic oeuvre are thus tested according to their value in elucidating the meaning and effect of individual poems.

The following chapter marks a caesura in the study. From an analysis of Nabokov's poetry and the identification of a lyric sensibility and voice, consideration moves to the permeation of that voice throughout other genres and works. The first genre to be treated is drama. The discussion of drama – as with the short story – offers concrete illustration of the thesis that Nabokov's artistic development was not characterized by the juvenile practice of poetry before transition to the 'adult' genre of the prose novel. Nabokov's entire career was distinguished by the simultaneous practice of various genres, from verse plays to the screenplay, all of which were marked by the specificity of Nabokov's lyric voice. Because Nabokov's drama is as little commented upon in the critical literature as his poetry, chapter 4 proceeds through a brief reading of the lyric imprint found in all of his plays before reaching the central focus of the chapter – examination of *Изобретение Вальса* (*Izobretenie Val'sa* / *The Waltz Invention*). Nabokov's perhaps most misunderstood play is shown to pivot on the formal and thematic function of poetry within the drama. Further justification for the choice of *The Waltz Invention* is its implicit thematic relation to *Pale Fire*, the subject of a later chapter.

Chapter 5 turns to Nabokov's lyric practice of short fiction. Analysis reveals that Nabokov's success in the form stems to a significant degree from the compatibility of the dominant conventions of short fiction with Nabokov's lyric sensibility and voice. Compactness, the creation of subjective mood, the substitution of pattern for plot, and the emphasis on lyricism in verbal expression are all shown to characterize Nabokov's short fiction, which, like his poetry, derived from a common lyric sensibility. Indeed, reference to rarely discussed short stories by Nabokov reveals the efficacy of a reading which emerges from awareness of the lyric quality of his prose writing, including his short fiction. The second half of the chapter addresses a detailed reading of Nabokov's short story 'Совершенство' ('Sovershenstvo' / 'Perfection'). This story is shown not only to illustrate the permeation of Nabokov's lyric sensibility in a prose form but, as a critical exercise in its own right, to release dimensions of meaning perhaps unperceivable without consideration of Nabokov's lyric voice.

Chapter 6 proceeds from short fiction to the novel form. Nabokov's *Дар* (*Dar* / *The Gift*), his ninth and final Russian novel, is famously about a young artist who progresses from poetry to prose genres throughout the course of the novel. *The Gift* suggests not only the possibility of indirect comment on the development of Nabokov's artistic gift, but, far more importantly, displays the essential role of Nabokov's lyric sensibility in the creation of a fictional universe. The informing themes of cosmic synchronization, inspiration, love, wonder at the trifles of life, and the otherworld all bespeak the presence of Nabokov's lyric sensibility in the novel, as does the demonstrably 'poetic' quality of his prose.

The final chapter of this study takes up Nabokov's most emphatically poetic novel, *Pale Fire*. In outlining the critical heritage of *Pale Fire*, it is suggested that the bulk of assessment has occupied itself with questions of relevance to the narrative structure of the novel. As an alternative to this, the present reading seeks consciously to emphasize the work's poetic achievement. This is postulated as more than a strategy of self-serving relevance natural to a study attempting to document the importance of Nabokov's lyric voice. A full reading of both the poem 'Pale Fire' and the novel *Pale Fire* is predicated upon interpretive sensitivity to the lyric sensibility which informs both. Denied this sensitivity, the poem may seem a mere hodgepodge of poetic references and styles, and the novel a virtuoso achievement of narrative playfulness. Such a reading is denied, and denies, the lyric depths that both poem and novel so abundantly harbour. Viewed through the lens of Nabokov's lyric sensibility, *Pale Fire*, as novel and poem, is shown to be a masterful formal achievement but also one of the most thematically moving and satisfying of Nabokov's works.

The conclusion of this study openly announces its incompletion as a critical project. The driving thesis of this study, the contention that a lyric voice informed the expression of virtually all that Nabokov wrote, cannot be contained within the necessarily foreshortened analysis of Nabokov's dramas, several of his short stories, and two novels. Not only are other – non-fictional – genres excluded, but the plethora of secondary topics which arise with consideration of the lyric are passed over. Even the potential insufficiency of a reading of Nabokov's poetry on the basis of five informing themes has to be acknowledged. Nonetheless, the first book-length study of Nabokov's poetry and lyric sensibility may justifiably claim to have offered, if nothing else, a comprehensive reading of Nabokov's poetry. A splendid ship of indisputable dimensions has been sighted in the harbour of Nabokov's oeuvre.

Note on Translations

Translation has been a necessity in the preparation of this study. Apart from one instance, the few citations of German and French sources are in my translations. With reference to Nabokov's Russian poetry, Nabokov's own translations have been used whenever possible; in these instances, the sole language of citation is English. With regard to Nabokov's prose, the literal English translations authorized by either Vladimir or Dmitri

Nabokov have been used in all citations, accompanied by page reference to the Russian source in *Vladimir Nabokov: Sobranie sochinenii russkogo perioda v piati tomakh*. Otherwise all prose and poetry translations are my own. My glosses of Nabokov's euphonically and stylistically rich verse are literal renderings only, capable of doing no more than conveying the essential meaning of the poems. If translations are indeed the post horses of civilization, then these humble creatures are but lowly pack mules – slow and stubborn, but ploddingly faithful in the transportation of their precious load. I alone am responsible for any infelicities or errors that may have occurred in the course of translation.

VLADIMIR NABOKOV:
POETRY AND THE LYRIC VOICE

1 Introduction: Locating Nabokov's Poetry

> Well, poetry, of course, includes all creative writing; I have never been able to see any generic difference between poetry and artistic prose. As a matter of fact, I would be inclined to define a good poem of any length as a concentrate of good prose, with or without the addition of recurrent rhythm and rhyme.
>
> — Vladimir Nabokov, *Strong Opinions*

Vladimir Nabokov was a poet. The statement would appear so self-evident as to render it banal, devoid of declarative meaning. The author of some of the most carefully crafted works of verbal art in the twentieth century, Nabokov may effortlessly claim for himself the title of poet. His mastery of the aesthetic potential of prose easily assumes the epithet *poetic*. Paradoxically, the assertion that Nabokov was a poet only provokes resistance and surprise when taken literally. So framed as to identify Nabokov as the author of an extensive corpus of verse, the claim is perhaps less self-evident and banal, though no less true. The writer admired above all as the author of *Lolita* and *Pale Fire* was also – if less famously – a Russian-language author and novelist, a cabaretist, screenwriter, biographer, autobiographer, essayist, critic, translator, short-story writer, dramatist, and – not least – a poet. By virtue of their artistic brilliance, but also the more accessible language of their composition, Nabokov's central English novels seem to overshadow an otherwise diverse and accomplished oeuvre. Awareness of specific works from the rest of this almost intimidating surfeit of genres is often as not dependent on the vagaries of individual reader awareness and audience availability than a measure of their intrinsic aesthetic merits. This is particularly so in the case of Nabokov's poetry. Indeed, the appending of poetry to the conclusion of a long list of genres highlights the very problem of recognition which hindered Nabokov's identity as poet. Consigned a place in the background of a stage crowded by more extroverted genres, Nabokov's poetry is present though unacknowledged and hence largely unexamined behind the bustling (English) novels of the foreground. Consequently, and despite the ubiquitous presence of poetry in his oeuvre, criticism has accorded Nabokov's poetry far less attention than his prose.

Nabokov himself can hardly be held responsible for the relative obscurity of his verse; a moment's reflection confirms the obvious importance he accorded poetry. Nabokov published hundreds of poems and wrote even more; a significant portion of his published criticism dealt with poetry; he was a translator of poetry or poetic prose; he wrote drama in verse; his prose is distinguished by the rhythm, cadence, and verbal precision of poetry; his novels and short stories are populated with poets and adorned with his own poetry, while his fiction regularly treats the subject of poetic creation; and lastly, Nabokov himself obviously considered his poetry important and himself a poet. It was in the poem 'Softest of Tongues' of 1941 that Nabokov marked his mid-career transition from Russian to English, from the 'softest of tongues' to 'clumsy tools of stone.' And it is perhaps no coincidence that Nabokov, as the master of symmetrically patterned fictions whose conclusions famously return readers to their narrative beginnings, contained his entire oeuvre within the matching bookends of two volumes of verse, one from 1916 and the other from 1979, both entitled *Cmuxu* (*Stikhi* / *Poems*).[1] The single genre which Nabokov never ceased practising throughout his long career as artist and which infuses all other forms of his writing demands closer examination. Few authors so pervasively display the imprint of poetry in their writing. Nabokov's poetry deserves to be seen.

The following introductory pages are intended to establish a broad two-part framework for the study of Nabokov as a poet. Here an attempt will be made to fix the context and scale of Nabokov's achievement as a poet. First to be established is a broad outline of the critical traditions which received and assessed Nabokov as poet and author. This will then be followed by a broad, descriptive cataloguing of the dimensions of Nabokov's poetic oeuvre. The overview to be proposed here is neither a history of Nabokov's reception as poet, nor an interpretive reading of his poetic writing – the explicit goals of chapters 2 and 3. Offered here instead is a superficial reading of the institutional conditions (and hindrances) that confronted Nabokov's poetry in both the Russian émigré and Anglo-American literary traditions, and an indication of the scope of Nabokov's poetic writing to require integration into the critical understanding of his artistry. The extent of these introductory comments is necessitated by the relative obscurity of Nabokov's verse to readers and the critical hypothesis that this obscurity is to a significant degree the result of the historical and institutional forces which determined its reception.

From the outset, it may be claimed in the purely empirical terms of quantity that Nabokov's poetry has received insufficient attention – either as a topic of its own or understood as a formative component of Nabokov's writing as a whole. Possible reasons for this relative neglect are close at hand. Foremost among these must be Nabokov's brilliance as a writer of prose. Despite the importance of poetry to Nabokov's artistry, and whatever the relative merits of his poetry – judging the aesthetic quality of his poetry is not an unproblematic undertaking – the startling quality of his prose contributes to the diminishing of his achievements in other artistic realms. Nabokov's poetry also suffers obscurity, in part, as a result of historical and linguistic circumstance. Published in Russian and often in émigré journals with limited circulation, much of Nabokov's poetry bore the same undeserved fate which afflicted the bulk of émigré Russia's astounding artistic output between the wars. In transferring the focus of his artistic activities to English and prose, Nabokov began the process of winning a larger audience for his art. In making this move, however, he seemed to leave behind the language and genre which helped to form his art and which introduced him to his first extended readership. Published in the context of émigré Russian literature, Nabokov's Russian poetry was cut off not only from a large audience but also from the continuing tradition of Russian-language poetry, a tradition which was damaged by both the imposition of socialist realism within the Soviet literary system in 1934 and the destruction of the once vibrant Russian émigré community in Europe by the onset of war in 1939. In the wake of these events, Nabokov the Russian-language poet was all but severed from an audience and hence denied the possibility of a subsequent critical heritage which might otherwise have emerged organically with the development of his oeuvre and career. Nabokov's much smaller body of English poems also suffered for reasons of an 'institutional' nature, though in a manner different from his Russian verse. Published in book form after the establishment of his reputation as an innovative master of English-language prose, Nabokov's English poems seemed a curio, an inexplicable, extraneous, and thus easily overlooked addition to the writings of an author abundantly enjoyed and studied for other reasons. As the reception of Nabokov's English poetry will show, critics conceptually prepared for the artistry of a 'postmodern' novelist found it difficult to see and hear a poet whose lyrics followed the aesthetic principles internal to his oeuvre, and not the externally imposed aesthetic dogma of literary schools and movements.

A still more complex source of the neglect of Nabokov's poetry most certainly resides in the complicated situation which arose out of the confluence of two central forces guiding his reception: first, the unusual trajectory of Nabokov's development as a multilingual author, and second, the demands and limitations native to the two central literary systems to which he belonged and so markedly influenced – émigré Russian literature and post-war Anglo-American literature. In order to appreciate the absence of critical treatment of Nabokov's poetry, it is necessary to review – however briefly – the dominant trends of Nabokov's reception as a writer. In the Russian émigré community, Nabokov was a writer identified above all according to his prose, which was not infrequently misunderstood and criticized as an imitation of the best of western European literature. Only later did his prose writing wrest from criticism the appreciation attendant to growing recognition of its independence and specificity. In the Anglo-American literary system, Nabokov's reception has also been subject to changes which derived from evolving critical expectations, rather than any alteration to the quality of his artistry. Nabokov's writing as an author within the Anglo-American tradition has gone through three central stages of assessment according to, respectively, aesthetic, ethical, and metaphysical criteria.[2]

That Nabokov's artistry should prove so challenging an object of critical consideration is not surprising. The very diversity and complexity of Nabokov's writing presents criticism with enormous difficulties, especially in the context of an attempt to develop a synoptic approach to his oeuvre. Nabokov produced thematically complex artistic texts in three languages and is recognized as a stylistic master in both the Russian- and English-language traditions. Apart from the inherent difficulty of distinguishing and assessing evidence of stylistic mastery across differing language traditions, the critical project of evaluating Nabokov's work is subject to the challenges attendant to the generic diversity of his oeuvre. Nabokov confronts scholarship with the unusually rare example of an author who excelled in all of the major and minor genres he turned to. Nabokov's oeuvre has proven to have been of such variety and expanse that changing scholarly trends have been unable to adapt.[3] No sooner fitted with the dress of a contemporary theoretical approach, Nabokov's oeuvre splits the seams, revealing the shoddy tailoring of mass-produced critical garments when draped over individual genius. From Realism to Modernism, Symbolism to Expressionism, Nabokov's writing has attracted and frustrated the

sartorial efforts of critics attempting to force him into the uniformed
fashion of literary schools.

Matters are only complicated when the attempt is made to classify
Nabokov's writing according to categories of thematic preference and national literary heritage. Over the length of his long career, Nabokov was
made to stand as representative for a variety of tendencies and movements
in both the Russian- and English-language traditions, with each new categorization not infrequently calling forth breathless praise and vitriolic
censure. Already in the 1920s and 1930s of his European period of exile,
Nabokov was castigated by a coterie of émigré critics for having failed
Russian literature in his supposedly epigonic adherence to western European
models of literary production and his refusal to treat themes expressive of
the Russian 'soul.' Nabokov was, in an infamous and repeated complaint,
'un-Russian.'[4] For others – Gleb Struve, for instance – the young Nabokov
was 'émigré Russia's greatest gift to Russian literature' (Struve 1930a, 3). In
a similar gesture of critical praise, Nikolai Andreev hailed Nabokov as the
standard-bearer of a national literary tradition that had been driven by the
Soviets out of Russia and into exile: 'In a formal sense, Sirin [Nabokov]
represents a synthesis of Russian sentiments and western European forms.
Sirin, more clearly and successfully than other writers, has fulfilled the
well-known principle of the late Lev Lunts – "To the West!" He has done
this (we repeat) while maintaining the fundamental direction of Russian
literature' (Andreev 1930, 6). The arc of Nabokov's gradual acceptance by
his émigré audience progressed from misunderstanding and rejection of
his earliest writing – poetry – to progressive appreciation of his prose. By
the time of his departure from Europe in 1940, Nabokov was acknowledged as one of the most important, if also most controversial and challenging, writers of an imperiled émigré community.

In the wake of Nabokov's reformation and transformation of himself as
an English-language writer in the early 1940s, the trajectory of the critical
reception of Nabokov changed once again. Nabokov's oeuvre has been the
object of three main trends of assessment since having entered into the
Anglo-American literary institution, with its own codes of reception and
criticism.[5] The first of these trends centred on Nabokov's skill as a technician,
a master of the aesthetic manipulation of language. Particularly following
Lolita's success, Nabokov was praised and prized for the aesthetic quality of
his writing and advanced by turns as a brilliant artist and, frequently in critical circles, an exceptionally vigorous exponent of an otherwise exhausted
form of literature.[6] Alfred Appel's statement from his introduction to *The
Annotated Lolita* is perhaps representative of the numerous critical voices to

champion Nabokov the author of metafiction: 'A future historian of the
novel may one day claim that it was Nabokov, more than any of his contemporaries, who kept alive an exhausted art form not only by demonstrating
new possibilities for it but by reminding us, through his example, of the
variegated aesthetic resources of his great forebears, such as Sterne and the
Joyce, who was a parodist rather than a symbolist' (*AnL* xx). Precisely because of its stylistic brilliance, and Nabokov's emphasis on the aesthetic
primacy of literature, Nabokov's writing seemed excellently suited for application in the development of critical definitions of then contemporary,
non-traditional, non-mimetic trends in literature.[7] Nabokov was thus identified as a harbinger of Postmodernism in American letters.[8] Maurice Couturier
is by no means alone in locating Nabokov's lasting contribution to American
letters in his role as the central animating figure of an 'extraordinary American
literary renaissance':

> Pourtant, près de dix ans après sa mort, il faut bien reconnaître que son pas-
> sage quelque peu fugitive à travers la littérature américaine a laissé durables. Il
> suffit, pour s'en convaincre, d'ouvrir les ouvrages de critique ou les revues con-
> sacrés à la fiction américaine contemporaine: Nabokov est sans aucun doute,
> et de loin, l'auteur de référence le plus souvent cité lorsque l'on évoque cette
> extraordinaire renaissance littéraire américaine, qualifiée par Ihad Hassan de
> 'postmoderne,' et qui va de John Barth à Donald Barthelme, de Robert Coover
> à William Gass, de John Hawkes et Gilbert Sorrentino à Don DeLillo, ou de
> Stanley Elkin à Thomas Pynchon. (Couturier 1986, 29)

> [Nonetheless, almost ten years after his death, it must be acknowledged that
> his somewhat fugitive passage across American literature has remained dur-
> able. To convince oneself of this, it is enough to open works of criticism or
> academic journals consecrated to contemporary American fiction. Nabokov
> is without doubt, and by far, the author of reference most often cited when
> that extraordinary American literary renaissance is being evoked – 'post-
> modernism' as qualified by Ihad Hassan – which extends from John Barth
> to Donald Barthelme, from Robert Coover to William Gass, from John
> Hawkes and Gilbert Sorrentino to Don DeLillo, and from Stanley Elkin to
> Thomas Pynchon.]

This first stage of reception within English-language criticism of
Nabokov as a writer of primarily aesthetic merit gradually gave way to
contributions from a second trend – the critical discussion of the ethical
and political dimensions of Nabokov's fiction. This second trend arose in

part as a counterbalance to the continued, frequently exclusive, emphasis on Nabokov's technique. Translation also most certainly contributed to this process. The increasing familiarity with Nabokov's Russian texts undoubtedly fostered growing interest in the thematic meaning of his writing; Nabokov's 'distance' from the world in favour of an exclusive, metaliterary form of aestheticism seemed less tenable as a critical paradigm in the context of several of his Russian novels.[9] In addressing the content of Nabokov's writing, worthwhile effort was made to probe the intellectual, thematic depths of a form of writing otherwise camouflaged by the virtuosity of its aesthetic form. Ellen Pifer in her *Nabokov and the Novel* of 1980, for example, offered a systematic investigation of the ethics presented in Nabokov's novels.[10] David Rampton's *Vladimir Nabokov: A Critical Study of the Novels* is a further example of this development. A synoptic study of Nabokov's oeuvre founded on intimate knowledge of Nabokov's Russian works, Rampton's study challenged the then prevailing interpretation of Nabokov the fabulist with an argument 'based on making a case for a view of Nabokov's art that places the emphasis squarely on ideas and human values and what his novels are "about"' (Rampton 1984, 5).

The third stage of reception is characterized by consideration of the metaphysical quality of Nabokov's oeuvre. And while not initiated by Véra Nabokov, she certainly decisively stimulated this approach in her identification of a single theme in her husband's writing. In the 1979 foreword to *Poems*, the first posthumously published collection of Nabokov's poems, Véra Nabokov referred to the theme of *potustoronnost'* (the otherworld), as a central theme which had purportedly saturated everything he wrote (*Stikhi* 3). Although the philosophical dimensions of Nabokov's oeuvre and aesthetic had been broached earlier in critical discussion, Véra Nabokov's remarks were responsible for revealing a very substantial, and yet previously unseen, figure in the carpet of Nabokov's writing. Indeed, for some, not only was a figure added, but the dimensions of the carpet itself were no longer the same. Recognition of the metaphysical quality of Nabokov's writing and assessment of the ramifications of Nabokov's putative belief in a transcendent sphere has led to a surge of new readings and contributed to a new understanding of the man and especially his work.[11] A writer previously understood first and foremost as a consummate fabulist, a virtuoso aesthetician, is increasingly being seen as a writer of new metaphysical heights and thematic depths. In terms of critical assessment, a metaphysical dimension has now been added to the ethical and all important aesthetic component of consideration of Nabokov's writing.

The addition of a metaphysical factor to an understanding of Nabokov has not been achieved without resistance. Richard Rorty, for instance, is perhaps indicative of a considerable number of accomplished readers and critics who continue to see Nabokov predominantly as a conjurer, a writer whose mastery in creating and then juggling worlds within the text radically complicates the clear identification of any mimetic connection to the external world, let alone a transcendent 'otherworld': '... for [Nabokov] the distinctions among art, religion, and metaphysics – like the distinction between inventing and intuiting – just don't matter' (Rorty 1992b, 126).[12] As a result, in the last several years Nabokov scholarship has been marked by a clear increase in the number of studies which address themselves to Nabokov's metaphysics, but also by those which resist this trend as a diminishment of Nabokov's value as a technical virtuoso and a distraction from the formal wonder of Nabokovian fiction.[13] In the prologue to a recent collection of articles devoted to Nabokov, for instance, two prominent Nabokov scholars, D. Barton Johnson and Brian Boyd, address the phenomenon of the emergence of an interpretive paradigm based on Nabokov's metaphysics and its relevance for Nabokov studies. For Johnson, the increase in scholarship devoted to the metaphysical dimension in Nabokov is essentially sound, though the threat remains that 'this dominant critical paradigm discourages critics and readers from attending to the very concrete details that constitute the basis of Nabokov's stature as an artist' (Johnson and Boyd 21). In his response, Boyd too cautioned against the pursuit of critical fashion, and yet clearly indicated that Nabokov's art forms a whole from which aesthetic considerations are not to be detached from the ethical and metaphysical (Johnson and Boyd 21–5). In identifying the essential interconnectedness of the differing dimensions of Nabokov's writing thus far addressed as strains of critical approach, Boyd parallels the suggestion made by Vladimir Alexandrov that 'the relationship among metaphysics, aesthetics, and ethics in Nabokov's works is so intimate that it might be visualized graphically as a ternary field with one of the terms labeling each of the apexes, and his works represented by points within the field. Thus, any work, or any aspect of a work, needs to be located in terms of metaphysical, ethical, and aesthetic criteria ...' (Alexandrov 1991, 6).

It is here, in this context of a debate concerning a composite approach appropriate to Nabokov's oeuvre in its entirety, and in light of failed consideration of the place of poetry in Nabokov's work, that fuller consideration of the role of poetry in Nabokov's writing gains critical urgency. While the need to assess Nabokov's artistry according to its aesthetic, ethical, and metaphysical ramifications has been acknowledged, criticism lacks an instrument equal to the task of consolidating these three disparate approaches while at the same time respecting both the continuity and inventiveness of Nabokov's literary achievement, both in individual works and across his oeuvre. It is the suggestion of this study that Nabokov's lyric sensibility – and the poetry which it expresses – guarantees the formal and thematic integrity of Nabokov's writing while simultaneously providing for its unique literary identity. The fundamental lyricism of Nabokov's artistic sensibility and voice forms the essential link connecting the aesthetic, ethical, and metaphysical dimensions of his art, and likewise provides the foundation for an oeuvre which is protean in shape yet consistently Nabokovian in expression. It is thus in consideration of poetry that I wish to take up Alexandrov's and Boyd's appeal to treat Nabokov's oeuvre in its metaphysical, ethical, and aesthetic entirety, both because the poetry in Nabokov's oeuvre deserves increased critical attention for reasons of its intrinsic quality, and also because, in fundamental ways, a comprehensive understanding of Nabokov the writer is not possible without an understanding of the role of poetry in his works.

Before turning in chapter 3 to a more detailed analysis which both describes Nabokov's poetry and lyric identity, and also attempts to link the aesthetic, ethical, and metaphysical dimensions of his writing, it will be necessary in chapter 2 to review the publication history and reception of Nabokov's poetry. A brief review of the existing scholarship regarding Nabokov's poetry will reveal the difficulties Nabokov had in finding an informed audience for his poetry and the limitations of the criteria used to assess his poetic work. It will be suggested that the failure of Nabokov's poetry mirrors the difficulties which confronted his early prose when Nabokov's independence of artistic expression met with stiff resistance before finding broad and lasting acceptance. While Nabokov's poetry certainly displays a degree of formal conservativism, as we will see, criticism was unable to see beyond the expectations conventionally associated with this formal quality. Purportedly anachronistic adherence to outmoded poetic models was thus discerned in his formal traditionalism rather than the depths of ethical and metaphysical content which is now more fully visible from the perspective of Nabokov's entire oeuvre. Prior to the essential tasks of reconstructing the problematic reception of Nabokov as poet and of proffering a synoptic reading of Nabokov's lyric identity, it will first be necessary to attempt an inventory of Nabokov's production. The goal of establishing a rough chronology of Nabokov's continuous, if intermittent, verse writing will also be to indicate the continual companionship of poetry throughout Nabokov's richly variegated career. Although not always seen, poetry was always a shaping presence in the expression of Nabokov's artistry.

Symptomatic of the difficulty of placing poetry within Nabokov's oeuvre is the fundamental problem of establishing a definitive corpus. Within the context of current scholarship, it is still not possible to say with certainty how many poems Nabokov wrote. At present, over five hundred Russian poems and some twenty-three English poems have seen publication. Even this substantial number, however, seems but a limited portion of those written. In the introduction to his collection of 1970, *Poems and Problems*, Nabokov referred to his poetic prolificacy of the 1920s and 1930s, indicating that the thirty-nine Russian poems of the volume 'represent only a small fraction – hardly more than one percent – of the steady mass of verse which I began to exude in my early youth, more than half a century ago, and continued to do so, with monstrous regularity, especially during the twenties and thirties, then petering out in the next two decades, when a meager output of a score or so hardly exceeded the number of poems I wrote in English' (*PP* 13). Andrew Field claims, albeit without concrete reference, that 'by 1928 Nabokov had written two novels, twenty-two short stories, and nearly a thousand poems' (Field 1986, 127). Although the mentioned number of a thousand poems seems exceptionally high, Brian Boyd reports that in August 1917 Nabokov 'began a thin notebook, the first of a continuous run of manuscript albums of verse stretching from 1917 to 1923, growing by a poem almost every other day' (Boyd 1990, 131). Boyd is also able to document Nabokov's selection process in 1918 for a volume of poetry which was never to appear, *Раскрытые окна* (*Raskrytye okna / Open Windows*). After rejecting 100 poems for this proposed volume, Nabokov was still left with 224, all written since 1916 (Boyd 1990, 142). Numbers such as these in reference to a single, unpublished collection of verse testify to the exceptional – 'monstrous' – volume of Nabokov's production as a young man.

Despite the difficulty in documenting the full corpus of Nabokov's poetic oeuvre, it is nonetheless possible to chart his development as a poet. An overview of the thematic and formal characteristics of his poetry may be gained on the basis of the poems gathered and published in his various collections, nine of which appeared throughout Nabokov's career. His first volume of poetry, *Poems*, was published in 1916 and contained sixty-eight poems written between August 1915 and May 1916. These adolescent poems were written for and dedicated to 'Lyussya,' Valentina Evgenievna Shulgin, Nabokov's first young love, the woman later to be stylized as 'Mary' in his first novel and 'Tamara' in his autobiography *Speak, Memory*.

Due to the very considerable financial means at his disposal as a result of a family inheritance, Nabokov was able to have *Poems* privately printed. The critical resonance for this work was almost exclusively negative. One of the leading symbolists of the time, Zinaida Gippius, went so far as to request Nabokov's father to inform the young poet that he 'would never, never be a writer.' In mute though decisive confirmation of this response, none of the poems from *Poems* was ever again republished in subsequent collections; Nabokov's self-criticism as recorded in *Speak, Memory* was correspondingly firm: 'my poems were juvenile stuff, quite devoid of merit and ought never to have been put on sale' (*SM* 238).[14] Nabokov's adult judgment of his adolescent verse is certainly correct; the poems are more poetastric than poetic, the sentiment expressed more conventional than considered, more enthusiastic than refined. While formally accomplished, the poems seem one-dimensional and lack the all-important aura of a second dimension which unmistakably marks Nabokov's more mature verse. Despite the legitimacy of this criticism, the poems are not entirely without interest, however, in consideration of Nabokov's subsequent development as an artist. The two epigraphs, one by Alfred de Musset – 'Un souvenir heureux est peut être sur terre / Plus vrai que le bonheur ...' – and the other by Wordsworth – 'Then fill the bowl! Away with gloom; / Our joys shall always last; / For hope will brighten days to come / And memory gild the past' – although perhaps demonstratively precious, nonetheless clairvoyantly foreshadow the theme of memory which was to emerge as one of Nabokov's central concerns. The epigraphs to his first book of poetry also indicate that the oft remarked upon Proustian theme in Nabokov's writing is in fact pre-Proust.[15] Also present here, as if in prescient anticipation of the future, is the optimism and emotional pleasure derived from sensual perception of the world, which would accompany Nabokov's life and artistry through even the most trying of times.

Upon being reminded of these early poems in a letter from his sister Helene Sikorski in 1945, Nabokov was less concerned with their stylistic deficiencies than with the wonder of being returned to a world lost to both memory and history: 'In your last letter you copied out my adolescent poems. Re-reading them very much engaged me. I had completely forgotten them. In those days I didn't search far for epithets' (*Pss* 27).[16] Perhaps it is because he had been returned by his sister to the 'charming' poems of his youth while preparing for the autobiography which would eventually emerge as *Speak, Memory*, that certain scenes descriptive of his courtship of 'Tamara' recall the poetry of 1916. The poem 'Осеннее' ('Osennee' / 'Autumnal') is very much reminiscent of one of the evening assignations with Tamara described in *Speak,*

Memory (*SM* 232–4).[17] The poetry of *Poems* is thematically weak and yet bears the germ of excellent versification and already points to the theme of memory and the precise, economical handling of descriptive scenes which will distinguish his later verse and prose.

Nabokov's next volume of poetry stems from the same poetic environment as *Poems*. In 1918 while in the Crimea, after a delay occasioned by the October revolution, Nabokov received from Petrograd a selection of poems written the previous summer at the family country estate, Vyra. Together with a schoolmate, Andrei Balashov, Nabokov published *Альманах: Два пути* (*Al'manakh: Dva puti / Almanac: Two Paths*), a slender volume containing eight poems by Balashov and twelve by Nabokov. Less the adolescent love poetry of *Poems*, *Two Paths* is dedicated more to nature, philosophical reflection, and budding awareness of the secrets of his poetic consciousness. Here arise the first references to such motifs as windows and bridges that will reappear throughout Nabokov's oeuvre. Likewise, *Two Paths* reveals the particular attention to the detail of nature – the sky as dark-blue wallpaper, for instance – which in later work will suggest an attitude and comportment through life indicative of awareness of the further depths and dimensions of experience. These poems also display the lyric happiness and confidence in the unfolding of life which distinguishes the tone of much of Nabokov's later verse. While the happiness expressed in the lyrics from *Poems* and here in *Two Paths* seems almost naive in its unabashed exuberance, any negative conclusions drawn from this hasty verdict are tempered by consideration that the same attitude informs later poetry and frequently arises as a theme in his prose. Even in poetry expressive of potentially tragic themes, an air of artless cheerfulness is present with a regularity which suggests a poetically expressed philosophy of life and a salient trait of Nabokov's authorial identity rather than mere juvenile naïveté. Still further, in perhaps the finest poem of the collection – 'У мудрых и злых ничего не прошу' ('U mudrykh i zlykh nichego ne proshu' / 'Of the wise and malicious I ask nothing') – Nabokov signals mysterious, confident awareness of the budding potential of his poetic gift. Already in his second volume of poetry, Nabokov is announcing the presence and growth of his artistic gift in poems which also indicate self-reflective awareness of the limitations and potential of that gift. In seeming comment upon what posterity would judge as the weakest examples of his poetry, the speaker of this poem indicates cognizance that he writes two types of poetry, one with his left hand, the other with his right. The poetry of his left hand is light and of limited substance – a youth with a cotton-batting soul and a girl with a cotton-batting face – while the poetry of his right hand comes from the depths of his being and deals with the secrets of the heart. This poem marks the early confluence of two themes in Nabokov's writing – self-conscious reflection on the state of his artistic abilities and awareness of the inner, secret rhythms of his being which were expressed in art. That Nabokov's poetry will also deal with things beyond appearance is thus already apparent in *Two Paths*. Much future poetry would come from Nabokov's right hand.

The poems of *Two Paths* were the last Nabokov would publish from Russia. Although, as indicated above, Nabokov had made a selection of poems intended for publication under the title of *Раскрытые окна* (*Raskrytye okna* / *Open Windows*) while still in the Crimea, the volume never appeared. The remainder of Nabokov's verse would stem from the stony though miraculously fertile soil of exile. For the next several years, Nabokov's steady rate of publication would be confined to journals. On 27 November 1920 the Russian émigré community was introduced to the poem 'Лес' ('Les' / 'The Forest') by a poet who was to become a prominent contributor to the pages of the new Berlin newspaper *Rul'* (*The Rudder*). Nabokov appended the name 'Cantab' to this early poem, though it was under the name 'Sirin' that he would become famous throughout the European émigré community until his transformation into an English-language author in America as Nabokov. Until the appearance of his first novel, *Машенька* (*Mashen'ka* / *Mary*), in 1926, Sirin/Nabokov would write hundreds of poems and publish many of them in *Rul'*, as well as the other journals located in the principal émigré centres apart from Berlin – Riga, Prague, and Paris. It was also during this period in the early 1920s that Nabokov undertook the translation into Russian of two books, both of which are characterized by their joyful, whimsical contents and the verbal inventiveness of their expression. The translation of Romain Rolland's *Colas Breugnon* was begun in the summer of 1920 and completed in March of the following year for publication a year later in November 1922; in the summer of 1922 Nabokov accepted the commission to translate Lewis Carroll's *Alice in Wonderland*, a task which was quickly accomplished to appear in March 1923. Significantly, the reviews of both books in *Rul'* emphasize the linguistic challenges posed by the texts and the poetic dexterity brought by Sirin/Nabokov to his translations: 'This is a delightful book about Colas Breugnon and its translation is likewise delightful and fresh. It would seem especially difficult to translate into Russian that entire play of words … at times rhythmic prose … The style and spirit of the book has been, I repeat, conveyed very successfully and in places brilliantly' (Ofrosimov 9). The review of *Alice in Wonderland* is still more explicit about the poetic abilities required for such a translation: 'The particular qualities of the book render it exceptionally difficult to translate, something to be mastered only by an individual who not only knows the English language, English life and English literature but especially someone who is capable of writing Russian prose and poetry' (V. 11). This review goes on to single out for praise the particular brilliance of the Russian poems created for inclusion into the text. Important about these early interludes as translator between stages of creative writing is the emphasis placed upon the qualities native to the poet. It is first and foremost the poet's concern for language which marks Nabokov's translation and criticism of translation from Pushkin to Rupert Brooke and Lowell.

Nabokov's third and fourth volumes of poetry fell in quick succession in late 1922 and early 1923. *Гроздь* (*Grozd' / The Cluster*), a slim volume of thirty-six poems, most of which were written between mid-1921 and the end of 1922, was published in Berlin by Gamaiun in December 1922. *Горний путь* (*Gornii put' / The Empyrean Path*) appeared in Berlin with Grani in January 1923. The poetry of *The Cluster* is divided into four sections, each in itself a cluster of thematically related poems. The first section is entitled 'The Cluster' and devoted largely to poetry and poets, and in particular, the consciousness of the poet. The second poem of both the volume and its first section, for instance, announces the unfolding of Nabokov's nascent poetic talent, his wings of 'weighty, silken fire,' in an image which makes indirect reference to Nabokov's pseudonym – Russia's mythical bird of paradise, the *sirin*.[18] In a further untitled poem from the opening section beginning with the line 'Туман ночного сна' ('Tuman nochnogo sna …' / 'The mist of a nocturnal dream …'), Nabokov mentions for the first time an essential characteristic of the poet's consciousness which will feature prominently in his own writing and in the personalities of the poets and artists of Nabokov's works – the tendency to be captivated and entranced by the details of existence. As the speaker of this poem says: 'Thus each trifle – we, children and poets, – / are capable of transforming into a wonder.' This quality is central to the lyric specificity of Nabokov's poetic identity and is one which this study will return to repeatedly in charting the relevance of poetry to Nabokov's work as a whole. In the opening poems of *The Cluster*, the young Nabokov announced the appearance of a poet with an independently formulated aesthetic which would distinguish itself through both attendance to the 'trifles' of the phenomenal world and sensitive appreciation of intimation of the supernal. The second cluster is entitled 'Ты' ('Ty' / 'Thou'). The poems of this section are tantalizingly ambiguous. At first blush poems about love, it becomes clear that the addressee – grammatically female – is never clearly defined. A desired lover perhaps, but just as likely, if not more, the muse; that which is so ardently sought after is inspiration and the writing of poetry rather than a particular woman or 'the cacodemons of carnal pain,' as Nabokov would describe in English half a century later in 'The Poem.' Love and poetry are cleverly combined in these poems, though not in the boy-desires-girl mode of Nabokov's first, juvenile volume of 1916, *Poems*. The poems of the third cluster are dedicated to 'Ушедшее' ('Ushedshee' /'Gone'). The dominant emotion of these eleven poems is the deep-seated, nostalgic sorrow for the irretrievable, departed things of the past. The locus of the past in these poems is frequently Russia, although it is not only the loss of Russia in itself which occasions sorrow but more a feeling of the transience of life and experience. The three poems of the fourth and final cluster – 'Движенье' ('Dvizhen'e' / 'Movement') – deal with trains and train stations. The 'movement' of these poems is not, however, so much movement through physical space as passage to altered realms of consciousness. In the poem 'В поезде' ('V poezde' / 'On a Train'), the speaker is rocked to sleep by the poetically rhythmic- sounding wheels of the train magically to be returned to a wondrous springtime setting in Russia. Upon awakening, the speaker finds himself plucked from a dream of a springtime past and abruptly returned to life's endless, directionless journey of the present, with the wheels of the train now a complaint 'like the tale of a fugitive about former prisons and torments.' The final poem of 'Movement,' and of the collection, is especially interesting for the motif of merger with, and dissolution into, the surrounding environment which it introduces into Nabokov's poetry. A central, poetry-based image of Nabokov's writing to be discussed in chapter 3 concerns the mysterious dispersal and dissolution of the poet out of the physical world into another realm of being. This motif, which occurs with intriguing frequency throughout Nabokov's oeuvre in relation to artists and especially poets, is introduced in the final poem of the collection in imagery which obliquely suggests the dissolution of the train the speaker is travelling on into the golden 'rapture of a sunset.' As will later be discussed, the imagery of metamorphosis and dissolution at a liminal moment in time – here sunset – and/or at a transitional point in space will reappear throughout Nabokov's poetry and provide his prose with its most mysterious, enigmatic, and magical moments.

Comprised of 128 poems written between early 1918 and June 1921, *The Empyrean Path*, published one month after *The Cluster*, was the more substantial of the two volumes. This collection was produced with the participation of Nabokov's father and the poet Sasha Chernyi, who undertook the selection of poems and oversaw the editing and proofreading of the volume while Nabokov was in Cambridge.[19] For the title, Nabokov had initially proposed a choice between *Светлица* (*Svetlitsa* / a well-lit room with connotations of lucidity and luminosity) as 'a symbol of light, height and solitude' and *Тропинки Божии* (*Tropinki bozhii* / *The Tracks of God*) as something 'somewhat more refined' before *The Empyrean Path* was settled upon.[20] With the absence of the clear divisions into sections which characterized the previous collection and with considerably more poems than that volume, the thematic character of *The Empyrean Path* is more difficult to determine than that of *The Cluster*. In *The Empyrean Path*, Nabokov displayed the breadth and variety of his expanding poetic genius while already introducing the central themes and motifs which would accompany him throughout a lifetime of literary creation. There are poems of love, although as in the love poetry of *The Cluster*, they are usually intended for an unspecified, frequently secret addressee, more likely than not, the muse. A selection of poems treats the memory of youth and Russia. The poems about nature are likewise often related to Russia. Many of the poems of different thematic matter are characterized by the role and treatment of consciousness. The poems describing the poet's happiness or wonder in the face of the detail of nature and the mystery of life and experience are simultaneously about the poet's sense of self-awareness while consciously registering this mystery and wonder. Related to the inclusion of consciousness are motifs of the transition of consciousness during such liminal states of being as dreams, daydreams, and memories. In these poems, the existence of another dimension and state of being is intimated. The most intriguing poems, however, are the many examples which treat themes related to the poetic calling and urge to create. Here the central topics of inspiration and the process of artistic creation are expressed. In these poems, as well, Nabokov's fascination with the nature of consciousness is of central importance, as the poet reflects on the very experience of writing poetry.

Characteristic of the poems of *The Empyrean Path* is also their plasticity and pictorial – at times narrative – quality. The first poem of the volume, 'Поэту' ('Poetu' / 'To the Poet'), is a call for poets to develop a new, Acmeist aesthetic based on clarity and precision and the rejection of Symbolist vagueness: 'Болота вязкие бессмыслицы певучей / покинь, поэт, покинь и в новый день проснись! / Напев начни иной – прозрачный и могучий' ['The viscous swamps of melodious nonsense / leave, poet, leave and to a new day awake! / Begin a different melody – clear and powerful']. In apparent response to his own call, Nabokov's poetry is resolutely non-abstract. This is not to suggest, however, that this poetry does not possess a philosophical quality. Indeed, it is the particular manner in which a philosophical, meta-physical dimension is expressed which marks this early poetry as the threshold to Nabokov's subsequent artistry. Set forth in clear, precise imagery, this poetry, like so much of Nabokov's mature art, intrigues by its ability – upon close reading – to convey the presence of unseen, inexpressible dimensions while maintaining the utmost fidelity to perspicacity of expression. In his study of Nikolai Gogol, Nabokov suggested that 'great literature skirts the irrational.' Further, he described the 'moments of irrational insight which simultaneously … disclosed a secret meaning' and which were the basis of Gogol's art (*NG* 140). It is this quality suggestive of a secondary, ineffable realm which distinguishes the two volumes of Nabokov's youthful poetry and presages the development of Nabokov's future works in this direction. Both the themes and the tantalizing indirect means of suggesting the presence of deeper, hidden dimensions which characterize *The Cluster* and *The Empyrean Path* provide an introduction to the thematic development of Nabokov's mature writing and aesthetic.

A hiatus of six years lasted until 1929 and the publication of Nabokov's next selection of poetry, the collection *Возвращение Чорба* (*Vozvrashchenie Chorba: rasskazy i stikhi* / *The Return of Chorb: Stories and Poems*). Along with the fifteen short stories of this collection, Nabokov selected 24 of the over 150 poems he had written in the last several years and presented them under the subtitle 'Стихи 1924–1928' ('Stikhi 1924–1928' / 'Poems 1924–1928'). In terms of Nabokov's development as a writer and his expansion into other genres, much had occurred since the appearance of *The Cluster* and *The Empyrean Path* which accounts for the modest number of poems contained in this volume. Essentially, Nabokov the writer was undergoing a transition, shifting the dominant – though not exclusive – mode of his artistic expression from poetic to prose genres, first with verse dramas and then with short stories and the novel form. In 1921, he published his first short story; in 1924, nine stories appeared, and five in 1925 (Tolstaia 644). In 1925, Nabokov also wrote *Mary*, his first of nine Russian novels. Although these developments signalled a progressive turning to prose between 1921 and 1925, Nabokov did not completely abandon verse forms in this period, even apart from the ever reduced number of poems written and published after 1923, especially after the appearance of *Mary* in 1926.[21] Indeed, in a review from 1929 of a collection by Ivan Bunin which combined poetry with prose in a single volume, Nabokov acidly commented that by portions of the 'reading public,' 'Bunin's poetry may not be held in esteem or, at best, regarded as the not entirely legitimate diversion of a person condemned to write prose' (*Ssoch* II, 673). In 1929, Nabokov, too, had published a volume containing poetry and prose – *The Return of Chorb*. The urge to defend the poetry of an author renowned primarily for his prose could well derive from consideration of his own career. Nabokov had begun a shift to other genres, but, as with Bunin, this implied no disparagement of his poetry. Before thoroughly dedicating himself to prose, though already seemingly intrigued by the narrative potential of extended forms, Nabokov set his poetic skills to the composition of five dramas in verse: *Скитальцы* (*Skital'tsy* / *The Wanderers*), *Смерть* (*Smert'* / *Death*), and *Дедушка* (*Dedushka* / *The Grand-dad*) in 1923; and *Трагедия господина Морна* (*Tragediia Gospodina Morna* / *The Tragedy of Mister Morn*) and *Полюс* (*Polius* / *The Pole*) in 1924 (Diment 1995, 587–8).

Perhaps as testimony to Nabokov's increasing interest in extended forms, the twenty-four poems of *The Return of Chorb* are markedly longer on average than the poems from his previous four collections. Fewer in number too are the smaller, compact poems which are more common to his earlier volumes and which compress emotion and the description of nature into a concentrate of poetic language and imagery. The poems of *The Return of Chorb* are not only longer and less often concerned with emotive descriptions of nature; almost all develop a narrative theme. These poems provide a context and then, with admirable economy, present a brief story. It is to the poems of this collection and this development in Nabokov's poetic that he refers in the 1969 introduction to *Poems and Problems* when, in hindsight, he identifies 'a period lasting another decade or so during which I set myself to illustrate the principle of making a short poem contain a plot and tell a story (this in a way expressed my impatience with the dreary drone of the anemic "Paris school" of *émigré* poetry)' (*PP* 14). This description coincides perfectly with a statement contemporary with *The Return of Chorb* wherein the poet Nabokov reveals poetic principles of relevance to his own art. In a 1927 review of émigré poetry, Nabokov suggested the importance of a lyric plot and its harmonious dénouement to successful poetry:

It has somehow fallen to me to discuss the way in which, in my opinion, a plot is just as important to a poem as to a novel. The finest lyric poems in Russian literature owe their power and delicacy to the manner in which everything in them agreeably proceeds toward an inevitable, harmonious dénouement. Poems in which there is no unity of imagery, no distinctive lyric plot but only a mood, are as incidental and short-lived as the mood itself. If, for example, the poet, having decided to describe his sadness, does not have a single definite image in which to embody that sadness, then something indistinct and irresponsible emerges; the poem is pointless, neither saying nor showing anything. That type of poem is boring. From such a poem an entire strophe may be removed and it will become neither better nor worse. (*Ssoch* II, 640–1)

During this period in his artistic development, Nabokov was visibly attracted by the narrative potential of longer forms, although concerned to see it artistically coupled with the precision and aesthetic potential of poetry. His reason for effecting this combination was likewise expressed in a review of poetry from 1927:

> In reading him [Gumilev] you realize, incidentally, that a poem cannot simply be a 'construct,' a 'lyric something,' an assemblage of chance images, a fog, a blind alley. Above all, a poem must be interesting.
>
> A poem must possess its own beginning, its own dénouement. The reader should begin the poem with curiosity and conclude it with agitation. It is as necessary to narrate lyric trepidation or a trifle as arrestingly as a journey to Africa. That a poem is absorbing is its best compliment. (*Ssoch* II, 639–40)

This concern for the narrative creation of arresting poetry regardless of the dimension of the subject matter is clearly reflected in Nabokov's poems of the late 1920s. And it is at least worth reflecting upon, whether Nabokov's shift in artistic mode during the 1920s was less a shift *away* from poetry as a shift into genres more congenial to the development of plot. Remaining to unite both modes is Nabokov's fundamentally lyric sensibility, itself derived from his poetry.

While the length and plot-based composition of the poems of *The Return of Chorb* represent further development in Nabokov's poetic practice, the central themes introduced in previous volumes remain essentially the same, although expressed now with greater command and precision. The theme of nostalgia for a lost homeland and past remains strong, as do poems expressive of the wonder and beauty of daily life and the natural environment. The theme of the poet and the specific quality of the poetic consciousness also figures prominently. Most intriguing about the poems of *The Return of Chorb*, however, is the creation of an atmosphere of mystery based on the presence of unseen forces. In even the most humble of the poetic settings depicted, the subtle though persistent rustle of another dimension is heard. A room, a seaside town, a beach, a circus tight-rope walker, a sun-lit village – the settings and related imagery of many of the poems are deceptively simple, and yet, within most, the felt but unseen presence of the paranormal is unmistakably registered. Precisely because of the conjunction of quotidian scenes from life with events and experiences of a mysterious nature, the rendered effect of these poems is all the more striking. Nabokov's control of a metaphysical element in these poems, while understated, is more pronounced because presented in the context of tightly controlled concentrates of narrative in poetic form. Wonder at the mystery of being in a world of infinite beauty and subtle complexity, a theme which in earlier poems was frequently simply stated, is, in *The Return of Chorb*, the subject of lyric depiction in poems which combine concise narrative development with the limpid precision of poetic language. As with much of Nabokov's writing, these poems are focused simultaneously both on things of the world and the realm beyond ordinary reality.

The poem 'Тихий шум' ('Tikhii Shum' / 'Soft Sound') of 1929, which Nabokov subsequently translated into English for inclusion in his later collection *Poems and Problems*, provides an excellent example of Nabokov's depiction of a humble experience which nonetheless reverberates with the whisper and hush of physically non-present forces, thanks both to the presentation of a concise plot and to the manipulation of the poetic potential of language. Both a depiction of the poet's personal experience and a direct invitation to the reader to share the same experience, 'Soft Sound' describes the speaker's ability at night by his window to hear the 'soft sound' of Russia contained within the murmur of the sea and the breaking of waves on the shore. Although the sounds heard are derived from unseen sources and, particularly, associations specific to the speaker, they may be heard by any 'soul that harkens unto them.' A poem about exile and loss and the haunting presence of the past and memory, 'Soft Sound' ends with the stillness of night and the calm reassurance that what has been lost to the past and exile is nonetheless ever present and undying: 'But in the compensating night, / in sleepless silence, one keeps listening / to one's own country, to her murmuring, / her deathless deep.' Composed in Russian in eight quatrains with an alternating *ABAB* feminine rhyme scheme, the most effective formal feature of the poem is the masterful implementation of sustained patterns of alliteration and assonance. Uncapturable in its full complexity in the English translation, the arrangement of whispering sibilants within Nabokov's language seems itself to mimic the sound of the sea and to communicate the quiet though relentless intensity of the poet's experience. In 'Soft Sound,' Nabokov creates a poem where 'the shades of voices' are miraculously heard in the whispering rendering of the alliteration and assonance of 'шум моря, дышащий на сушу' ('sh*u*m moria, d*y*shashch*i*i na s*u*sh*u*' / 'the sound of seawaves breathing upon land'). While describing a natural event, Nabokov's manipulation of poetic language and imagery allows hidden dimensions of experience literally to sound forth in expression of a physical event which is also something more.

Also to be drawn from the poems of *The Return of Chorb*, apart from Nabokov's development towards a poetics of narrative concision, is the further crystallization of a core of images and motifs which may be identified as essential to Nabokov's poetry and later fiction. These motifs, closely associated with the creation of wonder and what Nabokov called 'the sudden slanting of the rational plane of life' (*NG* 140) in connection with Gogol, emerged from Nabokov's poetry to serve across his oeuvre in the economical rendering of the mysterious and the everyday and the mysterious in the everyday. Although present in Nabokov's further collections of poems as well, their repetition and density of use in *The Return of Chorb* give first clear expression to their centrality to Nabokov's writing. It is to these motifs that Nabokov's poetry *and* prose will repeatedly return in evocation of veiled reference to the mysteries of a metaphysical dimension. Essentially, these motifs revolve around images of transition and enclosure. The motifs of transition are both spatial and temporal; those of a spatial quality are centred upon seashores, stairways, doorways, windows, mirrors, and bridges, while temporal transitions are marked, most prominently, by sunrise and sunset, dawn and dusk, and the on-coming of seasonal change, particularly spring and autumn. Nabokov's imagery of spatial enclosedness is expressed in such images as solitary rooms, beds, balloons, crystal balls, and hotel rooms. A further frequent refinement of these motifs of physical substance are those which concern altered psychological states, such as the intoxication of inspiration, dreams, and fever, and which emphasize psychological transition to other states of consciousness. Whether dealing with motifs of physical confinement or transition, or those concerning entrance into a modified state of consciousness, Nabokov's poetry foregrounds the notion that the physical world is but one layer of experience isolated from the many others that are available, though often unperceived, to humans. The poems of *The Return of Chorb* contain many of the above delineated motifs, often in complex patterns of combination, as in the above briefly discussed poem 'Soft Sound,' where an anonymous room, a seashore, and a night-time windowsill comprise the setting.

Exceptional to this volume from this catalogue of motifs, however, is the poetic rendering of dreams for a variety of thematic ends. Throughout Nabokov's poetic oeuvre, and as in the poetry of *The Return of Chorb*, dreams are effectively employed in the merging of motifs of transition and inclusion. Alone at night in bed, the poet falls into sleep and is granted access not merely to a realm where spatial and temporal distances are mysteriously overcome but also to the non-rational forms of understanding located there. The domain of dream is thus effectively contrasted with the realm of awakened, phenomenal reality, or in Nabokov's Russian, явь (*iav'*). Dreams and their irreplaceable worth in providing provisional consolation for the finality of time and experience figure prominently in such poems as 'Расстрел' ('Rasstrel'), translated by Nabokov as 'The Execution,' and the untranslated 'Сны' ('Sny' / 'Dreams'). 'Сновиденье' ('Snoviden'e' / 'The Dream'), for instance, describes the experience of a poetic narrator who, in seeking relief from fatigue in sleep, dreams of an encounter with a long-dead friend:

> To my alarm clock its lesson I set
> for next morning, and into the darkness
> I release my bedroom like a balloon,
> and step into sleep with relief.   (*PP* 37; ll. 1–4)

Enveloped in the darkness and the enclosed balloon of his bedroom, the narrator crosses into another state of consciousness where a range of emotions and events are experienced. The narrator meets with a deceased friend, laughs with him, and is afforded the sensation that death and the insult of mortal injury have been overcome: 'Without any astonishment I talk to him, / now alive, and I feel there is no deception / The once mortal wound has gone from his brow' (*PP* 37; ll. 13–15).[22] More intriguing, the dead friend attempts to whisper something in unstated explanation. But before the communication from the dead is possible, 'daylight breaks through my eyelids' and the world is returned to the forms of awakened experience. The narrator is left, not with concrete knowledge communicated from the dead, but something more interesting – the enchanting realization that 'unearthly powers' enable the dead to 'appear in one's sleep,' a realization which is of solace less to the mind than to 'one's shaken soul.' In 'The Dream,' no attempt is made to mystify the experience or to cloak it in mists of uncertainty; the events are clearly identified as having occurred in a dream, and it is this very sense of certainty coupled with the mystery of a dream which lends the poem its power. Even within the dominion of waking reality, missives from another deeper dimension of experience inexplicably make themselves felt. It is this awareness, clearly expressed in the poetry of *The Return of Chorb*, in part, by means of a core of important motifs, which will also be transferred to Nabokov's prose.

Nabokov's sixth volume of poetry appeared twenty-three years later in 1952 as a collection gathering poems from the intervening period of time since the publication of *The Return of Chorb*, as is reflected in the title, *Стиховорения 1929–1951* (*Stikhotvoreniia 1929–1951 / Poems: 1929–1951*). Released with the Parisian publishing house Rifma at a time when Nabokov was already located in the United States establishing himself as an English-language author, the fifteen poems of this volume are temptingly read as a farewell to the European period of his exile and to the genre associated with both his youthful artistry and his emergence as a poet and author in the émigré community. Nabokov's statement in the preface to this collection lends some weight to this reading. Referring to 'К музе' ('K muze' / 'The Muse'), the poem of 1929 which opens the volume, Nabokov claimed that 'with the first poem the period of my youthful creativity was concluded' (n. pag.). 'The Muse,' indeed, takes as its thematic matter the metafictional depiction of the poet's development of a more mature approach to artistic creativity and a subsequent change in writing. A poem to be examined in greater detail in chapter 3, 'The Muse' offers a retrospective interpretation of Nabokov's poetic development to that point and a tender lament for the loss of the youthful enthusiasm which animated his earlier verse.

Along with 'The Muse,' Nabokov included all fifteen of the poems from this volume in his own English translations in his subsequent volume *Poems and Problems*, his first American retrospective collection of Russian *and* English poetry. In the preface to this later volume, Nabokov returned again to the topic of stages within his poetic development, dating a final phase beginning in the period covered by *Poems: 1929–1951*: '… and finally, in the late thirties, and especially in the following decades, a sudden liberation from self-imposed shackles, resulting both in a sparser output and in a belatedly discovered robust style' (*PP* 14). Although it is certainly true that Nabokov's poetic production definitely waned at this time, never to recover the volume of his youthful verse writing, a qualitative change in the nature of his verse is not so easily distinguished. Rather, it would seem that the developments already entered upon within his poetics continued, as did the improvement of his poetic writing. Formally, the narrative-descriptive character of his verse was maintained, just as the average length of his poems increased. Thematically, the range of subject matter treated narrowed, with most poems centred upon the topics of Russia and the nature of poetry, the poet and the poetic consciousness. Within these poems, and others of isolated topics, the presence of a philosophical, metaphysical dimension is strongly felt. A soft but unmistakable breeze from realms of non-rational perception wafts consistently through these poems.

Prior to the publication of *Poems and Problems*, however, Nabokov released in 1959 the first collection of fourteen of his miscellaneous English poems in a volume entitled *Poems*, a title which in its simplicity echoed the Russian title of his first volume, likewise *Poems*.[23] Following his move to the United States in 1940, Nabokov began composing English poems again after a hiatus of approximately twenty years; while at Cambridge, Nabokov had in 1920 published two English poems – 'Remembrance' and 'Home' – and one in Berlin in 1923, 'The Russian Song.'[24] In October 1941, Nabokov returned to English verse with 'Softest of Tongues,' a poem which says 'goodbye' to the many things Nabokov had forsaken in émigré Europe – including the Russian language – with the euphonically similar Russian word *prashchai*. In publishing 'Softest of Tongues' in the *Atlantic Monthly*, Nabokov not only poetically marked his decision to start his career 'anew with clumsy tools of stone' – that is, the English language – but furthered his recent acquaintance with an American audience with a poem. His next English poem, 'The Refrigerator Awakes,' appeared in the *New Yorker*, the journal which would, until 1957, feature many of his poems, including twelve of the lyrics from *Poems*. The publication date of *Poems* deserves a moment of reflection. Released in August 1959, *Poems* is one of Nabokov's first publications after the financial and critical *succès de scandale* of *Lolita* in the autumn of 1958. Provided with financial independence and readerly curiosity, Nabokov was for the first time in his career in a position to capitalize upon and shape the future direction of his writing career according to his artistic interests alone. Famously, this success allowed him to undertake the translation of his Russian works, thereby introducing to an English-language public a brilliant portion of his oeuvre unjustly languishing in the obscurity of a language little known outside of Russia and a fading émigré community. As D. Barton Johnson perceptively claimed, this was 'a rare opportunity to define his *oeuvre* for posterity' (Johnson 1991, 312). It is significant, however, that Nabokov initiated that redefinition with his poetry. Once again, and now here in the context of an English-language audience, Nabokov sought the opportunity at a critical stage in his writing career to shift poetry from the periphery of his oeuvre to the centre.

Except for three unreprinted poems from the earliest stages of his career, all of Nabokov's English poetry derives from a more mature period. As such, this poetry has a corresponding feel of formal and thematic assurance. Although unblighted by the autumnal coolness Nabokov described as entering into his poetics in 'The Muse,' referred to above, the English poems are definitely characterized by a combination of multi-layered thematic density and verbal precision suggestive of a relationship with the muse which is more respectful and disciplined than impetuous and passionate. While Nabokov's English poetry seems to favour tight rhyme schemes and tetrameter measures – thereby alluding to Nabokov's poetic provenance in the Russian tradition – there are a number of formal innovations which suggest inventiveness and Nabokov's willingness both to expand his own writing and to shape a portion of a tradition he did not derive from. 'Lines Written in Oregon,' for instance, is composed of ten tercets of alternating masculine and feminine triple rhymes (*aaa BBB ccc DDD*). 'Exile,' a poem of 1942, is formed of two twelve-line stanzas of alternating amphibrachic tetrameter and trimeter lines (443 443) extending in tandem with a corresponding rhyme scheme (*aab ccb dde ffe*). Nabokov's final poem to first appear in the *New Yorker*, 'The Ballad of Longwood Glen,' is comprised of thirty-three jaunty, eerily comic rhyming couplets and perhaps best illustrates the 'robust style' that Nabokov claimed characterized his later poetry.[25] The narrative-descriptive inclination of Nabokov's later Russian poetry is preserved in his English verse, as is the tendency to combine thematic concerns in concise packages of poetic meaning. Limpid and light, these poems nonetheless contain overlapping layers of Nabokov's past poetic and fictional topics, the complexity of which is belied by the seemingly effortless exactitude of their combination. The long poem 'An Evening of Russian Poetry,' a stylized representation in poetic form of a modest lecture on Russian literature at a women's college, while pointing in the direction of the future *Pale Fire* with its inclusion of a paranoiac exile from a fairy-tale land, also looks to the past with reference to Russian poetry and Nabokov's own experience. The themes of nature, love of Russia, memory, the splintering of identity in exile, prosody, and the consciousness of the poet are all expressed in 'An Evening of Russian Poetry,' although the poem is most moving in its ability to suggest the constant throb and pressure of the exile's inexpressible pain. Simple in subject matter on the surface, 'An Evening of Russian Poetry' nonetheless expresses the presence of ineffable dimensions in the narrator's experience. Perhaps most arresting about the English verse of *Poems*, however, is the manner in which Nabokov takes up the – for him – familiar topic of poetry to combine it with the theme of the nature of poetic art of lasting value and the quality of the consciousness and poetics capable of producing such poetry. 'The Poem,' 'Restoration,' and even 'The Ballad of Longwood Glen,' with its generous portion of mysterio-comic occurrences, are all poems which set forth the key principles of a unique Nabokovian poetics which combines aestheticism and metaphysics. An informed reading of these poems is essential for a fuller understanding of Nabokov's artistry.

After the appearance of *Poems* in 1959, Nabokov all but ceased publishing previously uncollected English poetry; the short 'Lunar Lines,' the last English poem published during his lifetime, appeared in the *New York Review of Books* in 1966. Nabokov did not, however, discontinue his profound interest in poetry, Russian or English. In 1962, the 999-line poem 'Pale Fire,' probably Nabokov's most famous poem, was released as the masterful core and catalyst to the events of the eponymously titled novel. In 1964, Nabokov's monumental translation of Pushkin's novel in verse, *Eugene Onegin*, was accompanied not only by a controversial theory of translation but also his detailed study of Russian versification, *Notes on Prosody*. And in 1968, the collection of Nabokov's writing edited by Page Stegner, *Nabokov's Congeries*, appeared containing ten of the English poems previously collected in *Poems*.[26]

The next substantial volume of poetry, his eighth, was the retrospective collection Nabokov published in 1970. *Poems and Problems* is an unjustly ignored work of vital importance for a comprehensive understanding of Nabokov's oeuvre and poetics. Containing thirty-nine Russian poems with authorial English translations *en regard* and the fourteen English poems previously printed in *Poems*, as well as eighteen chess problems, this volume affords essential insight into the development of Nabokov's poetic oeuvre and identification of those poems – and their attendant themes – that the author himself obviously valued. While perhaps partially motivated by the urge to meet demanding contractual obligations with McGraw-Hill, *Poems and Problems*, Nabokov's first book after the furor of *Ada*, seems just as likely to have been an excellent means to divert audience attention to the language and genre which so influenced his career as a writer.[27] In *Poems and Problems*, the selection of Russian poems alone provides a broad sweep through Nabokov's poetic oeuvre, although emphasis in this volume rests on his later Russian verse: the collections *Two Paths* and *The Empyrean Path* were each represented with one poem; nine poems from *The Return of Chorb* were included, along with all fifteen from *Poems: 1929–1951*. Additional to these poems were eight published though previously uncollected examples spanning from the late 1920s until the late 1960s, and five previously unpublished poems ranging from 1917 to 1939. At the time of publication, *Poems and Problems* provided a panorama of Nabokov's entire career as a poet and writer. And in shaping this panorama, the poems collected in this volume grant a concise summation of the central themes to distinguish Nabokov's career – exile, Russia, nature, religion, memory, love, poetry, and the nature of the poetic consciousness are all represented. These are all themes which conspicuously contradict the one-sided identification of Nabokov as a 'self-indulgent' wordsmith – seemingly reconfirmed by the contemporary publication of *Ada* – and ought to have provoked at least a partial realignment of the critical understanding of Nabokov. The multi-layered combination of these themes in the poetry of *Poems and Problems* not only reveals Nabokov's infinite inventiveness and malleability as an artist but also provides essential insight into the character of his uniquely *lyric* sensibility, a fundamentally poetic approach to artistic creation which – as will be demonstrated in chapter 3 – combined aesthetic, ethical, and metaphysical qualities in a single artistic voice. With the poetry of *Poems and Problems*, Nabokov offered readers miniatures of a more complex representation of his artistry, while granting, in poems such as 'Слава' ('Slava' / 'Fame') and 'Restoration,' rare and privileged access into the intimate recesses of his creative consciousness. In this volume, the conjurer Nabokov note only entranced the audience with a display of his magic, but also conferred a stolen glimpse into the secret depths of the top-hat beneath the silken scarf.

Nabokov's ninth and final collection of poetry closed the circle of a lifetime of poetry writing. The final book Nabokov was to have initiated, *Poems*, was published posthumously in 1979, two years after his death; the title of this concluding work by Nabokov is identical to that of his first book published sixty years previous. The project had been instigated by the Nabokovs, who had contacted Carl and Ellendea Proffer of Ardis Publishers in early 1976 inquiring about the possibility of publishing either a small volume – fifteen or twenty patriotic poems previously deemed too topical for inclusion in *Poems and Problems* – or a longer retrospective collection of Russian verse. Nabokov undertook the process of selecting the poems appropriate for inclusion, but died on 2 July 1977 before completing a final, 'more rigorous review.'[28] Véra Nabokov, who wrote the foreword to *Poems*, records Nabokov's principles for selection:

> This volume is an almost complete collection of the verses written by Vladimir Nabokov. Not included are, first of all, his earliest poems, secondly, those poems which in terms of form and content were too similar to others and thirdly those in which he found formal deficiencies. The selection was made by the author himself. He intended to complete another more rigorous review, but did not succeed. (*Stikhi* 3)

Despite the unfortunate reason for its incompletion, it is perhaps providential for students of Nabokov's writing that he was unable to make his intended final review. As published, *Poems* contains 244 poems (including fragments from his novel *The Gift*). Of this number, 170 (or 73 per cent) are previously unpublished examples, most of which are derived from the earliest stage of his career between 1917 and 1925 and yet were not included in the volumes *The Cluster*, *The Empyrean Path*, or *The Return of Chorb*. Granting the proviso that he was unable to make his final selection, it is nonetheless apparent that the mature Nabokov returned specifically to some of his earliest work when assembling the material for his final book, the retrospective collection which would escort his oeuvre into posterity. Prior to analysis of the form and content of these individual poems, the very focus of this collection is worthy of note. With *Poems*, his final addition to an unusually expansive and multi-faceted oeuvre, Nabokov marked an explicit return to the genre which, like no other, accompanied his artistic development from beginning to end. And as if in imitation of the narrative strategy of many of Nabokov's texts whereby the narrative conclusion seamlessly returns the reader to the beginning to recommence a process of rereading and interpretive rediscovery, Nabokov's emphasis on the earliest examples of his poetry suggests, at the level of his entire oeuvre, that the reader re-examine his poetry in the interests of a fuller, synoptic reading of his subsequent works. The narrative development of Nabokov's oeuvre is concluded, as in so many of his fictions, with a return to its beginnings. This evidence of estimation and strategy on Nabokov's part is itself grounds for returning to his poetry for closer examination.

Since the publication of *Poems* in 1979, little has occurred substantially to alter the shape and perception of Nabokov's poetic oeuvre as it is known from the nine volumes reviewed above. The lifting of the political strictures imposed on the Soviet literary institution in the wake of Gorbachev's reforms in the mid-1980s has contributed to a realignment of Russian literature – Soviet and émigré – and a belated return of Nabokov to the mainstream of the Russian literary tradition. A portion of this process has been the growth in interest in the full breadth of Nabokov's previously inaccessible oeuvre, including his poetry, expressed in the release (rarely authorized) of numerous editions of works in Russia. The publication of an authorized five-volume collection of Nabokov's Russian works was initiated in 1999 and completed in 2000. This edition contains most, albeit not all, of Nabokov's poems, individual examples of which continue to surface occasionally, at times in translations by the author's son and main translator into English, Dmitri Nabokov. The qualities of Nabokov's body of

English-language poetry have remained essentially fixed in a limbo of limited regard on the part of critics and a lack of awareness on the part of a general readership, especially outside of Russia. The occasional inclusion of individual poems into anthologies of translated and English poetry, such as the recent *Poets of World War II*, edited by Harvey Shapiro, is as often as not accompanied by wonderment that Nabokov wrote poetry at all, a response which is as eloquently telling about reader awareness of the scope of Nabokov's writing as it is about the limited success of criticism in adequately disseminating knowledge about Nabokov's entire oeuvre. Indeed, it is my contention that this significant lacuna in the understanding of Nabokov's writing is partially the fault of an at times incomplete and at times misconstrued effort to encompass Nabokov's poetry in critical terms. It is to the essential project of reviewing and reassessing criticism of Nabokov's poetry that the next chapter will turn.

2 Reading Nabokov's Reception: Nabokov, Poetry, and the Critics

There are in emigration not a few people who deny that Nabokov is a poet and who value only his prose. Nabokov moved from verse to prose, although it would be wrong to say of his prose, as one may of the prose of Tsvetaeva, Osip Mandel'shtam, or Pasternak, that it is the prose of a poet. It would be perhaps more accurate to say that his poems are the poems of a prose writer.
– Gleb Struve, *Russkaia literatura v izgnanii*

In my opinion, he [Nabokov] is in general an unrealized poet. Yet, precisely because he is an unrealized poet he is a wonderful prose writer. It's always like that. As a rule, the prose writer without active poetic experience tends towards verbosity and bombast.
– Joseph Brodsky, 'New York: Peizazh poeta'

'Melodious existence' [*zvukovoe bytie*] is perhaps the most precise definition of Nabokov's lyricism. It is not a supplement to the writer's wonderful prose but something kindred to it.
– Vladimir Smirnov, 'Stikhi Nabokova'

'Few of those presently enraptured by *The Defense* likely know that Sirin began his literary course as a poet ...' (Struve 1930a, 3). Thus, the perhaps most comprehensive critic of Russian émigré literature, Gleb Struve, could baldly remark in 1930 upon the publication of Nabokov's third of nine Russian novels. Struve made his comment at a time when Nabokov had over four hundred poems in print, including those from *The Return of Chorb*, the widely reviewed collection published in 1929, one year previous to Struve's remark. Struve's observation is witness to the claim that even in the early stages of his career, Nabokov's unusual facility with prose served to the detriment of awareness of his poetry. In confirmation of this logic, and in the wake of a career as one of the greatest prose writers of the twentieth century, it is of little surprise that Nabokov is still poorly known as a poet, despite the voluminous critical literature devoted to the various aspects of his oeuvre. Thus, that Nabokov is poorly known as a poet may be legitimately ascribed – albeit with resignation – to a variety of circumstances, including his transition to English out of the language of the bulk of his poetry. That Nabokov is – in general – poorly regarded as a poet by the few critics and scholars who have addressed his poetic writing is another matter entirely. The first is the result of failed acquaintanceship with the poetry, the latter, in my opinion, a result of failed interpretative reading which, rather than being remedied by criticism, has its roots deep in the history of the critical response to Nabokov's poetry. Nabokov's estimation as a poet is a portion of his critical reception, a reception which has been shaped out of, and implicated by, the complex interplay of Nabokov's poetic production and ability, the expectations of criticism and scholarship, and the empirical circumstances of the appearance and assessment of Nabokov's poetry. It is to this troubled history of Nabokov's reception as a poet that the present chapter will turn. This is a matter of some urgency, and will be conducted with more than usual attention paid to a series of critical assessments over the course of Nabokov's reception, as the shortcomings of previous criticism must be identified and redressed in preparation for a new reading of Nabokov's poetry.

Despite the sustained interest in Russia since the early 1990s for Nabokov's verse, the amount of effort invested in developing a critical appreciation of Nabokov's poetry is dwarfed by that devoted to his prose. Although still too limited in quantity to qualify as a broad overview, much less a unified approach or consensus, enough studies have been conducted that general tendencies may be discerned. Central here is the rejection of Nabokov's efforts in verse. Indeed, apart from important isolated exceptions, the majority of critical responses to Nabokov's poetry are united in their varying degrees of negativity or, at best, hesitant, uncertain praise. This unanimity is in itself of interest and, as we will see, grounds enough for closer analysis. For although general agreement was achieved regarding the final normative assessment of Nabokov's poetry, rarely were the criteria for arriving at this conclusion consistent. Over the years since 1916, the critical reception of Nabokov's poetry has gone through a variety of stages, with analysis being conducted – particularly in the early years – less in accordance with the internal needs and requirements of Nabokov's poetry than by the strictures of critical tendencies blind to the specificity of

Nabokov's writing. Criticism of Nabokov's poetry has frequently functioned as a closed system of internal reference whereby the earliest un-
enthusiastic comments have been repeated – often down to the same
phrasing – with little evidence of willingness to address the poems as expressions of a unique poetic voice demanding of more than negative comparison to putative influences. In short, in the assessment of Nabokov's
verse, criticism has often fed on criticism rather than nourishing independent analysis. In the absence of a critical approach which accorded Nabokov
the same degree of freedom and individuality in creating a distinctive poetic voice as was eventually conceded to his development of a distinctive
prose poetics, Nabokov's poetry was judged to be deficient, not in terms of
principles of assessment derived from the poetry itself, but because it con-
formed either too closely or not closely enough to changing expectations
based on the writing of other poets. Keis Verkheil's comments on Nabokov's
early verse in an otherwise appreciative article are thus representative: 'In
the best and worst moments of his creative works, he [Nabokov] is dependent upon stronger colleagues' (Verkheil 139). This is likewise the upshot of
a comment by Maxim Shrayer, another critic very sensitive to Nabokov's
achievements who nonetheless reads Nabokov's poetry with an ear for
formal innovation though less with an eye for thematic independence:
'… Nabokov often sounds like a potpourri of the nineteenth- and twentieth-
century poetic repertoire, a Pushkin, a Fet, a Bunin, a Blok, and a Pasternak
all at once … Iurii Tynianov wrote in 1924 that "each *new* appearance in
poetry is marked first and foremost by a *novelty of intonation.*" Although a
profusely gifted poet, Nabokov did not find an original intonation'
(Shrayer 247). Moreover, Nabokov the émigré writer was frequently viewed
by critics very much concerned with the purported institutional needs of
exile literature. While in prose he was ultimately able to overcome the
critical resistance occasioned by his refusal to adopt standardized modes
of writing or to conform to generalized expectations, in poetry, Nabokov
failed to wrestle from criticism similar recognition of the specificity of his
lyric vision. As a result, Nabokov's poetic writing has but rarely been accorded assessment as a self-sufficient body of work related to, but also as
fiercely original as, his prose writing. Instead, Nabokov's poetry has been
frequently compared to external models of poetic writing and, in consequence, deemed either epigonic or outworn. Indeed, a wish to address the
failings of this general approach has served as a motivation for the present
study. Apart from illustrating the dimensions of Nabokov's poetic oeuvre
and the formative role of his lyric voice within his writing as a whole, a
reading of Nabokov's poetry will be proposed in the following chapter

which establishes the characteristics of his poetry according to the internal criteria of the poetry itself and Nabokov's artistic vision.

Although the critical response to Nabokov's poetry is characterized by general concurrence in terms of negativity of assessment – albeit with important exceptions – the history of the critical reception does not indicate a similar degree of uniformity with regard to the *justification* for this assessment. In keeping with the multi-staged nature of Nabokov's career, criticism has kept pace with four main phases of assessment of Nabokov's poetry. The first stage is devoted to Nabokov's Russian poetry of European exile and may be dated from the appearance of his collections *The Cluster* and *The Empyrean Path* in the early 1920s to the publication in 1956 of Gleb Struve's authoritative retrospective assessment of Russian émigré literature, *Русская литература в изгнании* (*Russkaia literatura v izgnanii / Russian Literature in Exile*). The second stage deals with Nabokov's English poetry and is distinguished less by the volume of response than by the difficulty critics experienced in attempting to respond to Nabokov's little-known poetry in the context of a prose oeuvre of increasing fame and critical acceptance. A third stage comprises a cluster of important academic criticism occasioned by the publication of *Poems* in 1979. These studies conducted by scholars intimately familiar with the totality of Nabokov's oeuvre sought to provide a synoptic overview which placed Nabokov's verse production within the framework of his entire body of work. A related fourth and still unfolding stage of academic criticism is less easily defined in either historical or thematic terms but seems, in my opinion, to coincide with the opening up of the Russian literary system. An altered institutional context has provided the impetus for a re-evaluation of Nabokov's oeuvre with particular reference to the Russian character of his work, which is of particular relevance to Nabokov's poetry. Thus postulated, these four stages form the basis of the following historically comprehensive, though inevitably incomplete, survey of the critical reception of Nabokov's poetry.

The Émigré Reading of Nabokov's Poetry

As reported in *Speak, Memory*, Nabokov's debut as a poet in 1916 was accompanied by a critical response which was as inauspicious with regard to the estimation of his poetic skill as it proved ironic in terms of his future development as a writer. As has previously been observed, upon receiving a copy of Nabokov's *Poems*, Zinaida Gippius requested in conversation that Nabokov's father pass on to the young poet the damning assessment that he 'would never, never be a writer' (*SM* 238).[1] Unfortunately for Nabokov, the negative tone of Gippius's evaluation of his poetry was to pursue him into exile, although, it ought to be recalled, the first references to Nabokov's poetry published in émigré journals was of 'a young poet of great lyrical strength which seems to be strengthening before our eyes, a poet with self-restraint and moderation' (Iakovlev 21). Nabokov's first two collections of poetry from late 1922 and early 1923, *The Cluster* and the more voluminous *The Empyrean Path*, reaped predominantly negative criticism, apart from isolated though illustrative exceptions. Of the two, critical reception of *The Cluster* was harsher than that of *The Empyrean Path*. The first review of *The Cluster*, printed in *Dni* (*Days*), chastised the young poet, not for his 'ultra aestheticism' alone, but for the poor quality of the aestheticism (Bakhrakh 17). Alexander Bakhrakh suggested that for Nabokov the world is 'blasphemous' and for this reason he attempts to create a separate world of refuge. Unfortunately, the poet lacks the necessary poetic independence and strength, and his world becomes but mediocre fluff. Nabokov's poetic images are said by Bakhrakh to be taken from the earliest symbolists, and many of the lines derived from Blok. They create, not a sense of wonder, but the impression of a cold and soulless toy, beautiful in its frivolity. Upon reading them, nothing remains but sweetness and operatic affectation. Despite the relative harshness of these criticisms, the author expresses the regret that the poems create the impression they do, as individual lines reveal that the poet is possessed of a poetic gift along with a sense of poetic culture and technique.

As one of the first in what would develop into a very long history of reception in both poetry and prose, Bakhrakh's brief review deserves particular attention. His appraisal is of interest, less regarding the result of its analysis than for the descriptive language and censured poetic characteristics which it introduced into Nabokov criticism; both would tenaciously follow Nabokov's prose and poetry throughout the émigré period of his writing. In terms of critical language, Bakhrakh lifted the image of a peacock from the conclusion of Nabokov's first poem in *The Cluster* to develop an impression of Nabokov's poetry.[2] Thus, the image especially of the 'peacock,' but also the 'tea-rose,' with its similar suggestion of exaggerated aestheticism and prissy artificiality and preciousness, was here first added to the compendium of terms available to critics to describe Nabokov's efforts to create an impression of emotion in poetry. In refining this impression, Bakhrakh attributes characteristics to Nabokov's writing which in the course of émigré criticism would become, in various forms of expression, touchstones of analysis: 'soulless' and 'cold.' In still further, now ironic, comment upon Nabokov's poetics and in pointed continuation of the 'ultra aestheticism' evoked in the review's first lines, Bakhrakh includes in his Russian text the semiotically charged French words *art poétique*. For a culturally conservative émigré community exceptionally concerned with maintaining its national identity while in exile, the inclusion of two otherwise innocent words unmistakably appeals to connotations both of foreignness and the characteristics already attributed to Nabokov – the 'peacock,' 'soulless,' and 'cold.' Thus, in one of the earliest of reviews dedicated to Nabokov, a foretaste of the essential features of an émigré assessment which would arise in later discussions of Nabokov's prose is first encountered in the context of Nabokov's poetry. The charge of soulless 'non-Russianness' and of resplendent, peacock-like artificiality would grow much stronger, beginning with the discussions of *King, Queen, Knave* in 1928. Although it would eventually give way as an appraisal of his prose to more subtle and informed judgments, the applicability of this appraisal to Nabokov's poetry was never systematically challenged. Apart from the critical terms of identification used by Bakhrakh, his review is also of exemplary interest in terms of its (mis)identification of a nascent Nabokovian poetics. Quoting two lines each from two poems, Bakhrakh correctly identifies one of the central features of Nabokov's poetics which, although first expressed in his poetry, would develop further over the course of his writing career to lend his entire oeuvre a particularly Nabokovian cast. The first is derived from an untitled poem beginning 'Туман ночного сна' ('Tuman nochnogo sna …' / 'The mist of a nocturnal dream …'), in which the poet identifies the unique capacity of poets and children to appreciate the trifles of daily life as wonders of existence: 'Thus each trifle – we, children and poets, – / are capable of transforming into a wonder.' The second quote – 'A star, a snow-flake, a drop of honey / I enclose in verse' – is likewise derived from an untitled poem, 'Есть в одиночестве свобода …' ('Est' v odinochestve svoboda …'/ 'There is in solitude freedom …'). Bakhrakh misreads these lines in illustration of his own thesis, what he has postulated as Nabokov's 'peacock-like' frivolity and preciousness. Lamenting that it is 'insufficient "to enclose" in verse even the most beautiful findings' (Bakhrakh 17), he seems to suggest that Nabokov was concerned solely with the creation of a beautiful image. Excluded by Bakhrakh's reading is the essential consideration that these lines, although meant to be aesthetically rendered in themselves, are just as importantly an expression of the theme of poetic consciousness. In this respect, they are undeniably suggestive of a fundamental portion of Nabokov's *art poétique*, here expressed in poetry – the faculty and facility essential to the artist of registering and appreciating even the most humble of things of the world. It is this central theme in Nabokov's poetics which first found expression in his poetry – indeed is defining of poetry and art for Nabokov – and which to a large degree lent his entire oeuvre its specificity. That Bakhrakh mistook an early expression of one of the central components of Nabokov's poetics for a form of poetic posturing is perhaps understandable given the early stage of Nabokov's career. Nonetheless, this misrepresentation of Nabokov's poetic intentions merits precise identification and rectification, for, as will be discussed below, Gleb Struve was to return to precisely these same lines in the formation of his influential, concluding assessment of Nabokov's émigré poetry in 1956.

It was Gleb Struve, but a few weeks after the analysis from *Dni*, who published the next review of *The Cluster* in February 1923 (Struve 1923). Struve's comments for *Russkaia mysl'* (*Russian Thought*) clearly indicate familiarity with his colleague's review, as is most significantly illustrated in his adoption of Bakhrakh's descriptive vocabulary. Commencing his assessment with the positive appraisal of Nabokov's formal abilities with which Bakhrakh had concluded his, Struve indicated that despite Nabokov's youth, a tremendous sense of poetic discipline and technical ability was to be felt. According to Struve, the presence of Bunin, Maikov, and the unnamed 'classics' of Russian poetry could be discerned in Nabokov. And in view of the poet's youth, a number of deficiencies could be forgiven, such as the occasional presence of sentimentality, excessive sweetness, and an overabundance of detail. Such faults were judged minor compared to Nabokov's supposed 'primary sin' of an excessively external approach to the world, a poverty of internal symbolics, the absence of authentic creative fire. Struve felt justified in using such harsh words in reference to Nabokov precisely because the presence of a tremendous poetic gift could be felt in Nabokov. Nabokov was judged to possess technical skill and a sense of language and imagery, although he needed in his poetry to free himself from the pressures of an oppressively heavy world, one at once cold and resplendent. Struve suggested that Nabokov attempt to break free from the overly logical approach which constrained his freedom of artistic movement; a reading of Nabokov's poetry, even the finest lines, was weighty and confining, leaving one wishing for some form of hiatus even at the cost of damaging the poetry's harmony. Despite these criticisms, Struve, cognizant of the poet's youth, remained optimistic about Nabokov's future development. This optimism was buttressed for Struve by the recent appearance of poems which were not included in *The Cluster*.

Significant about Struve's review is its essential concordance not only with Bakhrakh's earlier assessment, but its language. From the initial urge

to categorize Nabokov in relation to putative influences through the primary criticism of an overly 'external approach to the world' to the central
attributes of the world created by Nabokov – 'resplendent' and 'cold' –
Struve's comments seem at least in part based on Bakhrakh's. Although he
never claims with Bakhrakh that Nabokov's poetry is 'soulless,' along with
reference to 'coldness' and 'heavy and stuffy,' Struve does suggest that
Nabokov's poems are often 'lifeless.' The weight of indebtedness of this
critical impression is increased by the final image employed by Struve in his
comment concerning his confidence that Nabokov was not 'completely entangled in the nets of his *resplendent, peacock-like world*' (Struve 1923, 299;
emphasis added). And just as Bakhrakh revealed the limits of his interpretive reading in his misidentification of the place of poetically rendered trifles in Nabokov's poetry and poetics, Struve also demonstrated an inability
to perceive an important element contributing to the specificity of
Nabokov's lyric voice. Struve's final criticism concerns the supposed lack
of movement in the three poems comprising the fourth and final 'cluster'
of poems in the volume, entitled 'Movement.' Perhaps assuming the excessively 'external approach to the world' attributed to Nabokov's poetry,
Struve misreads the nature of the movement in these poems. Less about
physical movement, although the poems are based on images of trains, the
poetry of this section is devoted to the movement of consciousness in
dreams, memory, and, in the final poem, a mysterious transference into
another realm of being, a merging with the landscape being depicted in the
poem. This latter form of 'movement,' which was to provide the concluding image for so many of Nabokov's works, is also present in *The Cluster*,
though unseen by Struve and unfelt in his criticism.

   In startling contrast to the echoing assessments offered by Bakhrakh and
Struve, the next review of Nabokov's poetry by Vladimir Amfiteatrov-
Kadashev in *Segodnia (Today)* is resoundingly positive (Amfiteatrov-Kadashev
5). Foregoing vocabulary evocative of a 'soulless' 'peacock-like world' and the
urge to place Nabokov in the context of creative influences, Amfiteatrov-
Kadashev sees the verse of *The Cluster* as the youthful, optimistic response
to the chaos and disharmony in both the world and contemporary poetry.
And while the two previous critics censured Nabokov's purportedly external
approach to the world, Amfiteatrov-Kadashev, in language which skirts the
religiously ecstatic, suggests an almost metaphysical quality for Nabokov's
poetry. For Amfiteatrov-Kadashev, the central leitmotif of Nabokov's verse
is an 'infatuation with "the infant smile of the earth"' and a 'joyful reception
of the world' which pierces the variegated facts of existence to perceive a
'harmonious Unity,' a completeness which is 'indisputably an existing reality.'
While Amfiteatrov-Kadashev's casting of Nabokov's poetry in terms of an

exclusively metaphysical poetics and the near imputation to Nabokov of a conventional expression of faith seems forced, he nonetheless identifies a component of Nabokov's poetics which is, as will be shown in the following chapter, important to Nabokov's lyric sensibility and poetic writing. Certainly not to be miscategorized with any explicit confession of religious faith, Nabokov's poetry is, as the critic seems to indicate, suggestive of an optimistic approach and attitude to life – a particular configuration of the artistic consciousness – which renders the troubles of life bearable. Nabokov's poetry is, as Amfiteatrov-Kadashev indicates, frequently concerned with death, as well as the pain of exile, insecurity, and the loneliness of separation; the response to this is not only a poetic attitude which registers and responds to 'the sun, lilac and birches and the drops of rain on glistening crosses' but also a poetry which represents such trifles. Although Amfiteatrov-Kadashev seems overly receptive to the surface religiosity of isolated poems, his review is one of the few which correctly locates in Nabokov's poetry evidence of a specific poetic identity.

Unfortunately for Nabokov criticism, the next review of *The Cluster*, Konstantin Mochul'skii's discussion for *Zveno* (*The Link*), did not follow Amfiteatrov-Kadashev's lead in attempting to isolate and comment upon the salient features of Nabokov's nascent lyric voice. Elegantly, even slyly, written, Mochul'skii's review returns to the preoccupation introduced by Struve of attempting to intimate poetic influence and genealogy without ever demonstrating it, while, in this case, making insinuating reference to Nabokov's distinguished family background: 'Sirin [Nabokov] – one of the last descendants of a noble breed. Behind him stand great grandfathers and fathers: and Pushkin, and Tiutchev, and Fet, and Blok' (Mochul'skii 3). Mochul'skii's conflation of Nabokov's family and artistic heritage is more than a mere rhetorical device. It is intended to buttress his central contention that Nabokov's poetry is representative of not only an epigonic poetic tradition but, more importantly, a dying culture – a less than innocent insinuation in the context of the murderous class warfare then being waged in Nabokov's native land. Striking notes similar to those sounded by Bakhrakh and Struve of 'peacock-like' aestheticism and artificiality, Mochul'skii suggests an element of decadence not so much in Nabokov's poetry itself, but in the phenomenon of a young man of his class and background writing the type of poetry he does. Nabokov is granted to possess 'great artistic culture' and to have in his blood 'the rhythms and sounds of masters.' Ultimately, however, although 'his melody is refined, the rhythms solemn, the images noble … that splendour is not that of a sunrise but a sunset. Sirin's verse has a great past but no future' (Mochul'skii 3).

Mochul'skii's review is one of the most transparent of a type of criticism Nabokov would often be confronted with, where the phenomenon Nabokov – what he and his writing were assumed to represent – was the subject of analysis rather than the artistry in its own terms. In the instance of Nabokov's poetry, this may be seen to have had long-lasting results; succeeding generations of readers have been influenced by the negative assessment without contextualizing the critical method behind it.

Whereas each of the above critics sought to present even their frankest judgments of Nabokov's poetry according to the conventions of dispassionate analysis, Roman Gul''s review of *The Cluster* for *Novaia russkaia kniga* (*New Russian Book*) introduced an element of vitriol which would characterize a particular element of the later response to Nabokov in the community of émigré letters. Opening with the statement 'A small but very boring booklet,' Gul''s approximately twenty lines of assessment dismiss *The Cluster* in a sustained welter of sarcasm wherein even faint praise for the poet's technical skill is retracted: 'The rhythms are correct, the meters fitting, everything is in place. This is a fine example of a poet as "an excellent apprentice." Knowledge of poetic technique and the poetry of bygone poets is visible. Everything is printed off in threadbare clichés. Nowhere is there the beating of "his own" pulse' (Gul' 23). What is interesting about this review is certainly not its critical acumen, but rather the distinct impression created that the virulence of the review is being purposefully directed as a corrective to previous, overly positive responses. Even at this early stage, Gul' is obviously informed of Nabokov's career and makes comments which address less his poetry than Nabokov himself and earlier responses to his work. Such may be found, for example, in the following comment, where Gul' 'quotes' an earlier judgment of the quality of Nabokov's poetry only to correct it as he sees fit: 'Moreover, Sirin's "trifles" are neither "charming" nor "light" but boring in an old-fashioned manner.' That Nabokov is depicted as 'a poet of trifles' is relevant in this review, for in a gesture related to Mochul'skii's dismissive reference to Nabokov's social background, Gul' suggests that this characteristic of Nabokov is derived from his lack of experience of the world, his never having travelled beyond his 'blue drawing-room' (*golubaia gostinaia*). One of the central features of Nabokov's poetry – the appreciation of life's trifles – is thus again misread only to be tendentiously ascribed to a belittling sociology of the poet's privileged cultural background and the setting, though not subject matter, of several poems. The presumed aestheticism and artificiality first encountered in Bakhrakh's reference to peacocks and tea-roses is now overlain with a layer of class criticism.

Moving from critical response to *The Cluster* to the much longer collection *The Empyrean Path*, Iulii Aikhenval'd, one of the most prominent and accomplished of an older generation of Russian critics still active in the émigré community, discussed both volumes in a single review for *Rul'* (Aikhenval'd 1923). Of the two volumes, the critic immediately indicated his preference for *The Empyrean Path,* although – according to Aikhenval'd – it is in *The Cluster* that Nabokov indicates his devotion to Bunin's muse. Aikhenval'd grants the similarity to Bunin's style while suggesting as well that Nabokov's verse occasionally deviates from Bunin's clarity and precision in the direction of mannered refinement. Nabokov's verse shows refinement, and bears the mark of familiarity with Russian culture as well as the literature and artistic traditions of Europe. Persistent reference to motifs of Russia and separation from her are also noted. Aikhenval'd observes as well, however, that as a whole, Nabokov's poems do not ultimately deliver as much as they promise. Too often the poems are over-cluttered with words, in particular difficult and superfluous words. With persistent work, however, Nabokov's poems will definitely improve; like a sculptor chipping away superfluous material from a block of marble, the poet Nabokov will remove excesses of prolixity from his verse. Despite the balanced and generally positive tone of Aikhenval'd's review, the muted nostalgia of his perspective is to be felt in the focused reference to Bunin, Dostoevskii, and Russian nature in Nabokov's poetry. One senses that Aikhenval'd's expectations for poetry, in general, and Nabokov's poetry, in particular, are derived from established criteria, a critical point of departure which renders the critic more appreciative of Nabokov's general talent than his expressions of an independent aesthetic. Aikhenval'd's sole reference to poetic individuality is a lone example of alliteration from 'Ласточки' ('Lastochki' / 'Swifts'): 'в Назарете – на заре' ('v Nazarete – na zare' / 'in Nazareth – at sunrise').

Vera Lur'e's review of *The Empyrean Path* for *Novaia russkaia kniga*, apart from being the review which presumably provoked the 'corrective' assessment by Roman Gul' discussed above, is noteworthy in its crystallization of the fundamental difficulties Nabokov's first critics experienced in reviewing his poetry. Like Aikhenval'd, Lur'e begins her well-minded review by emphasizing the promise of the young Nabokov. Surprisingly, however, rather than elaborate further on the source of quality of the 'genuinely good poems' and the characteristics of Nabokov's indisputable gift as a poet, she abruptly reverses the direction of response to state that 'with the exception of several genuinely good poems, the collection *The Empyrean Path* is a boring book.' In proceeding from this contention, Lur'e's review does not seek to develop an interpretive analysis of Nabokov's strengths and a reading of the specifics of Nabokov's poetic voice, although in conclusion she does quote lines from 'На Голгофе' ('Na Golgofe' / 'On Golgotha') as evidence of the 'simplicity and strength' of Nabokov's verse. While not identified as such, the image quoted by Lur'e of the crucified Christ remembering the wood-shavings on the floor of his father's house illustrates a theme central to Nabokov's lyric voice. Discussion of this poem below will indicate how 'On Golgotha' exemplifies the Nabokovian facility in perceiving with heightened sensibility the irreplaceable details and 'trifles' of life. Weak in articulating and developing understanding of the identified strengths of Nabokov's poetry, this review is remarkably clear about its reading of his purported inadequacies: 'This [the boringness of *The Empyrean Path*] does not arise out of deficiencies in the author's talent; but it is simply not possible to pass by all contemporary artistic achievements and gains, to renounce all movements and schools and to use images which have long ago faded and ceased to be symbols' (Lur'e 23). Essentially, for Lur'e, the key to Nabokov's flaw is his total independence from contemporary achievements in poetry; in short, his striving for artistic originality. Lur'e's concise 'criticism' is but an inverted expression of the characteristics which would subsequently distinguish Nabokov's writing. The celebrated stylistic autonomy and disdain for the facilely symbolic, which would form the basis of Nabokov's later critical estimation, is in 1923, in the context of his poetry, a source of the censure that would doggedly pursue most subsequent assessments of his verse.

Read in the light of Lur'e's illuminating statement, the above discussed reviews of Nabokov's first two volumes of émigré verse may be seen to share similarities of assessment and to reveal the same (at this stage perhaps unavoidable) sources of critical myopia. Each of the reviewers acknowledged Nabokov's mastery of the formal elements of poetry; Nabokov is conceded to have manipulated the meter, rhythm, rhyme, and euphonic potential of poetry with accomplished adroitness. In formal matters, then, Nabokov is praised with *no* mention made of the purported formal 'conservatism' of his verse, a charge which will arise in later discussions of his poetry. Nabokov is criticized, however, for excessive identification with an astounding assortment of masters of Russian poetry. In the seven brief reviews discussed above, Nabokov is said to show the influence of Bunin, Maikov, Pushkin, Tiutchev, Fet, and Blok. In subsequent reviews, this list will be considerably lengthened, with the inclusion of a selection of still more disparate voices. It is less the range of these 'influences' which is remarkable, than the fact that they are attributed to a poet explicitly criticized for having renounced all 'movements and schools.' Rather than representing a seeming contradiction, however, Lur'e's observation undoubtedly points to a legitimate problem critics encountered in 'reading' Nabokov's artistry. In the absence of a contemporary poetic paradigm with which to evaluate and categorize Nabokov's verse, critics turned to the example of earlier poets, some of whom were indeed important to Nabokov in *individual* poems. Critics employed a similar strategy in normalizing Nabokov's first prose works. Upon the publication of Nabokov's first novel, *Mary*, in 1926, Gleb Struve perceived the influence of Turgenev and especially Bunin, while Dmitrii Shakhovskoi just as confidently (!) claimed that 'Sirin [Nabokov] is leaving Bunin ... and moving in the direction of Dostoevskii' (Shakhovskoi 173). Beginning with *King, Queen, Knave*, reference would be made to unspecified 'German expressionists,' and so on; the publication of each new work by Nabokov would see the continuation of this trend. The importance of these brief references to the early reception of Nabokov's prose is not to question the critical acumen of reviewers in individual instances, but rather to illustrate the genesis of a critical method which was as inadequate in judging Nabokov's poetry as his prose. Significantly, the critics who made no attempt to compare Nabokov with someone else – especially Amfiteatrov-Kadashev, but also Lur'e – were also the ones who specifically identified the tendency of Nabokov's poetry to emphasize the wonders and trifles of being and attempted to locate it, in a positive sense, in Nabokov's poetics. Those critics less disposed to reading originality in Nabokov's poetry, and hence more quickly inclined to comparison with other poets, accorded this feature importance, not as a central component in an emerging individual poetics, but as the attribute of a 'soulless' and 'cold,' 'resplendent' and 'peacock-like' approach to the world – a critical judgment which would follow Nabokov in various forms throughout his émigré period of artistic activity.

The following examples of émigré criticism related to Nabokov's poetry were produced in 1929–30 in response to the poetry and short stories contained in the volume of December 1929, *The Return of Chorb*. In the seven-year interlude since early 1923, Nabokov's oeuvre had expanded considerably, with the publication of a significant number of works in various genres; in contrast to the young poet of *The Cluster* and *The Empyrean Path*, Nabokov was now a known, if for some still controversial, quantity within the émigré community. The numerous reviews of *The Return of Chorb* display increased familiarity with Nabokov's writing and hence, with regard to his poetry, greater care and precision in principles of assessment. Significantly reduced are the facile comparisons to putative 'influences' except in those reviews transparently motivated by polemical goals.

In appreciation of the improvement in Nabokov's poetry and recognition of the emergence of a distinctive artistic voice, the reviews of *The Return of Chorb* are generally positive. Significant, however, is the generic division evident in Nabokov criticism. As a foretaste to the secondary role the assessment of poetry would take in the study of Nabokov's oeuvre, comment upon the twenty-four poems of *The Return of Chorb* is exceedingly modest in comparison to that expended on the fifteen short stories of the volume.

A response there was, however. Almost immediately upon its publication, A. Savel'ev reviewed *The Return of Chorb* in the final, December 31 edition of *Rul'* in 1929. After an enthusiastic discussion of the stories, Savel'ev turned his attention to the poems included in the volume. Before making his exceptionally positive remarks, however, Savel'ev proposed an emotional distinction between Nabokov's lyric and prose voices. This bifurcation is highly suggestive of the one which later critics would posit in claiming a fundamental division in Nabokov's oeuvre between his personal Russian poetry and his more impersonal English prose. Savel'ev contrasted the atmosphere of optimism and happiness that presided over the stories with the presence of personal emotion, the exile's 'quiet sigh,' found in the poems. For Savel'ev, this was anything but a criticism of Nabokov's 'wonderful, profoundly sincere [and] melodious poems.' The first review of *The Return of Chorb* concluded with a crescendo of praise for the formal and thematic perfection of Nabokov's poetry which acknowledges innovations introduced to Nabokov's poetry: 'Nabokov's poems are good not only in their singular and, in relation to this, unusual clarity and limpidity of form – in the domain of form many are at present successful; what makes them priceless rarities is that every one of his poems is, in terms of conception and plot, a completed work replete with [its own] subject matter' (Savel'ev 3). With the poetry of *The Return of Chorb*, Nabokov had attempted to develop a mode of poetry which introduced a brief though pronounced narrative dimension. In terms of Savel'ev's review, this innovation in Nabokov's poetry was unusually successful. Savel'ev thus provides another important example of a critic whose positive assessment of Nabokov's poetry was predicated upon willingness to concede the specificity of Nabokov's artistic goals and to tailor his criticism to this poetics rather than revert to forced comparison with other artists.

While Savel'ev's review validated Nabokov's explorations of the potential of short narratives within poetry, G.D. Khokhlov's assessment for *Volia Rossii* (*Will of Russia*) is indicative of the danger these innovations harboured for the reception of Nabokov's poetry. Criticism of Nabokov's artistry would keep parallel step to his intensifying interest in extended narrative and increasingly voice critical assessment framed in terms of extended prose forms, in particular, the novel form. Nabokov's poetry would be read as the verse of the innovative prose writer – and, in particular, novelist – Nabokov. This tendency is to be seen in Khokhlov's review of *The Return of Chorb*, where both the stories and poems are implicitly considered as indicants of the artistic style and ability which is best perceived in Nabokov's novels. The review of a collection of short stories and poems begins with the sentence: 'In order to see Nabokov in his full stature, it is necessary to read his novels' (Khokhlov 190). It is then immediately observed that *The Return of Chorb*, too, is an excellent introduction to an appreciation of the development of Nabokov's style, manner, and principles regarding the representation of reality. While the stories of this collection are accorded examination in the creation of a statement about Nabokov's artistic sensibility (for Khokhlov, Nabokov is a writer for whom the world is interesting on account of its outcasts and not in and of itself), the poems, which are not so easily fitted into this statement, receive cursory, purely formal and impressionistic, treatment. Khokhlov notes that Nabokov's verses are distinguished by the same care and precision in the use of language as his prose. Unfortunately, in Khokhlov's opinion, this quality of language – appropriate as it is to prose – produces an effect of excessive directness and dryness in poetry. Despite the formal accuracy and imagery of Nabokov's poetry, for Khokhlov, the effect created is ultimately one of rhythmic prose. In parallel to the unspoken assumption that Nabokov's poetry is an appendage to his prose, then, Khokhlov's review appends a non-specified assessment of Nabokov's verse which, without examining any individual poems, renders a verdict on Nabokov's poetry in its entirety. A universalizing pronouncement is allowed to substitute for specific analysis.

The review of *The Return of Chorb* published in *Sovremennye zapiski* (*Contemporary Annals*) by M. Tsetlin, while illustrative of the urge to read Nabokov's poetry through the lens of his prose, is indicative of still another critical blind spot born of Nabokov's increasing familiarity to readers and critics as a novelist. In confronting his émigré readership with indisputable innovations in prose and poetry, and as a consequence of his growing fame, assessment of Nabokov was increasingly framed in terms of bitter polemics regarding the phenomenon Nabokov. Tsetlin's review, although in general objective in tone, displays both tendencies. After briefly staking out his position with regards to the polemics revolving around Nabokov's 'non-Russianness' – a debate prepared for by Bakhrakh's review of *The Cluster* discussed above – Tsetlin demonstrates his urge to participate in the compartmentalizing of Nabokov's oeuvre into categories of genre and mode – short story or novel, poetry or prose. In commenting upon the stories included in *The Return of Chorb*, Tsetlin's assessment is grounded on the premise that they are, as venues for literary experimentation, somewhat weaker than Nabokov's novels. Continuing the reductivist, compartmentalizing logic, the discussion of the poetry is reduced to one sentence: 'Sirin's (Nabokov's) verses are less interesting and original than his prose' (Tsetlin 530). As weak as it is in concrete analysis, Tsetlin's review at least seems to have been concerned with examining Nabokov as a literary phenomenon. The same cannot be said of Georgii Ivanov and his infamous attack on Nabokov in his omnibus review of *Mary*, *King, Queen, Knave, The Defense*, and *The Return of Chorb* for the Paris journal *Chisla* (*Numbers*). Ivanov's deluge of *ad hominem* abuse was personally motivated and contains little reasoned critical assessment.[3] Nabokov's poems are dismissed here as 'simply vulgar' and then slightingly compared to a stream of second-rate versifiers. As a noteworthy, émigré assessment of Nabokov's poetry, the sole moment of interest in Ivanov's 'review' is its reference to secondary subjects of his vitriol, those critics who praised Nabokov on other occasions. Rather transparently, Ivanov's ire is raised as much by the unnamed critic who declared Nabokov 'an exceptional master of verse' (Ivanov 235) as by Nabokov's poetry itself. Interesting as well is the observation that Ivanov's review displays, albeit *in extremis*, the structural weaknesses of much émigré criticism of Nabokov, in particular, in reference to his poetry – the tendency to read Nabokov as fundamentally a novelist, to subject his work to assessment in terms of established models illustrated in unsubstantiated comparisons with other writers, and finally to present criticism in the service of tendentious polemics rather than critical enlightenment.

The next account of the poetry in *The Return of Chorb* to be examined here is one written in the context of a short article entitled 'Notes on Verses' by Gleb Struve for *Rossiia i slavianstvo* (*Russia and Slavdom*). Although non-polemical in tone and execution, Struve's article is nonetheless to be seen in the context of the literary polemics which gave rise to Ivanov's review discussed above. A measured and comprehensive critic, Struve seems to have been concerned to provide support for the young Nabokov besieged by the influential critic Georgii Adamovich and the circle of writers surrounding him. Struve offers analysis of Nabokov's poetry in direct contrast to the group of young 'Parisian Poets' associated with Adamovich and Ivanov. And while later discussion by Struve of Nabokov's poetry would be highly influential in fostering a negative opinion of it, in his review of 1930, Struve is exceptionally positive. Here Struve credits the central difference between Nabokov and the 'Parisian Poets' to the specificity of Nabokov's poetic voice, which is infused with a fundamental optimism and vitality. Opposed to the inertia and ennui of the 'Parisian Poets' discussed in the first portion of his article is the acuity of poetic vision felt in Nabokov's poetry: 'Clear-sightedness and perspicacity are the premises of Sirin's poetic relationship with the world' (Struve 1930b, 3). Struve's reference to the ocular aspect of Nabokov's poetry is not accidental; he explicitly isolates for comment a sensual, above all visual, quality in the verse of *The Return of Chorb* with which he correctly emphasizes the unusual plasticity of Nabokov's poetry. On the basis of a couple of representative examples, Struve quickly establishes the unique combination of formal perfection, linguistic virtuosity, and thematic interest which distinguishes Nabokov's poetry for him. It is above all Nabokov's enchanting mastery of versification which reveals his genius. Reversing the usual format of critical approach to Nabokov's poetry – from prose to verse – Struve suggests such features of Nabokov's poetry as the multiplicity of his creative cast along with the assurance, freedom, and lightness in which he approaches any topic as the characteristics which unmistakably reveal him to be a great writer: 'Astounding is the unusual multiformity of Sirin's artistic temperament, the unusual confidence and the light and courageous freedom with which he approaches any theme and compels any material to heed him' (Struve 1930b, 3).

C. Nal'ianch's review of *The Return of Chorb* for *Za svobodu* (*For Freedom*) on 4 August 1930 is the final assessment to be discussed here of a collection of poetry published during Nabokov's period of European exile. A mixed review of questionable analytical worth, Nal'ianch's brief discussion is nonetheless of interest as a telling illustration of the difficulties Nabokov's artistry posed for critics poorly equipped to recognize and evaluate its specificity. Nal'ianch's opinions are especially illustrative as he used the pages of *Za svobodu* less to discuss the qualities and weakness of the stories and poetry of *The Return of Chorb* than to advance his own quixotic views on the course and future trajectory of the Nabokov phenomenon. Intent on offering an overview of Nabokov's artistic development, Nal'ianch launched his review with a two-sentence summation of Nabokov's beginnings as a poet: 'About seven years ago Sirin (Nabokov) released several small collections of verse. On these poems is to be felt the considerable influence of Fet; they do not sparkle with originality, nor are they rich with profundity, interesting images, diverting themes' (Nal'ianch 3). Apart from the fact that Nabokov did not release 'several' collections of verse in 1923, the facile comparison to Fet is a strategy known to criticism of Nabokov's verse in the absence of analysis. Following this opening, Nal'ianch proceeds through a shortened version of the established critical narrative of the course of Nabokov's artistic development, an evolution claimed to have progressed through and out of the poetry of youth into the maturing prose of three novels.[4] Important to this narrative are the conflicting and mutually excluding roles played by poetry and prose. Supported with a statement such as 'in prose Sirin is a much greater innovator and revolutionary than in verse' (Nal'ianch 3), Nal'ianch indicates that he – like many future critics – places poetry in oppositional rather than complementary relation to Nabokov's prose. The assumed adversarial role of the two modes is understood as axiomatic, and is illustrated with reference to the critical debate then revolving around Nabokov: 'About Sirin (Nabokov), as with every talented writer who writes both prose and verse, people love to dispute about the nature of his true calling – poetry or prose' (Nal'ianch 3). Without immediately offering an opinion himself, Nal'ianch indicates that most critics welcomed Nabokov's conversion to short stories and novels. Indeed, in seeming refinement on this critical judgment, Nal'ianch suggests that *The Return of Chorb* proves that Nabokov is talented in the writing of both poetry and short stories. This Solomonic pronouncement is not intended as engagement with the topic, however, but rather as an opening for a critical innovation of Nal'ianch's own. For the critic, the issue of quality in Nabokov's writing is not one of prose or poetry, but of length. Nal'ianch's thesis is that whether in prose or poetry, Nabokov is at his best in short narrative modes; the short, lyric poems are better than the 'epic' poems and 'the author of the short stories in the collection *The Return of Chorb* is incomparably superior to the author of the novels *Mary*, *The Defense* and *King, Queen, Knave*.' Nal'ianch's subsequent explanation of this unusual assessment is revelatory of his distance from an understanding of Nabokov's lyric voice. Nal'ianch felt that in extended narratives, Nabokov was too easily enthralled by formal matters, narrative technique, and linguistic virtuosity, that 'the writer becomes a slave of trifles and details.' While in shorter forms, this enslavement to technique and detail had a formal function, in longer forms it revealed Nabokov's fatal superficiality, his lack of concern for the 'questions of being.' Indeed, for Nal'ianch, this perceived shortcoming was a prime concern: 'In this superficiality lies the main danger for the successful development of Nabokov's oeuvre.' In attempting in this short review to provide an overview of Nabokov's development up to 1930, Nal'ianch demonstrated, both with his factual errors and a facile comparison to Fet, lack of serious consideration of Nabokov' poetry, despite a certain generosity of predisposition. The placement of poetry in opposition to prose in the reading of Nabokov's development as a writer is likewise inadequate as an approach to the scholarly study of his poetry. Finally, the detection, but misidentification, of the importance of 'trifles and details' in Nabokov's poems and prose, while overlooking the connection of these very trifles to the demanded 'questions of being,' indicates that the nature of the sensibility expressed in verse has not been appreciated. It is precisely Nabokov's attention to the 'trifles and details' of life, and their expression in a manner attentive to linguistic inventiveness and narrative technique, which distinguishes Nabokov's lyric voice and reveals the indebtedness of the magic of Nabokov's prose to his poetry.

As Nabokov published no further collections of poetry during his European émigré period, the opportunity for sustained reflection regarding his poetry was limited. Comment on Nabokov the poet continued to rise in various incidental pieces, though such references were almost exclusively in the context of broader issues, such as the nature and quality of émigré Russian literature and, in particular, the future and abilities of young Russian writers in exile. These articles are of little use in assessing either Nabokov or his reception as a poet, as the references made are usually intended to support analysis, not of the writer, but of the critic's views concerning different issues.[5] Nabokov's brilliance as a prose writer, and in particular novelist, cast a long shadow which obscured his achievements in poetry for all but a few interested critics throughout the 1930s, his remaining years in Europe. His Russian poetry receded still further from the pages of émigré literary criticism upon his switch to English with *The Real Life of Sebastian Knight* and emigration from France to the United States in 1940. Moreover, Nabokov's move, not just to America but, more importantly, to the English language, undoubtedly cost him a portion of the Russian readership for his poetry. For not only were the numbers of Russian émigré readers with an interest in poetry declining with the advancement of time and the material difficulties of life in exile, but Nabokov's self-transformation into an American writer was judged by some as an expression of cultural apostasy, an abandonment of the cultural tradition which had fostered him (Andreev 1954).

Despite these important caesuras in Nabokov's career as poet and Russian writer, however, neither the publication of his final volume of poetry in European exile – *The Return of Chorb* of 1929 – nor his transposition to the Anglo-American literary system in 1940 may be regarded as a conclusion to the first, European period of Nabokov's reception as a poet. The termination of this period is best set at Gleb Struve's synoptic assessment of Nabokov the poet in his 1956 summation of the entire émigré cultural phenomenon in *Russkaia literatura v izgnanii*. Not only did Nabokov continue to write and publish isolated poems throughout the

1930s, but in 1952 he released *Poems 1929–1951*. It may only be speculated the extent to which the appearance of this volume functioned as Nabokov's conscious departure from Russian émigré literature, that Nabokov bid adieu to the émigré community with poetry, the genre with which he had introduced himself. Coming at a time when all future, original works would be written in English, the poetry of *Poems 1929–1951* turned attention once again to the genre most clearly expressive of the lyric voice at the centre of his oeuvre. The possibility of an element of leave-taking is strengthened by the central impression of nostalgia uniting the reception of Nabokov's Russian poetry after the war. Although most of the poems derived from the period before the war, the reading of them was conducted in an introspective, retrospective atmosphere where attention again seems as much directed at the cultural environment from which they stemmed as at the poems themselves.

The short positive review of *Poems 1929–1951* published in *Grani* (*Facets*) under the initials A.N. displays all of the hallmarks of the reception by a marginalized literary culture of Nabokov the former Russian writer and poet now living and writing as an English-language prose writer. The forlorn institutional conditions for émigré literature alluded to by the reviewer confirm the wisdom of Nabokov's difficult decision to adopt English as a language of publication. Referring to Nabokov's abandonment of his pseudonym and ironically commenting upon the relative limits of the émigré readership, the reviewer simultaneously notes that Nabokov the poet is less well known and that this may be as a result of his strengths as a prose writer. It is also observed that Nabokov is a 'difficult' poet, one whose 'astounding' gift in composition combines an accumulation of finely rendered images into intricate, authentic poems (A.N. 179). Although several of the themes of Nabokov's poetry are indicated, the emphasis of this nostalgic review is placed on the topic of displacement from Russia and Russian culture. The review concludes by stating that the publisher of this volume of poetry has provided the Russian reader with a wonderful gift.

A further, more substantial review of *Poems 1929–1951* by Ekatarina Tauber, which appeared three years later in *Vozrozhdenie* (*Rebirth*), is mixed in its assessment of Nabokov's poems. Like the previous review, Tauber's is expressive of profound concern for the maintenance of émigré Russian culture – in particular, poetry – and is thus above all occupied with the thematic field of Nabokov's poetry. Tauber renders Nabokov the indirect compliment of referring to the specificity of his poetic voice – absent from this review are the comparisons to other earlier poets or the superfluous suggestions of influence: 'And that particular approach to the theme [of

Russia] renders the collection of poems both incisive and unique. The same may be said of his manner of writing. In every poem there is something particular only to Nabokov' (Tauber 139). Tauber proposes that along with the theme of Russia, the themes of the double and artistic creation are central to Nabokov's poetry. In her reading of Nabokov's treatment of these themes, Tauber seems moved to a response which is both emotional and moral. Sympathetic to the depths of Nabokov's perceived feelings for Russia, Tauber nevertheless castigates him for the egocentricity of his approach; Nabokov is rebuked for his presumed lack of interest in the Russian people and their suffering and his concern only for his own memories. Tauber's last critical observation concerns 'la lucidité' she perceives in Nabokov's poetry; the final comment of the review itself, however, is devoted to a personal emotional response and indicative less of her reading of Nabokov's poetry than an interpretation of a troubled age: 'And you close his book with a heavy feeling of fear for our impoverished epoch, for the fate of the world and for the fate of that which is dearest to us – poetry' (Tauber 41). In both of the above discussed reviews of *Poems 1929–1951*, then, Nabokov's poetry is discussed primarily as a vehicle for comment on the state of Russian culture and only secondarily as artistic achievement. Perception of 'la lucidité' of Nabokov's verse is clouded by ill-defined fear for the age.

That the early to mid-1950s marked the waning of a once vibrant émigré community was indicated in more than the release of the final volume of Nabokov's unpublished Russian verse and the nostalgically framed response which received it. The passing of the period and community was still more clearly signalled with the publication of retrospective assessments by the important participants and observers of the émigré phenomenon – Georgii Adamovich and Gleb Struve. In 1955, Adamovich, the famous émigré critic and former foe of Nabokov's from the literary polemics of the 1930s, published his collection of essays *Одиночество и свобода* (*Odinochestvo i svoboda / Loneliness and Freedom*), which included a full essay on Nabokov wherein Adamovich attempted to come to terms with the artistic complexity of the Nabokov phenomenon. Although Adamovich's essay is mainly concerned with Nabokov's prose writing and its relationship to the Russian literary tradition, and in this sense conforms to the by then established trend of separating Nabokov's poetic oeuvre from his prose, Adamovich does offer a series of comments on Nabokov's poetry which indicate high critical estimation. In seeking to place Nabokov's poetry within a literary tradition, Adamovich suggests that Nabokov 'is, without doubt, the only authentic émigré poet who has studied Pasternak and learned something from him' (Adamovich 1955,

222). Adamovich sees in Nabokov's poetry the same rush and accumulation of words and images which characterizes Pasternak's poetry. For Adamovich, Nabokov's poetry revels in verbal innovation and combination and disparages the search for concision and simplicity. Despite having isolated supposed links to Pasternak, Adamovich makes no attempt to place him in the context of any specific school or trend, Russian or otherwise. Indeed, regarding possible links to the Russian poetic tradition, Adamovich suggests that Nabokov was far removed from what he identifies as 'the poetic canon established in the emigration' (Adamovich 1955, 227). Adamovich's final conclusions, however, written at a time when Nabokov was established as a major prose writer, recognize Nabokov as a poet and go so far as to indicate that Nabokov's artistic identity may be perceived in his poetry:

> However, Nabokov is a born poet, as is evident even in his search. Some of his poems are wonderful in the full sense of the word, and alone a single poem such as 'The Poets' or 'Will you leave me alone? I implore you! ...' would be enough to remove all trace of doubt in this regard. How fine they are! How astoundingly fine are the 'phosphoric rhymes' with the 'last, barely perceptible glow of Russia' on them! Here formal mastery is inseparable from feeling, the one flowing into the other. The author is clearly possessed of a complex personality and as an autobiographical document, the poem about 'Fame' is exceptionally characteristic and long; a poem in which everything appealing and confusing about Nabokov is woven into a fantastical symphony. (Adamovich 1955, 227)[6]

It is thus ironic that the final sentence from a once so powerful foe and defining voice of émigré literature should address Nabokov's poetry in a manner so in keeping with Nabokov's own aesthetic principles and thereby explicitly link Nabokov's poetry with the specificity of the sensibility it expressed: 'However, in literature as in life, there is room for contradictions of various kinds, and no principle, school or method, still less a "note," can claim a monopoly. Neither methods nor schools give life to poetry, but inner energy seeking an outlet: one has to be deaf to miss hearing it in Nabokov' (Adamovich 1955, 228). Despite Adamovich's clarion words, a certain hardness of hearing persisted.

One year later, in 1956, Gleb Struve published his study of Russian émigré literature in his seminal and still unsurpassed *Russkaia literatura v izgnanii*. In this book, Struve directed his encyclopedic knowledge of the topic to take stock of a cultural phenomenon which, although still relatively recent, had existed long enough to have developed distinctive contours of its own and which was ripe for synthesizing analysis. In his discussion of Nabokov, Struve divided his commentary into two sections – poetry and prose – and built upon both the body of critical material he had written regarding Nabokov over the years and his knowledge of the émigré reception of Nabokov. With the perspective of time and broad familiarity with émigré literature, Struve's analysis of Nabokov's poetic oeuvre posited a fundamental division between the early works, including the poetry published in various journals and the two volumes *The Cluster* and *The Empyrean Path*, and the later poetry published in *The Return of Chorb* and *Poems 1929–1951*. 'Rarely, in the context of any given poet has such an abyss existed between the poems of an early and late period as with Nabokov' (Struve 1956, 165). Struve's entire analysis is founded on this crucial caesura. The reasons for his strategic insistence on this 'abyss' later become clear, as it emerges that Struve's approach followed – and gave definitive expression to – the linear reading of Nabokov's oeuvre and development first articulated in the late 1920s. According to this reading, Nabokov's artistic course proceeded in a series of stages beginning with weak poetry, evolving into stronger poetry, and then on to its true calling in prose. Poetry is here interpreted as relevant to Nabokov, albeit primarily as a prelude to the related, though fuller prose.

Beginning with Nabokov's early poetry, Struve found little to merit positive criticism. Nabokov was conceded to have been a master of versification and capable of rendering unusual plasticity to images with his play of sound and visual acuity. Despite this evidence of mastery, the poetry of this early period was nonetheless felt to be marked by formal conservatism and overly strict adherence to the conventions of classical composition. Thematically, Nabokov's poetry from the early 1920s was at best imitative and banal and at worst sentimental and tasteless. Struve's evidence for this was based on two prime examples. For the latter charge of 'tastelessness' and even 'pretentiousness,' Struve refers to a genuinely weak poem by Nabokov, 'На смерть Блока' ('Na smert' Bloka' / 'On the Death of Blok'), a single poem which in future criticism will arise again and again in demonstration of otherwise unsubstantiated claims of vulgarity. More interesting is the poem referred to in substantiation of the claim of banality. The lines quoted are the ones brought forth by Bakhrakh in his critical review of *The Cluster*, the first assessment of Nabokov's poetry discussed above: 'Thus each trifle – we, children and poets, – / are capable of transforming into a wonder.' For Struve, these lines are a weak imitation of Blok, 'deprived of Blok's internal music and, somehow, banal and unchaste in their verbal composition' (Struve 1956, 168). Like Bakhrakh in

1923, Struve in 1956 is disinclined to see this as a thematic component in the poetic expression of Nabokov's lyric voice – a portion of Nabokov's aesthetic and ethical response to the world to be rendered into poetry.

Discussion of Nabokov's later poetry, while superficially affirmative, is ultimately guided by Struve's intriguing, though ultimately uncorroborated, thesis that Nabokov's artistic gift has its roots in parody (Struve 1956, 171). This is undoubtedly the source of his astounding array of comparisons with other poets. Nowhere does Struve's analysis suggest characteristics or principles derived solely from Nabokov's writing. The following lengthy citation provides an example of Struve's critical strategy of ever placing Nabokov's poetry in comparison with others:

> Along with Pasternak and Maiakovskii, in several of Nabokov's poems from this same collection, it is possible unmistakably to discern the voice of Khodasevich ... If one compares Nabokov's later poems with the earlier ones (1922–25) that went into his two first books or were published in newspapers, then it is of course possible to notice the change of themes, another system of images, and a new approach to the world (in the early poems, for instance, are very audible patriotic – at times sugary – and religious – obviously bookish – notes in which there is much sentimental longing for the homeland, 'birches' and polished description), though most striking is not that but the change of models. Instead of Pasternak, Maiakovskii, Khodasevich, and maybe sometimes Belyi and Mandel'shtam or even Poplavskii, who are heard behind the later poems, we find in *The Empyrean Path* in the best cases Fet and Maikov and in the worst – Ratgauz and in *The Cluster* and the later poems of the 1920s – Fet, Maikov, Shcherbina, Pushkin, Bunin, Bal'mont, Gumilev, and ... Sasha Chernyi (the poem about the 'poet-tadpole'). The early Nabokov is striking due to his skill in versification, his changeability and his failures in taste. Something about him is reminiscent of Benediktov. (Struve 1956, 166–7)

The manner in which any poet could encompass – and so quickly pass through – such a bewildering range of influences is left unremarked upon in Struve's critique, something which in itself suggests that Nabokov's poetry and poetic style are not being explicated but categorized.[7] Unlike Adamovich, moreover, who in claiming similarity to Blok nonetheless granted Nabokov the specificity of his writing, Struve's comparisons preclude – render unnecessary – serious analysis of Nabokov's poetry in its own terms.[8] The brief parenthetical reference in the above citation to Sasha Chernyi and the 'poet-tadpole' offers a convenient albeit brief example.

The fanciful anapestic poem from *The Cluster*, 'О любов, ты светла и крылата' ('O liubov', ty svetla i krylata ...' / 'O love, you are radiant and winged') (*Ssoch* I, 456–7), is indeed reminiscent of Chernyi with its whimsical comparison of a tadpole with a poet in love. Read, however, in the context of Nabokov's two-world metaphysics and his related proclivity for images of transformation (with the tadpole as a water-bound counterpart to the frequently used motif of butterflies), and, finally, mindful of the aquatic images employed by Nabokov in his influential contemporaneous study of Rupert Brooke as a poet of the otherworld, then the poem dismissed as a childish exercise in Chernyi's mode becomes a poetic vessel of potentially greater, if admittedly playful, depths. The poem may well be criticized, though preferably in the context of Nabokov's lyric oeuvre, and not simply as a touchstone of presumed influence.[9]

As questionable as Struve's critical method may have been, *Russkaia literatura v izgnanii* was influential less in terms of its categorization of Nabokov's poetry according to putative influence than with regard to another critical statement which continues to resonate through discussions of Nabokov's qualities as a poet. Building upon a comment from 1930 made in an assessment of Nabokov from *Rossiia i slavianstvo*, where he conjectured that Nabokov's move from poetry to prose was as a result of 'an absence of spontaneously singing inspiration which allowed one to think that perhaps Sirin ought to attempt prose' (Struve 1930a, 3), in 1956, Struve ventured a description of Nabokov's poetry in terms of a related though ultimately conflicting poetics of prose. Nabokov, he suggested, wrote the poetry of a prose writer:

> There are in emigration not a few people who deny that Nabokov is a poet and who value only his prose. Nabokov moved from verse to prose, although it would be wrong to say of his prose, as one may of the prose of Tsvetaeva, Osip Mandel'shtam, or Pasternak, that it is the prose of a poet. It would be perhaps more accurate to say that his poems are the poems of a prose writer. Some of his poems are wonderful (even amongst those he himself would now probably repudiate); they are capable of seizing and hypnotizing one, though in the final analysis there is something lacking in them, some element of final music. With Nabokov, there is a close relationship between prose and poetry. His poems were perfected in accordance with his mastery of the craft of story writing. (Struve 1956, 170–1)

Struve observed that the relationship between poetry and prose is close in Nabokov's artistry; his formulation, however, stresses and assumes the differentiation between the two modes of writing rather than their related-ness. Along with the steady growth in Nabokov's reputation as a writer of prose and his reduction in the amount of poetry written, this influential judgment by Struve undoubtedly contributed in casting the shape of later critical reception of Nabokov the poet. While this critical judgment has the advantage of being able to account for Nabokov's move from poetry to prose while observing legitimate appreciation for the development and progression of Nabokov's career as a whole, it does so at the risk of imply-ing that poetry was a distinct stage in Nabokov's art which he passed through and out of. As such, this view provides little room for an inter-pretation of poetry as an integral, ever present component of Nabokov's artistry and oeuvre.

With Struve's retrospective assessment of the émigré literary world and Nabokov's role in it, the first stage of Nabokov's reception as a poet was effectively closed. Renewed critical interest in Nabokov's Russian poetry would not arise again to any significant extent until after the posthumous publication of *Poems* in 1979. Unfortunately, however, and despite the fre-quency of analysis outlined above, the harvest of critical insight concern-ing Nabokov the poet remains disappointingly meagre. Although he was a visible presence as poet for both readers and critics, especially in the 1920s, criticism never developed an appropriate conceptual approach, or lan-guage, with which to address Nabokov's poetry. As a result, a predominant impression of negativity emerged from a series of reviews, all of which, paradoxically, praised the evidence of Nabokov's poetic mastery but were incapable of assimilating it according to standard models of reception. Significantly, and in strange parallel to Tolstoi's comment on families, each of the unhappy assessments of Nabokov's poetry was unhappy in its own way, with criticism being levelled in five central categories. First of all, Nabokov's poetic was tainted with the same ill-defined preciousness and evidence of 'foreignness' – expressed with the attributes 'coldness,' 'resplen-dence,' 'peacock-like,' and so on – later attributed to his prose. Secondly and in a manner literally *ad hominem*, Nabokov's poetry was claimed to suffer as a result of the weight of Nabokov's social past or, similarly, lack of authentic human experience. Thirdly, Nabokov refused acknowledg-ment of the movements, schools, trends, and symbolics of contemporary poetry; in striking contrast to this, Nabokov's poetry was derivative, based on an intimidating array of – in Struve's analysis quoted above no less than sixteen – discernible poetic influences. And finally is the fifth criticism, which developed in tandem with Nabokov's growing stature as a novelist – Nabokov wrote the poetry of a prose writer. Each of these criticisms is an appeal to external criteria of assessment; each is evidence of the inability to evaluate and normalize in a critical fashion Nabokov's poetry according to the autonomous principles of its composition and effect.

As the above overview of émigré response to Nabokov's verse reveals, greater unanimity was displayed by those reviews distinguished by their level of praise for Nabokov's poetry. These assessments are conspicuous by the absence of appeal to external criteria, and most strikingly the absence of comparison to poetic models. Rather, building upon the formal mastery conceded by even Nabokov's most virulent commentators, the positive assessments acknowledged the fundamental optimism and wonder at the world expressed by Nabokov's poetic rendering of trifles. From this arose appreciation of Nabokov's virtuosity in the command of language and imagery, the plasticity of his images, and the ability through verbal acuity to render language and description sensual. Ultimately, the uniting feature of the reviews receptive to Nabokov's poetry was their willingness, in Adamovich's sense, to lend their ear to Nabokov's poetry, to proceed from an acceptance of the nascent specificity of his lyric voice and thus develop a critical approach which engaged with the form and content of Nabokov's poetry.

Nabokov's English Poetry and the Critics

Unlike his émigré audience, which had both matured and waned in the 1920s and 1930s in concurrence with his poetry, Nabokov's English-language public was first introduced to his artistry via prose. In December 1941, Nabokov published 'Softest of Tongues' in the *Atlantic Monthly*, his first published English poem since his Cambridge efforts of twenty-one years previous. And although Nabokov would continue to publish isolated poems in journals until 1966, the second phase of reception of Nabokov as poet was based essentially on two slim volumes: first, the fourteen poems of the 1959 collection, *Poems*, and the 1970 *Poems and Problems*, a reprint of the fourteen poems of *Poems* along with thirty-nine of Nabokov's Russian poems with accompanying translations *en face*. In keeping with the slender corpus, the critical response to Nabokov's English poetry was correspondingly slight. At once regrettable and telling about this response, however, was not its lack of volume, but its inability, as witnessed in the reviews to be discussed below, to engage with the specificity of Nabokov's poetic voice without recourse to critical assumptions which hindered, rather than promoted, critical understanding. In the instance of his English-language reception, this fundamental incomprehension did not occasion negative responses, as it had with some émigré reviews of his Russian poems. Most of the reviews are benignly positive, though with a lack of critical specificity which suggests more enjoyment and formal admiration than comprehension of either the poems or their function as expressions of Nabokov's lyric voice. In announcing to Edmund Wilson the acceptance of his poem 'Softest of Tongues' with the *Atlantic Monthly*, Nabokov reported his displeasure at having his poem judged according to its 'sincerity.'[10] Although the purportedly 'amusing,' 'charming' quality of Nabokov's poetry would frequently be cited, a clearer influence would shape the taste of his English-language critics. Nabokov's poetry was read in the overpowering presence of his prose. Indeed, the very poetic quality of his prose, in part, predetermined the reception of his prose, without critics indicating any consciousness of the debt Nabokov's prose owed to his poetry. Edmund Wilson, for instance, in praising *The Real Life of Sebastian Knight*, Nabokov's novel written in English while still in European exile though published in the United States in 1941, would emphasize Nabokov's brilliance as a poet in English prose: 'I haven't really told you why I like your book so much. It is all on a high *poetic* level, and you have succeeded in being a first-rate poet in English. It has delighted and stimulated me more than any new book I have read since I don't know what' (*NWL* 56; emphasis in original). Paradoxically, this is commendation of a sort but rarely granted to Nabokov the poet.

   Poems appeared in 1959 in the shadow of the spectacularly successful *Lolita* – along with six other prose works – a circumstance which both created an expectant audience for Nabokov's less-known poetry and pre-established expectations for the poetry of such a writer as the creator of *Lolita*, as is clearly indicated in the critical response. Both James Wright's and Anthony Hecht's prompt reviews of *Poems*, for instance, make sparing reference to Nabokov's name and by then broad oeuvre to immediately establish connection to – in Wright's case – the author of 'such novels as *Lolita* and *Pnin*' and – in Hecht's – 'the author of a particularly celebrated novel' (Wright 378; Hecht 593). The interest in *Lolita*, moreover, seems as well to have extended from authorship to prurient expectations. Perhaps with the unusualness of *Lolita*'s central theme in mind, both brief reviews observe the putative strangeness of Nabokov's subject matter, with Wright referring to 'the very monstrosities which Mr. Nabokov likes to describe' and Hecht claiming that 'it is occasionally Mr. Nabokov's pleasure to take a particularly grisly subject and write about it in tripping anapests.' Apart from the phrasing of both critics, which suggests the repetition of themes at best rare in Nabokov's poetry, Hecht goes so far as to claim an authorial stance which is to be interpreted out of these supposed thematic occurrences in Nabokov:

'In every case, he stands at a polite remove from experience, and even when he deals with violence or madness or the grotesque it is always with flawless social poise' (Hecht 594). In turning from the implied broad themes of Nabokov's poetry and writing in general, both critics refer to the one Nabokov poem which was to be frequently singled out exclusively for praise – 'An Evening of Russian Poetry.' But while Hecht views the poem in thematic terms as 'touching and funny, dealing lightly with the failure of communication' (Hecht 594), Wright sees it from a linguistic perspective as 'an inspiring gift of shameless music, a heartening devotion to words themselves' (Wright 378). Positive in essence, neither description does justice to a complex poem about poetic artistry, but also about the inexpressible pains and contradictions of exile from one's language and cultural past. Of the two notices concerning *Poems*, Wright's is ultimately the more positive, with its candid admission of unparalleled enjoyment in Nabokov's poetry: 'In any case, I doubt if I have read in a long time a book of poems that gave me so much sheer pleasure in the experience of being entertained' (Wright 378). This is fine praise, though its effect is dampened by the suspicion that Wright's revelry in Nabokov's 'joy of words that glitter and jump delightedly all over hell's half-acre' (Wright 378) is incapable of proceeding past this important and undisputed component of Nabokov's poetry to more complex dimensions of meaning which, upon closer examination, are revealed to be most fully apparent in his poetry. Ultimately, upon rereading, both reviews encourage the misgiving that the then contemporary critical assessment of Nabokov the prose writer as exclusively a stylist and wordsmith was being applied to Nabokov the poet, thereby obscuring appreciation of the thematic depths of his poetry and precluding recognition of the scope and quality of his lyric voice.

Apart from the professional reviews accorded Nabokov's *Poems* in the *Hudson Review* and *Poetry* were the notices contained in the broader-based venues. Like their counterparts in the academic journals, these reviews indicate a modest span of response ranging from guarded admiration to puzzled censure. Nowhere is there apparent a confident assessment of Nabokov's poetic voice which is independent of assumptions derived from Nabokov's prose. The closest suggestion of the specificity of Nabokov's poetic voice comes in a review entitled 'Voices That Speak in Verse' by the poet Philip Booth for the *New York Times Book Review*, where the reviewer expresses admiration for the 'literate wit' and 'offbeat perception' of Nabokov's verse (Booth 6). Chad Walsh's review for the *New York Herald Tribune Book Review*, while seemingly positively minded, displays the inability of criticism to formulate a response to a poet identified foremost as the author of *Bend Sinister* and *Lolita*, but 'who now reveals himself as a poet with a sure and sometimes moving touch' (Walsh 4). The Nabokov being reviewed by Walsh is not identified even potentially as a poet with long-standing experience and a developed poetic voice, but as an author who 'appears to write poetry as *a byproduct of an active life*, and his verses have the charm of the intermittently kept journals of a highly civilized man' (Walsh 4; emphasis added). The clearest statement indicative of a critical inability to acknowledge Nabokov as a poet, and from thence to read his verse as the articulation of an independent poetic voice, is contained in Charles Tomlinson's review for the *New Statesman*. The entire review, cited below, bespeaks of criticism more responsive to Nabokov's reputation as a 'slick' wordsmith than as a poet of unseen depths:

> Nabokov's *Poems* are chiefly light-weight. They have a fluency that persistently treads on the edge of over-professional facility, and yet often redeems itself by some instinctive grace. 'On Translating Eugene Onegin' and particularly 'An Evening of Russian Poetry' contain good sketches, a controlled nostalgia, a wit that isn't morbidly slick. There are good jokes in 'The Ballad of Longwood Glen,' but others again are sadly New Yorkerish whimsy. By and large, words come to him too easily for us to believe he has ever known that resistant silence from which the deeper poetry emerges. (Tomlinson 674)

Attuned to an understanding of Nabokov as an author of 'over-professional facility' for whom 'words come too easily,' Tomlinson's review is incapable of hearing the 'resistant silence' contained within Nabokov's poetry. As will be discussed in the following chapter, poems such as 'The Ballad of Longwood Glen,' to follow Tomlinson's example, indeed sound the notes of 'deeper poetry'; it is simply unheard by critics anticipating, and thus hearing only, the surface jingles of whimsy. That it was in essence whimsy which was expected from Nabokov the poet is once again confirmed by Anthony Thwaite's review, which characterizes Nabokov's poems as 'short and slight, all of them ... extremely clever, sometimes over-clever' (Thwaite 770). For Thwaite, the only poem which rises above self-serving 'slickness' – in Thwaite's repetition of the negative attribute indicated by Tomlinson – is 'An Evening of Russian Poetry.' Here, too, it is not the voice emanating from Nabokov's poetry which is being heard, but the assumptions about Nabokov the author of verbally mischievous prose.[11]

In the decade-long interlude between the publication of *Poems* in 1959 and *Poems and Problems* in 1970, two academic assessments of Nabokov's poetry appeared which complicated the somewhat superficial appreciation of Nabokov's verse efforts by tempering evaluation of the poetry with awareness of wider dimensions of Nabokov's oeuvre. Indeed, both discussions bear witness to the explicit, educating urge to familiarize an English audience with the poorly acknowledged poetic and Russian depths of Nabokov's writing, while at the same time lending legitimacy and authority to his artistry through suggested comparisons with accepted masters of the modernist canon. Given the explicating function of studies by F.W. Dupee and Andrew Field with regard to Nabokov's oeuvre – if not always his poetry itself – these assessments offer a prelude to the academic criticism which will come in the wake of Nabokov's death and the posthumous publication of *Poems* in 1979. Despite the felt intention to direct critical interest to a level beyond the sensationalism of *Lolita*, Dupee's article 'Nabokov: The Prose and Poetry of It All' of 1963 nonetheless reveals a degree of captivity to the fame of *Lolita* which coloured the assessments of Wright and Hecht, as well as Tomlinson and Thwaite.[12] Dupee introduces his discussion of the poetic dimension of Nabokov's writing through reference to the 'occasional poetry' by Humbert Humbert contained within *Lolita*. Unlike Humbert, however, Nabokov is suggested by Dupee to be very serious in his uses of poetry, although in a consoling comparison to Joyce, the English poetry itself is ultimately judged to be minor albeit interesting:

> Like that other master of prose, James Joyce, Mr. Nabokov aspired in youth to be a poet. More than Joyce did, he has continued to write verse and to fill his novels with reflections on poetry. The reflections are often of major importance; the verse – the verse in English at least – is minor, as minor as verse could be and still remain interesting. (Dupee 1965b, 133)

Nonetheless, despite the suggestion of modest expectations for Nabokov's poetry and the clear placement of it in the context of a 'master of prose,' Dupee seeks, if still superficially, to read Nabokov's poetry against the backdrop of his émigré poetry and novels. Dupee offers a brief reading of Nabokov's novel *The Gift*, with perceptive reference to important themes and motifs of Nabokov's poetics. Furthermore, Dupee extends the adjective 'great' to Nabokov's 'An Evening of Russian Poetry,' while stating in general that 'the English poems do have a peculiar miniature excellence: perfect lucidity, precise wit, the glow of a lighted candle cupped in an expert hand against the windy verse roundabout' (Dupee 1965b, 139). Finally, in taking his cue from *Pale Fire*, where Nabokov the novelist and poet were called upon, and in marked contrast to the many critics who perceived a chasm between prose and poetry, Dupee suggests that Nabokov has united the two to make 'a team' of 'the poet and novelist in him' (Dupee 1965b, 141).

The explicatory function of Dupee's writing was much expanded in 1967 with the publication of Andrew Field's *Nabokov: His Life in Art*, which, along with Page Stegner's *Escape into Aesthetics: The Art of Vladimir Nabokov* of 1966, was one of the first book-length studies of Nabokov's art. Of the two, Field's study is unquestionably the more comprehensive, drawing as it does not merely on Nabokov's English or translated works but daring to offer a broad-based assessment of not only Nabokov the novelist, but Nabokov the poet, short-story writer, dramatist, critic, translator, lepidopterist, and so on. And although Field's later scholarship was frequently cast in the light of a subsequent polemic with his object of inquiry and suffered concomitantly in terms of balance and scholarly judgment, Field is to this day to be credited with the first and longest – if not most detailed or informative – account of Nabokov's Russian and English poetry in the context of his entire oeuvre.

Given that Field in 1967 was engaged in the pioneering activity of introducing the full breadth of Nabokov's oeuvre to an English audience most familiar with *Lolita*, it is perhaps understandable that his three-chapter discussion of Nabokov's poetry is far more descriptive than analytical. The discussion of Nabokov's émigré poetry, for instance, is less an end in itself than an important element in the creation of a composite picture of Nabokov's life and artistry in European exile. As a result, despite the frequent quotation of Nabokov's poetry in Field's translation, no clear critical statement regarding the poetry itself emerges. The central critical response concerns the issue of poetic influence, a perennial topic in criticism of Nabokov's poetry. Field's defence in principle of Nabokov's right to adopt poetic models derived from nineteenth-century Russian poetry, while a confirmation of 'Nabokov's view of an art which is above the tyranny of fashion' (Field 1967, 68), likewise suggests uncritical – and thus unacceptable – concurrence with the proposition that Nabokov was in fact epigonic in his poetic creation. As has been revealed in the above review of Nabokov criticism, this is a proposition which has often been made, though never demonstrated. In Field's analysis, rather than examining the proposition, he builds upon it:

> The real problem posed by *The Empyrean Path* is not its air of antiquity so much as the extraordinary diversity of the components of that cultivated classicism. Consider, for example, poems written in the manner of both Pushkin and Tiutchev ... Add to this the influence of a third poet, the Symbolist

> Aleksandr Blok, who is equally far removed from both Pushkin and Tiut-
> chev, with certain English poets in the background, and it at once becomes
> clear that no single poet could produce poetry in so many diverse keys and
> yet still in his own voice. (Field 1967, 69)

Quite apart from the vagueness of 'certain English poets in the background,' this is less an analysis of Nabokov's work than the contestation of
established opinion. Were it even accepted as a legitimate evaluation of
Nabokov's poetry, one asks oneself how it would be made to coincide with
the proposition concerning the parodic source of Nabokov's artistry or,
more contradictorily, 'the idiosyncrasy of the poet's vision' attested in
other unidentified poems. Likewise, Field's chapter-length analysis of eight
major long poems by Nabokov in both Russian and English is to be credited as an almost unique discussion of Nabokov's poetry from across his
oeuvre. Nonetheless, although certain themes as the return to Russia and
Nabokov's interest in the metaphysical mysteries of art and death are discussed, analysis frequently veers away from the poetry to the parallels between the poetry and Nabokov's life and writing. A composite, independent
reading of Nabokov's poetry had yet to emerge, notwithstanding the laud-
able effort to treat his verse as an important component of his oeuvre.

Despite the book-length studies of Nabokov's oeuvre by critics such as
Stegner and Field in the interregnum between the publication of *Poems*
and *Poems and Problems*, the response to the later volume continued to
bear the ballast of Nabokov's extensive and by now exceptionally famous
prose oeuvre. In 1970, the horizon of reader expectation for Nabokov's
poetry was crowded not only with *Lolita* but also *Pale Fire*, Nabokov's brilliant though controversial translation of *Eugene Onegin*, and most recently,
in 1969, the culmination of Nabokov's artistry and reputation, *Ada*. The
ripples and currents emanating from these works, as well as the persistent
tidal pull of an accumulated critical assessment which classified Nabokov
as a writer of metafiction, are all felt in the reviews to *Poems and Problems*.
Marianne K. Hultquist's brief comment on *Poems and Problems* is indicative of this trend: 'Although it is slyly deceptive, *Poems and Problems* emphasizes the deception and artifice of which Nabokov is capable both
through the translations of the Russian poems and the array of chess problems – a sort of metaphor for the chop-logic that characterizes fictional
worlds' (Hultquist 271). As a result, although some of the reviews are well-
meaning, all reveal limited comprehension of Nabokov's poetry – in, at
least one case, openly admitted – and in some cases misreading.

Howard Nemerov's review for the *New York Times Book Review* is marked by a tone of bemused puzzlement in the face of the chess problems and the Russian poems with translations. Despite the positive reference to three unquoted, unanalyzed English poems, Nemerov reveals that, for him, the poems are to be received as a curio produced by a great writer, but of little lasting interest. Indeed, proceeding from this perception, Nemerov erroneously suggests a similar degree of flippancy on Nabokov's part in writing, translating, and publishing them: 'Maybe it will be best to regard this book as a sort of souvenir for the author's many readers, the record of some diversions of a master' (Nemerov 5). Thus, out of an inability to assimilate the poems, either individually or within Nabokov's oeuvre, they are relegated to the periphery of his writing as a diversion. The reviews solicited one year later by the *Listener* and *London Magazine* were occupied almost exclusively with the eighteen chess problems included at the end of *Poems and Problems*. Despite the limitations of this specific focus, forays were made into assessment of Nabokov's poetry. In the absence of principles of critical analysis appropriate to poetry, much less Nabokov's poetry, however, these appraisals quickly fell back onto external criteria of assessment. Writing in *London Magazine*, Dickins contributes little more than to suggest that the poems 'possess an elegance similar to that of the chess-problems, including the wit and technical expertise' (Dickins 158); Wyndham likewise compares Nabokov's English poems to chess problems, while also imputing a negatively freighted sense of verbal trickery to Nabokov's writing of poetry: 'I can see some slight resemblance between Nabokov's problems and his *New Yorker* poems, which are full of witty ingenuities and cunningly planted shocks, slyly forcing the vernacular into a classic mode and refurbishing the banal with baroque elaboration' (Wyndham 116). According to this review, Nabokov's English verse is little more than the deceptive adornment of banality in classic poetic form – an advantage in chess problems but a deficiency in poetry.

The remaining reviews of *Poems and Problems*, while they promise greater professional competence in judging poetry, are little more successful in delivering an informed response directed at Nabokov's poetry rather than the author of *Lolita* or a controversial translation of *Eugene Onegin*. Indicative of the scope of Nabokov's familiarity to a mass audience not usually captivated by poetry, much less translated poetry, *Time* published one of the first reviews of the collection. Under the title 'Drinker of Words,' John Skow offered a mixed review of the Russian and English poetry, while constructing an argument presenting Nabokov according to the persona criticism had constructed for him as a cunning but ultimately frivolous and pedantic wordsmith, 'an expert poet' intoxicated by his own skills as 'a pleasing and self-pleased illusionist.' In this negatively framed variation of the image of author as metafictional wordsmith, Nabokov is rendered in an 'intoxicated' metaphor as 'primarily ... a prodigious drinker of language who does not always hold his words well' (Skow 68). The first quarter of the review opens with a discussion of Nabokov's English translations of his Russian poems that is reduced to the critic's dispute of Nabokov's use of a single word – caprifole for *zhimolost'* – an example meant to prove that the poet was capriciously obscure in his use of language. And although the original Russian poems 'are generally good, sometimes remarkable,' the unanalysed 'translations are generally flawed,' albeit in terms of unspecified criteria. Likewise, although an undetermined number of the unnamed English poems are judged to be 'splendid, of the high quality of the long poem in *Pale Fire*' (Skow 68), little concrete reference to individual poems is made, apart from the valued 'An Evening of Russian Poetry.' In a strange echo back to Nabokov's émigré reception, Skow praises the manipulator of form, while criticizing the poet. Nabokov's émigré critics occasionally accused him of the 'peacock-like' quality of his poetry; here, in Skow's review, the purported fault resides, essentially, in being 'peacock-like' in two languages: 'As a poet he is a master, divisively, sometimes awkwardly stretched between two land-mass languages. There are times when he appears as a provincial linguistic pedant. At other times he is an over-refined rhymester ...' (Skow 67).

The review from the *Hudson Review* by Richmond Lattimore, although critically the most sound, was also marked by a perception of Nabokov the persona and personality that coloured the reading of his poetry. Concluding his review with a positively intended citation from 'An Evening of Russian Poetry,' Lattimore balances his reading of this particular poem against a contrary understanding of the author with a comment that hinges on the 'nevertheless' of the final clause: 'Always the one-upman, Nabokov patronizes his imaginary audience and his reader: this poem is, nevertheless, mellow, beautiful, and wise' (Lattimore 508). Nevertheless, the review is a brief though serious appraisal of Nabokov's poems, albeit one which indicates uncertainty and thus seems incapable of a comprehensive reading of his poetic work, even in terms of the reduced number of poems offered in *Poems and Problems*. The opening portion of the two-part review deals with Nabokov's Russian poems and indicates awareness of, though lack of familiarity with, the body of verse behind this selection. The theme of nostalgia for Russia and childhood is noted, and the English translations criticized. The translation analysis is framed in the context of a counter-position to Nabokov's well-known views on translation and is, although exclusively negative and brief, supported with examples. The second section of the review, which deals with the English poetry, is more positive: 'In most of the English-composed poems (but not in the unaccountable "Ballad of Longwood Glen"), the awkwardness [of the translations] vanishes. Nabokov's virtuosity in English is manifest from his prose, tiresome as that can sometimes be' (Lattimore 507). Here too, however, praise is not only unsupported with examples, it is qualified. 'The Ballad of Longwood Glen' is deemed 'unaccountable,' and the superfluously referred to prose is judged 'tiresome' at times. Little more is revealed than that Lattimore is mystified by 'The Ballad of Longwood Glen,' a poem which will be later discussed as representative of Nabokov's lyric voice.

Nonetheless, Lattimore ultimately admitted that 'Ode to a Model' had long since charmed him and that his enjoyment of 'An Evening of Russian Poetry' was unreserved. The anonymous reviewer for the *Times Literary Supplement*, on the contrary, was unstinting in his censure. Starting from the premise that Nabokov 'is primarily a novelist,' the reviewer constructs out of selected quotes a 'straw-man poet' guilty of bad translations and bad English poems. Ultimately, it becomes clear that the target is not simply a novelist who, in presenting his poetry, is engaged in 'higher games, charades, impersonations, the evocation of the ghost of the author when he was young and somebody else' but Nabokov himself as the type of artist he is assumed to be. Here, it is the frivolous, gaming persona who is the object of attack and his poetry merely the instrument of attack: 'As with Joyce, the true poetry – i.e. the subtle and various exploitation of language to the end of expressing complex states of feeling and thinking – is reserved for the novels, where Nabokov's somewhat dated rhythms are justified by the ironic structures that surround them. You can always trust a murderer for a fancy style, says Humbert Humbert, and one may add to murderer pedant, fanatic, obsessive' (Anon. 1972, 984).

Konstantin Bazarov's brief review for *Books and Bookmen* retains the censorious tone of the *Times Literary Supplement* review, although here it is modified and the source of critical purchase on Nabokov's poetry and literary persona shifted from *Lolita* to Nabokov's translation of *Eugene Onegin*. In constructing his response to Nabokov's poetry on the basis of his controversial theory of translation practice, Bazarov returns to the criticism offered by John Skow in his review from *Time* the previous year, explicitly repeating and intensifying the central critique of that assessment. Using as an entrance point the quote from Nabokov's poem 'On Translating

Eugene Onegin' that Skow had ended his review with, Bazarov then picks up the very example of the translated word 'caprifole' (for *zhimolost'*) from 'The Rain Has Flown,' which Skow had addressed in documenting his criticism of Nabokov's self-translations. Throughout his review, Bazarov is more concerned with confronting the 'whole series of different problems about Nabokov both as a translator of his own and other people's work,' and less with Nabokov 'as an original creative writer' (Bazarov xii). As such, Bazarov's comments address neither Nabokov's Russian nor English versions of the poems *qua* poems but as unelucidated examples of a failed theory of translation. The hesitancy – by no means limited to Bazarov – in discussing Nabokov as a poet becomes clearer. For Bazarov, Nabokov is 'an intellectual puzzle-maker producing artefacts which are all clever construction and stylistic acrobatics' (xii). Only in the final paragraph of his assessment does Bazarov perfunctorily admit the possibility that the thematic concerns of Nabokov's poetry might entail a qualification of this all too common perception of Nabokov as literary gamester: '... the "tenderness" of which he often so apparently *inappropriately* speaks is a very real feature of much of his Russian poetry' (Bazarov xii; emphasis added). While unidentified later Russian poems are referred to as 'very fine indeed,' the later English poems are uncomprehendingly dismissed without analysis as 'in general much slighter, mere lighthearted squibs' (Bazarov xii). As with Skow (yet again), the sole positive reference in Bazarov's review comes in the final line to the poem 'An Evening of Russian Poetry.'

Common to all of the above reviews is a failure simply to read the poems for what they express themselves or for their parallels – formal or thematic – to Nabokov's prose. Instead, analysis of Nabokov's poems became an opportunity to stake out a position in the various critical debates that Nabokov's artistic oeuvre seems to have provoked – whether from theories of translation to the quality of his prose. Given this secondary emphasis, it is perhaps unsurprising that so little reference was made to concrete poems, apart from the repeated positive reference to 'An Evening of Russian Poetry.' This, too, seems witness to the thematic uncertainty Nabokov's poetry confronted readers with. Supportive of this suspicion, and startling in its contrast to the emphasis of some of the émigré critics, not a single mention is made to possible models or influences for Nabokov's poetry. Nabokov's renown as a fiercely independent artist seems to have reached the reception of his poetry, albeit at the price of an almost total inability of the critics to classify him other than in terms of a polemic interpretation of his artistic singularity as a prose writer.

Before concluding this survey of the second stage of critical response to Nabokov's poetry, a few remarks are owed to a single study which contradicted the general trend of English-language criticism of Nabokov's poetic work – Naomi Clark's dissertation 'The Jewel of a Bluish View: An Introduction to the English Poems of Vladimir Nabokov' of 1974. As Clark's work remained unpublished, it had little opportunity to affect Nabokov criticism. Nonetheless, her analysis offers an example of the type of scrutiny possible, though still lacking, in the history of Nabokov criticism. Clark's approach is determined by her acceptance of Nabokov as a poet deserving of serious consideration. Hence, in the lengthy, detailed analyses of individual poems contained in her study, Clark proceeds from the assumption that Nabokov's qualities as a poet extend far beyond that of a practitioner of 'light' or 'humorous' verse. The quality of Clark's approach includes as well her extensive efforts to draw parallels between Nabokov's verse and his prose, without compromising the specificity of his poetry. As Clark's focus is primarily on the explication of Nabokov's misunderstood or neglected poems, she does not strive towards the articulation of an encompassing poetic style or aesthetic which could be said to embrace all of Nabokov's writing. Her emphasis is placed more on the individual works than the principles which unite them. Nonetheless, in her readings of the poems, she correctly identifies such important central values of Nabokov's poetry as his fundamental optimism of approach to life and experience, the validation of plasticity and perspicacity in poetic imagery, the conquering of time through art, the function of parody in Nabokov's poetry, and the centrality of love to his verse and artistry. Although it does not include substantial consideration of Nabokov's Russian verse, Clark's study has the distinction of being the sole sustained, positive assessment of Nabokov's English poetry.

Nabokov's Russian Poetry and the Academics

The third stage in the history of the critical reception of Nabokov's poetry is in one respect a return to the issues and concerns of the first, émigré assessment of Nabokov's verse. Like the émigré reviewers of the 1920s and '30s, the Western university-based critics of the 1980s and early '90s are concerned primarily with Nabokov's Russian verse production. Nabokov's English poetry remains outside the purview of analysis. Here the similarity ends, however, for although the object of analysis remained the same, the context in which Nabokov was read was radically different. With the publication of each new volume of poetry, the earlier generation of reviewers thrashed out an opinion as contemporary readers of the emerging literary phenomenon of Nabokov in the pages of their various journals and newspapers; the later generation of critics discussed Nabokov's poetry in response to the retrospective and posthumously published volume of Nabokov's poetry, *Poems*, with the advantage of critical understanding of the full trajectory of Nabokov's oeuvre. And while the émigré critics read into Nabokov's poems their concerns for Russian literature in exile, the later critics were occupied with the character of a previously scarcely acknowledged facet of Nabokov's work. In this respect, the third stage of reception is essentially a university enterprise, with academic critics launching not simply an assessment but a *rediscovery* of a portion of Nabokov's oeuvre occluded by tremendous success in prose. And while the studies of this period are distinguished by exceptionally high quality and professionalism, they were characterized by the dual task of, firstly, reintroducing Nabokov's poetry to an academic audience largely unaware of its existence, much less scope, and, secondly, critically articulating a space for poetry in the oeuvre of a writer known for, and critically defined on the basis of, his – above all English – prose.

It may only be conjectured why the first three comprehensive critical responses to the challenge presented to Nabokov studies by the publication of *Poems* were completed in languages other than English, the language of Nabokov's fame as a novelist and the considerable bulk of his critical reception. The first two assessments appeared in 1980 in Russian and German soon after the publication of *Poems* in 1979. Keis Verkheil's article is entitled 'Malyi korifei russkoi poezii: Zametki o russkikh stikhakh Vladimira Nabokova' ('Russian Poetry's Minor Coryphaeus: Notes on Vladimir Nabokov's Russian Poems'). Published in self-translated form from Dutch into Russian, Verkheil's article is announced as intended for a non-specialist audience and was also almost certainly addressed to Russian 'friends' in Moscow and Leningrad who, although appreciative of Nabokov's prose, were acknowledged to know nothing of his poetry. Verkheil's article is approving of Nabokov's verse; it observes the importance played by poetry throughout Nabokov's life, suggests that poetry opens a new perspective on the transformation of the immigrant-student into a world-renowned author, proposes Nabokov's poetry as an excellent source for themes and images of his prose, and freely concedes that, even in the absence of such scholarly considerations, Nabokov's *Poems* makes for excellent reading. Despite these positive introductory remarks, for Verkheil, Nabokov is a 'minor poet': 'he is not an innovator, not the voice of a particular tradition, but a person who, inspired by the example of others, sometimes achieved something startling in verse form' (Verkheil 139). In addressing the thematic interests of Nabokov's verse, Verkheil immediately turned to the theme of the 'other-world' introduced by Véra Nabokov to Nabokov criticism in the context of his poetry. In following up Véra Nabokov's suggestion, Verkheil correctly notes that Nabokov's poetic interest in metaphysical topics was not religious in any traditional sense and that it was often to be related to such motifs as butterflies, dreams, and the Nabokovian treatment of travel through time and space. Verkheil's reference to the theme of the otherworld is one of the first of many examples where analysis of Nabokov's poetry and a theme clearly present there will spearhead investigation of the same theme in the rest of Nabokov's writing. Despite the guiding impression Verkheil creates in the introductory stages of his article concerning Nabokov's status as a 'minor' poet, the article remains positive to laudatory in its comments on Nabokov's poetry and concludes that some of the best characteristics of Nabokov's writing are manifest in his verse.

Appearing in the same year as Verkheil's more feuilletonistic discussion is the first of several assessments which bring a full scholarly apparatus into the synoptic, retrospective analysis of Nabokov's poetry, as it was then known. Vsevolod Setschkareff's authoritative article, 'Zur Thematik der Dichtung Vladimir Nabokovs' ('On the Themes of Vladimir Nabokov's Poetry'), begins with a concise *Bestandsaufnahme* of Nabokov's poetic production, observing that as a poet Nabokov was little known, despite his acclaim as author and critic. A critic exceptionally well versed in both the Russian literary tradition and Nabokov's Russian and English oeuvre, Setschkareff expends little critical energy in attempting to discern and demonstrate poetic influences, other than to note that Nabokov was exceptionally knowledgeable in several poetic traditions: 'Den echten, überwältigenden Einfluß übte die Gesamtheit der russischen Dichtung aus, die Nabokov zutiefst in sich aufnahm, und sicher Keats, Poe, Browning und die französischen Symbolisten' [The real, overwhelming influence was exerted by the entirety of Russian poetry – which Nabokov absorbed deeply – and certainly Keats, Poe, Browning, and the French Symbolists (Setschkareff 70)]. Instead, Setschkareff establishes principles of a reading which foreground the authorial specificity of Nabokov's poetic oeuvre, which Setschkareff sees as forming a unity. In terms of thematics, this entails the positing of four central thematic clusters:

Nabokovs Dichtung bildet thematisch und weitgehend auch stilistisch ein Ganzes. Sie lässt sich im Grunde zwanglos auf vier große Themen zurückführen:

eine eigenartige Metaphysik, die durch den Begriff der 'Jenseitigkeit' (potu-
storonnost') gekennzeichnet ist, und in Verbindung damit die dichterische
Berufung; dann das Erinnerungsvermögen, und in Verbindung damit–Russland.
(Setschkareff 71)

[Nabokov's poetry forms a thematic and, to a large degree, stylistic totality.
Essentially, it may be divided into four main themes: an idiosyncratic metaphysics which is characterized by the concept of the 'otherworld' (potustoronnost') and, in conjunction with that, the poetic calling; then the capacity to
remember and, in conjunction with that, Russia.]

Setschkareff then economically illustrates the presence of these four themes
– the otherworld, the poetic calling, memory, and Russia – in Nabokov's
poetry in a reading which identifies the thematic relevance of important
motifs within Nabokov's poetry and which draws parallels to his prose
writing as well. In formal, stylistic terms, Setschkareff's analysis records
neither the 'peacock-like' resplendence of the émigré critics nor the putative 'formal conservativism' of later critics. The critic judges Nabokov's
poetry to have been in accord with the ideals of a 'clear and powerful' style
set forth in Nabokov's first poem of *The Empyrean Path*, 'To the Poet':

Man könnte in diesen Anweisungen eine Charakterisierung von Nabokovs
eigener Dichtung erblicken: alle seine Gedichte haben klaren Sinn (mag seine
Philosophie auch ein Geheimnis bergen), und er vermeidet offensichtlich jede
Übertriebenheit in formalen Kunstgriffen. Auf das Klangbild achtet er sehr
genau, seine Verwendung der Lautwiederholung ist besonders wirkungsvoll
und dem Sinn genau angepasst. Seine Reime vermeiden das Banale, doch
sind sie auch nicht gesucht. Er strebt nach eindrucksvollen Formulierungen,
Vergleichen, Metaphern, doch sind sie nie weit hergeholt, nicht gewollt über-
raschend. (Setschkareff 83)

[In these instructions, one could discern a characterization of Nabokov's own
poetry: all of his poems have a clear meaning (although his philosophy may
conceal a secret), and he clearly avoids all exaggeration in terms of formal
technique. He is very particular in the creation of sound patterns; his use of
assonance and alliteration is particularly effective and very closely matched
to meaning. His rhymes avoid the banal, and yet are not forced. He strives for
impressive formulations, similes, and metaphors, though they are never excessive, never purposefully surprising.]

In the history of the reception of Nabokov's poetry, Setschkareff's is the fullest, most detailed analysis undertaken. It is also the first study which attempted to assess Nabokov's poetry according to criteria immanent to Nabokov's oeuvre; perhaps for this reason, Setschkareff's assessment was also the most positive as of 1980.

If Setschkareff's appraisal was descriptive in tenor, concerned primarily with refamiliarizing his literary audience with the thematic contours of Nabokov's poetic writing, then the next comprehensive discussion of Nabokov's poetry by Laurent Rabaté was intended to place analysis of Nabokov' poetry into a larger interpretive argument concerning Nabokov's oeuvre as a whole. 'La poésie de la tradition: Étude du recueil *Stixi* de V. Nabokov' ('The Poetry of Tradition: A Study of the Collection *Stixi* by V. Nabokov'), Rabaté's retrospective discussion of Nabokov's poetry, is thus both a reassessment and a fundamental component of his central hypothesis concerning Nabokov's artistic development. While Gleb Struve identified a central distinction between Nabokov's earlier and later Russian poetry, Rabaté takes the division a step further to claim that Nabokov's entire oeuvre may be divided into two halves as a 'double duality' comprised of, first, a linguistic duality (Russian and English) and, second, a formal duality (poetry and prose). According to Rabaté, Nabokov's writing is divided into two diametrically opposed halves which conform to these linguistic and formal dualities:

Il y a chez Nabokov constitution de deux pôles; l'un, qui représente à la fois la Russie et la tradition culturelle russe, est associé à la poésie; l'autre, caractérisé par la rupture avec la patrie, avec l'héritage russe, est associé à la innovation formelle, c'est-à-dire, pour Nabokov, à la prose. (Rabaté 398)

[With Nabokov, there are two poles: one, which represents at once Russia and the Russian cultural tradition, is associated with poetry; the other, characterized by a rupture with his homeland, with the Russian heritage, is associated with formal innovation, which is to say for Nabokov, with prose.]

Rabaté interpreted the presence of this generic fault line within Nabokov's work as a portion of the alternating dominance of poetry and prose in the Russian literary tradition. Whatever its source in Rabaté's structuralist reading of Russian literary history, the contestation of this division has important consequences for Rabaté's approach to Nabokov's poetry. First of all, because he sees it as an independent half of Nabokov's oeuvre,

Rabaté is required to accord Nabokov's poetry a status and independence on par with his prose. Rabaté thus promptly suggests that Nabokov's poetry was neither 'juvenilia' nor a secondary interest on the level of lepidopterology or the composition of chess problems, but a serious, lifelong pursuit – a 'partie intégrante de son oeuvre littéraire' – that entailed Nabokov's 'dialogue privilégié avec la tradition russe' (Rabaté 401). According to Rabaté, if for no other reason than this, Nabokov's poetry deserves evaluation according to its own criteria.

In support of his central argument concerning the duality of Nabokov's oeuvre, Rabaté's analysis of the thematic specificity of Nabokov's poetry focuses on the themes of Russia and the role of the poetry. Under the theme of Russia, Rabaté subsumes the two sub-themes of the dream and the voyage. Thus delineated, Rabaté then reads the cluster of themes related to Russia as expressive of a further dichotomy in Nabokov's art: 'L'antithèse fondamentale, rêve/réalité, est redoublée par deux oppositions coeur/raison, Russe/étranger, ou plutôt exil (izgnan'e) sans détermination géographique plus spécifique' [The fundamental antithesis, dream/reality, is redoubled by two oppositions – heart/reason, Russia/abroad, or exile (izgnan'e) without any more specific geographic determination (Rabaté 403)]. Poetry in Nabokov's œuvre is thus aligned along a central dream-heart-Russia axis. The formal qualities of Nabokov's poetry, in particular its purported conservatism, are likewise placed in the service of Rabaté's encompassing argument. In the creation of an influential line of argumentation to be adopted in later criticism, Rabaté suggests that Nabokov's conservatism is in essence an ideological choice, a conscious form of homage to, and preservation of, the lost Russian literary tradition:

> Si la poésie de Nabokov est, pour lui, signe de la Russie, si la forme poétique elle-même peut être lue comme gage de fidélité aux traditions russes, c'est pour une raison plus essentielle. La poésie est pour Nabokov le lieu de la tradition russe, car sa poésie est comme un conservatoire de toutes les formes canoniques, traditionnelles, de la lyrique russe.
>
> Contrairement à la poésie futuriste ou post-futuriste, très iconoclaste, souvent expérimentale, la poésie de Nabokov paraît, de prime abord, très traditionnelle ... Nabokov choisit une poésie de fidélité et de respect de la tradition. (Rabaté 408–9)

[If Nabokov's poetry, for him, signifies Russia, if poetic form itself may be read as a gauge of fidelity to Russian traditions, it is for a more essential reason. Poetry is for Nabokov the location of the Russian tradition, as this poetry acts as a conservatory of all the canonic, traditional forms of the Russian lyric.

Contrary to the futurist or post-futurist poetry – very iconoclastic, very experimental – Nabokov's poetry appears, above all, very traditional … Nabokov chose a poetry of fidelity and respect for the tradition.]

Given Nabokov's presumed fidelity to the canon of *traditional* Russian poetry, Rabaté is able to avoid detailed discussion of the influence on Nabokov of Blok and Pasternak, the two modernist poets frequently coupled with him. Suggesting that 'Nabokov rend homage, de manière éclectique, à tous les maîtres de la poésie russe' (Rabaté 409), Rabaté concentrates on the traces of traditional Russian poetry in Nabokov's verse. Indeed, in returning to the classics of Russian poetry, Rabaté introduces Zhukovskii to the daunting list of influences compiled during the course of the critical reception of Nabokov's verse.

Rabaté's calculated article has the advantage of an informed discussion of Nabokov's verse and the attraction of an intriguing interpretive argument. Through his reading of Nabokov's poetry, Rabaté is able to combine a synoptic discussion of Nabokov's poetry and an explanation for Nabokov's seeming abandonment of Russian and verse for English and prose. Unfortunately, however, in making an argument about Nabokov's poetry in the context of his entire oeuvre, Rabaté is required to underplay significant aspects concerning both Nabokov's poetry and his prose writing. Although Nabokov's poetry is seldom afforded critical treatment according to its own criteria, the treatment itself is framed within an a priori understanding of the relation between Nabokov's poetry and oeuvre. Practically, Rabaté's analysis is predicated upon a rupture within Nabokov's oeuvre and career between Russian and English, poetry and prose, and thus is unable to assimilate evidence of continuity. Disregarded are themes first articulated in Nabokov's poetry and which unite Nabokov's oeuvre across languages and genres. Likewise unaddressed is the phenomenon of Nabokov's English poetry and its relation to his Russian works. And lastly the very poetic quality of Nabokov's prose – Russian and English – is left unrelated to his poetry. In short, Rabaté's analysis leaves little space for the identification of a lyric sensibility and voice engendered in Nabokov's poetry which developed with his oeuvre into prevalence in each of the genres he practised, including his later poetry. In Rabaté's reading, Fyodor Godunov-Cherdyntsev of *The Gift* and John Shade of *Pale Fire* are perforce unrelated, and the novelistic universes they inhabit are not united by a shared lyric sensibility.

Both Rabaté and Setschkareff figure prominently in the English-language response to the reassessment of Nabokov's poetry called forth by *Poems*. In just over a decade after the appearance of *Poems*, the final issue of *Russian Literature Triquarterly* was devoted to Nabokov, with an excellent and important cluster of complementary articles treating Nabokov's poetry. The articles by Smith, Johnson, Connolly, and Rampton in 1991 represent the first extensive English-language analysis of Nabokov's (Russian) poetry. In general, these comprehensive articles are united by the desire to render due respect to the scope and accomplishment of Nabokov's poetic oeuvre and to read his poetry for signs of thematic specificity – especially the theme of the otherworld – which might prove useful in analysis of Nabokov's writing as a whole.

D. Barton Johnson's 'Preliminary Notes on Nabokov's Russian Poetry: A Chronological and Thematic Sketch' offers a computer-based overview of Nabokov's poetry according to chronological and thematic considerations. Johnson's chronological overview of the publication history of Nabokov's poetry is the fullest and most detailed to date. Accompanying the empirical publication history are numerous comments of an interpretive nature concerning Nabokov's poetry and oeuvre which are witness to close familiarity with Nabokov's writing and hence very useful. As valuable as these remarks are, however, the present study was constituted in response to one such observation made in the context of *Poems and Problems* but which seems to have been intended to carry general validity: 'Poetry and chess problems hold equal place as minor genres in his creative life' (Johnson 1991, 313). The premise of the current study is that poetry was an abiding interest in Nabokov's writing and may not be considered on par with chess problems, despite the parallels which may be drawn between them.

Johnson's thematic analysis consists of a structural model based primarily on assumptions derived from an analysis of the frequency of occurrence of selected words and, especially, the antonymic pairs formed by particular words. This structural analysis is motivated by Véra Nabokov's reference to the otherworld in her preface to *Poems* and the resulting research in Nabokov criticism concerning Nabokov's cosmology. Johnson sees the two-world dichotomy proposed by criticism in description of Nabokov's artistic cosmos reflected in a key series of antonyms within Nabokov's poetry: night/day, dream/reality, shadow/light, soul/body. Johnson applies these findings to an interpretation of Nabokov's oeuvre which corroborates Rabaté's claims concerning the dichotomy in Nabokov's writing between poetry and prose: 'Whatever else may be said about these two universes [indicated in the above pairs of words], one thing is certain:

the former term describes the realm of Nabokov's early lyric poetry; the latter, the world of his narrative poetry and prose' (Johnson 1991, 319). Proceeding out of these specific findings, Johnson proposed an expanded, highly evocative lexical model of Nabokov's poetic cosmology based on a series of oppositions with accompanying points of transition (Johnson 1991, 321). Johnson's structural analysis is exceptionally judicious and suggestive, though in its conclusion ultimately strengthens the impression – as suggested by Rabaté – of a dichotomy between Nabokov's poetry and prose with the two worlds of 'there' and 'here,' 'night' and 'day,' and so on forming an opposition complementary to the one proposed between Nabokov's poetry and prose: 'The novels offer a brightly-lit world brimming over with consciousness and physical sensation. They are filled with bright, precisely described detail that strongly contrasts with the shadowy vagueness of Nabokov's poetic universe' (Johnson 1991, 323). As the analysis of Nabokov's poetry below will demonstrate, the 'brightly-lit world brimming over with consciousness and physical sensation' is as much a legacy of Nabokov's poetry as is his evocation of the other world.

The otherworld is the explicitly identified topic of Julian Connolly's discussion of Nabokov's poetry. Enlarging upon Setschkareff's first discussion of this theme within Nabokov's poetry, Connolly sees the 'otherworldly' as 'subsumed under a larger thematic rubric – that of the "two-world" theme' (Connolly 1991, 330). In turn, the poems expressive of the two-world theme are identified by Connolly as comprising four categories: 'poems involving the poet's thoughts about his distant homeland; poems about the poet and a loved one; poems about art and the nature of inspiration; and poems about a supernatural "other" realm – a world that exists beyond our physical dimensions and that can perhaps be comprehended completely only after death' (Connolly 1991, 330). After briefly discussing and demonstrating Nabokov's poetic expression of the first three categories, Connolly's analysis is turned to the fourth category dealing with 'a supernatural "other" realm.' With economically chosen examples, Connolly successfully demonstrates both the prevalence of this theme but also its expression in selected examples of Nabokov's prose. Connolly also touches upon a central feature of Nabokov's poetry which arises in tandem with the otherworld and intimations of escape from the imperfections of the world to a transcendent realm of perfection: 'Although so many of his characters, both in his prose and in his poetry, feel constrained by the limitations they find in the world around them and strive to transform their environment or to escape from it, Nabokov himself remains fundamentally committed to exploring the beauty of the everyday world and to enshrining this beauty in his art' (Connolly

1991, 334). The otherworld is indeed an important expression of the meta-physical dimension of Nabokov's lyric voice, which is expressed both in his poetry and prose.

David Rampton's contribution to the Nabokov issue of *Russian Literature Triquarterly* turns attention from synoptic analysis of the thematic accents of Nabokov's poetry to an exceptionally suggestive reading of a particular trope within it. Observing that Nabokov's literary indebtedness to the mimetic and moral norms of nineteenth-century Russian literature – among other factors – renders him an awkward member of the pantheon of twentieth-century Postmodernist authors, Rampton proposes analysis of Nabokov's use of apostrophe in his poetry as a means of semiotically 'reading' the poetry and its relation to his fiction. Nabokov's early poetry is indeed distinguished by apostrophe, and following Jonathan Culler, Rampton is able to argue plausibly for a reading of the rhetorical function as Nabokov's self-conscious exploration of a specific form of poetic discourse. Most interestingly, Rampton sees Nabokov's use of a trope most often associated with highly conventionalized verse as an example of his lifelong refusal to submit his artistic vision to external standards of taste and convention. What critics such as Struve and others saw as 'vulgar' and 'sentimental,' and what Vera Lur'e criticized in 1923 as Nabokov's passing 'by all contemporary artistic achievements and gains, to renounce all movements and schools and to use images which have long ago faded and ceased to be symbols,' is for Rampton an indicant of Nabokov's poetic voice. For Rampton, Nabokov's use of apostrophe in invocation of the things of the world is a portion of his engagement through poetry with his environment and expression of his artistic vision:

> No doubt it was this kind of poem that made reviewers regard the early volumes as the product of a talent that was still immature, but their sentimentality should do more than make us condemn them out of hand. Apostrophe is always potentially sentimental because it conjures up a world in which nature is animate, whether in the form of talking dryads, articulate West Winds, responsive inkwells, or whatever. They are all the plausible inhabitants of a world that can be talked to ... Diminutives and naiveté may annoy the austere, yet they are a natural hazard in this kind of poetry which often mimes the childlike in search of consolation, and they are examples of what was to be, right through Nabokov's career, a systematic refusal to recognize conventional barriers of taste and mode. (Rampton 1991, 346)

Rampton's analysis of a particular trope in Nabokov's poetry serves as a plausible component in the identification of a poetic style which in fact engaged directly and exuberantly with the 'trifles' of the world and which both proclaimed and demonstrated the ability of poets and children to transform such trifles into wonder.

The last article to be discussed from the Nabokov edition of *Russian Literature Triquarterly* is Gerald Smith's authoritative study of Nabokov's prosody. Drawing upon an extensive corpus of Nabokov's known published poems, Smith provides an empirically based, descriptive analysis of the meter, rhythm, rhyme, and stanza form favoured by Nabokov in isolation from and in comparison with other Russian poets. Due to the precision of his analysis, Smith is able to make convincing descriptive statements concerning the formal properties of Nabokov's poetry. In terms of metrics, Smith's analysis reveals Nabokov to have had pronounced preference for iambic meters, in particular, the iambic tetrameter, and according to this indicator may be deemed 'quite clearly a formally conservative poet' (Smith 279). Although Nabokov altered his metric preferences at different times, the iambic measure remained prominent. Interestingly, however, Nabokov's preference for iambic meters is revealed to have been shared with his fellow émigré poets; indeed, Khodasevich indicated an even greater degree of preference for the iamb.[13] Despite the general metric conservatism of émigré verse, then, 'Nabokov is by no means an isolated case in terms of broad metrical typology' (Smith 279). Another interesting finding of Smith's analysis concerns the purported influence on Nabokov by the Symbolists – Nabokov is shown to have spurned both the long measures and dolniks favoured by the Symbolists. In terms of rhythm, Smith indicates that within the preferred iambic tetrameter measure, Nabokov used stress to ensure a high degree of rhythmic variety. Nabokov's use of rhyme is shown by Smith to have been very precise according to both grammatical category and declension in contrast to the Soviet poetry of 'the period of Blok and Maiakovski,' which saw a 'de-grammatizing' of rhyme. On the few occasions when Nabokov departed from exactitude in rhyme, he did so in the achievement of specific effects. With regard to the stanza, Nabokov is demonstrated to have been an exceptionally stanzaic poet with a marked preference for the rhyming *AbAb* quatrain, although other categories from couplets to terza rima were also employed.

Taken together, Smith concludes his analysis with the observation that 'in all these respects, Nabokov's choices resembled those made by other émigré poets of the inter-war period, with the marked exception of Tsvetaeva. His chief mentor in his earlier work was probably Balmont, and in his later work Bunin and Khodasevich' (Smith 302). From this observation, Smith draws a conclusion similar to that of Rabaté that Nabokov's rejection of formal innovation was the consequence of an ideological decision, an expression of his rejection of forms associated with poets of the left who either supported the revolution of 1917 or returned to Russia from exile. This may be. Another conclusion to be drawn from Smith's analysis, however, concerns the reception Nabokov received among his émigré peers. If his poetry was formally consistent with that of his fellow émigré poets, and even less 'conservative' than the admired Khodasevich, why was he singled out by some critics for censure as an overly traditional poet? The source of the irritation expressed in the early, authoritative responses to Nabokov's poetry seems to have resided, not in the formal qualities of his verse, but in the as yet un-normalized thematic and formal particularity of an emerging poetic voice.

A final article to be discussed from what has been identified here as the third stage of criticism in the history of reception of Nabokov as poet is Galya Diment's study 'Nabokov and Joyce: Portraits of Innovative Writers as Conservative Poets,' an article which makes the comparison between the two writers first suggested by F.W. Dupee. Written by a critic both highly knowledgeable of, and sympathetic to, Nabokov's artistry, Diment's article, as initially indicated by the title, perceives Nabokov's oeuvre as divided by a variant of the dichotomy posed by Rabaté, here between traditional poetry and innovative prose. The conclusion of Diment's article expresses the essence of this dichotomy: 'It was in his poetry that Nabokov experienced the most direct influence of others: Pushkin, Fet, Tyutchev, even Apukhtin; it is here that he borrowed, not stole. While his prose in both Russian and English is distinctly Nabokovian, no matter what the outside influences could have been, as a poet he does not have a strongly individual presence' (Diment 1991, 25). As in almost all the above discussed examples where external stimulus has been evoked, influence is here being attested without being demonstrated. This is both legitimate and possible as a hypothesis, though in the absence of closer study, it is insufficient as a critical finding. Given the dearth of a critical analysis to the contrary, the absence of a strongly felt 'individual presence' in Nabokov's poetry may be because one was never allowed to emerge in a history of reception that failed to read Nabokov's poetry according to its own criteria. With all due respect to an eminent scholar of Nabokov's writing, Diment's establishment of the conservatism of Nabokov's verse is in essence based on a reading of a single poem which makes little attempt to integrate the images discussed into a broader system of poetic meaning within Nabokov's writing. Nabokov's poem 'Ласточка' ('Lastochka' / 'The Swift') is instead examined as representative confirmation of a critical judgment derived from an émigré review (discussed above) from 1923 wherein Nabokov is criticized for refusing to conform to the poetic fashion of his time. Finally, in extending the structuralist reading proposed by Rabaté and forwarded by Johnson, Diment advances the binary oppositions poetry/prose, soul/body, as the ultimate source of the traditionalism of Nabokov's poetry in contrast to his prose:

> It is as if Nabokov and Joyce, while growing by leaps and bounds as prose writers, experienced but a stunted development as poets, and felt that they had to restrict their options in order to be in control of a medium which, unlike prose, was never quite 'theirs.' Feeling 'limited' as poets even as they were starting to feel 'limitless' as writers, they seem to have never grown out of the belief of their youth – shared by many amateur poets – that poetry should be used almost exclusively for the moments when 'the speech of the soul is about to be heard.'
>
>   Joyce's and Nabokov's poetry was so traditional, it seems to me, precisely because their notions of poetry remained so restrictive. Poetry, they felt, was unlike prose not only in form but also in essence: one came straight from one's soul, while the other relied on the experiences of one's body, and it was somehow more proper to be wily and playful with one's prosaic 'body' than with one's poetic 'soul.' (Diment 1991, 21)

Such a reading leaves little space for critical acknowledgment of, for example, the narrative quality of Nabokov's poetry or those poems which highlight the plasticity and physicality of the poet's relation to language and the natural environment or, much less, the – for Nabokov – central experience of cosmic synchronicity where in the distinction between body and soul is transcended in a moment of heightened consciousness and physical dissolution. Much of Nabokov's verse is traditional in form, as Smith, Diment, and others have shown, though this does not preclude dimensions of Nabokovian innovation in other realms.

Diment's article is of interest not only for its reading of Joyce's and Nabokov's poetic voices and the evidence it displays of an accumulation of some of the central observations made throughout the history of critical response to Nabokov the poet, but also for its command and knowledge of Nabokov's oeuvre in its entirety, including poetry. While assessment of Nabokov's poetry has not even begun to approach the dimension of response to his prose, by the 1990s poetry is recognized as a genre deserving of attention precisely because it had been unduly neglected in the past. The opening of the Soviet-Russian literary institution in the 1990s would hasten that process; Russian literature, in rediscovering Nabokov, would rediscover his poetry.

Russian Literature and the Rediscovery of Nabokov's Poetry

For the purposes of convenience, the fourth and current stage in the history of the critical reception of Nabokov's poetry may be dated with the changes initiated by the political collapse of the Soviet Union and the accompanying dissolution of official state domination over cultural and artistic expression. With the lifting of overt state control, the Russian literary institution was free to adopt instruments and principles other than that of ideological orthodoxy with which to fashion its cultural identity. A significant portion of the refashioning to have emerged out of this freedom has been the reintroduction of writers previously excluded from the Russian literary tradition by a system of censorship imposed and maintained by the Soviet government. Nabokov is an excellent example of this. Although he never ceased being an exceptional exponent of Russian literature for many, even Soviet, readers, he is now being reintegrated into the Russian literary institution by means of open publication and, especially, critical study.[14] Irina Prokhorova, for instance, the editor of the respected literary journal *Novoe literaturnoe obozrenie* (*New Literary Review*), has identified Nabokov as the father of the new Russian literature that emerged in the closing decade of the twentieth century.[15] Concomitant to Nabokov's importance as a literary model, the contributions of many excellent Russian-language scholars have invigorated Nabokov studies and have ensured renewed interest in Nabokov's – especially Russian – poetry.

As in the West, however, this interest is primarily of a historical, retrospective cast. Nabokov's poetry – whether Russian or English, only rarely together – is discussed as a portion of a larger, more significant oeuvre of prose works, with little attempt made to examine the similarities Nabokov posited between poetry and prose. The assessment of Nabokov's poetry made by Barry P. Scherr for *The Garland Companion to Vladimir Nabokov* is indicative of this tendency. Scherr's comprehensive study of Nabokov's poetry is a model of judicious review, a study which displays balanced familiarity with the existing critical literature, intimate knowledge of the Russian poetic, tradition, and genuine appreciation for the scope of Nabokov's accomplishment in poetry. And yet there is little direct engagement with Nabokov's poetry. This is undoubtedly due in part to the type of survey article demanded of Scherr in an encyclopedic volume of Nabokov criticism, and yet one wishes that he had levelled his expert eye at the poems in an analytical reading, rather than as citations intended to demonstrate critical claims also made elsewhere. In referring to Nabokov's use of rhyme, for instance, Scherr draws reference to the findings of Smith and suggests the potential for emphasis latent in repetend rhyme, but does not follow his finding into interpretive analysis: 'Smith points out that Nabokov, with his overwhelming preference for exact rhymes, tends to cluster his approximate rhymes in particular poems, with a specific purpose in mind each time. At the very beginning of "Evening [on a Vacant Lot]" Nabokov uses the most exact type of rhyme possible, repetend rhyme: *nébo-nébo* [sky-sky] and *oknóm-oknóm* [window-window]. Any repetend rhyme itself is unusual; to begin with two such rhymes immediately calls attention to the line endings' (Scherr 1995, 613). Scherr is correct that the repetend rhyme is unusual and in this instance, in the context of a mysterious meeting with a dead man, draws attention to the frequently used motif of windows and skies as boundaries between realms of being and thus an important link to the metaphysical theme of the poem (to be discussed below, in chapter 3). Thus, approximately forty years after the authoritative retrospective appraisal of Nabokov's émigré period by a critic as knowledgeable and sympathetic as Scherr – Gleb Struve – comes another appraisal which culminates with a reassertion of the supposition of the earlier critic: 'Struve's original judgment still holds: Nabokov, unlike, say, Mandelshtam or Pasternak, is not a poet who happened to write prose but a prose writer who happened to write verse. On several occasions Nabokov has been compared to Joyce; both were innovative, major prose writers who were conservative, minor poets' (Scherr 1995, 623).[16] That Nabokov was a conservative, minor poet is open to dispute; it may indeed be the case, although it may just as well not be. Beyond dispute, however, is the fact that as an appraisal, this claim has never been *demonstrated* in sustained interpretive analysis of Nabokov's poetry.

Similar to Scherr's comprehensive survey of Nabokov's body of poetic work is Th. Eekman's study, likewise of 1995, which essentially concentrates on a descriptive overview of the formal characteristics of Nabokov's verse. As Eekman is concerned primarily with Nabokov's versification, the issue of the potential relation between Nabokov's poetry and prose is not addressed and the thematic character of his poetry alluded to only in passing, with no mention made at all of the metaphysical dimension. In broaching the thorny subject of artistic indebtedness, Eekman places Nabokov in the traditional vein of Russian poetry and hence little influenced by contemporary models:

The molds into which the young Nabokov cast his verse are strictly traditional; one commentator even called his entire poetic oeuvre 'poetry of tradition.' He learned his trade from Pushkin, Lermontov, Tiutchev, Fet, and also from

more contemporary poets like Bal'mont and Blok ... Some other poets have
been mentioned to whom he was indebted: Zhukovskii, Blok, Bunin, Khodasevich. However, although it may be generally correct that 'his poetry, both in
Russian and in English, is playful, aristocratic, and is closer to that of Bunin
or Khodasevich (considered by Nabokov the greatest Russian poet of the
twentieth century) than to Pasternak or Akhmatova,' it should be noted that
his early poetry is not strongly influenced by, or close to, any of the modernist, contemporary poets of his day, but by the classics of the previous century.
(Eekman 89–90)

Eekman's study is very informed in its descriptive analysis of the formal
features of Nabokov's work, especially with regard to the Russian poems.
In moving to the discussion of Nabokov's English verse appended to the
end of Eekman's detailed article, the limits of his descriptive approach become more visible, however. In the absence of a thematic context within
the frame of either Nabokov's verse or oeuvre as a whole, the English
poems are reduced to interpretive suppositions based on their place of
publication: 'Unlike his Russian verse, these poems are all in a light, humorous vein; in fact, their atmosphere and tone remind one of the lighter,
ironic or humorous Russian poems. After all, they were intended for *The
New Yorker*. They are no great poetry, but evince wittiness and inventiveness and a true mastery of the language' (Eekman 98). Some of Nabokov's
English poems are indeed written in the comic vein – as was much of his
prose – though the thematic function of this mode is more complicated
than anything captured with the attribute 'light.' The dangers and difficulties of a reading of Nabokov's English poetry without a thematic context
are indicative of the hurdles which must be overcome in discussing
Nabokov's poetic oeuvre as a whole.

Moving from Scherr's and Eekman's more descriptively cast surveys of
Nabokov's poetry to the most recent – above all, Russian – studies, this
historical review of the critical reception of Nabokov's verse is taken to
the limits of a synthesizing reading. Since the lifting of official state control over literary production and reception in Russia, the interest in all
aspects of Nabokov's multi-faceted oeuvre has expanded dramatically.
Nabokov's (Russian) poetry is now an integral component of the rediscovery of his artistry by a Russian readership. The pages of Russian-language
journals reveal sustained interest in a multitude of topics related to the
form, subject matter, reception, and sources of Nabokov's poetry and its
relation to his prose.[17] Even those studies not primarily concerned with
Nabokov's poetry, but rather with other facets of his oeuvre, frequently

discuss relevant connections to the poetry, for instance, in the isolation of a particular motif or theme.[18] Interestingly, it is my impression that these more recent appraisals of Nabokov's poetry are more accepting of its qualities than preceding assessments and, in general, less inclined to compare Nabokov's poetry negatively to his innovative prose. Indeed, at least one critic, in confronting the dynamics of the Russian rediscovery of Nabokov's writing and especially his poetry, has gone so far as to invert the order of preference traditional to the history of Nabokov reception and place the poetry before the prose. Vladimir Soloukhin hazards the claim that Nabokov's lack of acclaim as a poet is less the result of the objective quality of his verse than his exceptional appeal as a writer of prose:

> And thus arose a particular injustice. With his numerous and exceptional novels, Nabokov eclipsed himself as a poet. Suppose that there lived in emigration a fine poet Khodasevich. Khodasevich and Nabokov each wrote poetry of comparable quality. I dare claim that Nabokov's poems, softly and delicately expressive, are no worse than Khodasevich's poems. Khodasevich, however, never wrote novels and exists in literature (in the consciousness of people) as a poet. When one begins to speak of Nabokov as a poet, one is sometimes questioned in surprise: 'What? Did he really write poetry?' Yes, Nabokov wrote wonderful poems. When the times changed and we began to re-examine our relationship to the parallel current of Russian literature of the twentieth century, our acquaintanceship with Nabokov began with the novels. The journal *Moskva* published *The Defense* and many other novels were rendered worthy for readers. People began to 'uncover' his poetry as well: here three, there four poems. I would like readers to be able immediately to gain a full impression of Nabokov as a poet. (Soloukhin 16)

Indeed, more than simply inverting the order of preference, another critic has addressed head-on two of the issues central to the negative reading of Nabokov's poetry: the purportedly subordinate position of Nabokov's poetry in comparison to both his own prose and the poetry of his contemporaries. On both counts, Vladimir Smirnov contends that the perspective of time has complicated the finality of past critical judgments to the credit of Nabokov's poetry:

> Nabokov's poetry is incomparably less known. It is located, as it were, 'in the shade' of his prose, essays, and translations. It was never particularly appreciated. Due to its old-fashionedness, almost archaic classicism, and noble restraint, it lost out to the sparkling novelty of Nabokovian prose. Even the

detractors of Nabokov's prose dared not to speak of his epigonism. Of his poetry, they often wrote thus.

It is as if Nabokov's poems were 'lost' against the background of the unusual flowering of Russian poetry of the twentieth century. After all, his contemporaries were Khodasevich and Georgii Ivanov, Kliuev and Esenin, Akhmatova and Tsvetaeva, Bunin and Voloshin, Maiakovskii and Khlebnikov, Pasternak and Mandel'shtam, Zabolotskii and Tvardovskii. Each of these poets is associated with innovation. In this company, Nabokov's poems appeared culturally second-rate, traditionally bookish. Nothing more. Yet, 'from the perspective of eternity' everything has turned out to be less simple and obvious.

In the 'longue durée' Nabokov's poetry has transformed into something indisputably precious, lively, and fascinating.

… 'Melodious existence' [*zvukovoe bytie*] is perhaps the most precise definition of Nabokov's lyricism. It is not a supplement to the writer's wonderful prose but something kindred to it. (Smirnov 9–11)

It remains to be seen whether the perspective of time will affect a transformation in the dominant critical appraisal of Nabokov's poetry, or whether the increasing frequency with which Nabokov's verse is confronted in Russian criticism will be matched in other critical traditions, particularly in English-language criticism. It is certain, however, that the potential of this occurring has been enormously advanced by the anthologizing of Nabokov's verse in accessible volumes. Throughout Nabokov's career, volumes of poetry have served as important milestones marking crucial moments in the development of his writing. Since the early 1990s, the publication in Russian of Nabokov's works – including the authoritative and authorized five-volume collected works in Russian in 1999–2000 – has provided readers with access to primary sources. In the case of Nabokov's poetry, such anthologies are not only vehicles for the transmission of Nabokov's poetry but also – as in the above quoted case of Smirnov – for comprehensive contemporary commentary on Nabokov's verse. The introductory notes to recent collections of Nabokov's poems are the latest contributions to the long history of reception of Nabokov's poetry.

The author of significant portions of the excellent explanatory notes contained within the five-volume collected works in Russian, M. Malikova is exceptionally qualified to introduce the fullest single-volume collection of Nabokov's poetry to date. Under the title 'A Forgotten Poet' ('Забытый поэт'), Malikova's approximately fifty pages of closely printed introduction is also the single longest treatment of Nabokov's poetry to date. Perhaps as a result of its introductory function, however, Malikova's survey is much stronger in reviewing the publication history and critical response to Nabokov's poetry than in offering an independent analysis of the verse. Thus, Malikova's work, while providing an admirably detailed overview of the critical response to Nabokov's poetry, is more indebted to the canonic perception of his verse than a (re-)reading of it. Not surprisingly, then, Malikova's survey ends with a contestation regarding Nabokov's poetry which, as so frequently in the course of Nabokov criticism, places it in a subordinate position in the 'shade' of his prose: 'We are not going to insist that Vladimir Nabokov (Sirin) is a great poet, although he is, undoubtedly, a forgotten poet. His emphatically conservative, traditionalist position of a "minor" poet at the early stage of a poetic evolution is surprising enough against the background of his originality and innovativeness in prose. The new – eclectic and uninhibited – poetics of a few verses and poems written by him since the beginning of the 1930s is certainly still far from having been appreciated and entirely unexamined ...' (Malikova 43–4).

A shorter though more analytical approach to Nabokov's poetry is to be found in Alexander Dolinin's introduction to the first volume of Nabokov's collected works in Russian. One of the most informed readers of Nabokov in both Russian and English, Dolinin is eminently qualified to comment on Nabokov's poetry in isolation and in the context of his entire oeuvre. Dolinin extends Struve's authoritative analysis of mid-century to read Nabokov's 'conservative' poetry essentially as a stage of apprenticeship in the process of becoming an innovative, modernist novelist. Dolinin accords the poetry due critical regard, as it is viewed as submerged within and hence integral to Nabokov's prose. In this, he qualifies Struve's mid-century reading, which seemed to suggest an opposition between the two genres rather than a complementary enrichment. In Dolinin's reading, Nabokov's position as an émigré writer is essential. In explanation of the purported 'conservatism' of Nabokov's poetry, he positions Nabokov with Khodasevich as one who could not bear the avant-garde 'with its program of a total, purifying destruction of tradition and the igniting of a new, hitherto unknown flame on the ashes of the former culture; his goal he saw as the "renewal of the mechanism" and not its destruction' (Dolinin 1999, 14). Hence the absence of perceivable influence from the modernizing voices in Russian poetry 'as if Pasternak, the futurists, Tsvetaeva, Mandel'shtam and even Annenskii and M. Kuzmin remained completely unknown to him' (Dolinin 1999, 15). The rejection of these figures for the influences previously identified by Nabokov's émigré critics – and the English 'Georgians' strangely unremarked upon by the émigré discerners of influence, though noted by Dolinin – is thus a staking out of ideological positions in the realm of émigré Russian literature. With this argument, Dolinin takes discussion to a level of analytical relevance higher than that frequently observed in critical commentary on what is identified as the conservatism of Nabokov's verse. With his own poetic practice, Nabokov indeed seems to have been repudiating a, for him, discredited aesthetic, while simultaneously participating in, and extending, a tradition reaching from Khodasevich back through Tiutchev and Fet to Pushkin. This argument is further buttressed by consideration of his choice of Russian poets for translation; as an accomplished translator, Nabokov sought to preserve (and shape Anglo-American understanding of) what he considered valuable in the Russian poetic tradition. While aesthetic-ideological considerations such as this offer a plausible explanation for his poetic conservatism, they also serve, however, to emphasize the great importance Nabokov placed on verse – including his own.

For Dolinin, as previously for Struve, individual examples of Nabokov's poetry of the 1920s belong to the second and third ranks of Russian émigré poetry because of their 'sentimentality' and 'tastelessness.' Rare in instance, even these failed examples of verse – not to speak of positive examples – are of interest to Dolinin, not for their intrinsic value, but as the source of Nabokov's developing narrative style:

> But then, from the point of view of the following evolution of the writer, they are of enormous interest. Firstly, the verse exercises of the young Nabokov played an important role in the formation of his narrative style, serving as a kind of conduit through which the images, intonation, tropes, techniques, and compositional principles of Russian classical and modernist poetry entered into his prose. (Dolinin 1999, 15)

In extending this essential notion of Nabokov's development out of poetry and into prose, Dolinin suggests, that Nabokov's prose style did not really unfold until it was released from the confines of verse:

> It is quite likely that Nabokov made the breakthrough to his individual style only when he began to write independent prose like liberated poetry, like a prose 'translation' of the images, intonation, and metaphors of his early poetry. Observing the young Nabokov's mastery of versification, G. Struve came to the conclusion that precisely this mastery fettered his style, which he defined in paraphrasing the following formulation from Coleridge: 'the best word in the best order.' The broad expanses of prose allowed Nabokov the

opportunity to free himself from the yoke of versification and finally quench
his thirst for the 'best word.' (Dolinin 1999, 17)

In the transformation from poet to prose writer, more was 'translated,'
however, than just the essentials of narrative style. In taking up the 'two-
world theme' previously identified in Nabokov criticism, Dolinin identifies
four thematic clusters which Nabokov adapted from his poetry to his prose:
the themes of consciousness, the journey, artistic creation, and 'the otherworld.' According to Dolinin, this entire complex of ideas ultimately derived from the silver age of Russian culture. Contained within poetic form,
Nabokov was constrained and hindered from finding his own 'intonation'
and 'poetics'; in prose, however, Nabokov found the space and freedom to
synthesize his own unique narrative style and poetics (Dolinin 1999, 20).

Although unsupported by concrete reference even to Nabokov's 'weak'
poetry and unleavened by consideration of the principles which distinguish
the positive examples of verse, Dolinin's assessment is, like Struve's fifty
years ago, both considered and authoritative. Thus, despite the presence of
opposing, positive assessments and the passing of several intervening dec
ades, criticism of Nabokov's poetry effectively ends where it began, with
the charge of being conservative and epigonic in character, a judgment
mitigated only by its purported function as a stage in the transition to
prose. This in reference at least to the Russian poetry. The English poetry,
which does not and cannot conform to this argument, as it was written
after the Russian prose and is less identifiable with the Russian tradition in
poetry, is simply ignored or, in the case of those critics who address it, dismissed as a bagatelle, a curio, further proof of the author's ludic, ironic
manipulation of readers and literary tradition. This, as has been indicated
above, is an unsatisfying state of affairs for several reasons. It leaves unan-
swered Nabokov's continued, career-long love affair with his poetic muse;
it smoothes over developments within the course of his poetic writing; it
leaves unaddressed the specifics of the role of poetry in Nabokov's prose;
and, most vexingly, it introduces the rough fissures of language (Russian-
English), genre (poetry-prose), and mode (conservatism-innovation) into
the perhaps most patterned and structured oeuvre of twentieth-century
letters. And lastly, as this review of criticism of Nabokov's verse has amply
demonstrated, it leaves Nabokov's poetry unexamined as a coherent body
of writing subject to analysis according to intrinsic principles of assessment. It is to such a reading – at once descriptive and interpretive – that the
following chapter will turn.

3 Nabokov's Lyric Voice: The Poetry of This World and Another

> But then, in a sense, all poetry is positional: to try to express one's position in regard to the universe embraced by consciousness, is an immemorial urge.
> – Vladimir Nabokov, *Speak, Memory*

A review of the reception of Nabokov's poetry has revealed that the central critical tradition has but incompletely addressed the single form of generic expression that Nabokov practised throughout his creative life. It has either, at worst, denied Nabokov a legitimate poetic identity with the charge of excessive identification with antecedent poetic models or, at best, insufficiently described the qualities of the lyric voice hesitantly attributed to him. The task of the present chapter will be to offer a synoptic reading of the dominant features of Nabokov's poetry as a means of arriving at a fairer and fuller representation of the specific tone and timbre of Nabokov's lyric voice. Given that Nabokov's poetic writing spanned approximately sixty years over nine volumes extending from juvenilia to a posthumously published retrospective with hundreds of poems, the intention of providing an overview of so broad a corpus of verse within a single chapter – however lengthy – seems at once presumptuous and naive. Matters would only seem worsened when to this descriptive intention an interpretive one is added. For an essential parallel objective of this chapter – and indeed the entire study – is the goal of advancing an interpretive argument demonstrating that poetry was not merely an offshoot of Nabokov's primarily prose oeuvre but the very root and trunk out of which his artistry expanded and grew. Rather than a protruding auxiliary activity, poetry forms the unseen – though always heard – thematic and formal core of his writing. In important ways, Nabokov's poetry is the first and final expression of the lyric voice which consistently sounds throughout the rest of his writing. The establishing of this identity, the unmistakable, idiosyncratic lyric voice resonating through his poetry, is thus integral to the identification and understanding of the distinctive voice which characterizes Nabokov's astounding artistic achievement in other genres.

Brian Boyd has, with Nabokov himself, observed that all of Nabokov's writing is ultimately occupied with the mystery and potential of consciousness (Boyd 2001a, 67). In taking up Boyd's claim, consideration of Nabokov's poetic approach to consciousness will form an entry point and guiding principle in the following reading of Nabokov's poetry. In furthering the interpretive power of my reading, and in support of my contention that poetry functions as a consolidating and unifying force within Nabokov's oeuvre, I intend as well to indicate the manner in which Nabokov's poetic approach to consciousness may be shown to illustrate the aesthetic, ethical, and metaphysical dimensions of Nabokov's writing, as announced in chapter 1. Hence, the following reading of Nabokov's poetry will be at once descriptive, in its attempt to survey the depth and breadth of Nabokov's Russian and English poetic oeuvre, and interpretive, in its explicit desire to foreground a specific understanding of Nabokov's lyric sensibility and poetic writing.

In fulfillment of this two-part goal, specific principles of selection will be required. As indicated in the previous chapter, such prominent scholars of Nabokov's poetry as Setschkareff, Connolly, Dolinin, and others have centred their discussions on thematics, focusing on what has often emerged as a four-part cluster of themes with which to encompass description of Nabokov's poetic writing. The present analysis will benefit from, though not follow, this strategy, not because, *pace* Sestschkareff's excellent study, for instance, the themes of metaphysics, the poetic calling, memory, and Russia are not discernible within Nabokov's poetry. They most certainly are. Rather, the dual descriptive and oeuvre-spanning interpretive function of this study demands a reading of Nabokov's poetry which accommodates identification of such themes within Nabokov's verse oeuvre, while also enabling a deeper, comprehensive reading which extends out of discussion of the individual poems into the rest of Nabokov's writing. At stake is both the poetic identity manifest in Nabokov's poetry and the lyric voice which derives from his poetry to find expression in other genres. Given this dual focus, a more inclusive instrument of comprehensive analysis will be sought. Furthermore, as was to be observed in the previous chapter, criticism – especially of Nabokov's English poetry – frequently censured Nabokov's poetry for its supposed lightweightedness, its presumed absence of spiritual and thematic depth. It is this charge which will be countered with a reading which accentuates the metaphysical and ethical depths of Nabokov's writing. And finally, in implicit contradiction of the claim that Nabokov's poetry was overly dependent on former models, the reading below will, while acknowledging Nabokov's intimate familiarity with a range of poetic styles, emphasize the individuality of Nabokov's poetic voice as it emerges over the long course of his poetic practice. The formal and thematic particularity discernible in all of Nabokov's writing, it will be suggested, rests on the lyric sensibility and voice which emerged and developed out of even Nabokov's earliest poetic works.

With this collection of disparate interpretive goals, care is required in the selection of a critical instrument which will do justice to the singular particularity of each of Nabokov's poems, while providing the analytical purchase necessary for a synoptic reading of his entire verse – and, ultimately, prose – oeuvre. Nabokov himself offered a solution. In the opening chapter of *Speak, Memory*, he suggested that 'the following of thematic designs through one's life should be ... the true purpose of autobiography' (*SM* 27). In modification of the generic focus of this claim from autobiography to an extensive body of writing, the following of thematic designs may also serve the true purpose of literary criticism. The assumed goal of following thematic designs is complicated, of course, by the generous profusion and intricate interweaving of a multitude of recurring themes and motifs in Nabokov's writing. Despite this embarrassment of thematic riches, however, it is nonetheless possible, as Gennady Barabtarlo has suggested in 'Nabokov's Trinity,' to isolate a concentrate of 'informing themes' from within Nabokov's work: 'When one scans all that Nabokov has written in two languages chronologically, one can discern a gradual change from a motley, exuberant, omnivorous profusion of "themes" ... to the more functional and concentrated ensemble of "informing themes," among which a few can be singled out as persistent' (Barabtarlo 1999, 111). The following will propose a cluster of key 'informing themes' with which to illustrate the specificity of particular poems, while asserting their connectedness as the individual products of a lyric voice which shaped them into a unique poetic oeuvre. Thus, starting from the Nabokovian approach to consciousness, and ever aware of the relevance to the aesthetic, ethical, and metaphysical dimensions of Nabokov's writing, the analysis of Nabokov's poetry will be conducted through reference to the following five thematic categories or, in Barabtarlo's coinage, 'informing themes': cosmic synchronization, inspiration, love, the otherworld, and, finally, the poetic expression of acute consciousness of the 'trifles' and natural wonder of existence. Consideration of this intricately interwoven ensemble of themes will reveal not only that Nabokov's poetic work represents a unified aesthetic – a poetic identity present in germ in Nabokov's first poetic expressions, though refined and developed over the course of his career – but that the awareness of this poetic identity is essential to a full understanding of Nabokov's entire oeuvre.

Before proceeding to analysis of Nabokov's poetry and the establishment of a five-part cluster of informing themes, however, the specificity of Nabokov's poetics calls for particular analysis of two fundamental, though controversial, topics: 'cosmic synchronization' and the related aesthetic dimension of Nabokov's individual brand of metaphysics. While Nabokov's lyric identity is composed of much more than an unusual experience of consciousness and a set of intimated, intuited philosophical beliefs, the specificity of both his poetry and prose is to a large degree derived from the play of these two little discussed – and at times actively resisted – principles. The critical compulsion of this analysis, however, runs deeper than mere description. The reception of Nabokov's poetry has frequently stumbled on the charge of imitativeness and epigonism and the related though separate charge of lightweightedness, while blindness to the pervasiveness of Nabokov's poetry and lyric interests throughout his writing has more than occasionally led to the mistaken identification of poetry as a minor concern within his artistry, an unprofitable sideline distracting him from the main business of prose. In my opinion, both sets of critical inaccuracy derive, to a significant degree, from insufficient attention to cosmic synchronization and the metaphysical strain within Nabokov's artistry. When identified in his poetry, Nabokov's non-dogmatic expression of metaphysical themes is too easily mislabelled as imitative of more dogmatic expressions; when not identified – as in his English poetry especially – Nabokov's poetry is represented as depthless. In the transition to analysis of Nabokov's prose and dramatic works, failed appreciation of these and other non-standardized, even anachronistic, principles intrinsic to his verse results in their obviation from the breadth of his oeuvre. The misrepresentation of the character of Nabokov's verse and the lingering critical insecurity regarding the metaphysical dimensions of Nabokov's writings may thus be seen to emerge from a common problem – insufficient knowledge of Nabokov's poetry.

The sources of this critical lacuna seem apparent. Although cosmic synchronization and an aesthetically trimmed metaphysics figure often and prominently in all of Nabokov's fiction – as subsequent portions of this study will amply demonstrate – Nabokov was not a writer of fiction-as-manifesto. Nabokov created fictional worlds which depict the intersections between consciousness and the world of experience; he did not espouse philosophical systems. Indeed, Nabokov's poetics, even though distinguished by philosophical concerns, is defined not simply by the evasion of, but the active resistance to, the conventions of philosophical exposition; herein lies its identity as an uncompromisingly aesthetic enterprise. Reference to the topics in Nabokov's various discursive texts – while they are always rewarding in their multi-dimensional, ultimately aesthetic suggestiveness – does not always explicitly form the formative link to Nabokov's poetry which I am suggesting either. It is out of this complex of almost contradictory forces – the non-dogmatic character of Nabokov's writing and the systemizing impulse of my own critical focus – that Nabokov's autobiographical account of his first poem in *Speak, Memory* emerges as the most promising entry point into discussion of cosmic synchronization and Nabokov's metaphysics. The insight to be gained from a rereading of Nabokov's lyric reconstruction of his paradigmatic first poem will more than repay the effort with knowledge into the source and function of Nabokov's poetic artistry. Nabokov's account of his first poem will here be shown to introduce the key concept of cosmic synchronicity, an essential source of interpretive purchase in subsequent discussion of Nabokov's poetry.

A Paradigmatic First Poem: Rereading 'The Rain Has Flown'

Speak, Memory might profitably be labelled a chronicle of Nabokov's experience of consciousness. It begins with Nabokov's coming into self-awareness as a child with the realization of time and concludes years – and pages – later with conjectures prompted by his infant son's awakening into consciousness. Contemplation of his son's growing experience of consciousness prompts consideration of one of the guiding themes of the book, the inclination that consciousness may eventually escape the prison of time in transition into still another 'special Space,' a dimension of unknown transcendence: '… if, in the spiral unwinding of things, space warps into something akin to time, and time, in its turn, warps into something akin to thought, then, surely, another dimension follows – a special Space maybe, not the old one, we trust, unless spirals become vicious circles again' (*SM* 301). The fate of consciousness – its potential to spiral into a fourth dimension – is thus central to *Speak, Memory*. It is against the background of the essential role of consciousness in Nabokov's life and artistry that the perhaps pivotal experience of consciousness for Nabokov *the writer* is contained. Nabokov's lyric description of his formative first encounter with

creative inspiration and poetic composition is more than just another experience of the mind; it is the awakening of the author as young man into
poetic consciousness. Nabokov's first poem marks the emergence of the
particular quality of consciousness that would determine the shape of his
life as artist. Chapter 11 of *Speak, Memory* relives the summer of 1914,
when the fifteen-year-old Nabokov was first overcome with 'the numb fury
of verse-making,' which was to serve as prelude to a life of verbal artistry
(*SM* 215–27).

As depicted in *Speak, Memory*, Nabokov's subsequent lifetime of artistic creation was inaugurated by this single July day at Vyra, the Nabokov
country estate, and this single poem. In an accumulation of imagery rendered in sumptuous prose, the autobiographer Nabokov takes the reader
back in time to an evocative setting and recounts the events of the day –
from the moment of initial inspiration to the poem's final recitation before
his enraptured mother. Rich as it is in superbly wrought detail and as redolent as it is of a particular moment, the events and poem described in
chapter 11 of *Speak, Memory* are, as Brian Boyd correctly indicates, 'a
considerable stylization' (Boyd 1990, 108). Nabokov neither began to write
poetry in 1914, nor was the poem described composed during that summer. In fact, Nabokov had 'for five years or so … been composing verse in
three different languages,' while the poem described, the lyrical 'Дождь
пролетел' ('Dozhd' proletel' / 'The Rain Has Flown'), was written in 1917,
three years after the event described in *Speak, Memory* (Boyd 1990, 108).
Despite the seeming inconsistencies in the incidentals of Nabokov's account, it would be mistaken to pass over this event as an inconsequential
fiction placed in Nabokov's autobiography for its aesthetic quality only. As
in all of Nabokov's writing, the self-conscious aestheticization of the events
described does not preclude the presence of deeper truth; rather, it confirms that the value of what is being communicated resides, as well, in the
manner of telling. Obviously, something is afoot in the recreation of this
poem. Although the poem discussed in chapter 11 of *Speak, Memory* is
not Nabokov's first in terms of historical chronology, it may be said to
mark the beginning of Nabokov's poetic canon and, by extension, the beginning of his career as a creative writer. In both *Poems and Problems* and
the posthumously published volume of selected Russian poetry from 1979,
Poems, Nabokov began with 'The Rain Has Flown,' indicating to posterity
that the trajectory of his career as poet and writer began with this poem.
Nabokov's autobiographical account of the inspiration for, and composition and delivery of, the poem 'The Rain Has Flown' is thus of importance
not alone for what it conveys about this one poem, but, more importantly,

for what it communicates regarding the creative process in general. As described from inspiration to recitation, this single poem encapsulates important elements of the experience of artistic consciousness and creativity:

> The rain has flown and burnt up in flight.
>   I tread the red sand of a path.
> Golden orioles whistle, the rowan is in bloom,
>   the catkins on sallows are white.
>
> The air is refreshing, humid and sweet.
>   How good the caprifole smells!
> Downward a leaf inclines its tip
>   and drops from its tip a pearl.   (*PP* 19)[1]

Itself a poem which brings sensual description to a minutely observed event from nature, Nabokov's subsequent reconstruction of his first poem begins with the luxuriously described physical world. With an abundance of detail, Nabokov brings into clear focus the time, place, and atmosphere of the setting which provoked the poem. Although not generally acknowledged as a writer of representational, mimetic fiction, it is to be noted that Nabokov's inspiration here derived from close observation of detail from the physical world and that Nabokov was careful to record the connection from visual setting to verbal rendering:

> A moment later my first poem began. What touched it off? I think I know. Without any wind blowing, the sheer weight of a raindrop, shining in parasitic luxury on a cordate leaf, caused its tip to dip, and what looked like a globule of quicksilver performed a sudden glissando down the center vein, and then, having shed its bright load, the relieved leaf unbent. Tip, leaf, dip, relief – the instant it all took to happen seemed to me not so much a fraction of time as a fissure in it, a missed heartbeat, which was refunded at once by a patter of rhymes: (*SM* 217)[2]

Not infrequently represented as an artist disparaging of the depiction of the physical world – in favour of pure fabulations – Nabokov's account of his first poem reveals that the inspiration to create art is born not out of avoidance but of heightened awareness of the world, in this instance the sight of a leaf tipping and dripping water after a storm at a particular time in a particular place.[3] In this, Nabokov shares a character trait with many of the most sympathetic of his characters – and in particular poets – who revel in observation and enjoyment of the 'trifling' wonder of the world. The poetic consciousness is a consciousness keenly attuned to the sensual and emotional pleasures of its environment. Rather than shunning contact with reality, the poet enlivens reality, takes the subject matter which has faded to 'average reality' through overfamiliarity and lack of specific attention, reshapes it with imagination and poetic reference to the sensual power of sight, sound, and smell into something physically revitalized through words. This is the purport of Nabokov's statement from *Strong Opinions* concerning the poet's relationship to reality: 'To be sure, there is an average reality, perceived by all of us, but that is not true reality: it is only the reality of general ideas, conventional forms of humdrummery, current editorials ... Average reality begins to rot and stink as soon as *the act of individual creation ceases to animate a subjectively perceived texture*' (*SO* 118; emphasis added). Rather than escaping into aesthetics, Nabokov suggests, the poetic consciousness is responsible for reanimating a world of experience that has become worn and faded. This is comparable to, though more than, the formalist project of *ostranenie*, for it also includes the important element of consciousness seeking out and reconfirming orientation in existence. Hence Nabokov's identification of the 'positional' impulse of poetry: 'But then, in a sense, all poetry is positional: to try to express one's position in regard to the universe embraced by consciousness, is an immemorial urge. The arms of consciousness reach out and grope, and the longer they are the better' (*SM* 218). In this configuration, poetry and all artistic creation is epistemological, driven by the need to exercise the limits of consciousness and expand the boundaries of awareness.

One of the central ontological coordinates of being is time. And Nabokov's autobiography literally begins with the coupling of time and consciousness in the form of Nabokov's reminiscence of his awakening into conscious thought as a child through his sudden awareness of his age relative to that of his parents. The experience is formative, leaving him feeling as if he had been 'plunged abruptly into a radiant and mobile medium that was none other than the pure element of time' (*SM* 21). Submersion in time heralds awareness of consciousness and the individual's ineluctable separateness from the surrounding human environment. Temporal duration also ensures human confinement in the 'prison' of time, a medium which constructs walls separating consciousness from the 'eternities of darkness' before birth and after death. Dissatisfied with this condition, Nabokov announced that throughout the course of his life he had repeatedly 'made colossal efforts to distinguish the faintest of personal glimmers in the impersonal darkness on both sides of life' and that 'this darkness is caused merely by the walls of time separating me and my bruised fists from the free world of timelessness' (*SM* 20). Nabokov's prison-break from time, a crossing out of the usual confines of life to another realm of time-space and consciousness, was in important ways a literary endeavour. Inspiration and the writing of poetry are thus an expression of Nabokov's banging of his fists against the walls of time, as may be gleaned from his autobiographical account of 'The Rain Has Flown.' In his description of its creation, Nabokov identifies the jolt of inspiration which occasioned his first poem with a disruption in the passage of time. This 'fissure' in the texture of time is a fundamental feature of inspiration and witness to the young Nabokov's experience of cosmic synchronization.

Poetic Consciousness

In his reconstitution of his first poem, Nabokov, through recourse to the fictional 'Vivian Bloodmark,' describes a process and feeling omnipresent in Nabokov's oeuvre, but most visibly experienced by many of the positive characters from Nabokov's writing, especially the finest poets of his fictional universe, Fyodor Godunov-Cherdyntsev and John Shade. 'Cosmic synchronization' is the term provided to depict the wondrous feeling when the fabric of time is rent and the individual is dispersed throughout time and space during an unusual moment of altered, expanded consciousness.[4] During such moments, consciousness slips the confines of time and space as conventionally known to enter a realm where temporal chronology and physical proximity are no longer of defining relevance. In such a state, simultaneity, rather than contiguity, governs the relationships between time and space; the individual undergoing such an experience is strangely aware of dissolving out of one contained realm and expanding into the infinite expanses of another. This new realm of being is characterized by the ability of consciousness, now expanded, to experience all time and space simultaneously in a single instant. Important to this experience is the act of transition, and throughout Nabokov's oeuvre the feeling of cosmic synchronization is associated with liminal states of being – fever, death, dreams, delirium, the emotional transport of love, and, above all, the trance of poetic inspiration – where consciousness is susceptible to a crossing-over from one state and realm of experience to another. Although also associated with fever and madness, cosmic synchronization is defining of the experience of love and creative inspiration when the creative consciousness perceives at an instant the potential and wondrous mystery of other realms of being. While depicted numerous times in Nabokov's writing – first in his poetry and then his prose – it was, significantly, in the reconstruction of his own first experience of poetic inspiration that Nabokov provided this phenomenon with a non-fictional name and narrative description:

> Vivian Bloodmark, a philosophical friend of mine, in later years, used to say that while the scientist sees everything that happens in one point of space, the poet feels everything that happens in one point of time. Lost in thought, he taps his knee with his wandlike pencil, and at the same instant a car (New York license plate) passes along the road, a child bangs the screen door of a neighboring porch, an old man yawns in a misty Turkestan orchard, a granule of cinder-gray sand is rolled by the wind on Venus, a Docteur Jacques Hirsch in Grenoble puts on his reading glasses, and trillions of other such trifles occur – all forming an instantaneous and transparent organism of events, of which the poet (sitting in a lawn chair, at Ithaca, N.Y.) is the nucleus. (*SM* 218)

Identified as it is with the fictional character Bloodmark, the phenomenon of 'cosmic synchronization' is not entirely free of suspicion regarding its validity. The possibility has to at least be acknowledged – though it would seem remote – that this is perhaps another instance of Nabokov the hoaxer leading credulous readers down the 'garden trail,' in this instance the garden trail at Vyra in 1914. Despite potential reservations, however, Nabokov's claim that 'a person hoping to become a poet must have the capacity of thinking of several things at a time' (*SM* 218) seems legitimate, while repeated depictions of cosmic synchronization across Nabokov's oeuvre lend it credence[5]. It is also a concept of a piece with Nabokov's comments on the creative process found in discursive texts ranging from 'The Art of Literature and Commonsense' to 'Inspiration.' What the mature Nabokov termed cosmic synchronization immediately recalls the phenomenon 'cosmic consciousness' discussed in William James's *The Varieties of Religious Experience* (James 344–6). As a creative artist, Nabokov's reference to cosmic synchronization seems to place him in the company of a long line of poets, though especially the Romantics, who described experience of what Abrams termed a 'revelatory and luminous Moment' (Abrams 387). William Wordsworth, for instance, famously recorded his experiences of 'unknown modes of being,' which appear similar to those found in Nabokov's autobiography and art. In Book 2 of *The Prelude*, Wordsworth describes one of his 'spots of time' in terms of a physical form of transcendence which corresponds to Nabokov's experience of cosmic synchronization and which seems equally relevant to the quality of Wordsworth's consciousness as poet:

I was only then
Contented when with bliss ineffable
I felt the sentiment of Being spread
O'er all that moves, and all that seemeth still,
O'er all, that, lost beyond the reach of thought
And human knowledge, to the human eye
Invisible, yet liveth to the heart   (ll. 418–24)

The generalized identification of Nabokov's experience with those associated with writers from Augustine to Stevens is of little service, however, in delineating its particular nature. Although the 'Moment' or 'spot of time' of cosmic synchronization is essential to Nabokov's poetics, this revelatory experience is not of central importance in and of itself, but for what it assumes – what intuited, irrational assumptions it entails for the poet and his art. The matter is worthy of further investigation. Most frequently associated with the experience of poetic inspiration, cosmic synchronization has obvious ramifications for Nabokov's aesthetics. It is also, moreover, to be linked with the ethical potential of literature and Nabokov's metaphysics. The cosmic synchronization Nabokov described as experienced during the rapture of inspiration is itself predicated upon the existence of another transcendent realm of being beyond the shared empirical world. The liminal quality of the phenomenon, with its references to a 'crossing-over,' suggests the existence of another, metaphysical realm which, in turn, supports belief in the essential goodness of the world. As will be seen below, the 'cosmic synchronization' experienced above all by creative artists, and especially poets, is linked by 'bliss' to Nabokov's metaphysics of an otherworld and, importantly, the ethics of love.

Exemplified via reference to the specific poem 'The Rain Has Flown,' Nabokov strengthens the importance of 'cosmic synchronization' by further describing it in his account of its occurrence during the writing of all his poems at the time. Struck by the inspiration that follows in the wake of intense perception of the physical world, the young poet Nabokov is launched into a trancelike state in which another quality of consciousness is lived, one in which the contiguous quality of time and space as usually experienced no longer reigns over understanding. Released into his 'private mist' (*SM* 223) of sole concentration on the completion of his poem, awareness of his surroundings ceased for the young poet Nabokov:

When I was irrevocably committed to finish my poem or die, there came the most trancelike state of all. With hardly a twinge of surprise, I found myself, of all places, on a leathern couch in the cold, musty, little-used room that had been my grandfather's study. On that couch I lay prone, in a kind of reptilian freeze, one arm dangling, so that my knuckles loosely touched the floral figures of the carpet. When next I came out of that trance, the greenish flora was still there, my arm was still dangling, but now I was prostrate on the edge of a rickety wharf, and the water lilies I touched were real... So little did ordinary measures of existence mean in that state that I would not have been surprised to come out of its tunnel right into the park of Versailles, or the Tiergarten, or Sequoia National Forest ... (*SM* 223)

In this state, not only were the usual confines of time and space removed, consciousness itself seemed to expand. Thus associated with the inspiration and composition of his poem, Nabokov once more confirmed and emphasized the nature of 'cosmic synchronicity' when recounting the recitation of his poem, the culminating experience of his first encounter with poetic creativity. Completing the recitation of his poem to his enraptured mother, the young Nabokov reached for the mirror offered by his mother:

Presently I finished reciting and looked up at her. She was smiling ecstatically through the tears that streamed down her face. 'How wonderful, how beautiful,' she said, and with the tenderness in her smile still growing, she passed me a hand mirror so that I might see the smear of blood on my cheek-bone where at some indeterminable time I had crushed a gorged mosquito by the unconscious act of propping my cheek on my fist. But I saw more than that. Looking into my own eyes, I had the shocking sensation of finding *the mere dregs of my usual self, odds and ends of an evaporated identity which it took my reason quite an effort to gather again in the glass.* (*SM* 227; emphasis added)

In the recitation of his poem, Nabokov's ego, his self, has been expanded and dissolved in a realm and state not governed by reason and the normal laws of physical experience. Returning out of this state to his usual self, Nabokov catches himself in the mirror returning to normality as his 'evaporated identity' is reassembled in the here and now of waking consciousness. The inspiration, composition, and recitation of his poem have initiated a crossing-over into another state of consciousness; the completion of the work brings him back to the conventional experience of time and space, returns his ego and consciousness, which had been released from the confines of physicality, to his mortal body. The fissure in time and conventional consciousness is closed. The prison-wall of time is once again erected.

The Metaphysical Nabokov and the Otherworld

The fundamentally metaphysical character of the experience of cosmic synchronization seems evident. Nabokov's experience of his first poem and cosmic synchronization presumes the existence· of a transcendent realm beyond, around, and prior to the physical world of time and space. This phenomenon, however, is likewise aesthetic; for the ultimate experience of consciousness – the breaking out of time and space – is associated with artistry, in this instance the composition of a poem. Indeed, the pinnacle of consciousness this side of death is artistic creation and the feeling of love. Finally, an ethical dimension is also intimately related to cosmic synchronization; love and cosmic confirmation of the 'goodness' of being are both synonymous with the 'bliss' and 'rapture' of heightened (aesthetic) consciousness.

Despite the unmistakable aesthetic and ethical dimensions of cosmic synchronization, both cosmic synchronization and Nabokov's poetry are firmly based on a uniquely Nabokovian metaphysics which has far-reaching consequences for the reading of his artistry. And here discussion is compelled to acknowledge the perhaps most controversial topic in Nabokov scholarship – despite its frequent rehearsal in Nabokov criticism. This compulsion is driven by the realization that Nabokov's poetry is clearly freighted with metaphysical import and because it is this dimension which comprises one of the two essential features of the lyric voice linking his poetic and prose writing in a composite whole. Despite the fundamental importance of the question of Nabokov's metaphysics, the following does not pretend to the status of a definite statement regarding the philosophical contours of Nabokov's oeuvre, the legitimate subject of an independent study. Rather, this discussion is intended foremost to offer initial clarification concerning the metaphysical dimension of Nabokov's artistry. Quite apart from serving in a descriptive analysis of Nabokov's poetic sensibility and voice, the issue is of considerable importance in confronting influential and yet foreshortened reservations about Nabokov's verse. As was observed above, Nabokov's poetry has been chided for its supposed reliance on other poets – many of whom are of a more explicitly metaphysical caste – but also its presumed religiosity (another topic to be addressed below). Clarity regarding the particular metaphysical quality of Nabokov's sensibility is essential for distinguishing it from assumed influence, but also for identifying an important feature of Nabokov's sensibility which lends his artistic expressions the monogram of individuality.

Although the metaphysical potential of Nabokov's writing had been the subject of earlier, albeit limited, comment,[6] it was not until the appearance of Nabokov's posthumously published volume of poetry *Poems,* with Véra Nabokov's foreword, that the topic received closer attention. In her opening commentary, Nabokov's wife indicated the centrality to Nabokov's life and work of a single theme of metaphysical import:

> ... I would like to direct the reader's attention to Nabokov's main theme. It has never, it appears to me, been remarked upon by anyone, although, incidentally, it pervades everything that he wrote; like a water mark, it symbolizes his entire oeuvre. I am speaking of the 'otherworld' as he himself called it in his final poem: 'Being in Love.'[7]

Given the poetry-based emphasis of this study, it is legitimate to observe already here the patterned 'symmetry' of Nabokov's identification of the otherworld in discursive texts treating his poetry. Nabokov's clearest programmatic identification of the mysteries of inspiration and cosmic synchronization occurred in *Speak, Memory* in his account of his *first* poem; it is thus appropriate that Nabokov should name this 'main theme' in his *final* poem and that both the poem and Véra Nabokov's comment should be contained within his final publication, a collection of poetry. It is also of significance that Véra Nabokov should credit Nabokov's awareness of this 'mystery' or 'secret' (тайна / *taina*) with his 'imperturbable love of life and lucidity even during the most terrible of tribulations.' Beyond its obvious literary importance to his writing, this central theme apparently also had ethical relevance to Nabokov, providing him – as Véra Nabokov observed – with reserves of confidence and perseverance in the face of life's difficulties.

In the wake of Véra Nabokov's revelations, and led by several prominent studies, scholarship has since undertaken a significant reassessment of Nabokov's writing. Among the earliest, most influential investigations to respond to Véra Nabokov's authoritative observations was D. Barton Johnson's *Worlds in Regression.* In this detailed study of selected texts from across Nabokov's oeuvre, Johnson develops a reading of 'an underlying "two-world" cosmology' in Nabokov's writing. Responding to the possibility that 'the aesthetic [two-world] cosmology that governs the novels was not without significance for his personal life' (Johnson 1985, 2), Johnson is above all at pains to reveal the aesthetic consequences of this belief for Nabokov's writing in both formal and thematic terms. Such features of Nabokov's fiction as 'mirroring,' 'doubling,' 'inversion,' 'self-reflectiveness,' 'pattern,' 'coincidence,' and 'involution,' as well as the complex play of references between *tut* and *tam*, 'here' and 'there,' are thus all synthesized by Johnson in a powerful argument underscoring Nabokov's aesthetic use of, if not personal belief in, another transcendent realm. Johnson's 'two-world' thesis was further expanded upon and implemented in the important examination of Nabokov's poetry for *Russian Literature Triquarterly* discussed in the previous chapter. In 'The Otherworldly in Nabokov's Poetry,' for instance, Julian W. Connolly adopted the two-world rubric to discuss Nabokov's verse according to four main categories, one of which subsumes 'poems about a supernatural "other" realm – a world that exists beyond our physical dimensions and that can be comprehended completely only after death' (Connolly 1991, 330). Building upon his important discussion of the related topic of consciousness in *Nabokov's 'Ada': The Place of Consciousness*, Brian Boyd in his two-volume biography of Nabokov repeatedly returned to the metaphysical dimension in Nabokov's life and writing. It was Vladimir Alexandrov in his *Nabokov's Otherworld*, however, who offered the most comprehensive treatment of the 'otherworldly' in Nabokov's writing. The power and importance of Alexandrov's discussion of the topic stems from his intention not simply to trace the theme in Nabokov's works, but to position it as the basis of an entirely new reading of Nabokov's oeuvre: 'The aim of this book is to dismantle the widespread critical view that Vladimir Nabokov (1899–1977) is first and foremost a meta-literary writer, and to suggest instead that an aesthetic rooted in his intuition of a transcendent realm is the basis of his art' (Alexandrov 1991, 3). Since the publication of Alexandrov's excellent investigation of the topic, numerous more recent studies have appeared which have likewise taken up the issue.[8] Indeed, as indicated above, for some critics, the topic of Nabokov's intuited belief in the 'otherworld' is threatening to choke out other subjects of discussion and investigation in Nabokov criticism. The issue now needs to be addressed with the aid of insights gained from a reading of Nabokov's poetry; for, as previously suggested, it is an understanding of Nabokov's poetry which accommodates the coexistence of the aesthetic, the ethical, and the metaphysical within a unified Nabokovian oeuvre.

In his formulation of a two-world model for Nabokov's universe – fictional and personal – D. Barton Johnson emphasized the duality of Nabokov's cosmology in his evocation of both Neoplatonism and Gnosticism (Johnson 1985, 2). Reference to two such codified systems of thought immediately conjures forth the hazards inherent in a discussion of Nabokov's metaphysics. As a poet and author, Nabokov was uninterested in, indeed emphatically avoided, identification with movements or schools of thought. Nabokov was most adamantly not a member of any school. Indeed, the rejection of formalized systems of philosophical assertion, even when treating topics of philosophical import, is a central feature of

Nabokov's artistry and of his understanding of the role of the artist. Despite the danger of seeming to force the autodidact Nabokov into an ill-fitting school uniform, however, reference to such systems may profitably serve criticism if only by providing a heuristic vocabulary and point of comparison with the specificity of Nabokov's poetically expressed example. As long as they serve the illumination of Nabokov's writing, they are, like reference to Nabokov's discursive writing, useful tools. Thus, in coming eventually to an analysis of the otherworld in Nabokov's poetry, it will be necessary to consider Nabokov's disparate comments in his discursive writing and to propose comparison to similar expressions of belief, especially when they relate to the creation of art.

The Platonism invoked by Johnson seems a relevant point of departure, not least because Nabokov himself referred to Plato. In discussing the process of writing, Nabokov suggested that his works came to him from another realm where they existed in an ideal form:

> I am afraid to get mixed up with Plato, whom I do not care for, but I do think that in my case it is true that the entire book, before it is written, seems to be ready ideally in some other, now transparent, now dimming, dimension, and my job is to take down as much of it as I can make out and as precisely as I am humanly able to. (*SO* 69)

As perhaps the last writer ever to contemplate rescinding the poet's *droit de cité*, as suggested in Book X of *The Republic*, it is not surprising that Nabokov was hesitant about identification with Plato.[9] Nonetheless, the (neo)Platonic quality of Nabokov's statement is apparent. Nabokov's artistry seems to stem from another transcendent realm, although the exact nature of this realm is not to be contained in descriptive language. As something clearly associated with the irrational, the essence of the otherworld could not be communicated in the language of common sense and experience according to the grammar of reason. Knowledge of this realm is intuited and, paradoxically, most convincingly confirmed for Nabokov by the absence of any other argument against it besides that mustered by common sense:

> That human life is but a first installment of the serial soul and that one's individual secret is not lost in the process of earthly dissolution, becomes something more than an optimistic conjecture, and even more than a matter of religious faith, when we remember that only commonsense rules immortality out. (*LL* 377)

Given the *sui generis* quality of the otherworld and the inability of finite human intelligence to conceptualize the infinite, Nabokov turned to the intuited knowledge of poetry. In this, Nabokov is not unlike the greatest poet of his fictional universe, John Shade. Confronted with a conundrum similar to the one facing Nabokov – the intuition of an otherworld which could not be rationally conceptualized – Shade utilized poetry's potential for metaphor, symmetry, and formal perfection to replicate and approximate the wonders of the otherworld, the realm from whence poetry comes:

> I feel I understand
> Existence, or at least a minute part
> Of my existence, only through my art,
> In terms of combinational delight;
> And if my private universe scans right,
> So does the verse of galaxies divine
> Which I suspect is an iambic line.   (*PF* 68–9; ll. 971–7)

Thus Shade, and through him Nabokov, effectively turns Plato on his head. Rather than function as a failed imitator of the 'truth,'[10] the poet-artist is alone capable of nearing representation of a transcendent beyond, albeit guided by the poet's sense of wondrous awe and trust in the irrational over dogmatic certainty.

Despite this partial reversal of Plato, the antecedents and correspondences to Nabokov's metaphysics of the otherworld are to be identified in the context of Neoplatonic traditions in literature, although none may justifiably be spoken of in terms of Nabokov's explicit adherence to a school of thought. Exceptionally well versed in a number of literary traditions, Nabokov was particularly close to Russian literature. And as Vladimir Alexandrov has indicated, features of Nabokov's linkage of poetry to metaphysics may be correlated with that of the Symbolists and, in particular, two of the Symbolist poets Nabokov openly expressed admiration for: Alexandr Blok and Andrei Belyi.[11] Central to the Symbolist aesthetic was a dualistic view of existence dividing human life on earth from a higher reality which could not be experienced in a direct, phenomenal manner but which was subject to intuited understanding.[12] Given the dual nature of being, poetry functioned as both vessel and instrument of understanding of the other, transcendental realm. Although Nabokov's writing suggests accordance with these central tenets, it is not Symbolist in any programmatic manner. Nabokov's aesthetic is not informed by the desire to establish poetic and metaphysical theories, as is the case with the Russian

Symbolists. Likewise, Nabokov's work, apart from isolated early poems, does not utilize, much less promulgate, a developed system of Christian iconography. Neither does Nabokov employ 'symbols' in expression of another universal realm of being or priorize music or 'correspondences' between different forms of artistic expression. Even the epiphanic experience of inspiration, so central to Nabokov's mysterious concept of cosmic synchronization, is not charged with the ecstasy of religious experience common to some of the Russian Symbolists. Indeed, in *Pale Fire*, the confusion between religious and artistic inspiration is lightly parodied. In short, although Nabokov's fictional and discursive writing certainly stresses the priority and autonomy of art and defends the value of the irrational in experience of the world and even emphasizes the multi-layeredness of reality, nowhere does it strive towards the status of an organized system of thought.[13] Quite the contrary: Nabokov's poetics is individual, inductive, and proceeding out of artistic engagement with the world of experience; it is not deductive, or an attempt to formulate poetic experience as the confirmation of abstract systems of thought. Nabokov's artistic and metaphysical ideals are revealed in his writing as an essential portion of their positional function.

Rather than appeal to the Symbolist aesthetic in the search for potential models for Nabokov's poetic practice and metaphysics, a more promising reference from within the Russian literary tradition seems likely in Acmeism, particularly as articulated by Nikolai Gumilev. For a variety of reasons, Gumilev seems to have been a figure more amenable to Nabokov. In the first poem of *The Empyrean Path*, for instance, Nabokov announced his almost programmatic rejection of Symbolist obfuscation for adherence to an Acmeist aesthetic of precision and directness. In 1927, in an omnibus review of poetry for *Rul'*, Nabokov took the opportunity both to praise Gumilev's artistry and memory and to indicate the narrative quality of his own lyric poetics: 'Of Gumilev it is impossible to speak without agitation. There will still come a time when Russia will take pride in him. In reading him you realize, incidentally, that a poem cannot simply be a "construct," a "lyric something," an assemblage of chance images, a fog, a blind alley. Above all, a poem must be interesting' (*Ssoch* II, 639). In 'The Art of Literature and Commonsense,' Nabokov documented his deep respect for Gumilev as poet and smilingly defiant martyr to Soviet repression. Gumilev, in an article of 1913, 'Наследие символизма и акмеизм' ('Nasledie simvolizma i akmeism' / 'Acmeism and the Legacy of Symbolism'), openly addressed the connection of poetry to an unknowable beyond, basing his poetics of Acmeism upon both the cognizance of this ineffable realm and the inability to express it. Symbolism, according to Gumilev, had defined itself in directing its attentions to the 'unseen,' but in doing so had, regrettably, overextended into the sphere of myth-making. Acmeism, in contrast, would with 'diamond coldness' register the presence of a mystical unknowable, but never seek to contain it in representational forms of discourse:

> The first thing that Acmeism may respond to that question will be to indicate that the unknowable, by the very meaning of the word, cannot be known. Secondly, that all attempts in this direction are unchaste. The full beauty, the entire sacred meaning of the stars resides in that they are infinitely distant from the earth and, despite all successes in aviation, will never become nearer. The poverty of imagination is revealed in those who continually imagine the evolution of personality in terms of time and space. How are we to remember our earlier existence (if that is not obviously a literary conceit) in an abyss where there are myriad different opportunities of being of which we know nothing other than that they exist? For each of them is reflected by our being and in turn reflects it. An agonizingly sweet, childishly-wise sense of our own incognizance – that is what provides us with the unknown ... Always remember the unknowable, though never insult one's conception of it with more or less plausible conjectures – that is the principle of Acmeism. (Gumilev 57–8)

The metaphysical, though intuited and non-dogmatic, dimensions of Gumilev's comments are obvious and concord with Nabokov's strivings to develop a poetic idiom based on crystalline perspicacity and underpinned by an ineffable two-world cosmology. Gumilev's reference to the wisdom of a child in the context of metaphysics is a further dimension to be explored more fully below.

Apart from Gumilev, reference to possible precursors to Nabokov's metaphysics may just as easily draw discussion to an earlier figure of influence for the Russian and French Symbolists, and a writer for whom Nabokov expressed measured admiration and acknowledgment in the form of frequent parody and complimentary reference, Edgar Allan Poe. Dale E. Peterson has elegantly and thoroughly described the similarities between Poe and Nabokov in terms of their 'militant aestheticism' and the manner in which Nabokov's parody of Poe was expressive of a deep affinity which derived from 'the perception that genuine poetry is inseparable from the spirit of parody' (Peterson 1989, 97). For Peterson, Nabokov and Poe shared a similar poetics of composition. The similarities identified by Peterson between their respective 'philosophies of composition' may also be extended to their metaphysics, though only to a limited extent. In his posthumously published 'The Poetic Principle' (1850), apart from excoriating 'the heresy of *The Didactic*,' Poe suggests a Neoplatonic source for the power and pull of poetry. According to Poe, rather than appealing to the human capacities of intellect and morality in the service, respectively, of truth and duty, poetry appeals exclusively to the sense of taste in expression of an instinctual appreciation of beauty. Significant for its Neoplatonic parallel to Nabokov's 'otherworld,' Poe located the source of beauty – what he termed 'supernal Loveliness' – in a transcendent realm which was to be approximated and glimpsed by art:

> An immortal instinct within the spirit of man, is thus, plainly, a sense of the Beautiful ... It is no mere appreciation of the Beauty before us – but a wild effort to reach the Beauty above. Inspired by an ecstatic prescience of the glories beyond the grave, we struggle, by multiform combinations among the things and thoughts of Time, to attain a portion of that Loveliness whose very elements, perhaps, appertain to eternity alone. And thus when poetry – or when by Music, the most entrancing of the Poetic moods – we find ourselves melted into tears – we weep then   not as the Abbate Gravina supposes – through excess of pleasure, but through a certain, petulant, impatient sorrow at our inability to grasp *now*, wholly, here on earth, at once and for ever, those divine and rapturous joys, of which *through* the poem, or *through* the music, we attain to but brief and indeterminate glimpses. (Poe 505)

The dominant emotional mood identified here through the vocabulary of 'an ecstatic prescience of the glories beyond the grave' and 'divine and rapturous joys' is already distant from Nabokov, whose approach to the otherworld, as expressed in his poetry, was one of wondrous awe and curiosity. Poe is also concerned with the *readerly* experience of transcendence, whereas Nabokov focuses on *authorial* intimation of a beyond. Neither did Nabokov revel in morbid identification with the abstractions of an ideal realm at the expense of consciousness and wonder of the phenomenal beauties of the world, as did, for example, Poe's Roderick Usher, of whose writings the narrator of 'The Fall of the House of Usher' claims: 'I fancied that I perceived, and for the first time, a full consciousness on the part of Usher, of the tottering of his lofty reason upon her throne' (Poe 147). The numerous figures in Nabokov's fictional universe who, like the unhinged Usher, fall into madness and despair are the distorted mirror images of the poet-artists of his oeuvre who, despite personal tragedy, maintain their equilibrium through love, appreciation of the natural world, and the solace of artistic creation. As will be illustrated below, the metaphysical, otherworldly dimension of

Nabokov's poetics is tempered by, and securely grounded in, precise attention to the realia of physical existence. Nonetheless, reminiscent of Nabokov's metaphysical realm is a transcendent sphere outside the limitations of time, a locus from which poetry mysteriously derives. For both, this metaphysical dimension was crucial to their poetics of inspiration, as writing was somehow a 'taking down' of the material available from another sphere; hence, the vital importance to Poe, and especially Nabokov, of formal perfection. The beauty and symmetry of poetry was both access to, and a reflection of, the perfection of a transcendent otherworld otherwise resistant to direct representation.

Stylistically distant from the Russian Symbolists, the Acmeist Gumilev, and the American Poe, but, like them, united as the object of Nabokovian fascination in the metaphysical potential of literature, are the Georgian poets Rupert Brooke and Walter de la Mare. As in his interest in individual Russian Symbolists and Poe, Nabokov himself identified his early affinity for the Georgians Brooke and de la Mare. In *Speak, Memory*, for instance, Nabokov claims to see in his early Russian verse the pernicious influence 'of various contemporaneous ("Georgian") English verse patterns that were running about my room and all over me like tame mice' (*SM* 266), while in a letter to Edmund Wilson, he suggests that the poetry of *The Empyrean Path* was 'strongly influenced by the Georgian poets, Rupert Brooke, De la Mare, etc., by whom I was much fascinated at the time' (*NWL* 87).[14] In the context of study of the metaphysical dimension of Nabokov's writing, recent scholarship has turned to examination of a potential connection between Nabokov and the Georgians. As the poet-critic Jonathan Borden Sisson has observed: 'Transcendence into another world is a vital theme throughout Nabokov's work, and a comparative study of Brooke's and Walter de la Mare's poems and Nabokov's essay and early poems could illuminate its first manifestations' (Sisson 1995, 531). In confirmation of Sisson's assumption, D. Barton Johnson has published informative articles concerning Nabokov and both de la Mare and Brooke.[15] As Johnson indicates, in the absence of all but the briefest of explicit references to de la Mare by Nabokov, it is difficult to establish more than the traces of echoes and congruences between the two authors. And although Nabokov complained of the influence of Georgian poets on his Russian verse, Johnson is quite correct in observing that what has subsequently been identified as the 'Georgian' strain in Nabokov's poetry predates Nabokov's familiarity with de la Mare and Brooke. Nonetheless, despite the difficulty in isolating specific, Georgian formal elements within Nabokov's writing, the theme of the otherworld so frequently associated with de la Mare is prevalent. As

Sisson states: 'Nabokov clearly reflects a general affinity with de la Mare (1873–1956). He shares de la Mare's fondness for alliteration and enchantment and his implicit "conviction," as W.H. Auden writes in an essay on de la Mare, "that what our senses perceive of the world about us is not all there is to know"' (Sisson 1995, 531).

Although of the two, de la Mare is more frequently associated with the metaphysical mysteries of the otherworld, it was Rupert Brooke for whom Nabokov indicated greater critical fascination, and it is in Nabokov's response to Brooke that the clearest traits of his own poetic identity are to be discerned. In 1921 Nabokov wrote his first critical article, to be published the following year in the Berlin journal *Grani*. Studded with lengthy translations of Brooke's poetry, Nabokov's article, 'Rupert Bruk,' is of interest not only as the location of Nabokov's first use of the term 'otherworld' (*potustoronnost'*) but for the perspective it offers on the thematic and stylistic aspirations which would help to form Nabokov's poetics (*Ssoch* I, 728–44).[16] Appropriate to Nabokov's idiosyncratically lyric approach to critical analysis, 'Rupert Bruk' begins not with empirical exposition but with the narrative depiction of Nabokov's rumination on minutely observed and poetically described fish in an aquarium. Contemplation of the fish swimming about in their 'pale-green eternity' brings Nabokov the young critic to thoughts of Brooke's poetry, in which 'the deep image of our being' may be felt (*Ssoch* I, 728). As Nabokov's introductory approach to his topic would suggest, his concern is less to systematically address the surface themes and stylistic preoccupations of Brooke's poetry than to attend to the deeper effect and metaphysical undertow of Brooke's writing.[17] As Johnson observes: 'The heart of Nabokov's essay focuses on Brooke's theme of death and the hereafter…' In Nabokov's words: 'No other poet has so often, with such tormented and creative perspicacity, gazed into the twilight of the otherworld' (*Ssoch* I, 731). The metaphysical inclination expressed in Brooke's poetry clearly attracted Nabokov and led him to statements indicative of his own proclivity to beliefs and poetry of a metaphysical quality: 'He [Brooke] very well knows that death is but a surprise; he is a bard of eternal life, tenderness, forest shades, transparent streams and fragrance; he need not have compared the burning pain of separation with heartburn and a belch' (*Ssoch* I, 738). While indicating his high estimation of the metaphysical strain in Brooke's poetry, in a manner already suggestive of his later statements, Nabokov demonstrated his impatience with conventional representations of the otherworld, that which is 'humanly imaginative' and thereby 'metaphysically limited': 'He so vividly feels the divine in the surrounding natural environment: of what interest to him that window-dressing eternity, Vrubel-like angels, that lord with the beard of cotton wool?' (*Ssoch* I, 742).

Nabokov is clearly attracted by the metaphysical depths of Brooke's writing and the force of its representation of the wonder and specificity of the world, although openly resistant to depictions of the transcendent in terms of the conventionally religious. It is not merely Brooke's expression of metaphysical themes which draws Nabokov's praise, however, but also Brooke's combination of an intimation of existence after death with aesthetically charged representation of his love for the realia of life and nature on earth: 'I repeat, Rupert Brooke loves the world with its lakes and waterfalls with a passionate, penetrating, dizzying love' (*Ssoch* I, 734). A sentiment essential to Nabokov's identity as a poet – as will be more fully discussed below – this quality within Brooke's poetry is presented as evidence of the poet's passionate love of life and the wondrous multiplicity of existence on earth (*Ssoch* I, 734). This love of nature, Nabokov saw not simply as a celebration of the living but as an integral portion of profound interest in the nature of existence after death. It is this same love of, and fascination for, the *thingness* of living existence which Nabokov expressed in his own poetry in combination with attraction for the realm intuited beyond the physical world. Indeed, from his discussion of Brooke's poetic probings of the otherworld and his sensuous depiction of the physical world, Nabokov expressed in critical terms what would subsequently develop into one of the central themes of his own poetry – the unwillingness to abandon the pleasures of life for the treasures of the beyond. As Nabokov would express it to dramatic effect in his play *The Waltz Invention* and in numerous poems, the beauty to be forsaken *here* on earth is but poorly compensated for by the supernal wonders intuited *there*: 'He [Brooke] knew, however, that although he may perhaps find an inexpressible wonderful paradise, he will necessarily leave forever his humid, living and expressive world' (*Ssoch* I, 734). This quintessentially Nabokovian theme, identified by Nabokov in Brooke's poetry, clearly predates his closer acquaintance with the English poet during his studies in Cambridge, as, for instance, indicated by the untitled poem of 1919 'Эту жизнь я люблю исступленной любовью' ('Etu zhizn' ia liubliu isstuplennoi liubov'iu …' / 'This life I love with an ecstatic love …').

Thus, although as Johnson has suggested, Nabokov's reading of Brooke is at times selective and thereby indicative of Nabokov's perceptions as much as Brooke's poetry and metaphysical beliefs, it is this very idiosyncrasy which reveals Nabokov's affinity for, though artistic independence from, Brooke. Nabokov was not influenced by Brooke in any discernible stylistic sense; hence, the absence of clearly Brookean tones in Nabokov's poetry. Nabokov was, however, clearly drawn to the features in Brooke's writing which confirmed the direction of his own developing aesthetic, as indicated by the example above. Here, it is two essential elements read by Nabokov in Brooke which merge into Nabokov's overarching obsession with consciousness – the mysteries of the otherworld and passionate affection for the unrepeatable uniqueness of life and the physical world. Full consciousness of this world is imperative for potential consciousness of the next. The Nabokovian poet is transfixed by both.

With regard to the metaphysical strain in his writing, Nabokov's relation to movements and personages as diverse as the Russian Symbolists, Nikolai Gumilev, Edgar Allan Poe, and Walter de la Mare and Rupert Brooke reveal two essential things. The metaphysical, Neoplatonic dimension of Nabokov's oeuvre may be compared to that exhibited in the fiction and discursive writing of a wide range of poets, all of whom may be clustered, if necessarily very loosely, under the rubrics of Romanticism and Neoromanticism. This is less than surprising. As Nabokov himself indicated, he was formed by poetry of the Silver Age of Russian literature, and intimately familiar with the writing of Vladimir Soloviev, Fedor Sologub, Konstantin Balmont, Viacheslav Ivanov, Andrei Belyi, and Alexandr Blok, to remain with the central figures of Russian Symbolism alone. As a wide and passionate reader of poetry, Nabokov was also knowledgeable of the writings of the French Symbolists and, through his deep admiration for such Russian poets of the nineteenth century as Fet and Tiutchev, the German romantics who had influenced Russian literature. Beyond a similar metaphysics, a belief in the existence of a higher, ideal reality, and the mysterious power of the poetic word to act as portal to other realms, however, little is to be gained in the attempt to identify Nabokov with this loosely defined tradition. The very diversity of Nabokov's poetic interests – the unlikely pairing of Brooke with Blok, for instance – suggests that the poet's *Wahlverwandtschaften* are at work here and not influence. Secondly, in the context of his metaphysics (and his ethics), Nabokov's is a lyric – rather than a discursive – voice. He drew primary inspiration from – and recorded his attraction to – the poetic practice of a wide range of poets, not from the manifestoes and systematized expositions of poet-theorists.[18] Likewise, what knowledge there is to be gleaned regarding Nabokov's metaphysics of an otherworld may be most profitably derived from his creative writing; it is in his poetic writing that Nabokov's metaphysics come to the fore in poetry which is expressive of a sensibility and not an ideology. While peerless in his defence of the highest aesthetic principles, in philosophical matters, Nabokov contends little, disdaining the compellent rigour of systemic, verifiable exposition for a mode of assertion dependent more on intimation and the mumbled speech of sleep than ex cathedra pronouncement. In conceptualizing Nabokov's non-discursive approach to the patently philosophical strain in his writing, above all poetry, it is perhaps illustrative to return to the arch-Romantic John Keats. In discussing Shakespeare, Keats famously identified the quality of 'negative capability, that is, when man is capable of being in uncertainties, mysteries, doubts, without any irritable reaching after fact and reason' (Keats 71). Nabokov's poetry seems eminently expressive of 'negative capability,' as witnessed in his creative ease in representing the ineffable without 'reaching after' the 'fact and reason' of organized systems of exposition. In a very real sense, it may be said that in communicating the depths of his aesthetic, metaphysical, and ethical beliefs, Nabokov wrote poetry, not prose. Analysis is thus perforce turned back to poetic practice.

Nabokov's Poetry: Five Themes

In acknowledgment of the emphasis displayed in the discussion of Nabokov's paradigmatic first poem and in support of the view that the fundamental concern of Nabokov's artistry is the exploration and expansion of consciousness, analysis of Nabokov's poetry will begin with Vivian Bloodmark's unusually Nabokovian concept of cosmic synchronization. This will be followed by a review of the themes of artistic inspiration, love, the otherworld, and lyric attentiveness to the trifles of being. Particular interpretive weight will be accorded the latter two themes; it is these two features which constitute the quintessence of Nabokov's poetry of this world and another. For although Nabokov's lyric sensibility is, in part, defined by an otherworldly component, it is equally marked by intense attachment to this world. In part instigated by intuitions of a beyond, poetry is nonetheless both of and about this world. Unavoidably, the following review will commit the Shelleyan murder of poetic dissection, for each of these five themes is to be isolated and distinguished from the unity of Nabokov's poetic corpus through the rationalizing violence of critical analysis only. In poetic form, they are interrelated in intricate patterns of effect and meaning. It is precisely the complex interweaving of these thematic threads which distinguishes Nabokov's artistic voice, lending his poetry the defining stamp of his lyric sensibility.

I. Cosmic Synchronization

Although first identified as a term in *Speak, Memory*, the concept of cosmic synchronization is a component of Nabokov's artistry which finds its fullest expression in poetic contexts within Nabokov's fiction and extends back to the earliest poetic sources of his oeuvre. Previous to its narrative depiction in *Speak, Memory* and a variety of other prose sources, the phenomenon may be identified in the lyric expression of his own early poetry. Of note here is *The Empyrean Path* of January 1923, Nabokov's fourth collection of poetry, which contains several poems descriptive of the sensations suggestive of cosmic synchronization which recur throughout his later writing. The early poem 'Поэт' ('Poet' / 'The Poet') of 1918, for instance, delineates the essential characteristic of a poet in terms of the specificity of his artistic consciousness. 'The Poet' describes the entranced consciousness of a first-person poet walking among the 'burnt-out ruins' and 'humiliating graves' that witness the destruction and insult of the world, while remaining untouched by even these, the most extreme of life's tribulations. Surrounded by the destruction of a troubled time, the poet is nonetheless able to wander full of life and strength, given over to yearnings not of this world. Gazing with 'inexplicable happiness' at the clear sky, he is literally oblivious; wandering with his 'invisible muse,' he is aloof in a state and space of spiritual contentedness where he needs of nothing but to sense the universe 'in his spiritual depths':

> Я в стороне. Молюсь, ликую,
> И ничего не надо мне,
> Когда вселенную я чую
> В своей душевной глубине.   (*Ssoch* I, 480)

[I am aloof. I pray, I rejoice, / and I require nothing, / when I feel the universe / in my spiritual depths.]

In this state and space of consciousness, the injustice and pain of the world 'are left somewhere far away.' The Russian wording chosen by Nabokov to describe this aloofness – 'Я в стороне' / 'Ia v storone' – is tantalizingly suggestive not only of psychological non-involvement but also of spatial distance, as if the poet were proceeding through life at a physical remove from his surroundings. Here, in the poet's 'spiritual depths,' which is simultaneously on the 'other side' in an unspecified physical sense, the poet converses with the waves and wind, and shares his pure dreams with the heavens:

То я беседую с волнами,
То с ветром, с птицей уношусь
И со святыми небесами
Мечтами чистыми делюсь.   (*Ssoch* I, 480)

[Now I converse with waves, / now with the wind, fly off with a bird / and with the sacred heavens / I share my pure dreams.]

Naive and willfully unsophisticated in both form and thematic content, 'The Poet' is nonetheless rescued from banality by its explicit self-consciousness and the deployment of images that would subsequently accompany Nabokov's literary development. More than an early example of cosmic synchronization, 'The Poet' is also an example of Nabokov's expression in early poetic form of one of the key themes in his writing – the conquering of the vulgar and intolerable in life through access to the superior facilities of the artistic consciousness.

In still another poem from the same collection, likewise entitled 'Поэт' ('Poet' / 'The Poet'), Nabokov strengthens the impression that the specificity of the poetic consciousness resides in its access to, and experience of, the wider realms of awareness associated with cosmic synchronization. In four quatrains of *AbAb* rhyme, 'The Poet' suggests that the poetic consciousness is defined by its awareness that the finite world of regular experience is one of illusion in comparison to the dimensionless wonders of other spheres. The poet is a poet, according to the opening lines, because of what he knows:

Он знал: отрада и тревога
и все, что зримо на земле, –
все только бред и прихоть Бога,
туман дыханья на стекле!   (*Ssoch* I, 540)

[He knew: delight and disquiet / and everything visible on earth – / all is but nonsense and the whim of God, / the steam of breath on glass!]

In contrast to the realm of life as a wide-awake dream is another more fundamental world 'infinitely dear' to the poet and which is experienced 'from oblivion to oblivion.' This other transcendent realm is a space entered during the intense heat of incessant inspiration, a place travelled to 'on the wings of a wondrous illness' and which is located in parallel sphere 'alongside the paths of everyday life.' Here Nabokov is deploying a motif which is frequently used within his writing of illness and fever as liminal states which function as fissures in the pattern of daily life and which allow expansion of consciousness into another more primal realm. Many of the 'poets' of Nabokov's fictional universe experience an illness as mysterious as the wonder of their artistic consciousness. In this space of expanded, inspired consciousness, the poet is able to pluck 'fragrant verse' from the depths of a 'passionate lily.'

It would seem significant to an appreciation of the importance of consciousness and poetry in Nabokov's writing that he attributed the fundamental experience of cosmic synchronicity to poets and provided artistic expression to the phenomenon in two poems both entitled 'The Poet.' Such early expressions were not left isolated, and throughout Nabokov's oeuvre, poetic depiction of cosmic synchronization and the mysterious expansion of consciousness has come in many forms. In 'Формула' ('Formula' / 'The Formula') of 1931, for instance, a poem later translated for inclusion in English in *Poems and Problems,* Nabokov takes up the topic again (*PP* 64–5). This poem is set temporally at the darkening of day and physically in a bare room. Both coordinates are relevant and repeated frequently in Nabokov's poetry of the metaphysically mysterious. Dusk, like dawn, is here a liminal time, a temporal cleft where the transformative potential of a cross-over is latent. Likewise, the bare room, or alternatively an anonymous hotel room, is an isolated space – a Platonic cave – enclosed within a much larger external realm of transcendent potential. In this setting, with a play of light which deceives the imagination, the poet's soul is carried by a draught (from another realm) into, presumably, a mirror, an open number of glass, 'one's soul has been blown / into a flowingly open / cipher of glass.' Allowed transfer into another space, the poet's soul is transformed and transfigured 'into thousands of rings,' at last to come to a stop 'in most crystal stagnation, / most excellent Nought.' 'The Formula' does not comment upon the dispersal and transformation of the poet's soul into an image of unity and self-enclosed perfection of an '0'; the mystery and wonder of the poem resides in the contrast between the bare humility of the modest setting and the wonder of the event.

A similarly mysterious, though still more tantalizingly suggestive, reference to the mystery of cosmic synchronization comes in Nabokov's long Russian poem of 1942, 'Слава' ('Slava'), translated for *Poems and Problems* as 'Fame' (*PP* 102–13). Since 'Fame' will form the object of fuller analysis below, comment here will be restricted to poetic reference to cosmic synchronization. 'Fame' recounts the confrontation between a poet-narrator and an intrusive nocturnal visitor who torments the exile poet with visions of his failings. Confronted with the defeatist mockery of his unwanted guest, the poet narrates his defensive response, which entails partial revelation of the fundamental 'secret' that allows him to rise above the transient concerns of daily life. The poet, although unable and unwilling fully to reveal the source of his cosmic-comic confidence, nevertheless discloses that he has overcome concerns about his mortal being through achievement of a higher, transcendent perspective: 'I admit that the night has been ciphered right well / but in place of the stars I put letters, / and I've read in myself how the self to transcend.' This transcendence of the self, although never explained, is indicated to assume a form of extra-body dispersal: 'Without body I've spread, without echo I thrive, / and with me all along is my secret.' Significantly, just as the young poet Nabokov of *Speak, Memory* saw at the conclusion of the recitation of his 'first' poem the dregs of his self in a mirror, and just as the poet-narrator of 'The Formula' has his soul swept into a mirror, so the narrator of 'Fame' descends deep into his being to see mirrored there the world, himself, and some ineffable secret:

> But one day while disrupting the strata of sense
>   And descending deep down to my wellspring
> I saw mirrored, besides my own self and the world,
>   Something else, something else, something else.   (*PP* 113; ll. 121–4)

With these and other examples from Nabokov's poetry – and from the poetry of Fyodor Godunov-Cherdyntsev of *The Gift* and John Shade of *Pale Fire*, to be discussed more fully in later chapters – the prevalence and poetic source of cosmic synchronization from even the earliest stages of Nabokov's writing seems established. Just as intriguing as this establishment of a transcendent realm of contiguous time and space within Nabokov's metaphysics, however, is the poetic use made of it. Cosmic synchronization is an essential portion of Nabokov's obsession with consciousness and the expansion of consciousness. And if poetry is, as Nabokov claimed, 'positional,' the urge 'to express one's position in regard to the universe embraced by consciousness' (*SM* 218), attendant questions immediately arise concerning what is reached for, what privileged feeling or experience is associated with the heightening of consciousness that is cosmic synchronization. A return to Nabokov's poetry indicates that the wonder of consciousness is repeatedly associated with aesthetics and ethics, or – synonymously in the thematic vocabulary of Nabokov's poetry – artistic creation and love.

II. Inspiration

The cluster of themes and motifs revolving around poetry, the muse, the poetic calling, and inspiration is one of the most extensive in Nabokov's writing and is especially prevalent in, and of relevance to, his poetry. The ·depiction of poetic inspiration offers synecdochic representation of the mystery and source of the creative urge which fuels artistry. Poetry for Nabokov is not only a vehicle of the representation of thought but simultaneously an expression and example of consciousness gripped by a force which assures access to, or visitation from, other dimensions. Thus, the relatedness of the poetic depiction of inspiration with the mysterious transports of cosmic synchronization. In an early untitled poem from *The Empyrean Path*, Nabokov described the complex process and experience of inspiration:

Вдохновенье – это сладострастье
   Человеческого «я»:
Жарко возрастающее счастье, –
   Миг небытия.   (*Ssoch* I, 544)

[Inspiration – that is voluptuousness / of the human 'I': / a fiery growing happiness – / an instant of non-being.]

While the first stanza suggests that inspiration is a sensation of rapture which envelops the poet's non-physical being and is thus expressed in vocabulary of absence ('non-being'), the second stanza – with conspicuous use of the second-person singular pronoun – describes a corresponding force, the voluptousness which is a form of inspiration to the body. Spirit and body – rather than remaining separate – affect each other complementarily. The central reference of this stanza is to the bodily senses and a sudden return of sight. The reference to physical sight, and related associations of epiphanic revelation referred to here, is a motif repeatedly returned to in Nabokov's artistry, most famously in *Pale Fire* in the image of the deceased poet John Shade staring, with open eyes, into the skies.[19] In this poem, inspiration is experienced as a sudden, transient illumination:

Сладострастье – это вдохновенье
    тела, чуткого, как дух:
ты прозрел, ты вспыхнул на мгновенье, –
    в трепете потух.   (*Ssoch* I, 544)

[Voluptuousness – that is inspiration / of the body, delicate, like a spirit / your
eyes are opened, you have flared up in an instant / expired in a flicker.]

Both in terms of its contents and cryptic, appositive formulation, the
second stanza also emphasizes abruptness and transience. Once the 'thunderous pleasure' of sudden inspiration has passed, what remains is 'living
life,' emotion ('heart'), or poetry. Significantly, the site of both is a 'secret
recess,' an internal wellspring that here remains mysterious and un-
described (as in other poems by Nabokov which treat the topic of the
creative urge):

Но когда услада грозовая
    пронеслась и ты затих, –
в тайнике возникла жизнь живая:
    сердце или стих ...   (*Ssoch* I, 544)

[But when the thunderous pleasure / has subsided and you have calmed down,
– / in a secret recess living life has arisen: / heart or verse ...]

This disarmingly direct encapsulation of the mystery of inspiration in
verse is not the only place where Nabokov described the psychology of
inspiration as the ecstatic dissolution of self in an instant of non-being.
Years later, in his essay 'The Art of Literature and Commonsense,' Nabokov
returned in discursive format, and as an internationally famous author, to
the phenomenon of inspiration so frequently broached in his verse. An
article essential to an understanding of Nabokov's lyric voice, one of its
most telling aspects is the insight it provides into the exercise of Nabokov's
creative consciousness. In language as surprisingly exuberant and 'naive' as
the imagery of his youthful verse, Nabokov observes that inspiration derives from the faculties of an associative frame of mind wherein disparate
elements from the poet's environment mysteriously merge to form in the
alembic of consciousness a unity of perfect, previously unforeseen sense:

A passerby whistles a tune at the exact moment that you notice the reflection of a branch in a puddle which in its turn, and simultaneously, recalls a

combination of damp green leaves and excited birds in some old garden, and the old friend, long dead, suddenly steps out of the past, smiling and closing his dripping umbrella. The whole thing lasts one radiant second and the motion of impressions and images is so swift that you cannot check the exact laws which attend their recognition, formation and fusion ... it is like a jigsaw puzzle that instantly comes together in your brain with the brain itself unable to observe how and why the pieces fit, and you experience a shuddering sensation of wild magic, of some inner resurrection, as if a dead man were revived by a sparkling drug which has been rapidly mixed in your presence. This feeling is at the base of what is called inspiration ... (*LL* 377–8)

In his discussion, Nabokov goes on to suggest that, as with cosmic synchronization, inspiration and the mysterious stimulation of the artistic consciousness are likewise marked by an abandonment of physicality and a crossing-over of the poet into a realm where the usual confines of time and space are overcome:

The inspiration of genius adds a third ingredient: it is the past and the present *and* the future (your book) that come together in a sudden flash; thus the entire circle of time is perceived, which is another way of saying that time ceases to exist. It is a combined sensation of having the whole universe enter you and of yourself wholly dissolving in the universe surrounding you. It is the prison wall of the ego suddenly crumbling away with the nonego rushing in from the outside to save the prisoner – who is already dancing in the open. (*LL* 378)

Intriguing as this account is of the workings of an inspired artist, Nabokov's discussion is also a catalogue of themes from his own poems. Not only does reference to 'the entire circle of time,' which marks the cessation of time, seem to suggest the 'most excellent Nought' at the conclusion of 'The Formula,' but the mysterious, imaginary rendezvous with a long dead acquaintance from the past is the subject matter of poems as diverse as the untitled 'Мне так просто и радостно снилось ...' ('Mne tak prosto i radostno snilos' ...' / 'I so easily and happily dreamed ...'), 'Сновиденье' ('Snoviden'e' / 'The Dream'), 'Вечер на пустыре' ('Vecher na pustyre' / 'Evening on a Vacant Lot'), and the late, untitled poem of 1967 'Сорок три или четыре года ...' ('Sorok tri ili chetyre goda ...' / 'Forty-three or four years ...'). Still more generally, however, the sudden falling into place of thought and disparate associations from out of another dimension is likewise treated in poems from across Nabokov's oeuvre. An early, untitled poem from *The Empyrean Path*, for example, reworks in poetic form the abrupt arrival of poetic inspiration described in 'The Art of Literature and Commonsense.' This poem, 'Разбились облака. Алмазы дождевые ...' ('Razbilis' oblaka. Almazy dozhdevye ...' / 'Clouds shattered. Rain-like diamonds ...'), begins with an image from nature of a sudden rainstorm whose impetuosity and force is suggestive of the unbidden arrival of inspiration (*Ssoch* I, 498–9). The spontaneity and release of the experience is itself mirrored in the choppy syntax of the poem's opening lines, which begin with imagery of a cloudburst and the falling of diamond raindrops, now fast, now slowly, from 'fragrant, agitated boughs.' The falling of raindrops is reminiscent of the manner in which 'the breath of being tears itself away,' and in the culminating image of the poem, each of the poet's songs 'melodiously falls into unearthly limits.' In this seven-line poem, it is clear that the inspiration for poetry and the resulting poetry mysteriously fall into being with the sudden luminosity, force, and sheer wonder of a crashing rainstorm.

Later in Nabokov's poetic career comes 'The Poem' of 1944, one of Nabokov's finest English poems. 'The Poem' provides direct insight into the demands and expectations of poetry and the metaphysical sources of inspiration and artistic creation, though now in the form of Nabokov's mature poetic artistry. Like the repeated use of the similar title 'The Poet,' the terse title 'The Poem' indicates the synecdochic relation of this particular poem to Nabokov's poetic oeuvre and, ultimately, the lyric voice which characterized his entire body of work. Particularly in reference to the role of metaphor in Nabokov's writing, 'The Poem' is fundamental to an understanding of Nabokov's artistry:

Not the sunset poem you make when you think
aloud,
with its linden tree in India ink
and the telegraph wires across its pink
cloud;

not the mirror in you and her delicate bare
shoulder still glimmering there;
not the lyrical click of a pocket rhyme –
the tiny music that tells the time;

and not the pennies and weights on those
evening papers piled up in the rain;
not the cacodemons of carnal pain;

not the things you can say so much better in plain
    prose –

but the poem that hurtles from heights unknown
– when you wait for the splash of the stone
deep below, and grope for your pen,
and then comes the shiver, and then –

in the tangle of sounds, the leopards of words,
the leaflike insects, the eye-spotted birds
fuse and form a silent, intense,
mimetic pattern of perfect sense.   *(PP* 157)

'The Poem' begins with the speaker's rejection of the conventional in poetry. In anaphoric repetitions, standardized subject matter such as sunsets, the formulaic lyricism of a conventional muse, social concerns, and carnal lust are all dismissed as 'the things you can say so much better in plain / prose.' Likewise rejected is the mechanized formal structure of such poetry – 'the lyrical click of a pocket rhyme' – here marked in the 'aloud-cloud' *consonne d'appui* rhyme appended to the 'think-ink-pink' rhyme of the poem's opening tercet. Opposed to this is the poem whose source is an external, transcendent sphere 'from heights unknown,' a source of inspiration, which, although seemingly extraneous, somehow emerges from 'deep below' in the poet's consciousness. The source 'deep below' of the preferred type of poetry is not only described in the text of the poem but also prepared for and illustrated in its prosody. Both an enjambment and, more skilfully, the anapestic stresses of the line 'when you wáit for the splásh of the stóne' enforce a 'wait' for the delayed revelation of 'deep below.' The subject matter of the ideal poem is not described; rather, emphasis is placed on its creation in metaphor and its revelatory effect. The final two quatrains of 'The Poem' implement the ideal of a perfect poem by utilizing metaphoric imagery which illustrates its goal rather than describing it. Through the use of metaphors of organic, exotic imagery, the final stanza enacts the perfect poem's epiphanic revelation of meaning, the conveyance of sense in a manner more immediate and compact – 'silent, intense' – than that available to the referential language of prose. And through the hastened accumulation of metaphors which conclude in a declarative statement, the very texture of experience is revealed and the mind allowed suddenly to see with perfect clarity, almost intuitively, the meaning previously camouflaged 'in the tangle of sounds, the leopards of words.' Significantly, the preferred poem ends in asserting renewed representational contact with the world of experience, a 'mimetic pattern of perfect sense.' 'The Poem' succeeds not only in describing the arrival of inspiration but also in allowing the reader to experience an analogous sense of lyric wonder and discovery in reading the poem. In this respect, 'The Poem' is also a statement on the nature of consciousness and the sudden, wondrous arrival of meaning which takes consciousness to a new level. It is thus less than surprising that Nabokov should use in *Speak, Memory* an image similar to the one concluding this poem when commenting on his supposition of a baby's first experience of consciousness: 'It occurs to me that the closest reproduction of the mind's birth obtainable is the stab of wonder that accompanies the precise moment when, gazing at a tangle of twigs and leaves, one suddenly realizes that what had seemed a natural component of that tangle is a marvelously disguised insect or bird' (*SM* 298). Attentively read, Nabokov's poetry likewise affords a 'stab of wonder.'

With the insight gained from these and numerous other examples of Nabokov's poetry – and confirmed through reference to Nabokov's discursive writing – it is apparent that inspiration, the wondrous source of the urge to artistic creation, is derived from the mysterious realm associated with cosmic synchronization and the heightening of consciousness. To this extent, the aesthetic and metaphysical dimensions of Nabokov's artistic persona are intimately related. The same is true of the ethical component of Nabokov's oeuvre. Like inspiration, the poetic treatment of love, with its clear associations with cosmic synchronization, is a further expression of the expansion and heightening of consciousness. Nabokov's extensive poetry of love is thus at once the expression of another form of expanded consciousness and demonstration of the presence of an all-important ethical dimension at the lyric source of Nabokov's oeuvre.

III. Love's Poetry

Love is, of course, present in a variety of dimensions from the very outset of Nabokov's writing career, beginning, indirectly, with the paradigmatic first poem 'The Rain Has Flown' described in chapter 11 of *Speak, Memory,* which was lovingly presented to his mother. As Nabokov claimed, this poem, as with all of the poetry of this early period, was essentially a sign that he had 'made of being alive, of passing or having passed, or hoping to pass, through certain intense human emotions' (*SM* 217). Love, as an intense human emotion, was eminently suited for expression through poetry, and much of Nabokov's earliest adolescent poetry records the experience of love in the trite, formulaic fashion mocked in Nabokov's remembrance of one such poem: '... as themes go, my elegy dealt with the loss of a beloved mistress – Delia, Tamara or Lenore – whom I had never lost, never loved, never met but was all set to meet, love, lose' (*SM* 225). This love, however, essentially an adolescent form of erotic love, is not of the order intended when the claim is advanced that Nabokov's poetry is suffused with an ethical dimension derived from love. Intended here is the love which is expressive of intense concern for the well-being of another and at the same time the sense of profound connectedness which unites individuals. Ultimately, this love provokes more than mere feeling, but, like poetry, an altering and expansion of consciousness. In the account of 'The Rain Has Flown' from *Speak, Memory*, this dimension is approached in Nabokov's reference to his mother, for this first poem is less *about* the stylized and literally fictional 'Delia, Tamara or Lenore' than *for* the fifteen-year-old's beloved mother. And hence the young poet's trepidation upon rushing to his mother to recite to her his poem: '... I did not doubt that my mother would greet my achievement with glad tears of pride ... Never in my life had I craved more for her praise. Never had I become more vulnerable' (*SM* 225). The adolescent Nabokov's mother here, as with the young Fyodor Godunov-Cherdyntsev's mother in *The Gift*, is a first, adored recipient and prompter of poetry who will later be not so much replaced as superceded by another muse, another prompter and recipient of poetry.

The essential connection of Nabokov's poetry to love is not in the first instance a matter of subject matter nor of addressee, however, although Nabokov's oeuvre contains a number of poems which represent the alteration of consciousness occasioned by the feeling of love. In the skilful overlapping of themes effected by these poems, the object of love is both a person and poetry; the artfully employed imagery combines description of the arrival of a woman ardently awaited for at a nocturnal rendezvous with that of the coming of the muse and the first stirrings of poetic inspiration.[20] The decisive connection between love and poetry is the similar effect both have on consciousness; both occasion a crossing-over and the experience of an intense feeling of bliss. In the concluding chapter of *Speak, Memory*, Nabokov describes the intensity of his feeling of love in terms of a stretching and expansion of his consciousness against and out of the usual confines of space and time in the conceptual vocabulary of cosmic synchronization initially referred to in the context of his first poem:

Whenever I start thinking of my love for a person, I am in the habit of immediately drawing radii from my love – from my heart, from the tender nucleus of a personal matter – to monstrously remote points of the universe. Something impels me to measure the consciousness of my love against such unimaginable and incalculable things as the behavior of nebulae (whose very remoteness seems a form of insanity), the dreadful pitfalls of eternity, the unknowledge-able beyond the unknown, the helplessness, the cold, the sickening involutions and interpretations of time and space ... When that slow-motion, silent explosion of love takes place in me, unfolding its melting fringes and overwhelming me with the sense of something much vaster, much more enduring and powerful than the accumulation of matter or energy in any imaginable cosmos ... I have to have all space and all time participate in my emotion, in my mortal love, so that the edge of its mortality is taken off, thus helping me to fight the utter degradation, ridicule, and horror of having developed an infinity of sensation and thought within a finite existence. (*SM* 296–7)

Such a feeling of love is more than an emotion; it is a swelling of consciousness and simultaneously an indication of, and participation in, something vaster than the mortal realm of time and space. Love and the intensity of emotion attending it can even effect a crossing-over into a form of existence beyond the physical world.

It is precisely this possibility which is expressed in Nabokov's poem 'Как я люблю тебя' ('Kak ia liubliu tebia' / 'How I Love You') of 1934:

> Kind of green, kind of gray, i.e.,
> striated all over with rain,
> and the linden fragrance, so heady,
> that I can hardly — Let's go!
> Let's go and abandon this garden
> and the rain that seethes on its paths
> between the flowers grown heavy,
> kissing the sticky loam.
> Let's go, let's go before it's too late,
> quick, under one cloak, come home,
> while you still are unrecognized, ·
> my mad one, my mad one!
>
> Self-control, silence. But with each year,
> to the murmur of trees and the clamor of birds,
> the separation seems more offenseful
> and the offense more absurd.

And I fear ever more rashly
I may blab and interrupt
the course of the quiet, difficult speech
long since penetrating my life.

Above red-cheeked slaves
the blue sky looks all lacquered,
and plumped-up clouds
with scarcely discernible jerks
   move across.
I wonder, is there nowhere a place there,
to lie low – some dark nook
where the darkness might merge
with a wing's cryptic markings?
(A geometrid thus does not stir
spread flat on a lichened trunk)

What a sunset! And once more tomorrow
and for a long time the heat is to last,
a forecast faultlessly based
on the stillness and on the gnats:
hanging up in an evening sunbeam,
their swarmlet ceaselessly jiggles,
reminding one of a golden toy
in the hands of a mute peddler.

How I love you! In this
evening air, now and then,
the spirit finds loopholes, translucences
in the world's finest texture.
The beams pass between tree trunks.

How I love you! The beams
pass between tree trunks; they band
the tree trunks with flame. Do not speak.
Stand motionless under the flowering branch,
inhale – what a spreading, what flowering! –
Close your eyes, and diminish, and stealthily
   into the eternal pass through.   (*PP* 79–81)

In this Russian poem translated into English for inclusion in *Poems and Problems*, the addressee of the poet's love remains tantalizingly indeterminate. Potentially an individual, the nominal and adjectival declensions of Nabokov's mellifluous Russian suggest neither a woman nor the (in Russian grammatically feminine) muse. More likely, the object of love is that portion of the poet's personality and being not constrained by the limitations of reason and common sense – 'my mad one' – and thus amenable to the liminal experience of crossing over. Equally indeterminate, moreover, is the source and identity of the poetic voice, the 'I' of 'How I love you.' What is apparent is the desire of the poetic consciousness to escape the beautiful, though cloyingly confining, garden of earthly life to merge with the addressee and thus end an 'offenseful,' perhaps Platonic separation in another 'eternal' realm where transcendent reunification and unity will be possible. The poetic voice seems forcefully constrained, self-consciously concerned not to 'blab' and 'interrupt' the lifelong communication – 'the quiet, difficult speech' – which has come from elsewhere to penetrate into and enrich his life. Desired is envelopment by darkness and the wish for transformation suggested by the moth on a branch at a splendorous, rapturously liminal moment of sunset.[21] The poem concludes with an ecstatic declaration of love and the impassioned invocation to surrender the ego and senses, thereby to experience and utilize the porous texture of nature to 'pass through' to another realm of being and state of consciousness. In 'How I Love You,' love is, like poetic inspiration, explicitly associated with the blissful experience of cosmic synchronization. In both instances, the individual's consciousness is raised to the very acme of sensitivity and receptiveness, then to cross over to another state in a process of rapturous transition.

Love is more, however, than merely a conduit to the other side. Love is also, and perhaps more importantly, the bridge connecting individuals, not just to other realms, but to other human beings as well and thus, through the experience of love, to other dimensions of consciousness. In her 'Shades of Love: Nabokov's Intimations of Immortality,' Ellen Pifer developed the ethic dimension of Nabokov's poetics of love and its connection to the transcendent, timeless realm witnessed by cosmic synchronization. She perceptively observed that in 'Nabokov's universe ... love is quite literally the power that exposes human beings to "alien worlds"; love opens them to the world of other people and to the even stranger realm of "the beyond," or "hereafter"' (Pifer 1989, 78). Concentrating on Nabokov's novels, Pifer demonstrates the liberating power of love for a variety of Nabokov's protagonists and the manner in which love revealed to their consciousnesses dimensions in their human and physical environments of which they were previously unaware. What Pifer establishes for Fyodor and Zina of *The Gift*, Adam and Olga of *Bend Sinister*, Humbert and Lolita of *Lolita*, and Hugh and Armande of *Transparent Things*, among others, is perhaps even more explicitly revealed in Nabokov's poetry, precisely because both poetry and love act as 'the "password," or medium of communication, between beings in "this world" and those who inhabit the "alien world" of the "hereafter"' (Pifer 1989, 85).

Indeed, in Nabokov's poetic universe, love is of such power as to conquer the boundary between this world and the next and to enable mysterious contact and communication between the living and the beloved dead. The perhaps most poignant expression of this conflation of poetry and love's power to transcend mortality comes in Nabokov's poem of 1932 'Вечер на пустыре' ('Vecher na pustyre' / 'Evening on a Vacant Lot'), which ends with the first-person poet meeting a person long-since dead, quite plausibly Nabokov's father.[22] The first stanza of the poem of seventy lines is set in an empty lot at sunset, an atmosphere suggestive of both a spatial void and a moment of temporal transition between day and night and thus redolent of liminal possibility. Like the poet-speaker of the first poem anthologized in *Two Paths*, who sees the 'dark blue sky' as wallpaper; and like the first-person speaker of the poem 'The Poet' of 1918 from *The Empyrean Path* who, set amid the terror of the world with its 'burnt-out ruins' and 'humiliating graves,' nonetheless wanders 'with inexplicable joy / looking at the clear sky'; and finally, like John Shade, who contemplated the sky as 'the painted parchment papering our cage,' concluding that 'we are most artistically caged' (*PF* 36, 37; ll. 106, 114); the poet of 'Evening on a Vacant Lot' similarly views the sky as a celestial division surrounding and separating human life from another dimension. Nabokov begins his poem with the repetend rhyme – sky-sky and window-window – to enforce the metonymic reminder that both sky and window are portals out of an enclosed space, both are a 'fiery window' in a 'black house':

> Inspiration, rosy sky,
> black house, with a single window,
> fiery. Oh, that sky
> drunk up by the fiery window!   (*PP* 69; ll. 1–4)

In contemplating the reddening light in the dark sky, the poet is both expectant of, and impatient for, poetic inspiration, the heralds from another realm. The release of artistic inspiration indicated here, however, is not simply desired as an aesthetic exercise but one of emotional necessity. Distraught and suffering, the poet nears a psychological condition which is as much that of a mental breakdown as that of the blissful dissolution of cosmic synchronization. The desire for the experience of inspiration is occasioned by the desperate need to counter the vulgarity and pain of the surrounding environment:

> What's the matter with me? Self-lost,
> melting in the air and sunset,
> muttering and almost fainting
> on the waste at eveningtime.
> Never did I want so much to cry.
> Here it is, deep down in me.
> The desire to bring it forth intact,
> slightly filmed with moisture and so tremulous,
> never yet had been so strong in me.
> Do come out, my precious being ...   (*PP* 69; ll. 9–18)

The world of the poet is identified as bleak and barren, redeemable only by the wonder of poetic inspiration. In the opening lines of an 'Evening on a Vacant Lot,' while the saving potential of poetry is registered, it is now of a decidedly more delicate, fragile order, something to cling 'to a stem, / to the window, still celestial, / or to the first lighted lamp' (*PP* 69; ll. 19–21). As tremulous as it may be, however, inspiration nonetheless provides the poet with the welcome harbour of a known good:

> Maybe empty is the world, and brutal;
> nothing do I know – except
> that it's worthwhile being born
> for the sake of this your breath.   (*PP* 69; ll. 22–5)

With the first stanza concluding with the consolation of inspiration, the second stanza laments the dwindling ability of the poet to unselfconsciously record its mystery in language. The youthful ease of inspiration is waning with age and the passage of time. What in 'presumptuous youth' was formerly a simpler activity – 'two rhymes – and my notebook I'd open' (*PP* 69; l. 27) – is now a less transparent process; the poet's soul, which was once capable of 'drifting to the very stars' on poetry 'that glided like a bridge' connecting realms, is no longer able to communicate the experiences undergone in the cosmic transports of inspiration. The poet's 'leaden-weighted words' seem now less capable of rendering the magic and wonder of the experience. The first two stanzas of the poem thus chart the poet's existential need for the assurance of inspiration, although the communicative power of his poetry is doubted. The remainder of the poem will raise the speaker out of his despondency to an experience which is more than the emotional release of poetic inspiration, but the triumph of reunion with his dead father.

Stanza three of 'Evening on a Vacant Lot' begins the poet's ascent out of his doubt and loneliness in a mental, three-stage process of association – from cognizance of natural beauty to cherished memories of the past to the perception of something wondrous and immutable. Bolstered by the beauty of the night sky reflected in the river and the associated memories of youthful poetry and a previous time and place, the poet is readied for a form of epiphanic insight that will come at a stage of altered consciousness. The poet describes 'the nearing of bliss' that arrives just before the onset of sleep, the state of consciousness that heralds receptivity to visions from the other side. '[A]ll that time had seemed to have taken' (*PP* 71; l. 55), all the memories, and – given the conclusion of the poem even individuals associated with a warmer, better time (at Vyra, the Nabokov country estate) are returned to the poet through a breech in the boundary to the other realm. The poet is left with the fortifying assurance that nothing has been, nothing may be, lost to memory, to consciousness. The fourth and final stanza of the poem returns to the vacant lot and sunset of the poem's opening lines. The dour, threatening atmosphere of the first stanza had culminated in the image of 'the skull of a borzoi.' Now the gloom of the setting is intensified and specified in further images of squalor. Surrounding the lone poet are 'fingerlike black stacks / of a factory,' 'weedy flowers,' and 'a deformed tin can.' Despite the debris, however, out of the physical detritus and clutter of despair, as if out of a fissure caused by the twilight, the poet-narrator sees a 'slender hound with snow-white coat' that seems to have resurrected the dead borzoi of the poem's beginning. Following the dog is a welcome figure radiating good health and vigour. The poet recognizes the individual, while the informal address and the man's friendly greeting of the poet suggest familiarity. Although the man is never identified, he most certainly stands emotionally close to the poet. The poem concludes with a wonder which is rendered all the more startling by the understatement of its expression:

> I recognize
> your energetic stride. You haven't
> changed much since you died.   (*PP* 73; ll. 68–70)

Of singular power here is the manner in which the seemingly impossible appearance of the dead man at the end of the poem, Nabokov's father, is rendered natural through the rhetorical force of the poem. In a few short lines, the man briskly strides into the poem, emerging from the despondency of the setting to convey the light and imagery of invigorating goodwill and confidence, dispelling the poet's – and poem's – gloom with a dog, a whistle, a call, and an energetic stride. Via the medium of language alone, 'the leaden-weighted words' so distrusted by the speaker of the poem, Nabokov has rendered a wonder believable. In the above discussed 'The Poem,' inspiration assumed through language 'a silent, intense, / mimetic pattern of perfect sense.' In 'Evening on a Vacant Lot,' inspiration shaped into poetic form has occasioned another manner of epiphanic revelation. Here the wondrous potential of poetry has been allowed to conquer the seemingly oppressive finality of life; poetry as a medium and expression of love has effected the reunion of the poet and his beloved dead, allowing memory, consciousness, and poetry to rise above oppressive reality.

The power of love to surmount the divide separating the living from the departed is a prominent theme in Nabokov's writing, and although 'Evening on a Vacant Lot' is a particularly powerful expression in poetic form, it is neither the earliest nor most explicit. In March 1923, one year after the emotionally cataclysmic death of his father, Nabokov wrote an exceptionally moving poem entitled 'Гекзаметры' ('Gekzametry' / 'Hexameters'). This poem granted Nabokov contact with his beloved father in imagery which he would return to frequently in his poetry and prose of the dead (*Ssoch* I, 601).[23] As in 'Evening on a Vacant Lot,' where poetic logic renders the dead more living and invigorating than sullen reality, 'Hexameters' reverses the standard hierarchy between the quick and the dead to grant death and the dead more substance than the living. It is the dead who are awake, while the living sleep. The poem's opening line establishes the reversal by describing death in imagery of renewal and life: 'Смерть – это утренний луч, пробжденье весеннее' ('Smert' – eto utrennii luch, probuzhden'e vesennee' / 'Death – that is dawn's ray, a spring awakening'). Although Nabokov's youthful poem employs an established Romantic trope, the turn of formulation is distinctly Nabokovian.[24] Here of relevance is not merely the ray of light marking the transition from night to day – 'dawn's ray' – which is common to Nabokov's poetry, but more pertinently the extensive play of meaning around sleep and dreaming. As has already been noted, dreams and sleep frequently serve in Nabokov's work as a liminal point where the potential for consciousness is rich. In 'Hexameters,' Nabokov suggests that his father, though 'submerged in the grave,' is nonetheless awake and free, an invisible, radiant presence walking among the living, who are merely sleeping until their appointed time. Nabokov, the assumed poetic speaker, describes himself asleep, arms outspread facing the stars, while a shimmering light flows from another, 'transparent' dimension. The very vocabulary of Nabokov's line "в сон мой втекает мерцающий свет, оттого-то прозрачны / даже и скорби мои ..." ['into my dream a shimmering light flows causing to become transparent / even my grief'] itself shimmers with essential imagery from Nabokov's writing, from the dream (a recurrent motif in Nabokov's poetry), through the draught from another dimension ('The Formula') and the shimmering light (the description of Zena, Fyodor's muse in *The Gift*), to the transparency of experiences associated with the dead (*Transparent Things*). In this dreaming state, he implores his father to incline over him so that he may benefit from the liminal potential of sleep to hear the communication emanating from his dream. Finally, in the last lines of the poem, he feels his father's breeze (ветер твой) softly kiss him on the eyelids and asks again that his father incline over him to hear what has been whispered in sleep – a name 'more sonorous than sobs, sweeter than any earthly song and profounder than a prayer.' The name is that of his fatherland. In its conclusion, then, 'Hexameters' becomes an elegy not only for his murdered father, to whom the poem is dedicated, but for his lost, politically murdered fatherland. This inclusion of homeland as the poem's final word serves to step back from the exclusively familial reference of the poem while adding an exile's sense of loss, although the power and pathos of 'Hexameters' surely derive from the breathtakingly open confrontation with death and the assured, supremely Nabokovian poetic demonstration that being is neither interrupted nor terminated by dream or death, but rather expanded.

The above selected references to Nabokov's poetic rendering of love are but a limited portion of a theme which is omnipresent in Nabokov's poetry. Here, love and its metaphysical dimension have been emphasized in accordance with both the goals of this study and the authoritative depiction of love Nabokov provided in the final chapter of *Speak, Memory*. Discussion of Nabokov's treatment of love could easily be expanded through inclusion of the numerous other themes repeatedly coupled by Nabokov with love throughout his oeuvre. For in this regard, individual critics of Nabokov's poetry are correct in stating that it is frequently concerned with love. They are mistaken, however, in suggesting that the poetic treatment of love was prominently the formulaic rendering of adolescent, erotic desire – a form limited almost exclusively to Nabokov's first collection of 1916. As Nabokov's poetic career proceeded, love developed into an essential theme in Nabokov's poetic universe, interwoven into numerous poems expressive of love of the natural world, love of art and the muse, love of memory and his youth and homeland, and finally – if here still somewhat bathetically expressed – love of the wonder and trifles of being.

Thus, in concluding a topic which is in itself a major theme in Nabokov's writing deserving of independent study, it seems fitting to turn to Nabokov's perhaps most intriguing poetic exploration of the mystery and power of love as it is found in the poem referred to by Véra Nabokov in her seminal identification of the theme of the otherworld in her husband's writing. Worthy of discussion in this context alone, 'Being in Love' is also an important poem for other reasons essential to this study of Nabokov's poetry. Thematically, 'Being in Love,' while occupied with the mysterious power of love, is not as explicit concerning the surmounting of the division between 'here' and 'there' (*tut* and *tam*) as the poems discussed above. Nor is the love of this poem focused on a particular object or abstraction, such as Russia or the wonder of being. The love of 'Being in Love' is essentially occupied with the particular quality of consciousness experienced by the individual in love. Apart from its thematic interest, 'Being in Love' effects a curious chronological completion of Nabokov's oeuvre. Just as the all-important theme of cosmic synchronization, with its metaphysical implications, was identified in *Speak, Memory* in Nabokov's account of his first poem, so, in the final poem of his career, Nabokov explicitly referred to the previously unobserved theme of the otherworld, as Véra Nabokov first indicated. Moreover, although 'Being in Love' was one of Nabokov's last poems, its composition in Russian and its placement at the end of Nabokov's long career, in his last, parodically autobiographical novel *Look at the Harlequins!*, seems almost to return Nabokov to the poetic source of his oeuvre and artistry. The poem is integrated into the narrative as the work of the novel's first-person narrator, Vadim Vadimych, a Russian émigré author who presents and explicates the poem to the object of his affections, a young English woman, Iris. 'Being in Love' unites a cherished emotional state of vulnerability with intimations of a transcendent realm, thereby identifying love with a wondrous metaphysical dimension. The transliteration and gloss, as presented by Vadim to Iris in the novel, merit full quotation:

My zabyváem chto vlyublyónnost'
Ne prósto povorót litsá,
A pod kupávami bezdónnost',
Nochnáya pánika plovtsá.

Pokúda snítsa, snis', vlyublyónnost',
No probuzhdéniem ne múch',
I lúchshe nedogovoryónnost'
Chem éta shchél' i étot lúch.

Napomináya chto vlyublyónnost'
Ne yáv', chto métiny ne té,
Chto mózhet-byt' potustoróronnost'
Priotvorílas' v temnoté.

'Lovely,' said Iris. 'Sounds like an incantation. What does it mean?'
'I have it here on the back. It goes like this. We forget – or rather tend to forget – that being in love (*vlyublyonnost'*) does not depend on the facial angle of the loved one, but is a bottomless spot under the nenuphars, *a swimmer's panic in the night* (here the iambic tetrameter happens to be rendered – last line of the first stanza, *nochnáya pániku plovtsá*). Next stanza: While the dreaming is good – in the sense of "while the going is good" – do keep appearing to us in our dreams, *vlyublyonnost'*, but do not torment us by waking us up or telling too much: reticence is better than that chink and that moonbeam. Now comes the last stanza of this philosophical poem.'
'This what?'
'Philosophical love poem. *Napomináyu*, I remind you, that *vlyublyonnost'* is not wide-awake reality, that the markings are not the same (a moon-striped ceiling, *polosatyy ot luny potolok*, is, for instance, not the same kind of reality as a ceiling by day), and that, maybe, the hereafter stands slightly ajar in the dark. *Voilà.*' (*LATH* 25–6)

Although oblique, as the poem's creator Vadim Vadimych suggests, 'Being in Love' very much characterizes Nabokov's poetics, demonstrating simultaneously both his linkage of love with another transcendent realm and his non-discursive, lyric approach to expressing thoughts of metaphysical depth.[25] Within the prose novel, it is a lyric poem which best carries the weight of philosophical thought. Thematically, the poem exemplifies Nabokov's central contention that poetry, although deriving from the poet's experience of the phenomenal world, is more than engagement with the sensual world; it is also, and much more, a positioning of consciousness. The opening lines remind the reader of the psychological essence of love, that 'being in love' is not simply a response to sensual matter, 'simply the angle of a face,' but much more a particular state of consciousness which arises out of, and ultimately subsumes, the original catalyst. Just as in 'The Poem,' poetry is more than 'the things you can say so much better in plain prose.' Being in love is triggered by the specific appeal of the loved one, but becomes a state of being, a feeling of vulnerability that comes from entrance into a new, unknown realm, 'the bottomless depths beneath water-lilies,' which in turn induces a psychological state, 'the night-time panic of a swimmer.' Like a dream, being in love – the lyric voice reminds us – is not the same state of consciousness as waking reality: 'I remind you that being in love / is not wide-awake reality.' When in love, the consciousness of the individual in love is expanded, opened to the depths and expanses of a transcendent realm: 'That maybe the otherworld / stands slightly ajar in the dark.' Ultimately, then, being in love brings about a state of consciousness that intimates the existence of, and functions like a door as passage into, another realm. By the conclusion of 'Being in Love,' both the poem and the lyric voice have moved from the specificity of a phenomenal thing of the world – the face of the loved one – to a glimpse of the otherworld and affirmation of the power of love to alter and extend consciousness.

IV. The Otherworld

Thus, Nabokov's final poem, 'Being in Love,' although about the pre-eminently human emotion of love, evolves into a philosophical statement concerning love's – like poetry's – transformative power over consciousness and makes explicit reference to what Véra Nabokov referred to as Nabokov's 'major theme,' the otherworld. Although rarely so openly identified as in 'Being in Love,' Véra Nabokov is nonetheless surely correct in observing that the theme of the otherworld is central to Nabokov's work, pervading his entire oeuvre like a watermark. This is demonstrably the case with regard to his poetry. The very omnipresence of this theme, however, while tantalizing for the careful reader, is for the purposes of scholarly analysis problematic. By its very nature, the otherworld is resistant to expository discussion, as Nabokov himself intimated in the few explanatory comments he made regarding the subject. Given that the concept of the otherworld lies outside of the boundaries of shared, empirical demonstration in the realm of intensely personal belief and experience, Nabokov seems to have been both unwilling and probably unable fully to apprehend the ineffable in discursive language: 'I know more than I can express in words, and the little I can express would not have been expressed, had I not known more' (SO 45). Nabokov's hesitancy about fixing the contours of a peculiar experience is, in itself, indicative of its mystic quality. William James, in attempting to provide a working definition of the mystical, settled upon the four following characteristics: ineffability, noetic quality, transience, and passivity. Of the characteristic of ineffability, James suggested that the mystical experience 'defies expression, that no adequate report of its contents can be given in words'; while in referring to the noetic quality of a mystical experience, James is in accord with Nabokov's frequent suggestions of a privileged form of consciousness: 'Although so similar to states of feeling, mystical states seem to those who experience them to be also states of knowledge. They are states of insight into depths of truth unplumbed by the discursive intellect (James 329). The attempt to communicate an essentially 'irrational' experience in rational words is to traduce the experience. This conundrum is well known in literature, Nabokov's métier. As cited above, Gumilev, for instance, spoke of the restraint required not to insult conceptions of the 'unknowable' through the resort to conjecture. Coincidentally (or perhaps not), one of the fullest expressions by Nabokov of this fundamental quandary is to be found in his translation of Fedor Tiutchev's poem 'Silentium':

> Speak not, lie hidden, and conceal
> the way you dream, the things you feel.
> Deep in your spirit let them rise
> akin to stars in crystal skies
> that set before the night is blurred:
> delight in them and speak no word.
>
> How can a heart expression find?
> How should another know your mind?
> Will he discern what quickens you?
> A thought once uttered is untrue.
> Dimmed is the fountainhead when stirred:
> drink at the source and speak no word.
>
> Live in your inner self alone
> within your soul a world has grown,
> the magic of veiled thoughts that might
> be blinded by the outer light,
> drowned in the noise of day, unheard ...
> take in their song and speak no word.   (*TRP* 33–4)

In the context of Nabokov's metaphysics, the proposition that 'a thought once uttered is untrue' has practical consequences for the examination of Nabokov's poetry of the otherworld. Explication is perforce turned back on interpretation in a manner more radical than in conventional literary analysis. The magic of Nabokov's 'veiled thoughts' may be conjectured and intimated but may never be revealed in empirical certainty. Indeed, the necessarily veiled and hesitant quality of all expression of the otherworld is the source of its particular amenability to lyric articulation, where conjecture is a legitimate mode, where the irrational may be given a persuasive and intelligible, if not rational, voice. This is, after all, in the Rabelaisean words to be punned upon in *Pale Fire* – *le grand peut-être*.

In response to this unusual situation and its inescapable methodological implications for study, the following analysis will proceed, not from the attempt to demonstrate the explicit identification of the otherworld in individual poems, as in 'Being in Love' – although this is possible in isolated instances – but through the development of an interpretive argument founded on the accumulation of examples which seem thematically united in Nabokov's oeuvre by their relation to the otherworld. Organizationally, my approach is prompted by the observation that, structurally, the otherworld is dependent upon a fundamental division between two spheres – the phenomenal world of human life in time and space and a transcendent, timeless realm of beneficence and perfection. In following the 'two-world cosmology' proposed by D. Barton Johnson between 'here' and 'there' (*tut* and *tam*), I intend to indicate that reference to the otherworld in Nabokov's poetry regularly occurs on the fault line of this structural division through emphasis on spatial enclosure and physical and temporal transition. The otherworld in Nabokov's poetry will be found, not in mimetic representation of that concept and realm itself, but in veiled suggestion of the mysterious, in the poetic working of the metaphoric potential of a depiction of separate realms and the division connecting them. The poet John Shade of *Pale Fire*, in grappling with a similar problem – the attempt to investigate the nature of life after death – arrived at the realization that secure knowledge of the hereafter could never be attained in empirical certainty, that intimation would only be achieved through attendance to the pattern and texture of life, which would offer a form of metaphoric enlightenment. So it is with Nabokov's poetry. As in 'Being in Love,' it is the chink of light, the moon-striped ceiling, and the open door which announce the presence of the otherworld. And it is on such poetic imagery, the lyric, metaphoric representation of the texture of being, that analysis must rely. Specifically, the following illustration of the presence of the otherworld in Nabokov's poetry will be based on demonstration of Nabokov's strategic deployment of central motifs consistently associated with separation from or passage to a transcendent realm. Two essential clusters of motifs – motifs of enclosure and those of transition – will be shown to announce the otherworld in Nabokov's poetry. These motifs will be demonstrated not only to have contributed to Nabokov's lyric expression of an ineffable metaphysical proposition; perhaps more importantly, in terms of an argument contesting the specificity of Nabokov's lyric voice, they will be revealed to have shaped the unique pattern and texture of Nabokov's poetic oeuvre.

In *The Gift*, Nabokov provided his clearest expression in prose form of the enclosedness of human life, in contrast to the openness of the otherworld, in his use of the metaphor of a house: '… we are not going anywhere, we are sitting at home. The otherworld surrounds us always and is not at all at the end of some pilgrimage. In our earthly house, windows are replaced by mirrors; the door, until a given time, is closed; but air comes in through the cracks' (*Ssoch* IV, 484; *Gift* 310). With this metaphoric statement, Nabokov is giving specific expression to a series of associations which arise frequently in both his poetry and prose where imagery of an enclosed house or domicile invokes intimations of death and the beyond. In the above discussed 'Evening on a Vacant Lot,' for instance, Nabokov invoked it in his allusion to the night sky at sunset as a 'black house, with a single window.' Nabokov provides evocative literary illustration of a mythic phenomenon described by Robert Pogue Harrison in *The Dominion of the Dead*, his study of the place of the dead in the world of the living. For Harrison, representations of house and home are always, at some level, depictions of mortality: '… it is by thinking the essence of a house that we will come to know what being is' (38).[26] The house of phenomenal life is surrounded always by the otherworld, and Nabokov's poetry, in taking up this metaphor, frequently evokes the presence of the otherworld through imagery of enclosed space.

One of the earliest and most radically contained of these spaces to be depicted in Nabokov's poetry of the otherworld is in the poem of 1918 'В хрустальный шар заключены мы были …' ('V khrustal'nyi shar zakliucheny my byli …' / 'In a crystal ball we were enclosed …') (*Ssoch* I, 482–3). Taking up the Platonic myth of the separation of soulmates at birth, this narrative poem of five quatrains of alternating *AbAb* rhyme describes two such souls enclosed within a crystal ball flying among the stars, slipping mutely 'from one splendour of blissful blue to another.' In this pre-earthly state, the inhabitants of the crystal ball were 'united by the rapture of eternity,' knowing neither the past nor a goal in flight. Unfortunately, however, their dimensionless eternity of bliss is disrupted; an earthly human sigh bursts their crystal ball and interrupts their endless kiss to cast them, separate, 'into the captive world.' On earth, much is forgotten of the previous state, to be remembered but rarely in sleep. Nonetheless, although the two rejoice and suffer separately on earth, the speaker is able to recognize the face of his soulmate on earth by the stardust remaining on the tips of the other's eyelashes. The beauty and specificity of this world is thus but a modest reminder of the splendour of a higher state of being experienced before the captivity of human life on earth. Less than new in terms of subject matter – the theme was immortalized in Russian literature in Lermontov's 'The Angel'[27] – it is not the bare treatment of the somewhat hackneyed, albeit mythic theme which appeals in this early example of Nabokov's poetic art. Rather, interest is aroused by the verve and precision of control over poetic form and verbal expression and, most strikingly, the unmistakable Nabokovian turn of the admittedly traditional subject matter. 'In a crystal ball we were enclosed …' contains an entire catalogue of otherworldly motifs which will appear in more artful form in Nabokov's maturer poetry. Enclosure in a hermetic space; the 'blissful-blue' firmament; the suspension of temporal constraints; the 'rapture of eternity'; veiled reference to human anguish – 'someone's sigh'; the living world as a place of captivity; a form of Platonic anamnesis; communication from another realm in sleep; the trepidation of deeply felt emotion; a wondrous rumble from the beyond; the mystery of love; and, finally, sensual focus on a telling, minutely observed detail from the phenomenal world – stardust on the tips of a loved one's eyelashes: each of these motifs is employed here, as they are throughout Nabokov's poetry, drama, and prose, in the creation of a singularly Nabokovian sentiment. In the course of Nabokov's poetic development, mastery over these motifs will become more assured, leading – except in isolated instances – to their more controlled and reticent use as representational images. Instead, they will be deployed in poetry which intimates the depths and dimensions of the otherworld without seeking empirically to depict it.

In the eerily powerful 'Как объясню? Есть в памяти лучи …' ('Kak ob'iasniu? Est' v pamiati luchi …' / 'How to explain? There are in memory rays …'), a poem of 1922, Nabokov returns to the Platonic theme of anamnesis, though here in reference to a strange house and the mysterious recollection of memories which may be earthly, or perhaps of still profounder provenance. Nabokov infuses this poem with the halting, troubled syntax and atmosphere of uncertainty concerning the nature and quality of the memories called forth by the unknown house and the poet's confidence in shaping them into verse. The poem begins with the poet-speaker reflecting on the awakening of memory and the conceptual difficulty discussed above of expressing the ineffable in poetry: 'О, муза, научи: / в понятный стих как призрак перельется' ('O, muza, nauchi: / v poniatnyi stikh kak prizrak perel'etsia?' / 'O, muse, teach [me]: / how is spirit to overflow into understandable verse?') (*Stikhi* 70). Standing in a strange city before a 'strikingly familiar' house, the poet-wanderer hears a 'mysterious singing' and suddenly recognizes every trifle about the building; he feels the 'shadow of his step' on the stairwell, senses another life, another fate, and 'knowing nothing' nonetheless recognizes everything about the building.[28] These concrete experiences of the first stanza lead in the second to reflections on the metaphysical, otherworldly source of such feelings. The poet reflects that his memory is of unknown depth, and his soul of an age and experience not fully known to him. Dreams, wanderings, and conjectures alone remain; his rambles through 'agitated streets,' while 'inclining towards the rumble of mirroring cities,' lead repeatedly back to 'the strikingly, strikingly familiar' house. In this poem, without the fissure to the otherworld actually being revealed, it is nonetheless conjured forth in the arousal of slumbering memories before a house that metaphorically recalls the realm which is home to vaguely intimated experiences and memories.

Although the house as home to another existence is redolent of the otherworld, it is not the only image of enclosedness within a larger space which evokes in Nabokov's poetry veiled comparison between earthly life and another transcendent realm. Train stations and trains as enclosed realms hurtling through space also figure frequently as suggestive locales where draughts from the otherworld are felt. The above discussed poem 'How to explain? There are in memory rays ...,' for instance, also includes suggestive reference to the poet's 'waiting in foreign parts for late trains.' As early as Nabokov's collection *Two Paths*, trains and train stations were used in Nabokov's poetry as vehicles with which to power the metaphoric potential of reference to travel and the unknown. The untitled poem 'Я незнакомые люблю вокзалы ...' ('Ia neznakomye liubliu vokzaly ...' / 'I love unfamiliar train stations ...') assembles the imagery of train stations in the creation of an atmosphere of the solitary, which is wondrous and eerie. Likewise the final three poems of the collection *The Cluster* take up the otherworldly potential of trains. The final stanza of 'В поезде' ('V poezde' / 'On a Train'), for instance, becomes more than a banal account of the speaker being rocked to sleep and dreaming while travelling by train when the frequent emphasis of Nabokov's poetry on the world as a place of captivity is recalled:

Дорога черная, без цели, без конца,
толчки глухие, вздох и выдох,
и жалоба колес, как повесть беглеца
о прежних тюрьмах и обидах.   (*Ssoch* I, 466)

[The path is black, no goal, no end, / the bumps faint, inhalation and exhalation, / and the complaint of the wheels, like the tale of a fugitive / about former prisons and torments.]

'On a Train' invites the synecdochic pairing of the train with the poet-speaker's bitter enclosure in exile. More oblique, though still suggestive, is the reference to mysterious workings in 'Крушение' ('Krushenie' / 'The Wreck'), a poem which describes the scene of a train crash and the strange coincidence of the conductor's daughter, who in a troubled dream sees two angels cause the wreck of a train (*Ssoch* I, 567–8).

Apart from houses and trains as metaphoric sites of identification with the otherworld are solitary rooms and, in particular, hotel rooms. Each space is an enclosed realm in a larger sphere, and Nabokov's poetry frequently employs the Spartan settings of rooms for intimation of another level of being. As with so many of the images more confidently manipulated in Nabokov's later artistry, the motif of the solitary room as a locus of mysterious wonder may be shown to reach back to the beginning of Nabokov's poetic career.[29] 'Номер в гостинице' ('Nomer v gostinitse' / 'Hotel Room') of 1919, while containing such suggestive imagery as a 'squinty looking-glass,' the speaker and his shadow, an open window onto a 'breathless' night, and the play of reflecting light, is but faintly evocative of the otherworld. The haiku-like simplicity and concision of the poem is derived from the contrast between the shabby, worldly setting of the hotel room and the strikingly inviting beauty of the moon and nighttime sky viewed from an open window:

Stirless, I stand there at the window,
and in the black bowl of the sky
glows like a golden drop of honey
       the mellow moon.   (*PP* 25)

Richer in suggestion of a transcendent realm which contrasts to the contained space of a room are two poems of the 1920s. 'Комната' ('Komnata' / 'The Room' [1926]) and 'Перешел ты в новое жилище ...' ('Pereshel ty v novoe zhilishche, ...' / 'You've moved to new lodgings ...'

[1929]) both suggest metaphoric connection between rooms and the spatial limitations and temporal transience of life on earth. 'The Room' begins with the bare shell of a room into which life is being infused by the speaker, the room's new tenant. Under the observation of a mirror, which looks with 'lucid madness' at the new and thus unfamiliar tenant, the speaker gradually makes his acquaintance with the room – 'the wonders of its keys' – until finally the room quivers and slowly becomes his own. Here, Nabokov's imagery and progressive verb forms bring noise and activity into the poem's descriptive language, but also mystery. Bumps in the night, draughts, and the silent, breathing presence of another tenant outside his room are heard. The light is extinguished, all is quiet, with the light falling on his feather bed transforming it into a crimson hill. The narrative first section of the poem thus ends with the closing of a day which has seen life and a life brought to the new room. The last two lines of the sixth quatrain conclude the setting: 'Все хорошо. И скоро я покину / вот эту комнату и этот дом' ['All is well. And soon I will leave / that room and that building'] (*Ssoch* II, 540). This thought leads to the second, more pensive atmosphere of the latter portion of the poem, where the poet regrets the transience of his abiding and decries the tendency to overlook and forget the humble simplicity of his temporary homes. The withered watercolour painting, the patterned walls, the cross by the window – all are to be forgotten: 'Но грустно мне: чем незаметней разность, / тем, может быть, божественней она' ['Though I am saddened: the less noticeable the difference / perhaps the more divine it is']. The final quatrain, in carrying the trajectory of this thought, concludes with the consideration that after death and the move to still another location, this forgetfulness will be regretted when nothing is available to decorate the new abode, a place that will have to be enlivened just like the room which began the poem:

И может быть, когда похолодеем
и в голый рай из жизни перейдем, –
забывчивость земную пожалеем,
не зная, чем обставить новый дом.   (*Ssoch* II, 541)

[And perhaps, when we have grown cold / and we move from life to bare heaven / this earthly forgetfulness we'll regret, / not knowing how to decorate [our] new home ...]

In 'The Room,' it is the temporal limitation of the transient abode which is evoked more than spatial enclosedness, although the draught, the window, and the unknown footsteps suggest dimensions beyond the room itself, as does the 'bare heaven' of the conclusion. In 'You've moved to new lodgings ...' the metaphorical associations of a room and lodgings are more explicitly related to the space of being and consciousness. The dedication of the poem 'On the death of Iu. I. Aikhenval'd' prepares the reader for weightier implications of the conceit of moving to new lodgings.[30] The quietly moving poem manages to portray the humble personality and literary interests of the dedicatee, while also overcoming sadness and ultimately celebrating his triumphant move to a new home. The pronoun (thou) of the first line indicates direct, informal communication with the dedicatee, before transforming to a more descriptive account of his life based on the central image of the room he inhabited. Contained within the opening quatrain are unadorned images which capture a sense of transience and unpresuming humility:

Перешел ты в новое жилище,
и другому отдадут на днях
комнату, где жил писатель нищий,
иностранец с книгою в руках.   (*Stikhi* 224)

[You've moved to new lodgings / and to another soon they will give / the room, where an indigent writer lived / a foreigner with a book in his hands.]

The alliterative sibilants of these lines in the Russian original lend a hushing sound to the poem, which is picked up and extended narratively in the second quatrain – 'тихо было в комнате: страница / изредка шуршала' ['it was quiet in the room: a page / rarely rustled']. The hushed silence of the scene, euphonically accentuated by the alliterative rustle of a page, is suddenly broken by an abrupt presence from a contrastive, external realm – the flash of blue light from a streetcar in the dark capital outside the room's window. The third quatrain, while first returning from the flashing blue light to the quiet room, then introduces two other images of enclosure which reflect on the nature of the room, a 'solid grave' and a container for 'broken glasses.' Rising out of the despondency of this imagery of the dead, the broken and the entombed, however, the poem indicates that within both the quiet room and the quiet man lived a concealed intensity. Although the neighbours never heard it, the dedicatee was addressed by a voice 'now like the rumble of swaying copper, / now like the trepidation of a swallow's wings.' The humble inhabitant of the solitary room conversed with the muses. And in a final image of both transcendence and commemoration, it is revealed that the voice of the muse has not ceased; rather, the dedicatee is being celebrated at an unearthly house-warming. The poem thus concludes with an affirmative image of the transition from an earthly room to another transcendent one.

Nabokov wrote a number of Russian poems which employ the metaphoric potential of rooms as sites of temporary abode, although few are as simultaneously direct and enigmatic as his English poem of 1950 'The Room' (*PP* 164–5).[31] Enclosed within a disconcertingly jaunty, almost comic form of expression, 'The Room' contains a cluster of themes and images which portend depths unseen beneath the deceptively simple vocabulary. The poem narrates the speaker's arrival in a mysterious hotel-room previously inhabited by a dying 'poet' and his unsuccessful attempt to reconstruct the former occupant's end on the basis of single line found 'in pencil, just above the bed.' Written in the iambic tetrameter of the entire poem, the line '"Alone, unknown, unloved, I die"' is both maudlin and rich in existential import, and acts as the fulcrum point of the poem. The opening quatrain announces the mixture of thematic weight – the temporal closure of nighttime and death – and surface lightness of approach which will be brought to bear in responding to this anonymous statement:

> The room a dying poet took
> at nightfall in a dead hotel
> had both directories – the Book
> of Heaven and the Book of Bell.   (*PP* 164)

The hotel room, although seemingly normal, is in fact only condescending 'to imitate a normal room' and is increasingly given the attributes of a human body – ribs, blood, a skeleton, and finally 'a ghostly thorax, with a heart.' The poem's speaker, upon arrival in the hotel room, identifies himself with the room's 'wheeling skeleton of light' as '[a] similar striped cageling.' Metaphorically a captive in the room as well, the poem's speaker seeks to learn the identity of the previous occupant but is unsuccessful. Rather than succumb to the despondency of the pencilled line or the banal artistry contained in the picture on the wall, however, the speaker reflects – optimistically – that the poet's death is final only on paper. The ultimate fate of the poet remains unknown, incomplete:

> Perhaps my text is incomplete.
> A poet's death is, after all,
> a question of technique, a neat
> enjambment, a melodic fall.   (*PP* 165)

According to the belief intimated throughout Nabokov's poetry, the anonymous line '"Alone, unknown, unloved, I die,"' ending as it does with the finality of 'I die,' is indeed incomplete; death is more accurately, and quite literally, 'a question of technique,' a process subtly contained within the image of 'a neat enjambment' – itself neatly replicated in the line of the quatrain. Death is a rupture, but also a continuation to another dimension, a carrying forth to the next line, the following strophe of being, the next stanza of consciousness. In the final quatrain of the poem, the word *death*, with its connotations of finality, is avoided. A life has changed, grown into a ghostly form, but not been left alone:

> And here a life had come apart
> in darkness, and the room had grown
> a ghostly thorax, with a heart
> unknown, unloved – but not alone.   (*PP* 165)

As in the conclusion of the Russian poem 'You've moved to new lodgings ...,' here, in 'The Room,' it would seem that departure from the temporarily inhabited room of life is quite probably but the poetic pause of an enjambment in consciousness, a prelude to habitation in another dimension.

The otherworld in Nabokov's poetry is thus subtly evoked by utilization of motifs and images of enclosure which are charged with metaphoric reference to a larger unknown dimension outside of their boundaries. A crystal ball, a cocoon, a train, a house, a room are but the most prominent of such motifs. The otherworld is induced in Nabokov's poetry not simply by enclosure, however, but with still greater diversity in a variety of motifs of temporal, spatial, and psychological transition. In such poems, Nabokov effectively infuses a sense of the texture and multi-dimensionality of being into poetic description by narrating events of the physical world and conventional psychological experience while ensuring that a slight though persistent draught from other realms is ever felt. The most prominent motifs of points of transition between spatial realms may be identified in the sky, seashores, watery surfaces, stairways, doorways, windows, mirrors, and bridges, while temporal transition are marked by sunrise and sunset, dawn and dusk. Further motifs of altered psychological states or levels of consciousness are contained in depictions of dreams, fever, passion, dementia, and, in physical beings – especially animals – that change from one form of existence to another.

Within Nabokov's artistry, the use of such motifs is rarely overtly transparent. The magic of his artistry and the source of the reader's 'radiant smile of perfect satisfaction, a purr of beatitude' – Nabokov's standard of achievement for 'true poetry' which expresses 'the mysteries of the irrational as perceived through rational words' – is his assured control over the correct balance of rational and irrational. Although the otherworld pervades Nabokov's poetry like a watermark, it never stains the page of his writing as the sole focus of representation. In this, Nabokov is to be distinguished from earlier, above all, Romantic practitioners of metaphysical poetry. Wordsworth, for instance, also gave poetic representation to the doctrine of anamnesis and the earthly recognition of precarnate knowledge, a topic frequently addressed in Nabokov's poetry. In Wordsworth, however, a poem such as 'Ode: Intimations of Immortality' provides a more discursive than imaginative approach to the topic, to become a philosophical meditation:

Our birth is but a sleeping and a forgetting:
The soul that rises with us, our life's Star,
    Hath had elsewhere its setting,
        And cometh from afar:
    Not in entire forgetfulness,
    And not in utter nakedness,
But trailing clouds of glory do we come
        From God, who is our home:
    Heaven lies about us in our infancy!
Shades of the prison-house begin to close
        Upon the growing Boy,
But He beholds the light, and whence it flows,
        He sees it in his joy ...   (Wordsworth 1985, 71)

Quite apart from the overt appeal to Christianity as the conceptual framework within which to embed the propagation of philosophical ideas, this poem is foreign in expression to Nabokov's artistry in its absence of pictorial force. Nabokov's poetry is predominantly a poetry of narrated experience captured in sensually affective imagery. The discursive value of his poetry may only be accessed via appreciation of the plasticity of his imagery. A poetically depicted apple, for instance, is an apple, though one which may also be transformed by a flick of the poet's imaginative knife into something else, a snowball. The attentive reader capable of feeling the texture camouflaged by the surface simplicity of a trifling image is rewarded with a 'radiant smile of perfect satisfaction' in recognition of still other depths. Indeed, Nabokov's progressive maturation as a poet may be measured to a significant degree by his control of this thematic multi-dimensionality, his ability unobtrusively to fold philosophical subject matter into innocent-seeming poems of narrated event by means of carefully freighted motifs. The most abrupt evidence of Nabokov's mastery of this dimension of his poetic art is the division between his adolescent collection of juvenilia, *Poems* of 1916, and subsequent volumes of poetry. As with his later writing, *Poems* too contains poetic representation of several of the motifs to be further illustrated below; nowhere in this first collection, however, does poetic representation achieve the thematic depth which distinguishes his later verse. And thus, although indicative of formal mastery and the germ of a pronounced lyric sensibility, this poetry remains on the surface of conventional love and nature poetry. Starting with *Two Paths*, however, mysteries of the otherworld have been consistently signalled through the use of motifs of temporal and spatial transition and intimation of subtle disruptions in the conventional experience of time and space. The progressive mastery of Nabokov's lyric voice is revealed in the increasingly intricate, though subtle, revelation of the chinks and folds in the texture of being.

Excellent examples of the slippage of time and space possible in everyday life are to be found already in selected poems of *The Cluster*. The final three poems of the volume contained under the heading 'Movement' are all less about physical movement – though each poem deals with train travel – than with other forms of mysterious passage. In the above referred to 'On a Train,' for instance, the first-person poetic voice, while travelling on a train at evening time in a foreign land, conquers time in sleep to return to intense sensual experience of his youth in Russia. In the third stanza, in preparation for the escape from the present to the past, images of transition are strategically introduced into the poem:

По занавескам свет, как призрак, проходил,
Внимая трепету и тренью
смолкающих колес, – я раму опустил:
пахнуло сыростью, сиренью!

Была передо мной вся молодость моя: (*Ssoch* I, 466)

[Light on the curtain, like a ghost, passed. / Heeding the trepidation and friction / of the quieting wheels, I lowered the window: / it smelled of dampness, lilacs. // Before me was my entire youth:]

Through an open window and a curtain which announces the presence of the mysterious in the ghostly passage of a breeze, the speaker is magically lifted from the drab present to be afforded Proustian experience of the past. The young Nabokov here illustrates in poetic form the secret to the recapturing of lost time that he would later identify in a discursive manner in his discussion of Proust's *À la recherche du temps perdu* : 'In short, to recreate the past something other than the operation of memory must happen: there must be a combination of a present sensation (especially taste, smell, touch, sound) with a recollection, a remembrance, of the sensuous past ... In other words, a nosegay of the senses in the present *and* the vision of an event or sensation in the past, this when sense and memory come together and lost time is found again' (*LL* 249). The window of the train in 'On a Train' thus signals the subjugation of time, not in passage to a transcendent realm, but in the rediscovery of lost time.

In similar fashion, though here in terms of space rather than time, the final poem of *The Cluster*, 'Как часто, как часто я в поезде скором ...' ('Kak chasto, kak chasto ia v poezde skorom ...' / 'How often, how often I on a fast train ...'), depicts the poetic speaker's experiences of a wondrous merging with the surrounding physical environment (*Ssoch* I, 467). Sitting, in the first stanza, in a train marvelling at the 'swimming spaciousness,' the speaker leans his head against the glass separating his compartment from the coiling, dissipating physical environment outside the train 'beside the wide, rumbling windows.' It is the window which offers him a vista out of his physical space onto a wonder which announces its delirious irrationality as 'the meadow distance / blissfully rotates in blue delirium.' Continuing the poem and journey into the second stanza, the central image of transition of the first, the window, is replaced by a sunset. The speaker claims experience of sunsets of such magnificence that the train seems to have loosened its ties to the earth to fly, as if transformed into an angel, 'along coloured cliffs' 'in the rapture of the sunset.' Both of these early poems of movement pivot on images of separation and transition – curtains, windows, a sunset – which, while narrating conventional physical passage, also obliquely announce the temporal and spatial wonder, the irrationality, of a conquest of time and space through their dispersal.

Nabokov's exploitation of the suggestive, metaphoric potential of the central cluster of images of transition within his oeuvre is varied in quality, extending beyond statements regarding the generalized meaning of their use in his poetry. Windows and doorways, sunsets and seashores, are not in Nabokov's poetry *symbols* freighted with fixed abstract meaning. They are instead signs of the presence of another realm and the possibility of transition which is in each poem different and thus adaptable to varying representations. Selected examples may be offered which are united only in the thematic effect they produce in Nabokov's poetry and not in the demonstration of final meaning. The following poem, despite its brevity and concision, is exceptionally rich in subtle suggestion of a journey set to leave the map of contiguous reality. Dedicated to Nabokov's mother, 'Людям ты скажешь: настало!' ('Liudiam ty skazhesh': nastalo! ...' / 'To people you will say: it's time! ...') is at once about the exile's longing to return to Russia, but also the radical transition required to complete a journey of this sort. The specificity and understated beauty of this poem hinge on its ability to suggest much while employing minimalist forms of verbal and syntactic expression. Here, the combination of metaphysical suggestion and linguistic precision is all:

> Людям ты скажешь: настало!
> Завтра я в путь соберусь …
> (Голуби. Двор постоялый.
> Ржавая вывеска: Русь.)   (*Ssoch* I, 558)

> [To people you will say: it's time! / Tomorrow I intend to take to the road. /
> (Pigeons. An inn. / A rusty sign-post: Rus.]

The first quatrain, with its address to humans, begins in the profane sphere of earthly time and space – tomorrow and Rus. The second quatrain, with its address to God, already suggests a different dimension where, although the speaker has arrived home, much time has passed:

> Скажешь ты Богу: я дома!
> (Кладбище. Мост. Поворот)
> Будет старик незнакомый –
> вместо дубка, у ворот …   (*Ssoch* I, 558)

> [You will say to God: I am at home! / (A cemetery. A bridge. A turning point.) /
> There will be an unknown elderly man / Instead of the young oak at the gates.]

Both stanzas are about travel – the first spatial and the second temporal – with the essential movement expressed in the troikas of images concluding each stanza. Employing here in poetry a rhetorical manoeuvre which he would later deploy in his prose, Nabokov makes a statement and then illustrates it with three parenthetically contained images of metonymic force. Real in themselves, each image carries with it as well a rich field of associations concerning the journey of time and experience. The images of the second quatrain especially are redolent of the extra-temporal and -spatial journey required to return to Russia. Death and the cemetery are the bridge and turning point to the only possible final return home. It is in these images that the texture of the poem is most suggestively and intriguingly expressed.

The perhaps most frequent motif of spatial transition in Nabokov's poetry is the window. Throughout Nabokov's poetic oeuvre, in poems from 'Soft Sound' to 'Restoration,' windows function as images suggestive of portals to other dimensions. And given the ubiquity of windows across his writing career, the proposed title for what was to be Nabokov's second independent volume of verse – the never published collection *Раскрытые окна* (*Raskrytye okna / Open Windows*) – indicates that even as a young writer, Nabokov was conscious of his manipulation of this image in consistently suggestive fashion. It is also in the context of the above enumerated images of enclosure and transition – and especially windows – that Nabokov's self-description of his émigré persona Sirin gains added interest. In *Speak, Memory*, Nabokov claims that émigré readers 'were impressed by the mirror-like images of his [Sirin/Nabokov's] clear but weirdly misleading sentences and by the fact that the real life of his books flowed in his figures of speech, which one critic has compared to "windows giving upon a contiguous world … a rolling corollary, the shadow of a train of thought"' (*SM* 288). 'Windows upon a contiguous world' – underscored in the inverted commas of a fabricated critical comment – is indeed an apt appraisal of the otherworldly presence within Nabokov's writing. It is, simultaneously, coy reference to one of the central images utilized in the artistic creation of this presence, as in the above discussed poem 'How often, how often I on a fast train …' The preponderance of windows may be fixed in numbers, as well; six of the thirty-eight poems of *The Cluster*, for instance, contain imagery of windows. Frequently windows are associated with nighttime and the transition of consciousness in, especially, dream, as in 'Для странствия ночного мне не надо …' ('Dlia stranstviia nochnogo mne ne nado …' / 'For nocturnal travel I require …'), a poem which explicitly links the magic of dream-travel in time and memory and the open entry-point of a window:

Для странствия ночного мне не надо
　　ни кораблей, ни поездов.
Стоит луна над шашечницей сада.
　　Окно открыто. Я готов.　　　　　　　　　　(*Ssoch* II, 597)

[For nocturnal travel I require / neither ships nor trains. / The moon hangs above the checkerboard of the garden. / The window is open. I am ready.]

Likewise, in 'Сон' ('Son' / 'The Dream'), the speaker is granted by the Lord a dream whose coming arises out of the rain drumming on his windowsill:

Однжды ночью подоконник
дождем был шумно орошен.
Господь открыл свой тайный сонник
и выбрал мне сладчайший сон.   (*Ssoch* I, 637)

[Once at nighttime the windowsill / was noisily irrigated by rain. / The Lord opened his secret book of dreams / and selected for me the sweetest of dreams.]

Lulled by the sound of rain at his window, the speaker falls asleep and is transported by a dream along a 'blue route' from exile and his 'house shaking with the sobs of the night' to an idyllic, rural setting where he lies sprawled on his back on the top of a wagonload of hay. As the sound of the rain by his 'breathing window' merges into the creaking wheels of the wagon beneath him, dream and reality are inverted and the speaker is left wondering which is more real, the 'fateful foreign land' where he sleeps by a rain-washed window or the sensually perceived reality of his dream with its fragrant 'camomile flower in the warm hay / right by my lips, right there.'

It is not only dreams and intriguing draughts from transcendent realms which waft through Nabokov's poetry and windows, bringing with them intimations of transition and other realms. In the single-sentence, untitled poem 'Сам треугольный, – двукрылый, безногий …' ('Sam treugol'nyi, dvukrylyi, beznogii…' / 'Himself triangular, two-winged, legless …'), a moth, a 'frightening little one, a heavenly cripple,' flits through the speaker's window to flutter about the room. Disturbed by the winged presence, the speaker wishes only that the moth would leave the enclosed space of the room for another wondrous place of metamorphosis:

Только бы вылетел, только нашел бы
это окно и опять, в неземной
лаборатории, в синюю колбу
сел бы, сложась, ангелочек ночной …   (*Ssoch* III, 671)

[If only he would fly away, if only he would find / that window and again, in the unearthly / laboratory, in a deep blue retort / come to rest, enfolded, a nocturnal angel.]

An agitated cripple in the speaker's room, the moth, in flying out the window into the night sky – here described in imagery of enclosure as a 'deep blue retort' – will come to rest metaphorically transformed by the poem's selective imagery into an angel.

Thus, with the moth, still another example of a preferred image of transition between levels of being flits into Nabokov's poetry. Nabokov's poetry is studded with instances of poetry containing animals which are comparable in their magical power for transformation and sudden displays of splendour. *The Cluster*, for instance, Nabokov's first volume of poetry released under the name Sirin, is populated with various animals, beginning with two poems containing a peacock and an unidentified bird suggestive of the *sirin*, a wondrous bird of paradise. The same volume contains the untitled poem 'О любовь, ты светла и крылата …' ('O liubov', ty svetla i krylata, – ' / 'O love, you are radiant and winged '), a deceptively simple poem, which in a complex play of imagery describes the transformation of the speaker from an unformed aquatic being as blank page into a 'tadpole poet.' It is to be inferred that the tadpole will develop into something else as the page of his skill grows with poetic expression.[32] Likewise, in *The Cluster* is the poem 'В зверинце' ('V zverintse' / 'In the Menagerie'), a despondent poem about the speaker's visit to an exhibit of animals, which are considered by the speaker not beasts but gods. The speaker's attention is especially drawn to a solitary animal randomly plucked from its native realm to be placed in captivity, a lone jerboa, in whose eyes, loneliness, and caged condition the speaker sees a reflection of his own disconsolate state. Immediately following 'In the Menagerie' is 'Ночные бабочки' ('Nochnye babochki' / 'Nocturnal Butterflies'), a lyric poem of the 'rapture of memory' and the speaker's sensuously described reminiscences of catching butterflies at night as a youth in Russia. Although there are still other intriguing examples of Nabokov's metaphysically suggestive poetry of animals, it is the butterfly in Nabokov's poetry – indeed, throughout his oeuvre – which serves as the most suggestive motif of transformation to another, more splendorous stage of being. The earliest and perhaps most explicit use of the motif of the butterfly in Nabokov's oeuvre comes in 'Нет, бытие – не зыбкая загадка!' ('Net, bytie – ne zybkaia zagadka!' / 'No, existence is not an unstable riddle!'), a brief poem of 1923 whose wonder resides in the

contrast between the verbal and imagistic simplicity of the poem and the
metaphysical reverberations of its tacit implications. Rendered concise by
the controlled consistency of the *AbAb* rhyme scheme of the two quatrains, the poem begins with an emphatic counter-assertion to an unstated
claim about the nature of being. Existence is something tremulous and
beautiful, a natural stage in preparation for a further transformation:

Нет, бытие – не зыбкая загадка!
Подлунный дол и ясен, и росист.
Мы – гусеницы ангелов; и сладко
въедаться с краю в нежный лист.   (*Stikhi* 105)

[No, existence is not an unstable riddle! / The moonlit dale is both clear and
dewy. / We are the caterpillars of angels; and pleasurable / [it is] to eat from
the periphery into a tender leaf.]

The second stanza proceeds, not into discursive abstraction, but with a
single extended metaphor of illustrative strength which, after an initial
profusion of verbs, unfolds into a single revelatory image:

Рядись в шипы, ползи, сгибайся, крепни,
и чем жадней твой ход зеленый был,
тем бархатистей и великолепней
хвосты освобожденных крыл.   (*Stikhi* 105)

[Dress up in thorns, crawl, bend, grow strong, / and the meaner your green
course was / the more velvety and magnificent / the tips of [your] freed
wings.]

This poem seems an uncommonly clear expression of belief regarding the
nature of existence, though it contends nothing in conventional argumen-
tative form. Any declarative power residing within the poem rests solely on
the image of the caterpillar as a forestage of the butterfly, and the suggested comparative potential of humans engaged in the profane business
of earthly survival ultimately to metamorphose into divine form. The relevance of the poem's central image is forcefully stated, albeit articulated
poetically in a metaphor, thereby retaining Nabokov's persistent adherence
to a lyric form of expression. A brief text of metaphysical import, it nonetheless remains a poem, as if – *pace* Tiutchev's 'Silentium' – any other form
of expression would be a lie.

A reading of Nabokov's poetry which is sensitive to central motifs of enclosure and transition thus reveals an important device in Nabokov's poetic expression of his 'major theme,' the otherworld. While lyric articulation of the otherworld seems demonstrable in houses, rooms, and trains and in windows, dreams, and animals, it is important to observe that, as with the above discussed poem about the caterpillar-butterfly/human-angel, the aesthetic primacy of poetry is never sacrificed to discursive goals, however weighty they may seem. Rather, the intuited, suggestive potential of poetry – and especially the metaphor – is exploited to its full potential in the expression of subject matter which, by its nature, falls outside the realm of empirical exposition. Nabokov's poetry is not only expression of 'the mysteries of the irrational as perceived through rational words' (*NG* 55), it is witness to the unique power of poetry to articulate the shades of experience and thought inaccessible to the rational. Likewise, although Nabokov's poetry may be shown to be occupied with themes and subject matter of aesthetic, ethical, and metaphysical import, rarely is one sphere accorded primacy over the others. Perhaps nowhere is this interwoven character of Nabokov's poetry more apparent than in his poems dealing with the wonders of the poetic calling and, in particular, in an important sub-theme, the arrival of the muse. In these poems, dimensions of the aesthetic, ethical, and metaphysical are interwoven in a complex web of inter-dependent themes and images centred in the figure of the muse, who combines the aesthetic primacy of poetry, the ethical demands of love, and the metaphysical wonder of poetry's source in a mysterious, transcendent realm. Nabokov's poetry about the appearance of the muse is thus worthy of brief discussion as a concluding illustration of the mysterious quality of Nabokov's poetry of the otherworld as it merges with the theme of love.

As with so many of the themes and motifs which characterize Nabokov's oeuvre, the encounter with the muse is one first expressed in his poetry, from whence it developed into variegated forms of expression in a lifetime of subsequent writing. As with the depiction of animals, Nabokov's first collection of poetry as Sirin, *The Cluster*, introduces the muse into his poetry. Nabokov's earlier collection with Andrei Balashov, *Two Paths*, contained poetry dealing with the poetic calling, though it is not until his first independent volume that the muse appears in mysterious form bearing the central metaphysical characteristic of much of Nabokov's poetry and subsequent writing. In *The Cluster*, the cluster of poems entitled 'Ты' ('Ty' / 'Thou'), the second of four, is devoted to poetic apprehension of a loved one who, although occasionally shaded with the contours of human erotic interest, is as much and more a supernal presence. Love of artistry and the muse fuses with love of a young woman in Nabokov's poetic alembic. Vladimir Alexandrov has convincingly suggested the youthful Nabokov's indebtedness to Alexandr Blok in the development of this theme in his poetry, in particular, in the relatedness of Nabokov's muse to Blok's figure of the 'prekrasnaia dama' (the 'wonderful lady') (Alexandrov 1991, 215– 17). Indeed, in a two-poem cycle dedicated to Blok in *The Cluster*, Nabokov indicated his familiarity with Blok's collection *Stikhi o prekrasnoi Dame* (*Verses about the Wonderful Lady*) through direct reference to the floating arrival of the 'wondrous lady.' Alexandrov is also correct in pointing out the unmistakable imprint left by Blok's example on the imagery, lexicon, and rhythms of the young Nabokov's poetry of the muse.[33] Perhaps more intriguing than this evidence of poetic affinity is the delineation of characteristic differences at this still early stage in Nabokov's poetic development, differences which indicate the germ of an independent lyric identity. In this regard, Alexandrov notes that Nabokov's poetry 'eschews the apocalyptic undertones derived from Vladimir Soloviev that underlie Blok's verse' and, in contrast to 'the mood of mystical despair or abandonment' in Blok's poetry, 'Nabokov's poems are filled with hope' (Alexandrov 1991, 216). Related to this, it is also to be noted that Nabokov's poems of the muse do not strive to carry the symbolic weight freighted in Blok's poetry and drama. As figures representative of a symbolic composite combining the eternal feminine and personages of mythic-religious significance, Blok's 'wonderful lady' and her sister-in-verse the 'unknown woman' (*neznakoma*) are abstractions of primarily philosophical relevance. Nabokov's 'wonderful lady' is, in contrast, associated first and foremost with the artistic development and refinement of his *individual* skill as a poet. The muse's presence is never felt without conscious reflection on the state of Nabokov's poetic genius. In this, the muse in Nabokov's poetry is inspiration and poetry personified; metaphorically, she is the fleshly embodiment of both the unknown source of inspiration and the poetry itself.

Apart from these differences of temperament, however, is also a central stylistic difference. Nabokov's poems seem more vivid and dramatic in the verbal staging of scenes. Although Nabokov is drawn to, and draws upon, the Blokian imagery of mysticism and the indeterminacy of a mysterious being and experience, his poetry is also marked by the precision and plasticity of the scene created. Even such potentially ethereal topics as cosmic synchronization and the wonder of inspiration and the otherworld are always ballasted with, indeed derive from, precise imagery of the world. Nabokov's depictions of the muse seem as much concerned with the waking reality of the poet as with the half-lit dreamworld of the muse, and thus often contain a pronounced narrative element in combination with the depiction of lyric experience. Indeed, the skill of the poetry is in part to be located in the maintenance of a sense of indeterminacy which is derived from this dual representation and the manner in which final clarity is suspended regarding what is being referred to in the figure of the 'wonderful lady' – an erotic interest of human flesh and blood or the mysterious muse or, somehow, both. Metaphor forms the bridge between the two. Indeed, the occasionally encountered dismissal of Nabokov's youthful poetry as juvenile love poetry or epigonic mimicry of Blok undoubtedly arises from the inclination of some readers to read but one layer of the poems, as if blinded to the subsidiary layers by the perspicacity of depiction of the real. Although related, the Blokian and Nabokovian muses are two different women. Blok's 'wondrous lady' may look like Zina of *The Gift* and Sybil of *Pale Fire*; however, the latter two are related via the bloodline of Nabokov's lyric sensibility.

Nabokov's poetry frequently turns to the muse. The first two poems of the second section of *The Cluster*, for instance, describe the poet's first encounter(s) with a lover/muse. In the poem 'Когда, туманные, мы свиделись впервые …' ('Kogda, tumannye, my svidelis' vpervye …' / 'When, obscure, we saw each other first…'), the poet, upon meeting the object of his enchantment, recedes into the seclusion of his studio in the attempt to capture her appearance in artistic form (*Ssoch* I, 451–2). Although unsuccessful in this endeavour, the poem ends with the artist's conviction that at some time he will tear aside the curtain separating him from the object of representation to reveal her spirit, his purest artistic achievement. In this poem about the urge to engage in artistic representation, it is perhaps paradoxical that the object of representation is the most vaguely depicted element in the poem. Cast in the mysterious, ill-defined vocabulary of 'obscurity,' 'a haze of dimness,' 'and 'the ghost of [a] inclined face,' the object of representation is never actually identified in terms of physical or psychological characteristics; rather than submit to depiction, she 'melts away behind mists,' thereby eluding capture in artistic form in either Nabokov's poem or the sculpture attempted within the poem. Likewise indeterminate is the 'mute and bright studio' of the artist and the exact place and duration of the attempt to sculpt an image of the woman. Despite the non-specificity of the woman and the artistic process, however, the poem is replete with sensual imagery which extends beyond the heightened sense of psychological urgency in the artist's desire to create. The whitening of a god in sunlit dust, two bronze statues with swollen muscles and shiny backs, a lump of clay which is blue, damp and soft, and the tactile precision of hands which carefully outline a face by memory – each is a concise verbal appeal to the senses and a sign of the phenomenal reality of a layer of the poem. Ultimately, the poem never reveals whether the object of depiction in sculpture is a woman or the muse to be represented in metonymic form in both the clay of the planned sculpture and the lines of the poem. More forcefully depicted than the woman/muse herself is the intensity of the wish to create. Indeed, in shifting interpretive focus again, it seems possible that neither a woman nor the muse is the focus of representation; rather, that the poem depicts the psychology of artistic creation and the rapturous, sensual surrender to inspiration during the forming of art. In Nabokov's above discussed autobiographical description of his first poem in *Speak, Memory*, he describes the experience known to the poets Fyodor Godunov-Cherdyntsev of *The Gift* and John Shade of *Pale Fire* of cosmic synchronization and the poet's loss to consciously experienced time and space while in the grip of inspiration. This seems equally the case in the present poem, with 'the mute and bright studio' a metaphor for the mind and the acting of sculpting, metaphoric expression for the writing of poetry:

> И вновь тебя я встретил,
> и вновь средь тишины высокой мастерской,
> забыв наружный мир, с восторгом и тоской,
> я жадно стал творить, и вновь прервал работу …
> Чредой сияли дни, чредой их позолоту
> смывала мгла ночей. Я грезил и ваял …   (*Ssoch* I, 451)

[And again I met you / and again amidst the silence of the high studio / oblivious to the external world, with rapture and yearning / I greedily began to create and again interrupted the work / In succession shined the days, in succession their gilding / was washed away by the mist of night. I dreamed and sculpted …]

Oblivion to the surrounding environment and the unnoticed melting away of time are the recognizably Nabokovian features of the psychology of inspiration, as is the rapture and will to create. One of Nabokov's first poem's of love of a woman/muse is thus also readable as a depiction not simply of the source of inspiration but the very experience of it.

In a similar manner, the following untitled poem from *The Cluster*, beginning with the line 'Мечтал я о тебе так часто, так давно …' ('Mechtal o tebe tak chasto, tak davno …' / 'I dreamed of you so often, so long ago …'), takes on further shades of unexpected meaning in the context of Nabokov's account in *Speak, Memory* of his first poem. Here again, Alexandrov is correct in reference to this poem in observing the echoes from Blok's 'О доблесиах, о подвигах, о славе ...' ('O doblestiakh, o podvigakh, o slave ...' / 'Of attainments, of great deeds, of glory ...') (Alexandrov 1991, 216). Into Nabokov's poem, however, steals an element of self-parody just as, in the poem, 'the night stole into the window / and the candles winked at one another.' The silent collusion of the winking candles prepares the poem for a depiction of the established theme of the muse's arrival and, likewise, parodic treatment of the conventions perhaps all too easily employed in the representation of this theme. The poet-speaker describes awaiting the arrival of a woman/muse known to him in general form through his browsings in 'books about love, about the haze above the Neva, / about the bliss of roses and the misty sea' (*Ssoch* I, 452). Although thus studied and keenly awaited, the muse fails to appear. 'Years' pass within the young poet's still short life: 'I called for you, I waited. Years passed. I wandered.' Finally, after undergoing the trials common to the Romance convention, the muse 'lightly arrived.' Rather than depicting the range of emotions to be expected after so long and ardent a wait, the poem coolly records, not the encounter, but, at a second remove, memory of the encounter. Disturbing the fulfillment of the meeting are the poet's troubling and inescapable thoughts concerning its authenticity, as he 'remembers superstitiously, / how those deep assonant-mirrors / faithfully predicted you.' The poet's 'superstitious' remembrance of how his muse's image all too closely accords with the images learned in the conventional guides to poetastery perused in his youth introduces the suspicion that Nabokov is both utilizing and gently mocking the theme. If so, then this early poem coincides with Nabokov's gentle self-parody in *Speak, Memory* when he notes that the subject matter of his first – artistically weak – elegy 'dealt with the loss of a beloved mistress – Delia, Tamara or Lenore – whom I had never lost, never loved, never met but was all set to meet, love, lose' (*SM* 225). Likewise in 'I dreamed of you so often, so long ago,' it seems that Nabokov's depiction of the arrival of the muse was also subject to parodic manipulation in a manner suggestive of a degree of conscious control of poetic subject matter rarely acknowledged in Nabokov the young poet.

In another of the several poems from the second cluster of *The Cluster* which invoke the muse, Nabokov personifies love of artistic creation and inspiration through the figure of an adored muse-like woman, thereby bending the artistic theme of the coming of the muse to the specifics of Nabokov's aesthetic. 'Позволь мечтать. Ты первое страданье ...' ('Pozvol' mechtat'. Ty pervoe stradan'e ...' / 'Allow me to dream. You are my first torment ...'), a brief double quatrain poem with an insistent *AbAb* rhyme scheme, identifies inspiration as a 'first torment and a final bliss' in an informal address directed to the muse: 'I feel the movement and breath / of your soul ...' In an enjambment which extends across the quatrains, the address to the muse becomes an apostrophic plea to poetry itself – expressed metaphorically as 'a pure string' – to allow the poet to believe in rapture and the hope 'that life, like you, is but full of music' (*Ssoch* I, 453). Inspiration, the muse, and poetry are allowed to merge with one another in a poem which concludes on the very Nabokovian note of optimism that life itself is a work of art. Despite the buoyancy expressed at the end of this poem, the arrival of the muse is not always marked with confidence. In 'Ты войдешь и молча сядешь ...' ('Ty voidesh' i molcha siadesh'...' / 'You will enter and wordlessly sit down...'), Nabokov employs several motifs of transition – evening time, a door, a curtain, the glass of a window, and the shimmering light of dawn – to strengthen the atmosphere of separation from the muse after an unsatisfying encounter in which the poet vainly attempted to complain of the conditions of his life (*Ssoch* I, 473). Most frequently, however, the coming of the muse is an experience wondrous in physical and emotional dimension, as in 'О, встречи дивное волненье!' ('O, vstrechi divnoe volnen'e! ...' / 'O, wondrous agitation of a meeting! ...'), 'Часы на башне распевали ...' ('Chasy na bashne raspevali ...' / 'The clock on the tower sang out ...'), 'С восьми до полночи таюсь в будке тесной ...' ('S vos'mi do polnochi taius' ia v budke tesnoi, ...' / 'From eight until midnight I hide in a small booth ...'), and 'Тоска, и тайна, и услада ...' ('Toska, i taina, i uslada ...' / 'Yearning, and mystery, and delight ...'). In each of these poems, love and the otherworld are combined in poems which are intrinsically of aesthetic relevance in their reflection on the coming of inspiration and the writing of poetry.

That Nabokov's poetry of the muse was the poetry of his youth, despite the importance of its formal and thematic composition in formatively shaping his lyric identity, is in essence the subject matter of Nabokov's poem of 1929 'К музе' ('K Muze' / 'The Muse'). Subsequently translated for inclusion in *Poems and Problems*, 'The Muse' first appeared in the volume *Poems: 1929–1951*, where it was identified in Nabokov's brief preface as the poem which concluded his 'period of youthful creativity' and, as such, a pivotal work in the history of his poetic development.[34] With this prefatory statement and, more importantly, with the poem itself, Nabokov indicates that his poetry of the muse was at once a demonstration of poetic facility with an established theme and also a self-reflexive comment on the changing state of his poetic sensibility. 'The Muse,' in reflecting on Nabokov's changed relations with the muse, marks the culmination of the youthful stage in his artistic maturation. Composed of six quatrains of, in Russian, alternating masculine and feminine rhymes (*aBaB*), the poem begins in a retrospective mode to recreate, in the past tense, an illustrative pastiche of the images indicative in earlier poetry of the psychological and physical setting associated with the wondrous arrival of the muse:

> Your coming I recall: a growing vibrance,
> an agitation to the world unknown.
> The moon through branches touched the balcony
> and there a shadow, lyriform, was thrown.   (*PP* 57)

The second stanza indicates the type of poetic sentiment which once moved Nabokov and clearly identifies the muse as the personification of his own poetry, in this instance, in an image which also suggests both the innocence and slightly tawdry effusiveness of the overly forthcoming poetic style of his youth – 'with the red lips of its rhyme it smiled':

> To me, a youth, the iamb seemed a garb
> too rude for the soft langor of your shoulders;
> but my imperfect line had tunefulness
> and with the red lips of its rhyme it smiled.   (*PP* 57)

Despite these shortcomings, however, the poet-speaker in the third quatrain acknowledges the dreamy happiness and creative ardour of his previous infatuation. With the fourth quatrain of the six-quatrain poem, a temporal caesura is marked; while the first three quatrains of 'The Muse' are cast in the past tense, with images of night and indeterminacy predominating, the final three return to the present and the clear light of day. And whereas the past is characterized by heedless fervour, the present is taken up with the practical and mundane:

> I am expert, frugal, intolerant.
> My polished verse cleaner than copper shines.
> We talk occasionally, you and I,
> across the fence like two old country neighbors.   (*PP* 57)

Thus, an encounter which was once marked by the poetry of mystery, wonder, and tender trepidation has become a prosaic relationship of friendly
gossip, familiar, though no longer infused with tremulous intimacy. The
deflating contrast between the romance of the past and the familiarity of
the present is intensified via Nabokov's subtle, self-parodying reference to
a previous poem about an exotic muse-like figure collected in *The Empyrean
Path*. In this poem, 'Сторожевые кипарисы …' ('Storozhevye kiparisy…' /
'Sentinel cypresses …'), in the enchanting half-dusk of a star-lit garden,
the poetic speaker feels the penetrating gaze of a wondrous woman from
across a fence:

> И чья-то тень из-за ограды
> упорно смотрит на меня,
> …
> А там, – глаза Шехеразады
> в мой звездный и звенящий сад
> из-за белеющей ограды,
> продолговатые, глядят.   (*Ssoch* I, 486)

[And someone's shade from behind the fence / is intently looking at me / …
And there – Sheherazade's eyes / into my starry and sonorous garden / from
behind the whitening fence, / elongated, peer.]

The fence between muse and poet in both poems – what in the youthful
poem once maintained a veil of nighttime indeterminacy and mystery –
has become a place of daytime meeting, while the muse herself has meta-
morphosed from an exotic, fairy-tale figure into a familiar, country
neighbour. In the final quatrain, 'The Muse' turns, as so often in Nabokov's
poetry of the muse, to explicit commentary on the state of his artistic development. Turning again to the Nabokovian rhetorical trope of a metonymic image followed by three illustrating metaphors, Nabokov comments
on the quality of mature art; for with his changed relationship to the muse,
the type of poetry written by him has been correspondingly transformed:

> Yes, ripeness is pictorial, agreed:
> leaf of grapevine, pear, watermelon halved,
> and – top of artistry – transparent light.   (*PP* 57)

As in Nabokov's case, the poet of 'The Muse' observes that his poetry has
become pictorial, although still transfused with a luminosity emerging

from a hidden source: the 'top of artistry – transparent light.' Although accorded the consolation of polished verse and controlled, confident artistry, the poet is nonetheless left in the final line of the poem to bemoan the oncoming coolness of maturation: 'I'm feeling cold. Ah, this is autumn, Muse!' (*PP* 57).

Thus, analysis of Nabokov's poetry, which has thus far emphasized the metaphysical underpinnings of a lyric identity tempered with ethical and aesthetic dimensions, concludes with a poem of self-conscious reflection on Nabokov's altered relationship to the muse and his poetic voice. Although the otherworld, and in general a metaphysical aura, will continue to infuse Nabokov's poetic artistry, it increasingly assumes a subtler form with the above discussed motifs of transition being substituted for more indirect, diffuse forms of expression. To adopt the imagery from 'The Muse,' a fence separating realms is exchanged for transparent light emanating from another space. And just as Nabokov indicated in 'The Muse' heightened interest in the phenomenal specificity of the world and experience – 'leaf of grapevine, pear, watermelon halved' – so the present study will turn to the fifth and final element to be proposed here as defining of Nabokov's poetic voice – attention to the enchanting detail and specificity of the phenomenal world.

V. A Poet of the World – the Poetry of Trifles

Thus far, the comprehensive reading of Nabokov's poetic oeuvre offered here has concentrated on the thematic clusters of cosmic synchronization, inspiration, love, and the otherworld. This strategy was chosen in the attempt to achieve synoptic breadth of analysis, while simultaneously indicating that Nabokov's lyric identity resides in his deployment of these themes in poems of multi-layered, thematically interrelated complexity. Analysis based on these thematic categories, however, necessarily foregrounds the metaphysical dimension of Nabokov's poetry and runs the risk of imposing an inappropriate degree of uni-dimensionality on his lyric sensibility. As previously noted, D. Barton Johnson has warned of the dangers of formulating a critical paradigm of the 'metaphysical' Nabokov which 'discourages critics and readers from attending to the very concrete details that constitute the basis of Nabokov's stature as an artist' (Johnson and Boyd 21). From the perspective of Nabokov's poetry, and in seeming contradiction to the predominance thus far accorded the metaphysical Nabokov in this study, Johnson is correct, indeed doubly correct; attentiveness to details is not only an imperative of critical analysis of Nabokov's writing, it is in itself a crucial element 'of Nabokov's stature as an artist.' Indeed, in his article of 1941 entitled 'The Lermontov Mirage,' Nabokov emphasized the necessity of the artist-poet's attentiveness to both this world and the other: 'To be a good visionary you must be a good observer. The better you see the earth the finer your perception of heaven will be; and, inversely, the crystal-gazer who is not an artist will turn out to be merely an old bore' (34). As the following review of this quality of Nabokov's poetic identity will indicate, Nabokov invested attention in the specificity and wonder of phenomenal life with a degree of relevance and reverence which defined his artistry. For Nabokov, the capturing in poetic form of the 'trifles' of life was not simply a question of subject matter but an issue of consequence to the aesthetic, ethical, and metaphysical character of his artistry. Sight, seeing, perception, the visual, sensual apprehension of the humble wonder of the world is as essential to the Nabokovian creative consciousness as is sensitivity to the light breezes blowing into experience from the beyond. It is also a matter of aesthetic relevance, as suggested in a critical statement from a poetry review of 1927 linking sight and language in Nabokov's sensory poetics: 'Gusev's poems are boring because the author does not use his gift of sight. If he says "door" or "stone" or "sunrise," then they are only symbols of something and never simply a door, a stone, a sunrise. A ruinous path!' (*Ssoch* II, 641). Nabokov's later statement of 1937 from 'Pouchkine ou le vrai et le vraisemblable' ('Pushkin, or the Real and the Plausible') provides similarly clear expression of his art as the 'pittoresque du vrai,' an artistry which draws aesthetic and existential sustenance from quotidian life which is seen:

> If at times life appears pretty dim to us it is because we are nearsighted. For someone who knows how to look, everyday existence is as full of revelations and delights as it was to the eyes of the great poets of the past. Who on earth, one asks oneself, can be this artist who suddenly transforms life into a small masterpiece … One would therefore like to think that what we call art is, essentially, but the picturesque side of reality: one must simply be capable of seizing it. And how entertaining life becomes when you put yourself into the frame of mind where the most elementary things reveal their unique luster. (42)

It is no exaggeration to claim that only through attentiveness to Nabokov's aesthetics of the detail and specificity of life is it possible to know his 'faith' as an artist. The following demonstration of the practice of this aesthetic principle within Nabokov's poetry will thus not only balance the prevalence given to metaphysical topics, but also round out critical understanding of the characteristic features of Nabokov's poetic voice by moving discussion from the mysteries of the otherworld to the quotidian, though no less miraculous, wonders of this one. As with the metaphysical in his writing, the acute attentiveness to detail may be illustrated to have emerged from Nabokov's poetic writing to infuse his entire oeuvre with distinctive traces of his lyric temperament.

As is to be recalled from Nabokov's account of his first poem in *Speak, Memory* and from the poem itself, heightened interest in the phenomena of the surrounding natural world is imperative to Nabokov's aesthetic. Given that 'all poetry is positional,' an expression of the urge to place oneself in a universe embraced by consciousness – as Nabokov suggested – attentiveness to the detail and texture of the surrounding world is assumed. In apparent illustration of this, the poem chosen by Nabokov as his first seems important less for the merits of its thematic matter than as a demonstration in verse of sensual apprehension of a minutely observed natural setting. This quality extends from the particular poem 'The Rain Has Flown' to include all of the poems from the early volume in which it was first published, *Two Paths*. Described by Nabokov himself as 'a collection of juvenile poems,' *Two Paths* is nonetheless of interest for the predominant atmosphere of wonder, optimism, and enjoyment in nature, which is a crucial segment of Nabokov's poetry of trifles (*PP* 19). From the opening metaphor of the collection's first line, comparing the sky to dark blue wallpaper, Nabokov's poetry revels in sensual enjoyment of the environment, while simultaneously indicating the self-conscious pleasure and psychological invigoration that comes of recording that enjoyment in verse. The twelve poems written by Nabokov for this volume record the poet's physical delight in the sensual perception and poetic representation of the surrounding world, what Wordsworth in Book 8 of *The Prelude* called 'the circumambient World / Magnificent' (ll. 47–8). Spring is rendered in the image of a 'shy linden tree waving an emerald handkerchief'; a barrel-organ sings in a courtyard; the trunk of a birch tree is as white as porcelain; rain drops burn up in flight; a leaf 'drops from its tip a pearl' of water; after rain 'the grass is coated with silver'; 'the entire world sparkles, the entire world smells fragrantly,' and amid this natural bounty is the poet:

В душе поет восторг безбрежной воли …
Весь мир в лучах! Вся жизнь передо мной!
Как сердце, бьется огненное поле
Под лаской ветра, буйной, молодой.

(*Ssoch* I, 439)

[In (my) soul is singing the rapture of a boundless will … / The entire world is
in sunbeams! The entirety of life before me! / Like a heart beats the fiery field
/ beneath the caress of a breeze, tempestuously, youthful.]

The enthusiasm for nature in itself and the sensuous experience of nature
are unabashed and unqualified and thus, on first reading, in danger of
leading the poet into the banality of effusive poetastery. This admittedly
youthful, exuberant poetry is nonetheless to be saved from this criticism
by both the perspicacity of the images chosen and the self-consciousness
of the poetic voice behind them. This is not poetry of an abandonment of
consciousness to nature, but the poetic celebration of precise awareness of
nature's effect on the mind. Even at this early stage of his writing career,
Nabokov signals conscious attentiveness to the nature of his response to
the environment and his capturing of that response in poetry. Both are part
of a temperament which draws strength not simply from nature but the
conscious awareness and observation of nature even in trifling form. In the
poem 'Гроза растаяла. Небо ясно …' ('Groza rastaiala. Nebo iasno …' /
'The storm has melted away. The sky is clear …'), for instance, Nabokov
bluntly declares 'Я буду радостен и бесстрашен' ('I will be cheerful and
fearless'), a statement which draws added resonance with the knowledge
that this was a defining feature of Nabokov's personality throughout a
subsequent lifetime of at times exceptionally trying circumstances.

That appreciation of this intense relationship with the specificity and
wonder of the natural world was paralleled by self-conscious understanding of his poetry is revealed in the final poem of *Two Paths*. Written by a
poet not yet twenty years of age, 'У мудрых и злых ничего не прошу …'
('U mudrykh i zlykh nichego ne proshu …' / 'Of the wise and malicious I
ask nothing …') is remarkable in its display of calm self-awareness regarding Nabokov's relationship to the world, his sense of self, and his poetry. Contented with himself and his independence from both the wise and
the malicious, Nabokov describes himself smiling and looking through the
window, while writing with his left hand sonnets about – as is revealed
after the pause of the enjambment – a rose. The self-conscious, almost self-
parodic, whimsy of the scene is revealed through the rhetorical question
addressed to the reader immediately after the anti-climactic revelation of
subject matter:

> Гляжу, улыбаясь, в окно
> И левой рукою сонеты пишу
> О розе … Не правда ль, смешно?   (*Ssoch* I, 442)

[I gaze, smiling, through the window / And with my left hand write sonnets / About a rose ... Is this not amusing?]

The second quatrain resumes the whimsy and stock quality of the scene with the stated awareness that what is written with his left hand will be read by 'some youth with a cotton-batting soul / and a girl with a cotton-batting face.' For the 'quietly laughing,' unperturbed poet, the seeming triteness and formulaic conventionality of this poetry – 'About a rose, about a thunderstorm I write unhurriedly' – is of secondary importance. That which really matters, that which 'lives by the golden gates / by my fiery goal,' is written with his *right* hand. Nabokov's final poem for a collection which exuberantly announces ecstatic love of existence and nature thus purposefully disrupts and challenges the interpretive tendency to dismiss such poetry as unimportant. Through gentle parodic reference to his own writing of the left hand – formulaically rendered storms and roses – Nabokov nonetheless signals that his poetry of the right hand retains depths not immediately visible. The poems of *Two Paths* likewise indicate that minute attention to the physical world is as much a part of Nabokov's aesthetic as the secretive, metaphysical writing of his right hand. Indeed, both combine to form the fundamental feature of Nabokov's lyric voice.

The self-conscious constructedness of Nabokov's artistry, with its exceptional attention to thematic and verbal patterning – what was later construed as the source of his metafictional poetics – may thus be seen to have originated in this early example of Nabokov's self-awareness regarding his poetic intentions. This awareness Nabokov immediately carried over into subsequent volumes of poetry. As has already been observed, the arrangement alone of *The Cluster*, in clusters of thematically related poems, indicates patterning. The first introductory cluster, which also announces the unfolding of Nabokov's poetic wings as a *sirin*, is a call to re-perceive and re-experience the wonder of the natural world. The reader is invited with the poet through his poetry to bathe in physical appreciation of the trifles of the surrounding environment. The opening poem begins with a declarative, questioning address – 'Кто выйдет поутру? Кто спелый плод подметит?' ('Kto vyidet poutru? Kto spelyi plod podmetit?' / 'Who will go out in the morning? Who will notice the ripened fruit?') – and then leads the reader via imagery and alliteration into sensual cognizance of the setting. The dripping, dropping of juice from 'heavy pears' and 'purple cherries' is alliteratively reproduced in the tok-tok sound of Nabokov's Russian: 'то словно каплет на песок ... пахучий сок' ('to slovno kaplet na pesok ... pakhuchii sok' / 'as if fragrant juice drops onto the sand'). The melting shadows on arched trunks are euphonically stretched and drawn out in the repeated *t*'s and languorous vowel sounds of 'цветные тени тают' ('tsvet-nye teni taiut' / 'coloured shadows melt'), while the use of recurring sibilant *s*'s in combination with *l*'s captures the buzzing sound of wasps on plums:

> Деревья спят, и осы не слетают
> С лиловых слив.   (*Ssoch* I, 443)

[The trees sleep, and wasps refuse to fly / from the lilac plums]

The final quatrain of the poem returns to the beginning line, though now with a shift in setting from morning to evening, to ask:

> Кто выйдет ввечеру? Кто плод поднимет спелый?
> Кто вертогада господин?   (*Ssoch* I, 443)

[Who will go out in the evening? Who will take up the ripened fruit? / Who is the lord of this orchard?]

The final questions are answered with an image which, in contrast to the unadorned manner of expression, is alive with mottled light and varie-gated colour:

> В тени аллей, один, лилейно-белый,
> живет павлин.   (*Ssoch* I, 443)

[In the shade of the path, alone, lily-white / lives a peacock.]

A poem which both calls on and evokes appreciation of the natural mag-nificence of the world thus ends with an animal which stands in metonymic relation to the entirety of the environment; both are defined by explosive displays of hidden, then revealed, natural splendour.[35]

    The naturalness of Nabokov's poetic peacock-display of the beauty of the world is something consciously executed without resort to systemized philosophical discourse. Nabokov's wonder at the trifles of the world is meant to be childlike and trifling, and thus the conscious simplicity of much of his subject matter: 'A star, a snow-flake, a drop of honey / I enclose in my verse.' Here arises the seeming naiveté of Nabokov's verse, which was re-peatedly criticized during Nabokov's period of émigré reception. Both

Alexander Bakhrakh and Gleb Struve, for instance, criticized Nabokov for the following lines, seeing them not as the expression of an alternate form of consciousness of the world, but as examples of the 'banality and lack of chastity' of Nabokov's verse (Bakhrakh 17; Struve 1956, 168):

> Так мелочь каждую – мы, дети и поэты,
>   умеем в чудо превратить,
> в обычном райские угадывать приметы,
>   и что ни тронем – расцветить …   (*Ssoch* I, 446)

[Thus each trifle – we, children and poets, – / are able to transform into a wonder, / in the usual [we are able] to decipher heavenly signs, / and whatever we touch – to cause to flourish …]

The lines are indeed childlike, though the intention is anything but banal; they are one of the first expressions of a central component of Nabokov's poetics, which derives out of a particularly Nabokovian understanding of the essential beneficence of being to extend into, and shape, Nabokov's artistic representation of the world with growing consistency throughout his oeuvre. In his reading of Charles Dickens, Nabokov paused for editorial comment upon imagined criticism of a charge of evocation of the trifling similar to Bakhrakh's: 'Some readers may suppose that such things as these evocations of trifles not worth stopping at; but literature consists of such trifles. Literature consists, in fact, not of general ideas but of particular revelations, not of schools of thought but of individual genius. Literature is not something: it is the thing itself, the quiddity' (*LL* 116). In this regard, Nabokov's temperament is consciously childlike in its willed desire to construe the world as positive, as in the poem 'Плывут поля, болото мимо …' ('Plyvut polia, boloto mimo …' / 'The fields, the swamp sail by …'):

> Весь мир – как детская улыбка,
> Все ясным кажется, нетрудным …   (*Ssoch* I, 437)

[The entire world is like a child's smile. / Everything is comprehensible, it seems, uncomplicated …]

A fundamental appreciation of the goodness of the world, which has – as will be indicated below – ethical dimensions, takes on aesthetic dimensions to become a key element in Nabokov's poetics.

That a poetics of 'trifles' and a 'childlike' perspective on the world are essential to Nabokov's artistry and were born in consideration of poetic practice is made evident by a series of critical statements delivered by Nabokov throughout the length of his career. Nabokov's early poetic identity was formed in the writing of poetry and in his response to other poets. Critical concern for close attention to the detail of nature, which he would seek to capture in his own poetry of 'trifles,' is revealed as early as Nabokov's first published article, his above discussed introduction of Rupert Brooke to an émigré public in 'Rupert Bruk' of 1921. In this article, Nabokov demonstrated his early admiration for Brooke not only as a poet of the 'otherworld,' but, just as importantly, a poet of the physical wonder of this world, especially things aquatic: 'That Tiutchev-like love for everything streaming, rippling, and sparkling-cool is expressed so clearly, so convincingly, in the magic of his verses that one wants not to read them but to suck them through a straw, press them to one's face like dewy flowers, plunge into them as into the freshness of an azure lake' (Ssoch I, 729). In developing his argument regarding Brooke's interest in the otherworld as an inverted reflection of his attachment to this one – the things to be dearly missed in the afterlife – Nabokov described Brooke as sensing his death and drawing up a list of the things 'he loved on earth. And he loved a lot: white saucers and tea-cups, cleanly sparkling, gilded with fine blue; pinnate, transparent dust; wet roofs in the light of lamps; the hard crust of friendly bread; and multi-coloured food; rainbows; and blue bitter woodsmoke; and shining drops of rain sleeping in the cold corollas of flowers; and the flowers themselves wavering in the ripple of sunny days and dreaming of nocturnal butterflies who drink from them beneath the moon ...' (Ssoch I, 735). The list goes on in great length, and Nabokov's reproduction is a *tour de force* revealing both his sensuous appreciation of Brooke's 'trifles' and his artistic skill in transmitting it in the poetic language and imagery which would distinguish his own verse. In a similar, though now more declarative, fashion, Nabokov stated in a review of 1924 that 'the muse of the poet lives in those ages when people wrote on wax and were inclined to attribute epic relevance to the trifles of life and nature' (Ssoch I, 748).

Already in the early 1920s, then, Nabokov was formulating in his criticism and poetic practice a poetics which sought to invest representation of the detail of life with far-reaching thematic significance. The extent of that significance into spheres of metaphysical, ethical, and aesthetic relevance is most clearly indicated in the important essay 'The Art of Literature and Commonsense,' where Nabokov identifies the relatedness of the trifles of his life and his poetic sensibility. Reminiscent of his validation of Gogol's poetry of the irrational, Nabokov's 'The Art of Literature and Commonsense' is a defence of the primacy of the irrational, the illogical, and the detailed over the rationality of common sense, or, as Nabokov put it, 'sense made common.' Nabokov's espousal of the variegated thingness and detail of the world derives from an ultimately metaphysical sense of the essential goodness of the world, an 'irrational belief' which constitutes a kind of leap of faith itself prompted and witnessed by the manifold specificity of life. This 'irrational belief' in a cosmic goodness demonstrated by the phenomena of 'the lovely and lovable world,' in turn, has ethical ramifications insofar as this belief allows 'goodness' to become the basis of life: '... the irrational belief in the goodness of man (to which those farcical and fraudulent characters called Facts are so solemnly opposed) becomes something much more than the wobbly basis of idealistic philosophies. It becomes a solid and iridescent truth. This means that goodness becomes a central and tangible part of one's world ...' (*LL* 373). In language which reflects the vocabulary and imagery of his early poetry, Nabokov enumerates precisely his support of the irrationally specific over the rationally general:

> What exactly do these irrational standards mean? They mean the supremacy of the detail over the general, of the part that is more alive than the whole, of the little thing which a man observes and greets with a friendly nod of the spirit while the crowd around him is being driven by some common impulse to some common goal ... This capacity to wonder at trifles – no matter the imminent peril – these asides of the spirit, these footnotes in the volume of life are the highest form of consciousness, and it is in this childishly speculative state of mind, so different from commonsense and its logic, that we know the world to be good. (*LL* 374)

'"[G]oodness" is something that is irrationally concrete' (*LL* 375), Nabokov later claims in the same article. Nabokov formed a similar link between a fundamental 'goodness' and the perspective of a child in *The Defense*: '... childhood, the time when the soul's instinct is infallible' (*Def* 105). In aesthetic terms, this defence of the childish and illogical likewise assumes the poet's willingness to take 'sides with the irrational, the illogical, the inexplicable, and the fundamentally good' (*LL* 377), what Gumilev described as the 'childishly wise' (Gumilev 58). Poetry that displays this partisan alliance with the irrational reflects its provenance at the acme of consciousness, itself characterized by a disinterested, childishly speculative capacity 'to wonder at trifles.' Against this background, Nabokov's insistent focus on the trifles of being which 'children and poets are able to transform into a wonder' takes on levels of meaning unacknowledged by the émigré critics of Nabokov's poetry.

Attentiveness to Nabokov's poetics of 'trifles' and the 'childishly specu-lative state of mind' is not only of value in righting a critical disservice to Nabokov's poetry. It also sheds light on the nature of the connection be-tween Nabokov's uncompromising assertion of the primacy of the aes-thetic function in all art and the ethical quality of his own writing. Awareness of Nabokov's poetics of acute perception of the world is essen-tial to understanding the relationship between the aesthetic and ethical in his writing. This poetics was first developed in Nabokov's poetic practice and is a defining element of his lyric sensibility. A man of strong and often volubly stated opinions, Nabokov the writer nevertheless steadfastly re-fused to allow his writing to be identified with any form of moral or reli-gious message, especially one which could be harnessed to the stone-boat of ideology. Nabokov was insistent that the value of his writing lay within the aesthetic realm and that any message it might contain was impervious to mass propagation. As he vividly stated in *Strong Opinions*: 'As an artist and scholar I prefer the specific detail to the generalization, images to ideas, obscure facts to clear symbols, and the discovered wild fruit to the synthetic jam' (*SO* 7). This fundamental emphasis on the aesthetic pri-macy of his writing has led many to presume that Nabokov was categoric-ally unmoved by the things of the world and his environment in the creation of art. This claim may be documented at various stages in the history of his reception as a poet, beginning with the attestation of peacock-like dis-dain for the world raised in his first émigré reviews. It has been assumed that Nabokov was concerned only with worlds of words, with which he maintained cool 'aloofness' from the external world – a charge which Nabokov himself countered:

> My aloofness is an illusion resulting from my never having belonged to any literary, political, or social coterie. I am a lone lamb. Let me submit, how-ever, that I have bridged the 'aesthetic distance' *in my own way* by means of such absolutely final indictments of Russian and German totalitarianism as my novels *Invitation to a Beheading* and *Bend Sinister*. (*SO* 156; empha-sis added)

Of importance here is Nabokov's claim that he in fact 'bridged the "aes-thetic distance"' in his writing *in his own way*, that his response to issues of the world – in this case totalitarianism – was conducted according to his individual vision and artistry. As the above cited quotation from 'Pushkin, or the Real and the Plausible' makes amply clear, Nabokov the poet and artist was not averse to the representation of the surrounding world and its related ethical issues; he merely, albeit vehemently, insisted that his representation of that world was made according to the demands of his individual artistic consciousness and that its reception by individual readers not be predetermined through adherence to a supposed message. For Nabokov, the difficulties of representing reality in fiction were of an epistemological nature and not the product of the kind of ontological predicament fabricated by theorists of non-referential art. It was not that the external world was mere mirage, thus leaving the artist nothing more than the product of his own imagination for fictional representation, but that knowledge of the surrounding world could never be exhausted and that for the artist, depiction of the world could only be realized according to the potential of the artist's individual talent and through the medium of language:

> Reality is a very subjective affair. I can only define it as a kind of gradual accumulation of information; and as a specialization. If we take a lily, for instance, or any other kind of natural object, a lily is more real to a naturalist than it is to an ordinary person. But it is still more real to a botanist. And yet another stage of reality is reached with that botanist who is a specialist in lilies. You can get nearer and nearer, so to speak, to reality; but you can never get near enough because reality is an infinite succession of steps, levels of perception, false bottoms, and hence unquenchable, unattainable. (*SO* 10–11)

Nabokov's insistence on the subjectivity of reality and, in turn, the subjectivity of his artistic vision is of key importance in understanding the ethical potential of his writing, for the entire issue of the representation of thematic matters of ethical import ultimately rests on the fundamental question as to how the poet positions himself in relation to the world – as indicated by Nabokov in his account of his first poem in *Speak, Memory,* where he contested the 'positional' quality of poetry. Rather than an escape from the world, the act of writing poetry is the poet's subjective act of clarifying and expressing his place within the universe, the peeling away of yet another level of perception. Essential to Nabokov, however, is the subjectivity and specificity of this act. Because it is personal, because it is an individual act of positioning, of reanimating 'average reality,' any ethical or metaphysical 'message' to be derived is closed to mass communication as a message. The operative relationship is between the individual creative consciousness, the poet, and the individual reader. Nabokov saw the creation and reception of literature at the level of the individual; hence, the source of his claim in *Strong Opinions*: 'A work of art has no importance whatever to society. It is only important to the individual, and only the individual reader is important to me' (*SO* 33). This individual contact between poet and reader does not preclude either the author's artistic formulation or the reader's identification of a 'message,' ethical, political, or otherwise; it does, however, preclude the mass proselytizing of a message, as the fixing of such a message would impinge upon the freedom crucial to the poet-reader relationship. The potential ethical or moral value of fiction is realizable alone in individual contexts. The ethical value of literature cannot be ideological in the usual sense, as this assumes a group base and the intention of mass propagation, a descent from the open potential of the individual imagination to the enforced strictures of a mass understanding of common sense.

For Nabokov, the creation and reception of meaning in the world is always individual. Literature emanates from the individual poet's positioning of himself in relation to external reality and is received by the reader on the basis of aesthetic pleasure in reading of that positioning. An ethical reading of Nabokov's writing is not to be excluded and may even be welcomed, but it can neither be assumed nor forced. Thus the capacity of the creative imagination – epitomized in the transformation of the 'trifling' detail of the world into poetry – is not simply a matter of aesthetics but of recognition of, and participation in, the goodness of the world. It is along this continuum, from appreciation and poetic recreation of the trifle and detail of the world to acknowledgment and verification of its essential goodness, that Nabokov saw his own transformation from 'frivolous firebird' to 'rigid moralist': '... I believe that one day a reappraiser will come and declare that, far from having been a frivolous firebird, I was a rigid moralist kicking sin, cuffing stupidity, ridiculing the vulgar and cruel – and assigning sovereign power to tenderness, talent, and pride' (*SO* 193). Through language and the aesthetic potential epitomized by poetry, Nabokov the poet recharged the details and trifles of the world to reintroduce them, transformed by metaphor, to the reader as defamiliarized and hence new. Nabokov's writing invites the reader to sharpen consciousness, to re-experience the world, to revel in its plasticity and wonder, and finally to allow 'goodness' to become 'a central and tangible part of one's world' through recognition of 'the irrational belief in the goodness of man' (*LL* 373) which comes of sensual apprehension of the beauty of the world. Rather than enforcing a separation, Nabokov's adherence to aesthetics leads to an ethical response. Aestheticized, poeticized consciousness of the world is the central proof and demonstration of this goodness and, in turn, a call to participate in it through the cultivation of a sensibility responsive to the beauty of trifles. Beauty, as Nabokov indicated in *The Real Life of Sebastian Knight*, is ultimately not a category of an object to be represented, but a product of consciousness: '… that real sense of beauty which has far less to do with art than with the constant readiness to discern the halo around a frying-pan or the likeness between a weeping-willow and a Skye terrier' (*RLSK* 81).

Here, against the background of an ethics based on adherence to the specific, the illogical, and the transformative power of art, it is possible to return to Nabokov's poetry to clarify misperceptions about disputed religious imagery in Nabokov's early verse. Analysis of Nabokov's poetry indicates the manner in which imagery commonly associated with religion is not used in validation of religious belief as conventionally understood, although it is deployed in a poetics of trifles which has ethical value. Andrew Field, for instance, has written in *The Life and Art of Vladimir Nabokov* that Nabokov's poems previous to the death of his father in 1923 'enact a ritual of prayer, grace, purity, radiance, and the unity of the poet's soul with all creation and the Creator' (Field 1986, 79).[36] Field attributed this supposedly religious temperament and poetry to the religious and artistic tastes of his parents: 'But such poetry was also the poetry that his father and mother loved and knew by heart. Although each tended to keep religious faith at a little distance from institutionalized religion, both his father and mother were devout. It is hard to see any reason their son would not have joined with them in their faith …' (Field 1986, 80). Nabokov, in responding to suppositions such as this, claimed in the preface to *Poems and Problems* that the scattered religious references in his early poetry are to be understood as 'Byzantine imagery' which some readers have mistaken 'for an interest in "religion," which beyond literary stylization, never meant anything to me' (*PP* 13–14). With all due suspicion of the predilection of artists to veil their intentions and cover past tracks, the weight of textual evidence clearly supports Nabokov's claim. There is, in examples of Nabokov's poetry of the 1920s, a prevalence of religious imagery, though it is in no way expressive of any systematized religious thought, nor is it even close to the doctrinal intensity suggested by Field. Indeed, Nabokov's scattered comments on the topic, from his scholarly writing on Rupert Brooke and Nikolai Gogol – where the tendency to conceptualize God in conventional form is criticized – to the steadfast refusal to adopt religious explanations for acknowledged metaphysical beliefs – as in his interview with Alvin Toffler – to the enigmatic statements of such fictional characters as the French philosopher Delalande of *The Gift*, who prefers an enigmatic metaphor of a house to describe existence after death, or Falter of 'Ultima Thule,' who seems to have secret, privileged knowledge of God's existence, all suggest that John Shade is a better guide to an understanding of the religious quality of Nabokov's metaphysical beliefs.[37] In his refusal to imagine a god and life after death, the poet of *Pale Fire* was discouraged, not by the topic, which fascinated him, but by his realization that the limited human mind is constrained from adequately imagining the transcendent:

> It isn't that we dream too wild a dream:
> The trouble is we do not make it seem
> Sufficiently unlikely; for the most
> We can think up is a domestic ghost.   (*PF* 41; ll. 227–30)

Add to this the systematized, doctrinal nature of organized religion, and the grounds for Nabokov's rejection of standard understandings of religion was complete, what he described as '[his] indifference to organized mysticism, to religion, to the church – any church' (*SO*, 39). Indeed, elsewhere, Nabokov made explicit the negative connection between religion and regimentation as the source of his resistance to organized religion: 'I suppose that my indifference to religion is of the same nature as my dislike of group activities in the domain of political or civic commitments' (*SO*, 48). Nabokov described this sentiment perhaps most clearly in his poem 'Fame': 'I prefer to stay godless, with fetterless soul / in a world that is swarming with godheads.' The cumulative force of Nabokov's verse, moreover, suggests another more satisfying explanation for the presence of the religious imagery in Nabokov's poetry falsely attributed by Field and others to conventional religious belief. This imagery is indeed used 'figuratively,' as Nabokov suggested, in illustrating the wonder of participation in the magnificence of existence through conscious perception of its details, and the attainment of godlike heights in the capture of that magnificence in poetry. Nabokov's poetry of religious imagery is ultimately less about confirmation of doctrinal abstractions than poetic attentiveness to the detail and trifling wonder of the world.

Nowhere is this more apparent than in two poems of the 1920s containing the figure Christ. The effect of Christ's presence in these poems is not the confirmation of his divinity as god, but the narrative demonstration of godlike awareness of the details and trifles of life, including the

ugly. In a poem written on the anniversary of Dostoevskii's death, 'Садом
шел Христос с учениками …' ('Sadom shel Khristos s uchenikami …' /
'Through the garden walked Christ with disciples …'), Nabokov portrays
Christ with his disciples in a sun-mottled garden coming upon a dead and
decaying dog, whose white incisors are to be seen beneath the black folds
of its jaw. While the disciples are described as repulsed by the scene and
agreed in their condemnation of a vicious dog whose death is loathsome,
Christ is recorded in the final line of the poem observing nothing more
than the wonder of a detail: '"Зубы у него как жемчуга …"' ['"His teeth
are like pearl …"'] (*Ssoch* I, 448). In this poem, Christ's perspective is not
that of a religious divinity but of a poet-god transforming decay into
something startlingly vivid and precious with a simile. In the poem 'На
Голгофе' ('Na golgofe' / 'On Golgotha'), the last thoughts of Christ on the
cross are recorded. Rather than reflect on issues of doctrinal relevance,
Christ is moved by remembrance of the trifling beauty of his modest
though beloved home:

> Да,   с умилепьем сладостным и острым
> (колени сжав, лицо склонив во мглу …)
> он вспомнил домик в переулке пестром,
> и голубей, и стружки на полу.   (*Ssoch* I, 546)

[Yes – with emotion sweet and sharp / [knees compressed, face hanging in the
gloom] / he remembered the little hut in the mottled lane, / and doves, and
wood-shavings on the floor.]

In a closely religious sense, this poem borders on the blasphemous in its
use of a scene symbolically laden with religious significance while resolutely avoiding consideration of the divine. Furthermore, while religion is
absent in any conventional sense, the events of the poem are touched by
wonder.[38] Christ here, although not explicitly sacred, is extraordinary.
Eminently human in his fragility and suffering, Christ is redeemed as
exceptional in his ability 'to wonder at trifles no matter the imminent
peril' – as Nabokov expressed it in 'The Art of Literature and
Commonsense.' It is, in short, Christ's heightened consciousness which
raises him above the suffering condition of his body. The humble though
wondrously concrete imagery of the final lines raises both Christ and the
poem out of the cramped gloom of the scene. Christ's assumed nobility
of soul is founded, not on doctrine and myth, but the perspicacity of his
vision and imagination.

A further poem illustrative of Nabokov's deployment of religious imagery in poetry which demonstrates his poetics of heightened attentiveness to the phenomena of the world is the untitled poem 'Блаженство мое, облака и блестящие воды …' ('Blazhenstvo moe, oblaka i blestiashchie vody …' / 'My blessedness, clouds and sparkling waters …'). In this poem, the speaker is presented literally bathing 'in the colours and sounds of the many-faced earth.' Standing beneath the stars in an open field, the poet experiences a form of merger with all of existence in perception of a drop of honey and a dewdrop, both circled images of unity and perfection:

и в капле медвяной, в росинке прозрачно-зеленой
я Бога и мир и себя узнаю   (*Ssoch* I, 546)

[and in a drop of honey, in a translucent-green dewdrop / I recognize God and the world and myself]

In this state, the poet is himself transformed metaphorically into a lord intoxicated by the fullness of his own trifling paradise, a 'drunken moth' inhabiting an apple and refusing to substitute the wondrous plenitude of his world for the 'other' heaven.

In still other poems of religious imagery, the poet himself becomes a god. In his writing on Dostoevskii in *Lectures on Russian Literature*, for instance, Nabokov suggested that 'man comes nearest to God through becoming a true creator in his own right' (*LR* 106). It is something approaching this that is suggested at the conclusion of the intriguing poem 'Нас мало – юных, окрыленных …' ('Nas malo – iunykh, okrylennnykh …' / 'We are few – the young, the winged …'). This poem records the tribulations of youths (poets) born to a violent century, which hangs over them 'vulgar and large.' Rather than despair at the thunderous noise of the age, however, the first-person plural voice of the poem contends their position in a state – suggestive of cosmic synchronization – where they are on a level with God:

мы целомудренно бездомны,
и с нами звезды, ветер, Бог.   (*Ssoch* I, 447)[37]

[we are chastely homeless, / and with us the stars, the wind, God.]

In still another significant cluster of thematically related poems, Nabokov employs religious imagery of paradise and angels in poetry descriptive of experience at, or after, death: 'Эту жизнь я люблю исступленной любовью …' ('Etu zhizn' ia liubliu isstuplennoi liubov'iu …' / 'This life I love with an ecstatic love …'); 'Смерть' ('Smert'' / 'Death'); 'В раю' ('V raiu' / 'In Paradise,' 1920); 'В раю' ('V raiu' / 'In Paradise,' 1927); 'Вершина' ('Vershina' / 'The Summit');[40] 'Когда я по лестнице алмазной' ('Kogda ia po lestnitse almaznoi …' / 'When I on the diamond staircase …'); 'О, как ты рвешься в путь крылатый' ('O, kak ty rvesh'sia v put' krylatyi' / 'O, how you strive for the winged path') and 'Об ангелах' ('Ob angelakh, 1' / 'Of Angels, 1'). Often employing the conceit of the poet-speaker recounting his experiences in paradise after death, they are united in their absence of curiosity about the nature and setting of life after death. Instead, these poems represent the specificity of life on earth and yearning to share again in the splendour of the 'emerald sphere.' Illustrative of this thematic complex is an untitled poem Nabokov wrote in 1919 while still in the Crimea, 'Эту жизнь я люблю исступленной любовью …' ('Etu zhizn' ia liubliu isstuplennoi liubov'iu …' / 'This life I love with an ecstatic love …'), which describes the torments of the first-person lyric voice imagining his feelings of imprisonment when, in heaven, he looks down upon the earth – 'the emerald sphere / in the stripe of fiery rain!' Disconsolate in the divine though lifeless setting of heaven – 'a silent God' and 'pale angels' – the poet recounts in the final two stanzas of the poem his plea for release from the captivity of 'paradise':

И я вспомню о солнце победном,
    и о счастии каждого дня.
Вдохновенье я вспомню и ангелам бледным
    Я скажу: отпустите меня!   (*Ssoch* I, 495)

[And I will reminisce about the sun, about the triumphant sun, / and about the happiness of every day. / Inspiration I will remember, and to the pale angels / I will say: release me!]

Despite the assumed splendours of paradise, existence with the 'pale angels' is anemic, devoid of the vibrancy of a sun-infused life of inspiration. Here the poet is imprisoned:

Я не ваш. Я сияньем горю беззаконным
    в белой дымке бестрепетных крыл,
и мечтами я там, где ребенком влюбленным
    и ликующим богом я был!   (*Ssoch* I, 495)

[I do not belong to you. I am afire with a lawless radiance / in a white haze of dauntless wings, / and in my dreams I am there, where a child in love / and a rejoicing god I was!]

Passionate affection for the unrepeatable uniqueness of life and the world is not to be substituted with the colourless attractions of paradise, while the poet's divinity is manifest in the love of a child and the daily wonder of life on earth.

It is the same sense of reluctant loss of earth-bound divinity which distinguishes Nabokov's poem of 1939, 'Око' ('Oko' / 'Oculus'). In this poem, the 'omnipotent vision' accorded consciousness after life on earth is presented as a weak alternative to a world 'monogrammed' with particularity during life. The poem opens with an image of a fleshless, faceless, and hence unspecific and characterless eye which humans become after death:

> To a single colossal oculus,
> without lids, without face, without brow,
> without halo of marginal flesh,
> man is finally limited now.   (*PP* 101)

Here, Nabokov's inspired choice of the word *oculus* in his English translation for *Poems and Problems* captures the literal meaning of the Russian word *oko* (eye), while reverberating with the metaphysical connotations associated with his oft-employed imagery of transition out of enclosed spaces. The oculus is not only an eye but also a circular opening, here not out of an architectural structure but onto the universe. The above-quoted opening quatrain is not only *unheimlich* in its depiction of a featureless face, but expressed in vocabulary of limitation and reduction. Deprived of the living flesh that had acted as a 'halo,' 'man is finally limited.' Against this fleshless image of unity and expansiveness is contrasted the earth, a being personified as a familiar face warmed with a smile. To the earth the oculus looks:

> And without any fear having glanced
> at the earth (quite unlike the old freak
> that was dappled all over with seas
> and smiled with the sun on one cheek),
>
> not mountains he sees and not waves,
> not some gulf that brilliantly shines,

and not the silent old cinema
of clouds, and grainfields, and vines,

Seeing all, the eye is nonetheless conscious of nothing of the marvel of life:
Gone, in fact, is the break between matter
and eternity; and who can care
for a world of omnipotent vision,
if nothing is monogrammed there?   (*PP* 101)

Although death has brought the dissolution of the boundary separating eternity and matter and hence conferred a measure of omnipotence, the advantage is doubtful if the stamp of particularized life is not to be seen.

In these and other poems, then, Nabokov demonstrates that his religiosity, if at all existent, is not based on traditional metaphysics and conventional belief systems. Nabokov's striving for transcendence is a striving to take consciousness to new levels; his scripture is not the codified thought of prosaic belief but acute, poetic perception of the 'monogrammed' wonder and detail of the natural world. The perhaps most astonishingly declarative statement of Nabokov's 'trifle-based' faith is contained in a poem of June 1922, 'Знаешь веру мою?' ('Znaesh' veru moiu?' / 'Do You Know My Faith?'). This crescendo, in poetic form, of the texture, sound, colour, and movement of nature is taken beyond conventional protestations of love of a natural setting by its inclusion of an impassioned offer of love. Proclamation of love of the world merges into love of an individual who shares the same perceptivity of consciousness, the same poetic temperament. The poem begins with the image of an oriole flown in from Nabokov's 'first' poem, 'The Rain Has Flown,' to exemplify in 'Do You Know My Faith?' the singing, fluttering heart of the speaker. In an urgent questioning appeal to an unspecified addressee, the speaker seeks confirmation whether the addressee senses and shares the speaker's sensibility: 'Слышишь иволгу в сердце моем шелестящем?' ['Do you hear the oriole in my rustling heart?']. Rather than define that sensibility, the speaker illustrates it with a list of trifling things from the natural world:

Голубою весной облака я люблю –
райский сахар на блюдце блестящем, –
и люблю я, как льются под осень дожди,
и под пестрыми кленами пеструю слякоть …
Есть такие закаты, что хочется плакать,
а иному шепнешь: подожди!   (*Ssoch* I, 588–9)

[During the blue spring I love the clouds, / heavenly sugar on a sparkling saucer; / and I love the way towards autumn the rain pours, / and the mottled slush beneath mottled maples. There are sunsets such that one wants to cry / and to others you will whisper: wait.]

Here is a list which demonstrates allegiance to a world which is 'illogical' – in the Nabokovian sense outlined in 'The Art of Literature and Commonsense' – in its detailed specificity and dependency upon the subjective perception of the individual. Captured in metaphors of personal association and united by nothing more than the speaker's use of the preposition 'под' (*pod*: here meaning *towards* and *beneath*) and the whim of changing emotion, the details of nature are rendered in imagery which is both particular and private. After illustrating the character of his sensibility with regard to the trifles of nature, the speaker asks confirmation of a similar temperament on the part of the addressee as a condition of love. Assuming the addressee's love of a further catalogue of disparate details of nature, the speaker promises love, confident of future demonstrations of a poetic sentiment like that of the speaker:

Я тебя полюблю, как люблю я могучий,
пышный шорох лесов, и закаты, и тучи,
и мохнатых цветных червяков; –
полюблю я тебя оттого, что заметишь
все пылинки в луче бытия,
скажешь солнцу: спасибо, что светишь …

    Вот вся вера моя   (*Ssoch* I, 589)

[I will love you as I love the powerful / luxurious rustle of forests, and sunsets and storm-clouds, / and furry colourful caterpillars; – / I will love you because you will notice / all the specks of dust on a sunbeam of existence, / you will say to the sun: thank you for shining.[41] // That is my faith in its entirety.]

The seemingly naive quality of the sentiment expressed, especially at the conclusion of the poem, is deceptive. Effusive and unguardedly enthusiastic, the sentiment is also reminiscent of 'the childishly speculative state of mind' identified by Nabokov as the pinnacle of consciousness. In thematic terms, it is this apparent artlessness which encapsulates the depth of the poem. An unadorned declaration of faith and a poem which unashamedly records its 'position in regard to the universe' (*SM* 218), 'Do You Know

My Faith?' is a rare expression of a poetic sentiment based on the detail of the world which Nabokov would bring from his poetry to the full extent of his artistry.

'Do You Know My Faith?' is a not inappropriate place to conclude a review of the thematic features which characterize Nabokov's poetry. A proclamation of belief, the convictions are asserted, nevertheless, not in the doctrinal form of a manifesto, but in the quintessentially Nabokovian packaging of a poem which illustrates in lyric form its unabashed, 'child-like' appeal for love and the sharing of an aestheticized appreciation of the wondrous specificity of the world. Thus, although one of the earliest from his poetic oeuvre, this poem bears – and even announces – traits of the poetic sensibility that would distinguish both Nabokov's poetic and later prose writing until the end of his career. In this respect, 'Do You Know My Faith?' is also an open challenge to the critical reading which would bifurcate Nabokov's oeuvre into juvenile Russian poetry and mature English prose. In an interview response to a question concerning the putatively traditional and derivative quality of Nabokov's early poetry, Véra and Dmitri Nabokov offer a differentiated response which grants Nabokov's poetic writing dimensions of changing quality and development: 'But to say that his early poetry is consistently traditional and derivative is an exaggeration. While some of Nabokov's early poems should be discounted as part of his apprenticeship, others are highly original ... As for Nabokov's later poems, we consider many of them on the same artistic level as his mature prose' (Johnson and Proffer 76–7). Nabokov's poetry and lyric sensibility unquestionably underwent refinement and development, though it is the conviction of this study that essential traits which were to mature into defining elements were present in germ when the seventeen-year-old Nabokov wrote 'The Rain Has Flown,' the poem which has been codified as his first. The above analysis has concentrated on the presence of the conceptual clusters of cosmic synchronization, inspiration, love, the otherworld, and, finally, the poetic expression of acute consciousness of the 'trifles' and natural wonder of existence in poetry from across Nabokov's lengthy poetic oeuvre. Conscious effort has been made not merely to reveal the presence of these defining features in six decades of poetry but to suggest the manner in which Nabokov's poetry, as the most immediate expression of his distinctive lyric sensibility, combines aesthetic, ethical, and metaphysical meanings. The formulation of this portrayal of the foundation of Nabokov's lyric sensibility was thus based on five clusters of 'informing themes' which are clearly to be discerned in Nabokov's poetry. Others, such as exile, memory, and Russia, for instance, could have been added. This freely admitted possibility of granting greater emphasis to still other thematic clusters does not affect, however, the essential parallel argument being forwarded as a consequence of this representation of Nabokov's poetry. Nabokov's verse was the source and first expression of the lyric sensibility which would mark his artistry even when not writing poetry. Indeed, it is my contention that the crucial traits of Nabokov's poetic voice are to be found in the key clusters of the otherworld and Nabokov's poetics of the trifles and minutiae of the natural world. It is especially these two latter features of Nabokov's poetics which lend his poetry its specificity and independence – its identity – even in the face of affinity with previous poetic models, and which contributed to the unique quality of his prose.

Four Poems

Rather than concluding this extended chapter with a summation of the contentions that have been frequently illustrated above in references to Nabokov's poetry, analysis will return once again to Nabokov's lyric practice. In fulfillment of the two-part goal of this chapter – to both describe the salient features of Nabokov's infrequently discussed poetry and, on the basis of this, to offer an interpreting reading of Nabokov's poetic oeuvre as the source of the lyric voice which distinguished his entire body of writing – the following will proffer a representative reading of four poems from across the history of his poetic writing. This brief discussion of two Russian and two English poems will demonstrate the validity of the claims raised in the above reading of Nabokov's poetry about the five 'informing themes' proposed here as defining of Nabokov's lyric voice. The insights derived from this chapter ought thus to culminate in a fuller understanding of four brilliant, though rarely discussed, poems which simultaneously illustrate the deceptive simplicity and yet thematic density of Nabokov's poetry and, ultimately, lyric sensibility.

i. 'The Swift'

'Ласточка' ('Lastochka' / 'The Swift'), the chronologically first poem to be discussed, is a poem which first appeared in *Dar* (*The Gift*), Nabokov's ninth émigré novel, serialized in *Sovremennye zapiski* in 1937 and 1938. Within the novel – which will be discussed in greater length below – 'The Swift' serves as an example of the verse written by the central protagonist of the novel, a young, aspiring expatriate poet-author who shares central characteristics with Nabokov during his émigré period in Berlin. Apart from including this poem from his greatest of Russian novels in the 1979 collection *Poems*, Nabokov referred to this poem as 'probably [his] favourite Russian poem' (*SO* 14) on the occasion of an interview subsequently reprinted in *Strong Opinions*. Despite the prominence this poem was accorded by Nabokov himself, criticism has been slow to plumb the potential depths that it may contain, either as a single poem or as one representative of his lyric sensibility, although it has been discussed in Galya Diment's article 'Nabokov and Joyce: Portraits of Innovative Writers as Conservative Poets.' While the following reading will not share her assessment of the poem as a traditional 'love lyric,' the poem indeed contains several of the conventional elements of sentimental love poetry identified by Diment: a young couple in the evening, a swallow – as second choice to the even more traditional dove – and seemingly obligatory reference to 'evening,' 'grave,' and 'tears.' Rather than remaining with an interpretation restricted to the traditional, however, it is also possible to discuss the poem while being mindful of the traits identified above as defining of Nabokov's poetic voice. Such a reading allows this poem of love to reverberate from sources deeper within Nabokov's lyric sensibility, and echo with meaning beyond that of a traditional love lyric.

The title of the poem, 'The Swift,' is in itself of importance.[42] Birds swoop through Nabokov's poetry frequently, beginning with the orioles of his first poem, 'The Rain Has Flown,' one of which flitted into 'Do You Know My Faith?' in an image describing the speaker's agitated heart. In an early poem entitled 'Ласточки' ('Lastochki' / 'Swallows') of 1920, swallows are described swooping about a monastery, contracting the time and space from sunset and sunrise between Tsaregrad and Nazareth with their speed and the alliteration of poetic expression: 'В Цареграде – на закате, / в Назарете – на заре' ['In Tsaregrad at sunset, / in Nazareth at sunrise'] (*Ssoch* I, 534).[43] In this poem as well, the images of transition between day and night are highlighted. Perhaps most famously, however, it is a waxwing, in connection with a pane of glass, which forms the quintessentially Nabokovian image of transition through death and a point of cross-over to expanded consciousness in another, otherworldly realm in the opening lines of the poem 'Pale Fire.' In the poem 'The Swift,' the swallow brings with it concrete manifestation of shared sentiment and love between two people in their mutual appreciation of the trifles of being, in this instance, embodied in a particular bird in flight. The swift also brings a sense of fleeting transience, the temporal contraction of a lifetime to that of a single event within the momentary swoop of a swallow. That Nabokov wished to portray the idea of speed within the image of a swallow seems confirmed in his use of the word 'swift' in his English translation of *lastochka*:

One night between sunset and river
On the old bridge we stood, you and I.
Will you ever forget it, I queried,
 – that particular swift that went by?
And you answered, so earnestly: Never!

And what sobs made us suddenly shiver,
What a cry life emitted in flight!
Till we die, till tomorrow, for ever,
You and I on the old bridge one night.   (*Ssoch* IV, 277; *Gift* 94)

This brief narrative poem in its Russian form contains two quatrains of *AbAb* rhyme hinged by a middle, fifth line, which records the sole response of the addressee. The spatial and temporal setting of the poem contributes to the evocation of a momentary departure from the contiguity of time. Through Nabokov's use of motifs of transition – at sunset on a bridge – the individuals in the poem are presented as suspended in a liminal space where they are allowed briefly in their love, and the identification of a shared lyric temperament, to escape the earthly coordinates of time and space. That the two share a particular sentiment – Nabokov's 'childlike' appreciation of the trifles of nature – is illustrated in the poet's query whether his companion will remember 'that particular swift.'[44] Connected to the shared attention to this single fleeting vision is the related unification that comes through the mutual possession of a future memory. The poetic question 'Will you ever forget it' and the emphatic response is thus also a declaration of unity which will not be worn by the passage of time. United in temperament and love, and the conquest of time, the two are shaken by emotion, a premonition of the expansiveness that is love, as the entire trajectory of their life together passes in an instantaneous swoop and cry of the swallow. In Nabokov's Russian, the poetic embedding of the swallow into the flight of life is strengthened through the euphonic potential of the language chosen. The use of вскрикнула (*vskriknula* / to cry out) in the lines 'как вскрикнула жизнь на лету … / До завтра, навеки, до гроба, –' ('kak vskriknula zhizn' naletu / Do zavtra, naveki, do groba' / 'What a cry life emitted in flight! / Till we die, till tomorrow, for ever') itself replicates phonetically the shrieking sound of swallows in flight. Incorporated into this poem, then, are motifs of transition (sunset and bridge) and the contraction of time (Till we die, till tomorrow, for ever'), wonderment at the 'trifles' of nature (*that* swallow), the expansiveness of the ecstasy of love ('what sobs made us suddenly shiver'), and exemplary compactness of form and verbal dexterity. While a 'conventional' love poem on the surface, 'The Swift' is also at deeper levels a concise exemplification of Nabokov's lyric voice.

ii. 'Fame'

Fear for the posterity of that voice and an adequate response to worries concerning the longevity of one's poetic art are the subject matter of one of Nabokov's most intriguing and accomplished poetic works. Nabokov's Russian long poem of 1942 'Слава' ('Slava' / 'Fame') (*PP* 102–13) was written in the United States after Nabokov's abandonment of the Russian language for English – the 'softest of tongues' exchanged for 'clumsy tools of stone,'[45] a circumstance which, although associated with terrible loss, also 'caused [Nabokov's] Russian poetry to improve rather oddly in urgency and concentration' (*SO*, 54). Urgent and concentrated, 'Fame' is, in part, Nabokov's expression of the trauma of exile, the uncertainty of life and artistic achievement in a new environment, and, finally, the triumph of psychological and artistic independence over the lure of public success. The poem is divided into two parts and comprised of 124 lines. The narrative first section of 96 lines begins with the nighttime arrival – in a cacophony of alliterative *k* sounds – of a strange 'waxlike, lean-loined' (*PP* 103, l. 2) figure who taunts the poet regarding his lack of public fame in Russia, his native land. In parodic reversal of the motif of the arrival of the muse – the 'wonderful lady' – the poet's unwelcome guest brings, not the transport of inspiration and 'illogical' poetry, but the leaden ballast of doubt and 'logical' concern for the world. The 'garrulous' guest is never identified, but only described in a series of shifting images, beginning with such comparisons as 'like a spy, like a hangman, like an evil old school-mate' (*PP* 103; l. 9). In one sense, 'like an adverb,' 'like a mockery of conscience in a cheap drama,' the intruder seems to emerge from bad art to become an image of the poet's weakened will, the personified voice of reason and common sense which bullies 'the burry-R'd meek heart,' which feels and intuits but which has 'no words and no fame' and hence seems defenceless. As 'conscience' and common sense, he is also a figure representing the rational force of generalized thought and accepted ideology, an individual whose group identity is announced by the wearing of uniform-like hats:

For my visitor speaks – and so weightily, folks,
and so cheerfully, and the creep wears in turn
a panama hat, a cap, a helmet, a fez:
illustrations of various substantial arguments,
headgear in the sense of externalized thought?   (*PP* 105; ll. 26–30)

The intrusive guest is thus a composite of particular images from life and
art representing the general, the conventional, and the banal, in short, the
negation of Nabokov's aesthetics of the individual and specific.[46] The negative link to Nabokov's poetics is further indicated by lyric evocation of
Nabokov's homeland and his poetic conquest of the temporal and physical
distance of his past through poetry. For after being subjected to the guest's
mocking reference to the poet's forced 'changing [of] countries like counter-
feit money,' the poet contradicts the taunt with poetic description of his
poetic return to Russia:

It is far to the meadows where I sobbed in my childhood
having missed an Apollo, and farther yet
to the alley of firs where the midday sunlight
glowed with fissures of fire between bands of jet.
But my word, curved to form an aerial viaduct,
spans the world, and across in a strobe-effect spin
of spokes I keep endlessly passing incognito
into the flame-licked night of my native land.
To myself I appear as an idol, a wizard
bird-headed, emerald gloved, dressed in tights
made of bright-blue scales …   (*PP* 105; ll. 37–47)

In the self-identifying imagery of the *sirin*, Nabokov's émigré pseudonym,
the poet thus alludes to the wondrous transition offered by poetry – 'my
word' – as an 'aerial viaduct' (in Nabokov's Russian, 'bridge') to other
realms. Unmoved by this suggestion of a form of transcendence through
poetry, the jeering guest attempts in 43 lines of layered direct speech to
brutally return the poet to the earth and 'reality' of his failings. The poet is
reminded by the anti-muse, in the precise poetic imagery characteristic of
Nabokov's own writing, that he will fade into émigré obscurity, deprived of
his land, his language, and an audience:

Who, some autumn night, *who*, tell us, please, in the backwoods
of Russia, by lamplight, in his overcoat,

amidst cigarette gills, miscellaneous sawdust,
and other illumed indiscernibles – who
on the table a sample of *your* prose will open,
absorbed, will read *you* to the noise of the rain,
to the noise of the birch tree that rushes up window-ward
and to its own level raises the book?   (*PP* 107; ll. 65–72)

In the absence of public accolades and material success, the philistine visitor suggests, the poet is a failure, his artistry a waste.

Rather than succumb to despair in the face of this attack, however, the
poet responds in the first lines of the lyric second section of the poem with
the twin defences of laughter and poetry:

Then I laugh, and at once from my pen nib a flight
   of my favorite anapests rises ...   (*PP* 111; ll. 97–8)

In Nabokov's cosmology, the two – laughter and artistry – are frequently
linked as responses to the pain and vulgarity of the world, especially insofar as both derive from wellsprings of confidence based on the fundamental 'goodness' of the world and the presence of an otherworld. This linkage
and the serene confidence it engenders are hinted at, though extend beyond, Nabokov's statement in *Nikolai Gogol* that 'the difference between
the comic side of things, and their cosmic side, depends upon one sibilant'
(*NG* 142). Likewise, in 'The Art of Literature and Commonsense,' Nabokov
located reserves of strength for the artist in the absurd, what 'commonsense would dismiss as pointless trifles or grotesque exaggerations in an
irrelevant direction.' This power of the poetic sensibility secure in its awareness of the comic-cosmic was forcefully, if tragically, illustrated for
Nabokov by the example of the Russian poet Gumilev:

One of the main reasons why the very gallant Russian poet Gumilev was put
to death by Lenin's ruffians thirty odd years ago was that during the whole
ordeal, in the prosecutor's dim office, in the torture house, in the winding
corridors that led to the truck, in the truck that took him to the place of
execution, and at that place itself, full of the shuffling feet of the clumsy and
gloomy shooting squad, the poet kept smiling. (*LL* 376–7)

Likewise, in 'Fame,' girded with secret knowledge, the first-person lyric
voice rises to a smiling repudiation of the commonsensical philistinism of
his intrusive guest. Fortified with a form of radiance that derives from his

merging of poetry and secret knowledge of the transcendental, the poet overcomes profane worries of readers and glory – an 'empty dream' – or even exile. The final lines of the poem conclude in a powerful, though mysterious, statement which indicates that both the poet's cosmic confidence and his poetry emanate from a common metaphysical source impervious to the torments of worry of fame:

Today

   I am really remarkably happy.
That main secret tra-tá tra-tá-ta tra-tá –
   and I must not be overexplicit;
this is why I find laughable the empty dream
   about readers, and body, and glory.
Without body I've spread, without echo I thrive,
   and with me all along is my secret.
A book's death can't affect me since even the break
   between me and my land is a trifle.
I admit that the night has been ciphered right well
   but in place of the stars I put letters,
and I've read in myself how the self to transcend –
   and I must not be overexplicit.
Trusting not the enticements of the thoroughfare
   or such dreams as the ages have hallowed,
I prefer to stay godless, with fetterless soul
   in a world that is swarming with godheads.
But one day while disrupting the strata of sense
   and descending deep down to my wellspring
I saw mirrored, besides my own self and the world,
   something else, something else, something else.   (*PP* 111; ll. 103–24)

The assertive force of this series of declarative sentences belies the mystery of their contents and stands in striking contrast to the opening lines of the poem, where the personification of worldly care was shrouded in non-defining comparisons. Poetry and the illogical are not merely impervious to the blandishments of the commonsensical, the logical, they are also more precise. From the perspective of Nabokov's poetic sensibility, it is the profanely commonsensical which lacks substance.

   'Fame' thus presents an unusually suggestive, though still secretive, expression of Nabokov's poetics of the otherworld, a realm of consciousness which is accessed through acute self-awareness of the self and the experience of cosmic synchronization – 'without body I've spread, without echo I thrive' – and witnessed by poetry – 'in place of the stars I put letters.' That the 'secret' of the otherworld is ineffable is less an indictment of its reality than indication of its radical foreignness from standardized experience, from, in short, the commonsensical and logical. Furthermore, with 'Fame,' and in demonstration of his independence as a 'fetterless soul,' Nabokov poetically expressed his distance from conventional representations of religion in 'a world that is swarming with godheads,' while simultaneously indicating the importance of his understanding of a metaphysical realm for his life and writing, as the prominent use of the first-person pronoun in section two of the poem indicates. What began as an *exegi monumentum* for an oeuvre threatened by the worldly exigencies of exile and linguistic change concludes as a celebration of the metaphysical source of Nabokov's artistry. Nabokov translated 'Exegi Monumentum,' and with 'Fame' he seems to have corroborated the final stanza of Pushkin's famous poem:

> Obey thy God, and never mind, O Muse,
> the laurels or the stings: make it thy rule
> to be unstirred by praise as by abuse,
>   and do not contradict the fool.   (*TRP* 5)

iii. 'Restoration'

Nabokov's English poem of 1952 'Restoration,' though it begins with the mysteries of consciousness, expands thematically out of the otherworldly sources of poetry and cosmic confidence treated in 'Fame.' 'Restoration,' one of Nabokov's most accomplished poems, suggests that poetry is allied to consciousness in its ability to reveal unseen facets about both this world and a beyond.[47] Less a lesson than a revelation or discovery, poetry is divulged in this poem to afford entrance into the mystery of existence, to act as a portal to an otherworld of expanded consciousness. Divided into six five-line stanzas of iambic tetrameter with alternating *aabba* rhymes, the first three stanzas allude to the mysterious, ineffable sources of poetry, while the second half of the poem returns to the mundane yet ever wondrous realia of life and the world to become an *ars poetica* of Nabokov's poetics of metaphor and wondrous revelation. At once a meditation on the mysteries of an intuited beyond and an identification of the investigative, epistemological function of poetry, 'Restoration' pivots on the revelatory potential of art to shock and expand consciousness:

To think that any fool may tear
by chance the web of when and where:
O window in the dark! To think
that every brain is on the brink
of nameless bliss no brain can bear,

unless there be no great surprise –
as when you learn to levitate
and, hardly trying, realize
– alone, in a bright room – that weight
is but your shadow, and you rise.

My little daughter wakes in tears:
She fancies that her bed is drawn
into a dimness which appears
to be the deep of all her fears
but which, in point of fact, is dawn.

I know a poet who can strip
a William Tell or Golden Pip
in one uninterrupted peel
miraculously to reveal,
revolving on his fingertip,

a snowball. So I would unrobe,
turn inside out, pry open, probe
all matter, everything you see,
the skyline and its saddest tree,
the whole inexplicable globe,

to find the true, the ardent core
as doctors of old pictures do
when, rubbing out a distant door
or sooty curtain, they restore
the jewel of a bluish view.   (*PP* 167–8)[48]

'Restoration' opens with an invocation of the mysterious fragility of the
veiled boundary – 'the web of when and where' – separating physical existence and the expanses of a transcendental realm, the fourth spiral in the
helix of being described by Nabokov in *Speak, Memory* as 'a special Space'

(*SM* 301). In the third-line apostrophe, 'O window in the dark!' Nabokov explicitly draws on the image of a window as a motif of transition prevalent in his poetry; here it is evoked to convey the simplicity of the shift to a blissful state of consciousness. Referred to is a conquering of the physical laws of being via an act of consciousness; in the enclosed space of a room, the earth-bound weight of the body is overcome, allowing the body to rise: '– alone, in a bright room – that weight / is but your shadow, and you rise.' The brink to nameless bliss is a transition as potentially innocuous as the windowed aperture from the house of being to the unknown, dark expanses outside. The move to another dimension is as simple, or as surprising, as levitation.[49] Nabokov's poetry is replete with instances of mysterious travel in the rapture of consciousness altered by, for example, inspiration and love; and here the expression of the unexpected simplicity of a 'solution' to the restraints of time and space is reminiscent of that offered in 'Chto za-noch'' of 1938, a Russian poem translated for inclusion in *Poems and Problems* as 'What Happened Overnight':

A simple, elegant solution.
(Now what have I been bothering about
so many years?) One does not see much need
in getting up: there's neither bed, nor body.   (*PP* 91)

In 'Restoration,' this levitating escape from the physical to an entrance into another state may appear frightening in its strangeness, in the radical change it portends – 'a dimness which appears / to be the deep of all her fears.' Rather than a depth and the end of being, however, this dimness is actually a transition to another dimension of consciousness; in the metaphoric terms of time and an awakening from the sleep of physical being, it is a form of Platonic anamnesis, a new beginning at 'dawn.'

The beginning of the transitional, fourth stanza redirects the movement of the poem from the metaphysical to the aesthetic, with abrupt reference to poetic practice. And here, as so often in Nabokov's poetry, the uniquely lyric qualities of children and poets are coupled. In stanza three, it is the speaker's young daughter, a child, who intuits and instinctively senses without conscious reflection the thinness of the boundaries of time and space, 'when and where.' In stanza four, it is the poet with the conscious dexterity of his artistry who purposefully effects this transformation. Nabokov illustrates the function of poetry in a multi-layered metaphor about the ability of a poet to peel an apple – itself metaphorically named – suddenly to reveal, after the delay of accumulating descriptive phrases and an enjambment at a stanza-break, the apple's metaphoric likeness, a snowball. The poet magically removes a thin boundary, an apple peel, to disclose, not what is expected, but something transformed by poetry and metaphor into another object. This, the poem suggests, is the epistemological potential unique to poetry. Stanza five, in particular, with its accumulation of verbs of tactile exploration, ending with 'see,' re-enacts Nabokov's often repeated emphasis on the positioning function of poetry – from his account of his first poem in *Speak, Memory* to his frequent coupling of imagery of sight with poets. Poetry harnesses and utilizes the creatively associative, conjunctive power of metaphor to initiate a process of discovery and disclosure leading to revelation of the specificities and mysteries of 'the whole inexplicable globe,' and beyond. In 'The Art of Literature and Commonsense,' Nabokov suggested that the goal of metaphors is to 'follow the course of their secret connections' (*LL* 373). And in a manner analogous to the frequent thematic motifs of transition within Nabokov's writing, though now on the formal level, metaphors are more than rhetorical embellishments on the surface of writing, but vehicles of transition between parallel associations. It is metaphor which allows Nabokov to unite in a single poetics his fascination for an intuited, ineffably metaphysical dimension *and* wonder at the specificity and quiddity of phenomenal existence. Metaphor and poetry encourage renewed, sharpened awareness not only of the multi-layered texture of reality but of previously unperceived correspondences to further dimensions of consciousness. For the poet not only probes the phenomenal world, but removes the 'distant door,' the 'sooty curtain,' the barriers hindering access to previously unperceived realms of experience. Nabokov's poetics of the metaphor is not so much the modernist project to 'make it new' as a self-reflective exercise in ornamental brilliance, but the Nabokovian one to 'make it revelatory,' transformative; poetry is both a product of artistic consciousness *and* an enhancement of consciousness; poetry is a response to the world *and* its transformation. In this regard, 'Restoration' provides concise illustration for Robert Alter's essential comment made in reference to *Ada*, though of relevance to Nabokov's entire creative project:

> Nabokov has often been celebrated for his brilliance as a stylist; but it is important to recognize that this brilliance … is not ornamental, as in some of his American imitators, but *the necessary instrument of a serious ontological enterprise*: to rescue reality from the bland nonentity of stereotypicality and from the terrifying rush of mortality by reshaping objects, relations, existential states, through the power of metaphor and wit, so that they become endowed with an arresting life of their own. (Alter 1979, 105–6; emphasis added)

The 'restoration' of Nabokov's title assumes an added layer of significance in the context of Alter's identification of the urge in Nabokov's
writing to reshape the world in an act of aesthetic engagement. The poetry
of Nabokov's lyric sensibility is thus capable of uncovering and granting
access to the quintessence of being, 'the ardent core,' while metaphor, in
'rubbing out a distant door / or sooty curtain,' removes the boundaries of
the physical, and containment in the literal, to afford vistas onto something beyond, a 'jewel of a bluish view.' 'Restoration' thus not only con-
fers perspective onto the mysterious source of Nabokov's poetry, 'the
ardent core,' but also illustrates the metaphor-based linkage between the
two fundamental elements of his poetic sensibility, the metaphysical dimension of the otherworld and the physical specificity of the natural
world. Poetry, with its surprising even irrational leaps of association, takes
consciousness to dimensions closed to what Nabokov referred to in 'The
Poem' as 'plain prose.'

iv. 'The Ballad of Longwood Glen'

The final poem to be approached with the critical awareness gained from
an interpretive review of Nabokov's poetic oeuvre is a poem which brilliantly illustrates both the independence and specificity of Nabokov's poetic sensibility and the critical incomprehension with which it is frequently
confronted. Apart from the testimony of the puzzled responses which
greeted 'The Ballad of Longwood Glen' in the reviews of *Poems* and *Poems
and Problems*, the publication history of the poem is itself witness to
Nabokov's tenacity in foregrounding his poetry in the face of miscomprehension of his poetic sensibility and artistry. First submitted to, and rejected by, the *New Yorker* in 1953, Nabokov returned the reworked poem
to Katherine White in 1957 with an urgent appeal for reconsideration:
'With my usual modesty I maintain it is the best poem I have composed –
far superior, for instance, to the *Evening of Russian Poetry*' (*SL* 208–9). A
poem written at the height of Nabokov's artistic prowess, and deemed the
best of his poetic oeuvre, must legitimately bear the right of closer analysis.[50] Doubly so, as 'The Ballad of Longwood Glen' may also be shown to
bear the defining traits of Nabokov's lyric sensibility.

One of Nabokov's longer poems, 'The Ballad of Longwood Glen' is a
ballad of sixty-four lines of thirty-two couplets in predominantly masculine, but also feminine, rhyme, a form which lends the poem the distinct-
ively jaunty tone characteristic, as Nabokov said, of the 'robust style' of
his later poetry. The poem narrates the story of Art Longwood, a florist,

who visits a local glen with his wife, his two sickly children, and his father, stepfather, and father-in-law. Entreated by his wife to play ball with his crippled son, Paul, Art tosses a ball in the air only to have it lost in a nearby tree.[51] Art climbs the tree in retrieval of the ball but never returns. A crowd gathers, a search conducted, the tree felled, but Art is never found. After the loss of her husband and the subsequent death of her remaining children, Paul and Pauline, Art's wife remarries and regularly returns as a tourist to the glen, now as Mrs Deforest, with four old men. The poem invites the irrational boldly to intrude into the everyday, then quietly to recede. This coupling of the bizarre subject matter with the comic tone of the rhyming couplets and narrative reference to grotesque imagery and events lightly treated creates a destabilizing effect which renders the poem resistant to confident interpretation. The reader is left suspended between a reading of the poem as a metaphysical exercise or a poetic jest of predominantly parodic, comic effect. It is presumably this indeterminacy – along with assumptions derived from the poem's first publication in the *New Yorker* – which led early critics of *Poems* and *Poems and Problems* to settle on the designation 'light verse' and forego further analysis.[52] Anticipating this response, Nabokov in his letter to Katherine White urged that she 'please stick to it as long as you can bear, and by degrees all kinds of interesting shades and underwater patterns will be revealed to the persevering eye.' Indeed, 'The Ballad of Longwood Glen' reveals a variety of shades and patterns recognizable from Nabokov's poetic oeuvre.

The poem begins in movement, with Art Longwood crossing over a creek to enter into a glen. As with much of Nabokov's poetry of metaphysical ramification, the setting of the 'The Ballad of Longwood Glen' draws upon images of transition and enclosure, with passage over a bridge into the enclosed realm of the glen. From the first couplet of the poem, Art Longwood is in transition. Immediately identified after the establishment of a portentous setting are the central characters of the poem: 'Art Longwood, a local florist, / With his children and wife (now Mrs. Deforest)' as well as 'Art's father, stepfather and father-in-law.' Art's name and profession and the future name of his wife, Mrs Deforest, are rich in rhyming potential, but they also convey something of the characters. Arthur is not only the small-town American unpresupposingly known as Art, he is also, as a florist and one presumably captivated by the aesthetic potential of flowers and conscious of the beauty of nature, an artist in his own right. He is also an individual; as Art 'Longwood,' he is a specific tree set off from the surrounding forest of Deforests. The sole instance of direct communication from Art – '"I never climbed trees in my timid prime," / Thought

Art; and forthwith started to climb' – comes in the form of a privately held thought about memory and the past which manages also to suggest that Art Longwood 'long would' achieve a feat appropriate to his temperament of artistic attention to the trifles of existence. This potential is confirmed by the single narrative allusion to Art's psychology. Art's character is rendered, not in generalizing editorial comment, but via illustration of an act specific to Art, the intent observation of an insect: 'Silent Art, who could stare at a thing all day, / Watched a bug climb a stalk and fly away.' Watching a bug climb a stalk and then fly away is more than a foreshadowing of what Art himself will do in climbing the tree, then to disperse into another realm; it is much more Nabokov's granting to Art a fundamental characteristic of a heightened, artistic consciousness. Art is demonstrating his inherent allegiance to what Nabokov described in 'The Art of Literature and Commonsense' as 'the supremacy of the detail over the general, of the part that is more alive than the whole, of the little thing which a man observes and greets with a friendly nod of the spirit while the crowd around him is being driven by some common impulse to some common goal.' Like the young Nabokov in his poem 'The Rain Has Flown,' or Christ in the poem 'Through the garden walked Christ with disciples ...,' or the young lover in 'Do You Know My Faith?' – to select illustrations from the beginning of Nabokov's poetic oeuvre – Art Longwood reveals his all-important 'capacity to wonder at trifles.'

Upon climbing the tree in search of his son's lost ball, Art takes this capacity to new heights and is literally lost in nature:

Now and then his elbow or knee could be seen
In a jigsaw puzzle of blue and green.
Up and up Art Longwood swarmed and shinned,
And the leaves said *yes* to the questioning wind.
What tiaras of gardens! What torrents of light!
How accessible ether! How easy flight!
His family circled the tree all day.
Pauline concluded: 'Dad climbed away.'
None saw the delirious celestial crowds
Greet the hero from earth in the snow of the clouds.   (*PP* 178)

Art achieves divestment. His dispersal into another realm in a tree at a point of intersection between earth and sky with accompanying imagery of 'torrents of light' and 'delirious celestial crowds' is rendered in terms evocative of 'cosmic synchronization,' the key experience of the artistic consciousness rapturously granted release from the temporal and spatial boundaries of earth. The dispersal and dissolution of Art's body is captured in the 'jigsaw puzzle of blue and green'; in Nabokov's poetry, green is almost exclusively identified with the physical earth, while blue is the colour of the immeasurable expanses of a beyond, whether of the sky and universe or the depths of water. Nabokov's oeuvre is populated with characters of heightened sensitivity and consciousness – observers of the trifles of life – who, when overcome by the pain and vulgarity of their earthly lives, dare merger into the wonder and perfection of their chosen realms. The dealer in butterflies Paul Pilgram (a name echoed in the tree, 'the green pilgrim,' into which Art climbs) of the short story 'The Aurelian' dies into his long-held dream of departing on a butterfly hunting expedition; the poet Vasiliy Shishkov seems to vanish into his own verse at the conclusion of the eponymous short story, just as 'the forgotten poet' Perov returns after an absence of years from out of his poetic reputation; the sensitive, modest bachelor Vasili Ivanovich of 'Cloud, Castle, Lake' begs to be 'let go' after his realization that he no longer possesses the strength to belong to mankind; Martin Edelweiss of *Glory* transcends the boundary exiling him from the lost Russian homeland of his youth, while the chess-master Luzhin of *The Defense* 'drops out of the game,' committing suicide by throwing himself from a window onto the chessboard-patterned tiles on the ground below; and Ivanov of the short story 'Perfection' achieves the perfect knowledge of cosmic synchronization in his death in the shallow water of a seashore. Like these and other figures in Nabokov's writing, Art Longwood transcends the deficiencies of life by taking consciousness to a higher stage through merger into his earthly obsession; appropriately for a florist and a man capable of watching a bug on a stalk, it is a tree which aids Art in his ascension and dissolution into another stage of consciousness. That the green earth, despite its beauty, was also a place of suffering is only hinted at by his children and the suggested philistinism of his wife. Especially Art's children – the asthmatic Pauline and crippled Paul, both of whom eventually die – indicate that as multi-faceted and wondrous as the earth is, it is also visited and indeed defined by physical infirmity and death, both of which are only to be conquered at another stage of consciousness.[53] As in Nabokov's poem 'Restoration,' Art Longwood discovers how simple – 'How accessible ether! How easy flight!' – the transition and escape to another otherworldly realm is during his tree-ward ascent; in the imagery of 'Restoration,' Art learns how easy it is to tear 'the web of when and where' separating earthly life from the 'nameless bliss no brain can bear.'

Art thus accomplishes his glorious feat of metaphysical acrobatics, achieving rapturous release into another expanded stage of consciousness. Upon his mysterious slippage through a fissure in reality, however, the other members of the earthly picnic are left behind, puzzled in thwarted comprehension on the hard ground of rationality. Precisely because Art has allowed the illogical and irrational to triumph over the physically possible, it is alone Art's daughter who, from her child's perspective, is able to proffer an adequate explanation: 'Pauline concluded: "Dad climbed away."' Unannounced, the mysterious, illogical, and irrational has happened. The remaining adults of the poem, however, all identified in such imagery of conventional group activity as card-playing, conventioneers, and fishermen, insist on rational explanations, arriving ultimately at the negative pinnacle of mass insistence on the commonsensical. In 'The Art of Literature and Commonsense,' Nabokov not only described the artistic sensibility of solidarity with the irrational, he also noted its opposing force, the spirit of common sense, which seeks to enforce allegiance to sense made common:

> Commonsense has trampled down many a gentle genius whose eyes had delighted in a too early moonbeam of some too early truth; commonsense has back-kicked dirt at the loveliest of queer paintings because a blue tree seemed madness to its well-meaning hoof; ... Commonsense at its worst is sense made common, and so everything is comfortably cheapened by its touch. Commonsense is square whereas all the most essential visions and values of life are beautifully round, as round as the universe or the eyes of a child at its first circus show ... *Stranger* always rhymes with *danger*. The meek prophet, the enchanter in his cave, the indignant artist, the nonconforming little schoolboy, all share in the same sacred danger. (*LL* 372)

With Art's affront to the rational in his refusal to descend from the tree, the spirit of common sense and common response is driven ultimately to the desperation of threatened violence and sensation:

> Cars on the highway stopped, backed, and then
> Up a rutted road waddled into the glen.
> And the tree was suddenly full of noise,
> Conventioners, fishermen, freckled boys.
> Anacondas and pumas were mentioned by some,
> And all kinds of humans continued to come:
> Tree surgeons, detectives, the fire brigade.
> An ambulance parked in the dancing shade.

A drunken rogue with a rope and a gun
Arrived on the seen to see justice done.
Explorers, dendrologists – all were there;
And a strange pale girl with gypsy hair.
And from Cape Fear to Cape Flattery
Every paper had: Man Lost in Tree.   (*PP* 178–9)

'The Ballad of Longwood Glen' thus contains a catalogue of the ever more desperate responses of the mass spirit of common sense to disallow the irrational. Ultimately, the stately tree is felled under compulsion of reason and the urge to conquer the irrational, while the once paradisiacal glen is reduced to a commercial site, a monument to philistine culture, literally and figuratively a toilet in a beautiful, natural setting:

And the sky-bound oak (where owls had perched
And the moon dripped gold) was felled and searched.
They discovered some inchworms, a red-cheeked gall,
And an ancient nest with a new-laid ball.
They varnished the stump, put up railings and signs.
Restrooms nestled in roses and vines.   (*PP* 179)

In his article 'Philistines and Philistinism,' Nabokov diagnosed a figure and temperament which finds expression in a material, insouciant form of culture diametrically opposed to the ineluctably individual artistry of the poetic sensibility: 'A philistine is a full-grown person whose interests are of a material and commonplace nature, and whose mentality is formed of the stock ideas and conventional ideals of his or her group and time (309). 'The Ballad of Longwood Glen,' after narrating the commercialized demise of the wondrous site of a wonder, concludes with the anticlimactic legacy of the marvellous event personified in the fate of Art's philistine wife:

Mrs. Longwood, retouched, when the children died,
Became a photographer's dreamy bride.
And now the Deforests, with *four* old men,
Like regular tourists visit the glen;
Munch their lunches, look up and down,
Wash their hands, and drive back to town.   (*PP* 179)

Mrs Deforest takes her place in a crowded forest of trees, substituting the precision and observant accuracy of Art's florist's apprehension of the world for the distant, visually mediated, and brutally mimetic form of the photographer. Nonetheless, the Deforests, although occupied with their bodily needs and ablutions, seem somehow vaguely cognizant of the mysterious achievement of a lone tree in their frequent return to the glen. A shadow of Art Longwood's experience of cosmic expansion seems to lie on the uncomprehending consciousnesses of the Deforests.

In similar fashion, Nabokov's poetry – as in the specific example of 'The Ballad of Longwood Glen' – affords fleeting glimpses of the potential of the artistically charged consciousness. Andrew Field, in analysing Nabokov's English poems, including 'The Ballad of Longwood Glen,' suggested that 'they have no equivalents among Nabokov's Russian poems' (Field 1967, 99). The above, admittedly superficial, overview of Nabokov's Russian and English poetry reveals this statement to be one of a number of misconceptions regarding Nabokov's poetry which arise from insufficient attention to the characteristics of Nabokov's poetic identity. The two late poems from Nabokov's poetic oeuvre, 'Restoration' and 'The Ballad of Longwood Glen,' for instance, reveal differences from his earlier poetry in terms of tightness of thematic representation and narrative control; the latter poems are visibly the product of a mature artist. Nonetheless, it may be claimed with equal justice that these poems also demonstrate characteristics which defined Nabokov's poetic voice from its first expressions as an adolescent in the country estate at Vyra. Over the course of several decades, and hundreds of poems, crystallized a form of poetic expression based on the twin pillars of intuited belief in an otherworldly realm and intense sensitivity to the variegated patterns and textures of the physical world. Cognizance of both realms is accessible through the potential of heightened consciousness; poetry, in turn, is at once expression and exercise of the wondrous promise of consciousness. Out of this foundational emphasis on consciousness, Nabokov's poetry extends into essential themes such as love and the poetic calling, as well as others, to provide concrete expression to the aesthetic, metaphysical, and ethical import of his poetry. It is this complex – forged in poetry – which lends all of Nabokov's writing the distinctive features of a poetic sensibility. Demonstration of the presence of this poetry-based sensibility across the breadth of Nabokov's artistry will be the object of the following chapters.

4 Staged Lyricism: The Play of Poetry and Dream-Logic in Nabokov's Drama

... the best plays are generally a combination of both action and poetry.
– Vladimir Nabokov, 'Playwriting'

The esteemed critic Gleb Struve, in his retrospective analysis of Nabokov's émigré writing, suggested in *Russkaia literatura v izgnanii* that Nabokov's transition to prose was prompted by the intrinsic character of his artistic temperament, that, ultimately, 'his poems are the poems of a prose writer' (Struve 1956, 171). Struve's interpretive claim has often been repeated, perhaps because it seems to explain the mounting emphasis in Nabokov's oeuvre of prose over poetry as well as the increasingly narrative character of the verse he continued to write, however sporadically. As a critical statement of explanatory potential, however, these limited gains are only to be purchased at the inflated price not just of subordinating Nabokov's lyric sensibility to prose but also of eliding over the generic variety of his writing in the 1920s and 1930s. Nabokov did not undergo an early, adolescent apprenticeship in poetry – as this foreshortened narrative of artistic development might seem to suggest – and then abruptly graduate to prose mastery in the short story and novel.[1] Between the appearance of his first volume of poetry, *Poems,* in 1916 and his first novel, *Mary*, in 1926, Nabokov produced more fictional writing than the twenty-odd stories, poems, and translations of the period; he also conducted his first experiments in playwriting. The outcome of his efforts in this genre was an original and not inconsiderable – albeit rarely studied – body of dramatic writing extending from the early 1920s until the late 1930s. In different ways and to different degrees, each of these dramatic works illustrates the workings of Nabokov's poetic temperament and demonstrates the metamorphosis of poetic material into other generic forms. Both in terms of formal expression in verse and poetic imagery, and with regard to the quintessentially lyric quality of themes dealing with the inner workings of individual human lives, Nabokov's drama is reflective of his lyric sensibility. The present chapter will pause to examine the expression of Nabokov's lyric voice in drama, with particular attention accorded the example of *Изобретение Вальса* (*Izobretenie Val'sa / The Waltz Invention*), before the consideration in later chapters of his prose.

Before taking up *The Waltz Invention* as the culminating example of Nabokov's expression of his lyric voice in drama, a brief review of his central dramatic works is in order as preliminary demonstration of the workings and transformations of his poetic sensibility. While the following discussion makes no claim to comprehensiveness in terms of a general formal and thematic analysis of Nabokov's dramaturgy, it will be sufficient to highlight indisputable features of his defining lyric voice as they arise in drama. Viewed through the lens of his poetic writing, Nabokov's drama takes on contours of meaning otherwise unseen. Cognizance of Nabokov's lyric sensibility not only fosters awareness of the relatedness of his poetry and drama but also provides essential interpretive leverage in the understanding of his dramatic works.

With but minor exceptions, the bulk of Nabokov's dramatic writing was composed in two clusters at the opposing poles of the European period of his émigré career.[2] This temporal division is paralleled by a fundamental change in the form of his dramatic writing. The early plays of 1923–4 tend to be shorter, one- or two-act works composed in verse, with the exception of the single five-act drama of this period, *Трагедия господина Морна* (*Tragediia gospodina Morna / The Tragedy of Mister Morn*). Beginning with a single play in 1926 and followed twelve years later in 1938 with two further works, the remaining plays are extended prose dramas intended for conventional stage production.

Nabokov's first published play, *Скитальцы* (*Skital'tsy / The Wanderers*), was written in 1921 and appeared in Sasha Chernyi's almanac *Grani* in 1923 as the alleged translation of the first act of a four-act tragedy of 1768 by the 'obscure' English dramatist Vivian Calmbrood, an anagram for Nabokov's name.[3] This rhymed romantic drama tells the story of two long-separated brothers – one a world-weary traveller and the other a drunken brigand – who meet in a tavern in the presence of an innkeeper's daughter who feels reciprocated attraction for the turbulent highway man. *The Wanderers*, which is set at night in the enclosed space of a tavern described as a 'grave' and which asks whether life is not a 'disturbed dream,' is laden with luxuriously voiced reference to the two-world cosmology expressive of much of Nabokov's poetic writing. The dialogue between the two long-separated brothers is replete with mists, the stars, transparent sunrises, and 'beyond the window mirrory murk'; while the characters – the weary world traveller and the tempestuous brigand – are themselves rich in the Romantic associations of elements of Nabokov's verse. Especially Eric, the traveller, articulates the poetic sensibility native to Nabokov's verse in his acute sensitivity to the details of existence and his desire to conquer time in a return to the home of childhood memory. His longed-for return is similar to that invoked in Nabokov's poem of 1922 'Как объясню? Есть в памяти лучи …' ('Kak ob'iasniu? Est' v pamiati luchi …' / 'How to explain? There are in memory rays …'), as well as the numerous other poems in which a physical sensation associated with memory evokes sensual, Proustian contact with the past. Eric's first speech after recognizing his long-lost brother, for instance, rushes to a description of arrival home expressed in the motifs of temporal and spatial transition familiar to Nabokov's poetry:

> Мнится,
> уж вижу я – на светлой полосе
> родной зари – чернеющую крышу
> родного дома; мнится мне, уж слышу
> незабываемый сладчайший скрип
> поспешно открываемой калитки …   (*Ssoch* I, 662)

[It seems / I already see – on the illuminated stripe / of a native sunrise – the blackening roof / of [my] native home; it seems to me I already hear the unforgettable voluptuous squeak / of the hastily opening wicket-gate …]

A precisely remembered physical sensation literally opens the gate – here a wicket-gate – to arrival home and a past captured in memory and sensual depiction.

Eric's brigand brother Robert, though superficially less a man of consciously articulated lyric sensitivity, also gives representation to an essential theme from Nabokov's poetry in his keenly felt, though roughly expressed, dissatisfaction with life perceived by him as a nightmare inversion of a better existence. For reasons he is unable to conceptualize, Robert is tormented by the pain of life, conceived by him in images of purification. For Robert:

> Доблесть – бред,
> день – белый червь, жизнь – ужас бесконечный
> очнувшегося трупа в гробовом
> жилище …   (*Ssoch* I, 664)

[Valour – nonsense, / day – a white maggot, life – the unending horror / of the regaining of consciousness of a corpse in sepulchral / lodgings ...]

The impassioned Robert appears coiled for the creative release or violent explosion of energy dormant in his being. The conflicting potential of that release is suggested at the conclusion of the first and only act of *The Wanderers* by an argument and mysterious appearance which intimate the dramatic thrust of the remaining, ostensibly still untranslated, tragedy. The volatile Robert and the innkeeper, Colvil, become embroiled in a violent struggle as Robert reveals his desire to marry the innkeeper's daughter, Silvia, a muse-like figure perhaps capable of opening 'the tender flower sleeping' within him. Just as Robert is about to kill Colvil because of the latter's unwillingness to release his daughter, Silvia enters in the delirium of sleepwalk to deliver a speech replete with such motifs of Nabokov's metaphysical poetry as the delirium of somnolence, moonbeams, a key, and a locked door:[4]

> O/ бедный мой, о, бедный ...
> Как холодно, как холодно ему
> в сыром лесу осеннею порою! ...
> Тяжелый ключ с гвоздя сейчас сниму ...
> Ах, не стучись так трспстно! Открою,
> открою, мой любимый ... Ключ
> держу в руке ... Нет! Поздно! Превратился
> он в лилию ... Ты – здесь, ты возвратился?
> Ах, не стучись! Ведь толко лунный луч
> в руке держу, и эту дверь нет мочи
> им отпереть ...   (*Ssoch* I, 672)

[O my poor one, o poor ... / How cold, how cold it is to him / in the damp autumn forest! / The heavy key I will now take from the nail ... / Ah, don't knock so anxiously! I'll open it / I'll open it my love ... The key / I hold in my hand ... No! It's too late! He has changed / into a lily ... Are you here, have you returned? / Ah, don't knock! Nothing more than a moonbeam / I hold in my hand, and there is no power able / to unlock that door to them ...]

Unlike the young author Fyodor with his muse Zina only temporarily locked out of their new lodgings at the conclusion of *The Gift*, the first act of *The Wanderers* ends with the intimated tragedy of barred transition. Silvia's premonitory inability to open a door locked to Robert portends disaster. Despite its limitation to a single act, the curious *The Wanderers* is

fully Nabokovian, not only in terms of setting, theme, and language but
also in its exercise, and (self-)parodic acknowledgment of, images and motifs characteristic of Nabokov's poetic voice.

Смертъ (*Smert' / Death*), Nabokov's next theatrical work, is a two-act
play first published in 1923 which dramatizes the metaphysical implications of life, love, and death in a dialogue between a Cambridge don,
Gonville, and his young student, Edmond. Learning of the death of
Gonville's beautiful young wife, Stella, Edmond hastens to his mentor to
offer and seek commiseration. Edmond, it transpires, is inexplicably disconsolate at Stella's death and announces his desire to end the 'illness' of
existence in suicide, for which he will require the poison in Gonville's possession. Gonville, who had suspected an affair between his wife and a student, offers Edmond not the required poison but a potion which will loosen
Edmond's tongue and elicit a confession without killing him. Deceived
into believing that he is dead, in act two of *Death*, Edmond recounts his
experiences of existence beyond the grave. In subject matter, *Death* explicitly dramatizes the thematic concerns at the core of Nabokov's metaphysical poetry. The play functions as a rumination on anamnesis and the
otherworld, essentially ineffable subject matter which is nonetheless rendered representable due to the strategic inclusion of Gonville's cruel hoax
within the plot. The metaphysical and dramatic effect of *Death* hinges on
the suspension of final assurance regarding the certainty of Edmond's
death, as all claims about the transcendent and otherworldly are thereby
relativized and released from the compulsion of certitude. As in Alexander
Chernyshevski's rejection of an afterworld in *The Gift* on the basis of a
mistaken belief that it is raining outside his hospital room, and John
Shade's erroneous confirmation of life after death as a result of a misprint
in the words *mountain* and *fountain*, the very possibility that Edmond's
claims are nothing more than his delusions grants *Death* narrative space
for treatment of the indescribable.

Like so much of Nabokov's writing, *Death* is a meditation on the dimensions of consciousness and the potential of a pre- and after-life of awareness. In accordance with the tenor of Nabokov's lyric sensibility, which
validates the wondrous and illogical as the pinnacle of consciousness, the
topic of the fate of consciousness after death is staked out early in the
drama through identification with divergent, character-specific positions.
A contrast is thereby dramatized between the irrationality of Edmond's
love and possible experience of the otherworld and the cruel and calculat-
ing rationality of Gonville's profane science. Asked by Edmond what death
is, Gonville dryly replies:

... быть может, удивленье,
быть может – ничего. Склоняюсь, впрочем,
к последнему ...   (*Ssoch* I, 678)

[... perhaps it is a surprise / perhaps – nothing. I tend, incidentally, / to the latter ...]

Edmond's position is opposed to this view, and the weight of dramatic representation within *Death* is lent to the depiction of his metaphysical experience, which may or may not be real. While not a poet or even an artist, the cumulative effect of Edmond's reported experiences and the imagery of his self-expression indicate that he is a superior individual moved by the unsettling wonder of his own consciousness, which is itself inexplicably moved by his love for Stella. Stella herself, like the muses of Nabokov's poetry and novels, is enveloped in the imagery of a mysterious entity capable of releasing something wondrous in Edmond's poetic being. Her name associates her with the stars, as is likewise suggested in further imagery related to her. To Edmond 'she always walked in darkness ... Stella / a flickering name in a murky vortex.' Convinced that his soul is 'imprisoned' in the hollow shell of his body, Edmond attempts vainly to find release in the certainties of Gonville's science. Despite these efforts, however, Edmond remains subject to alterations in consciousness described by him as a 'wondrous illness' and which are reminiscent of the experiences of cosmic synchronization felt by various of Nabokov's figures of poetic temperament:

Но, с темнотой, чудовищный недуг
меня опять охватывает, душит:
средь ужаса и гула звездной ночи
теряюсь я; и страшно мне не только
мое непониманье, – страшен голос,
мне шепчущий, что вот еще усилье
и все пойму я ...   (*Ssoch* I, 679)

[However, with the darkness, a frightening illness / again seizes, suffocates me: / amongst the torment and rumble of the starry night / I lose myself; and terrifying to me is not only / my incomprehension, – terrifying is the voice, / whispering to me that a little more exertion / and I will understand all ...]

Like Art Longwood, who suddenly discovered a lightly veiled secret – 'How accessible ether! How easy flight!' – Edmond seems prepared to tear 'the web of when and where' leading to the 'nameless bliss no brain can bear' of Nabokov's poem 'Restoration.' For Edmond, the sole cure for his 'wondrous illness' is to be found 'behind the black curtain' of death accessed through self-poisoning. Soon after his self-induced 'death' and transition to another stage of consciousness, Edmond is induced by Gonville to describe the nature of his love for Stella. Here, too, Edmond's experiences are rendered in the imagery of Nabokov's poetry. Starting with the image of a window as a point of transition and metaphysical potential, Edmond relates how, by a window opened to an 'entire sky awash in stars,' Stella suddenly appeared by his side to stare at him with eyes of 'reflected eternity.' To Gonville's subsequent surprise, Stella's and Edmond's relationship was chaste, indeed literally Platonic. Staring into each other's eyes, the two soulmates sprouted wings to be united again in mysterious, momentary flight:

и вот концы серпчатых крыльев наших, –
пылающие длинные концы –
сошлись на миг ... Ты понимаешь, – сразу
отхлынул мир; мы поднялись; дышали
в невероятном небе   (*Ssoch* I, 691)

[and then the tips of our crescent wings – / flaming long tips – / joined together in an instant ... Do you understand – immediately / the world swept away; we arose; breathed / in the unbelievable sky]

Analogous to the narrator of 'In a crystal ball we were enclosed ...,' who was interrupted in rapturous flight with his soulmate by a human sigh, Edmond is brought back to the captivity of life by the closing of a 'distant door,' which seems to suggest the sealing of a fissure to the beyond. Shaken by his experience and a world rendered intolerable by his separation from Stella, Edmond seeks the death which motivates his consumption of poison and the action of the play.

Gonville's attempt at the end of the play to convince Edmond that he is not dead is inconclusive, for the audience and especially for Edmond. And in final confirmation of the potential implications of death for consciousness, Edmond describes what he takes to be his death in terms of the creative release and expansion of his consciousness:

Под муравой лежу я, ребра вздув,
но мысль моя, мой яркий сон загробный,
еще живет, и дышит, и творит.   (*Ssoch* I, 694)

[Beneath the grass I lie, [my] ribs bloated, / but my thought, my vivid dream
of the next world / still lives, and breathes, and creates.]

Death concludes with the forestalled appearance of Stella – the lone figure
capable of rupturing Edmond's dream of death or, indeed, taking it to
another level – an ending which leaves the play with the mystery of the
otherworld imaginatively illuminated though empirically intact. Experience
of the ineffable has been intimated, though not conclusively confirmed.
Infused like *The Wanderers* with the light wash of (self-)parody, *Death* announces its conscious manipulation of the distant temporal and physical
settings and conventions of the romantic tale and such plays as Calderón's
La vida es sueño; nonetheless, shining through the ludic inventiveness are
the unmistakable traces of the themes and imagery which define all of the
artistry derived from Nabokov's lyric sensibility. The play of uncertainty
regarding the death of a central character is something that Nabokov
would develop still further in *The Eye* and *Transparent Things*.

Nabokov's following dramatic work, Дедушка (*Dedushka* / *The Grand-
dad*), a verse drama in one act, was first published in October 1923. Set in
early nineteenth-century France, *The Grand-dad* recounts a noble (in character and in social rank) Frenchman's foiling of death and fate on two occasions – once as a young man during the tumult of the French Revolution
and second, years later, as an old man during a chance repeat encounter
with the now senile artist-executioner of the terror. Like the above discussed *The Wanderers* and *Death*, *The Grand-dad* is characterized by the
same telling reference to the distinctive themes and imagery of Nabokov's
poetry. And like these two plays, *The Grand-dad* maintains focus on the
metaphysically freighted theme of the mystery of life and fate, while further complicating the use of poetic themes and imagery through oblique
reference to the second thematic pillar of Nabokov's lyric sensibility – his
poetics of trifles and conscious appreciation of the wonder and detail of
life. It is with reference to these central features of Nabokov's lyric sensibility that the drama takes on fullest meaning.

The Grand-dad begins with an aging French nobleman's taking of shelter
during a sudden thunderstorm in the home of a prosperous peasant family.
The nobleman, de Mérival, approvingly surveys the humble comforts of
the house, observing a carved chest in the corner of the room. As if
prompted by the natural drama of the tempestuous rainfall witnessed
through the prominently staged windows, the assembled characters fall
into a discussion of the wonder of nature, a conversation which reveals
their various perceptions and conceptions of the natural world. While the

nobleman de Mérival is enchanted by the 'golden smoke' created by the
sudden appearance of the sun after the rain,[5] the peasant farmer indicates
another, more prosaic understanding of nature and the environment.
Although likewise expressed in sensual imagery, the farmer indicates that
his perception of the environment is not filtered through a refined consciousness appreciative of the beauty of detail, but rather by his unmediated proximity to, and fearful dependency on, the land:

> See – you, sir,
> can marvel at it, but what about us?
> We *are* the land ... And our thoughts are the land's
> own thoughts ... We do not need to look, but sense
> the swelling of the seed within the furrow,
> the fruit becoming plump ... When, from the heat,
> the earth begins to parch and crack, so, too,
> the skin upon our palms starts cracking, sir.   (*USSR* 293)

Ultimately, however, it is in an aside by the farmer's wife that the most
immediate, most intense, and thus most poetic, relation to nature is seemingly reported. Living with the farmer and his wife and daughter is an
unnamed 'grand-dad,' an agèd, now senile old man graciously taken in
and cared for by the farmer and his family. The grand-dad, in his dementia, seems to enjoy the most mysterious and childishly intimate relation
with the natural world:

> Grand-dad, too, awaits
> assiduously some kind of revelation,
> pressing his ear first to the bark, then to
> a petal ... He believes, it seems to me,
> that dead men's souls live on in lilies, or
> in cherry trees.   (*USSR* 294)

Against the example of the farmer in his fearful dependency on the environment and the grand-dad in his dementia, it is alone de Mérival who
exercises consciousness in his appreciation of the natural environment. It
soon emerges that de Mérival's capacity for consciously experienced sensual love of the external world is predicated upon the very tumultuousness
of his life and its suggested hardships, in particular, his miraculous escape
from the scaffold and execution during the terror. As a twenty-year-old,
de Mérival had been sentenced to execution at the hands of a renowned

executioner, an 'artist' in his grim trade. De Mérival describes in minute detail to his peasant audience the meticulous preparations of the executioner-artist and his own feelings upon being taken to, and mounting, the scaffold; his curious attention to 'various trivial details'; his presentiment of death; and, suddenly, his miraculous escape in the tumult of a fire.[6] Freed from death, which is vividly described in Nabokovian imagery of physical transition and passage, de Mérival nonetheless undergoes a change reminiscent of the expansion of awareness occasioned by contact with the otherworld and the attainment of consciousness of a higher stage. De Mérival's perception is awakened, and he becomes keenly attentive to the trifling beauty – 'the colored specks of our precious life' – of this world:

> – Thus I escaped, and suddenly
> it seemed my eyes were opened: I'd been awkward,
> unfeeling, absent-minded, had not fully
> appreciated life, the colored specks of
> our precious life but, having seen so close
> that pair of upright posts, that narrow gate
> to nonexistence, and those gleams, that gloom ...   (USSR 298)

Coincidentally, it is also 'colored specks' which, indirectly, lead to the second foiling of death and the curious denouement of the drama. Concluding the brief history of his tumultuous and difficult though rich life, the drama veers in the direction of the pastoral as de Mérival makes appreciative comments about the peasant family's expected grandchild and the 'dreamy air' surrounding the second child, the grand-dad, in his second childhood as he tenderly caresses lilies in the sunshine of the garden. Viewed through the window, de Mérival concludes that the grand-dad, with his delicate flowers named after duchesses and marquesses, has lived a 'life in peace' far 'from civil and from other tumults' (USSR 301). Rupturing this idyllic scene is Juliette, the peasant farmer's pregnant daughter, who enters to announce in innocent laughter that the grand-dad has inexplicably seized and thrown into the river her basket for collecting cherries. In subsequent conversation between the two elderly men, the grand-dad resists de Mérival's attempts to have him describe his beautiful lilies. Instead, the grand-dad playfully, though ominously, requests that de Mérival lie face down on a table to peer through a keyhole into the carved chest, 'an enchanted wardrobe.' Here, The Grand-dad turns to the motifs of enclosure and transition of Nabokov's lyric voice. The enclosed space of the wardrobe viewed through a 'chink' to the other side renders it indeed enchanted, though as a second passage to death and the otherworld analogous to his near passage to death through 'that narrow gate' on the scaffold; hence, de Mérival's earlier presentiment of death felt as an 'eerie ... troubled feeling.' The senile old grand-dad is, of course, the inverted artist-executioner of years before. As de Mérival had vaguely intuited, the cherry-stained basket had awoken in the grand-dad associations with his executioner's blood-stained basket and cast him back in time to the decreed completion of his unfulfilled duty. Thus, building upon the imagery and themes developed in Nabokov's poetry and constitutive of his lyric sensibility, *The Grand-dad* offers in the figure of the eponymous grand-dad early expression of a strong subsequent motif in Nabokov's writing – the acute and perspicacious, though nonetheless damaged and perverted, consciousness. Both Robert of *The Wanderers* and the grand-dad of *The Grand-dad* introduce to Nabokov's oeuvre characters suggestive of a mirrored inversion of the lyric temperament. In characters such as these is to be seen the shade of Kinbote, the mad commentator of *Pale Fire*.

In the words of Brian Boyd, Nabokov's next dramatic work, *Трагедия господина Морна* (*Tragediia Gospodina Morna* / *The Tragedy of Mister Morn*), was in 1924 'by far the most significant work Nabokov had yet written in any medium ...' (Boyd 1990, 222). Despite the promise of this high praise, which has more recently been echoed in Barabtarlo's claim that this play is Nabokov's 'very first major work' (Barabtarlo 1999, 122), *The Tragedy of Mister Morn* was not published in extended, though still perhaps incomplete, form until 1997.[7] This five-act play written in unrhymed iambic pentameter tells the story of Morn, a good man who wisely and prosperously rules an unnamed European country incognito and basks in the love of the populace and Medea, his lover. Morn's happiness is disrupted by the return of Medea's husband, Ganus, resurrected as if from the dead after four years in prison. Ganus, in his rage, forces Morn into a failed duel and then the cutting of a deck of cards to decide who will die. Although Morn loses, and is thus honour-bound to commit suicide, out of love for life and Medea, he chooses to flee his fate rather than confront it. Later pursued by the memory of this moment of personal weakness and shame, Morn's relationship with Medea cools and she leaves him. After her departure, Morn yearns for the arrival of the wrathful Ganus to free him from his shame. Ganus ultimately learns of Morn's hiding place, searches him out, and shoots him. Wounded, though not killed, Morn returns to his kingdom to resume rightful control of the state after an insurrection has removed the powers who usurped control after Morn's departure. In the final act, however, rather than return to the public love and political power that would be restored to him, Morn commits suicide.

More fully than even the three previous plays, *The Tragedy of Mister Morn* reads like a lexicon in dramatic form of Nabokov's poetry of the early 1920s. Beginning with the opening lines, the play self-consciously incorporates the staging of themes, motifs, and stylistic devices from his poetry:

Сон, лихорадка, сон; глухие смены
двух часовых, стоящих у ворот
моей бессильной жизни …   (*TGM* 9)

[Dream, fever, dream: the mute changes / of the two sentinels standing at the gates / of my impotent life …]

A metaphysical comment on the nature of life as a fever interrupting the dream preceding and following after conscious existence, the opening lines also suggest almost chorus like comment on the passion staged in the imagination of the playwright. In the opening and closing scenes of the play, a mysterious figure – иностранец (*inostranets*, 'stranger' or 'foreigner') – slips in and out of the action of the drama. A *somnitel'nyi somnambula* or 'dubious sleepwalker,' he is clearly from twentieth-century Russia and the author of the play. Like the poets of Nabokov's verse composing by an open window (for instance in 'Сон' ['Son' / 'The Dream']), he is dreaming the play and slips out of the action only when temporarily awakened into the living reality beyond the realm of the play:

Я просыпался. Ветер разбудил.
Оконницу шарахнуло. С трудом
заснул опять …   (*TGM* 26)

[I woke up. A breeze awoke [me]. / The window-sash banged. With difficulty / I fell asleep again]

This appearance of self-identified authorial agency in the action of the play is representative of the central innovation of this play. *The Tragedy of Mister Morn* demonstrates not merely the expression by Nabokov of the themes and imagery of his poetry in dramatic form, but the conscious assimilation of the defining principles of his lyric voice into the drama as functioning agents. Vladislav Khodasevich documented this unusual feature of Nabokov's artistry in his retrospective assessment of 1937:

But this catches one's eye because Sirin not only does not mask or hide his techniques as most usually do – and in which Dostoevskii, for instance, achieved startling perfection – but the opposite. Sirin himself exhibits them in full view like a magician who, having amazed his audience, immediately reveals the laboratory of his wonders. This, it seems to me, is the key to all of Sirin. His works are populated not only with functioning characters but also with innumerable techniques which, like elves or gnomes scurrying amongst the characters, perform an amazing amount of work: they saw, cut, nail, and hammer beneath the eyes of the audience setting up and clearing away those stage sets in which the play is performed. They construct the world of the artistry and themselves appear as indispensable figures in it. Sirin thus does not hide them because one of his central goals is precisely to show how his techniques live and work. (Khodasevich 1937, 9)

Khodasevich's suggestive turn to the metaphor of drama and the stage is appropriate, for it is with Nabokov's dramaturgy that the principles of his lyric sensibility achieve more than thematic expression to take on, as it were, speaking roles in his artistry. As essential features of Nabokov's lyricism, inspiration and the love of the trifles of life and nature, for instance, are not merely expressed in *The Tragedy of Mister Morn* but embodied in figures who personify both the fulfillment – and negative inversion – of these qualities in character form. A noble 'poet' of life, Morn expunges the shame of his flight from death in his final embrace of it. In this, he is in contrast to the Maiakovskii-like poet Kliian, who is an ignoble coward. Morn is associated with and expressive of love, peace, and happiness; Ganus, as his mentor Tremens observes, will 'spread fire and coldly strange / torturous disease: murderous / revolts; mute destruction / blessedness; emptiness; oblivion' (*TGM* 18). Especially Dandilio – in contrast to the cold, murky figure Tremens – seems an important personification of qualities essential to Nabokov's lyric love of the pulsing world. A 'happy dandelion,' as his name would suggest, Dandilio is an inspirational force of good in the play. Someone who has frequently been dreamed by the 'foreigner,' the author of the play, in his childhood, Dandilio combines transcendent knowledge with love of nature and the world acutely expressed in Nabokovian images of trifles:

> Да, к мелочам случайным
> мой глаз привык, исследуя прилежно
> ходы жучков и ссадины на теле
> старинной мебели, чешуйки красок,
> пылинки на полотнах безымянных.   (*TGM* 77–8)

[Yes, to random trifles / my eye is accustomed, examining diligently / the movements of beetles and the scratches on the body / of old furniture, scaling paint / specks of dust on anonymous paintings]

Within the world of Nabokov's characters, Dandilio, with his quiet love of trifles, seems a distant relative of, among many others, Art Longwood from 'The Ballad of Longwood Glen.' Responding to the question regarding death put to Gonville in *Death*, Dandilio admits that he loves everything in life, including, by extension, its transformation in death, which he concedes is 'curious' (*TGM* 81). Dandilio's association with Morn suggests that it is into this transcendent state of consciousness that Morn will resurrect after his death.

It is in Morn's death in the final scene of the play that *The Tragedy of Mister Morn* dramatizes another central theme derived from Nabokov's poetry and formative of his lyric voice. Against expectations, Morn commits suicide at the conclusion of the play, even though return to his kingdom seems assured. In this, he demonstrates with his life the iron consequentiality of a rule first learned by speakers of Nabokov's lyric poetry and then by such characters as Ganin of *Mary*, Chorb of 'The Return of Chorb,' Martin of *Glory*, Humbert Humbert of *Lolita*, Kinbote of *Pale Fire*, and even, presumably, Eric of *The Wanderers*. This is the existential tragedy of Mr Morn. The past, a wondrous kingdom of love and fulfillment, remains a foreign country which may never be returned to physically. Only through the exercise of consciousness in the conjuring forth of memory and the creation of art, and perhaps in death, is the lost kingdom of the past to be regained. This bittersweet lesson Waltz, too, will learn.

Nabokov's final verse drama, Полюс (*Polius* / *The Pole*), was published in August 1924. This one-act play offers a fictional reconstruction of the death of Robert Falcon Scott and his company of explorers during their attempted return from an expedition to Antarctica in 1912. In basing *The Pole* on a dramatic confrontation with death, Nabokov emphasizes, among other themes, the topic of nobility of character, subject matter already suggested in both de Mérival of *The Wanderers* and Morn of *The Tragedy of Mister Morn*. In terms of reference to Nabokov's poetic writing, *The Pole* is clearly occupied with the theme of the otherworld, of comportment in this world at the point of transition to the other. The play is set within the enclosed space of a tent during a blizzard in conditions where passage to the outer space assures fatal divestment in the sense experienced by the hero of *Pnin*: 'Stay inside or you perish. Death is divestment, death is communion. It may be wonderful to mix with the landscape, but to do so is the end of the tender ego' (*Pnin* 20). Inside the tent, the four individuals –

Captain Scott, Fleming, Kingsley, and Johnson – prepare for divestment, each in his own way. Johnson, the first to die in a manner later described by Scott as 'valorous,' indicates his proximity to death in an early speech which emphasizes the division and awaited metamorphosis of his consciousness:

> It seems as if I'm split into two parts –
> one is myself, strong, lucid ... while the other's
> scorbutic, drowsy ... a real sleepyhead ...   (*USSR* 270)

While Johnson's physical body is falling into a somnambulant state, the quintessence of his being, his consciousness, remains strong and lucid. His feet swollen and blackened with frostbite, Johnson recalls a dream from youth wherein his feet were those of an elephant and which now seems a presentiment of the future, his current state. In this state, he willingly leaves the enclosure of the tent to die and thus selflessly spare food and resources for the others. Kingsley, the next to die, is also – like Johnson – already in a liminal state at the play's beginning. Suffering in a delirium which indicates that his mind has returned to his love for his fiancée and the remembered games of youth, he dies alone as Fleming and Scott exit the tent to search for Johnson. His final speech is a description of the passage to death:

> ... So – this is what death means: a
> glass entrance ... water ... water ... it's all clear.   (*USSR* 276)

The words of a delirious man witnessed by no one, the clarity of what Kingsley sees – whether water, the secret of transition into death, or both – is not to be determined. Nonetheless, his ravings describe watery entrance into another dimension, providing early expression to the aquatic associations of the otherworld likewise frequently articulated in poetry by Nabokov, for instance, his poem of love and the otherworld, 'Being in Love,' and the short story 'Perfection,' to be discussed below. The relevance of aquatic associations to the otherworld is further intensified through connection of Scott to Rupert Brooke, a poet of critical interest to Nabokov in the early 1920s. The source of his first discursive reference to the otherworld, Nabokov's article 'Rupert Bruk' of 1922 is studded with aquatic imagery, as the young critic read in Brooke's poetry of water 'the deep image of our being' (*Ssoch* I, 728). In the article, Nabokov also records seeing Scott's diary in the British Museum alongside a sonnet by Brooke: 'His [Brooke's] rough draft is preserved under glass in the British Museum between a manuscript by Dickens and captain Scott's notebook' (*Ssoch* I, 733).

Left alive are the two men who in their lengthy speeches narrate the most conscious engagement with the trifling wonder and delight of physical existence. Fleming, with no one waiting for him in England, reveals that his past life has been one of Romantic wandering and the tribulations of an unsettled life: 'Few have been the peaceful nights, / the happy days I've had from life' (*USSR* 274). Despite, or indeed because of, this dearth of happiness in his past, Fleming, like de Mérival of *The Grand-dad*, feels an intense urge to live, expressed in the desire to enjoy what amount to the 'simple' trifles of life:

> And yet I've an unbearable
> desire to live ... Yes, to pursue a ball,
> a woman, or the sun or – still more simply –
> to eat, to eat a lot, to tear the plump
> sardines in golden oil out of their tin ...
> I want to live so much, it maddens me,
> it hurts to live somehow ...   (*USSR* 274)

Still strong – a 'burning, bursting mote' of energy – Fleming decides in agreement with Scott to leave his captain and to set out in search of help. After Fleming's exit, the lone Scott is the fourth and final character to reflect on his divestment. As explorer-scientist and leader of the expedition, Scott unites the positive traits of disinterestedly pursuing further understanding of the natural world and also of channelling the hopes and aspirations of his entire crew. The superiority of his almost artistic temperament is reflected in his overriding wish to observe, reflect upon, and record experience regardless of the circumstances, as represented in his meticulous note-taking. Concerned earlier in the play that in sleep he might 'slip' over into death, and having experienced a 'radiant, fearful dream,' Scott is left alone with these presentiments of death following Fleming's departure. Leafing through his journal, which reads as a chronology of the demise of Kingsley and Johnson, Scott remains with one final entry to make – the final circumstance of his own end. Appropriately, as he sees it, his pencil breaks, and he is left with his last thoughts, which turn to love in the form of a sun-lit vision of his beloved son in London. Slipping into a delirium, which now seems a fulfillment of his earlier 'radiant, fearful dream,' Scott sees the departed Fleming in a hallucination which elides into a release and dispersal of his body and consciousness suggestive of something approaching the mystery of cosmic synchronization:

> Everything's quiet.
> I picture Fleming on the vast, smooth plain –
> he walks, moving his skis ahead
> so steadily – one, two … he's disappearing …
> And I'm no longer hungry … Such great weakness,
> such quietude is rippling through my body … (*pause*)
> It's probably delirium … I hear …
> I hear … Can it really be possible?   (*USSR* 281)

Despite the passage into delirium and the quiet rippling of his body, what Scott seems to hear is not the mysterious rumble of the otherworld, but the returned Fleming come back to await rescue or die with his friend and captain. The concluding imagery of the sudden dying down of the blizzard and the beauty of the outside world all aglitter in snow, however, leaves open the possibility – as in the open ending of *Death* – that Scott has died and that Fleming's return and his offer of a knife to sharpen Scott's pencil is but expression of the continuation of Scott's consciousness in another dimension.

Aside from the in various ways exceptional *The Tragedy of Mister Morn*, Nabokov's early verse dramas thus reveal a variety of similarities which invite comparison with one another and Nabokov's poetry. More than their verse form alone, thematically, and in imagery, these plays carry into dramatic form the central concerns of Nabokov's verse. In their fidelity to the two central themes of the otherworld and the keen appreciation of the trifles of life, they provide a first demonstration of the extension of key poetic themes and images from Nabokov's verse into a lyric sensibility practicable in other genres. Indeed, given the limited development of character psychology and the almost plot-less representation of subject matter, each of the plays seems almost a continuation of Nabokov's narrative poetry by other generic means. Despite the obvious narrative quality of each work, however, the essential drama of these plays – the confrontation and mastery of death and fate – is essentially lyric in character. Each drama depicts a conflict which is quintessentially individual, and not collective, a play of consciousness and metaphysical speculation, rather than societal forces. Nabokov's later prose plays, while maintaining close relation to the issues of Nabokov's verse, extend the expression of his lyric sensibility into other dimensions. The formal transition of these plays – the shift from verse to prose writing – marks the conveyance of his lyric sensibility in the direction of traditional drama and the representation of socio-historical reality.

This is immediately apparent in Nabokov's first prose drama, *Человек из CCCP* (*Chelovek iz SSSR* / *The Man from the USSR*). Successfully staged in Berlin in 1926, only the first act of this five-act play was published in Russian in January 1927; the play did not appear in its entirety until the publication of Dmitri Nabokov's translation into English in the collection *The Man from the USSR and Other Plays* of 1985. Unlike the distant Romantic temporal and physical settings of Nabokov's verse plays, *The Man from the USSR* signals its proximity to the more prosaic communal concerns of his Berlin émigré audience. Populated with a disparate cast of exile characters, the play is about émigré life in Berlin and the underground efforts of the central character, Kuznetsoff, to 'return' to Russia in an effort to destabilize the young Soviet regime. On one level prosaic in its depiction of the web of individual and social associations and ramifications extending out from Kuznetsoff's machinations, the play is also shot through with scenes and imagery which emphasize its self-consciously artistic qualities and, in particular, its provenance in Nabokov's lyric sensibility. Accompanying Kuznetsoff's *always* offstage preparations for a return to Russia, the *real* plot of the play unfolds in what are ostensibly its secondary plots, as it moves through five settings representative of various aspects of the fate of the exile Russian community: a submerged, almost grave-like basement tavern, from which the parallel life of Berlin may be seen passing by; a foyer to a lecture hall, as focal point of émigré cultural life; the lobby of a film studio, where the exile community's native Russia is 're-created' in the banality and vulgarity of stereotypic images; and finally, two scenes in the quintessentially émigré setting of a bare room in an impoverished boarding house. *The Man from the USSR* displays frequent Nabokovian touches of detail which challenge and reward the attentive audience member / reader: for instance, Kuznetsoff's act-two gazing at a photograph of a man who is revealed in act five to have been one of his co-conspirators coldly sacrificed to a Soviet firingsquad for the good of his cause; the use of film and stage imagery in the repeated self-reflective reference to the dream-like artifice of the lives of the émigré characters who seem to be stage extras in the play of history; Olga Pavlovna's articulation of her love for Kuznetsoff in the image of wished-for eternal co-containment in a jail; and, finally, Olga's validation of conscious appreciation of the trifles of life – a silly dance tune – as an expression of the love uniting two characters.

The at once most poignant illustration of émigré fate and perhaps clearest parallel to Nabokov's poetry arises in the figures of Mr and Mrs Oshivenski and their changing of living quarters. The play begins with Victor Oshivenski – like Chernyshevski of *The Gift* – a tenderly portrayed figure from the pantheon of Nabokovian characters who have been mauled by fate and yet manage to confirm their essential humanity in the experience.

Oshivenski's physical and existential pain opens *The Man from the USSR* as he slams his thumb with a hammer in the first scene of the play. Struggling to eke out an existence in his subterranean tavern, Oshivenski seems already to have one foot in the grave. It soon emerges that Oshivenski and his wife are being broken by the loss of their property and status in Russia, the death of their son to the Soviets, and the intolerable material and spiritual deprivation of émigré life. In the opening lines of act one, Victor Oshivenski suspects he may soon have to move; in the final act of the play, the setting is the Oshivenskis' modest room as they prepare to depart to an unknown new location. As in Nabokov's poem 'You've moved to new lodgings ...,' however, repeated suggestion is made that, against his expectations, Oshivenski's move will be to Russia/death. Prompted by the intolerability of life in their current lodgings, Oshivenski sardonically suggests to his wife that 'we'll move straight into the Kingdom of Heaven. At least there you don't have to pay the rent in advance' (*USSR* 102). Later, their friend Fyodor Fyodorovich informs them that he has found modest lodgings at a suggestive address presided over by an angel: 'Five Paradise Street, care of Engel; courtyard entrance, fifth floor. Unpresupposing but extremely cheap room' (*USSR* 112). Ultimately, it is not the material poverty of their existence which so troubles the Oshivenskis; it is the impossibility of a return to Russia which moves them: 'I'm so homesick I could die, ... I'm dying to see Russia, it's true' (*USSR* 117). In their pain, the Oshivenskis are representative of each of the characters of the play, all of whom are suffering individual loss directly related to the common loss of Russia. The full dimension of the Oshivenskis' move – the changing of lodgings, a return to the past, arrival in the land of their son's grave – will be accomplished only in death. In manipulation of Nabokov's frequent association throughout his oeuvre of metaphysical themes with imagery of a home and lodgings, the Oshivenskis will both return home and gain a new home in death. The Oshivenski plot-line thus illustrates the play's real subjectmatter. Ostensibly a play about a man from the USSR preparing to return to Russia, the play resolutely consigns this 'central' theme to offstage development, instead to concentrate on the ramifications of this return to 'secondary' characters. It is they who act out the concerns of Nabokov's lyric sensibility through allusion to the elements of his poetic voice. The world of émigré experience is movingly depicted, but in a poetic rather than prosaic-political mode. *The Man from the USSR* concludes with a speech by Kuznetsoff indicating that his own return to Russia is in fulfillment of an ideal, though hardly realizable, goal of importance to all: 'Olya, I'm going to the USSR so that you will be able to come to Russia. And everybody will be there ... Old

Oshivenski living out his days, and Kolya Taubendorf, and that funny Fyodor Fyodorovich. Everybody' (*USSR* 122). The only move and return to Russia possible is on the plane of fictional/fairy-tale reality or the transcendent, both of which are accomplished in Nabokov's art.

Nabokov's second prose play, the three-act Событие (*Sobytie* / *The Event*), was both first staged and published twelve years after *The Man from the USSR*, in the spring of 1938.[8] While ostensibly set in a contemporary émigré environment, unlike *The Man from the USSR*, the location of the action of *The Event* is not to be definitively placed in any specific socio-cultural context. Described by Nabokov as 'a dramatic comedy,' the sources of *The Event* are to be found in a range of works by Gogol', Pushkin, Chekhov, Goethe, and Ibsen, as well as in the real-world dilemma and drama of émigré life. Tying all of the features together and lending the place its distinctive Nabokovian quality is its recourse to the lyric sensibility underlying the entire play. Indeed, it is this quality which lifts the play out of its localized social and familial context to grant it broader ramifications, as Iurii Annenkov, the play's first director and set designer observed. Important in this poetry-based discussion of Nabokov's drama is Annenkov's identification of the decisive role of a lyrical component in the achievement of Nabokov's success:

In my opinion, *The Event* is the first play written according to the needs of great art in the last [several] years of Russian literature. Russian writers have unlearned the ability to write lovingly for the theatre. Sirin has made the breach. His play, with a change of names, could be played on any stage in any language with the same success ... *Our lives are composed not only out of realist facts but also out of our relationship to them, out of our dreams, out of the tangle of our memories and associations*, and yet from the dramatist for some reason only one-sided extensions are required – either entirely realistic or openly fantastical. Sirin combined the one and the other in a single mass and thus achieved the greatest humanity. (Vakar 4; emphasis added)

The Event treats a suspenseful day in the lives of the painter Aleksei Troshcheykin and his wife, Lyubov', as they fearfully await the 'event,' the arrival of Lyubov''s former lover, Barbashin, a man just granted early release from prison after serving six years of a sentence for the attempted murder of Troshcheykin and Lyubov'. The threatened possibility that he may return to accomplish his task exerts the external force necessary to reveal the hidden cracks and imperfections in the lives of, and relationship between, Troshcheykin and Lyubov'. Troshcheykin is a public failure as an artist and a passive cuckold and coward, while Lyubov' regrets her marriage to the 'safe' Troshcheykin rather than the passionate Barbashin. Both, above all else, mourn the death of their infant son three years previous. It is this death which constitutes the real, though subterranean, 'event' of the play and constitutes the key to the thematic and formal composition of *The Event*.

The progressive protrusion of the theme of the boy's death through the surface action of the play indicates not only its life-shaping importance to Troshcheykin and Lyubov', but reveals the textured, multi-layered facade of the play's organization. Before distinguishing between these layers, however, it is important to recall a division of ontological magnitude in Nabokov's theory of dramaturgy. In his article 'Playwriting,' Nabokov emphasized the strict division of labour established by the theatre's inviolable fourth wall separating fiction from audience. For Nabokov, the spectators of a play are granted spiritual awareness of the events onstage, though constrained to physical non-intervention in them; while the players are granted the ability to emotionally move the audience, though they may indicate no awareness of the audience's presence. Complementary in their dependence on each other, the two spheres' division is sacrosanct:

> Sight and hearing but no intervention on one side [the audience] and spiritual intervention but no sight or hearing on the other [the players] are the main features of the beautifully balanced and perfectly fair division drawn by the line of footlights. It may be proved further that this convention is a natural rule of the theatre and that when there is any freakish attempt to break it, then either the breaking is only a delusion, or the play stops being a play. (*USSR* 315–16)

This clearly stated principle is essential to forestall erroneous conclusions regarding a Postmodernist merging of realms of fiction and reality in Nabokov's dramaturgy. As in *The Event* and *The Waltz Invention*, Nabokov plays with addresses and explicit references to the audience, though these in no way assume the conscious participation of the characters functioning in their world of fiction. In *The Event*, this is illustrated in the complementary layering of the play on either side of the footlights. For the audience, *The Event* is an artistic construct which self-consciously announces its fictionality through numerous literary allusions and the accumulation of self-parodic references to its own fictional essence as a play. Far more important, however, is the layering of events in the internal, fictional world of *The Event*. Here dramatic action unfolds on the surface level of prosaic public reality, where events are causally motivated by the external, interpersonal obligations of the characters, and the interior, lyric level of individual consideration, where the forces of intensely personal memory and associations hold sway. As in *The Man from the USSR*, where Kuznetsoff's real-world, though always offstage, preparations for a return to Russia cede importance to the private loss of the individual characters, in *The Event* the public realm of realist activity recedes to emphasize the importance of the inner world of the characters. Parallel to this development, commencing with the appearance of Mrs Vagabundov and Eleonora Shnap midway through the play, is the increasing intrusion of the grotesque, the self-consciously theatric, into the otherwise realist unfolding of events on the stage. The entrance of these two fictional depictions of Death initiates the rubbing through of the lyric subterranean level of the subjective worlds of Troshcheykin and Lyubov' into the public action, thereby shaping a drama arising out of the tangle of private memories and associations. This – according to Annenkov – is the essential subject matter of this play.

In supporting this quintessentially lyric development, *The Event* draws extensively on the themes and motifs of Nabokov's poetry. Troshcheykin, for instance, experiences the artist's wonder of inspiration, a physical sensation akin to sickness which he is incapable of expressing even to his wife: 'I don't know what's happening to me … All kinds of thoughts, too – my eyes are closed, but there is such a merry-go-round of colors spinning in the head I could go insane' (*USSR* 132) His dream inspired idea for a great work of art which would remove an ontological 'wall' and allow depiction of a black abyss with an audience full of the faces of all the people he has known is, for lack of ability to express it verbally, dismissed as 'just a fleeting image seen in a semidelirious state, a surrogate for insomnia, sickroom art' (*USSR* 132–3). The proximity of Troshcheykin to this 'abyss' of altered consciousness is emphasized by repeated reference to the stoppage of time suggested by his broken watch. Unlike her husband, Lyubov' is plagued less by the transcendent than by her acute experience of this world, unbidden associations with her deceased son, and precisely recalled memories of the past and abandoned passion. In the climactic scene of act two, just after the arrival of Death in the figures of Vagabundov and Shnap and before the arrival of a messenger figure named Shchel' – which in Russian means 'fissure' – the partition separating the consciousness of man and wife is rent, and Troshcheykin and Lyubov' are granted privileged access to the subjective being of the other. During a delirium invoked by the recitation of a short story by Lyubov''s mother, Troshcheykin and Lyubov' are separated off from the actions of the other figures on another plane of linked, intersubjective consciousness. This separation is itself marked in the stage directions. All of the other onstage characters freeze while the two communicate directly and without rancour. Despite the promise of a possible union, Lyubov' correctly states that they 'are two solitudes, and each is a closed circle' (*USSR* 214). Troshcheykin is frozen in fear and cast back to a now distorted version of his previous idea for a work of art: '... Alone on this narrow, lighted stage. Behind us, the old theatrical frippery of our whole life, the frozen masks of a second-rate comedy, and in front a dark chasm full of eyes, eyes, eyes watching us, awaiting our destruction' (*USSR* 214). Lyubov', for her part, is consumed with regret and the ghostly presence of her dead son: 'Our little son broke the mirror with a ball today. Hold me, Alyosha. Don't loosen your grip' (*USSR* 214). Unfortunately for both, Troshcheykin is unable to 'hold' her, and both slip from the 'marvelous ... momentary heights' of a wondrous state of shared consciousness to re-enter life and reality again. Despite this privileged glimpse into the 'closed circle' of the other, husband and wife are as separate as before. The most poignant scene of the following, third act has Troshcheykin and Lyubov' argue on a conscious level in a manner which mirrors in tragic inversion the understanding achieved in their delirium. Throughout the remainder of the final act, their lives are overcome with increasing reference to the fictional and irrational in the form of conventionally 'theatrical' exchanges between 'real' characters who comport themselves like actors onstage; the accumulation of doubles; farcical plot developments; the reading of palms; and a denouement based on a 'double' and a coincidence. Beginning in the real and the verisimilitudinously represented, *The Event* concludes with the comedic triumph of the irrational over the real, the lyric over the prosaic.

This tilting of the action in the direction of the unconventional, culminating in the roles of the bizarre figures Meshaev Two and Al'fred Barboshin – doubles to Meshaev One and Barbashin – is presaged by the strategic appearance of the play's first pair of doubles, Mrs Vagabundov and Eleonora Shnap, and, significantly, the accompanying introduction of verse into the narrative of the prose play. Andrei Babikov, in discussing these characters in his unusually insightful article '*The Event* and the Main Thing in Nabokov's Theory of Drama,' records Khodasevich's consternation, expressed in a review of *The Event*, that Mrs Vagabundov should speak in rhymed verse (Babikov 152). Both components, Vagabundov and Shnap at the level of characterization and rhymed verse at the level of narrative form, portend the arrival of the otherworldly and the irrational into the play. Both Vagabundov and Shnap are closely associated with death, in particular the unspoken central event of the play, the death of Lyubov''s and Troshcheykin's son. Eleonora Shnap, Lyubov''s midwife of five years previous, mistakenly believes that the birthday party is for the – in fact, dead – child. She also suggests to Mrs Vagabundov that the child was from Barbashin, the source of the current threat of death: 'Speaking betveen me und you, now I am kvite sure the child wass hiss ...' (*USSR* 198). Mrs Vagabundov is sitting for a portrait by Troshcheykin, as is a little boy to be depicted with five balls. Together the two subjects of his art suggest Troshcheykin's treatment of his son's death three years previous at age two, hence his anger at the loss of the balls necessary for the painting. Two balls, paralleling two years, are present while three others have vanished: the green and speckled balls – in the art of Nabokov's lyric sensibility the colours of life and the world. Vagabundov, whom Troshcheykin is depicting 'in a white dress against a Spanish background, and [who] does not understand what a horrid, lacy grotesque that makes ...' (*USSR* 130), is, as Babikov convincingly demonstrates, the character Death transposed into Nabokov's drama from Russia's *balagan* tradition of folk puppet shows (Babikov 153). In keeping with her folk-art source, she speaks in verse and offers chorus-like commentary on the events of the play. Her rhymed speech, as Nabokov's recourse to verse, is more than a sign of her folk-drama roots; it is also the signalling of a switch in the narrative to the lyric and irrational. This rending of the narrative texture of the play is analogous to Troshcheykin's lyric address to a mental audience in the delirium shared with his wife. The plot-shifting appearance of Death is thus paralleled by an alteration in narrative format. It is this form of strategic inclusion of verse, along with themes and motifs from his own poetry, that Nabokov would develop still further in *The Waltz Invention*.

The Waltz Invention: The Lyric Consolation of Fantasy

The preceding overview of Nabokov's plays is intended to exemplify the metamorphosis of Nabokov's poetic interests into drama, both as a demonstration of the versatility of his lyric sensibility and as illustration of the critical necessity of awareness of the character of his lyric voice as a prerequisite for full understanding of his too rarely discussed body of dramatic works. The same critical goal and intended interpretive outcome applies doubly well to Nabokov's next and final full-length play, *The Waltz Invention*. First published in November 1938, *The Waltz Invention* was composed by Nabokov in the wake of the astounding success of *The Event* for production with the Parisian 'Russian Theatre,' again under Iurii

Annenkov's direction and set design. Unfortunately, a conflict between Annenkov and the 'Russian Theatre,' and the onset of the Second World War, led to the abandonment of the project and the failure to mount a production for Nabokov's émigré audience. The play was eventually translated by Dmitri Nabokov for publication in English in 1966 and first produced, in Russian, at Oxford in 1968.[9] Thanks undoubtedly to its early translation into English, *The Waltz Invention* is one of the best known of Nabokov's in general little known plays. Despite the greater amount of commentary accorded it – relative to Nabokov's other dramatic works – increased familiarity has not guaranteed attendant critical understanding, much less acceptance.[10] Galya Diment is certainly representative in her reading of *The Waltz Invention* when she suggests that 'it is, perhaps, the weakest of his longer plays' (Diment 1995, 594). The 'perhaps' in Diment's statement is not inappropriate; for *The Waltz Invention* trails a history of tentative responses which, as often as not, reach in their interpretive uncertainty for comparison with other works as sources of interesting, though necessarily indirect, interpretive purchase rather than detailed analysis. Georgii Adamovich, writing in *Poslednie novosti* (*The Latest News*) in 1938, for instance, proposed Blok's *Балаганчик* (*Balaganchik / The Puppet Show*) as the source and superior model for the conception of Nabokov's play:

> Precisely at the end of the play, remembrance of the very kinship which Sirin himself would likely deny arises of its own accord. What is it similar to? To what is that return of sound thought to its rights after its long ordeal close to? To *The Puppet Show,* of course. *An entirely different tone, much less lyricism, much more concession to topicality*, but the techniques are the same. (Adamovich 1938, 3; emphasis added)

Despite the listed differences between the two plays, Adamovich allows the negative comparison to stand without elucidating its critical worth for an understanding of Nabokov's play. In a letter of 1943 to Nabokov, Edmund Wilson recorded his disappointed reading of *The Waltz Invention* – in an unattributed English translation – in a statement which, more than indicating a differentiated response, betrays the irritation of miscomprehension: 'The first scenes amused me, but I don't think there is enough to the idea to make it last through three acts – also, the unreality of everything gets on the reader's nerves before he understands that it is all a fantasy in the madman's mind; when he does find that out, he feels sold' (*NWL* 108). Andrew Field, in *Nabokov: His Life in Art*, described the play as both 'political' and Gogolian, 'a play about mistaken intention, political and sexual' (Field 1967,

210) best discussed through comparison to Shakespeare's *Twelfth Night*. Brian Boyd, in *Vladimir Nabokov: The Russian Years,* sees '[a] lightweight nightmare, a study in insanity, a succession of comic one-liners and dramatic sight gags, and a fable about the puerility of political or any other dreams ...' (Boyd 1990, 489), which owes something to the Nighttown scene from Joyce's *Ulysses*. Simon Karlinsky's article 'Illusion, Reality and Parody in Nabokov's Plays,' which described *The Waltz Invention* as 'major and typical Nabokov,' is distinguished as the fullest discussion of the play to date and the only one which attempts to place it within a system of references derived from Nabokov's artistry rather than purported external influences.

The critical consternation and attendant collection of hesitant, qualified interpretations elicited by this play is understandable; *The Waltz Invention* is a challenging and highly unusual play. It is also, however, one of Nabokov's finest artistic achievements and certainly his greatest play. It is also a play which most fully unfolds through awareness of Nabokov's lyric sensibility. Brilliant in its verbal manipulations and expressions of the manic energies of the farcical and the subdued pain of a broken consciousness, *The Waltz Invention* in its original Russian achieves the paradoxical effect of a representation of unspoken tragedy via recourse to comic instruments. Parallel to the creation of a tragic-comic symbiosis in the play's language is the thematic merging of the harrowing and the ludic in the representation of 'external' slap-stick stage action which simultaneously depicts the 'internal' drama of a man caught suffering in the quagmire of his own memories and consciousness. To a degree greater than either *The Man from the USSR* or *The Event*, Nabokov in *The Waltz Invention* achieves subtle representation of an essential subterranean theme through skilled reference to scenes visible through the semi-transparent surface texture of the play. Shining through the farce of Waltz's onstage antics is the submerged tragedy of Tourvalski's life. In this masking of the pitiable in the comic, *The Waltz Invention* seems an important forerunner to *Pale Fire*. While in particulars the play is comparable to Calderón, Shakespeare, Blok, Strindberg, Joyce, and others, critical understanding is only supported, not significantly furthered, by reference to works external to Nabokov's oeuvre.[11] Reference to the socio-political reality exterior to the play is likewise of marginal value in assessing it. Despite the presence of inviting geopolitical allusions extending from Stalin to a – in 1938 – prophetic atomic bomb, Nabokov may confidently be taken at his word when in the foreword to the English translation he claims the absence of any political message: '... I wish to point out most emphatically that not only is there in my play no political "message" (to borrow a cant word from the jargon of quack reform) but that publication of its English version today has no topical import ...' (*WI* i). The import of the play is of the non-discursive form native to poetry. Nabokov's sole request voiced in the same foreword was that future productions – and, presumably, readers – of the play 'take into account the *poetry* and the *pathos* underlying the bright demented dream' (*WI* iii; emphsis added). It is the explicit claim of the following reading that *only* through attentiveness to the poetry and pathos of Nabokov's lyric voice is the play able to release its full artistic effect.

Retreating from the social and familial setting of his two previous plays to the enclosed, private space of consciousness, the three-act *The Waltz Invention* recounts the fantastical adventures of poet-inventor Salvator Waltz. Waltz begins the play awaiting an audience with a minister of war to inform him of his invention, a fabulous machine capable of causing tremendous explosions anywhere in the world. Initially rebuffed and demeaned as crazy, Waltz, by virtue of his personal control over his machine, first destroys the beautiful mountain visible from the window of the minister's office; then, with the help of an androgynous factotum, Trance (in Nabokov's original Russian, Сон / *Son*, or Dream), Waltz proceeds to seize absolute power in his non-specified homeland with the intention of subduing a warlike neighbouring country and of inaugurating a new era of freedom and creativity the world over.[12] Rather than exercising his dictatorial power in the realization of his dream of a new age, however, Waltz abuses his power in the fulfillment of his increasingly capricious and sordid personal desires, which have progressively descended from the heights of ideal achievements to the fulfillment of base physical urges. Unable to fulfill his final wish, the seduction of the seventeen-year-old daughter of General Berg, Waltz's entire world collapses; his trusted aide, Trance, abandons him, and the game abruptly ends with Waltz awakening from his phantasmagoria to find the mountain returned to its place and himself seated in a waiting room pleading an audience with the minister of war. The events of the play have returned full circle to their beginnings and are revealed to have been nothing more than the delusions of a deranged man, who, in the final scene, is forcibly removed to an insane asylum. Waltz, in effect, concludes his mental *tour de valse* to 'awake' from the dream of the play to the, for him, nightmare of reality.

This brief introduction can do little to convey the bizarre atmosphere of comedy, tragedy, and insanity evoked in Nabokov's play. Laconically deemed a 'Drama' by Nabokov, *The Waltz Invention*, with its grotesque combination of lyrical poetry, subdued emotional pain, and manic, farcical activity, approximates the absurdist dimensions of an Ionesco or Beckett.

Indeed, given the form and breakneck pace of this play, it would be possible to argue that Nabokov was already in 1938 practising a form of Theatre of the Absurd, *avant la lettre*. As in theatre of the absurd, events transpire in an indeterminate setting where levels of being – dream and reality – seem to merge and part randomly. Moreover, like the characters of much absurdist drama, the dramatis personae of *The Waltz Invention* are figures of radically indeterminate status. Apart from the recognizably human characters Waltz, the Minister of War, his aide the colonel, and General Berg, a cast of less conventional characters populate Nabokov's stage: among them Waltz's helper, the androgynous figure 'Trance,' an invisible President of the republic, and a succession of suggestively named generals, who appear throughout the play in various roles – Berg, Brig, Breg, Gerb, Grob, Grab, Grib, Gorb, Burg, Brug (of these, one is dumb, while the final three are literally stuffed dummies).[13] Completing the cast of characters is also General Berg's mysterious, fairy-tale-like daughter, Annabella. Furthermore, as in theatre of the absurd, language in *The Waltz Invention* occasionally slips the referential moorings tying signifier to signified to become less a medium of rational communication than, at best, a locus for puns and play, and, at worst, the source of failed communication and incomprehensibility. The ludic puns and linguistic acrobatics – for the characters of the play, often a frustrating source of misunderstanding – provide the audience with unexpected access to dimensions of meaning foreclosed to literal denotation. The events of the play themselves seem beyond the realm of discernible, rational motivation, stemming instead from the highly subjective experience of the main character, Salvator Waltz. The plot of the play proceeds, not according to a system of naturalistic, causal development, but more as the externalization of Waltz's personal fears, memories, and megalomania.[14] Despite these similarities, Nabokov nonetheless diverges from the characteristics of the theatre of the absurd as developed by critics in reference to post-war playwrights in his typically Nabokovian refusal to admit abstract, meta-critically formulated theories of being in explanation for the state of affairs depicted in his play. For Nabokov, the inability of his characters to communicate is not a comment on the nature of language, but the individually determined problem of one person. Similarly, the intimations of tragedy suggested by Waltz are not the result of some inchoately felt existential angst, but the residual effect of painful experiences and the memory of deep, personal loss. In short, it is not the loss of God or other abstract 'meta-narratives' of belief which makes Waltz's life intolerable, but the pain of living in a world unresponsive to the depth and specificity of his intensely individual, and hence incommunicable, experience. *The Waltz*

Invention depicts, not an irrational world, but a world gone irrational for
one man, with lyricism forming the portal to the metaphysical depths signalled by the irrationality of the play.

That Nabokov should associate poetry with the depiction of the irrational in *The Waltz Invention* is consistent with the predominant characteristics of his poetic identity, which priorized the irrational, and with
various discursive statements made by Nabokov concerning both poetry
and a poetics of the theatre. Nabokov's dramaturgy indicates clear parallels to the sensibility which emerges from his verse writing. In reference to
the poetry of Gogol's *The Inspector General*, for instance, Nabokov famously conflated poetry and Gogol's drama to 'poetry in action, and by
poetry I mean the mysteries of the irrational as perceived through rational
words' (*NG* 55). In an article entitled 'The Tragedy of Tragedy,' Nabokov
specified still further his ideals concerning a poetics of the theatre, in a series of statements which seem highly significant to both his poetic practice
and *The Waltz Invention*: 'The highest achievements in poetry, prose, painting, showmanship are characterized by the irrational and illogical, by that
spirit of free will that snaps its rainbow fingers in the face of smug causality' (*USSR* 326). In the same essay, Nabokov goes on to suggest the mixing
of the grotesque and the tragic in the form of 'dream-plays,' which he held
to be the summit of dramatic production:

> I doubt that any strict line can be drawn between the tragic and the burlesque,
> fatality and chance, causal subjection and the caprice of free will. What seems
> to me to be the higher form of tragedy is the creation of a certain unique pat-
> tern of life in which the sorrows and passing of a particular man will follow
> the rules of his own individuality, not the rules of the theatre as we know
> them. (*USSR* 341)

In his mature dramatic works, Nabokov was striving for a form of theatre
wherein the events on the stage would slip the chains of causality and deter-
minism to dramatize the 'tragedies of real life [which] are based on the
beauty or horror of chance' (*USSR* 341). Furthermore, Nabokov sought to
effect the inclusion of poetry into dramatic art by bringing to his drama not
merely verse form but the concern for irrationality and the metaphysical
along with the acute attention to the minutia of life which characterize his
own poetic practice. These principles of a *lyric* poetics of the theatre
Nabokov implemented to fullest effect in *The Waltz Invention*. For the
Nabokov of the article 'Playwriting,' '… the best plays are generally a combination of both action and poetry' (*USSR* 319), and in the absence of

awareness of the function and presence of poetry in his drama, the action of the play seems incomprehensible. The influence of Nabokov's poetry and lyric sensibility is to be distinguished in *The Waltz Invention* at two levels: in the equation of essential features of Nabokov's poetic identity with the thematic concerns which lend the play its deceptive depth; and in the strategic inclusion of verse within the prose text of the play. The narrative shifts to examples of formal poetry drive the plot forward by indicating lesions in the levels of reality imagined by the increasingly delusional central protagonist, while the lyric sensibility embedded within the play's thematics indicates the workings of a creative consciousness, here twisted and tormented to destruction by memories of suffering. A reading of *The Waltz Invention* attentive to the 'poetry and the pathos underlying the bright demented dream' is necessarily returned to Nabokov's lyric sensibility.

As with so much of Nabokov's writing, the central point of entrance into the play is the topic of consciousness, here the consciousness of the central character, Waltz. In one of the at once earliest and most prescient – and by now most famous – statements regarding Nabokov, Vladislav Khodasevich suggested that Nabokov's writing is dominated by a central theme – that of the nature of the creative imagination and, similarly, the fundamental loneliness of the individual or artist possessed of such creativity (Khodasevich 1937, 9).[15] In pursuing this idea, Khodasevich further suggested that the artists in Nabokov's works often wore a mask of sorts disguising the nature of their creativity. Both comments seem particularly apt with regard to Salvator Waltz of *The Waltz Invention*. For in this play, it becomes apparent that the drama, the tragedy of the central protagonist's life, is his inability to reconcile his abilities and desires with the blunt forces of reality, those forces which have inverted the dream of life into a nightmare and have produced the experiences of deprivation and pain intimated in the play. And like a host of other creative individuals from Nabokov's works who find themselves confronted with a hostile, nightmarish world – a world which has become 'an unending horror,' in Robert's phrasing from *The Wanderers* – the artist *manqué* Waltz seeks refuge first in a comforting counter-dream – the misdirected art and action of the play. When this too fails, he threatens simply to explode the 'device' behind both his marvellous weapon and the play – his imaginative consciousness.

That Waltz is an author and thus possessed of an artist's sensibility is suggested at various levels in the play. In the listing of the dramatis personae for the English translation, Nabokov identifies Waltz explicitly as 'a haggard inventor; a fellow author.' Apart from this authorial intervention by Nabokov, however, there are a host of other indicators which suggest

Waltz's creative occupation. Waltz designates himself an inventor; he pointedly demonstrates a love of verbal precision; his factotum, Trance, identifies him as a fellow artist; he is offended by the very suggestion that the product of his imagination could be contained within blueprints; and, most importantly, he admits to the authorship of poems, in particular, those which intrude with dramatic effect into the play's narrative. The secret to Waltz's identity resides less in the mere designation author, however, than in the artistic turn of his sensibility. From the beginning speeches of the play, delivered in the 'rather arcane' mode of Waltz's expression, he demonstrates his peculiar perspective on existence – 'Everything is odd in this world, Mr. Minister' (*Ssoch* V, 523; *WI* 10). Waltz literally sees the world differently than others. Beginning with the play's comic opening scene, which has the colonel attempting to remove a speck from the minister's eye, *The Waltz Invention* is interspersed with a series of puns and suggestive references to impaired and enhanced vision, all of which derive from Waltz's experience. As a child, Waltz suffered a form of the 'wondrous illness' endemic to Nabokov's creative heroes. In this instance, the shock to perception was occasioned by a case of 'optical glow' caused by the lodging of something in his eye, with the result that 'for a whole month everything I saw was a beautiful pink, as if I were looking through the stained-glass windows of the church of St. Rose' (*Ssoch* V, 523; *WI* 10). Waltz's speech describing his descent into 'a beautiful pink' not only has him employ a window motif central to Nabokov's poetry, but indicates that due to his youthful infirmity, he has experienced the mysterious privilege of wondrous sight, an outlook and temper derived from an uncommon perspective on the world. As the events depicted onstage are the product of Waltz's consciousness, both the minister and the audience are compelled to view and enact the world *as Waltz sees it*. Vision on both sides of the stage lights is at once enriched and blinded by the stardust cast by Waltz's fancy. The mysteries of perception and sight, a trait central to Nabokov's lyric sensibility, are of defining relevance to *The Waltz Invention*.

Attendant to the exceptional faculties suggested by his history of 'optical glow' is Waltz's control of time. In suggestion of the Nabokovian creative consciousness suspended outside of time, the three-act traffic of time on the stage is revealed in the last scene to have been but a moment in Waltz's imagination. In *The Event*, the pivotal scene of the play occurs in the interconnected minds of Lyubov' and Troshcheykin in the time it takes Ryovshin to open the bottle of champagne wedged between his legs; in *The Waltz Invention*, fantasy is suspended between Waltz's act-one comment on the mountain seen from the window to the colonel's third-act opening of the same window out onto the mountain. It is the window which provides an aperture to another time and mental space. Within the universe of the play as well, however, Waltz contests his mastery of time. In response to the time-pressed minister of war, Waltz thunders that he controls the advance of time: 'Don't you dare talk to me of time! It is I who am in charge of time...' (*Ssoch* V, 526; *WI* 15). Waltz's personal mastery over time and space – his machine can access any point on the globe – is but the pinnacle of the artist's subjugation of the rational, the scientific, the rules of nature. Waltz thus appropriately advises the minister and the colonel to deflect their reason, to surrender their reason to him (*Ssoch* V, 527; *WI* 15). And when Waltz succeeds in achieving the impossible in his destruction of the mountain, it is generally to be conceded with Trance that 'Mr. Waltz has tripped Mother Nature and made her fall flat on her face' (*Ssoch* V, 538; *WI* 33). The minister of war, the colonel, and their servants may frantically search for geographical explanations for the disappearance of the mountain and seek comfort in the listing of facts related to the event, but it remains that Waltz has made the irrational real. And finally, in strengthening the assumption that Waltz's is a creative consciousness in a Nabokovian sense, is the presence of Trance. Upon the recognition that Waltz has subdued rationality in the destruction of the mountain, there appears from the enclosed space of a closet a figure who is half inspirational muse, half facilitator. One of the 'stage-helper' embodiments of Nabokov's artistry in the sense identified by Khodasevich, Trance seems, in her mysterious comings and goings, a personification of inspiration and the creative process, a muse of sorts.[16] Throughout the play, Trance repeatedly arrives to serve Waltz's fantasy when the further development of his dream seems threatened. Conversely, at the end of the play, Waltz's dream explodes when Trance is no longer able to satisfy his wishes. *The Waltz Invention* thus displays many features derived from a Nabokovian conception of the artist which combine to assure Waltz's identity as a poet-artist. As an author-inventor, the convalescent of a 'wondrous illness,' the master of time and space, and a sovereign served by Trance, Waltz, although an artist, is also a kind of freak in his idiosyncrasy and particular form of madness. This, too, is a designation understood by Nabokov as a portion of the artist's difference, and described by him in 'The Art of Literature and Commonsense' as follows: 'The meek prophet, the enchanter in his cave, the indignant artist, the nonconforming little schoolboy, all share in the same sacred danger [of the mob's displeasure]. And this being so let us bless them, let us bless the freak ...' (*LL* 372). Waltz is an artist made indignant, literally driven mad, by the strokes of fate.

The Waltz Invention blesses, or at least pities, Waltz as a poet-freak, a 'dreamer' given over to 'irrational and divine standards during the darkest and most dazzling hours of physical danger, pain, dust, death' (*LL* 373). And it is in the particular shape of Waltz's dream, and its disintegration into delusion, that the specificity of his history is told, the subterranean focus of the play. As in *The Event*, where the secondary 'event' of the death of a child protrudes into the foreground of action, likewise in *The Waltz Invention*, the play's quiddity lies in the tragedy of Waltz's unexplained personal history shining through the semi-transparent surface of farce.[17] Of central importance here is Waltz's first dramatic exploit, the destruction of the mountain viewed from the minister of war's window. A violent act carried out in the fantasy of a deranged man, the motivation for this deed may only be presumed, and yet, within the distorted logic of the play, a rationale may be perceived which is based on Waltz's personal tragedy, his assumed experience of 'dazzling hours of physical danger, pain, dust, death.' Waltz's heartfelt sympathy for those whose worlds have crumbled about them, the accumulation of veiled reference to memories of past psychic pain, his obsession with changing the world, and the pronounced linguistic counterplay between '*gora*' and '*gore*' (in Russian, 'mountain' and 'woe') invite the interpretation that the mountain he has destroyed at exactly twelve o'clock noon is a metaphor for the brute, unmovable reality which seems to have been the source of his suffering.[18] In his desperation and anguish, Waltz is erasing, blowing up, subjecting to his control, the implacable reality which has determined his fate and rendered his life unbearable.

The exact nature of Waltz's suffering is never clearly identified, though from within the cocoon of his protective dream, references are made to terrible privations which have pursued him there in the form of memory. After the destruction of the mountain of woe and his decision forcefully to subordinate reality to his will, for instance, Waltz expresses his sympathy with the sufferers of the world in a speech of lyric imagery which suggests the desperation of his enterprise:

… I am a humane man, much more humane than you can even imagine. You say that you have endured many things in your lifetime. Allow me to say that *my* life has consisted of such material privations, of such mental torments that now, when everything is about to change, I still feel behind my back the raw cold of the past as, after a stormy night, one still feels an ominous chill in the morning shadows of the glistening garden. I feel sorry for you, I sympathize with the stabbing pain that every man experiences when his habitual world, the familiar order of life, crumbles around him. However, I must carry out my plan. (*Ssoch* V, 535; *WI* 47)

Besides containing reference to a liminal state in the poetic imagery of dawn, Waltz's confession, in its pronounced shift to lyric expression, indicates that it is motivated by experience which occurred at a level of reality different from that of his grandiloquent fantasy, which is voiced in a different register. Moreover, it suggests that his 'plan,' his descent into the escape of fantasy, is a final desperate attempt to escape the furies of memory and real-world experience. More focused instances of the shining through of real deprivation into his protective dream are the frequent appearances of 'trifles' planted in the play's narrative. Unmotivated even by the internal logic of Waltz's fantasy, these extraneous details derive from a different level of experience and are united in their suggestion of painful associations with childhood and/or a child. In the course of the play, Waltz finds an atlas, recognizable by a stain, which belonged to him as a boy and, on three occasions, has his fantasy interrupted by the appearance of toys. The final memory provoked by the unbidden association with a toy is so strong and disturbing that Waltz, in his self-protective megalomania, orders the closing of all toy stores. The fantasy dictator Waltz wishes to take action to blot out all associations with toys suggesting a painful memory of either his own youth or a child.[19] Apart from the trifles of childhood, however, the most intriguing and powerful indication of the tragedy of Waltz's past is his troubled interaction with Annabella.

First mentioned in a first-act telephone conversation regarding the death of Perrault, a teller of wonderful fairy tales, Annabella is the seventeen-year-old daughter of General Berg.[20] A mysterious character, she too is associated with a lyric sensibility in her uniting of love of the world, the recognition of the triflingly wondrous and magical in it, and her possible association with Waltz's youth.[21] In the concluding scene and speech of act one, Annabella confronts Waltz concerning the implications of his destruction of the mountain. Waltz may have destroyed reality's mountain of woe, though along with it he has also sacrificed an irreplaceable embodiment of reality's wonder, 'an old enchanter and a snow-white gazelle' (*Ssoch* V, 540; *WI* 37). Annabella reinforces a perception characteristic of Nabokov's poetry that the frightening world of insult and injury is also home to splendour. Both Annabella and her father, General Berg, are subsequently to pursue Waltz throughout the play as his interest in the seventeen-year-old develops into an obsession. By the end of act three, when Waltz has exhausted all the potential of his dictatorial desire, he insists on possessing Annabella erotically. General Berg's refusal to release her to him; his insistence that she is hidden 'abroad' in a place he will never gain access to; the confused insinuation that she may indeed be dead and 'in the next world'; and finally the suggestion that she is hidden as well as his machine or, in other words, resident only in his consciousness, combine finally to rend the delicate fabric of Waltz's three-act dream. Annabella's permanent disappearance, Trance's inability to conjure her forth, and General Berg's refusal to recall her from 'abroad' lead – more than anything else – to the definitive puncturing of Waltz's fantasy. Annabella's eternal, inexplicable absence seems both the summit of Waltz's earthly, real-world despair and, internal to his fantasy, the catalyst for a final climax ruinous to his dream-world: 'I can't stand it any longer … Where is she, where is she, where is she?' (*Ssoch* V, 582; *WI* 108). Recognition that she is equally inaccessible in both realms – the real and the fantastical – grants disastrous evidence of the supremacy of the real over his dream. Death intrudes into his phantasmagoria. No longer immune from the pain of the world, Waltz's fantasy collapses. Trance, too, is powerless against death, and her comment 'Alas, the game is up' (*Ssoch* V, 582; *WI* 109) applies equally to Waltz's fantasy and the play. Waltz is promptly returned to the vulgar reality of his life as an insignificant little man waiting for an interview with the minister of war. Sitting in a waiting-room, he gazes out through the window to a resurrected mountain. General Berg, whose German name means mountain, seems with his refusal to release Annabella to have exhumed the exploded mountain of blunt reality and Waltz's inability to reverse the brute pain, the woe, of life, embodied here in the permanent absence and possible death of a young girl.[22]

The thematic relevance of Annabella's presence in the play is mirrored further in the most direct examples of the presence of Nabokov's poetry and lyric voice in *The Waltz Invention*. Beyond the play's deployment of themes and motifs suggestive of a specifically Nabokovian approach to artistic consciousness and the lyric representation of both the suffering and wonder of the world, the inclusion of verse into the prose narrative demonstrates the centrality of poetry to an understanding of this play. In parodic acknowledgment of the Platonic division of the levels of reality, *The Waltz Invention* takes place on three planes of being. The cave of Waltz's disturbed consciousness forms the central stage of the action, with the offstage world of reality glimpsed through troubled associations with childhood forming another level, and the megalomaniacal dream of a better world comprising still another. While Waltz's fantasy is composed in prose, access to the other two realms of being is represented in and by verse. It is thus in the strategic inclusion of verse within the play that narrative fissures are opened allowing the revelation of thematic material from unseen depths within the play.

The first example of evidence of the thinning of the material separating Waltz's fantasy and the reality of his bitter experience is contained in a poem which reaches back to reality to illuminate Waltz's delusion. In act two, during a farcical conference convened by the generals to evaluate the ramifications of Waltz's power, Gerb, one of the generals, abruptly steps forward and recites a poem, 'To My Soul':

My soul, how fierce is your impatience,
How gladly home you would have flown,
Out of the marvelously fashioned,
But much too narrow cage of bone!

Your home I do not know, believe me!
Even the way there, is not clear,
And when you fly, how shall I follow
With so much booty taken here?   (*Ssoch* V, 548; *WI* 50)

The poem is discovered to have been assigned to General Gerb as a form of homework. The poem is by Tourvalski, Waltz himself, for Waltz admitted to having written poetry and, more importantly, his is the controlling consciousness behind all of the events of the 'dream-play' and thus the only figure capable of 'assigning' tasks to the characters. Like Annabella's implied rebuke at the end of act one regarding the enchanter and gazelle destroyed by Waltz in his destruction of the mountain, 'To My Soul' by Tourvalski/Waltz is a clear example both of Nabokov's metaphysical poetry and the dilemma tormenting the benighted Waltz. 'To My Soul' presents a Platonic vision of the body as a cage of bone imprisoning the spirit in a form of profane exile from a transcendent state. And while consciousness sympathizes with the soul's urge to return to its native realm, the loss of the booty collected in the living world is also feared. Although a place of pain and suffering, the world is also home to treasures of consciousness, the trifling memories and impressions of life. The poet Waltz-Tourvalski may wish to subdue and escape the torments of life, but in destroying the 'mountain of woe,' he will also be forced to forego the enchanting beauty of the pied and pulsing world. 'To My Soul' seems a belated plea from and for the three-dimensional world of Tourvalski's reality before his fantasy as Waltz takes flight.

Further explicit use of poetry in *The Waltz Invention* comes in Waltz's description of the era he wishes to inaugurate on earth after his seizure of total control. Upon clarifying that he intends nothing less than personal control of the world, that the power he wields will not be released to others, Waltz announces the start of a new world order: 'Attention, Gentlemen! I now declare / The start of a new life. Be welcome, Life!' (*Ssoch* V, 557; *WI* 65). Following his announcement, Waltz describes the era he intends to enforce in extended speeches of blank iambic verse. Reminiscent of the *belle époque* presided over in Zembla by Charles II, alias Kinbote, of *Pale Fire*, the dream of a better world Waltz describes, while nobly intended, reveals itself to be an almost hysterical mixture of utopian vision and random authoritarian *dictat*, a hybrid of lyric poetry and a socialist realist paean to a future decreed shining. The world Waltz has ordained in his poetic manifesto will be a place where labour, games, poetry, and science thrive, but also a place where people, like children, are forced into obedience and acts of good will by the knowledge that Waltz is capable of destroying them. In essence, Waltz's blank verse manifesto is a promise to institute a civic order reminiscent of Plato's plans from *The Republic*.[23] This grotesque poem is not merely a momentary shift to another level of fantasy from within Waltz's dream, it is also a perversion of Nabokov's lyric sentiment. Parodic of Nabokov's poetic voice in its deployment of, for instance, imagery of a window and its depiction of access to metaphysical mysteries during the transports of poetic inspiration, Waltz's blank verse form is an inversion of Nabokov's lyricism. Not only is Nabokov's beloved memory of the past threatened in Waltz's regime, but the wonder of artistic consciousness is used, not in the celebration of individual perception, but in the forced imposition of common understanding. The following partial citation indicates both the source in, and distortion of, Nabokov's lyric voice:

> Gone is the old and musty world. Now Spring
> Through Time's wide-open window rushes in,
> And I who stand before you, am today –
> Though yesterday a pauper and a dreamer –
> Master omnipotent of every land.
> I have been called to renovate the world
> And roll away toward the nearest exit
> The ashcans of the Past. Oh, blissful toil!
> ...
> Oh, blissful toil! Long have I tried to solve
> The problem of your world – that problem – bristling
> With such uncertain data, spectral numbers,
> And obstacles, and traps for a man's mind!
> Long have I tried to solve or give it up
> Till suddenly the live spark of the 'X'

Burst into flame and furnished the solution.
Now all is clear to me. My secret engine
Is surer than hereditary crowns,
Popular vote, or a dictator's fury.
Not that I wish to sop my reign in kindness:
A threat can work much better with a child
Than any persuasion; lessons based
On fear are lessons rammed into the marrow.
...
                A ghost alone is free,
But men should always feel a boundary,
Material fences that affirm existence.   (*Ssoch* V, 557–9; *WI* 66–8)

The threatening, megalomaniacal undertone of this 'poem' foreshadows the direction Waltz's reign subsequently takes immediately after the delivery of his blank verse speech and the abdication of the invisible president of the republic. The inclusion of this poem thus not only reflects upon the troubled state of Waltz's controlling consciousness but drives the action of the play forward.

In the third and final act of the play, Waltz's reign of dictatorial power is revealed to be less than the paradise he expected. In an attempt to attain the heights of lyric idealism, Waltz is mired in the prosaic concerns of the state under his dictatorial control. Not only is he forced to attend to the workings of the nation, which has suffered since his takeover; his aide, the colonel, insinuates that he is both incompetent and mad; an assassination attempt is made on him; he is driven to the destruction of the significantly named city 'Santa Morgana' in a warlike demonstration of his power; and, finally, his aide Trance does not always appear when needed. Waltz's fantasy of power ebbs and he seeks, within his dream, a form of physical flight which mirrors his mental escape. Waltz prepares to leave for the contained and isolated space of a paradisiacal island, Palmora Island. Before going, however, Waltz demands the fulfillment of a series of desires which reveal the degradation of his noble plans for the inauguration of a new world to the base satisfaction of animalistic urges. Waltz commissions Trance to assemble for him thirty of the most beautiful, desirable women of the realm. Instead of producing beauty, Trance delivers two prostitutes and three physically grotesque women. As Waltz correctly recognizes, these women are a vulgar profanation of what he wished for, which is the unacknowledged quintessence of Annabella's attraction: 'What good is such trash to me? I asked you for youth, beauty, innocence, tenderness, languor, peach bloom, fragility, grace, dreaminess ...' (*Ssoch* V, 579; *WI* 103). The deterioration of Waltz's fantasy is heightened when one of the 'hags' – the inversion of Annabella – begins to recite a doleful convict's song, which Waltz recognizes as his own verse. The intrusion again of Tourvalski's verse into Waltz's dream represents a third inclusion of poetry into the narrative and a further alteration in Waltz's consciousness. In this instance, the song is an imitation of a *tsyganskii romans* (gypsy romance) set to the melody of A.I. Beshentsov's popular 'Romans.'[24] Steeped in parody, the inclusion of this strange song about arrest and exile also suggests the incursion of Waltz's actual past as Tourvalski into his by now fading dream and thus the shining through of reality into the protective cocoon of his delusion. All that is left is the previously discussed refusal of Waltz's desire for the return of a possibly dead girl to effect his ejection from what was once the pleasant dream-space of an inspired though delusional fantasy to the nightmare of reality. With the reassertion of the mountain of woe's implacable presence in both Waltz's life and fantasy, Tourvalski's *tour de valse* is ended. The play's last scene has Waltz forcibly removed to an insane asylum by Grib, Grab, and Grob (in Russian, fungus, pillage, and grave) in a manner reminiscent of Robert's comparison of life to 'the unending horror / of the regaining of consciousness of a corpse in sepulchral / lodgings' in *The Wanderers*. Confronted with this living burial in the nightmare of reality, Waltz is left threatening that he will explode. The fantasy has ended, the play is over.

Waltz's exiting threat that he is capable of exploding is the final motif from *The Waltz Invention* which connects the benighted Waltz to a distinguished brotherhood of poets and failed artists from Nabokov's fictional universe who escape the pain of existence through retreat to another realm. *The Waltz Invention*, however, is more than the drama of a failed poet. Like all of Nabokov's dramas, *The Waltz Invention* reveals the play of Nabokov's lyric sensibility in a non-poetic genre. It is no exaggeration to claim that the innovation and specificity of Nabokov's various plays – although perhaps also the source of their relative misunderstanding and neglect – is born of the workings of his lyric interests. Formally, and especially thematically, Nabokov's poetic concern for the wonder of this world and the mystery of the otherworld merged into his practice of dramaturgy to lend his expressions of the form the unmistakable imprint of his lyric sensibility and voice. It is an imprint also to be found on his prose.

5 Nabokov and the Short Story: The Lyric Heights of a Small Alpine Form

... puerile, perishable poems, which, by the time the next were printed, would
have been certain to wither as had withered one after the other all the previous
ones written down in the black exercise book; but no matter: at this moment I
trust the ravishing promises of the still breathing, still revolving verse, my face
is wet with tears, my heart is bursting with happiness, and I know that this
happiness is the greatest thing existing on earth.
– Vladimir Nabokov, 'Torpid Smoke'

In 1939, less than a year before his departure for America and English prose,
Nabokov wrote his final Russian short story, 'Vasiliy Shishkov,' as the culminating instalment of an elaborate literary hoax born of his own poetic
practice and begun with a poem. Irked by the refusal of crudely tendentious
critics to grant his verse a non-partisan reading, Nabokov had published
his poem 'Поэты' ('Poety' / 'The Poets') in *Sovremennye zapiski* under the
pseudonym Vasiliy Shishkov. Recognizing the appearance of accomplished
verse when he saw it, the influential émigré critic and Nabokov's literary foe
Georgi Adamovich swallowed Nabokov's carefully set bait; in his subsequent review of the journal, Adamovich praised the poem and asked:
'... who is this Vasiliy Shishkov? Where does he come from? It is quite possible that in a year or two everyone to whom Russian poetry is dear will
know his name.'[1] In answer to Adamovich, and as the revelatory climax to
his hoax, Nabokov published a short story which provided the fictitious
poet with an equally fictitious, and quintessentially Nabokovian, past. The
story 'Vasiliy Shishkov' tells the tale of the narrator's brief acquaintance
with a curious though gifted émigré poet, the fictional Shishkov. In despair
at the failure of his venture to establish a journal and despondent about the

prospects of languishing in obscurity despite his genuine talent, Shishkov – to the considerable perplexity of the first-person narrator – simply vanishes at the conclusion of the story, returning as it were to the fictional realm from which he had emerged. 'Vasiliy Shishkov' concludes with the narrator's musings about the mystery of the departed poet's dissolution and two lines of his verse:

> But where the deuce did he go? And, generally speaking, what did he have in mind when he said he intended 'to disappear, to dissolve'? Cannot it actually be that in a wildly literal sense, unacceptable to one's reason, he meant disappearing in his art, dissolving in his verse, thus leaving of himself, of his nebulous person, nothing but verse? One wonders if he did not overestimate
> *The transparence and soundness*
> *Of such an unusual coffin. (Ssoch V, 413; Stories 419)*

For readers of Nabokov's verse, who are thereby familiar with its lyric acceptance of things 'unacceptable to one's reason,' the poet Shishkov's dissolution into another realm is mysterious, though certainly not unprecedented. In the startling finality of his departure from a troubled world of insult and vulgarity, Shishkov joins a select fraternity from Nabokov's writing, including such poets as Waltz, who threatens to explode at the end of *The Waltz Invention*, and Konstantin Perov of 'A Forgotten Poet,' who also mysteriously disappears, albeit to return years later. Ultimately, however, interest in the story extends beyond its thematic contents and the context of its inception as a further episode in the spirited polemics of the émigré community. 'Vasiliy Shishkov' also invites reading as a form of self-commentary by Nabokov on the state of his literary identity as a poet at a crucial stage in his artistic career.

It is indeed intriguing that at the time of his immanent departure from émigré Europe and the Russian language, Nabokov should have concluded his final Russian story with the comparison of an accomplished though poorly acknowledged corpus of verse with a coffin. Nataliia Tolstaia, in her comprehensive article 'Russian Short Stories,' reads the conclusion to 'Vasiliy Shishkov' as a reference to Nabokov's perception of himself as a Russian and poet: 'This is the unusual way in which Nabokov parts with Russian poetry, and, more broadly, with all of Russia; he buries his Russian past and erects a gravestone of verses over himself as a poet. He considers this gravestone transparent enough to allow the poet himself – and the secret essence he expressed in his poems – to be seen' (Tolstaia 658).[2] In the following chapter, I intend to take up and modify Tolstaia's enticing observation as the catalyst for discussion of the shift of Nabokov's lyric sensibility from verse to prose. 'Vasiliy Shishkov,' at the end of Nabokov's corpus of Russian stories, functions not merely to mark the resting place of his verse, but to signal its unusual burial in another generic form. Previous to the individual story 'Vasiliy Shishkov,' the quintessence of Nabokov's lyric voice – what Tolstaia refers to as 'the secret essence he expressed in his poems' – was located in the very genre he deployed in announcing his departure from Russian verse. Rather than verse marking the passing of Shishkov (and Nabokov) from Russian poetry, it is the form of short fiction, and prose in general, which comprised 'such an unusual coffin' for Nabokov's quintessentially lyric temperament. In short, in countering the unremittingly linear reading of Nabokov's artistic development, which sees him progressing by stages out of a juvenile interest in poetry through several experiments in drama to artistic maturity in prose – first the short story and then the novel – I wish to suggest that Nabokov's success with the short story was based, not in rejection of his poetry, but in its continuation in, and unmistakable colouring of, his prose. Poetry, and the themes Nabokov first explored in his poetry, provide the primary colours which cast virtually everything he subsequently wrote in unmistakably lyric hues. Such a reading not only better conforms to the historical realities of Nabokov's artistic development, which was distinguished by the simultaneous practice of disparate genres throughout his career, but provides a source of interpretive purchase on a prose oeuvre characterized by the recurrence of a core of themes, motifs, and a particular stylistic voice, the traits suggestive of Nabokov's unified lyric identity as an artist.

Nabokov's first published short story, 'The Wood-Sprite,' appeared in the Berlin émigré newspaper *Rul'* in January 1921; his final (English) story, 'Lance,' was published in the *New Yorker* in February 1952. Within the intervening span of thirty-one years lie approximately seventy short narratives. The establishment of a conclusive corpus of stories is rendered difficult not only by the vagaries of an oeuvre produced and preserved under difficult personal and historical conditions,[3] but also by questions of generic definition and classification; hence, the resort to the noncommittal term, short narrative. As in so much of his writing, Nabokov's practice of the short story form complicates understanding of the structural stability of the genre itself. Various of Nabokov's narratives, while short, are not in the first instance short stories. 'Ultima Thule,' 'Solus Rex,' and 'Scenes from the Life of a Double Monster,' for instance, are portions from unfinished larger works. Similarly, 'Krug' ('The Circle') is reported by Nabokov to have separated itself off from the main body of *The Gift* to revolve around his greatest Russian novel like 'a small satellite.' The more overtly autobiographical 'Mademoiselle O,' after first publication in French, was translated into English and revised for inclusion as chapter 5 in Nabokov's autobiography

Conclusive Evidence.[4] Equally problematic as closely defined short stories, albeit for different reasons, are such beautifully composed, though almost plotless, narratives as, for instance, 'Gods' and 'A Guide to Berlin.' The inventive manipulation of form comprises a significant portion of Nabokov's originality as an artist, which necessarily complicates the discussion of genre in his work. It is likewise for this reason that Charles Nicol and Gennady Barabtarlo, in the introduction to their edited collection of essays, judiciously chose 'short fiction' as the subtitle of their book *A Small Alpine Form: Studies in Nabokov's Short Fiction*.

In confronting the difficulties of generic taxonomy, Nabokov himself seems – at first glance – to offer but modest help. His central authorial statement regarding the short story appears to promise little in terms of classificatory elucidation, although, as will be indicated below, it is essential to an understanding of his artistic practice. Asked by Stephen Jan Parker if he would 'care to venture a definition of the short story as a distinctive genre,' Nabokov made the following response:

> Many widespread species of Lepidoptera produce small, but not necessarily stunted, races above timberline. In relation to the typical novel the short story represents a small Alpine, or Polar, form. It looks different, but is conspecific with the novel and is linked to it by intermediate clines. (Parker 69)

For a practising author famously unmoved by restraining considerations of genre, school, or ideological motivation – in contrast to individual expressions of artistic achievement – Nabokov's disinclination to descend into the particulars of exclusive generic distinctions is both understandable and consistent. It is of a piece, for instance, with his famous refusal to mark a clear distinction at a more fundamental level of generic abstraction between poetry and prose: '... poetry, of course, includes all creative writing; I have never been able to see any generic difference between poetry and artistic prose' (*SO* 44). It also recalls the more dramatic instance of generic cross-identification suggested in his claim from 'Good Readers and Good Writers' that 'great novels are great fairy tales' (*LL* 2). Quite apart from his partisan critical perspective as an author understandably unwilling to concede restrictions of a generic nature on his writing, Nabokov is certainly not alone in seeing similarities as well as differences between the two prose forms of novel and short story. The critical tradition concerning short story theory admits of the possibility that no defining distinction is to be made between short story and novel. Suzanne C. Ferguson, for instance, has tendered the legitimate proposition that 'there is no large and distinguished corpus of short story theory because the short story does not exist as a discrete and independent genre' (Ferguson 13). Further to this, she proceeds to claim that 'there may be no rational way to distinguish "short story" from other narratives in the same mimetic mode: *all* stories, short and long, have certain required properties of narrativity – characters, place, events, a "beginning, middle, and an end," and coherence among the parts' (Ferguson 14). In seeming confirmation of this view, Nicol and Barabtarlo, in discussing Nabokov's conception of the short story genre, likewise allow a degree of conspecific similarity across all of Nabokov's fictions, whether long or short. Nonetheless, despite concessions of cross-generic similarity, they also delineate the means by which Nabokov's practice in short fiction reveals differences not merely of size but also of narrative quality, to the extent that it is possible to speak of a 'mode of artistic expression' different from his novels. In illustrating this claim, Nicol and Barabtarlo correctly emphasize differences between Nabokov's short stories and novels in terms of (1) unity of time and action, (2) narrative self-containedness, and (3) narrative voice, elements which, taken together, seem to suggest continuity with Nabokov's central artistic interests but a discernibly separate narrative manner in expressing them. The bamboo bridge connecting all of Nabokov's writing in its various generic expressions – to adopt a metaphor from Nabokov – is his lyric sensibility.

Thus the importance of critical awareness of Nabokov's lyric voice. The apparent conundrum born of the intrinsic generic indeterminacy of the short story form, of Nabokov's critical statements, and of the nature of his artistic practice across genres is less intractable when viewed from the perspective of Nabokov's poetic writing. Seen through the lens of his poetry, the ostensible discrepancy between theory and practice is less a Gordian knot to be cut – in this instance, with a slice of the critical knife irrevocably separating short story from novel and poetry from prose – than further demonstration of Nabokov's ingenuity in consistently deploying his central artistic vision – and voice – to weave a Nabokovian work of art, regardless of the generic strands being bound together. Sensitivity to the quality of Nabokov's lyric sensibility thus serves critical analysis of the fundamental consistency and distinctiveness of Nabokov's writing across a widely variegated oeuvre. The short story provides excellent illustration of this point, as examination of Nabokov's lyric manipulations of the short story form reveals the implementation of his poetic voice within prose. And it is with illustration of the presence of Nabokov's signature poetic voice in his short fiction that the remainder of this chapter will be concerned: first with a discussion of the structural parallels between the dominant conventions of the short story form and Nabokov's lyric voice; secondly, through a brief overview of the pervasive presence of those qualities previously isolated as definitive of Nabokov's lyric identity within selected examples of his short fiction; and thirdly, by means of a reading of the story 'Perfection' as a single illustration of how amenable Nabokov's lyric voice is to the generic principles of the short story. As in the case of Nabokov's facility in dramatic forms, his achievements in short fiction will be shown to be an extension of his poetic writing via other, in this instance prose, means. Nabokov's short prose narratives, I suggest, are most fruitfully read, not with critical focus fixed on questions of genre, though they certainly partake of conventions common to the short story, but as the expansion of his poetic sensibility into prose.

It was briefly observed above that the attempt to define the short story form is a critical task beset with perhaps insurmountable difficulties and, for Nabokov, a matter of secondary importance. In this context, the comments below are not intended as a contribution towards a structural definition of the short story but rather the delineation of those conventions shared by the short story in general and Nabokov's poetry, and thus further expressive of his lyric identity. That Nabokov should excel in the short story is to no small degree a function of the conspecificity of the form's generic essence and his lyric sensibility. Alberto Moravia, for instance, has suggested that the quintessence of the form is based in its defining lyricism: '... the principle qualities of the short story ... an exceedingly complex charm, deriving from a literary art which is unquestionably purer, more essential, more lyrical, more concentrated and more absolute than that of the novel' (Moravia 151). In seeking to distinguish the narrative source of this lyric density, most commentators on the short story, from Edgar Allan Poe onward, focus discussion on the form's manipulation of the unities of time and action.[5] Regardless of the physical length of stories in terms of words, compactness is essential to the form, with an impression of concentratedness being created through the narrative restriction of temporal and thematic scope. As Nicol and Barabtarlo indicate, this is also generally the case with Nabokov's short fictions: '... unlike his novels, most of Nabokov's short stories maintain a relative unity of time and almost all, of action' (Nicol and Barabtarlo x). Although unmentioned by Nicol and Barabtarlo, the unity of space is also a prominent feature of Nabokov's stories and a primary vehicle of their distinctive lyric quality, as will be discussed below. From the essential compactness of this form of narrative extend ramifications for plot, character, and language. The plot of the short story, for instance, is less concerned with the mimetic depiction of life in syncretic, representational fullness than with the creation of a prominent mood or atmosphere, the importance of which is frequently illustrated in a culminating revelatory moment of epiphany. Alterations in the function of short story plot, in contrast to longer narratives, affect its narrative development as well. Rather than proceed as a process of accumulation, the short story promotes 'the transformation of plot into pattern' (Rohrberger and Burns 6). Given the structural relevance of pattern to plot, the short story accentuates the importance of carefully placed motifs and the creation of plot layers, with a deceptive, surface layer camouflaging a second, metaphoric level which is accessible only upon rereading and the full disclosure of pattern.

Nabokov's stories are indeed to be categorized by the formal specificity of their plots and by their meticulous deployment of motifs in the creation of intricate patterns and plot layers.[6] The temporal and thematic unity of Nabokov's plots is maintained, as Nicol and Barabtarlo indicate, though it is in the creation of the unity of space that the importance of motifs and Nabokov's poetry is revealed. Throughout Nabokov's stories, the same motifs of containment and transition discussed in chapter 3 in reference to his poetry frequently serve as well the creation of lyrical tone and atmosphere in his stories. The world of Nabokov's stories repeatedly makes use of such spatially contained settings as lonely nighttime rooms with a single window (e.g., 'The Wood-Sprite,' 'The Thunderstorm,' 'Terror'), hotel rooms ('Wingstroke,' 'The Seaport,' 'The Return of Chorb,' 'An Affair of Honor'), trains ('A Matter of Chance,' 'The Passenger,' 'A Dashing Fellow'), boarding-rooms ('The Doorbell,' 'A Busy Man,' 'Terra Incognita,' 'The Reunion,' 'Torpid Smoke'), as well as bedrooms, studies, bars, a museum, and even a cave. Likewise, parallel to the motifs derived from his poetry which mark experience of psychological, physical, and temporal transition, the 'epiphanic' moments or conclusions of Nabokov's stories are figuratively illustrated in, for example, such liminal settings as a sunrise or sunset (e.g., 'Sounds,' 'Gods,' 'Details of a Sunset') or a seashore division between land and water at twilight ('Perfection,' 'Lik'). Many of Nabokov's most accomplished stories are characterized by the formation of elaborate patterns of meaning based on the strategic placement of motifs within the narrative ('The Visit to the Museum,' 'Spring in Fialta,' 'Signs and Symbols,' and 'The Vane Sisters'), with particular stories building implicit thematic meaning out of the creation of patterns of motifs paralleled in his poetry.

The 1924 story Катастрофа ('Katastrofa'), for instance, which was renamed 'Details of a Sunset' in English translation and subsequently used as the title story for Nabokov's collection of 1976, *Details of a Sunset and*

Other Stories, not only highlights a motif of temporal transition in its title but also builds upon a series of images and motifs recurrent in Nabokov's poetry. The story's crucial imagery of a dream of a deceased father, of the electric blue light of a streetcar, and a vacant lot is familiar to such poems as 'Hexameters,' 'You've moved to new lodgings …,' and 'Evening on a Vacant Lot,' and evocative of a similarly mysterious and lyrical atmosphere. In confirmation of the short story's generic propensity to transform plot into pattern, the plot of 'Details of a Sunset' is relatively simple, dealing with the death of a young man who is hit by a bus upon jumping from a streetcar on the very day that, unbeknownst to him, his beloved fiancée abandons him for a former lover. The lyric power of the story arises, not from the plot, but from the meticulous orchestration of contrasting motifs and imagery of enclosure and transition which allows the reader, with knowledge superior to that of Mark, to escort the doomed (or blessed) protagonist to a level of bliss other than that which he experienced in the waking world of the story. Throughout 'Details of a Sunset,' the story's hero, Mark Standfuss, insouciantly negotiates his way between dark and ominous images of enclosed space, such as moving vans 'like enormous coffins,' oakwood trunks, 'the heavy skeleton of a double bed,' 'the flat cardboard boxes' in which Mark packs ties, and the tram which carries him to his death.[7] Against these repeated motifs foreboding death are images of physical, temporal, and psychological transition: a stairway in the dark of night, 'a rain-streaked bridge,' puddles which 'reflected the soft incandescence of the evening,' and, finally, 'the flush of a fiery sunset.' Mark himself is recorded throughout the story in various states of altered consciousness – intoxicated by drink, a dream, the bliss of love for his fiancée, and finally his death. His death, and at least potential transition into another space, is prepared less by the plot of the story itself, which culminates in a final sentence – 'Mark no longer breathed, Mark had departed – whither, into what other dreams, none can tell' (*Ssoch* I, 147; *Stories* 85) – than by the arrangement of the story's imagery and motifs. 'Details of a Sunset' thus provides an excellent example of Nabokov's use of motifs from his poetry which ensures the unities of time, action, and space so essential to the economy of the short story, while at the same time creating in their patterned arrangement a symbolic order crucial to the atmosphere and meaning of the story.

The creation of layers of plot as an important structural feature of the short story is a further element which distinguishes Nabokov's practice in the genre and which is at once related to the lyric quality of his artistry as a whole. Nabokov himself identified the layered quality of his stories in a famous letter to Katherine White of the *New Yorker*: 'Most of the stories I am contemplating (and some I have written in the past ...) will be composed on these lines, according to this system wherein a second (main) story is woven into, or placed behind, the superficial semitransparent one' (*SL* 117). Although Nabokov identified this structural feature in reference to a late English story, 'The Vane Sisters,' it seems to parallel the essential metaphysical character of his poetics as the structural, narrative expression of a two-world cosmology. Prevalent in numerous short stories (and novels), it also distinguished the plots of, for instance, the previously discussed plays *The Event* and *The Waltz Invention*. In the above referred to 'Details of a Sunset,' approximately one-third of the narrative transpires after the death of the central protagonist; upon first reading, however, this is not clear until the end of the story and not ultimately to be verified until a second reading of the story when the narrative signals of the main story – Mark Standfuss's death – are revealed under the transparent story of Mark's expectant visit to his fiancée. Nabokov's 1931 story 'Terra Incognita' is based on the conceit of a layered plot whereby the main story – a delirious man in his room is progressively allowed to protrude from behind the surface level of a story of drama and adventure in an exotic jungle.[8] The epiphany of the story, however, rests on still another assumed layer of being. The narrative ultimately suggests that both the delirious fantasy of escapades in the jungle and the more prosaic experience of fever in a European room are layers equally fictitious from the perspective of death, a still higher level of plot in the marvellous fiction of existence: 'Everything around me was fading, leaving bare the scenery of death – a few pieces of realistic furniture and four walls. My last motion was to open the book, which was damp with my sweat, for I absolutely had to make a note of something; but, alas, it slipped out of my hand. I groped all along the blanket, but it was no longer there' (*Ssoch* III, 571; *Stories* 303).

Another important feature of the short story form and its lyric practice by Nabokov is the nexus of subjectivity of mood and characterization. In arguing for a shift in the interpretation and representation of reality in the late nineteenth and early twentieth centuries, Ferguson has explicitly argued for the importance of subjectivity, claiming that in short stories 'imitation of how things "feel" or "seem" to the characters became the preferred subject of fiction rather than the imitation of "how things are" in the "real" world ... and the exploration of subjectivity became the elusive "object" of fictional imitation' (Ferguson 15). This emphasis on subjectivity, with its ramifications for characterization, also conforms to Nabokov's short story practice and seems a further element uniting his poetic practice with his prose writing and thereby guaranteeing the lyric quality of his short fiction. Important to the establishment of a subjective mood is narrative mode; Nabokov's stories are predominantly – and increasingly throughout the development of his oeuvre – written in the lyric first-person voice. Furthermore, in this choice of narrative mode, as Nicol and Barabtarlo correctly observe, Nabokov drew experience which would extend into his innovations in the novel form – 'In this practice [first-person narration] the short stories blaze the trail the novels will follow' (Nicol and Barabtarlo xii) – thereby providing further confirmation of one source of the lyric tone in Nabokov's novels. Composed in the present tense and in the first person, the sense of subjectivity of many of the stories is further heightened by the emphasis on the individual impressions and internal psychological workings of the minds of Nabokov's protagonists, particularly as expressed in memories. In stories such as 'A Letter That Never Reached Russia' and 'The Admiralty Spire,' and especially in 'Spring in Fialta,' the predominant mood of the stories grows out of a representation not merely of reminiscences but of the ineluctably individual mechanisms of consciousness whereby trifles of the external world trigger the memories which define the character of the respective protagonists.

Nabokov's much vaunted use of detail in narrative promotes the creation of subjective moods still further. In Nabokov's stories, the particulars of surroundings are frequently delineated more for their value in characterizing the perceiving consciousness, and thereby heightening the mood of subjectivity, than in describing the external world and narrative setting. Even in third-person narratives, as in 'Lik,' for instance, the accumulation of detail is placed at the service of characterization and the inexorable washing of the protagonist's subjective mood into the narrative as a whole:

> His illuminated room was antiseptically white compared to the southern darkness framed in the open window. He crushed a red-bellied mosquito on the wall, then sat for a long time on the edge of the bed, afraid to lie down, afraid of the palpitations. The proximity of the sea whose presence he divined beyond the lemon grove oppressed him, as if his ample, viscously glistening space, with only a membrane of moonlight stretched tight across its surface, was akin to the equally taut vessel of his drumming heart, and, like it, was agonizingly bare, with nothing to separate it from the sky, from the shuffling of human feet and the unbearable pressure of the music playing in a nearby bar. He glanced at the expensive watch on his wrist and noticed with a pang that he had lost the crystal; yes, his cuff had brushed against a stone parapet as he had stumbled uphill a while ago. The watch was still alive, defenseless

and naked, like a live organ exposed by the surgeon's knife. (*Ssoch* V, 382; *Stories* 466)

In this passage – which deploys in miniature, as in 'Soft Sound,' the quint-essentially Nabokovian setting of an enclosed room with a sole aperture onto the night and a seashore – each detail of the protagonist Lik's sur-roundings contributes to an oppressive mood indicative of his undefined feelings of exposure and trepidation. The crushed, heart-red mosquito, the sea with nothing but a thin 'membrane of moonlight stretched tight across its surface,' as well as the watch without its crystal covering and the organ exposed to the surgeon, cumulatively suggest the vulnerability that Lik, with his hereditary heart problem, feels but does not consciously articulate. While Lik's watch is still functioning, his time seems to be ticking to its end; the danger of physical divestment looms. Thus, quite apart from the particular composition of this passage, which in itself obliquely reflects the imagery and thematic concerns of Nabokov's lyric discourse (the lonely room, the expanse of a nighttime sea), the details narrated here serve in the creation of a mood of subjective thought and in this respect contribute to the lyrical quality of the story.

The above passage is lyrical, however, not just in terms of thematic con-cern or the narrative creation of atmosphere. The arrangement of the words themselves into figurative language is characteristic of the precision and compression of poetical expression associated with the short story form. Poetic language use is not exclusive to the short story form, though the predominance of a lyric narrative mode and the premium placed on concision and the creation of plots of patterned motifs common to the short story promote the foregrounding of style and poetic imagery. Ferguson has noted the predominance of short story writers known for their lyric prose style:

> By and large – except for Lawrence – the great short story writers have reputa-tions as outstanding stylists, and much of the praise for their style, in terms of its 'jewelling' or 'polish,' arises from a sense of care lavished in the search for *le mot juste* … The attribution of 'lyricism' to the story also comes in large measure from the attention to style, the deliberation that is so apparent in manipulating diction, figuration, and syntactic and phonemic patterning to achieve precise tonal effects. (Ferguson 21–2)

As Ferguson herself suggests, this general comment about the nature of language use in the short story applies directly to Nabokov. Added to

Nabokov's stylist's care for *le mot juste* as an expression of the short story's demand for concision is abundant evidence of his poet's sensitivity to the euphonic and rhythmic potential of language as well as the affective, sensual force of figurative language molded into simile, metaphor, metonymy, and so on. The formal quality of the language deployed in Nabokov's stories is of relevance at even the level of structural composition, and hence his occasional inclusion of formal verse in his prose narratives. Used at the thematic level as textual illustrations of lyric subject matter, the insertion of poetry into the narrative reinforces the creation of a lyric tone in the world of the story ('The Admiralty Spire,' 'Vasily Shishkov,' 'A Forgotten Poet,' 'The Vane Sisters') or, in cases of doggerel ('Cloud, Castle, Lake,' 'Tyrants Destroyed'), illustrates its negation or absence. Indeed, Nabokov's identification with the lyric potential of the short-story form has at times been so complete as to cause him difficulty with important readers who, with certain justification, read his stories as prose poems. Brian Boyd recounts, for instance, Nabokov's unsuccessful attempt to sell 'a brief sketch' to prominent British and American journals with the quoted example of a rejection from *Esquire* which thought the text 'poised, frequently distinguished writing – but a prose poem' (Boyd 1990, 510–11).

In terms of such structural elements as (a) the unity of time, action, and space, (b) the delimitation of plot in favour of patterns of motif and layered plot, (c) the preference for first-person narration, (d) the creation of an atmosphere of subjectivity, (e) the delineation of character through the individual perception of details of setting and memory, and (f) the adoption of a lyric style in language use, Nabokov effectively exploits the lyric potential of the short story form. While his manipulation of each of these above-enumerated structural conventions is decidedly Nabokovian, the achievement of a lyric quality in the stories is derived from properties immanent within the genre as much as Nabokov's poetic practice. This is insufficient as an explication of the lyricism of his stories. The particular lyric quality of Nabokov's stories goes much further than the manipulation of generic conventions. The unmistakable imprint of his lyric temperament on the short story form has its origins in sources deeper within Nabokov's artistry and oeuvre; it derives from his own poetic practice. Nabokov's use of motifs of enclosure and transition derived from his verse writing has already been observed. Further to this, however, is the recurrent deployment of the 'informing themes' identified in chapter 3 as the subject matter of his stories. Cosmic synchronization, inspiration, love, the otherworld, and appreciative awareness of the trifles of life – the central themes of Nabokov's poetry and what Tolstaia referred to as 'the secret essence he expressed in his poems' – are repeatedly found in Nabokov's stories and represent a reanimation of Nabokov's lyric voice in prose.

Recognition of the role played by subject matter formulated in poetry in the short stories is more than a demonstration of the lyric shadings of Nabokov's oeuvre; it is also an issue of relevance to a fuller understanding of many of the stories. Andrew Field, for instance, has referred in *Nabokov: His Life in Art* to a 'minor line' in Nabokov's artistry that includes three novels and numerous Russian stories (Field 1967, 150). And while Field remains respectful of the achievement of even this secondary strain in an opus as accomplished as Nabokov's, the impression remains that, with regard to the stories, Field is making a qualitative distinction with insufficient consideration of what distinguishes the stories. What troubles Field about the short stories of this 'minor line' is precisely their lyricism and especially their seeming lack of plot, as is apparent in his discussion of 'Beneficence.' In reference to this story of 1924, for instance, Field suggests that 'Beneficence' '... is a soliloquy addressed to a lover with whom the narrator has quarreled; the story leaves something to be desired since a great deal of what is said in the narrator's "mental letter" to his lover is obviously "background information" unnecessary to anyone but the reader' (Field 1967, 141). In his description, though not in his resulting analysis, Field is correct. The early story 'Beneficence' is in fact an excellent, if economical, example of Nabokov's manipulation of the short story's potential for layered plot in combination with the deployment of the poetic subject matter which distinguishes all of his lyric writing.

Like many of the later stories, 'Beneficence' functions in layers; in this instance, the first realist layer of plot about a lover's quarrel and an attempt at reconciliation is quickly shed to reveal the main focus of the story, which concerns a lyrical, Nabokovian expression of the bliss, the beneficence, that comes of conscious perception of the whimsical wonder of the world. With but a single detail – a cigarette butt – Nabokov unobtrusively documents the sexual betrayal which is the source of the narrator's quarrel with, and separation from, his lover and the prelude, two weeks previous, to the rendezvous and awaited reconciliation at the Brandenburg Gate, the event which seems the motivation for the story. This 'background information' – to adopt Field's wording – is indeed quickly discarded by the story to become, not a conventional love story, but an excursus into the consolation of heightened consciousness and an exclamation of love, *not* for a woman, but for conscious human existence as a precondition for the creative consciousness. In several respects, the story functions as a reworking of the lyric material from a poem from *The Cluster*, 'When, obscure, we saw each other first ...' In this poem, the sculptor's studio, the elusive woman as muse, and the tribulations of the artist occasioned a poem about inspiration and the urge to create; in 'Beneficence,' similar thematic material is taken further into another sphere of Nabokov's poetic discourse – the appreciative cognizance of the trifles of existence as an essential portion of the creative consciousness. Expectantly awaiting his lover, the narrator of 'Beneficence' is led from reflections of the woman who will *not* appear to the modest and yet miraculous wonder of the surrounding environment. The cold, windswept street, an impoverished old woman selling her modest wares, and an unprompted act of quiet kindness between the old woman and a soldier are all recorded in sensuous detail in Nabokov's prose. The accumulation of loving perceptions of the alternatingly raw and warm detail of life engulfs the narrator's consciousness and spills over into a larger epiphanic revelation:

> Here I became aware of the world's tenderness, the profound beneficence of all that surrounded me, the blissful bond between me and all of creation, and I realized that the joy I had sought in you was not only secreted within you, but breathed around me everywhere, in the speeding street sounds, in the hem of a comically lifted skirt, in the metallic yet tender drone of the wind, in the autumn clouds bloated with rain. I realized that the world does not represent a struggle at all, or a predaceous sequence of chance events, but shimmering bliss, beneficent trepidation, a gift bestowed on us and unappreciated. (*Ssoch* I, 113–14; *Stories* 77)

A lyric declaration foreshadowing the passage in *Speak, Memory* wherein Nabokov describes love as a kind of radiating swelling of consciousness (*SM* 296–7), this moment in 'Beneficence' prepares for the story's denouement, the narrator's mental and sensual preparation for artistic creativity: 'There was no point in waiting any longer... I captured and collected all of it. The oblique, plump raindrops grew more frequent, and I recalled the cool coziness of my studio, the muscles, foreheads, and strands of hair that I had modeled, and felt in my fingers the subtle tingle of my thought starting to sculpt' (*Ssoch* I, 114; *Stories* 78). Nataliia Tolstaia, in referring to 'Beneficence' and this latter passage, is certainly correct in her suggestion that 'this is also one of the first stories where the writer treats the theme of creation: the mysterious, magical inception of the future child within the depths of the artist's personality, the theme of the first shiver of a sprout inside a grain' (Tolstaia 649), although – as this study would contest – the theme was previously explored in Nabokov's poetry. The reconfiguration in prose form of thematic material from, for instance, 'When, obscure, we saw each other first …' and the emphasis of several themes which distinguish Nabokov's poetic writing – the trifles of existence, love, and inspiration – strongly suggest the lyric quality of 'Beneficence' and illustrate the importance of cognizance of this quality in assessing the stories.

Several of Nabokov's earliest, almost plotless stories function in a manner illustrated by the example of 'Beneficence,' where a narrative, surface plot is pared down to its essentials to concentrate on the core of the story, which is expressed in the minimalist dramatization of a lyric theme conveyed in the form of subjective reflection. The story 'Sounds' of 1923, for instance, is a semi-autobiographical account of a youthful, adulterous love affair which extends beyond the human complications of physical love to become an elaborate prose poem illustrating the mystery of cosmic synchronization, here in the form of a youthful, exuberant urge to merge with all of nature.[9] The external plot of the story, such as it is, recounts the final day of a romantic relationship as the first-person narrator wordlessly prepares his distraught lover for the end of their affair. The surface plot is laden with the lovingly remembered detail of an enchanted moment and country-estate locale, including – for nostalgic effect – discreet reference to Sarajevo and the distant rumble of a world-historical event which would end it all. The potential for a rich secondary plot is gently mooted in the figure of Pal Palych, a lovingly drawn individual who, like many of the positive characters populating Nabokov's fictional world, betrays both a childlike love of the minutia of life and a secret, perhaps tragic passion. The main plot of 'Sounds,' however, unfolds not in the explicit development of the dramatic potential derived from either the characters or the location but entirely within the mind of the narrator. Thus, the real story is shaped out of the narrator's various and variegated interactions with the entirety of his world, including his lover, his friend Pal Playch, the other minor figures, and the whole surrounding environment. The depth and relevance of these interactions is not registered in terms of experience shared between one individual and another, however, but solely with regard to their subjective value for the narrator himself. In his response to a range of experiences, from the feel of a 'fiery' raindrop falling onto his lip to his wordless rejection of his lover's declaration of love, each event accrues importance according to its subjective worth to the narrator, who self-consciously records its effect with delirious pleasure.

From the perspective of the radical subjectivity of the perceiving narrator, the entirety of the world in both time and space seems to centre on his experience of the world – in one instance, his listening to his lover playing the piano: 'And suddenly it was supremely clear to me that, for centuries, the world had been blooming, withering, spinning, changing solely in order that now, at this instant, it might combine and use into a vertical chord the voice that had resounded downstairs, the motion of your silken shoulder blades, and the scent of pine boards' (*Stories* 17–18). Out of this extreme subjectivity arises an early expression of cosmic synchronicity to form the lyric central theme of the story's main plot. Throughout the day, the narrator revels in the wonder of his senses and the conscious assimilation of all that occurs in the world surrounding him, including interaction with his lover and with Pal Palych. These two, although appreciated and even loved by the narrator, are ultimately of little importance, however, not as a result of blind egotism but because they are eclipsed by an order of experience which is much greater and far more inclusive. The emotion he feels for his lover – the catalyst for the story – is quickly superseded by a much stronger order of experience which subordinates everything else he perceives during the day. The narrator experiences a mysterious sense of unity with the entire natural world:

> I realized that you had no power over me, that it was not you alone who were my lover but the entire earth. It was as if my soul had extended countless sensitive feelers, and I live within everything, perceiving simultaneously Niagara Falls thundering far beyond the ocean and the long golden drops rustling and patterning in the lane. I glanced at a birch tree's shiny bark and suddenly felt that, in place of arms, I possessed inclined branches covered with little wet leaves and, instead of legs, a thousand slender roots, twining into the earth, imbibing it. I wanted to transfuse myself thus into all of nature, to experience what it was like to be an old boletus mushroom with its spongy yellow underside, or a dragonfly, or the solar sphere. I felt so happy that I suddenly burst out laughing, and kissed you on the clavicle and nape. I would even have recited a poem to you, but you detested poetry. (*Stories* 15–16)

Although 'Sounds' in its dramatization of the inexplicable, subjective experience of a form of cosmic synchronization does not draw the connection between this feeling and artistic creation – as will be the case in later treatments of the theme – the all-embracing quality of the creative consciousness is being established. 'Sounds' is thus one of the first prose treatments of an exemplarily lyric theme associated foremost with Nabokov's poetry, for instance, the later poem 'How I Love You' of 1934.

A form of consciousness similar to that celebrated in 'Sounds,' though now in narratively far more tightened circumstances, pervades the 1923 story 'Gods.' An intense, densely composed story of desperate emotion and mental triumph, 'Gods' is unusual within Nabokov's oeuvre and for perhaps this reason waited until 1995 for publication. Boyd has referred to it, in contrast to 'Sounds,' as a failed piece of 'experimental fiction' primarily because of its emphasis on what he terms 'the wayflights of fancy' and the 'attempt to see everything originally' (Boyd 1990, 219). Boyd is undoubtedly correct in identifying this as the story's dominant theme, although it is open to dispute whether the story is in fact 'unlike anything else Nabokov wrote.' A reading of the story mindful of Nabokov's lyric sentiment reveals that it is like much of what he wrote. 'Gods' takes up a theme predominant in Nabokov's poetic writing – the perception of the extraordinary in the ordinary – and makes of it the core of an early piece of prose. The story recounts in a single voice the first-person narrator's attempt to soothe his loved one after the death of their infant son. As in 'Sounds,' in 'Gods' two plot-lines unfold on possibly two narrative levels. The submerged, catalytic plot involves the recent occurrence of a tragedy, an unstated event which is only to be discerned by the reader through careful attention to the narrative details, which accumulate to suggest a child's death, the type of tragedy that broke Waltz's mind.[10] The main plot arises from this unspoken death and depicts the narrator's endeavour to counteract the pain and mute sorrow of his partner during their visit to the cemetery, presumably where their son lies buried. At this level of plot, the narrator attempts to convey through illustration a quintessentially Nabokovian understanding of human strength, whereby the creative consciousness is equipped with the wherewithal to integrate and assimilate all experience, even the blows of fate, into something miraculous. Whether these two plots occur on a single narrative level, or on two, is not easily determined. The story opens with a clear identification of at least one narrative plane, as the narrator reveals that his internal dialogue is prompted as a response to emotions read in his wife's eyes. The story begins with 'Here is what I see in your eyes right now…' (*Stories* 44), and it is possible – even probable – that the entire 'action' of 'Gods' occurs within the narrator's mind and the enclosed borders of his wife's eyes. In this reading, which heightens the subjectivity of the story, the references to his addressee's eyes dispersed throughout the narrative function as markers maintaining reference to this plane. On this plane, the entire journey to the cemetery is nothing but a fantasy. Whether only mentally or within the extended space of a fictional universe, however, the story narrates movement – first out onto the balcony of the young couple's apartment and then into the street and on to the cemetery – which concludes in an essential realization.

During the course of this probably mental journey, the narrator provides
a commentary on everything that crosses his field of perception, demonstrating how even the trifles of existence may be transformed into wonders
and – of still greater consolation – the art of fable received and appreciated
by their departed son: 'He can hear my fable, there's no doubt at all he can
hear it. It is to him that it's addressed. Words have no borders' (*Stories* 49).
Of the pedestrian wonders to be observed is, for instance, a travelling circus
performing, among other things, a high-wire act and leading exotic animals
through the streets.[11] The marvellous incongruity of dreamy camels plod-
ding through the urban streets seems a blunt rejoinder to death and the
depressing memory of loss: 'How can death exist when they lead camels
along a springtime street?' (*Stories* 46). An airplane crossing the sky spontaneously prompts the narrator to the effortless composition of a marvellous fable. Each visual impression, every mental move, is redirected by
consciousness to become an act of creativity and hence of triumph over
existential pain. Mastery of the world, the narrator suggests, is achieved not
so much through an act of will translated into physical action, as, more
precisely, through the exercise of consciousness. The story's epiphanic moment comes at its conclusion when the narrator remains alone in reflection
as his wife passes through a wicket-gate to enter the cemetery:

> The wicket-gate squeaked, then banged shut. I sit alone on the sparse grass. A
> short way off there is a vegetable garden with some purple cabbage. Beyond
> the vacant lot, factory buildings, buoyant brick behemoths, float in the azure
> mist. At my feet, a squashed tin glints rustily inside a funnel of sand. Around
> me, silence and a kind of spring emptiness. There is no death. The wind comes
> tumbling upon me from behind like a limp doll and tickles my neck with its
> downy paw. There can be no death.
>   My heart, too, has soared through the dawn. You and I shall have a new
> golden son, a creation of your tears and my fables. Today I understood the
> beauty of intersecting wires in the sky, and the hazy mosaic of factory chim-
> neys, and this rusty tin with its inside-out, semi-detached lid. The wan grass
> hurries, hurries somewhere along the dusty billows of the vacant lot. I raise
> my arms. The sunlight glides across my skin. My skin is covered with multi-
> colored sparkles. (*Stories* 50)

Death was defeated on a vacant lot in Nabokov's 1932 poem 'Evening on
a Vacant Lot' by memory of home and the past; in the short story 'Gods,'
the transformation of pedestrian, quotidian events and experiences into the
miraculous by force of creative consciousness makes of humble sufferers

gods. 'Gods' may be read more conventionally as a mental dialogue tran-
spiring during an actual trip across the city or, still more complexly, as an
entirely mental dialogue in which the action is read in the eyes of the narrator's addressee, in which case the theme of the story – the mastery of
reality through imagination – is reflected in the manner of telling. The narrator has created a story and altered his world through an act of consciousness prompted by nothing more than the emotion read into his wife's eyes.
In narrative terms, 'Gods' is an indeterminate story not least because
Nabokov seems to have been experimenting with the means of expressing
in prose one of his central lyric themes, while at the same time suggesting
via the narrative mode deployed the heightened subjectivity of the topic. It
seems apparent, however, that Nabokov sought to adopt the potential of
prose and the short story form to express his central lyric theme of the
wonder of worldly trifles.

It is Nabokov's lyric theme of the unusual worth of life's humble events
and impressions which provides the thematic core of another early, formally unconventional story. Nabokov's story 'A Guide to Berlin' was first
published in 1925 in *Rul'* and subsequently collected twice by Nabokov
for inclusion in short story collections – first in Russian in *Vozvrashchenie
Chorba* (*The Return of Chorb*) and later in English translation in *Details
of a Sunset and Other Stories*. Described by Nabokov as 'one of my tricki-
est pieces,' 'A Guide to Berlin' foregrounds perhaps more directly than any
of his other writing – apart, of course, from poetry – the essential theme
of the appreciation and conscious transformation of trifles in Nabokov's
opus. In reference to this story, Brian Boyd has perceptively written of the
perspicacity of Nabokov's artistry and its exceptional attention to detail
as it transforms the realia of existence into the unique and exceptional:
'No great artist accepts the world blandly, and least of all Nabokov. His
curiosity was alert to everything: a quirk of psychology, a play of light, a
tree, a tram. No generalization could account for the stray fact, no category could catch the individual, no explanation for this planet or anything
beyond it would satisfy him as more than merely possible. Everything was
full of wonder and beauty, everything could be turned around another
way to release the surprise of life' (Boyd 1990, 250). However, in illustrating his claim that 'A Guide to Berlin' 'marks the boldest advance yet in
Nabokov's art' (Boyd 1990, 250), Boyd sets the innovations of the story in
contrast to Nabokov's earlier poetry, suggesting that the story supersedes,
rather than advances in a new form, the thematic concerns previously
charted in verse.[12] This, although the story may profitably be read with the
lessons of Nabokov's poetry.

With regard to formal features, 'A Guide to Berlin' seems more a prose poem than a short story. The story has almost no plot, consisting instead of a series of five vignettes of Berlin addressed by the first-person narrator to his drinking companion in a pub. In a prefatory statement, the narrator announces both the objects of his observations and the importance of the things to be described in a manner which seems ironic, given the seeming discrepancy between the mundane quality of the things depicted and the value attributed to them: 'We sit down and I start telling my friend about utility pipes, streetcars, and other important matters' (*Ssoch* I, 176; *Stories* 155). As announced, these vignettes of 'important matters' concern minutely, lovingly drawn descriptions of pipes about to be laid into the street at a construction site; a streetcar with its conductor; the work being performed by construction workers, a baker, a postman, and a butcher; a city zoo; and finally, a pub. From the quotidian humility of a streetcar to the mysterious exoticism of a Galápagos tortoise, each object is invested with a sense of the quiet wonder that comes from its ineluctable specificity and its intrinsic phenomenal attraction for the ever curious artist. Referring to a descriptive tour of sites very different in scale and meaning from public tourist locations laden with the abstractions of history and communal relevance, the story's title – 'A Guide to Berlin' – assumes shades of irony announced at the story's beginning, as the account serves less as a 'guide' to Berlin than a guide to the narrator's individual poetics of appreciatively wrought trifles:

> I think that here lies the sense of literary creation: to portray ordinary objects as they will be reflected in the kindly mirrors of future times; to find in the objects around us the fragrant tenderness that only posterity will discern and appreciate in the far-off times when every trifle of our plain everyday life will become exquisite and festive in its own right: the times when a man who might put on the most ordinary jacket of today will be dressed up for an elegant masquerade. (*Ssoch* I, 178; *Stories* 157)

The trifles observed and described are obviously less in scale than the conventionally admired monuments of architectural wonder, but also more than randomly perceived *objets trouvés* unlinked by any syncretizing principle. That they are different from the usual objects of comment for a customary guide to a city is confirmed by the negative response of the narrator's uncomprehending companion (and, perhaps, the inattentive reader): '"That's a very poor guide," my usual pot companion says glumly. "Who cares about how you took a streetcar and went to the Berlin

Aquarium?"' (*Ssoch* I, 180; *Stories* 159). That they are indeed 'important matters' nonetheless – each alike in their relevance as subject matter for the artistic consciousness – is suggested by the story's final vignette, set in the pub.

Present in the pub with the narrator and his drinking companion is a small child sitting alone under a mirror after having been fed by the publican's wife. The narrator observes both the child and the details of what he sees and arrives at a modest, and yet important, realization:

> Yet there is one thing I know. Whatever happens to him in life, he will always remember the picture he saw every day of his childhood from the little room where he was fed his soup. He will remember the billiard table and the coat-less evening visitor who used to draw back his sharp white elbow and hit the ball with his cue, and the blue-gray cigar smoke, and the din of voices, and my empty right sleeve and scarred face, and his father behind the bar, filling a mug for me from the tap.
>
> 'I can't understand what you see down there,' says my friend, turning back toward me.
>
> What indeed! How can I demonstrate to him that I have glimpsed somebody's future recollection. (*Ssoch* I, 181; *Stories* 159–60)

The above-quoted English translation of the original passage includes a single detail not present in the Russian. The passing reference to 'my empty right sleeve and scarred face' within the final lines of the story was added to the English version as the sole item of narrator self-description. Consistent with Nabokov's later artistic practice of composing layered plots, this oblique allusion seems the kind of detail which suggests the un-explored vistas of a second, submerged plot-line concerning, potentially, the traumatic brush with death (as in *The Grand-dad*, for instance) which has led the narrator to his exceptionally appreciative perspective on the small wonders of life. It is also, as will be discussed below, an important detail in the all-important composition of a child's memory. Although the translation of 'A Guide to Berlin' is able to alter the texture of the plot in this passage, it cannot replace the poetic, linguistic texture of Nabokovian alliteration lost to the English in such phrases as *sizyi dym sigar* (the blue-gray cigar smoke), *gul golosov* (din of voices), or *nalivavshego iz krana kru-zhku piva* (filling a mug for me from the tap).

In both English and Russian, the story highlights the erasure of time and the validation of subjective perspective – regardless as to what is being per-ceived – through imagined access to a future memory, that of the child. In the context of Nabokov's poetic practice and its place in his subsequent oeuvre, however, of still greater significance is the pairing of the perspective of an observing artist and a child. Through self-inclusion into the narrative – as the bearer of an 'empty sleeve and scarred face' – and the child's field of vision, the narrator assures transcendence of his own time and space. Like an 'ordinary object' that 'will be reflected in the kindly mirrors of future times,' as per the above-quoted ideal of the narrator's poetics, the man with the scarred face will live on in the future memory of a child. This form of transcendence, although here in the form of enclosure in a more conventional bearer of memory, is likewise the subject matter of Nabokov's 1927 poem 'Снимок' ('Snimok' / 'The Snapshot'). This poem, subsequently translated for inclusion in *Poems and Problems*, recounts the poetic speaker's chance inclusion in a photo taken by a man on the beach of his family – 'radiant mother' and 'stirless child.' The speaker, an 'accidental spy,' imagines the family opening a photo album in the depths of a future winter to return to summer's blissful memories 'and in that album there will be a snapshot, / and in that snapshot I shall be' (*PP* 40–3). The poet is able secretly and silently to live on in the dimension of other people's memories. In terms of Nabokov's poetic practice, however, the elision of a child's and artist's perspective relates directly to still another essential feature of Nabokov's lyric voice – the quality of consciousness receptive to the exquisiteness of trifles. By his own admission in the penultimate line of the story – 'I can't understand what you see down there' – the narrator's uncomprehending companion is capable neither of *understanding* nor *seeing* what is seen, understood, and thus shared by the child and the narrator. The creation of a wonder out of a trifle is shown to be a quality of consciousness not shared by all, but here reserved to the poet and the child of the story. And it is in this identification of artist and child that analysis of both 'A Guide to Berlin' and Nabokov's lyric voice is returned to one of Nabokov's early poems, 'The mist of a nocturnal dream ...,' which explicitly thematized the approving perception of trifles common to poets and children as a feat of consciousness:

Так мелочь каждую – мы, дети и поэты,
умеем в чудо превратить ...   (*Ssoch* I, 446)

[Thus each trifle – we, children and poets, – / are able to transform into a wonder ...]

It is to be recalled that Nabokov the poet was criticized for the sentiment of these very lines as first expressed in his earliest poetry and yet, as 'A Guide to Berlin' indicates, they form a core element of his artistry. Julian Connolly, in writing of 'A Guide to Berlin,' states that 'this sketch is the only one of the period to have an overtly programmatic orientation' (Connolly 1992, 27).[13] In 'A Guide to Berlin,' Nabokov offers an early prose working of the theme of cognizance of the beneficence and quiddity of existence as exhibited in the trifles of life. Expressed in a story which is itself distinguished by its lyricism, the theme is both derived from his poetic practice and in itself expressive of the lyric sentiment at the core of Nabokov's artistry.

Nabokov's short story oeuvre is replete with examples which may be read as the prose expressions of his lyric voice. The lyricism is achieved through the skilful manipulation of the formal conventions of the short story form in terms of plot, mood, and language use; through the foregrounding of subject matter representative of poets and poetic creation; and via the focused re-implementation of 'informing themes' derived from his own verse production. As one convenient example, for instance, Nabokov's rarely discussed story 'Tiazhelyi dym' ('Torpid Smoke') of 1935 provides a masterful example of the exploitation of these interlocking modes of lyric potential.[14] 'Torpid Smoke' dramatizes a young poet's progressive submission to poetic inspiration in a story which foregrounds such themes as cosmic synchronization, the trance of inspiration, the poet's loving attention to the details of being, and the conscious registration of future memories, while simultaneously deploying such Nabokovian motifs of containment and transition as the writer's study and desk at dusk and, especially, the liminal, transformative possibility latent in the doorways placed throughout the narrative. Rather than examine the more transparently 'poetic' story 'Torpid Smoke' in closer detail here, however, attention will be turned to 'Perfection' as exemplary of a different form of the transposition of Nabokov's lyric voice to prose. The subject matter of 'Torpid Smoke,' with its representation of the creative labours of a young poet, will be returned to in analogous form in the following chapter, devoted to Nabokov's novel *The Gift*. Recommending 'Perfection' as the culminating example of the present examination of the lyricism of Nabokov's short stories is, paradoxically, its apparent distance from the subject matter of poets and poetic creation. One of Nabokov's greatest achievements in the genre, 'Perfection' is a masterful short story and approaches perfection precisely because of its marrying together of the lyric potential of the short story genre and the lyric quintessence of Nabokov's voice as artist.

Finding 'Perfection': Nabokov's Lyricism and the Short Story

Written in Berlin and first published in the Parisian daily *Poslednie novosti* in 1932, 'Perfection' is a story of transcendence and divestment, the conquering of the division separating an individual being from the totality of the surrounding world. The hero of the story, Ivanov, is an impoverished émigré eking out a tentative existence in Berlin as a tutor to a young boy, David. Engaged to accompany David to a seaside resort in Pomerania, Ivanov finds perfection at the story's conclusion in his death by drowning in the Baltic Sea. True to Nabokov's propensity to layered plots, 'Perfection' is more than the story of the death of an impoverished émigré and former gentleman. A man of exceptional sensitivity, Ivanov has spent his life oppressed by a feeling of alienation which results from his inability to experience the world in full, unmediated immediacy. 'Perfection' is also, then, the story of the metamorphosis of an individual consciousness; and Nabokov's narrative takes full advantage of the formal means available to the short story genre to develop the extreme subjectivity intrinsic to his theme. Augmenting the lyricism latent in the form and content of 'Perfection' is Nabokov's use of themes and motifs from his poetry.

That the narrative focus of 'Perfection' is devoted to the inner yearnings and transformations of an individual consciousness rather than the external world of shared experience is apparent in Nabokov's handling of temporal and spatial setting. As befits a story of one man's experience of the world, the temporal and physical settings of 'Perfection' are subordinated entirely to the central character's perceptions of space and time. While the story is physically set in Berlin and Pomerania, these locations are of limited importance in terms of their familiarity on the map of shared human reality. Both are described in relatively general terms in comparison to the sharp focus of Ivanov's memories and fantasies of places which, although distant to events of the narrative, are nonetheless cherished as more real and immediate to him. Apart from the story's quintessentially Nabokovian setting of the beach, which will be discussed in greater detail below, the spatial setting of the story is of relevance primarily as a spur to Ivanov's subjective perceptions. Nabokov's molding of temporal setting is similar. 'Perfection' is framed almost exclusively in the past tense. The contemporaneity of the events depicted within the narrative seems indeterminate, with neither the date of the summer proceedings nor their chronology fixed. Only through indirect reference is it possible to plot the progression of the action of 'Perfection' from late spring into summer in approximately 1930. Far more sharply delineated and exactly recorded in the narrative than the here and now of Berlin and Pomerania are various past settings of personal importance to Ivanov – from the marvellous history depicted in maps of ancient Alexandria and a Russian monk's travels to Jerusalem to the more recent past of a trip to the sea at Hungerburg, Estland, in 1912, and, still more recently, the cherished memory of swimming in the river Luga near St Petersburg before the revolution. These, rather than the events of the narrative present, are the touchstones of Ivanov's life. Ivanov is in enthrallment to the memories of the past, which he feels with more immediacy and splendour than his diminished present. Fed by nostalgia for the life and privileges enjoyed before exile and impoverishment, Ivanov's temporal dislocation from the events of the present goes beyond, however, mere longing for lost material pleasure. Ivanov's relation to time is far more an expression of his existential condition and a central indicator of his fundamental alienation. Indeed, his death at the conclusion of the story will offer transcendence into another dimension of time and space, where all temporal and spatial divisions are conquered – a dimension where the parallel lines skilfully introduced into the story's narrative at its beginning will finally meet.

In terms of characterization, then, 'Perfection' is manifestly a story which conforms to the short story form's tendency to emphasize the subjective perception of the world as opposed to realist representation of it. Although written in the third person, Nabokov's narrative is extraordinarily successful in colouring all external happenings in the wash of Ivanov's exceptional, subjective perspective. The following description from the narrative's beginning is a *tour de force* lyric delineation of the central protagonist's existential condition which, as will be discussed below, simultaneously prepares the narrative for the epiphanic culmination of the story's conclusion:

During those first warm days everything seemed beautiful and touching: the leggy little girls playing hopscotch on the sidewalk, the old men on the benches, the green confetti that sumptuous lindens scattered every time the air stretched its invisible limbs. He felt lonesome and stifled in black. He would take off his hat and stand still for a moment looking around. Sometimes, as he looked at a chimney sweep (that indifferent carrier of other people's luck, whom women in passing touched with superstitious fingers), or at an airplane overtaking a cloud, Ivanov daydreamed about the many things that he would never get to know closer, about professions that he would never practice, about a parachute, opening like a colossal corolla, or the fleeting, speckled world of automobile racers, about various images of happiness, about the pleasures of very rich people amid very picturesque natural surroundings. His thoughts fluttered and walked up and down *the glass pane which for as long as he lived would prevent him from having direct contact with the world*. He had a passionate desire to experience everything, to attain and touch everything, to let the dappled voices, the bird calls, filter through his being and to enter for a moment into a passerby's soul as one enters the cool shade of a tree. His mind would be preoccupied with unsolvable problems: How and where do chimney sweeps wash after work? Has anything changed about that forest road in Russia that a moment ago he had recalled so vividly? (*Ssoch* III, 593; *Stories* 339–40; emphasis added)

As the representation of an almost childlike consciousness that delights in the bounty of existence, the above passage also provides lyric expression of the dilemma of Ivanov's character. Ivanov is shown to be attracted by the shared trifles of life unfolding during 'those first warm days.' The mode of expression which, for instance, transforms the everyday occurrence of trees shedding their pollen into 'green confetti that sumptuous lindens scattered every time the air stretched its invisible limbs' simultaneously enhances the poetry of the narrative while lending lyricism and subjectivity to Ivanov's characterization. Entranced by the world, Ivanov is nonetheless revealed to be distanced from it, unable to achieve the degree of communion with existence that he yearns for – 'lonesome and stifled in black.' It seems indeed likely that 'as long as he lived,' Ivanov would not be able to achieve the cosmic synchronization he desires, though the inference is likewise introduced that with death, transcendence of the division between self and world is possible. That it is cosmic synchronization which is wished for is made apparent by Ivanov's desire to overcome the limitations of all spatial and temporal boundaries, to know everything of the physical, animal, and human world. In this passage from 'Perfection,' Nabokov seems to be rehearsing a sentiment that he would express in poetic form in the poem of 1934, 'How I Love You.' Here, too, merger with the song of birds and the cool of trees is yearned for as the lifting of an artificial separation: '… But with each year, / to the murmur of trees and the clamor of birds, / the separation seems more offenseful / and the offense more absurd' (*PP* 79). Regardless as to its relation to a particular future poem, in 'Perfection' the central passage describing the protagonist's character combines subjectivity with the theme of cosmic synchronization, which is of primary relevance to Nabokov's poetic imagination.

In the absence of the causality born of temporal chronology and spatial contiguity, and with representational focus levelled on the subjective workings of the protagonist's consciousness, the plot of 'Perfection' depends on an alternative set of narrative features for development. Rather than depict a series of objective, external events unfolding in mimetic regularity until the conclusion of the story, Nabokov deploys the patterning potential of the short story genre to subtly prepare for the unfolding of the conclusion. To this end, recurrent motifs are strategically dispersed throughout 'Perfection.' Central examples relate to clothing, Ivanov's physical infirmities – in particular, his vision – and the seashore. The motif of Ivanov's clothing is essential to the story and an excellent place to begin examination of Nabokov's use of patterned motifs in the creating of meaning. Throughout 'Perfection,' repeated mention is made of the state of Ivanov's attire. In the first instance, reference to his clothing highlights a central feature of the surface plot of the story concerning the deprivation and want of the impecunious émigré's life:

> Throughout a dozen years of émigré life, mostly in Berlin, he had remained faithful to starched collars and cuffs; his deteriorating shirts had an outdated tongue in front to be buttoned to the top of his long underpants. Of late he had been obliged to wear constantly his formal black suit with braid piping along the lapels (all his other clothes having rotted away); and occasionally, on an overcast day, in a forbearing light, it seemed to him that he was dressed with sober good taste. Some sort of flannel entrails were trying to escape from his necktie, and he was forced to trim off parts of them, but could not bring himself to excise them altogether. (*Ssoch* III, 592; *Stories* 339)

It becomes progressively apparent that repeated indication of Ivanov's clothing serves more than mimetic proof of his reduced financial state. These are more than the bedraggled remnants of a gentleman's past. A further reading of Ivanov's attire is already suggested in the above mention of his having 'remained faithful' to formal clothes and his inability to 'excise them altogether.' Ivanov's sartorial conservatism is evidence of his deep allegiance to the past in general. Ivanov is literally clad in the past, and his loyalty to the apparel of a foregone age offers metonymic expression of his inability to function successfully in the here and now, which is in turn evidence of his feelings of disassociation and alienation. Robert Grossmith has observed Ivanov's 'Nabokovian longing for communion and divestment, for self-transcendence' (Grossmith 1993b, 74). Ivanov's gradual disrobing of the accoutrements of the past provides literal expression of the divestment identified by Grossmith, which will culminate in the self-transcendence of his death. Ivanov's shedding of his clothes is a dress rehearsal for the shedding of his body in death, as is indicated in his first venture into the sea. Feeling compelled by the wishes of his young charge, Ivanov purchases a bathing suit and strips himself of his clothing to enter the water:

That very day Ivanov took extraordinary measures: he acquired a black bathing suit and, on reaching the beach, hid in the cabana, undressed gingerly,
and pulled on the cheap shop-smelling garment ... He went in up to his knees,
splashed some water on his head, then walked on with outspread arms, and
the higher the water rose, the deadlier became the spasm that contracted his
heart. At last, closing his ears with his thumbs, and covering his eyes with the
rest of his fingers, he immersed himself in a crouching position. The stabbing
chill compelled him to get promptly out of the water. He lay down on the
sand, shivering and filled to the brim of his being with ghastly, unresolvable
anguish. (*Ssoch* III, 597; *Stories* 344)

The 'ghastly, unresolvable anguish' Ivanov feels is a foretaste of the total
divestment which will come first of the shedding, not of his clothing but
his body, and then of entry, not into the sea, but another dimension of
consciousness at death.

The bodily discomfort Ivanov experiences upon entering the water is
illustration of another series of interlocking references made to Ivanov's
physique and physical health which will culminate at the conclusion of the
story in the abandonment of Ivanov's corporeal being. From the first narrative description of Ivanov as 'lanky, swarthy, none too young, with a
permanent shadow cast on his face by a black beard that had once been
permitted to grow for a long time' (*Ssoch* III, 592; *Stories* 339), he is described as one beset by a series of minor physical infirmities which accentu-
ate his discomfort in life. Ivanov is plagued by a sense of disassociation
from the world, an inability to enjoy the communion with his surroundings
which he desires. This feeling of being cut off from the world by a 'glass
pane' is extended to his perception of himself as a physical being. Ivanov
sees 'himself from the outside' in a manner which both demonstrates a
form of displacement from his own body and provides a self-description
which extends to the weak heart which will cause him discomfort throughout the story before failing him entirely at his death:

He saw himself from the outside – a blotchy complexion, a *feu du rasoir* rash,
a shiny black jacket, stains on its sleeve cuffs – and caught his own falsely
animated tone, the throat-clearing noises he made, and even that sound which
could not reach David – the blundering but dutiful beat of his long-ailing
heart. (*Ssoch* III, 593–4; *Stories* 340)

Although it is this weak heart which seems to provide synecdochical representation of Ivanov's precarious physical being, almost every reference

to his body signals vulnerability. This instability of health signalled by the motif of physical infirmity is a further sign of immanent, radical divestment and places Ivanov in the company of such other Nabokovian protagonists as, for instance, Captain Scott, Fleming, Kingsley, and Johnson of *The Pole* (1924), the actor Lik of the eponymous short story (1939), Pnin of the likewise eponymous novel (1957), and John Shade of *Pale Fire* (1962). Lik, it is to be recalled, felt 'like a live organ exposed by the surgeon's knife' (*Ssoch* V, 382; *Stories* 466), and it is a similar degree of vulnerability which is recorded in the repeated reference to Ivanov's heart spasms, the 'acute discomfort in his chest,' his clammy neck, his 'blotchy complexion,' his sunburned skin, the 'hot tingling' over the top of his head, his weak legs, the low rumble in his head, his difficulty breathing, and his dulled eyesight. The latter indicant of his physical health is particularly prominent, as it is returned to in a series of images related to vision which will culminate in Ivanov's sudden ability to see all in a dimension of being unconstrained by physical limitations. As will be noted below, the moment of Ivanov's death and transition to a state of transcendent consciousness is signalled by the sudden clearing of his vision. In the language of Nabokov's poem 'Restoration,' Ivanov will tear 'the web of when and where.'

The motifs of clothing and physical infirmity unobtrusively, though strategically, placed in the narrative of 'Perfection' as a replacement to a causally developing plot are in keeping with the potential of the short story form to convert plot into pattern. They assist in the creation of a mood of lyricism in that they function according to suggestion and accumulated inference, instead of direct reference, and focus on subjective perception of the world, rather than imitative recreation in realist specificity. In such manner, these motifs promote the lyricism of 'Perfection'; however, they are not motifs derived from Nabokov's poetic practice.[15] In this respect, they differ from the recurrent images of the sea and twilight likewise positioned to lyric effect in 'Perfection.' As motifs of spatial and temporal transition, the sea(shore) and twilight are frequent in Nabokov's poetry and, as in 'Perfection,' suggestive of transferal to the otherworld.

The sea and seashore referred to in 'Perfection' are repeatedly brought into association with twilight and Ivanov's experience of the acute physical discomfort which portends his impending death and transition to another stage of consciousness. The radical divestment which will erase the 'glass pane' separating him from the entirety of the world is foretold by his experience of the sea. Upon David's and Ivanov's initial arrival at the seaside town where they are to vacation, they quickly unpack and, at David's urging, immediately proceed to the beach as the sun begins to set:

> David was in a hurry. He could not wait to get a look at the sea. The sun had
> already begun to set.
>   When they came down to the beach after a fifteen-minute walk, Ivanov in-
> stantly became conscious of an acute discomfort in his chest, a sudden tight-
> ness followed by a sudden void, and out on the smooth, smoke-blue sea a
> small boat looked black and appallingly alone. Its imprint began to appear
> on whatever he looked at then dissolved in the air. Because now the dust of
> twilight dimmed everything around, it seemed to him that his eyesight was
> dulled, while his legs felt strangely weakened by the squeaky touch of the
> sand. (*Ssoch* III, 595–6; *Stories* 342)

Clad in funereal black himself, Ivanov seems identified with the small black
boat 'appallingly alone' on the expanse of the sea; the weakening of his
vision in the twilight seems to presage a change in his sensual perception.
Chastened by this first contact with the sea, Ivanov nonetheless dares to
shed the threadbare clothing of his past and enter the water, only to suffer
the deadly spasms which contract his heart and fill 'his being with ghastly,
unresolvable anguish.'

Ivanov's third and fatal contact with the intimidating expanse of the
vastness of the sea comes during a final, morning-time trip to the beach
with David. In the logic of Nabokov's poetic motifs, the immanence of
Ivanov's death and transition to another realm of consciousness is prepared for in the narrative by representation of discomforting dreams and
the donning of glasses which alter his vision. Nabokov's verse contains
various examples of poems in which dreams provide privileged – though,
for the conscious mind, incomplete – access to another sphere of being,
where the laws of nature are suspended, the dead communicate, and the
mysteries of the otherworld are lifted.[16] In a poem of 1927, 'The Dream,'
for example, the poetic speaker records the astonishment of the 'shaken
soul' at what may occur in dreams – in the instance of this poem, 'that the
dead can appear in one's sleep' (*PP* 39). In 'Perfection' as well, awaking on
the morning of his death, Ivanov is both intrigued and troubled by the
mysterious communication of a memory or dream which he is unable to
see, incapable of fixing in conscious perception:

> ... but Ivanov was not feeling well; he longed to stay in bed and think of re-
> mote and vague semievents illumined by memory on only one side, of some
> pleasant smoke-gray things that might have happened once upon a time, or
> drifted past quite close to him in life's field of vision, or else had appeared to
> him in a recent dream. (*Ssoch* III, 598; *Stories* 345)

As in 'Details of a Sunset,' where Mark Standfuss's disquieting dream and drunkenness suggest liminal states of consciousness before death, Ivanov is being prepared for the transition of death at the spatially intermediary location of a seashore. That a temporal context of transition is also being prepared – if only subjectively – is indicated when, before leaving the house for the beach, Ivanov puts on David's sunglasses '… and the morning light upon the porch steps acquired *a sunset tinge*' (*Ssoch* III, 599; *Stories* 345; emphasis added). At the beach, Ivanov is psychologically agitated, his thoughts in flux as he reflects that he has 'lived neither very long nor very well' and yet that 'it would be a shame to complain; this alien world is beautiful, and I would feel happy right now if only I could remember that wonderful, wonderful – what? What was it?' (*Ssoch* III, 599; *Stories* 345–6). The world is indeed alien to Ivanov. His alienation seems to be of a fundamental sort, reminiscent of the strain of metaphysical thought prevalent, most explicitly, in Nabokov's poetry of the otherworld and anamnestic intimation of a realm prior to conscious life.[17] Ivanov's control of his physical senses is also indeterminate; he is unable to ascertain whether he feels hot or cold: '"Somehow I can't decide."' He remains lost in thought, plagued by imprecise images on the edge of his mental field of vision which refuse to assume clear shape. David's cries from the waves and his jesting imitation of drowning abruptly draw Ivanov from his reveries and prompt his fatal attempt to save the young boy:

> 'I'm coming,' he shouted. 'I'm coming. Hold on!' He splashed through the water, lost his footing, his ice-cold trousers stuck to his shins … He started to swim trying to catch sight of David. He felt enclosed in a tight painfully cold sack, his heart was straining unbearably. All at once a rapid something passed through him, a flash of fingers rippling over piano keys and *this* was the very thing he had been trying to recall throughout the morning. He came out on a stretch of sand. Sand, sea, and air were of an odd, faded, opaque tint, and everything was perfectly still. Vaguely he reflected that twilight must have come, and that David had perished a long time ago, and he felt what he knew from earthly life – the poignant hot tears. (*Ssoch* III, 600; *Stories* 346)

Ivanov's death is presented here in the sudden remembering of a previously intimated sensation and a coming out on a beach at twilight. The moment of death – a vaguely remembered experience of transition to another shore.

The association of swimming and the *unheimliche* sensation of being enclosed in a restricted space – here a 'tight painfully cold sack' – was previously prepared at the beginning of the narrative in the comparison

Ivanov makes between the feeling of physical transformation one has when suspended in the abyss of an elevator and a swimmer's feet: '… he went up in the elevator, he would have a sensation of slowly growing, stretching upward, and, after his head had reached the sixth floor, of pulling up his legs like a swimmer' (*Ssoch* III, 593; *Stories* 340).[18] Likewise, Ivanov's reservations about swimming are caused by his need 'to feel underfoot the presence of bottom.' Each of these associations between swimming and the mystery of an altered physical state, and even death, is reminiscent of Nabokov's poetic invocation of the otherworld and swimming at night in his final poem, 'Being in Love.' Of still greater interest because of its suggestion of the early provenance of this theme in Nabokov's writing is a poem from *The Empyrean Path* entitled 'Вдали от берега, в мерцании морском …' ('Vdali ot berega, v mertsanii morskom …' / 'Far from shore, in the marine shimmering …'):

Вдали от берега, в мерцании морском,
я жадной глубиной был сладостно влеком.
Я видел небосвод сквозь пену золотую,
дрожащий серп луны, звезду одну, другую …
Тускнел далекий свет, я медленно тонул.
Манил из глубины какой-то чудный гул.
В волшебном сумраке мой призрак отражался.
В блестящий траур волн я тихо погружался.   (*Ssoch* I, 479)

[Far from shore, in the marine shimmering, / I was blissfully attracted by the avaricious depths. / I saw the firmament through the golden foam, the trembling sickle of the moon, one star, another … / The distant light grew dim, I slowly sank. / A wondrous rumble beckoned from the depths. / In the magical twilight my spirit was reflected. / Into the shining mourning of the waves I quietly submerged.]

Albeit in a less artful, more transparent form, this early poem invokes the imagery and mood of seduction to be rendered to more refined metaphysical effect in 'Perfection.'

It is not only the mystery of the otherworld and the passage to death and another stage of consciousness which is dramatized in 'Perfection' through the deployment of motifs of psychological, temporal, and physical transition. This story also takes up another of the themes central to Nabokov's lyric temperament – the 'this-worldly' theme of wonder at the multifarious phenomenality of the world acknowledged and appreciated especially by children and individuals of heightened consciousness. Although Ivanov feels psychically stranded and inexplicably lonely in earthly life, he also acknowledges that 'this alien world is beautiful' and devotes his attention to developing this awareness in David, his young charge. Ivanov's insatiable curiosity about all the phenomena of life has already been referred to with regard to his desire to breach the 'glass pane' separating him from the world. In his discussions with David, Ivanov attempts to demonstrate to the boy the rich rewards of loving attention to the world and the transformative powers of a creative consciousness. Ivanov's confidence in David's receptivity to the wonder of the world's trifles is based on his observations of the boy and the simple proposition that he is a child and hence perfect: 'One might construct the following syllogism: a child is the most perfect type of humanity; David is a child; David is perfect' (*Ssoch* III, 594; *Stories* 341). As a child, David is not only perfect, as per Ivanov's syllogism, but has the access to perfection of unmediated consciousness. First programmatically articulated in Nabokov's poetry and later in such prose works as 'A Guide to Berlin,' the child David of 'Perfection' provides illustration of an exceptional, in this case childlike, form of consciousness and further illustration of an essential component of Nabokov's lyric sensibility. Children, in their openness and freedom from the constraints of reason, are capable of what artists achieve through the agencies of memory and imagination, transcendence of the limitations of time and space, what Ivanov would recognize as the penetration of the 'glass pane' separating self from world. As a child, David has the gift of direct apprehension of the world of experience.

During a walk in the woods undertaken as respite after the fiasco of his first attempt to bathe, Ivanov endeavours to initiate David into the wonders of nature and observation:

> 'While admiring nature at a given locality, I cannot help thinking of countries that I shall never see. Try to imagine, David, that this is not Pomerania but a Malayan forest. Look about you: you'll presently see the rarest of birds fly past, Prince Albert's paradise bird, whose head is adorned with a pair of long plumes consisting of blue oriflammes ... the point is that with a bit of imagination – if, God forbid, you were someday to go blind or be imprisoned, or were merely forced to perform, in appalling poverty, some hopeless, distasteful task, you might remember this walk we are taking today in an ordinary forest as if it had been – how shall I say? – fairy-tale ecstasy.' (*Ssoch* III, 598; *Stories* 344–5)

Ivanov's loving attention to the nature of the here and now – 'at a given locality' – seamlessly merges into expression of his yearning for physical apprehension of the world, including those places he would never see. This rare capacity to activate the imagination in the conquering of space is mirrored in the defeat of time, in this instance through the exercise of memory. Through the activation of memory, the individual attentive to the beauty of the world is granted rescue from even the most desolate of future contexts via magical return to the past. Thus, throughout 'Perfection,' Ivanov imagines his role in the creation of David's future memories, just as he finds consolation in his own recollections of the past. Attention to the beauty of the phenomenal world – what was identified in Nabokov's poetry as the trifles of being – is the key to transcendence of both time and space, the warders of human experience. Attendant to both is the sensation of 'fairy-tale ecstasy,' which marks escape from the prison-house of human limitation into the infinity of consciousness.

The conclusion of 'Perfection' gathers all of the central motifs into a culminating epiphanic event which illuminates the patterned structure of the story's plot while releasing Ivanov into the delirium of cosmic synchronization. Following his heart attack on the beach, the narrative records in a single sentence the expanding field of perceptions revealed to Ivanov. This blossoming of Ivanov's sensual capacity is announced by the lifting of the glasses that both obscured his vision – 'Only then were the clouded glasses removed' – and placed a 'glass pane' between him and the world:

> The dull mist immediately broke, blossomed with marvelous colors, all kinds of sounds burst forth – the rote of the sea, the clapping of the wind, human cries – and there was David standing, up to his ankles in bright water, not knowing what to do, shaking with fear, not daring to explain that he had not been drowning, that he had struggled in jest ... and a bewildered David was being led away by a fat woman in a pince-nez, the wife of a veterinarian, who had been expected to arrive on Friday but had had to postpone his vacation, and the Baltic Sea sparkled from end to end, and, in the thinned-out forest, across a green country road, there lay, still breathing, freshly cut aspens; and a youth, smeared with soot, gradually turned white as he washed under the kitchen tap, and black parakeets flew above the eternal snows of the New Zealand mountains; and a fisherman, squinting in the sun, was solemnly predicting that not until the ninth day would the waves surrender the corpse. (*Ssoch* III, 600–1; *Stories* 347)

The expansive grasp of Ivanov's consciousness is indicated by his privileged access to not only David's feelings but also to otherwise unknowable details from the life of the woman administering to David and that of her veterinarian husband with his delayed travel plans. That Ivanov has also finally bridged the ineluctable self/world divide of the human condition is suggested by the final images, each of which previously defined the alienation of his earthly life. The Baltic Sea sparkles from the seaside resort in Pomerania of the story's concluding action to the resort in Hungerburg, Estland, where he had last bathed in the sea in 1912, thereby connecting Ivanov's present to past in a shoreless sea of time and space; Ivanov now knows how chimney sweeps wash after work and is able to visualize the beloved 'forest road in Russia' of a recent memory; and lastly, he is able to experience the splendour of marvellous birds in untravelled-to distant lands. The fisherman squinting into the sun reappears in the narrative as the story's final image, after two previous occasions when he was associated with the sea and sunset. An enigmatic figure, the fisherman is perhaps Nabokov's authorial presence presiding over the metaphysical goings-on from a dark corner of the story's canvas;[19] the fisherman's solemn claim that the sea would release Ivanov's body in nine days is, however, no more authoritative than his earlier mistaken claim that it would rain the morning of Ivanov's death. The sole incontrovertible information to be derived from the fisherman's reported claim is that Ivanov's body has disappeared. Like Vasily Shishkov and like Art Longwood, to name but two poetry-related examples from Nabokov's oeuvre, Ivanov has slipped from the page of life to another realm.

The narrative of Nabokov's story 'Perfection' begins with an item of reported speech by Ivan during his tutoring of David: "'Now then, here we have two lines,'" he would say to David in a cheery, almost rapturous voice as if to have two lines was a rare fortune, something one could be proud of' (*Ssoch* III, 591; *Stories* 338).[20] The delight in Ivanov's voice is appropriate: the two lines are not only components of an exercise in mathematics, they are much more a representation of the planes of time and space which constitute reality, life in a world, which is 'a rare fortune.' The rapture betrayed in Ivanov's voice is surely anticipatory of the bliss of consciousness that Nabokov frequently associated with the state of cosmic synchronization, a stage of consciousness where all the lines meet. In *The Gift*, to be discussed below, the poet-hero of the novel yearns for sentiment and artistry which partakes of transcendence to perfection – 'I search beyond the barricades (of words, of senses, of the world) for infinity, where all, all the lines meet' (*Ssoch* IV, 504; *Gift* 329). In a manner less consciously self-aware than Fyodor Godunov-Cherdyntsev, Ivanov, too, sought communion with the totality of existence and found experience 'beyond the barricades' after his death. With the example of 'Perfection,' Nabokov may be shown to have brought the central thematic preoccupations of his poetry to the short story form, utilizing the potential of that genre as a prose forum serving the needs of his lyric sensibility. The same lyric sentiment is responsible for the distinctive character of Nabokov's novel writing, as the following chapter on *The Gift* will demonstrate in its representation of the growth of a young poet's voice.

6 Lyricism and the Novel: Nabokov's Gift for Prose

> By the way, I've read your very remarkable collection of poems. Actually, of course, they are but models of your future novels.
>
> — Vladimir Nabokov, *The Gift*

Ivanov of the short story 'Perfection' ultimately surmounted the subject-object impasse of human existence, though only in death, a transcendence of the physical self which brought him transition to a blissful sphere of being 'where all, all the lines meet.' Fyodor Godunov-Cherdynstev, the poet-protagonist of *Дар* (*Dar* / *The Gift*), likewise seeks a form of unmediated experience of the world. Unlike Ivanov, however, Fyodor is not seeking removal of the 'glass pane' separating him from the world or through which John Shade's waxwing flew. As a gifted young poet-artist, Fyodor's striving for existential fulfillment finds realization in artistic expression, a merger of subjective inspiration with external world, what he describes as the attainment of a 'living connection between my divine excitement and my human world' (*Ssoch* IV, 334; *Gift* 153). Blessed with creative consciousness, Fyodor is afforded the 'perfection' of verbal artistry and love – in Nabokov's lyric poetics, the two alternate experiences of the voluptuous bliss of transcendence available to sentient humans this side of death. *The Gift*, which both recreates and celebrates the gift of a young poet's artistic genius, is, if not Nabokov's fullest, then certainly his most direct, exploration of the workings and wonder of artistic consciousness and an exceptional example of the fusing of Nabokov's poetry and lyric sensibility in the prose of the novel form.

One of the greatest works of twentieth-century Russian literature, Nabokov's ninth and final Russian novel is one of many gifts. Serialized in the Parisian émigré journal *Sovremennye zapiski* in 1937–8, *The Gift* first appeared in truncated form, due to the refusal of the journal's editorial board to publish the novel's fourth chapter, the controversial biography of the nineteenth-century radical critic N.G. Chernyshevskii.[1] *The Gift* did not appear in Russian in unexpurgated form until after the war with publication by the Chekhov Publishing House in 1952. An English translation undertaken with Nabokov's authorial collaboration appeared in 1963 in the wake of Nabokov's fame as the writer, behind, above all, *Lolita, Pnin*, and *Pale Fire*. Although *The Gift* enjoys the almost unanimous recognition of scholars as Nabokov's finest Russian novel, it has not garnered the critical response it so abundantly merits.[2] Of relevance to Nabokov's Russian audience, Alexander Dolinin has noted the pertinence of the novel's belated, unbowdlerized appearance in the diminished, post-war world of émigré letters at a time when Nabokov himself had already decamped to the more promising Anglo-American literary institution. Even after translation into English, the critical and readerly response that would have been expected for one of the greatest exemplars of twentieth-century letters was muted. The relative silence of the potentially large English-language audience quite possibly stemmed, as Dolinin has also observed, from the novel's intimidating array of intertextual references to Russian literature (Dolinin 1995, 138). Nabokov's claim in the introduction to the English translation that the novel's heroine is Russian literature is more than rhetorical, and the deep familiarity with an entire tradition assumed in the novel may have seemed an almost insurmountable hurdle to the nonspecialist reader.[3] Further to these factors is the formal density and complexity of the novel. A portrait of the young artist as poet, *The Gift* makes tremendous demands on the interpretive capabilities of the reader to normalize the encyclopedic rush of formal and thematic elements into a single whole. While exceptionally rewarding as a textured work of art, *The Gift* is equally demanding as a text to be read. Required as a prerequisite to unlock the fullest possible understanding of *The Gift* is a readerly key, an overarching principle of interpretive approach capable of gathering the thematic multiplicity and formal diversity of the novel into a unity. In short, awareness of the lyric identity of Nabokov's most complex Russian work is urgently required. If, as Gleb Struve has suggested, *The Gift* is the key to Nabokov's oeuvre, then the key to Nabokov's *The Gift* is critical understanding of his poetry and the place of his lyric sensibility in his prose. The following discussion will thus be devoted to a reading of poetry as both the key to, and source of, the artistry of *The Gift*.

The previous chapter of this study sought to exhibit the affinity of Nabokov's lyric voice to prose and the short story form. Nabokov was shown not only to have utilized the lyric potential inherent to the genre, but to have expressed in his stories thematic concerns demonstrably derived from his poetry and lyric sensibility. Beginning with his first novel, the same may be said of Nabokov's resourceful manipulations of the novel form, from *Mary* in 1926 to *Look at the Harlequins!* a half-century later in 1974. This applies equally well to the novels antecedent to Nabokov's last Russian émigré novel. For the reader attuned to the voluble presence of Nabokov's poetry, each of the eight novels previous to *The Gift* bears the subtle though unmistakable imprint of Nabokov's lyric sensibility: from, in *Mary*, the use of Nabokov's poetry-based motifs in such scenes as Ganin's curious suspension in the enclosed quarters of a darkened lift and his conception of the image of a future love during the delirium of a fever to his narrative progression through the individual rooms of a boarding house before, at novel's end, his departure on a train for the liberation of the sea;[4] to, in *Invitation to a Beheading*, Cincinnatus's intimation that he is a prisoner in the world and the coincidence of his childhood awareness of 'how to make letters' and a fateful fall into consciousness from his liminal perch in a window, a location itself described in images of contrast and transition as the 'white nook of the sill, sharply marked off by the shadow of the half-open casement' (*Ssoch* IV, 103; *IB* 96). The young poet Fyodor is informed in *The Gift* by an unusually perspicacious – imaginary – reader that his poems 'are but the models of [his] future novels' (*Ssoch* IV, 256; *Gift* 71). The statement applies equally to Nabokov. As in Nabokov's Russian short stories, and as the above randomly chosen and easily multiplied illustrations from his novels suggest, critical demonstration of the imprint of Nabokov's lyric sensibility within his prose is conveniently achieved through reference to each and all of his novels prior to *The Gift*.

The lyricism of *The Gift*, however, is of this order and more. The presence of Nabokov's poetry and related expressions of his lyric voice achieved a quantitatively and qualitatively new dimension in his final Russian novel. In *The Gift*, Nabokov advanced beyond the strategies hitherto used to distinguish his prose writing with the stylistic markers of his distinctive artistic voice – a verbally inventive writing style which exhausts the full aesthetic potential of prose while reaping the lyric potential of individual themes and motifs derived from his poetry. *The Gift* is a *Künstlerroman* which recounts the experiences of a young émigré poet-writer in Berlin, Fyodor Godunov-Cherdyntsev, as he lives a life of reduced material resources, though exceptionally rich mental and creative experience, from 1 April 1926 until 29 June 1929. In thus concentrating his story on a poet-hero's artistic maturation, Nabokov added a plot-line which centres on a poet-writer and thereby explicitly thematizes the development of a lyric sensibility.[5] Furthermore, in the narrative process of representing this intrinsically lyric subject matter, Nabokov marshalled the full elasticity of the novel form to weave poetry and poetic forms into the very texture of the novel's prose. During an imagined conversation between the protagonist and an admired fellow poet, Fyodor approvingly quotes a line from his poet-interlocutor which effectively expresses Nabokov's achievement in *The Gift*: "'Yes, some day I'm going to produce prose in which «thought and music are conjoined as are the folds of life in sleep»'" (*Ssoch* IV, 256; *Gift* 71). This is the achievement of *The Gift*, and, for critical purposes, to separate the folds of poetry from prose, it is necessary to understand the character of Nabokov's poetry and lyric voice.

The Gift is famously awash in a multitude of narrative voices and alternating perspectives. Equally prolific, however, are the narrative types within the novel. Embedded within *The Gift* is a library of narrative modes extending from the fictional forms of 'album-type' poetry, short story, drama (in parody), and novel to the non-fictional forms of biography, book review, and letters. Each of these modes – and especially the novel they all coalesce to form, *The Gift* – is derived from, and illustrative of, the poet-protagonist's, and author's, poetry and lyric sensibility.[6] A statement by Nabokov from the foreword to the English edition of *The Gift* provides authoritative evidence of the cumulative importance of poetry to the thematic and structural development of the novel:

> The plot of Chapter One centers in Fyodor's poems. Chapter Two is a surge toward Pushkin in Fyodor's literary progress and contains his attempt to describe his father's zoological explorations. Chapter Three shifts to Gogol, but its real hub is the love poem dedicated to Zina. Fyodor's book on Chernyshevski, a spiral within a sonnet, takes care of Chapter Four. The last chapter combines all the preceding themes and adumbrates the book Fyodor dreams of writing some day: *The Gift*. (*Gift* ii)

Further to Nabokov's statement are the claims of critics. Scholars from Salehar to Johnson have directly and indirectly focused on the literary expressions of the protagonist's artistic talent – one of the gifts of the title – as a central component of the novel. Anna Maria Salehar, for instance, extends beyond Nabokov's above-quoted statement to claim that the poem at the centre of chapter 3 is 'clearly more' than the hub of a single chapter, as Nabokov suggested: 'It comes to be the core of the novel as well. For as the reader identifies the evolving verse he experiences Fyodor's artistic workshop in operation and gains insight into the material of poetry and the nature of Fyodor's gift' (Salehar 71). D. Barton Johnson identifies two main plot-lines within the novel: the gradual meeting and coming together of Fyodor with his muse and lover, Zina Mertz, and the maturation of Fyodor's artistic talents (Johnson 1982, 190–1). Johnson is less forthright than Salehar in his emphasis on the thematic importance of poetry in the novel, though it is apparent that narrative expression of both these two plot-lines is strategically encapsulated in poetic form. *The Gift* is clearly saturated with poetry as both structural component of the narrative and thematic emphasis within the plot.

The most immediately accessible entrance into the poetry of Nabokov's prose in *The Gift* is the prose itself. As was observed above, *The Gift* is a novel woven out of a variety of strands of narrative type, from critical biography to literary reviews, lyric poetry to reported speech. Regardless of the particular type of narrative format used, however, each is characterized by the highly aesthetic, self-conscious use of language which distinguishes Nabokov's prose. Nabokov the poet is always present behind Nabokov the novelist. Replete with alliteration and assonance, rhythm and rhyme, metered prose and startling metaphors, Nabokov's prose famously exhausts the aesthetic potential of expository prose. Examples of this type of writing are legion within *The Gift* – as in all of Nabokov's prose texts – and may be illustrated here with several convenient examples. For instance, in parodic commentary on a weaker poet's proclivity for imitating qualities discerned in two poets, Esenin and Blok, Nabokov's narrative succeeds in folding the music of alliteration into clever reference to the overly imitated qualities of their respective poetics. In the Russian of Nabokov's original, the concision and wit of even a brief passage – 'есенинскую осень, голубизну блоковских болот' ('eseninskuiu osen', golubiznu blokovskikh bolot') – is but partially rendered in the English of the translation: 'autumn scenes à la Esenin, the smoky blue of Blok-ish bogs' (*Ssoch* IV, 225; *Gift* 38). Attention to rhythm is effectively captured in a Russian line of anapests that concludes a lyric depiction of Fyodor's first meeting with his beloved mother and their mutual defeat of time in luxurious recollection of the past: 'как бывало когда-то в Россий, как бывало и будет всегда' ('kak byválo kogdá-to v Rossíi, kak byválo i búdet vsegdá' / 'as it had once been in Russia, as it had been, and would be, forever' (*Ssoch* IV, 270; *Gift* 87). The penultimate paragraph of the novel, the concluding depiction of Fyodor, has him composing a poem during the course of his final interior monologue (*Ssoch* IV, 541; *Gift* 366).[7] All are examples of Nabokov's exploitation of the aesthetic function of prose. Nabokov consolidates and protracts the lyric effect of briefer passages such as these with the accumulation of sumptuous imagery and affective syntax in the numerous extended passages of descriptive brilliance which adorn his novel. The following paragraph-length extract captures the wrought verbal and represented beauty of an enchanting memory in the form of a prose poem:

> The rain still fell lightly, but with the elusive suddenness of an angel, a rainbow had already appeared. In languorous self-wonder, pinkish-green with a purplish suffusion along its inner edge, it hung suspended over the reaped field, above and before a distant wood, one tremulous portion of which showed through it. Stray arrows of rain that had lost both rhythm and weight and the ability to make any sound, flashed at random, this way and that, in the sun. Up the rain-washed sky, from behind a raven cloud, a cloud of ravishing whiteness was extricating itself and shining with all the detail of a monstrously complicated molding. (*Ssoch* IV, 260–1; *Gift* 77)

The passage continues for several hundred words as the verbal portrayal of Fyodor's sensually enacted recreation of a remembered scene from the past. Ivanov of the short story 'Perfection' had attempted to initiate his child-charge, David, into awareness of the powers of a sensually recollected memory to offer consolation for the sensual poverty of the present. As if in achievement of the state of consciousness referred to by Ivanov as 'fairy-tale ecstasy,' Fyodor conquers the shabbiness of *his* present – he is sitting on a Berlin tram – through the loving recollection of the details of a memory.[8] Fyodor's reverie proceeds, and thanks to this trick of consciousness, he is transported back to a setting which occupies all of his senses. Among the reminiscences and associations lovingly re-experienced by Fyodor are a series of detailed scenes, including the memory of an anecdote told by his explorer-naturalist father of once having stepped into the enchanted space of a rainbow and Fyodor's walk through muddied fields after a thundershower. Intriguing about this *tour de force* of descriptive writing is not only its formal brilliance as a piece of iridescent prose, but its imagistic provenance in Nabokov's earliest poetry. The entire extended passage of lyric prose, and Fyodor's memory-induced prose poem within it, contains images tantalizingly similar to imagery from Nabokov's earliest poetry. The above-quoted citation, for instance, with its description of raindrops evaporating in flight, begins with the Russian words 'Eshche letal dozhd" and thus echoes the words and opening image from Nabokov's paradigmatic 'first' poem – as presented in *Speak, Memory* – 'The Rain Has Flown,' which begins 'Дождь пролетел и сгорел на лету' ('Dozhd' pro-letel i sgorel na letu' / 'The rain has flown and burnt up in flight') (*Ssoch* I, 438–9). The poem translated by Nabokov as 'The Rain Has Flown' first appeared in *Two Paths* of 1918 and is followed in that collection by the untitled poem 'The storm has melted away. The sky is clear' (*Ssoch* I, 439), which likewise contains imagery paralleling Fyodor's walk through a rain-drenched rural landscape and Fyodor's father's wondrous experience with a rainbow.

This is not the sole example of luxuriously rendered prose scenes from *The Gift* echoing startling imagery and settings from Nabokov's poetry. Early in the novel, the narrative describes a summer morning's rush of sen-sual impressions, sounds, and sights that draw the young poet out of his room into a world of humble and yet wondrous activity. The luxuriously described feast of sensations nourishing Fyodor's eagerly receptive con-sciousness occurs in the unlikely setting of a Berlin square. This scene paral lels the creation of an atmosphere of radiant, sun-infused joy and detailed imagery likewise found in another early poem from *Two Paths*, 'Темно-синие обои …' ('Temno-sinie oboi …' / 'Dark-blue wallpaper …') (*Ssoch* I, 437). Like the poem, this scene from *The Gift* features carpets, sunlight, and a barrel-organ (*Ssoch* IV, 245–6; *Gift* 59–60). These references to echoes of descriptive scenes and imagery from Nabokov's lyric juvenilia in his mature prose are proffered here not to suggest direct correlations as Nabokov's at-tempt to restructure individual poems in his later prose. Rather, they are proposed as further illustration that Nabokov's lyric prose emerged out of an artistic sensibility which first found expression in the verse exercises and themes of his earliest poetry. Although this type of verse was ultimately abandoned as inadequate in formal terms, the lyric sentiment and sensibil-ity remained to be transposed and transferred to other forms, including prose. Just as Nabokov in *Speak, Memory* criticized, without repudiating, his earliest efforts in verse, Fyodor in *The Gift* describes the formal weak-ness, though artistic purity, the inspiration, of his first poems.

Each of the above examples of Nabokov's poetic use of prose – exam-ples which could be multiplied at will – serves as little more than a brief allusion to the wondrous concision and musicality of Nabokov's writing and can, as in the case of the latter example of a prose poem, at best be but indirectly traced back to Nabokov's poetic practice. This type of lyricism is native to Nabokov's prose and as such is a hallmark of his dazzling style, an issue of the formal texture of his writing; here, the folds of music and thought have been all but seamlessly conjoined. As in drama and the short story form, however, there are throughout *The Gift* other indicants where the specificity of poetry and the lyric representation of experience are accentuated in the narrative to reveal the thematic texture of a novel informed by a lyric sensibility. In these instances, the workings of Nabokov's lyric sensibility rise up out of stylistic technique to assume the form of those themes and motifs which provide the novel with its thematic shape. The reception of these lyric elements of the novel assumes the interpretive participation of the reader and an awareness of the lyric identity of Nabokov's writing. In reading *The Gift* as a novel informed by a lyric sensibility, the thematic emphases of Nabokov's poetry – inspiration, cosmic synchronicity, the otherworld, love, and the appreciation of trifles – will be shown to be of defining importance, as is the play of motifs of enclosure and transition. These are, as has been suggested, the keys to and source of *The Gift*. Entrance into the novel, Fyodor's artistic gift, and awareness of the lyric foundation of Nabokov's prose novel is first achieved through a reading of his experience of inspiration.

The Gift: A Portrait of the Novelist as a Young Poet

Chapter 1 begins the novel with an excursus into the mysteries of inspiration and the creative consciousness. Centred on Fyodor's mental review of the inspiration for, and aesthetic qualities of, his previously published poems, the chapter also dramatizes the arrival of a fresh surge of inspirational energy, out of which will emerge – after a laborious process of composition – a new poem. This new poem, whose emergence is captured in the prose narrative, may in turn be read as self-reflexive comment on the inscrutability of inspiration and the enigmatic wonder of Fyodor's growing poetic gift. Woven into this segment of plot development are several of the multiple themes and motifs which will expand to shape the novel's narrative while accompanying and thereby documenting the progressive development of Fyodor's creative talents. The first of these themes, and one central to Nabokov's lyric sensibility, is the theme of movement from lodging to lodging, with the related motif of a room. Fyodor is introduced to the narrative as he stands reflecting on a moving van parked in front of the house he is about to move into. The first-paragraph description of the moving van is not only a literary tip-of-the-hat to the opening scene of Gogol's *Dead Souls*, but a means of announcing the self-reflexivity of the young artist observing the scene in the role, as it were, of the two *muzhiki* from Gogol's novel. For although the laterally shaded blue letters on the side of the truck catch Fyodor's eye as 'a dishonest attempt to climb into the next dimension,' and thereby recall the otherworldly associations of the furniture and coffin-like moving vans seen by Mark Standfuss of 'Details of a Sunset,' the narrative abandons the setting after having recorded its relevance to the both conscious and unconscious artist in Fyodor: 'Some day, he thought, I must use such a scene to start a good, thick old-fashioned novel. The fleeting thought was touched with a careless irony; an irony, however, that was quite unnecessary, because *somebody within him, on his behalf, independently from him, had absorbed all this, recorded it, and filed it away*' (*Ssoch* IV, 192; *Gift* 4; emphasis added). The scene has, of course, just been used to begin a thick, though not particularly old-fashioned, novel – the kind Fyodor will feel the first tugs of inspiration about at the novel's end. Just as importantly, however, the novel has announced the presence of an artistic consciousness greedily alive to the creative nourishment of all forms of stimuli. Much will be absorbed, recorded, and filed away during the course of *The Gift*.

Fyodor proceeds to his new home. The boarding-house room which Fyodor is to occupy is first referred to in the context of the keys left for him by his landlady, a narrative detail which introduces the motif of keys within the novel. In *The Gift*, Fyodor's adventures and misadventures with rooms and keys will accompany him as he develops as an artist, gradually to accrue importance as metonymic reference to both the stages of his creative writing and proximity to his muse.[9] The room Fyodor takes possession of is described in the manner of many across Nabokov's prose, but most explicitly in the recurring motifs of his poetry – an uninspiring, enclosed space with a sole window and a prescribed view that will take on life only as it is inhabited by the artist who breathes the soul of artistic inspiration and creation into its physical limitations: 'It would be hard, he mused, to transform the wallpaper (pale yellow, with bluish tulips) into a distant steppe. The desert of the desk would have to be tilled for a long time before it could sprout its first rhymes. And much cigarette ash would have to fall under the armchair and into its folds before it would become suitable for traveling' (*Ssoch* IV, 195; *Gift* 8). Despite the enclosure of four walls, the presence of mirrors, windows, and fissures ensures the portals of Nabokovian creative escape. Fyodor's imaginative consciousness, mysteriously compelled to transcendence of the here and now in flights of inspiration, will not be contained by drab walls.

That the room is associated with a setting for inspiration and artistic creation is immediately demonstrated in the narrative. Having just arrived in his new room, Fyodor is called to the phone and is informed (falsely – it transpires – in the context of an April Fool's joke) that his recent book of poems has been warmly reviewed and that he may read the entire review during attendance that evening at a soirée being held by his caller, Alexander Yakovlevich Chernyshevski. Overjoyed by the positive news, Fyodor is immediately cast into a different state of consciousness. The change overcoming Fyodor is not remarked upon with direct narratorial comment, though it is observed in narrative detail. Fyodor is revealed in the narrative to mistake the yellow and blue design of the wallpaper for the print of his landlady's dress and to perceive the movements of her cat separately from the stripes of its fur. Fyodor's consciousness has begun the process of shifting to another plane. Locking himself in his room to await his evening appointment, he surrenders himself to a personal review of his poetry. The lengthy passage recording Fyodor's bliss is a virtuoso mélange of narrative voice and mode, combining third-person narration with Fyodor's personal thoughts, as well as representative examples from his poetry and excerpts from the expected critical review which Fyodor himself imagines into existence. Fyodor's loving mental review of his own poetry is exceptional for its account of the source of his inspiration in memory and also for its demonstration of poetry's capacity, in the present, to conquer time and distance to return the poet to the sentient source of his poem's creation. Fyodor rereads his poetry and is transported to the past:

> In other words, as he read, he again made use of all the materials already once gathered by his memory for the extraction of the present poems. And reconstructed everything, absolutely everything, as a returning traveler sees in an orphan's eyes not only the smile of its mother, whom he had known in his youth, but also an avenue ending in a burst of yellow light and that auburn leaf on the bench, and everything, everything. The collection opened with the poem 'The Lost Ball,' *and one felt it was beginning to rain.* (*Ssoch* IV, 197; *Gift* 9–10; emphasis added)

Reading his poem 'The Lost Ball,' Fyodor is mentally transposed to another space and time and thereby allowed to re-experience the oncoming of rain, as the mid-sentence shift in syntax indicates.

The purview of his poetry, both from the perspective of Fyodor as character and the 'external' perspective of the review he is imagining, allows Fyodor to gauge the strengths and weaknesses of this type of juvenile 'album poetry' in terms of his growing gift. It is revealed that in writing this poetry Fyodor sought to capture the very quiddity of his childhood experience in verse, that the verbal arrangement of his poems was intended to recreate in mimetic perfection the sensual impressions of youth as they were really felt. Despite the fact that each of the poems seems brilliantly executed – as Fyodor's imagined critic puts it, 'Each of his poems iridesces with harlequin colors' (*Ssoch* IV, 214; *Gift* 27) – the threat of solipsism looms large. At a later stage of his artistic maturation, in a different room and with a different muse, Fyodor will reflect back on these poems and censure those which failed, because they sought to represent individual experience in formulaic linguistic combinations, while retaining those which remained vivid as examples of 'a pleasant exercise.' The verse reviewed in Fyodor's slim volume *Poems*, though it will eventually be surpassed, is nonetheless presented as the font of an artistic gift which will grow throughout the novel.

Regardless as to Fyodor's subsequent estimation of individual poems, in terms of his developing artistic abilities, what remains of his early experiences of poetry writing – and what is relived in rereading them – is the excitement of 'true inspiration.' Fyodor's purview of his poems also serves as an anatomy of inspiration. For Fyodor, the psychological deformation that takes place when one is in the grip of inspiration is akin to a dangerous illness and is described in terms strongly reminiscent of cosmic synchronization, as described in Nabokov's account from *Speak, Memory* of his first poem and as illustrated in several of his early poems. The poet experiences the mysterious loss of control over the rational faculties and undergoes a transformation which is physically felt as an expansion and contraction:

> … I nevertheless knew true inspiration. The agitation which seized me, swiftly covered me with an icy sheet, squeezed my joints and jerked at my fingers. The lunatic wandering of my thought which by unknown means found the door in a thousand leading into the noisy night of the garden, the expansion and contraction of the heart, now as vast as the starry sky and then as small as a droplet of mercury, the opening arms of a kind of inner embracement, classicism's sacred thrill, mutterings, tears – all this was genuine. (*Ssoch* IV, 334; *Gift* 153)

The narrative repeatedly describes Fyodor's experience of inspiration in terms which reflect the transformation of his consciousness: 'a kind of drunken trance' (*Gift* 61), 'versificatory illness' (*Gift* 150), 'a kind of bliss' (*Gift* 195). The closest analogous condition, however, is the delirium of fever. Fyodor, in recalling the inspiration for his poetry, folds into his narrative memory of a childhood illness that parallels the expanded state of consciousness which is experienced during inspiration. Perilously close to death during a bout of pneumatic fever, the young poet as child experiences the sensation of lucidity and release which recalls the psychological state of inspiration and the super-sensory expansion of cosmic synchronization:

> The fever had ebbed away during the night and I had finally scrambled ashore. I was, let me tell you, weak, capricious and transparent – as transparent as a cut-glass egg. … As I lay flat in bed among bluish layers of indoor twilight I felt myself evolving an incredible lucidity, as when a distant stripe of radiantly pale sky stretches between long vesperal clouds and you can make out the cape and shallows of God knows what far-off islands – and it seems that if you release your volatile glance just a little further you will discern a shining boat drawn up on the damp sand and receding footsteps filled with bright water. In that minute, I think, *I attained the highest limit of human health*: my mind had been dipped and rinsed only recently in a dangerous, supernaturally clean blackness … (*Ssoch* IV, 209; *Gift* 22–3; emphasis added)

Fyodor as poet thus undergoes the mysteriously liminal experience of fever to be recorded by John Shade of *Pale Fire* and Nabokov himself in *Speak, Memory*. Although submerged in illness, Fyodor's consciousness ascends to the highest limit humanly possible. In further identification with the characteristic imagery of Nabokov's lyric sensibility, the experience is described in the transitional imagery of an expanse of water and shoreline and the visual lucidity that comes with a twilight setting.

Very close to *The Gift*, both in terms of its compositional history and subject matter, is 'Torpid Smoke,' a short story of 1935 which recounts the transitory psychological state of Grisha, a young poet ensconced in his Berlin room while grappling with the blissful arrival of inspiration. In keeping with Nabokov's practice of the short story form, the textured plot of 'Torpid Smoke' arises out of the patterned arrangement of motifs key to his lyric voice. Dusk, the privately inhabited space of study described here as a 'room's cosmos,' the play of light through a window, the psychological and physical barriers separating individuals and spaces – all coalesce to form the story. At its very centre, however, is a study of the oncoming of inspiration felt by Grisha, which is described in the unmistakable imagery of cosmic synchronicity:

> And in the same way as the luminosity of the water and its every throb pass through a medusa, so everything traversed his inner being, and that sense of

fluidity became transfigured into something like second sight ... To move was, however, incredibly difficult; difficult, because the very form of his being had now lost all distinctive marks, all fixed boundaries. For example, the land on the other side of the house might be his own arm, while the long skeletal cloud that stretched across the whole sky with a chill of stars in the east might be his backbone. Neither the striped obscurity in his room nor the glass of the parlor door, which was transmuted into nighttime seas shining with golden undulations, offered him a dependable method of measuring and marking himself off ... (*Ssoch* IV, 553; *Stories* 397)

Later, Grisha will have difficulties recognizing 'his proper confines and countenance' as he views himself in the mirror. Like the adolescent Nabokov, whose reason, it is recorded in *Speak, Memory*, had difficulty assembling the features of his 'evaporated identity' after the recitation of this first poem, Grisha in the trance of inspiration has experienced a form of divestment. This divestment is the 'жарко возрастающее счастье, – / миг небытия,' the 'fiery growing happiness – / an instant of non-being,' described in Nabokov's early poem 'Inspiration – that is voluptuousness ...'

For the poets Nabokov, Grisha, John Shade, and Fyodor, it is divestment from the physical contours of the body which entails the wonder and the risk of inspiration. Released from the physical limitations of the body, the consciousness of the poet is free to experience an expansion which enables super-sensory perception of the world. In the throes of his inspiration-like fever, Fyodor is granted the gift of a genuine experience of clairvoyance; he is able to observe his mother buying a gift for him and even perceive the presence of individuals unseen by his mother. It is for this reason of disassociation with the physical limitations of the body that Fyodor will slip the confines of spatial limitations while writing of his father to sensually enter the exotic geographical settings of his father's explorations and later, when writing of Chernyshevskii, to lose track of time, to the chagrin of Zina. However, leaving the physical room of the body is not without risk to life. Ivanov's experience of cosmic synchronization, for instance, was achieved only in death. Thus, the physical strain of divestment will cause Fyodor to describe the composition of a poem as 'ardor dangerous to life' (*Ssoch* IV, 247; *Gift* 56). Indeed, upon its completion, Fyodor, in looking in the mirror, will find himself 'examining and not quite recognizing himself' (*Ssoch* IV, 242; *Gift* 57), and thereby again record an experience much like that discussed by Nabokov in the account of his first poem in *Speak, Memory*. This poem, whose composition is followed in the narrative of *The Gift*, and which released its 'certain meaning' to Fyodor – and the narrative – only after its completion, itself merits further consideration both as a comment on the workings of Fyodor's poetic gift and as an illustration of Nabokov's folding of verse into the prose of his novel. The first poem composed within *The Gift* grants entrance into Fyodor's creative consciousness as it wrestles with the creation of new poetry, not as the reformulation of a past experience, but as the poetic assimilation of contemporary experience – the first verse product of a new room and home.

Concluding his day-long submersion into the poetry of the past, Fyodor resurfaces to attend the Chernyshevski soirée he has promised to attend. Clutching at what he thinks are the keys to his new boarding house, he proceeds to the party. Still enveloped in the pleasure of his poetry-driven return to the past and anticipating the confirmation to be provided by a (non-existent) review that his gift is appreciated by other readers, Fyodor walks in thoughts of his future fame. Suddenly, as if out of nowhere, the first lines of a poem mysteriously, bird-like, flit into his consciousness:

> But what do I care whether or not I receive attention during my lifetime … And yet … I am still a long way from thirty, and here today I am already noticed. Noticed! Thank you, my land, for this remotest … A lyric possibility flitted past, singing quite close to his ear. Thank you, my land, for your most precious … I no longer need the sound 'oticed': the rhyme has kindled life, but the rhyme itself is abandoned. And maddest gift my thanks are due … I suppose 'meshes' waits in the wings. Did not have time to make out my third line in that burst of light. Pity. All gone now, missed my cue. (*Ssoch* IV, 216; *Gift* 29–30)

Pursued by the fragments of an unbidden poem taking shape in his consciousness, Fyodor ambles oblivious to time and space yet acutely sensitive to the sensual detail of his surroundings. Aimlessly crossing streets without regard for cars, Fyodor is described like a drunk; the hands of clocks seem to slow in comparison to his movements. Fyodor's thoughts are occupied at the party by other matters, and the poem remains imperfect and incomplete for the remainder of the evening. Upon returning home several hours later, Fyodor discovers that although he had keys in his possession, they were not the right ones. Those in his possession were the keys to a former room and the inspiration from a previous set of poetry, the poetry of his memories of adolescence in Russia presided over by an earlier muse, not his life in Berlin exile. Fyodor is locked out of his new 'room,' the space associated with his contemporary existence in Berlin, in need of different keys, new inspiration, a new muse, and a new poetry with which to assimilate his present experience. Unbeknownst to Fyodor, his new muse is hovering in the margins of his life, almost ready to make an appearance. Looking at a park bench, Fyodor imagines that he sees a beautiful young woman sitting there, but on closer inspection discovers that it is only the shadow of a tree; later, Fyodor will learn that Zina – his future lover and muse – often came to his building, where she quite likely sat waiting for her acquaintances in fulfillment of Fyodor's vision. Shuffling about in the half-light, half-shadow of a street-lamp, he returns to the poem begun hours before and falls again into the trance of inspiration. He is, as in Nabokov's poem of 1918 'The Poet,' 'в стороне,' aloof, beside himself in a parallel mental space:

> He was somnambulistically talking to himself as he paced a nonexistent sidewalk; his feet were guided by local consciousness, while the principal Fyodor Konstantinovich, and in fact the only Fyodor Konstantinovich that mattered, was already peering into the next shadowy strophe, which was swinging some yards away and which was destined to resolve itself in a yet-un-known but specifically promised harmony. (*Ssoch* IV, 240; *Gift* 55)

Allowed into the building by an exiting visitor – an acquaintance of his future muse – Fyodor reaches his room and completes his poem, a poem which documents a further stage of development in his maturation as an artist and which echoes his experiences of being entranced in the creation of poetry about and for Russia while in Berlin:

> Thank you, my land; for your remotest
> Most cruel mist my thanks are due.
> By you possessed, by you unnoticed,
> Unto myself I speak of you.
> And in these talks between somnambules
> My inmost being hardly knows
> If it's my demency that rambles
> Or your own melody that grows.   (*Ssoch* IV, 242; *Gift* 56)

The first poem represented as written within the temporal frame of the narrative assembles Fyodor's concerns and experiences of inspiration and poetic creation, his nostalgic desire to write of and for Russia and his uncertainty whether his 'demency' is debilitating madness or the swelling music of genuine poetic talent. Fyodor will ramble and somnambulate in the throes of inspiration, he will know the demency of reason's release into cosmic synchronization, though just as surely the melody of his artistry will grow.

Inspiration, cosmic synchronization, the intimations of love and the appearance of a new muse, the motif of a humble room, thus all emerge out of the first chapter of *The Gift* and later reappear throughout the narrative in reference to the maturation of Fyodor's gift and in confirmation of the external lyric authorial sensibility orchestrating the form and contents of the novel. Like inspiration and cosmic synchronization, a further, related theme from Nabokov's poetic writing plays an essential role in *The Gift*. The theme of the 'otherworld' is central to Nabokov's lyric sensibility, and as a theme associated with poetry-related motifs, it functions as a central intersection within the novel, connecting still other themes and motifs which flesh out the plot of the novel. The initial manifestation of the theme of the otherworld within the novel is in relation to Fyodor's poetry and experience of inspiration; here, the theme has clear aesthetic ramifications. From this aesthetic background, the theme of the otherworld branches out further to encompass important implications regarding metaphysics and ethics, dimensions which are likewise expressed in poetic contexts.

The review of Fyodor's poetry which begins *The Gift* and first provides direct narrative manifestation of the novel's underlying lyric sensibility is shown to have emerged from Fyodor's earliest childhood memories. The linkage of memory and poetry is noteworthy. Through poetry, his consciousness as poet and his awakening into consciousness as a child are rendered coterminous; they both emerge from the same wellspring. As Fyodor the émigré poet recalls, the childhood scenes evoked through reference to balls, a nurse, and the perspective of a child are all his 'very earliest memories, the ones closest to the *original source*' (*Ssoch* IV, 198; *Gift* 10–11; emphasis added). Poetry, it is suggested, has its source in memories from life, but also, in a deeper sense, in the memory of an original source of consciousness antecedent to life and, presumably, subsequent to death. The writing of poetry, the straining of memory to 'taste' prenatal nonexistence, is thus in part an effort to probe the otherworld:

> My probing thought often turns toward that original source, toward that reverse nothingness. Thus the nebulous state of the infant always seems to me to be a slow convalescence after a dreadful illness, and the receding from primal nonexistence becomes an approach to it when I strain my memory to the very limit so as to taste of that darkness and use its lessons to prepare myself for the darkness to come ... (*Ssoch* IV, 198; *Gift* 11)

Given Fyodor's own experience of the liminal experience of fever, the comparison of an infant's 'nebulous state' with convalescence after an illness is unsurprising. Equally unsurprising to readers of Nabokov's poetry and the prose expressions of his lyric sensibility is Fyodor's association of children with poetry and the mysteries of artistic consciousness. Poems of 'The Lost Ball' and 'The Found Ball,' which begin and end Fyodor's collection of poetry, bring to *The Gift* more than thematic closure through repetition. The last poem to be reviewed by Fyodor, 'The Found Ball,' not only rounds out the collection but also offers submerged reference to the theme of physical change and domestic movement which will parallel the development of his talent throughout the novel. The final poem from his first volume of poetry – a collection devoted to childhood – is also about talent's 'home' and, significantly, concludes with commotion in the house of youth and the end of childhood:

> Only pictures and ikons remained
> In their places that year
> When childhood was ended, and something
> Happened to the old house: in a hurry
> All the rooms with each other
> Were exchanging their furniture,
> Cupboards and screens, and a host
> Of unwieldy big things·
> And it was then that from under a sofa,
> On the suddenly unmasked parquet,
> Alive, and incredibly dear,
> It was revealed in a corner.   (*Ssoch* IV, 215; *Gift* 28–9)

In the year that 'childhood was ended,' something happened 'to the old house.' The disruptions and shifting of furniture signal fundamental changes in the poet's life and the state of his talent. The ball with which Fyodor associates the awakening of his artistic gift in 'A Lost Ball' has been found to be taken to another house and room.

The ball which connects the first and final poems of Fyodor's collection *Poems* is itself an image of childhood which bounces through Nabokov's entire oeuvre: from Fleming's expression of an urge to live in *The Pole*, to the balls which function as silent reminders of a dead child in *The Event*, through the ball David unpacks at the seaside resort in 'Perfection,' and the ball Pnin presents to his beloved 'son,' and on to the ball which becomes lodged in the tree as the indirect catalyst for Art Longwood's mysterious divestment in a poetic glen. Nabokov repeatedly correlated the consciousness of a poet and that of a child in his earliest poetry. Indeed, for precisely this sentiment – as has already been observed – Nabokov's poetry was explicitly censured by émigré critics unaware of what would emerge as an almost programmatic feature of his writing. This association between child and poet, first articulated in Nabokov's poetry and later repeated in his drama and short fiction, takes on fuller meaning in *The Gift* in the context of the dualistic world view assumed in representation of the otherworld. In Nabokov's oeuvre, children, like poets, are not only more amenable to the fairy-tale suspension of reason in the daily appreciation of the miracle of life, but also, and perhaps more importantly, they are closer to direct experience of 'the original source' of all artistry. Poets and children retain the gentle imprint of the otherworld. With regard to the workings of inspiration, the poet is somewhat like the strangely defective toy of Fyodor's youth, a mechanical Malayan songbird which, although wound up with a special key, refused to sing because of a malfunctioning mechanism – only then, days or weeks later, to begin unexpectedly to 'emit its magical warbling' (*Ssoch* IV, 199; *Gift* 12). The poet, too, as demonstrated by Fyodor in all of his writing – his poetry, his study of his father, and his biography of Chernyshevskii – was wound up by the key of inspiration only later to begin to sing.[10] Mnemosyne's gifts are unpacked in the artistic consciousness at the most unexpected of moments.

That inspiration arrives to the poet from an otherworldly 'original source' is also openly maintained by Fyodor. On several occasions, Fyodor expresses his intuited, though firmly held, conviction that artistry and inspiration descend from a transcendent realm of perfection. His interest in chess problems, for instance, stems from a belief that the solving of a problem is analogous to the writer's taking down of a scheme that 'already existed in some other world, from which he transferred it into this one' (*Ssoch* IV, 352; *Gift* 171).[11] In conversation with his muse, Zina Mertz, he is still more explicit in identifying the otherworldly source of his artistry: 'I seem to remember my future works, although I don't even know what they will be about. I'll recall them completely and write them' (*Ssoch* IV, 374; *Gift* 194). Fyodor's understanding of the transcendent source of artistry is one which accords not only with other poets from Nabokov's oeuvre, but with Nabokov himself when he suggests in *Strong Opinions* that '... I do think that in my case it is true that the entire book, before it is written, seems to be ready ideally in some other, now transparent, now dimming, dimension, and my job is to take down as much of it as I can make out and as precisely as I am humanly able to' (*SO* 69). As Alexandrov appositely notes, this is 'a conception of authorship and inspiration that is distinctly anachronistic' (Alexandrov 1986, 25). It most closely resembles, as Alexandrov also observes, the poetics of the Symbolists and, before them, metaphysically inclined Romantics. The relevance of this neo-Romantic strain in Nabokov's poetics has, despite its distinctiveness, garnered relatively little critical comment. It is, it would seem, difficult first to see and then to explain the affinity of one of literature's most distinctive voices to an 'anachronistic' poetics of inspiration, until it is realized that the two are mutually supportive rather than exclusive. The earliest critics of Nabokov's poetry were, in a way unknown to them, correct in criticizing his poetry, as did Vera Lur'e in 1923, for passing 'by all contemporary artistic achievements and gains, [and renouncing] all movements and schools' (Lur'e 23). What is most visible in Nabokov's poetry – and hence has most frequently been the object of the criticism of consternation – is, when taken to other genres, the source of the unmistakable in Nabokov's writing. As the transcendent source of Fyodor's artistic gift, the otherworld has clear implications for the aesthetic dimension of *The Gift*, just as it does for his poetry and the rest of an oeuvre founded on Nabokov's lyric sensibility.

The theme of the otherworld is of relevance to more than the aesthetic principles underlying Fyodor's – and Nabokov's – oeuvre. It also carries philosophical import. As a theme of metaphysical implication, the otherworld is likewise directly related to Nabokov's lyric sensibility; it is frequently expressed in themes suggestive of the poetic consciousness and presented in artistic form in motifs derived from Nabokov's poetry. In *The Gift*, the metaphysical connotations of the otherworld are most fully explored in the context of Fyodor's friends, the Chernyshevskis – Alexander Yakovlevich, his wife, Alexandra Yakovlevna, and their deceased son, Yasha. The Chernyshevskis, as the similarity of their Christian names and patronymics suggests, form a spiritual unity which has been severely damaged by the suicide of their only son, a death which has especially affected the mental and physical health of Alexander Yakovlevich. At the literary soirée held by the Chernyshevskis, Fyodor is bored and disappointed upon learning that the review which had given wings to his memory and imagination throughout the day was nothing more than a hoax, an April Fool's joke. As a mental diversion, Fyodor imagines the presence of the dead son among the guests as he, Fyodor, imagines Alexander Yakovlevich must be imagining his son. At the bidding of Fyodor's creative imagination, Yasha's shade thus arises within the world of the novel at the third imaginative remove from reality. Yasha, as Fyodor imagines him at the

party, and as the narrative presents him in Fyodor's short story–like reproduction of his final days, is revealed to be a strangely inverted version of
Fyodor himself. Physically similar in appearance and comportment, Yasha
is also a poet who loves literature as much as Fyodor. Yasha's aesthetics,
however, are different, perhaps fatally different, from Fyodor's. Romantic,
dreamy, and moonstruck, Yasha seems the proponent of a defeatist, passive lyric poetics that Fyodor disapproves of to the same degree that
Nabokov disapproved of the Parisian School of his own émigré literary
polemics. Elsewhere in the novel, Nabokov's parodic reference to Georgii
Adamovich in the fictional figure of the critic Christopher Mortus is a
further instance of this polemic. It was Adamovich who functioned as the
figurehead of a school of émigré poetry and criticism much at odds with
Nabokov.[12] As depicted, Yasha seems solipsistic and introverted, an individual given to mawkish Romantic excesses, character deficiencies mirrored in his trite, bloodless poetry:

> As a poet he was, in my opinion, very feeble; he did not create, he merely
> dabbled in poetry, just as thousands of intelligent youths of his type did ...
> Besides patriotic elegies, Yasha had poems about low haunts of adventur-
> ous sailors, about gin and jazz (which he pronounced, in the German way,
> as 'yatz'), and poems about Berlin, in which he attempted to endow German
> proper names with a lyric voice in the same way, for instance, as Italian street
> names resound in Russian poetry with a suspiciously euphonious contralto;
> he also had poems dedicated to friendship, without rhyme and without meter,
> full of muddled, hazy and timid emotions, of some internal spiritual bicker-
> ings, and apostrophes to a male friend in the polite form (the Russian 'vy'),
> as a sick Frenchman addresses God, or a young Russian poetress her favorite
> gentleman. (*Ssoch* IV, 224–5; *Gift* 38–9)

More than simply clichéd in thought and unsound in form, Yasha's leaden
metaphysical excesses in poetry and life are unleavened by appreciation of
the specificity and endless wonder of life, what Fyodor recognizes as the
gift of existence in a world of myriad sensual impressions. He is as distant
from Fyodor's character and artistic vision on the side of Romantic form-
lessness and insipidness as Nikolai Gavrilovich Chernyshevskii, the Russian
materialist critic of the nineteenth century, is distant in the opposing direction of ideological and didactic over-determinism. The two unrelated
Chernyshevskis, Yasha and Nikolai Gavrilovich – one a maudlin poet, the
other a materialist critic – are both negations of Fyodor's lyric sensibility,
with Yasha especially providing the illuminating contrast of a dark shade
to the brightness and optimism of Fyodor's character and poetics.

It is not foremost as an independent character, however, that Yasha furthers the metaphysical thematics of the otherworld in the novel. In this regard, Yasha is of greater relevance in the evocation of considerations of the otherworld on the part of his father, who, like the narrator, Fyodor, and a fictional French philosopher, will return to a cluster of metonymic motifs related to the house, room, and door to describe the beyond.[13] The deceased Yasha is first introduced to the narrative from the perspective of Fyodor's musings of how Yasha's father must be imagining him. In the inverted logic which saw the entranced, inspired Fyodor as more substantial than the 'local consciousness' that merely guided his physical movements down the street, the ghost of Yasha which presides over his parents' party is perceived as more corporeal than the living guests:

> The boy [Yasha] who looked like Fyodor (to whom the Chernyshevskis had become so attached for this very reason) was now by the door, where he paused before leaving the room, half turning toward his father – and, despite his purely imaginary nature, how much more substantial he was than all those sitting in the room! The sofa could be seen through Vasiliev and the pale girl! Kern, the engineer, was represented only by the glint of his pince-nez; so was Lyubov Markovna; and Fyodor himself existed only because of a vague congruity with the deceased – while Yasha was perfectly real and live, and only the instinct of self-preservation prevented one from taking a good look at his features. (*Ssoch* IV, 221; *Gift* 35)

First described seated at a writing table, Yasha occupies the space of the room in a manner parallel to that of Fyodor's spiritual occupation of his room. In the above passage, Yasha pauses by the door before leaving the room – and this stage of the narrative – just as, at the conclusion of the paragraph, the narrative shifts perspective from a depiction of Yasha's movements to Fyodor's thoughts. The motif of the door as division between realms of being is invoked, moreover, with more than Yasha's movements alone. Upon Yasha's death, his father begins to suffer the mental illness which signals his own transition to another form of consciousness. Alexander Yakovlevich's descent into madness is signalled by his continuing visions of Yasha and metaphorically described with the imagery of doorways, partitions, and the draughts from the beyond rippling the makeshift curtain separating this world from the other:

> Yasha's death had its most painful effect on his father ... the partition dividing the room temperature of reason from the infinitely ugly, cold ghostly world into which Yasha had passed suddenly crumbled, and to restore it was

impossible, so that the gap had to be draped in makeshift fashion and one tried not to look at the stirring folds. Ever since that day [Yasha's death] the other world began to seep into his life; but there was no way of resolving this constant intercourse with Yasha's spirit ... (*Ssoch* IV, 235–6; *Gift* 49–50)

The matrix of interrelated motifs – key, door, room, house, life – reaches its culmination as a reference to the otherworld in Fyodor's last conversation with Alexander Yakovlevich before the latter's death. In a *tour de force* of narrative indeterminacy, Alexander Yakovlevich's half-sane, half-delirious reflections on his approaching death emerge out of what at first seems a mélange of potential perspectives, including that of Fyodor, the narrator, and the French philosopher Delalande, author of *Discours sur les ombres*. The fictional philosopher Delalande shares with Nabokov, his creator, a proclivity for turning to metaphor as the means of illustratively suggesting – rather than proclaiming – his intuited insight into the ineffable.[14] His preferred extended metaphor of house and door is likewise Nabokovian in its recourse to lyric redolence rather than expository dogma in discussing the experience of death and the hereafter:

I know that death in itself is in no way connected with the topography of the hereafter, for a door is merely the exit from the house and not a part of its surroundings, like a tree or a hill. One has to get out somehow ... the unfortunate image of a 'road' to which the human mind has become accustomed (life as a kind of journey) is a stupid illusion: we are not going anywhere, we are sitting at home. The other world surrounds us always and is not at all at the end of some pilgrimage. In our earthly house, windows are replaced by mirrors; the door, until a given time, is closed; but air comes in through the cracks. (*Ssoch* IV, 484; *Gift* 309–10)

Delalande is further credited with describing consciousness after death as 'supersensory insight into the world accompanied by our inner participation,' which conforms well with the description of consciousness in the inspired state of cosmic synchronization. Locked in the grip of fever, Alexander Yakovlevich himself is adamant that 'there is nothing afterwards.' His despairing conclusion comes as the culmination of a series of images linking human life to an enclosed space separated off from a larger space: notes in the margin of a larger page, life as a womb, and a lonely, haunted room. Falling into what is described as a 'twilight' state, Alexander Yakovlevich's final moment of ambiguous lucidity comes moments before his death. Chernyshevski emphatically asserts that nothing awaits consciousness after death; this he states with the same empirical certainty with which he can refer to the rain he 'sees' falling outside the window. Chernyshevski does not know that instead of rain splashing onto the window out of his room, the tenant above is watering the flowers on her balcony. *The Gift* thus demonstratively steps back from lending narrative authority to the perspective of either a sympathetic character or a fictive philosopher. The mystery of the other-world as a category of metaphysical certainty remains shrouded in ineffability (much as in Nabokov's early play *Death*), though the topic itself has been allowed to colour the narrative with the tones of Nabokov's lyric sensibility.

In *The Gift*, the informing themes drawn from Nabokov's lyric voice – inspiration, cosmic synchronization, and the otherworld, as well as their metaphoric expression in the cognate cluster of motifs related to keys, doors, and rooms – wash imperceptibly into an ethical dimension represented by the theme of love. The relatedness of love to the otherworld and cosmic synchronicity is, in terms of recognizable models from Nabokov's poetic practice, most explicitly suggested in Fyodor's dream of reunion with his departed, presumably dead, father, the naturalist explorer Konstantin Kirillovich Godunov-Cherdyntsev. Less conventionally ghost-like than Yasha, the spectre of Konstantin Kirillovich may nonetheless be said to haunt both Fyodor's consciousness and the narrative. Fyodor's father is a figure of unfathomably deep respect for Fyodor, and his presence in the young poet's memory and artistry extremely nuanced. Konstantin Kirillovich is a man of poetic qualities in his unshakeable dedication as a gifted naturalist to refined awareness and respect for the awesome multiplicity of the phenomenal world. Disdaining the worldly imposition of the First World War, Konstantin Kirillovich departs on a research expedition to Tibet, a project which conventional opinion is recorded to have regarded as 'a wild caprice, a monstrous frivolity,' in short, a demonstration of a love of trifles and the artist's consciousness.[15] Konstantin Kirillovich is last reported alive in 1917, before the narrative time span of *The Gift*. Within the world of the novel, his inexplicable absence is rationally explained in terms of the ravages of war, the perils of the revolution, and the hazards of travel; within the world of Nabokov's oeuvre, however, Konstantin Kirillovich takes his place alongside a range of other 'artists' who simply disappear without leaving a trace. Unlike Fyodor, whose defining space is the room and writing table from which he is launched into flights of inspiration, Konstantin Kirillovich's domain is the entire Eurasian land mass from the Urals to China. It is here that he is described experiencing the inexhaustible wonder and diversity of the natural world he passionately adores, it is here that he achieves such miracles as stepping into a rainbow, and it is into this geographical realm that he enters, as Fyodor intimates, 'not so much to seek something as to flee something, and that on returning, he would realize that it was still with him, inside him, unriddable, inexhaustible' (*Ssoch* IV, 298; *Gift* 115). And finally, it is here that Konstantin Kirillovich perhaps rids himself of this existential itch by experiencing, like Art Longwood, the transcendence of unmediated contact with the natural world he had previously assiduously described in learned studies. Fyodor's desire to write of his father is a project launched out of love for his father, but also for his mother, who likewise shares with Fyodor the deep intimacy of mutual loss.

A constant presence in Fyodor's life, Konstantin Kirillovich finally exits the narrative as the central personage in an event which is the climax of Fyodor's second last day in the novel. Having spent a day in Grunewald forest dreamily engaged in activities rich in associations with psychological and physical liminality – physical dissolution under the warmth of the sun, a swim of indeterminate duration in the 'warm opacity' of a lake before emerging 'on the other shore,' a visit to the secluded forest site of Yasha's suicide, an imagined conversation about literature with Koncheyev – Fyodor returns to his lodgings and bed to dream of his father. In his dream, Fyodor is awakened from sleep in his current boarding-house room to be returned to his previous boarding house and the room from which he had attempted to write a book about his father. The room itself has magically adopted features associated with Konstantin Kirillovich. The wallpaper of pale yellow with blue tulips recounted in the first narrative description of the room has now become one of swans and lilies, the ceiling decorated with Tibetan butterflies. Within the world of his dream, Fyodor feels himself at the verge of a death that will bring liberation: 'His heart was bursting like that of a man before execution, but at the same time this execution was such a joy that life faded before it …' (*Ssoch* IV, 529; *Gift* 354). Rather than death, Fyodor awaits in his dream-room only to have the door thrown open and his father revealed to him standing on the threshold. As an apparition, Konstantin Kirillovich cannot, of course, cross the threshold separating the otherworld from the enclosed 'room' of Fyodor's physical life; neither can the two directly communicate, and Fyodor is left hearing only the incomprehensible words of his father and, in the background, the rapturous laughter of his mother. Fyodor's attempt to embrace his father is the contact which ruptures the fragile bubble of his dream, leaving him awake and alone in his room by a half-open window, though with a residual, indescribable feeling which suggests the 'non-being' of the otherworld:

I have woken up in the grave, on the moon, in the dungeon of dingy non-being. But something in his brain turned, his thoughts settled and hastened to paint over the truth – and he realized that he was looking at the curtain of a half-open window, at a table in front of the window: such is the treaty with reason – the theater of earthly habit, the livery of temporary substance. He lowered his head onto the pillow and tried to overtake a fugitive sense – warm, wonderful, all explaining – but the new dream he dreamt was an uninspired compilation, stitched together out of remnants of daytime life and fitted to it. (*Ssoch* IV, 530–1; *Gift* 355)

In the language of Nabokov's poetic practice, Fyodor's narrative farewell to his father is – apart from the lyric framing-setting of a room by a window – most like two poems translated for inclusion in *Poems and Problems*. As in Fyodor's dream-world reunion with his father, the poem 'The Dream' of 1927 narrates the wondrous and yet mysteriously incomplete experience of encounter with a dead friend in a dream inevitably ended by the onset of waking reality. Of still greater resonance to the poet Fyodor is the poem 'Evening on a Vacant Lot' of 1932, which recounts the poetic speaker's reunion with a deceased loved one and his rescue from despair and artistic sterility.

The braiding of the thematic strands of love and poetry includes, however, much more than the sub-theme of Fyodor's father. Next to poetry, which fulfills both a formal and thematic function within *The Gift*, love is the most prevalent subject of the novel; indeed, in many respects the two themes are so tightly interwoven as to become indistinguishable. Alexander Dolinin has claimed that 'Nabokov associates creativity with *agape*' (Dolinin 1995, 165), an assertion whose plausibility is strengthened by the thematic developments of *The Gift*, but also by the fact that Nabokov in *Speak, Memory* depicted both poetry and love in the descriptive imagery of cosmic synchronicity.[16] Love in its multiple manifestations fills the plot of *The Gift*, from Fyodor's filial love for his mother and father and later erotic love for his muse and lover, Zina; through the pained love of the Chernyshevskis for their dead son and the solipsistic, despairing love nurtured in the doomed triangle of Yasha, Rudolf Baumann, and Olya G; to Fyodor's passion for literature and his appreciative love of the manifold beauty of the world and all its curious, intrinsically fascinating inhabitants. The expression of love which most perfectly gathers the various themes of the novel into a single bundle is, of course, Fyodor's love for Zina Mertz. It is here that the second major plot-line of the novel – Fyodor's joining with his lover and muse – merges with the first, the development of his artistic gift. The love between

Fyodor and Zina is, in turn, both expressive of, and expressed through, the idiom of Fyodor's, and Nabokov's, lyric voice.

The maturation of Fyodor's artistic talent throughout *The Gift* is paralleled by the search for his muse, a woman who will hold the keys to, and act as the inspirational source of, his future works. Chapter 1 of the novel granted Fyodor access to a new room and, after a brief lockout, the inspiration to poetry (itself about inspiration and the growth of his gift) and a form of artistry which would take him beyond the writing of his juvenile verse. However, despite the love and support of his mother, Fyodor was still without a muse; his artistic development would not remain at this stage, nor could he remain in that – in a sense, keyless – room. As if in corroboration of the temporary nature of Fyodor's stay in this room, the central artistic work undertaken at this address, the book about his father, remained unfinished, although the labours on it left rich deposits of imagery to be mined for later use. The thematic proximity being suggested here between Fyodor's room and the relevant stage of his artistic development is more directly suggested in the narrative organization of chapter 2. Immediately after informing his mother of his unwillingness to carry on with the project about his father, the narrative breaks to the concluding theme of the chapter, the machinations of fate directing Fyodor's move from the creative interregnum of 7 Tannenberg to the artistic potential of 15 Agamemnonstrasse.

Chapter 3, the fulcrum of the novel, begins in Fyodor's new room with the corporeal presence of his (as yet unidentified) muse and the composition of poetry. The narrative hints at the artistic efficacy of the new domestic arrangement in Fyodor's life – 'Quite often now he began the day with a poem' (*Ssoch* IV, 328; *Gift* 147) – before proceeding to an extended description of the maturing poetics which will carry Fyodor forward to new creative output. Fyodor compares the achievement of his present verse with that of an earlier stage – to the pronounced disadvantage of the 'forgotten' latter – and arrives at a description of his earlier muse, the woman who had presided over the inspiration for his youthful poetry. The charms of this 'poorly educated and banal' woman reflect the relative worth and shortcomings of his earlier poetry. Possessed of an intensity of emotion, which Fyodor does not disavow, this poetry was nonetheless marked by poverty of lasting effect, which he does reject. The volume of poetry with which Fyodor was introduced to the novel, *Poems*, is recalled as 'a pleasant exercise' from which Fyodor, now at an advanced stage of artistic maturity, is liberating himself. The trajectory of Fyodor's future development is suggested in a lengthy description of Fyodor's enthusiastic experiments – and failures – in prosody, as well as the descriptive and normative discussion of poetic models from Pushkin, Fet, and Tiutchev to Blok and Belyi. This critical reading of his own poetics takes its place in the novel, along with Fyodor's imagined conversations with his admired fellow poet Koncheyev, as an excellent introduction to Fyodor's and, at least in part, Nabokov's aesthetic values.[17] Paramount for the future of Fyodor's growth as an artist is his certainty in the strength of his maturing gift and the awareness of his almost physical need to write, coupled with his confidence that words and poetic form are equal to the task of representing emotion:

> The oft repeated complaints of poets that, alas, no words are available, that words are pale corpses, that words are incapable of expressing our thing-ummy-bob feelings (and to prove it a torrent of trochaic hexameters is set loose) seemed to him just as senseless as the said conviction of the eldest inhabitant of a mountain hamlet that yonder mountain has never been climbed by anyone and never will be; one fine, cold morning a long lean Englishman appears – and cheerfully scrambles up to the top. (*Ssoch* IV, 335; *Gift* 154–5)

Concrete expression of Fyodor's expanding gift is folded into the prose of the narrative. Lying in the familiar enclosed space of his room, in the 'womblike warmth' of his bed, Fyodor descends into the physically insensate, spiritually rapturous state of inspiration: 'His euphoria was all-pervading – a pulsating mist that suddenly began to speak with a human voice' (*Ssoch* IV, 337; *Gift* 156). Emerging as the lyric issue from this state of inspiration is a virtuoso poem embedded in, and distributed throughout, approximately twenty pages of prose narrative. Surviving a series of Coleridge, 'Kubla Khan'–like interruptions, the poem is shown surfacing in perfected form from its prose environment, much as poetry derives for Fyodor from a transcendent space of perfection to be taken down in verse form. The poem acquires shape throughout the day (and narrative) to result in a celebration of inspiration and poetry and, above all, a declaration of love to Zina Mertz. In the poem, Zina is finally identified as Fyodor's new muse, surreptitiously within the poem and then conclusively at its end. The forty-five-line love poem, what Nabokov described as the 'real hub' of the chapter, is distributed across three sections of multiple quatrains of (in the Russian) iambic pentameter *aBaB*, masculine-feminine, rhyme. Nabokov's translation, with line breaks included, runs as follows:

I

Love only what is fanciful and rare:
What from the distance of a dream steals through;
What knaves condemn to death and fools can't bear.
To fiction be as to your country true.

Now is our time. Stray dogs and cripples are   5
Alone awake. Mild is the summer night.
A car speeds by: Forever that last car
Has taken the last banker out of sight.

Near the streetlight veined lime-leaves masquerade
In chrysoprase with a translucent gleam.   10
Beyond the gate Baghdad's crooked shade,
And yon star sheds on Pulkovo its beam.

Oh, swear to me –

II

What shall I call you? Half-Mnemo*syne*?
There's a half shim*mer* in your surname too.   15
In dark Berlin, it is so strange to me
To roam, oh my half-fantasy with you.

A bench stands under the translucent tree.
Shivers and sobs reanimate you there,
And all life's wonder in your gaze I see,   20
And see the pale fair radiance of your hair.

In honor of your lips when they kiss mine
I might devise a metaphor some time:
Tibetan mountain-snows, their glancing shine,
And a hot spring near flowers touched with rime.   25

Our poor nocturnal property – that wet
Asphaltic gloss, that fence and that street light –

Upon the ace of fancy let us set
To win a world of beauty from the night.

Those are not clouds, but star-high mountain spurs;   30
No lamplit blinds, but camplight on a tent.
O swear to me that while the heartblood stirs,
You will be true to what she shall invent.

III

Within the linden's bloom the streetlight winks.
A dark and honeyed hush envelopes us.   35
Across the curb one's passing shadow slinks:
Across a stump a sable ripples thus.

The night sky melts to peach beyond the gate
And water gleams, there Venice vaguely shows.
Look at that street – it runs to China straight,   40
And yonder star above the Volga glows!

Oh, swear to me to put in dreams your trust,
And to believe in fantasy alone,
And never let your soul in prison rust,
Nor stretch your arm and say: a wall of stone.   45

The poem develops over the course of Fyodor's Bloom-like peregrinations throughout the day and embraces both the self-reflexive mental considerations of the poet as well as details from the visual perception of his physical surroundings. It includes the remnants of imagery from Fyodor's musings about his father's explorations and coalesces into a lyrically formulated credo in affirmation of a life of creative, inspired consciousness. And finally, from its morning beginning in perception of Zina's proximity to its conclusion at nine during a secluded evening assignation with her, the poem is suffused with its addressee's presence.

The first unit of the poem begins and ends with an invocation. David Rampton, in building upon Jonathan Culler's discussion of apostrophe in *The Pursuit of Signs*, has convincingly demonstrated the relevance of this trope to Nabokov's poetry from *The Cluster* and *The Empyrean Path*

(Rampton 1991). Here in *The Gift*, too, Fyodor's apostrophic invocation seems to suggest metonymic representation of the very passion that caused it, as well as sheer sensual enjoyment in the rhetorical, creative act of de-claiming in verse. The object of invocation will eventually be identified as Zina, and, upon conclusion of the poem, she will dutifully emerge in the time-honoured tradition of the invoked muse. It was earlier remarked that Nabokov's various poems of the muse always contain self-reflective refer-ence to the state of his creative development, and at this early stage of Fyodor's poem, too, something more is being evoked as well. The poet is also calling forth a sensibility which, although associated with the aes-thetic, is ultimately a form and practice of consciousness which provides the basis of creativity. Fyodor's poetry, like Nabokov's, derives from the transcendent, and the opening lines explicitly invite allegiance to things not of the commonsensical but of the imagination, to the '… fanciful and rare: / What from the distance of a dream steals through.' In the poem, the guardians of the rationally quotidian, cars and bankers, have retreated, leaving a setting rich in the potential of a super-sensory dimension con-necting Baghdad to Pulkovo. With the spatial limitations of reason con-quered in the translucent, expectant atmosphere of an evening setting, the irrational is possible. Or, in the vocabulary of Nabokov's poetic oeuvre, in the play of light and shadow, *iav'* (waking reality) is magically erased by *son* (dream). The trope of the apostrophe is associated with the emotion-ally naive, ecstatic, and idealistic, and this is precisely the allegiance to a sensibility and poetics being programmatically evoked in the poem.

The second section of the poem further extends the association of muse and poetics. The first quatrain begins with Fyodor's folding of the phonetic identification of his muse, Zina Mertz, into the naming of his creative gift. Transcription of Nabokov's Russian reveals more clearly than the English the embedding of the name Zina Mertz into Fyodor's attempt to name the source of his artistry: 'Как звать тебя? Ты полу-Мнемозина, полумерцанье в имени твоем" ("Kak zvat' tebia? Ty polu-Mnemo*zina*, polu*merts*an'e v imeni tvoem' / 'What shall I call you? Half-Mnemo*syne*? There's a half-shim*mer* in your surname too' [*Ssoch* IV, 337–8, ll. 14–15; *Gift* 157; empha-sis added]). Etymologically, Zina Mertz is Fyodor's muse as the daughter of Zeus – her name means daughter of Zeus – and of Mnemosyne, the goddess of memory. And indeed, Fyodor's poetry springs from memory in both a worldly sense, as the reformulation of remembered emotions and settings from life, and in an otherworldly sense, as the anamnestically re-called impressions from another dimension. Poetry and Zina shimmer into being in the liminal atmosphere of Fyodor's evening-time wanderings. At the time of the composition of Fyodor's first poem within the narrative of *The Gift*, he was represented locked out of his room, deceived by the play of shadow and light into believing that he saw a beautiful young woman seated on a bench beneath the shadow of a tree. In this present love poem to Zina, Fyodor is finally able to 'reanimate' the figure he previously saw, now to depict her in exotic imagery also derived from his writings on his father. The reanimation goes further. In the final two quatrains of the poem's second section, the speaker moves from the first-person to the second-person pronoun to suggest the merging of the two figures. Together, the two will implement a form of consciousness in the harnessing of the potential of fancy and imagination to 'win a world of beauty from the night,' to transform quotidian reality into wondrous invention.

The third section of the poem reverts from the first- and second-person plural address of the second to a more descriptive mode. The poem's concluding section of three quatrains centres on the transcendence of physical and spiritual boundedness. Throughout the poem, repeated reference is made to transition beyond the physically contained: dreams steal through 'from the distance' (l. 1); the last banker has been removed 'forever' from sight (ll. 7–8); Baghdad's shadow lies 'beyond that gate' (l. 11); a 'fence' forms a portion of the poet's 'nocturnal property' (ll. 26–7). In the process of referring to these images of containment, however, the poet likewise emphasizes the porousness of earthly limits and the capacity of the heightened consciousness artistically to transform and transcend them in the act of creativity. Clouds are thus imaginatively converted into 'star-high mountain spurs' and the blinds of lamp-lit windows into 'camplight on a tent' (ll. 30–1). This is the transformative power of poetry and metaphor – the turning of an apple into a globe discussed in the examination of Nabokov's English poem 'Restoration' at the conclusion of chapter 3. In the concluding quatrains of the poem, this transformative potential is developed to its programmatic conclusion. Fyodor's use of metaphor underlines this potential as, in the liminal setting of twilight, the streetlight flickers and 'winks,' while the passing of a human shadow 'slinks' across the curb, as does a sable across a stump in the forest. The narrative portion of the poem culminates into 'details of a sunset' in the visual splendour and liminal promise of day's metamorphosis into night. The conventional parameters of physical space are shown to dissolve before the combined force of the temporal and physical setting and, especially, the imaginative power of the poet and his muse. The night sky literally 'melts' into the variegated colour of peach 'beyond that gate' separating world from beyond. The wet, puddled asphalt of the street gleams, reflecting the peach fire of the sunset and showing the contours of Venice to those who can see it. The street itself crosses all boundaries to extend to China, while the star shining in the evening sky connects Berlin with the flowing distant Volga. The transcendence of space and the demonstration of the power of imagination enacted in the first two quatrains of the poem's concluding section develop in the final quatrain into an apostrophic declaration of allegiance to the principles of the lyric consciousness. Dreams and fantasy are the mainstay of life. The creative soul is never to be left to rust in the prison of reason and empirical limitation, nor the quotidian reality within arm's reach allowed to become 'a wall of stone' irrevocably separating the physically apparent from the imaginatively possible. The world is always more than it appears, awaiting creative enrichment and transformation. The poem thus ends with apostrophic affirmation of the creative consciousness which transcends all boundaries and which has been demonstrated throughout the poem.

Zina Mertz is obliquely identified in the poem as Fyodor's muse and central addressee; she is the 'you' of the apostrophic entreaty to remain true to the life of the imagination. Thus invoked by Fyodor's poem, upon its completion, she finally appears in the prose narrative to take physical shape after a series of previous indirect references distributed throughout the novel. Appropriately, within the prose of the narrative, Zina emerges from out of a passage of blank verse.[18] Provided with line breaks, the poem describing Zina's introduction runs in Nabokov's translation as follows:

> She always unexpectedly appeared
> Out of the darkness, like a shadow leaving
> Its kindred element. At first her ankles
> Would catch the light. She moved them close
> together
> As if she walked along a slender rope.
> Her summer dress was short, of night's own color,
> The color of tree trunks and of shining pavement –
> paler
> Than her bare arms and darker than her face.   (*Ssoch* IV, 357; *Gift* 177)

Zina's appearance as muse in Fyodor's verse is not the sole example within Nabokov's oeuvre of the coupling of this theme with verse. Nabokov's poetic writing is rich in the treatment of the muse, and individual poems offer clear parallels to the novel and suggest important insight into the thematic development of *The Gift*.

Nabokov's poem of 1923 'Встреча' ('Vstrecha' / 'The Meeting') begins with the emergence of a woman from her 'kindred element,' although in this instance on the liminal setting of a bridge:

> Тоска, и тайна, и услада …
> Как бы из зыбкой черноты
> медлительного маскарада –
> на смутный мост явилась ты …   (*Ssoch* I, 610)

[The longing, and mystery, and delight … / as if from the swaying blackness / of some slow-motion masquerade / onto the dim bridge you came.][19]

The mysterious woman who meets the poet 'beneath lindens, along the canal' is mysteriously felt to be his 'fate' and destined, as in Fyodor's instance, to influence his verse. Still more striking in terms of its parallels to the imagery of Zina's appearance in *The Gift* is Nabokov's poem of 1923 'Я помню в плюшевой оправе …' ('Ia pomniu v pliushevoi oprave …' / 'I remember within velvet frames …'), which contains a veritable catalogue of imagery descriptive of Nabokov's lyric experience of inspiration and the muse.[20] Thirteen quatrains of *AbAb* rhyming verse, this poem also recounts the arrival of a feminine, muse-like figure – an 'erect and slender shadow' – from out of the mists and play of light in an evening of wet streets shining like amber mirrors. With the arrival of his muse, the world itself changes to become a place of wonder and Hoffmanesque magic, a fairy-tale realm with a woman shod in glass:

> Да, правда: город угловатый
> играет жизнью колдовской
> с тех пор, и, как на улицу вошла ты
> своей стеклянною стопой.
>
> И в этом мире небывалом
> теней и света мы один.
> Вчера нам снились за каналом
> Венецианские огни.   (*Stikhi* 116)

[Yes, it is true: the angular city / plays with magical life / since you entered into the street / with your glass foot. // And in this fantastic world / of shadow and light we are alone. / In the evening we dreamed beyond the canal / of Venetian lights]

Important to the lyric speaker of this poem – as with Fyodor in *The Gift* – is the ineffable intimation that the muse shares a sensibility which draws her into immediate, speechless proximity with the poet. The poem records this silent communication in images of verse and language:

> Гадая, все ты отмечаешь,
> все игры вырезов ночных,
> заговорю ли – отвечаешь,
> как бы доканчивая стих.
>
> Таинственно скользя по гласным,
> Ты шепчешь, замираешь ты,
> И на лице твоем неясном
> Ловлю я тень моей мечты.

(*Stikhi* 116)

[Surmising, you notice everything, / all the games of nighttime excisions / should I begin to speak – you answer / as if finishing a verse. // Secretly gliding on vowels, / you whisper, you fade away, / and on your indefinite face / I catch the shade of my dream]

The play of shadow and light, images of containment and transcendence, a woman in a black dress, allegiance to the fantastical, Venetian lights reflected in water, and the association of the muse with the formal stuff of poetry are all themes and images which offer intertextual witness to the claim that Nabokov's poetry, like Fyodor's, is the basis for his later novels. If the earlier poem is more descriptive of the relevance of the muse to the lyric speaker in 'I remember within velvet frames ...,' in the later poetry contained with *The Gift*, parallel imagery is used programmatically to announce the tenets and values of a lyric sensibility which will unite Fyodor and his lover. More than indicating the lyric source of Nabokov's prose oeuvre, however, awareness of the thematic preoccupations of Nabokov's poetry promotes understanding of his novels, in this instance, the thematic thrust of the inter-character relations between Fyodor and Zina. In *The Gift*, Fyodor's love poem to Zina embodies in narrative form and content the interplay of love and lyricism which informs Nabokov's poetic sensibility; and, as in 'The Swift,' the love between the two is itself born out of a meeting of sensibilities.

After finally emerging fully formed on a tide of verse midway through the narrative, Zina, and her relationship to Fyodor, is described in a manner likewise suggestive of the metaphysical, lyric inclinations displayed in

Nabokov's poetry. Zina and Fyodor appear to be soulmates, somehow strangely acquainted with and matched to one another:

> In talking to her one could get along without any bridges, and he would barely have time to notice some amusing feature of the night before she would point it out. And not only was Zina cleverly and elegantly made to measure for him by a very painstaking fate, but both of them, forming a single shadow, were made to the measure of something not quite comprehensible, but wonderful and benevolent and continuously surrounding them. (*Ssoch* IV, 358; *Gift* 177)

Like Fyodor's poetry, their love seems to derive from a sphere 'not quite comprehensible, but wonderful and benevolent.' Fyodor's relationship to Zina also complicates and reflects upon his relationship with, and understanding of, others close to him. Fyodor's fierce devotion to artistry, and his realization that despite his love for Zina, 'he was incapable of giving his entire soul to anyone or anything: its working capital was too necessary to him for his own private affairs' (*Ssoch* IV, 359; *Gift* 178), clarifies understanding of his father's awareness of the 'innate strangeness of life' (*Ssoch* IV, 303; *Gift* 119), expressed in the naturalist's fierce dedication to his explorations, despite extended separation from his beloved wife and children. Zina's love of the poem by Fyodor 'about the swallow that cried out' signals her proximity in terms of sensibility to Fyodor's mother, who also loved – like Nabokov – 'The Swift.'[21] Fyodor's mother was associated with the room and inspiration for his abandoned book about his father. It is clearly Zina as muse who holds the keys to, and is the source of, Fyodor's future works. His first encounter of erotic potential with Zina takes place in a quintessentially Nabokovian setting of transition, a doorway at the foot of a set of stairs in the shade and contrast of poor lighting. In close proximity to the woman who would be his muse, Fyodor feels a kind of magic, the hint of the otherworld associated with love and poetry. 'Fyodor suddenly felt – in this glassy darkness – the strangeness of life, the strangeness of its magic, as if a corner of it had been turned back for an instant and he had glimpsed its unusual lining' (*Ssoch* IV, 363; *Gift* 183). The primary source of Zina's attraction for Fyodor, however, is their sharing of a quality of consciousness, the form of lyric sensibility expressed in what Fyodor calls 'multifaceted thought.' Zina's first explicit appearance in the narrative as Fyodor's lover and muse is in his poem; the reader subsequently learns, however, that Zina had first presented herself to him as a secret admirer of his poetry, in particular, the volume *Poems*, which opened the novel. In a very real sense, Fyodor's early poetry called forth his future

312 Vladimir Nabokov: Poetry and the Lyric Voice

muse. Their similarities go further. The narrative representation of Fyodor's and Zina's previous missed encounters, their mutual cognizance of the workings of fate, their whimsical measuring of the metaphysical worth of such trivial things as a 'fence' and a 'blurry star,' their love of colours and different art forms, their unforced, unembarrassed reflections on the other-world and the nature of genius while mutually observing a moth circling a lamp, all of these are markers of the heightened consciousness they share. Within Nabokov's narrative, these and other references to the trifling wonder of life are also evidence of Nabokov's lyric sensibility at work at the basis of this novel. After inspiration, cosmic synchronization, the other-world, and love, the narrative representation of the love of trifles is final indication of Nabokov's lyric voice in *The Gift*. As within Nabokov's poetic oeuvre, in *The Gift*, lyric sensitivity to the wonder of life is represented as a key to the artistic consciousness.

Throughout the three years of Fyodor's life depicted in *The Gift*, the young poet is presented as an artist not simply by virtue of his writing of poetry or even his suggestions of an intimated transcendent sphere, but, more fundamentally, because of the nature of his consciousness. Fyodor is presented throughout the novel as an individual greedily imbibing all sensory impressions from his environment. His every movement in life is rewarded with the harvest of consciously – and unconsciously – registered sensual curios which decorate his life and feed his talent. Reconnoitering his new street at the beginning of the novel, for instance, Fyodor is shown imaginatively rearranging the landmarks of his environment – tobacco shop, pharmacy, greengrocery – into aesthetic patterns. Events as humble as a frustrated trip to the tobacconist's followed by a walk across the street yield the harvest of mental riches granted the receptive mind:

The type of store that he entered can adequately be determined by the presence in a corner of a small table holding a telephone, a directory, narcissi in a vase, and a large ashtray. This shop did not carry the Russian tipped cigarettes that he preferred, and he would have left empty-handed if it had not been for the tobacconist's speckled vest with mother-of-pearl buttons and his pumpkin-colored bald spot. *Yes, all my life I shall be getting that extra little payment in kind to compensate my regular overpayment for merchandise foisted on me.*

As he crossed toward the pharmacy at the corner he involuntarily turned his head because of a burst of light that had ricocheted from his temple, and saw, with that quick smile with which we greet a rainbow or a rose, a blindingly white parallelogram of sky being unloaded from the van – a dresser with mirror across which, as across a cinema screen, passed a flawlessly clear reflection of boughs sliding and swaying not arboreally, but with a human vacillation, produced by the nature of those who were carrying this sky, these boughs, this gliding façade. (*Ssoch* IV, 193–4; *Gift* 5–6; emphasis added)

Ricocheting from a third-person to a first-person singular and then first-person plural perspective, the above scene pivots on the conscious appreciation of the compensations of the mind, which are emphasized in the sudden intrusion of a first-person response. Fyodor's review of the verse from his volume *Poems* and their genesis in remembered scenes and sensations of childhood indicates that the birth of this faculty is coincident with his awakening into consciousness. The proclivity of Fyodor's consciousness to artistic expression is displayed, however, in more than the production of finished verse. Throughout the narrative, he is revealed to have the natural capacity and propensity to perceive the world in metaphoric images. A rainbow of oil on the street becomes 'asphalt's parakeet,' a public toilet becomes 'Baba Yaga's gingerbread cottage' (*Gift* 53), the objects in his room appear in the pale light of dusk 'like people come to meet someone on a smoky railroad platform' (*Gift* 57), the singing of sparrows in ivy becomes 'big recess in a little school' (*Gift* 57), the muddy puddles of a country road appear 'full to the brim with thick café crème' (*Gift* 77), the objects of an abandoned room take on a series of funereal attributes (*Gift* 144). The examples may be extended at will. In one respect, this form of metaphoric language is unexceptional; it is native to Nabokov's style, a hallmark of his literary identity. Within the text, however, this particularly lyric mode of describing the world also fulfills a narrative role. Presented from Fyodor's perspective as the product of his artist's consciousness at work normalizing the sensory impressions of his environment, the aesthetization of experience illustrates a further component of Fyodor's character. Fyodor is shown to be an artist not only or even primarily in what he writes, but in the very way he perceives the world. This intense sensitivity to the impressions of the surrounding world is an essential characteristic Fyodor shares with Wordsworth and his description of the particular quality of the poet's sensibility from Book 13 of *The Prelude*:

> ... they build up greatest things
> From least suggestions, ever on the watch,
> Willing to work and to be wrought upon,
> They need not extraordinary calls
> To rouze them, in a world of life they live ...   (ll. 98–102)

This ability to transform even the most humble forms of experience into art is a salient feature of the Nabokovian poet and reaches its apogee in his fictional universe in John Shade of *Pale Fire*.

The acuity and inventiveness of Fyodor's 'Acmeist' perception of the world is a telling indicant of his lyric sensibility and a central feature of his nature as an individual. This quality in Fyodor is especially highlighted in the narrative through contrastive comparison with three other individuals in the novel. Within *The Gift*, Yasha Chernyshevski, Konstantin Kirillovich Godunov-Cherdyntsev, and Nikolai Gavrilovich Chernyshevskii are all accorded lengthy descriptive passages. Fyodor's father, Konstantin Kirillovich, and the radical critic Nikolai Gavrilovich each have chapters devoted to them. Although rich in a variety of thematic strands which feed into the novel, the portraits of each of these individuals are also important in terms of their reflections upon Fyodor's aestheticized relationship to the phenomena and experience of the world. Yasha Chernyshevski, tormented by unsatisfied homosexual desires and seemingly compelled to fulfill the 'poet's' clichéd role of submission to ill-defined sorrows, dies the solipsistic death of suicide. The two young men are poets of a different order; Fyodor's love of the world and people stands in contrast to Yasha's 'agitated, neoromantic' love of abstractions. Nikolai Gavrilovich Chernyshevskii, a far more complex figure of historical weight, is representative of many ills, perhaps most damningly of propagating a world view which has led 'Russia to become so shoddy, so crabbed and gray' (*Ssoch* IV, 356; *Gift* 175). Fyodor's (much abused) dissection of the 'great' materialist critic is, in essence, an analysis of the man's metaphysics and ethics viewed through the all-telling prism of his aesthetics. Chernyshevskii is unremittingly cramped and formulaic in his perception of art and hence of all other forms of experience. Unlike the 'Symbolist' Yasha, the 'materialist' Nikolai Gavrilovich castigated all poetry which did not fulfill a didactic function. In his representation of Chernyshevskii's views, Fyodor ironically adopts the critic's undifferentiated, communal perspective of sense made common with its sinister tones of normative insistence: 'We too, with equally stolid seriousness, are annoyed at poets, at healthy fellows who could be better doing nothing, but who busy themselves with cutting trifles "out of very nice colored paper." Get it clear, trickster, get it clear, arabesquer, "the power of art is the power of commonplaces" and nothing more' (*Ssoch* IV, 417; *Gift* 239). Chernyshevskii's denunciation of 'trifles and baubles,' his reproval of Pushkin, Gogol, Fet, and others is cast – in Fyodor's wording – in language which contrasts directly with Fyodor's and Nabokov's poetics of trifles lucidly rendered. Fyodor diagnoses the source of Chernyshevskii's materialist failings in his insistence on theorizing about the relations *between* things at the expense of perceiving *things themselves* in the full wonder of their physicality and noumenal specificity: 'Our overall impression is that materialists of this type fell into a fatal error: neglecting the nature of the thing itself, they kept applying their most materialistic method merely to the relations between objects, to the void between objects and not to the objects themselves, i.e. they were the naivest of metaphysicians precisely at that point where they most wanted to be standing on the ground' (*Ssoch* IV, 420–1; *Gift* 242–3). Yasha and Nikolai Gavrilovich are entangled in abstraction; the poet Fyodor is enraptured by the tangible, sensual manifestations of the world.

It is thus the two forms of abstractions, Yasha's and Nikolai Gavrilovich's, which lead away from the world and proceed through bad aesthetics to destructiveness. Enthralled by the multifariousness and splendid originality of the natural world, Fyodor's father is both a contrast to the two unrelated Chernyshevskis and, although not a versifier, a poet in his own right, a model of the form of consciousness that nurtures the artist that Fyodor wishes to be. Significantly, Fyodor's difficult decision to abandon the study of his naturalist father is motivated by his desire to not debase the 'poetry' of his father's work through imperfect literary representation. A 'seeker of verbal adventures,' Fyodor comes to realize 'the impossibility of having the imagery of his travels germinate without contaminating them with a kind of secondary poetization, which keeps departing further and further from that real poetry with which the live experience of these receptive, knowledgeable and chaste naturalists endowed their research' (*Ssoch* IV, 321; *Gift* 139). Poetry is born out of the quiddity of experience. Artistry could not emerge for Fyodor from the distance of his father's genuine experience.

Fyodor's sensual apprehension of the world, his delight in perception of the minutia of experience, is analogous to Nabokov's poetics of trifles and illustrated in more than contrastive comparison to other characters within the novel. Fyodor himself is conscious of the 'gift' of the perception of even quotidian objects. Indeed, he sees it as a form of aesthetic offering presented especially to him. The following lengthy passage deserves extended quotation as a virtuoso catalogue of the staged wonder presented to Fyodor by the humble reality of a Berlin street. Arising on an inviting summer morning, Fyodor leaves his room for a day of sunbathing and swimming to find the street buzzing with the miracle of accumulated trivia:

A turned-back doormat held the door in a wide-open position while the janitor energetically beat the dust out of another mat by slapping it against the trunk of an innocent lime tree: what have I done to deserve this? The asphalt was still in the dark blue shadow of the houses. On the sidewalk gleamed the first, fresh excrements of a dog. A black hearse, which yesterday had been standing outside a repair shop, rolled cautiously out of a gate and turned down the empty street, and inside it, behind the glass and among artificial white roses, in place of a coffin, lay a bicycle: whose? why? The dairy was already open, but the lazy tobacconist was still asleep. The sun played on various objects along the right side of the street, like a magpie picking out the tiny things that glittered; and at the end of it, where it was crossed by the wide ravine of a railroad, a cloud of locomotive steam suddenly appeared from the right of the bridge, disintegrated against its iron ribs, then immediately loomed white again on the other side and wavily streamed away through the gaps in the trees. Crossing the bridge after this, Fyodor, as usual, was gladdened by the wonderful poetry of railroad banks, by their free and diversified nature: a growth of locusts and sallows, wild grass, bees, butterflies – all this lived in isolation and unconcern in the harsh vicinity of coal dust glistening below between the streams of rails, and in blissful estrangement from the city coulisses above, from the peeled walls of old houses toasting their tattooed backs in the morning sunshine ... Where shall I put all these gifts with which the summer morning rewards me – and only me? Save them up for future books? Use them immediately for a practical handbook: *How to Be Happy?* Or getting deeper, to the bottom of things: understand what is concealed behind all this, behind the play, the sparkle, the thick, green greasepaint of the foliage? For there really is something, there is something! And one wants to offer thanks but there is no one to thank. The list of donations already made: 10,000 days – from Person Unknown. (*Ssoch* IV, 502–3; *Gift* 327–8)

For an individual of Fyodor's sensibility, a dingy railroad bank is as rich in wonder as a Tibetan meadow for his father; and, indeed, at the end of Fyodor's walk to the forest, the spirit of his naturalist father is appropriately invoked.[22] Fyodor's narrative about Konstantin Kirillovich was never granted direct access to his father's reflections on the sources of nature's magnificence. Fyodor, however, is here recorded reflecting, in a metaphor of the stage, on the reality 'behind the play, the sparkle, the thick, green greasepaint of the foliage.' There is, of course, no answer to Fyodor's grateful and yet frustrated musings. Fyodor is left with nothing more than the conviction that 'there really is something' behind it all, a belief itself derived from the beauty and perfection of what he sees. This is not a conventional expression of faith, but one which could be understood by the Christ from 'Through the garden walked Christ with disciples ...,' where Christ is observed not expounding on dogma but observing the white incisors in the jaw of a decaying dog, or 'On Golgotha,' where the crucified Christ recalls the sun-mottled lane of his carpenter father's home with its wood shavings. In Nabokov's poem 'Do You Know My Faith?' the poet swears his love to another, not on the basis of eroticism or conventional physical attractions, but out of a sharing of a sensibility regarding the natural world: 'I will love you because you will notice / all the specks of dust on a sunbeam of exist-ence, / you will say to the sun: thank you for shining.' It is this intuited confidence in the 'goodness' of the world as a result of its beauty which Fyodor will share with Zina and which unmistakably suggests the proven-ance of his poetic gift in Nabokov's lyric sensibility.

The unconfirmable, though deeply felt, faith in the goodness of the world comes from the poet's sensibility, his captivity to the trifles and man-ifold detail of the world. This quality, along with experience of cosmic synchronization, inspiration, love, and the otherworld, make of Fyodor a poet and the novel *The Gift* the product of Nabokov's lyric voice.

7 A Novel Snatched from the Sun: Nabokov's *Pale Fire*

Let us turn to our poet's windows. I have no desire to twist and batter an un-ambiguous *apparatus criticus* into the monstrous semblance of a novel.

– Vladimir Nabokov, *Pale Fire*

In *The Gift*, Fyodor makes of his lyric abilities an offering – a gift – freely granted to promote the development of his poetic art into prose; his poems, like Nabokov's, are the models of his later novels and proof of the singular quality of his artistic consciousness. In contrast to *The Gift*, the plot of *Pale Fire* rests on the theft of a poet's gift, the stealing of a poem to create a prose commentary and novel. The pilfered booty – the resulting novel – is evidence, however, to more than a single crime. Perhaps more overtly than any of his other works, *Pale Fire* exemplifies the intertextual 'thievery' responsible for the unmistakably lyric quality which defines Nabokov's writing. The Shakespearean image of the moon's stolen fire does more than provide Nabokov's fifth English-language novel with a title luminous with associations; at still deeper levels of suggestion, it alludes to the lyric exchange operative throughout the totality of his oeuvre:

> … I'll example you with thievery:
> The sun's a thief, and with his great attraction
> Robs the vast sea: the moon's an arrant thief,
> And her pale fire she snatches from the sun.   (*Timon of Athens*, act IV, scene iii)

Nabokov's poetry and lyric sensibility seems a vast sun to have illuminated everything he wrote; and in snatching the lyric fire of John Shade's poem to fuel the fantastical narrative of his prose commentary, Charles Kinbote was acting out an eminent example. *Pale Fire*, the focus of the present chapter and Nabokov's most formally unconventional novel, reflects the poetic energy of its author's lyric sensibility. Indeed, due to the particular relationship of poetry and prose which is this novel, *Pale Fire*, like perhaps no other work by Nabokov, illustrates the critical necessity of attending to his lyric sensibility when reading his works. Read against appreciation of Nabokov's poetry and the lyric tenor of all his writing, the assessment of *Pale Fire* wins unforeseen contours of meaning and profundity; confronted *without* the exegetical support of awareness of his lyric voice, the novel can seem – as it has for many – a spectacular though ultimately depthless display of formal virtuosity. The present discussion of *Pale Fire* will review the limitations of critical approaches which have largely passed over the poetry of the novel to attend instead to issues of narrative structure. In reversal of this form-based methodology, a detailed reading of *Pale Fire* will be offered which locates the novel's persistent glow in the five informing themes of Nabokov's poetry, the pale phosphorescence of his lyric sensibility.

If, as was suggested in the previous chapter, *The Gift* is a work that long remained largely unsung in criticism, *Pale Fire* is the novel which has assured Nabokov the most intensive scholarly attention, and guaranteed a form of continuous close scrutiny denied even *Lolita* and *Ada*.[1] Since first publication in 1962, *Pale Fire* has sustained unbroken readerly and, especially, critical interest. Mary McCarthy famously opened 'A Bolt from the Blue,' one of the first and still most often quoted reviews of the novel, with the exclamation that '*Pale Fire* is a Jack-in-the-box, a Fabergé gem, a clockwork toy, a chess problem, an infernal machine, a trap to catch reviewers, a cat-and-mouse game, a do-it-yourself kit' (McCarthy 1970a, 15). Despite the ludic potential suggested by McCarthy's list of games and gadgets, it has been less *le plaisir du texte* that has garnered *Pale Fire* sustained regard, than the interests of more abstract, academic import suggested in the culminating statement of her review: 'Pretending to be a curio, it cannot disguise the fact that it is one of the very great works of art of this century, the modern novel that everyone thought was dead and that was only playing possum' (McCarthy 1970a, 34). Both more and less than a pleasure to read, *Pale Fire* was to be construed as an event of literary history, the avatar – for better or worse – of the novel in its then modern form.

For many of the earliest reviewers, Nabokov's innovations seemed decidedly a development for the worse, and *Pale Fire* to be decried for its presumed threat to the 'great tradition' of the novel. Stranger, as Nabokov observed, rhymes with danger. Saul Maloff, for instance, rang a frequently heard alarm bell, claiming that '… for all its cleverness and dexterity, its brilliance of play and maneuver, Nabokov's novel raises disturbing questions precisely about his practice of the novel.' Ultimately, the exuberance and play of the novel constituted for Maloff nothing more than '... a constellation of elegant and marvelous *bibelots*, an art which is minor by definition' (Maloff 542). Alfred Chester's prognosis regarding the health of the novel was still more pessimistic. Reviewing *Pale Fire* for *Commentary* in an assessment entitled 'Nabokov's Anti-Novel,' Chester began with the sentence 'The novel is having a hard time' (Chester 449) and continued to an amazing reconstruction of Nabokov's intent, not simply in writing *Pale Fire*, but with regard to *the* novel as genre: 'Nabokov, in *Pale Fire*, tells us that there is no novel at present, and he offers this book in its place' (Chester 450). Andrew Riemer's reading of *Pale Fire* occasioned reflections on the very applicability of the designation novel in relation to so heterogeneous a 'work of fiction.' For Riemer, the meaning and significance of *Pale Fire* called forth a new category of classification. Taking his cue from Northrop Frye, Riemer proposed the genre 'Anatomy' as the form most appropriate to a full understanding of the book: '[*Pale Fire*] must be read as an "Anatomy," a compendium of erudition, mythology, sociology, literary parody and many other things, all of which are bound together by Nabokov's exuberant satire' (Riemer 45).[2] Despite the critical challenges and consternation provoked by the novel upon publication, however, for an increasing majority of critics, the structural innovations and challenges posed by the narrative form of *Pale Fire* were gratefully seized upon as illustration of the potential and promise of the novel form in its post-war, Postmodern incarnation.[3] With *Pale Fire*, Nabokov seemed for many both to have written himself an authorial identity as American Postmodernist and to have provided a predominantly national literary tendency with cosmopolitan credentials. As Maurice Couturier has noted in his retrospective 'Nabokov in Postmodernist Land,' '... it was Nabokov's least democratic novel, *Pale Fire*, which was most frequently mentioned with admiration by the postmodernists ...' (Couturier 1993, 249). And when Couturier claims that the establishment of the Postmodern identity of the author of *Lolita*, *Pale Fire,* and *Ada* is not 'an idle question,' but one of relevance to 'the very definition of postmodernism itself' (Couturier 1993, 247), he is making a pertinent assertion about both Nabokov and literary criticism. With his central English novels, and especially *Pale Fire*, Nabokov not only consolidated recognition for a half-century of artistic achievement, but, willy-nilly, helped shape the critical understanding of post-war twentieth-century literature and the rejuvenating potential of the novel form.

Even as 'one of the most complex novels ever written' (Kermode 144), however, the mass of criticism subsequently engendered by *Pale Fire* has been provoked less by concern for the fate of the novel form or the development of a then contemporary literary mode in American letters and its putative place within a broader literary tradition – the 'question' of Postmodernism – than by the more localized issues deriving from the composition of Nabokov's novel itself. Central in this regard has been the explication of the profusion of literary allusions offered by the novel and – especially and most intractably – the identification of the novel's narrator. Of the two, the latter topic has been the most prominent in Nabokov scholarship. The bedevilled question of the internal authorship of *Pale Fire* has engendered a voluminous debate centred on four dominant positions: Charles Kinbote is the sole author of poem and *apparatus criticus*; John Shade is both the author of his poem and the creator of an imagined critic and commentary; sole authorship by one of the main characters is possible though ultimately indeterminable on the basis of narrative evidence; within the fictional world of the narrative, Shade is Shade, the author of his poem, and Charles Kinbote is Charles Kinbote, the author of the commentary.[4] Consumed with unravelling the question of fictional authorship from a tangle of textual evidence, the critical response to *Pale Fire* has, as often as not, focused on the intricacies of the novel's narrative structure rather than the thematic riches of its contents.[5] As early as 1975, the accumulation of critical commentary devoted primarily to the narrative questions posed by the novel drew the following response from Robert Alter:

> ... I am afraid the novel has inspired its own Kinbotian commentators among Nabokov's critics. Exegetes of the novel, it seems to me, have tended to complicate it in gratuitous ways by publishing elaborate diagrams of its structure (which is, after all, clear enough in its main outlines), by devoting learned pages to wondering who – Nabokov, Shade, or Kinbote – is responsible for the epigraph, by exerting their own ingenuity to demonstrate dubious theses, like the one in which both the poem and the poet are argued to be Kinbote's inventions. This novel is not a Jamesian experiment in reliability of narrative point-of-view, and there is no reason to doubt the existence of the basic fictional data – the Poem and its author, on the one hand, and the mad Commentary and *its* perpetrator on the other, inverted left hand. (Alter 1975, 185–6)

Alter's grievance, formulated in a book subtitled 'The Novel as a Self-Conscious Genre,' was certainly not motivated by a desire to foreclose theoretical analysis; rather, his legitimate concern seems to have been that excessive emphasis on narrative structure hinders consideration of the *functional* point of such formal innovations and fosters the tendency '... merely to uncover intricate patterns of the novel's formal games and then to assume that intricacy itself is sufficient evidence of masterful imaginative achievement' (Alter 1975, 186). In fundamental sympathy with Alter's concern of over thirty years ago, the present analysis of *Pale Fire*, without disparaging the essential insights enabled by attention to structure,[6] will effect a realignment of critical interest from narrative form to artistic effect, from the prose of structure to the poetry of meaning. This approach is born of the conviction that examination of questions of narrative form is best conducted when linked to the totality of the novel's 'masterful imaginative achievement,' and of the related critical assumption that the wellspring of this achievement – in both formal and thematic terms – is John Shade's poem. For Kinbote within the world of the narrative – as for the reader of *Pale Fire* without – the source of all thematic meaning and subsequent critical response is 'Pale Fire.' The entire work is illuminated by the light of meaning emanating from the novel's poetry. The poem is the sun, the novel the moon.

The project of reading *Pale Fire* in the context of Nabokov's poetry and lyric sensibility is thus not simply a matter of further illustrating a general argument about the nature of Nabokov's artistry, but of complicating and deepening understanding of a complex and fascinating novel. Apart from the preponderance of appreciative studies devoted to the formal structure of the novel, a review of the critical literature reveals a range of responses strenuously resistant to *Pale Fire*, particularly in the years immediately following publication.[7] The dangers of inadequately reading *Pale Fire*, of admiring the intricacy of the structural weave without attending to the lyric pattern of meaning it forms, of insufficiently acknowledging the poetry of 'human reality' radiating out from poem to novel, has led, on the part of negatively disposed critics, to disparagement of the novel's very real achievement and, on the part of some proponents of Nabokov's artistry, to skepticism and frustration. Page Stegner effectively expresses the nagging doubts of an early sensitive critic, supportive of Nabokov's achievement, but stymied in his attempt to see beyond the 'surfeit' of structural pyrotechnics:

One wishes that critics like Mary McCarthy who find significant 'moral truth' in *Pale Fire* would somehow demonstrate where they found it, and how, and what it is ... Until it can be demonstrated that *Pale Fire* does deal in some way with moral truth or valid experience, I can admire the poem and the language and humor of Kinbote's commentary, and be amazed by its complexity, but

I must remain skeptical about its greatness and, in fact, its durability. (Stegner 131–2)

Stegner's appeal – although now dated – retains some urgency both because it states in relatively understated tones the reservations of many critics of Nabokov and *Pale Fire* (and Nabokov's English poetry) who complain of technical 'self-indulgence' – what Maloff described as 'a constellation of elegant and marvelous *bibelots*, an art which is minor by definition' – and also because it has only been rarely directly addressed. This, too, is a portion of the motivation for the present approach. The thematic depths of the novel are inextricably bound up with its poetry.

Before proceeding to *Pale Fire*'s play of poetry and prose, however, it is necessary to address one dimension of the complex subject of literary allusions in the novel, the second central focus of previous scholarly inquiry into the poetry of the novel. Beginning with McCarthy's review, much of the criticism devoted to the poem has been occupied with the intriguing task of explicating the myriad allusions to poetry woven into the fabric of Shade's poem and Kinbote's commentary. For numerous early critics, Nabokov's peppering of *Pale Fire* with learned literary references was clearly a case of over-spicing the broth; for others, a question of taste, a significant portion of the intellectual pleasures of a brilliant literary *pot-au-feu*. Such literary detective work has also been made to yield significant interpretive understanding. Brian Boyd's *Nabokov's 'Pale Fire': The Magic of Artistic Discovery*, for instance, integrates a very close reading of the poem, including its myriad literary references, into a provocative discussion of the novel, indicating that the discovery of such references may reveal much about the literary texture of the novel.[8] In cataloguing the literary allusions of *Pale Fire*, however, few critics have been as thorough as Gérard de Vries, who, in 'Fanning the Poet's Fire: Some Remarks on Nabokov's *Pale Fire*,' has identified a library of above-all English poets in *Pale Fire*. Less intent upon assessing the significance of such allusions than in locating their sources – though his study is larded with interpretive insight as well – de Vries assembles an impressive list for presentation in alphabetical form: 'Arnold, Browning, Butler, Byron, Crashaw, Donne, Eliot, Flatman, Goldsmith, Hardy, Housman, Johnson, Keats, Marvell, Milton, Pope, Shakespeare, Shelley, Southey, Swift, Tennyson, Wordsworth, and Yeats' (de Vries 1991, 249–50). The imprint of Scott, MacDiarmid, Frost, Sandburg, and Kipling is also observed and could be extended to include such internationals as Goethe and Pushkin. The often ingenious findings by de Vries and others lift a considerable burden of literary detective work from the present study, which is consciously intent less on identifying other poetic voices – a topic which has been investigated – than in isolating the echoes and tones of Nabokov's lyric voice in *Pale Fire*, a topic which has *not* been investigated. As Vladimir Alexandrov has observed, 'The poem *Pale Fire*, a moving and skillfully wrought stylization of Pope and Wordsworth that has not been sufficiently appreciated on its own terms, is a virtual pastiche of Nabokov's most important themes from fictional and discursive works of his Russian and English periods' (Alexandrov 1991, 187). The following is an attempt to read *Pale Fire* 'on its own terms,' in the certainty that the 'pastiche of Nabokov's most important themes' is most clearly illustrated in the context of Nabokov's poetry and lyric sensibility.

The identification of poetic allusions in 'Pale Fire' contains further dimensions of relevance to Nabokov and poetry. Although a legitimate exegetic tool of great value in sounding the poem's subterranean thematic echoes, critical concentration on such references may distract from sufficient grasp of 'Pale Fire' at other levels. The interpretive over-determination of the thematic and stylistic function of literary allusion leads easily to the same form of failed critical appreciation of Nabokov's poetic achievement that characterized portions of his reception as a Russian poet. In the overview of Nabokov's reception as émigré poet, it was observed that all too often criticism of Nabokov's poetry stopped short of analysis of the intrinsic qualities of Nabokov's verse to satisfy itself with general observations about its putative debt to other poets and poetic styles. The same threat applies in the reading of *Pale Fire* and may be forwarded as a reason for the insufficient appreciation of the poem 'Pale Fire' noted by Alexandrov. The abundance of alluring literary references in the poem has proven a more promising – and accessible – field of literary investigation than Nabokov's own verse. Alvin Kernan, for instance, has been led on the basis of his identification of the 'elaborate intertextuality' of 'Pale Fire' to far-reaching statements about the nature of Shade's – hence Nabokov's – poetry and poetic voice:[9] 'Shade is almost a parody version of what Harold Bloom has called the "weak" poet, the belated writer who has no authentic voice of his own but merely echoes earlier stronger writers, and "Pale Fire" can be read as an extended and amusing spoof on romantic and modern poetry, particularly on Frost' (Kernan 103). The echoes heard by Kernan in Shade's poem extend beyond Frost, however, to become a cacophony of poetic voices:

... the Frostian tone dominates 'Pale Fire': regular metrical system, rhyme, a plain, almost folksy note, a mixture of everyday trivia with sudden terrors

lying below the surface, and a search for metaphysical meaning in the ordinary. Nabokov does not, however, entirely suppress his own signature, and
the Frostian tone is complicated by a good deal of light mockery, burlesque,
and ironic self awareness. But Nabokov's is not the only other poetic voice
we hear, for though Frost's style dominates, Shade's style and subject matter
are a literary conglomerate containing, among many other poetic echoes, the
mock-epic tones and heroic couplets of Pope, Wordsworthian spots of time
and a sense of identity with nature, the lyricism of Goethe, the somnambulis-
tic sounds of Poe, touches of Browning's monologues, the linguistic dandyism
of Stevens, the rhythms of Yeats, and Eliot's sinister sounding banalities of
ordinary speech ... (Kernan 103)

The bewildering diversity of this roll call of English-language poets
(apart from Goethe) immediately recalls the range of influence attributed
to Nabokov by the émigré critic Struve, among others, in the context of
his Russian poetry. In that instance, from *Russkaia literature v izgnanii*,
discussed in chapter 2, sixteen Russian poets were clustered into a single
paragraph-length discussion of Nabokov's poetry. A further parallel to
the émigré reception of Nabokov's poetry is the conspicuous absence of
direct reference to Nabokov's published verse, a lacuna made strikingly
obvious by the very framing of the criticism of Nabokov's poem and
putatively imitative voice. With statements such as 'his own signature'
and 'Nabokov's is not the only other poetic voice we hear,' Kernan signals identification of a poetic identity, though he immediately equates it
with Frost rather than acknowledging even the possibility of a source in
Nabokov's voluminous corpus of poetry.[10] A similarly unsubstantiated,
though briefer, gesture of critical foreshortening is suggested in Philip
Toynbee's claim that 'Pale Fire' the poem 'is about as good as brilliant
pastiche can ever be, and, in the opening stanza, perhaps a little better
than that. There is something of Pope here, something of Donne, something of Meredith's "Modern Love," something of Wallace Stevens and
Robert Frost. But these influences are not fused and transformed by any
novelty of poetic vision or technique' (Toynbee 24). Nabokov is indeed
possessed of, in Kernan's terms, 'his own signature,' or, in Toynbee's
words, a distinctive 'poetic vision' which may be heard throughout the
poem and novel, though it is too rarely alluded to – much less explored
– in criticism devoted to *Pale Fire*.[11] Neither Kernan nor Toynbee indicates any awareness of Nabokov's poetry, a startlingly 'visible' blind spot
in a form of criticism which overtly accentuates speculation regarding
the provenance of Nabokov's poetic identity. As a result, the light of a

much brighter sun is all too easily mistaken for the pale fire of various lesser moons also present in Nabokov's poetic universe. As will become clearer below, the project of reading *Pale Fire* – the poem and the novel – without adequate consideration of Nabokov's lyric voice is fraught with danger; *Pale Fire* is a thoroughly Nabokovian novel and thus requires a reading attentive to the lyric sensibility which informs all of his writing.[12] Shade's prosody may appear Popean, his physical appearance and lifestyle Frostian, and his autobiographical interests Wordsworthian, but his poem 'Pale Fire' is unmistakably Nabokovian. Indeed, before turning to 'Pale Fire' itself, the critical relevance and interpretative potential of attendance to Nabokov's own poetic oeuvre may be briefly but forcefully demonstrated by reference to his most popular – and critically successful – English poem apart from 'Pale Fire.'

An exceptional work in its own right, Nabokov's narrative poem of 1945 'An Evening of Russian Poetry' is also an intriguing pre-text to *Pale Fire*. The poem most often praised in positive assessments of Nabokov's poetic abilities (in English), this 143-line narrative poem assumes the form of a public lecture addressed to an audience of undergraduates on the theme of Russian poetry. 'An Evening of Russian Poetry' thus resembles *Pale Fire* in its playful mimicking of a non-fictional prose genre in its choice of external form. The parodic, comic potential of the poem's apparent generic form is tempered, however, with a sustained undertone of intense, though muted, poignancy, leaving the unpresupposing prose façade of 'An Evening of Russian Poetry' to house, at subsidiary levels, the lyricism of a brilliant poem.

The poem begins with the identification of the ostensible topic of the 'lecture' – Russian poetry – and quickly proceeds to the identification of the speaker:

> My little helper at the magic lantern,
> insert that slide and let the colored beam
> project my name or any such-like phantom
> in Slavic characters upon the screen.
> The other way, the other way. I thank you.   (*PP* 158)

The confusion indicated in the inverted projection of the lecturer's 'phantom' name in Slavic characters introduces the slippage in both identity and theme which will transform a lecture into lyric expression of muted despair.[13] The central speaker of the poem, the invited lecturer expounding on Russian poetry, is revealed to be not a single poetic voice but the composite of three identities each with its own accent: a lecturer, an exiled monarch, and a poet. The controlling voice is that of the lecturer who expounds upon the charms of Russian prosody to his ill-informed audience and who patiently answers innocent questions about poetry:

> Yes, Sylvia?
>   '*Why do you speak of words*
> *when all we want is knowledge nicely browned?*'
> Because all hangs together – shape and sound,
> heather and honey, vessel and content.   (*PP* 158)

The restrained, pedagogical perspective of this figure is interrupted, however, by the more desperate voice of the exiled poet-monarch, who intercedes to continue discussion of Russian poetry with a quiet, personalized lament expressed in the lyric language of fairy-tale imagery:

> Beyond the seas where I have lost a scepter,
> I hear the neighing of my dappled nouns,
> soft particles coming down the steps,
> treading on leaves, trailing their rustling gowns,
> and liquid verbs in *ahla* and in *ili*,
> Aonian grottoes, nights in the Altai,
> black pools of sound with 'l's for water lilies.
> The empty glass I touched is tinkling still,
> but now 'tis covered by a hand and dies.   (*PP* 159–60)

In anticipation of *Pale Fire*'s Kinbote – a would-be monarch-in-exile pursued by the 'shadow' Jakob Gradus (alias d'Argus) – this speaker from 'An Evening of Russian Poetry' is tracked by the shades of artistry and time past – the abandoned remnants of inspiration and the lingering intimations of half-remembered memories:

> My back is Argus-eyed. I live in danger.
> False shadows turn to track me as I pass
> and, wearing beards, disguised as secret agents,
> creep in to blot the freshly written page
> and read the blotter in the looking glass.
> And in the dark, under my bedroom window,
> until, with a chill whirr and shiver, day
> presses its starter, warily they linger
> or silently approach the door and ring
> the bell of memory and run away.   (*PP* 160–1)

Exiled by time from the past, and by space from the kingdom of his native language, the poet-lecturer is left alone with the partial consolation of memory and physical sensation, faculties of consciousness which are occasionally able, unbidden and briefly, to collapse time and space in a Proust-like return to the past:

> And now I must remind you in conclusion,
> that I am followed everywhere and that
> space is collapsible, although the bounty
> of memory is often incomplete:
> once in a dusty place in Mora county
> (half town, half desert, dump mound and mesquite)
> and once in West Virginia (a muddy
> red road between an orchard and a veil
> of tepid rain) it came, that sudden shudder,
> a Russian something that I could inhale
> but could not see. Some rapid words were uttered –
> and then the child slept on, the door was shut.   (*PP* 162)[14]

The 'bounty of memory' is necessarily a private boon, as cryptic as a child's speech in sleep and hence impervious to conveyance to an uncomprehending audience. During the course of the address, the public prose of the scholar's lecture has given way to the lyricism of the poet's private emotion. The evening of Russian poetry concludes with the merger of academic and poet in a macaronic statement which returns to the language of his past to express the inexpressible pathos of his situation. In responding to a well-intended question, which nonetheless bites in its very insouciance and banality, the speaker answers in the personal, unspeakable language of his inconsolable grief:

> '*How would you say "delightful talk" in Russian?*'
> '*How would you say "good night"?*'
>   Oh, that would be:
> *Bessónnitza, tvoy vzor oonýl i stráshen;*
> *lúbov moyá, otstóopnika prostée.*
> (Insomnia, your stare is dull and ashen,
> my love, forgive me this apostasy.)   (*PP* 162–3)

The translation in parentheses which concludes the poem not only provides painfully ironic comment on the futility of the entire enterprise – the attempt to communicate in an evening's lecture the essence of Russian poetry. In the manner of so many of Nabokov's narratives, it also opens up a cleft, a slight fissure, which exposes the subterranean subject matter of the poem submerged beneath the surface structure. Lines untranslated and thus, in a sense, uncommunicated within the poem nonetheless serve as the poem's most powerful statement.

'An Evening of Russian Poetry' is above all a poem about psychological dissonance and physical separation, about exile from the language of the past and the confounding inexpressibility of personal grief, but also about the private consolation of memory. And although 'An Evening of Russian Poetry' and *Pale Fire* share a series of common images and themes – academic setting, the configuration of poet, lecturer, and exile in a single, first-person character, theories of prosody, exile from a fairy-tale past, pursuit by 'shadows,' and so on – the incidentals of theme do not provide the fundamental linkage. The decisive parallel between the two is the maintenance of a delicate tonal balance between the wonder and consolation of art and the muffled pain of a damaged life. In his published lecture on Kafka's *Die Verwandlung*, Nabokov suggested that '*beauty plus pity* – that is the closest we can get to a definition of art' (*LL* 251; emphasis in original). It is the lyric rendering of 'beauty plus pity' which distinguishes 'An Evening of Russian Poetry,' and it is this combination which will be observed in *Pale Fire* as it emerges out of the thematic emphases that comprise Nabokov's poetic voice.

'Pale Fire' and the Poet's Pattern: Novelistic Text and Poetic Texture

Pale Fire is a novel characterized by its semblances and differences, its mirror images and contrastive reversals. Its narrative exterior is famously that of a four-part scholarly edition of a fictional text with Foreword, 999-line poem, a line-by-line critical Commentary, and Index. The self-parodic reference to Nabokov's own four-volume translation, with commentary, of Pushkin's *Eugene Onegin* is obvious, though ultimately of limited interpretive substance.[15] The primary reference point for understanding of *Pale Fire* comes not from without but from within the text, from its lyric substrata in John Shade's poem.[16] As Alexandrov has observed, the 'exegetic anchor' of the novel is the poem 'Pale Fire,' with its fictional author John Shade (Alexandrov 1991, 187). At 999 lines, 'Pale Fire' is the longest poem in Nabokov's poetic oeuvre.[17] Beginning with the heroic couplets which form the basic unit of its composition, 'Pale Fire' is a masterpiece of structural symmetry. Four cantos divide the poem: the outer cantos, one and four, mirror each other in length at 166 lines, while the poem's inner cantos, two and three, are twinned at 334 lines each. In harmony with imagery contained within the poem, the physical shape of 'Pale Fire' – two flanking smaller sections connected by two larger inner sections – resembles two lemniscates, or ampersands, placed side-by-side or, still more promisingly, given Kinbote's descriptive language of 'twin wings of five hundred verses each' (*PF* 15), a butterfly. The poem's form is thus suggestive of both eternity and metamorphosis. The conclusion of canto two at line 500 marks the half-way point of the poem. The missing final line and conclusion to the 500th couplet is rendered with a repetition of the poem's opening line, which both completes the poem and returns it to its beginnings. The poem begins in imagery of transition redolent of metaphysical wonder; line 500 brings death at the poem's fulcrum; the conclusion ends 'Pale Fire' in neither transition nor death, though *suggests* both. The very architectonic fullness of the poem seems a rock of stability within the shifting sands of the novel's narrative layers, although, as will be discussed at greater length below, the patterned symmetry of the poem has a thematic function as well.

   Pale Fire, the novel framing and containing the poem, is marked by an elaborate system of inversions and oppositions extending from the generic contrast between an 'autobiographical' poem and a *märchenhaft* prose commentary; between the aging 'fire-side' poet John Shade, a universally beloved, domestically contented heterosexual man at home in his local Appalachian environment, and his cosmopolitan, homosexual *pendant*, a man robust in physical health, though imprisoned in the loneliness of exile and the caustic disdain of all but Shade in his social environment; between a poem which reaches outward to find faint confirmation of the life of consciousness after death in love and the artistic apprehension of life, and Kinbote's solipsistic (re-)creation of a fantasy past where love is found only in the fantasy realm of dream and where life is threatened with suicide in a lonely room. In contrast to the inversions of the novel, the poem 'Pale Fire' is distinguished by layers of formal and thematic patterning. In *Pale Fire*, John Shade's poem offers a template of relative narrative stability and thematic focus. Although mediated by a mad commentator who for better or worse has 'the last word' – as he proprietarily asserts – any claims to be advanced regarding the thematic import of the novel are ultimately derived from the poem, whether directly, in terms of its form and contents, or indirectly, in terms of the manipulations it is subjected to as the object of Kinbote's commentary. To read the novel *Pale Fire* is to assimilate the lyric beauty and force of John Shade's poetic meditation on life and death, love and art, then to read Charles Kinbote's distortion of the same. Kinbote's redaction provides a form of pleasure derived from its comedy and beauty, but also negative confirmation of the lyric wisdom of Shade's poem as its example shines through the chinks in Kinbote's pitiable fantasy. In short, understanding of Nabokov's novel is thrown back on reference to the beauty of Shade's poetry and the pity of Kinbote's tortured commentary.

'Pale Fire' begins with a quintessentially Nabokovian form of perfection, its first twenty lines expressive of the formal and thematic density of his poetry:

> I was the shadow of the waxwing slain
> By the false azure in the windowpane;
> I was the smudge of ashen fluff - and I
> Lived on, flew on, in the reflected sky.   (*PF* 33; ll. 1–4)

Ivanov of Nabokov's short story 'Perfection' was able to remove the 'pane of glass' separating him from direct contact with the external world only in death, a brief caesura or an enjambment in the poem of being (cf. 'The Room') which led to the blissful expansion of his consciousness on a higher plane of transcendence. Thanks to the creative turn of his perceptive powers, John Shade, the speaker of these lines, is able to project himself into an ineffable beyond. Shade remains alive on 'the inside,' short of the total divestment which is death, but imaginatively experiences in his art the flight which presumably greets him at his death and the conclusion of the poem, when his first line provides the final, missing, one-thousandth line, granting both Shade and his poem a new beginning:

> And from the inside, too, I'd duplicate
> Myself, my lamp, an apple on a plate:
> Uncurtaining the night, I'd let dark glass
> Hang all the furniture above the grass,
> And how delightful when a fall of snow
> Covered my glimpse of lawn and reached up so
> As to make chair and bed exactly stand
> Upon that snow, out in that crystal land!   (*PF* 33; ll. 5–12)

Apart from the metaphysical thematics at this point still only implicit in the poem's opening scene (more of which below), the imagery deployed is subtly suffused with references to Nabokov's poetry. Distant but perceptible is the combination of a pane of glass and a trick of visual perception, an echo which is contained not only in the story 'Perfection,' but in the early poem 'How often, how often I on a fast train …' (*Ssoch* I, 467), where the poet-speaker travelling on a train leans his forehead against the window and seems to merge with 'the rapture of a sunset.' Likewise familiar is the mysterious flight of one of the many songbirds swooping through Nabokov's verse and descriptions of inspiration. More visibly present from various examples of Nabokov's poetry, however, is the imagery of the writer's modest room furnished – as in 'Pale Fire' – with a lamp, a chair, and a bed, all to be transformed by the night and a window. Significantly, it is not only the speaker who is both reflected back upon himself and released into the beyond by the mysterious properties of the window; the 'dark glass' division also marks a transition between the enclosed space of the poet's room and the open expanses of 'that crystal land' beyond the glass.

   Further to the themes and imagery being evoked and alluded to here is the euphony of the lines, which also bears the stamp of Nabokov's thematic concerns. The thematically relevant play of division and reflection is taken into the very prosody of the poem, allowing sound to recapitulate meaning:

> Retake the falling snow: each drifting flake
> Shapeless and slow, unsteady and opaque,
> A dull dark white against the day's pale white
> And abstract larches in the neutral light.
> And then the gradual and dual blue
> As night unites the viewer and the view,
> And in the morning, diamonds of frost
> Express amazement …   (*PF* 33; ll. 13–20)

Within the rhymed unity of each couplet, a complex series of internal rhymes reflects against the divisions formed by caesuras and line breaks in an intricate play of mirrored and duplicated sound. *Retake/flake* mirror each other euphonically within line 13; *snow/slow* are reflected across the line-break of the couplet in lines 13 and 14. The same form of rhyming pattern is formed with dark *white* / pale *white* and *dark/larches*, as well as *gradual/dual* and *night unites / viewer and the view*. Nabokov's manipulation of form supports his thematic ends; experience is patterned and re-formed in art as his words are made with rhyme and assonance to mimic the reflection they are describing. *The Gift* began with the young poet Fyodor absorbing and recording a street scene for future transformation into art. Charles Kinbote in the Foreword which opens *Pale Fire* records his witnessing of 'a unique physiological phenomenon: John Shade perceiving and transforming the world, taking it in and taking it apart, re-combining its elements in the very process of storing them up so as to produce at some unspecified date an organic miracle, a fusion of image and music, a line of verse' (*PF* 27).

The famous opening scene of 'Pale Fire' is likewise an illustration of the poet transforming his environment, while simultaneously investing it with the meaning definitive of Nabokov's lyric sensibility.

John Shade's 999-line poem is thoroughly Shadean in its autobiographical orientation on the individual particulars of the poet's life and experiences. It is also quintessentially Nabokovian; beneath the narrative structure adopted out of adherence to the trajectory of Shade's life lies the constellation of lyric themes that define Nabokov's poetic sensibility. The poetic representation of Shade's life and experience is shot through with the lyric concerns of Nabokov's poetry. 'Pale Fire' is thus not only the longest poem in Nabokov's oeuvre, it is also the fullest, most densely articulated expression of cosmic synchronization, inspiration, the otherworld, love, and the sensual appreciation of the manifold wonder of nature. The following will offer a reading which establishes the 'moral truth,' the poignancy and pity, the metaphysical consolation, and the artistic wonder of *Pale Fire* as it emerges out of Nabokov's lyric sensibility. Confident that Nabokov's artistry is best read with an ear attentive to the imagistic echoes and thematic cadences of his lyric voice, the approach will proceed through the poem 'Pale Fire' to follow closely the traces of the informing themes defining of Nabokov's poetic voice. As in each of the genres and texts so far discussed in this study, critical consciousness of the lyric core of Nabokov's artistry will intensify cognizance of the exceptional 'imaginative achievement' of *Pale Fire* as both poem and novel, while further illustrating the centrality of Nabokov's lyric sensibility in the shaping of his artistry.

Central to Nabokov's lyric poetics is the mystery of cosmic synchronization. Not surprisingly, then, John Shade is also depicted as someone marked in his life and artistry by a mysterious experience of transcendence. John Shade's first experience of cosmic synchronicity came – as for Fyodor of *The Gift* – in boyhood and is placed in the poem at the conclusion of canto one as the most significant experience of childhood. Shortly after his eleventh birthday, Shade lies prone on the floor to observe a 'clockwork toy – / A tin wheelbarrow pushed by a tin boy' (*PF* 38; ll. 143–4) – that has, like the ball in Fyodor's first poem from *The Gift*, rolled under a piece of furniture. While looking at his toy, Shade feels an explosion of light in his head followed immediately by total darkness. Rather than seeming a frightening experience, Shade's collapse – the pain and tug of 'playful death' – is associated with a wondrous feeling of dispersal through time and space:

> The blackness was sublime.
I felt distributed through space and time:

One foot upon a mountaintop, one hand
Under the pebbles of a panting strand,
One ear in Italy, one eye in Spain,
In caves, my blood, and in the stars, my brain.
There were dull throbs in my Triassic; green
Optical spots in Upper Pleistocene,
An icy shiver down my Age of Stone,
And all tomorrows in my funnybone.   (*PF* 38; ll. 147–56)

Along with his photographic memory, the strangely liminal experience of cosmic synchronization is, in accordance with the contours of Nabokov's lyric sensibility, the first evidence of the specificity of Shade's consciousness, the first unmistakable sign of a form of consciousness which will also know the blissful expansion of love and artistic creation. It is also an experience which seems to foreshadow the shock and wonder of death, the presumably final experience of consciousness and the central concern of Shade's poem and much of his creative life. Unbeknownst to Shade himself, albeit in implicit confirmation of his belief in the divinely patterned structure of life, this first, childhood experience of cosmic synchronization will find completion in his death by shooting and is rehearsed in alternate forms at key points throughout his life and poem. Shade's first return to the experience, now linked more closely with death (both his own and his daughter's), occurs in canto two on the evening of his daughter's suicide. Watching television in expectation of Hazel's return home, Shade's wife plays 'Network roulette' (*PF* 49; l. 465). She impatiently selects a channel and just as impatiently turns it, cancelling the actions taking place in another spectral dimension, among them the raising of a gun:

An imbecile with sideburns was about
To use his gun, but you were much too quick.
A jovial Negro raised his trumpet. Trk.
Your ruby ring made life and laid the law.
Oh, switch it off! And as life snapped we saw
A pinhead light dwindle and die in black
Infinity.   (*PF* 49–50; ll. 468–74)

As Kinbote will assert in his commentary, and as an instance of art foreshadowing life, an imbecile with a gun ultimately robs Shade of his life before being struck down himself by a 'jovial Negro.' In canto three, a more explicit repetition of the fainting fit, and more pressing dress rehearsal of death, occurs. Lecturing, like the speaker of 'An Evening of Russian Poetry,' on the topic of poetry, Shade is confronted by a questioner:

One of those peevish people who attend
Such talks only to say they disagree
Stood up and pointed with his pipe at me.   (*PF* 58; ll. 688–90)

The threatened weapon is only a pipe; nonetheless, Shade is struck by 'the attack, the trance, / Or one of my old fits' and suffers an abrupt change of consciousness, which once again brings him perilously close to death. In this instance, 'the trance' is felt by Shade to be the crossing-over of – after a well-placed enjambment – a border, a threshold into a realm of interconnected-ness and unity dominated by the vision of 'a tall white fountain':

                    I can't tell you how
I knew – but I did know that I had crossed
The border. Everything I loved was lost
But no aorta could report regret.
A sun of rubber was convulsed and set;
And blood-black nothingess began to spin
A system of cells interlinked within
Cells interlinked within cells interlinked
Within one stem. And dreadfully distinct
Against the dark, a tall white fountain played.   (*PF* 59; ll. 698–707)

The image of a tall white fountain in the context of a changing and expan sion of consciousness is itself reminiscent of the experience recorded in Nabokov's poetry of the poet's glimpsing of a mysterious 'something else, something else, something else.' Nabokov's poem 'Fame' of 1942 records the first-person experience of a poet who has read in himself 'how the self to transcend.' One day, 'while disrupting the strata of sense,' the poet des-cends down to his 'wellspring' (*kliuchevoe*) to see mirrored there the in-effable 'something else.' Similarly, in 'The Paris Poem' of 1943, the poet-speaker records a life 'rich in patterns' and his revisiting of his 'foun-tainhead' there to unravel himself

as a gift, as a marvel unfurled,
and become once again the middle point
of the many-pathed, loud-throated world.   (*PP* 123; ll. 126–8)

Shade subsequently learns of another individual's seeming confirmation of his vision of a fountain glimpsed during his penultimate experience of the transformation of cosmic synchronization. An article in a newspaper reports of a woman's near-death experience and her vision of a 'fountain.'

Upon interviewing 'Mrs Z,' however, Shade learns that she had not seen the 'wellspring,' the 'fountainhead,' or the 'fountain' of Nabokov's poets (as in 'Fame'), but rather a 'mountain' which was mistakenly transformed into coincidental confirmation of Shade's experience by a journalist's misprint.[18] Despite the initial disappointment, the quiddity of Shade's vision is left intact, and he is brought to a fundamental realization:

> *Mountain* not *fountain*. The majestic touch.'
> Life Everlasting – based on a misprint
> I mused as I drove homeward: take the hint,
> And stop investigating my abyss?
> But all at once it dawned on me that *this*
> Was the real point, the contrapuntal theme;
> Just this: not text, but texture; not the dream
> But topsy-turvical coincidence,
> Not flimsy nonsense, but a web of sense.
> Yes! It sufficed that I in life could find
> Some kind of link-and-bobolink, some kind
> Of correlated pattern in the game,
> Plexed artistry, and something of the same
> Pleasure in it as they who played it found.   (*PF* 62–3; ll. 802–15)

As will be further discussed below, within the context of Shade's life and poem, *mountain* and *fountain* provide him with evidence of the 'contrapuntal theme' of life, a fundamental existential insight which offers the consolation of at least 'faint hope' in confronting the mystery of death and life's meaning. At the narrative level of the novel *Pale Fire*, however, Shade's penultimate experience of cosmic synchronization and the realization of the 'contrapuntal theme' in life also provide an important principle of the novel's composition. It is also the 'contrapuntal theme' developing out of Kinbote's narrative kinship to Shade which provides *Pale Fire* its 'correlated pattern.' The 'plexed artistry' of *Pale Fire* – its 'texture' and the 'web of sense' seemingly woven from the 'flimsy nonsense' of Kinbote's commentary – is also based on Kinbote's reflected and inverted depiction of Shade's experience, which appears, now distorted, in the fantastical story of his own life. While Shade narrates the *text* of his life in his poem, Kinbote provides it *texture* as further dimensions of Shade's experience shine through the interstices of Kinbote's distorted retelling. The beauty and inspiration of Shade's telling is served by the psychic pain and anguish which motivate Kinbote's retelling.[19]

Kinbote, too, undergoes a recurrent liminal experience which parallels – though inverts – Shade's mysterious, multiple experience of cosmic synchronization. In the narrative recreation of his fairy-tale existence in the kingdom of Zembla, Kinbote recounts – like the *poète manqué* Waltz of *The Waltz Invention* – the delicate beauty of his reign, a *belle époque* purportedly distinguished by the 'harmony' owed to the beneficent influence of its sovereign (*PF* 75). Despite the apparent boon of Kinbote's benevolent governance, however, a coterie of revolutionaries usurp his power to introduce a regime of vulgarity and anti-aestheticism, substituting a reign 'once redolent of carnation and lilac' for the 'smell of leather and goat' (*PF* 120). Kinbote, imprisoned by the insurgents in an abandoned room of his palace, is returned by memory to an event of his childhood three decades previous. Then, as a young boy, Kinbote had sought out a toy in an abandoned room: not the 'tin wheelbarrow pushed by a tin boy' of Shade's experience, but 'an elaborate toy circus contained in a box as big as a croquet case' (*PF* 124). Finding at first a 'dusty black trunk,' Kinbote also disturbed a piece of 'black velvet' and discovered a hidden door, which, as 'the threshold of a secret passage' (*PF* 125), formed the transition point to an unknown space which was as mysterious as the coffin-like imagery of the trunk which announced it. With his boyhood friend Oleg, Kinbote descended into the tunnel-like passage to walk its 1,888 yards before emerging at a green door, behind which threatening sounds suggestive of sexual aggression are heard. In fear, the boys hurriedly returned through the passage to the castle to take up their own sexual explorations. Years later as a deposed, imprisoned king awaiting an uncertain fate, Kinbote recalls the secret passage, which grants him escape after passing through the terminal 'green door' and the dark folds of a heavy dark curtain.

While Shade opens his poem expansively, projecting himself out of the confines of a glass pane into a larger external expanse beyond, Kinbote inverts the experience by describing his attempts to intrude into the enclosed space of Shade's home through nighttime windows. An analogous inversion of Shade's experience of a childhood toy and mysterious expansion in cosmic synchronization occurs in Kinbote's experience of the tunnel. Whereas Shade's consciousness was expanded in a death-like experience, Kinbote's is enclosed in the dark tunnel of his narcissism; and whereas Shade's presumed final encounter with cosmic synchronization and the releasing of his consciousness in a form of transcendence at the moment of his death is accompanied by thoughts of love for both his wife and deceased daughter, Kinbote's release is associated with the frolicking 'sport' of adolescent sexual activity and the confusing, frightening uncertainty of a violent heterosexual encounter (in fact, an exchange between two actors). Shade's experience presages death as a form of release and expansion; Kinbote's experience is entwined with the altering of consciousness in carnal release, delirium, death, and forgetting:

> Soon after the discovery of the secret passage he almost died of pneumonia. In his delirium he would strive one moment to follow a luminous disk probing an endless tunnel and try the next to clasp the melting haunches of his fair ingle. To recuperate he was sent for a couple of seasons to southern Europe. The death of Oleg at fifteen, in a toboggan accident, helped to obliterate the reality of their adventure. (*PF* 128)

Even the numerical associations of Kinbote's experience express solipsism rather than expansion. The number 1,888 refers both to the date of death of Iris Acht, former mistress to Kinbote's grandfather and an actress whose former dressing-room concluded the secret tunnel, and the number of yards connecting the palace lumber-room and dressing-room. The triple lemniscates of the three eights suggest an eternity introduced by the singularity of a one. Kinbote's consciousness seems trapped in the exitless, eternal return of solipsism. His escape is not a release but an enclosure.[20] Shade, in contrast, will die at the cusp of line 1,000 of his poem, a place where, in the language of Fyodor's poetics in *The Gift*, all the lines meet.

In life, before the divestment of death and the removal of a glass pane separating him in his domestic enclosure from an external expanse – as with Ivanov in 'Perfection' – Shade is granted the earthbound extension of consciousness in love and artistic inspiration. Both figure prominently as 'informing themes' in the characterization of Nabokov's lyric sensibility, and both figure prominently in Shade's life and art. Canto four of Shade's poem, which will conclude his life and verse, begins with a disquisition on forms of composition and inspiration, of which Shade counts two:

> Two methods of composing: A, the kind
> Which goes on solely in the poet's mind,
> A testing of performing words, while he
> Is soaping a third time one leg, and B,
> The other kind, much more decorous, when
> He's in his study writing with a pen.   (*PF* 64; ll. 841–6)

Shade's discussion of the theme central to Nabokov's poetry and his prose representations of artists and artistic consciousness is conspicuous in its

similarity to Nabokov's lyric description of the poet's mind. 'I am aloof,'
Nabokov wrote in his early lyric 'The Poet,' which described the poet's dis-
connectedness from waking reality when in the grip of poetic inspiration.
Shade, too, describes himself as somehow aloof or beside himself, an 'au-
tomaton' deprived of his waking will, when engaged in the creative
process:

> ... which no effort of the will
> Can interrupt, while the automaton
> Is taking off what he has just put on
> Or walking briskly to the corner store
> To buy the paper he has read before.   (*PF* 64–5; ll. 856–60)

Fyodor in *The Gift* had described composition as an 'ardor dangerous to
life' when producing the poem which self-reflectively illustrated the workings of his gift, the 'demency that rambles' (*Ssoch* IV, 242; *Gift* 56);
for Shade, too, composition is 'agony' and leads to the 'demency' known
to Fyodor:

> Dressing in all the rooms, I rhyme and roam
> Throughout the house with, in my fist, a comb
> Or a shoehorn, which turns into the spoon
> I eat my egg with. In the afternoon
> You drive me to the library. We dine
> At half past six. And that odd muse of mine,
> My versipel, is with me everywhere,
> In carrel and in car, and in my chair.   (*PF* 67–8; ll. 941–8)

Fyodor of *The Gift* and Grisha of 'Torpid Smoke,' poets who are subject
to the dissipation and expansion of consciousness during the throes of inspiration, are also explicitly described in terms of their bodies. For these
poets, as with numerous other protagonists from Nabokov's oeuvre associated foremost with the mysteries of consciousness, emphasis on the physical deficiencies and failings of the body repeatedly provides an unspoken
contrast across the spirit-body divide to the strengths and mysterious
flights of the mind. A pinched shoe and the razor burn around Fyodor's
Adam's apple suggest that his spirit is caged in an impermanent prison, but
also that the needs of the body are subordinated to the attention of the
creative consciousness when swept up in inspiration. Nabokov described
the same phenomenon in his article 'Inspiration': 'A prefatory glow, not

unlike some benign variety of the aura before an epileptic attack, is something the artist learns to perceive very early in life ... As it spreads, it banishes all awareness of physical discomfort – youth's toothache as well as the neuralgia of old age' (*SO* 309). Shade, too, is body or – in his incarnation as waxwing – ashen fluff left behind in the flights of inspiration. Shade depicts himself in the bath preparing to shave:

> The more I weigh, the less secure my skin;
> In places it's ridiculously thin;
> Thus near the mouth: the space between its wick
> And my grimace, invites the wicked nick.
> Or this dewlap: some day I must set free
> The Newport Frill inveterate in me.
> My Adam's apple is a prickly pear:
> Now I shall speak of evil and despair
> As none has spoken. Five, six, seven, eight,
> Nine strokes are not enough. Ten. I palpate
> Through strawberry-and-cream the gory mess
> And find unchanged that patch of prickliness.   (*PF* 66; ll. 895–906)

Along with his weak heart and unsteady gait, the daily procedure of shaving intimates the divestment from the 'ridiculously thin' hull of his body that Shade will leave, much like the 'empty emerald case' of a cicada he found on a tree trunk on the day of his beloved aunt's death.[21]

In 'Pale Fire,' Shade's curious discourse on shaving is more than reference to the vulnerability of the physical hull surrounding his spirit. It also leads to a description of the physical pleasure of inspiration, the bliss of what Fyodor termed the 'divine stab.' Shade parodies the commercial advertisements for shaving cream which depict the pleasure of effortless shaving. In his poem 'Ode to a Model' of 1955, Nabokov describes a model in advertisements as a reversal or negation of authenticity, beautiful but a sham.[22] Here, in 'Pale Fire,' the inauthenticity of an advertisement is made to serve as an image of the corporeal pleasure of inspiration, what Nabokov described in 'The Poem' as the shiver of delight when thought and expression 'fuse and form a silent, intense, / mimetic pattern of perfect sense.' The voluptuousness of inspiration is real and leads to a physical response more intense than the ersatz reaction of commercial feeling:

> Now I shall speak ... Better than any soap
> Is the sensation for which poets hope

When inspiration and its icy blaze,
The sudden image, the immediate phrase
Over the skin a triple ripple send
Making the little hairs all stand on end
As in the enlarged animated scheme
Of whiskers mowed when held up by Our Cream.   (*PF* 67; ll. 915–22)

That Shade is contrasting authentic inspiration and artistry from false forms – as in Nabokov's poem 'The Poem' – is made apparent in Kinbote's commentary to line 922, the final line of this passage. Here, Shade's demented exegete, Kinbote, records two of the poet's discarded variants. Rather than mere poetic dross, the two variants emphasize the contrast Nabokov is making between real inspiration and poetry and their sham forms. Both variants decry the vulgarization of public life and, especially, art in a manner which draws direct parallels to the imagery and themes of 'The Poem':

England where poets flew the highest, now
Wants them to plod and Pegasus to plough;
…
And all the Social Novels of our age
Leave but a pinch of coal dust on the page.   (*PF* 270)

Ultimately, the coupling of inspiration and the mundane care of the body in daily ablutions also suggests that the creative consciousness is operative at all times. What Kinbote correctly describes as 'a unique physiological phenomenon' (*PF* 27) – the poet's transformation of perception of the world into art – is a process that is incessant and knows no hierarchy in terms of the relative value of sensual input. In his Foreword, for instance, Kinbote records observing Shade as the poet looked 'from the terrace (of Prof. C.'s house on that March evening) at the distant lake' (*PF* 27) and correctly assumed the profundity of Shade's transmutation of experience into art, though he could not have known – as does the reader only upon *rereading* the novel – that Shade is undoubtedly thinking of the private tragedy of his daughter, drowned on a March night in that distant lake. Central to Nabokov's artistic sensibility, however, is the realization that inspiration and art also spring from the more humble, trifling realms of experience, including shaving. Appropriately, then, Shade's rumination on composition and inspiration concludes at the end of the poem's narrative description of his shaving with the germ of an idea for later development, an idea which will serve Kinbote in the composition of *Pale Fire*:

Man's life as commentary to abstruse
Unfinished poem. Note for further use.   (*PF* 67; ll. 939–40)

Kinbote himself provides unbidden confirmation of the force and practice of inspiration in the poet's life according to the two modes identified
by Shade. Spying through his window into the enclosed, private space of
Shade's study, Kinbote observes the 'blaze of bliss,' the 'contours of his
inspiration' (*PF* 88), as the poet, seated at his desk, engages in the second
of the two modes of composition, the 'other kind, much more decorous,
when / He's in his study writing with a pen' (*PF* 64; ll. 845–6). Kinbote also
observed Shade consumed by the 'penless work' of composition 'when the
poet paced back and forth across his lawn, or sat down for a moment on
the bench at the end of it, or paused under his favorite hickory tree' (*PF*
89). Significantly, Kinbote clutches for the conventional in attempting to
rationalize the mystery of Shade's creative ability and mistakenly attributes
divine guidance as the source of the poet's inspiration. In the prison of his
narcissism, Kinbote is unable to imagine the actual source of inspiration to
fuel the creative gift of the greatest of Nabokov's poets – love. An informing
theme definitive of Nabokov's lyric sensibility, love also figures prominently in Shade's life and poem.

Throughout the breadth of Nabokov's lyric oeuvre, inspiration and love
are co-joined as the related forms of transcendence available to humans
before physical divestment and the intuited release of consciousness in cosmic synchronization. Likewise, throughout Nabokov's lyric oeuvre, inspiration and love as themes are frequently united and personified in the figure
of the muse. In 'Pale Fire,' too, Shade's discussion of inspiration seamlessly
blends in canto four into a loving tribute to his wife and muse, a figure who
is depicted in poetry-based imagery as literally a portion of his artistry:

And all the time, and all the time, my love,
You too are there, beneath the word, above
The syllable, to underscore and stress
The vital rhythm. One heard a woman's dress
Rustle in days of yore. I've often caught
The sound and sense of your approaching thought.
And all in you is youth, and you make new,
By quoting them, old things I made for you.   (*PF* 68; ll. 949–56)

Shade's reference to the traditional associations of the muse in mentioning
the rustle of a woman's dress accentuates her provenance in a lengthy literary

tradition and her partial conformity to the demands of literary convention. Even in her archly literary role as muse, however, Sybil Shade is quintessentially Nabokovian in her independence as a character. Emergent from the long line of inspirational women in Nabokov's poetry, during her metamorphosis into the unique character in *Pale Fire*, she brings with her the primary traits of the lyric muse of Nabokov's poetry. Central to the specificity of the Nabokovian muse is the quality of sharing with the poet the unspoken unity of thought – itself the hint of a Platonic prehistory. Wordless communication, the shared, unspoken perception of experience, characterizes the muses and lovers of Nabokov's poetry from Sybil of *Pale Fire* back through Zina Mertz of *The Gift* and the nameless woman of the poem 'The Swift' in *The Gift* to the various 'dark ladies' of Nabokov's early poetry and, for instance, the nameless feminine addressee of 'Do You Know My Faith?' where the poet's declaration of love is born of a shared love of the trifles of nature. More than a lover of erotic appeal, the muse shares the poet's sensibility and encourages his gift, making of artistic creation an act of love.

Intellectually, John Shade is transfixed by the spectre of death and its silent, ineffable mystery; in the daily conduct of life, however, Shade is powered by love. Love in all of its dimensions envelopes him. Shade loved his aunt, was wracked by a love powerless to soothe his tormented daughter, was sustained by his love for nature, his art, and his wife. Indeed, Shade goes to his death at the end of his poem and life accompanied by lyric expression of his love for nature – the garden, the shagbark tree, and a 'dark Vanessa' wheeling in the light of dusk – as well as reassuring thoughts of his daughter and his wife. Inspired and loving, Shade's consciousness is enriched with gifts entirely lacking to Kinbote. In this, more than in the previously listed oppositions contrasting the two men, Shade is fundamentally all that Kinbote is not. Kinbote, Shade's inverted *semblable*, is inspired, not by appreciation of the beauty and inexplicably patterned goodness of being which seems confirmed by love, but by naked fear and the intractable loneliness which both plagues and feeds upon his self-absorption. Even Kinbote's homosexual erotic adventures – love's physical manifestation – are described, not in terms of emotion, but repeatedly in the vocabulary of bodily exertion and sport, what Kinbote terms 'copious but sterile pleasures' (*PF* 173). As expressions of love, these exertions are inauthentic, as distant from love as, in Nabokov's 'The Poem' of 1944, the poetry describing 'the cacodemons of carnal pain' is from 'the poem that hurtles from heights unknown.' In Kinbote's upturned world, the closest he can come to Shade's experience of love is an adaptation and inversion of the poet's relationship with his daughter and wife. Within his fantasy life, Kinbote is married to Queen Disa, Duchess of Payne and Mone, a woman who seems a composite of Judge Goldsworth's daughter Dee – whose photograph hangs in the house Kinbote rents – Shade's daughter Hazel – for whom the words 'pain' and 'moan' are used in description on lines 351 and 355 of Shade's poem – and especially Sybil Shade as lovingly described by her poet husband. Significantly, Kinbote notes the similarity between Sybil and his wife Disa in Shade's poem, but accords the greater reality to his imagined projection and not the intensity of Shade's love:

> Now the curious thing about it is that Disa at thirty, when last seen in September 1958, bore a singular resemblance not, of course, to Mrs. Shade as she was when I met her, but to the idealized and stylized picture painted by the poet in those line of *Pale Fire*. Actually it was idealized and stylized only in regard to the older woman; in regard to Queen Disa, as she was that afternoon on that blue terrace, it represented a plain unretouched likeness. I trust the reader appreciates the strangeness of this, because if he does not, there is no sense in writing poems, or notes to poems, or anything at all. (*PF* 207)

Significant as well, in the mirrored, inverted world created by Kinbote, proximity to the feelings of love and pity and an escape from the emotional eternal return of narcissism are possible only in a dream:

> His dream-love for her exceeded in emotional tone, in spiritual passion and depth, anything he had experience in his surface existence. This love was like an endless wringing of hands, like a blundering of the soul through an infinite maze of hopelessness and remorse. They were, in a sense, amorous dreams, for they were permeated with tenderness, with a longing to sink his head onto her lap and sob away the monstrous past. They brimmed with the awful awareness of her being so young and so helpless. They were purer than life. (*PF* 210)

Kinbote glimpses the consolation of love which arises out of a deep feeling of tenderness for Disa, but is agonizingly denied its experience outside of dreams, the soothing sleep of his tortured reason. In life, Kinbote is unable to love, caught instead in 'an infinite maze of hopelessness and remorse.' Kinbote is alone, a matter of dire consequence for his fragile identity.

'Solitude is the playfield of Satan,' observes Kinbote, and 'that cold hard core of loneliness which is not good for a displaced soul' (*PF* 95) becomes the poisoned wellspring of his desperate fantasy. Ensconced in the house rented from Judge Goldsworth, the liminal 'turning point of dusk' – so frequently associated in Nabokov's writing with lyric potential – resembles for Kinbote 'the nightfall of the mind' (*PF* 96). Kinbote is nightly prey to the delusions which pursue him to the point of suicide: 'At times I thought that only by self-destruction could I hope to cheat the relentlessly advancing assassins who were in me, in my eardrums, in my pulse, in my skull ...' (*PF* 97). Even the house, which as metaphor for the enclosed cosmos of a human life ought to have offered him protection from premature divestment of the body, seems porous. Despite checking the doors and window-shutters before bedtime and sleep – the harbinger of the transformation of consciousness – each morning revealed to Kinbote 'something unlocked, unlatched, a little loose, a little ajar, something sly and suspicious-looking' (*PF* 97). It was as response to the threat to his own mind and 'house' that Kinbote 'got used to consulting the windows of [his] neighbor's house in the hope for a gleam of comfort' (*PF* 96). Like Waltz of *The Waltz Invention*, whose life, as he declaimed, 'has consisted of such material privations, of such mental torments' (*Ssoch* V, 535; *WI* 28) that he was driven to delusional fantasies, Shade claims to 'have suffered very much, and more than any of you can imagine' (*PF* 300). And like Waltz, who substituted memory of an inexpressible tragic past and an intolerable present for a grandiloquent fantasy of limitless power, Kinbote, too, seeks to overcome the pull of 'death's fearful shadow' at his door in the creation of a more reassuring and gregarious identity composed in images of romance and vigour.

It is here that Kinbote's actual identity is suggested within the fictional universe of *Pale Fire*. The muted despair of the Russian émigré Botkin is revealed through the ragged fabric of Kinbote's frayed identity. As in the case of Waltz in the *The Waltz Invention*, the narrative of *Pale Fire* does not explicitly represent Kinbote's trauma but intimates its power as a catalytic experience for Kinbote. Botkin-Kinbote's fabrication of a past and identity out of Shade's poem is an act of despair. Within the combinational, patterned logic of the novel, it is not necessary that Kinbote be decisively identified as Botkin, only that his pain and despair be registered.[23] The pity evoked by Kinbote's desperate assumption of an identity rests, not in identification of its 'real' source at still another narrative level within the novel, but in recognition of its precariousness, its sense of wretched necessity, and, lastly, its containment in the inexpressible privacy of an exile's irrevocably 'foreign' experience. The exile-speaker of 'An Evening of Russian Poetry' does not translate the private language and thought of his final words into speech his well-meaning audience can understand; he does not because he cannot, which is itself the crowning insult to an exile's despair. There are no suitable words. In the language Kinbote has created for himself, Zemblan, the word *kinbote* means regicide, which is, as he says, itself another word for someone who has sunk 'his identity in the mirror of exile' (*PF* 267). As an exile in America, Botkin-Kinbote *is* existentially 'foreign'; he comes from a foreign land, speaks a foreign language, and harbours memories from a now forever foreign world. And finally, in adopting the imposed identity of a new land – in sinking 'his identity in the mirror of exile' – he has deposed his former self and thereby committed a form of regicide.

As Shade – and seemingly only Shade – realizes, if Kinbote is misguided, it is the 'madness' of suffering. In defending his benighted neighbour from the charge of madness levelled by a less charitable acquaintance, Shade graciously and perceptively diagnoses Kinbote's terribly private predicament: '"That is the wrong word," he said. "One should not apply it to a person who deliberately peels off a drab and unhappy past and replaces it with a brilliant invention. That's merely turning a new leaf with the left hand"' (*PF* 238). Like the speaker of 'An Evening of Russian Poetry,' the Russian émigré lecturer V. Botkin – alias Kinbote, alias Charles Xavier Vseslav II – is desperately shedding 'a drab and unhappy past,' adopting a new identity in his Waltz-like escape from the intolerable indignities of past experience. In this psychic turning of 'a new leaf,' there is a portion of the poet's creativity and commitment to the fantastical identified by Shade as the province of the poet. In Shade's community is an elderly man who 'thought he was God and began redirecting the trains'; judged a 'loony' by others, Shade demurs to term him 'a fellow poet' (*PF* 238). It is to Shade's belief in the centrality of pity in the governance of human conduct and to his Nabokovian belief in the allegiance of the poetic to the illogical that Kinbote owes his tenuous 'friendship' to the famous poet. Kinbote is able, at least temporarily, to master the pain and loneliness of his existence through recourse to his imagination. As an artist, however, although possessed of a Hubert Humbert–like 'fancy prose style,' Kinbote's abilities remain unleavened with the love and inspiration which help to make of Shade both a poet and a kind and perceptive man.

Loved, loving, and inspired, Shade approaches the moment of his sudden end reasonably certain that death will bring to consciousness a surprise as wonderful as life. Kinbote has no such consolation; in this, he is not unlike another metaphysically uninspired character from Nabokov's oeuvre, Gonville of *Death*. The logic of inversion and semblance uniting Kinbote and Shade provokes questions as to Kinbote's end 'beyond the skyline of the page.' At the conclusion of his commentary, Kinbote asserts that he 'shall continue to exist,' that in various possible disguises and in various possible contexts he will carry on until overtaken by a pursuer who will confront him at the threshold of the house of life: '… and presently he will ring at my door – a bigger, more respectable, more competent Gradus' (*PF* 301). Despite Kinbote's trust in the uncertain prospects of this contingent form of existence, he himself alludes to suicide, which seems a more likely end: 'God will help me, I trust, to rid myself of any desire to follow the example of two other characters in this work' (*PF* 300). Kinbote, of course, is referring to Hazel Shade and Jack Grey, both of whom take their lives. Suggesting the continuation of their negative example, Nabokov claimed in an interview reprinted in *Strong Opinions* that 'Kinbote committed suicide (… after putting the last touches to his edition of the poem)' (*SO* 74). Although Nabokov's authorial intervention need not be considered final, suicide nonetheless seems a demise plausible for Kinbote, given the trajectory suggested by the internal evidence of the novel. The likelihood of suicide is still further strengthened through allusion to Nabokov's poetic practice. Shade, for one, seems to have intuited his neighbour's death, as Kinbote perceives. In his commentary to 'Pale Fire,' Kinbote notes a variant of four lines in canto two at a point in the poem where Shade is writing of the hereafter in response to the dementia and subsequent death of his aunt:

> Strange Other World where all our still-born dwell,
> And pets, revived, and invalids, grown well,
> And minds that died before arriving there:
> Poor old man Swift, poor   , poor Baudelaire   (*PF* 167)

With subdued misgivings, Kinbote notes that, given the meter of the line, the missing name of the dash must – like the name Kinbote – be a trochee; he likewise muses on the 'prophetic scruple that prevented [Shade] from spelling out the name of an eminent man who happened to be an intimate friend of his' (*PF* 168). Shade, it seems, judges Kinbote a mind 'that died,' foreshadowing imminent death, as was the case with his Aunt Maude. Added to this is the coincidence of Swift's death on October 19, the date appended by Kinbote to the conclusion of his Foreword. The matter is of sufficient consternation to Kinbote to merit two references in his index, each with the compulsion and laconicism of a private obsession: once under '*Kinbote, Charles, Dr.*' as 'poor who? *231*' (*PF* 308); and again under '*Variants*' as 'poor old man Swift, poor — (possible allusion to *K*), *231*' (*PF* 314).

Further evidence of Kinbote's suicide is to be found in his commentary to line 493 of 'Pale Fire,' which identifies Hazel Shade's 'accidental' death as suicide. Although announced as anything but 'an apology of suicide,' Kinbote's entry dealing with Hazel emphasizes the positive aspects of what he terms 'the transition' of death, and simultaneously reveals several clues suggesting the 'intolerable temptation' of suicide for Kinbote. Of the various possible forms of self-destruction, Kinbote prefers falling: 'Of the not very many ways known of shedding one's body, falling, falling, falling is the supreme method ...' (*PF* 220). Significantly, Kinbote claims that 'the ideal drop is from an aircraft, your muscles relaxed, your pilot puzzled, your packed parachute shuffled off, cast off, shrugged off – farewell, *shoot-ka* (little chute)' (*PF* 221). *Shootka* does not mean 'little chute' but is Russian – as Botkin knows – for joke, suggesting that Kinbote's casting off of his mortal coil is a farewell to, and shedding of, the cosmic joke of a body which has imprisoned his spirit in metaphysical and political exile. Kinbote later claims to have entered the United States via parachute, indicating that a transitory escape by falling is pressing on his mind. That Kinbote perceives the body, the *shootka*, as a disposable husk surrounding an immortal essence is also revealed in his comments about the welcome home of death: 'Ecstatically one forefeels the vastness of the Divine Embrace enfolding one's liberated spirit, the warm bath of physical dissolution, the universal unknown engulfing the miniscule unknown that had been the only real part of one's temporary personality' (*PF* 221). The most direct expression that Kinbote will end his life in 1959, however, comes of a combination of his discourse on death by falling and repeated allusions to Nabokov's poetry of a lone suicide's death in an anonymous, rented room. In his discussion of the preferred modes of falling to death, Kinbote suggests the possibility of rolling out of a hotel window from 'room 1915 or 1959' (*PF* 220). Coincidentally – or not – 1915 is the year of Kinbote's birth, and 1959 the probable year of his end.

Kinbote's allusion to the fatidic room numbers of his birth and probable death and, in more general terms, an anonymous hotel room invites consideration of further evidence of his suicide derived from Nabokovian poetry external to 'Pale Fire.' The image of the anonymous room as an enclosed space surrounded by larger expanses has already been discussed in this study as a motif frequently deployed in Nabokov's poetry. In *Pale Fire*, as well, this theme arises in a cluster of references to three motifs from Nabokov's poetry and prose contained in lines 589 to 611 of 'Pale Fire' – a dream, a noble death, and a death in a hotel room. The theme of dream-world contact with the dead as it is perhaps most explicitly treated in Nabokov's poem 'The Dream' is taken up in lines 589 to 596; lines 597 to 608 recast a theme exemplified by Gumilev in Nabokov's article 'The Art of Literature and Commonsense' and Fyodor's father in *The Gift*, that of the artist's bravery in the face of violent sanction at the hands of self-designated guardians of common sense and order, all those incapable of appreciating

'Empires of rhyme, Indies of calculus' (*PF* 55; l. 602). Of relevance to Kinbote's fate as a probable suicide, however, is the allusion to the third theme contained in the lines from 'Pale Fire' which echo 'The Room,' a poem of 1950 (discussed in chapter 3) which meditates on the death of a poet alone in a hotel room (*PP* 164–5). In canto three, Shade's poem ominously identifies a dying exile:

> Nor can one help the exile, the old man
> Dying in a motel, with the loud fan
> Revolving in the torrid prairie night   (*PF* 55; ll. 609–11)

In his commentary to these lines, Kinbote notes a variant by Shade which, in its fourth line, alludes to the imagery of striped, coloured light which figures prominently in 'The Room' as 'the darkness where / rain glistened and a shopsign bled' and a 'wheeling skeleton of light.' The discarded variant is, as Kinbote senses, ominous:

> Nor can one help the exile caught by death
> In a chance inn exposed to the hot breath
> Of this America, this humid night:
> Through slatted blinds the stripes of colored light
> Grope for his bed – magicians from the past
> With philtered gems – and life is ebbing fast.   (*PF* 234)

Kinbote observes that 'this describes rather well the "chance inn," a log cabin, with a tiled bathroom, where I am trying to coordinate these notes' (*PF* 235). Kinbote, as Botkin, is also an 'exile' of the variant's first line, which connects a string of disconcerting references suggesting death as the end of an exile's life 'ebbing fast.'

Ultimately, however, the inevitability of Kinbote's death seems sealed at another level of textual compulsion. The three central actors of the novel – Shade, Gradus, and Kinbote – are connected to one another at various levels. Shade and Kinbote share the same birthday, July 5th; while Kinbote and Gradus share the same year of birth, 1915. Each of the three also owes his presence in the novel, his fictional being, to Shade and his poem. Shade as the author of 'Pale Fire' is the animating artistic force, the original sun or *primum mobile* granting them all movement and life within the text; Kinbote, Shade's *semblable*, functions in his distorted, creative madness as a pale moon, the commentator to a poem who depends for his existence on the poet and poem. Jack Grey, as Gradus, Kinbote's fabrication within the commentary, is placed at a further third remove from Shade's artistic source. As a factotum within Kinbote's fantasy devoted to a poem, Gradus, too, is dependent upon the poem for his existence. According to the misdirected logic established by the commentary, Kinbote is correct when he states that 'the force propelling him [Gradus] is the magic action of Shade's poem itself, the very mechanism and sweep of verse, the powerful iambic motor' (*PF* 136). Shade and Gradus/Grey perish at the end of the poem which has sustained them, and it would seem that Kinbote, the figure to have connected them, will share a similar fate.

The figure of Gradus is of relevance at still another level to the lyric, Nabokovian poetics established by the novel. If Kinbote, related to Shade by a shared birthdate and a creative 'madness' unfortunately unleavened to true artistry by inspiration and love, is a misshapen semblance of the artist Shade, then Gradus, at a still further remove from Shade, is his artistic inversion, the negation of the aesthetic and ethic epitomized by the poet. Gradus represents the opposite of the lyric sensibility exemplified in Nabokov's poetry and in the figures who embody it in his prose. In *The Waltz Invention*, Waltz was beset by puppet-like generals and functionaries who personified the carnage and destruction to have beset the failed poet's life; in *The Gift*, the materialist critic Nikolai Gavrilovich Chernyshevskii, with his emphasis on the functional and utilitarian, seems the opposite of the aesthetic championed by Fyodor. In *Pale Fire*, it is gray Gradus, dressed in brown and walking with his simian gait, who functions as the antipode to Shade's achievements of heightened consciousness: 'Spiritually he did not exist' (*PF* 278). Unmoved by interest in the unique in life and driven by a crude ideology of class conflict and the subordination of the individual to the masses, Gradus – as depicted by Kinbote – appears to have surrendered his individuality to the will of the group:

Mere springs and coils produced the inward movements of our clockwork man ... He called unjust and deceitful everything that surpassed his understanding. *He worshiped general ideas and did so with pedantic aplomb. The generality was godly, the specific diabolical.* If one person was poor and the other wealthy it did not matter what precisely had ruined one or made the other rich; the difference itself was unfair, and the poor man who did not denounce it was as wicked as the rich one who ignored it. People who knew too much, scientists, writers, mathematicians, crystallographers and so forth, were no better than kings or priests: they all held an unfair share of power of which others were cheated. A plain decent fellow should constantly be on the watch for some piece of clever knavery on the part of nature and neighbor. (*PF* 152; emphasis added)

Expressed in Kinbote's cadences and trimmed to his socio-political interests as a deposed monarch, Kinbote's diagnosis of the fundamental destructiveness exemplified by Gradus is correct. The driving belief that 'the generality was godly, the specific diabolical,' is an exact reversal of Nabokov's plea for the illogical and irrational made in 'The Art of Literature and Commonsense,' which prioritized 'the supremacy of the detail over the general, of the part that is more alive than the whole' (*LL* 373). Gradus's materialist article of faith forms the programmatic substrata of a world view which is as inimical to Shade's aesthetics, ethics, and metaphysics as it is to Kinbote's imaginary political legitimacy. Gradus represents death to both. His presence in the narrative, albeit as a product of Kinbote's fantasy, is nonetheless a further instance of Kinbote providing the texture of a negative example to the text of Shade's sensibility.

Gradus's reversal of Shade's lyric celebration of 'the supremacy of the detail' returns discussion to a further feature of Nabokov's poetic identity, the fourth 'informing theme' present in Shade's poem. Characteristic of Nabokov's poetry and lyric identity is acute attention to the trifling specifics of the natural world. In his behaviour, as recounted by Kinbote and in the narrative of his poem, Shade is shown to share this passion for his natural environment in ways which carry implications for his aesthetics, ethics, and metaphysics. Born the child of scientist-ornithologists, though raised by the poet and painter Aunt Maud, Shade is excellently placed to unite the skills of the poet Fyodor and his naturalist father or, in Nabokov's words from *Strong Opinions*, to effect the merger 'between the precision of poetry and the excitement of pure science' (*SO* 10). Shade's love of nature is identified relatively early in the poem as a driving force in his life. It is of sufficient power, even at a young age, to supplant faith in conventional religion. Shade's 'God died young' (*PF* 36; l. 99) leaving him unconstrained by dogma, like the speaker of 'Fame' who chooses 'to stay godless, with fetterless soul / in a world that is swarming with godheads' (*PP* 111). Replacing theolatry for Shade was a sensually experienced love of nature:

> How fully I felt nature glued to me
> And how my childish palate loved the taste
> Half-fish, half-honey, of that golden paste!   (*PF* 36; ll. 102–4)

Shade's world was not devoid of metaphysical speculation, however, and as a youth, the child Shade learned to read in his natural surroundings the signs of impermanent enclosure within a larger space:

My picture book was at an early age
The painted parchment papering our cage:
Mauve rings around the moon; blood-orange sun;
Twinned Iris; and that rare phenomenon
The iridule – when, beautiful and strange,
In a bright sky above a mountain range
One opal cloudlet in an oval form
Reflects the rainbow of a thunderstorm
Which in a distant valley has been staged –
For we are most artistically caged.   (*PF* 36–7; ll. 105–14)

Shade's sensual apprehension of his surroundings is articulated in the aesthetic terms of mottled colour and stage design, a delicate imagery of containment lending the passage a patina of metaphysical wonder. Suggestive, too, of the continuity of Nabokov's poetic voice and the place of Shade's poem in Nabokov's lyric oeuvre is the use in this passage of an image from one of Nabokov's earliest poems. The lyric which opens Nabokov's almanac of 1918, *Two Paths*, with its clear echoes of a 'gypsy romance' and its headlong exuberance, is of a fundamentally different order than the poetry of 'Pale Fire.' Nonetheless, the poem's opening image of 'Темно-синие обои / Голубеют' ('Temno-sinie oboi / Golubeiut' / 'Dark-blue wallpaper / Growing lighter blue' [*Ssoch* I, 437]) and its unabashed revelry in the beauty of a dawning day are reminiscent of the 'painted parchment papering our cage' and Shade's 'childish palate' that loved the taste of nature.

Likewise evocative of Nabokov's early poetry and witness to Shade's love of nature is the presence in 'Pale Fire' of a menagerie of birds and animals distinguished, liked those of Nabokov's youthful verse, by the aesthetic and metaphysical potential of external transformation and metamorphosis. The waxwing of the poem's opening lines, the pheasant of 'torquated beauty, sublimated grouse' (*PF* 33; l. 25), the white butterflies that 'turn to lavender' (*PF* 35; l. 55), the mockingbird, the trilling crickets, the singing cicada (later identified by its abandoned emerald envelope), an ant lodged for eternity in amber, the 'dark Vanessa' butterfly, the wood duck 'richly colored' in 'emerald, amethyst, carnelian, with black and white markings' (*PF* 184), and other animals are but some of the creatures that recall the peacocks, butterflies, tadpoles, cranes, moths, and swallows of Nabokov's early poetry. Additional to the various animals is the selection of natural phenomena – from waterfalls to moondogs – that make of Shade's modest Appalachian environment a garden of earthly delights, an Arcadia of pastoral wonder apparent to the lyric sensibility that perceives it.

In aesthetic terms, the Nabokovian emphasis on the bounty of nature is manifest in the poem's inclusion of imagery of the trifles of nature. In ethical terms, the relevance of nature is also stressed through its association with love. Shade's love for his wife, Sybil, and his deceased daughter Hazel, for instance, is cast in poetically rendered settings of nature and trifles. Shade fell in love with Sybil during a high-school field trip to a local waterfall. Shade's poetic recreation of the event emphasizes the way in which a potentially banal event was miraculously transformed by a trick of refracted light and Sybil's presence into something magical:

> We luncheoned on damp grass.
> Our teacher of geology discussed
> The cataract. Its roar and rainbow dust
> Made the tame park romantic.   (*PF* 42; ll. 250–3)

For Shade, Sybil is identified with the Nabokovian animal *par excellence*, a 'dark Vanessa, crimson-barred' butterfly. And although the temporal measure of their love is calibrated in the domestic image of the family clock and 'free calendars' hanging on the kitchen door, the quotidian homeliness of their shared, private experience is what renders it unique:

> I love you when you're standing on the lawn
> Peering at something in a tree: 'It's gone.
> It was so small. It might come back' (all this
> Voiced in a whisper softer than a kiss).
> I love you when you call me to admire
> A jet's pink trail above the sunset fire.
> I love you when you're humming as you pack
> A suitcase or the farcical car sack
> With round-trip zipper. And I love you most
> When with a pensive nod you greet her ghost
> And hold her first toy on your palm, or look
> At a postcard from her, found in a book.   (*PF* 43; ll. 281–92)

Sybil, with a sylvan-sounding name, is also, like her daughter Hazel, bound up in associations with trees – an evocation of the otherworld in Nabokov's lyric writing, from Silvia's name in *The Wanderers* to the leafy medium of Art Longwood's transcendence in 'The Ballad of Longwood Glen.' At the poem's conclusion, Shade will see Sybil's shadow near his favourite shagbark tree, the one which once held his daughter's swing and to which

Kinbote observed him gravitate while in the throes of poetic inspiration. In the above passage, however, his love for her is manifest in her relation to shared specific, ineluctably private, experiences, both trifling and tragic. It is these experiences which emboss his life with the watermark of the unique. And it is, in turn, the uniqueness of life which renders it irreplaceable.

Here, the trifles, coincidences, and particulars which form a significant portion of Nabokov's poetic identity are also revealed to bear a metaphysical dimension. Throughout 'Pale Fire,' John Shade is shown to be exceptionally concerned with the mystery of death and the nature of being after death. Shade has discarded religion, not because he has an alternative theology with which he wishes to replace it, but because the communal, shared quality of organized religion and its mythologies of the afterworld seems too convenient, too commonplace, too unimaginative to capture the quiddity of life. As a portion of his love of the trifling and unique in nature, Shade observes that life on this side of death is 'impossible, unutterably weird, / wonderful nonsense' (*PF* 41; ll. 219–20). With this realization, Shade naturally questions why the hereafter should be less magnificently unexpected:

> So why join in the vulgar laughter? Why
> Scorn a hereafter none can verify:
> The Turk's delight, the future lyres, the talks
> With Socrates and Proust in cypress walks,
> The seraph with his six flamingo wings,
> And Flemish hells with porcupines and things?
> It isn't that we dream too wild a dream:
> The trouble is we do not make it seem
> Sufficiently unlikely ...   (*PF* 41; ll. 221–9)

Moreover, Shade contests that the trifling wonder of life with its stamp of the specific is not to be traded for the domesticated visions of religion:

> And I'll turn down eternity unless
> The melancholy and the tenderness
> Of mortal life; the passion and the pain;
> The claret taillight of that dwindling plane
> Off Hesperus; your gesture of dismay
> On running out of cigarettes; the way
> You smile at dogs; the trail of silver slime
> Snails leave on flagstones; this good ink, this rhyme,

This index card, this slender rubber band
Which always forms, when dropped, an ampersand,
Are found in Heaven by the newlydead
Stored in its strongholds through the years.   (*PF* 53; ll. 525–36)

Shade's list of irreplaceables runs through disparate sources of beauty and
pity in human life – from melancholy and tenderness through the particu-
larities of Sybil's habits and the trifles of nature to images of art and eternity. In assembling this catalogue, Shade is likewise revealing his participation
in a prominent theme from Nabokov's poetry. From 'In Paradise' to 'Oculus,'
among other examples, Nabokov's poetry repeatedly addressed the dilemma of the meagre gains of heaven, conventionally conceived, when traded
against the wonder and specificity of human existence, or, as expressed in
the final lines of 'Oculus': 'and who can care / for a world of omnipotent
vision, / if nothing is monogrammed there?' (*PP* 101). In 'Pale Fire,' Shade
thus expresses a theme more tragically exemplified in the example of the
mad Salvator Waltz/Tourvalski and more dramatically stated in the final
lines of his poem 'To My Soul':

Your home I do not know, believe me!
Even the way there, is not clear,
And when you fly, how shall I follow
With so much booty taken here?   (*Ssoch* V, 548; *WI* 50)

And, finally, it is this central idea that the young Nabokov associated with
Rupert Brooke – likewise in connection with reflections on Brooke's death
and the beyond – when he wrote: 'He [Brooke] knew, however, that although
he may perhaps find an inexpressible wonderful paradise, he will necessarily
leave forever his humid, living and expressive world' (*Ssoch* I, 734).

Waltz's fellow sufferer, Kinbote, shares neither Waltz's nor Shade's love
of the irreplaceable trifles of life which monograph existence; he thus again
emphasizes both his distorted relation to the poet and his negative embodiment of the lyric sensibility illustrated by Shade. Kinbote suffers and certainly knows 'passion and pain.' The compensating expressions of his
imagination, however, emerge not from loving observation and appreciation of the external world but from solipsistic centredness on the workings
of his own obsessed mind. In his commentary, Kinbote repeatedly reveals
his inability to occupy himself with anything unconnected to the private
fantasy born of his personal grief. The forms of his self-absorption are
numerous in *Pale Fire* and, indeed, frequently serve the novel's strong

undercurrent of humour, though they just as often reveal the emotional poverty of a deranged man. Kinbote, for instance, delivers to the Shades the third-class mail he himself ignores; he wishes a heart attack on John Shade as a pretext to administer 'Zemblan herbal receipts' to the grateful poet; he insouciantly interrupts the Shades as they tearfully read Shade's poetic recreation of their daughter's death; he misinterprets the disdain of his colleagues and neighbours for awe; he disparages Shade's lyric representation of Hazel, seeing in it material 'expanded and elaborated to the detriment of certain other richer and rarer matters' (*PF* 164); after the shooting, he first hides Shade's manuscript before attending to his 'friend'; and, as a final example from many, he denies identification with, or even representation of, the awesome pain of Sybil's grief after Shade's murder with the laconic remark: '... and then there was the awful moment when Dr. Sutton's daughter drove up with Sybil Shade' (*PF* 295). Kinbote's perhaps most eloquently telling misreadings of his environment come, however, in his failure to appreciate those details which provide Shade's life the stamp of the specific and which suggest the metaphysical depths of his poem and life. In his note to line 137, for instance, Shade's reference to a 'lemniscate' is judged to have 'no real meaning' (*PF* 136); Shade's reference to a 'Toothwort White' butterfly has Kinbote assuming 'folklore characters, perhaps? Fairies? Or cabbage butterflies' (*PF* 184). And in the commentary to line 238 and the allusion to the 'empty emerald case' of a cicada, which in the poem is sighted on the very day of Aunt Maud's death and thus becomes an image of transformation, Kinbote complains of the loving attention to natural detail which distinguished Shade and served his art:

> ... my friend had a rather coquettish way of pointing out with the tip of his cane various curious natural objects. He never tired of illustrating by means of these examples the extraordinary blend of Canadian Zone and Austral Zone that 'obtained,' as he put it, in that particular spot of Appalachia where at our altitude of about 1,500 feet northern species of birds, insects and plants commingled with southern representatives. As with most literary celebrities, Shade did not seem to realize that a humble admirer who has cornered at last and has at last to himself the inaccessible man of genius, is considerably more interested in discussing with him literature and life than in being told that the 'diana' (presumably a flower) occurs in New Wye together with the 'atlantis' (presumably another flower), and things of that sort. (*PF* 168–9)

For Shade, in ways Kinbote is constitutionally unable to understand, the trifles of nature are the individual, monogrammed stamp of existence and, in their specificity, proof of the goodness of life; their sensual appreciation is demonstration of the poet's heightened consciousness and illustration of both the poet's and poem's provenance in Nabokov's poetic sensibility.

Cosmic synchronization, inspiration and love, and the trifles of nature are all defining motifs of Nabokov's poetic identity; they are also all present in *Pale Fire* in positive form in the character of John Shade and, especially, his poem; their negative affirmation is effected by Kinbote and Gradus. The fifth of the 'informing themes' constitutive of Nabokov's poetic identity – the otherworld – is also present in 'Pale Fire,' is, indeed, its central theme and hence to be discussed last in this reading of the poem. And if appreciation of the poetic achievement of *Pale Fire* has been obscured by insufficient acknowledgment of the novel's debt to Nabokov's lyric sensibility, then the reception of 'Pale Fire' has been doubly occluded by blindness to the relevance of the 'otherworld' in this novel. The 'otherworld,' while not the sole theme in Nabokov's writing, is central to his poetic identity and the lyric sensibility that shaped his artistry. The delineation of this theme of metaphysical import in 'Pale Fire' is thus essential in achieving full understanding of the novel and also in establishing the lyric continuity of all of Nabokov's writing.

Shade, as was previously observed, is surrounded by death, and it is the theme of 'consciousness beyond the tomb' (*PF* 39; l. 176) which becomes the focus of his life, just as it is a central emphasis of his poem:

And finally there was the sleepless night
When I decided to explore and fight
The foul, the inadmissible abyss,
Devoting all my twisted life to this
One task.   (*PF* 39; ll. 177–81)

'Pale Fire' is a retrospective, autobiographical poem composed in the last twenty days of Shade's life. The obsession with the mystery of the otherworld, the 'fight' with the 'inadmissible abyss,' which moves Shade, is, at the time of writing, resolved in the consolation of 'faint hope' born of the natural beauty of life, love, and the patterned example of his own art. 'Pale Fire' is an artistic text but also, in a literal sense, the culminating expression of, and proof for, Shade's hope. Shade's poem begins in the past tense – he *was* the 'shadow of the waxwing slain' – suggesting that the rereading of the poem compelled by the completion of the final couplet in a return to the poem's beginning is 'faint' confirmation of the legitimacy of Shade's hope. By the time the poem's beginning is returned to, Shade has flown on.

In Nabokov's 'The Room,' a poet's death is, after all, 'a question of technique, a neat / enjambment,' a pause before continuation on the next line of being.

'Pale Fire' abounds in the Nabokovian imagery of the otherworld identified throughout his poetic writing. Motifs of enclosure within a restricted space separated off from a larger expanse extend from Shade's metaphor of the firmament as the 'painted parchment papering our cage' (*PF* 36; l. 106), to moondogs, the 'iridule,' and Aunt Maud's 'paperweight of convex glass enclosing a lagoon,' through the architectonic references to the windowed houses and rooms of the poem, to, finally, the anatomical enclosure of an ant encased in amber, Shade's 'ridiculously thin' body – the 'hive' he feels himself 'locked up' in (*PF* 40; ll. 216–17) – and the 'ashen fluff' of a bird which 'lived on, flew on, in the reflected sky' of a window. Imagery of physical and temporal transition arises in the deceptive glass of the window pane which opens 'Pale Fire,' in the sunset glow on a tree at the beginning (*PF* 34; l. 51) and conclusion (*PF* 69; l. 994) of the poem, and in reference to the seaside where Hazel was conceived and the 'ice half drowned' (*PF* 51; l. 498) of the lake where she died during a transitional March thaw which suddenly brought spring to winter. The animal imagery of 'white butterflies [that] turn lavender' (*PF* 35; l. 55), a cicada that has abandoned its 'empty emerald case' (*PF* 41; l. 238), and a favourite species of butterfly all suggest the potential of metamorphosis and the transformation to another state, just as the repeated *8*'s, lemniscates, and ampersands invoke the eternal. The alteration of consciousness into liminal states which likewise presage a more radical transition is captured in Shade's boyhood fainting spells, Aunt Maud's dementia, the near-death of a heart attack, the dream of sleep-walking which is and is not a dream (*PF* 65; ll. 874–85), and finally the strange trance of artistic inspiration.

'Pale Fire' is thus laden with the imagery of enclosure as well as of physical, temporal, and mental transition which characterizes Nabokov's lyric, intimated representation of an otherwise ineffable otherworld. The specificity of the treatment of the theme in 'Pale Fire' arises, however, not in the identification of a structural type of imagery, but in its implementation in a unique fiction. The theme is most visibly present in the linked figures of Aunt Maud and Hazel Shade, and in Shade's own reflections on his life and art. The poet and painter Aunt Maud is characterized in the poem through the furnishings of her room, which reveal an interest in the trivial and wondrous, 'realistic objects … and images of doom' (*PF* 36; ll. 88–9). Her real force in the poem as referent of the otherworld comes, however, with her decline and death. Shortly before her death at eighty – a

number composed of the eternity of an ampersand and the enclosed perfection of a naught – Maud's mind slips into dementia, and the woman of
previously vigorous intellect is left 'to reason with the monsters in her
brain' (*PF* 40; l. 208). The collapse of Maud's mind, 'fading in the growing
mist' (*PF* 40; l. 202), provokes Shade's first concrete reflections on the transience of being and the possibility of an afterlife, but also the futility of
attempting to reason into existence the image of an essentially ineffable,
indescribable phenomenon. The outcome of Shade's reflections coalesces
in images of poetry, what will become by the end of 'Pale Fire' the lynchpin
in a strategy for imaginatively intuiting – it not rationally fixing – understanding of the otherworld. The first of the references to verse as the most
appropriate of instruments for representing the ineffable comes of Shade's
comparison of the difference between 'poetry divinely terse' and 'disjoint-
ed notes' and the futility of attempting to make a private experience conform to a 'public fate,' as expressed in the imagery of the afterworld
standardized in conventional mythologies (*PF* 41; ll. 231–4). The second
reference comes of Shade's spotting a cicada's 'empty emerald case' on a
tree. The connection to metamorphosis seems clear and is strengthened in
Kinbote's commentary to lines 90–3, where he notes a variant by Shade
which brings 'a Luna's dead and shriveled-up cocoon' in relation to Maud.
However, the cicada's 'envelope' is more than mere mute confirmation of
the possibility of transformation to another level of being. Beside the cicada's case viewed by Shade is a 'gum-logged ant' (*PF* 41; l. 240) fixed
forever in a preserved single state of future amber. Shade interprets the
natural scene connecting Lafontaine's *cigale* and *fourmi* as a refutation of
the famous fable:

> Lafontaine was wrong:
> Dead is the mandible, alive the song.   (*PF* 42; ll. 243–4)

While the ant remains fixed, the cicada has emerged and flown on to sing,
suggesting, as Alexandrov indicates, that '"the song," or art, is linked to
transcendence, while utilitarian efforts are not' (Alexandrov 1991, 197).
The references to artistry and verse, however opaque, are here in relation to
Maud part of the texture of Shade's understanding which will find confirmation of transcendence and the otherworld in his art.

Aunt Maud's manifold associations with the otherworld assume more
mysterious dimensions in relation to Shade's daughter, who invokes the
suggestion of continuity with his aunt, who, it is observed in the poem,
'lived to hear the next babe cry' (*PF* 36; l. 90). Hazel Shade is both a delicate

and wrenching figure within 'Pale Fire.' At one level, she is, as Nabokovian character, sister to the deceased, unnamed baby of the short story 'Gods,' to Troshcheykin's and Lyubov''s dead son in *The Event*, to Albinus's daughter Irma in *Laughter in the Dark*, to Yasha of *The Gift*, to the dead, baseball-playing son of the barber of Kasbeam in *Lolita*, and to various other children whose lives are thwarted by fate in Nabokov's fictional universe. At this level, she is the specific embodiment of an existential dimension latent in Nabokov's highly aesthetic representation of the grief and bliss of life – what Shade terms the 'melancholy and the tenderness / Of mortal life; the passion and the pain' (*PF* 53; ll. 526–7), which he will not deny in either life or art. Unlike Ivan Karamazov's two-dimensional accusation of God, Hazel is a human portrait in flesh and blood of the heart-rending tenderness and pity of life, tragic evidence of the ever unique quality of lived experience in all its lyric beauty and pain. For Shade, she is first and foremost his 'difficult, morose' darling, but also a manifestation of the uniqueness of his experience, an expression of life's monograph, which, however painful, forms a significant portion of the wondrous pattern of life to be transformed into the text of art. Kinbote may inopportunely blunder into the cocoon of intimacy Sybil and John Shade establish for themselves during a reading of Shade's poetic working of their daughter's life and death (*PF* 91), and he may literally spy through the poet's windows into the space housing Shade's inner world, but he will never know the depth of Shade's emotion – in bliss and pain – and thus never really understand his art.

Hazel's experience, as depicted by Shade in his poem and as expanded upon by Kinbote in his commentary, also reveals the working of Nabokov's aesthetic of the otherworld. The link between Hazel and the otherworld is prepared in 'Pale Fire' before her actual appearance as a living presence in the poem's narrative. Shade's first poetic references to his daughter are in the spectral imagery of a ghostly presence – 'The phantom of my little daughter's swing' (*PF* 35; l. 57) and 'When ... you greet her ghost' (*PF* 43; l. 290). Only later is she depicted in terms of the spirit's corporeal *pendant* from across the spirit/body divide. And when finally depicted in the poem's narrative as a living presence, Hazel Shade is defined by the negative traits of her body. Overweight, myopic, and 'scratching her head,' she seems imprisoned in a body of 'swollen feet' and 'psoriatic fingernails' (*PF* 45; ll. 354–6). What ought to have been the consolation of her heightened intelligence – the source of the 'prizes won / in French and History' and her Maud-like love of strange words and palindromes – is but confirmation of her separateness, her exclusion from the company of her peers. Tellingly cast in the role of 'Mother Time' (*PF* 44; l. 312) in the school play, Hazel is cruelly excluded from the fairy tale of youth and adolescent love evoked in Shade's imagery of 'elves and fairies' and a princess in a 'dream of gauze and jasmine' (*PF* 45; l. 335). Like the physically frail Ivanov of 'Perfection,' whose vision is impaired before descent into water and a mysterious, revelatory transition into another state of consciousness, Hazel Shade is also associated with water, blindness, and eternity. John Shade, it is recalled, marked his recovery from the fainting spells of youth with physical activity, in particular, learning to swim (*PF* 38; l. 160). He fell in love with his wife by a waterfall, and his daughter was conceived during the same trip to the sea which had him overhear an Englishman commit the verbal equivalent of the misprint which turned the watery *fountain* of Shade's otherworldly vision into Mrs Z's *mountain*. The English tourist of dubious linguist abilities unwittingly raised reference to the cicadas of art's transcendence while feeding seagulls at the seaside in Nice (*PF* 41, 48; ll. 241–4, 440–1). The associatively rich element of water is also central to Hazel. After her seaside conception (*PF* 48; l. 435), Hazel's emergence in the poem from out of a cluster of images revolving around water and blindness, but also eternity, begins with Shade's poetic reversal of a fairy-tale plot. His thwarted hope that his 'dingy cygnet' of an infant daughter would emerge into a resplendent 'wood duck' (*PF* 44; ll. 318–19) not only sharpens an image grown dull with use, but tailors its use to the specificity of his Appalachian vision in the evocation of waterfowl. The evening of Hazel's disastrous 'blind' date is also awash with water. The 'azure' glass of the door and entrance to the bar is not crossed, and Hazel remains outside, where 'puddles were neon-barred' (*PF* 47; ll. 397–8) as if in suggestion of her imprisonment. Travelling home alone, Hazel descends from the bus to cross a half-frozen stretch of ice, which is described as a misty, liminal space where stars and ground meet in water:

> Black spring
> Stood just around the corner, shivering,
> In the wet starlight and on the wet ground,
> The lake lay in the mist, its ice half drowned.
> A blurry shape stepped off the reedy bank
> Into a crackling, gulping swamp, and sank.   (*PF* 50–1; ll. 495–500)

Prior to the final description of Hazel's death at line 500 – the halfway point of the poem – Sybil and John Shade are shown engaged in activities which eerily foreshadow Hazel's drowning. A fork in the poem's development enables the narrative splitting of time and the representation of simultaneity. While Hazel is shown groping through the humiliation of her 'blind' date, Sybil and Shade are depicted spending a quiet evening at home watching television. The imagery deployed in the representation of the Shades' scene of domestic humility abounds in figural suggestions of the infinite – the number 8 – as well as birth, swimming, and eternity. The Shades thus unknowingly embody the imagery which parallels the return of Hazel to the water of her conception, the closing of the 'giant wings' of 'Infinite foretime and / Infinite aftertime' (*PF* 37; ll. 122–3). Out of the separate though linked activities of parents and child emerges a 'correlated pattern' of imagery and reference which suggests to the reader the same kind of 'web of sense' that Shade will ultimately recognize in reading the 'plexed artistry' of his life.

At home, the Shades turn on the television, introducing a third dimension into the poem which will mediate their experiences with those of their child. Commentary on the weather across a televised map reveals 'from Florida to Maine / The curving arrows of Aeolian wars' (*PF* 47; l. 409); the Aeolian winds presage both 'a night of thaw, a night of blow, / With great excitement in the air' (*PF* 50; ll. 494–5), which will accompany Hazel to her death five lines later but also, in a foreshadowing detail, Shade to his almost-death during the question period after his lecture a year later during 'a year of Tempests [when] Hurricane / Lolita swept from Florida to Maine.'[24] Shade retreats to his study to proofread the galleys of his book on Pope and to introduce to his poem reference to the eighteenth-century poet's condemnation of opulence and garish beauty (*PF* 47–8; ll. 413–16) from 'The Rape of the Lock.' It is this very understanding of beauty criticized in Pope's poem, vulgarized still further through twentieth-century commercialization, which is the bane of his daughter and, at one level, the cause of her death. Shade is called from his work on Pope to watch reference to himself on a television documentary on poetry – shown on Channel 8 – where he is mentioned 'as usual just behind / (one oozy footstep) Frost' (*PF* 48; ll. 425–6). The reference is to more than superficial similarities of poetic style. An oozy footstep will subsequently betray Hazel as she steps from a reedy bank into 'a crackling, gulping swamp' at a location where more robust individuals are able to negotiate the crossing of water 'on days of special frost' (*PF* 50; l. 490). In a play of trinities which bind the three agents together, a televised travelogue returns the Shades to the French seaside where Hazel was conceived 'in thirty-three, / Nine months before her birth' (*PF* 48; ll. 434–5); the March night depicted in the documentary is, like their present one, foggy. The sight of the familiar seaside evokes recollection of several images of solitude and exclusion which revolve around birds: a 'flock of

sails' viewed on the distant sea reveals a lone blue one which 'clashed queerly with the sea,' while a single 'dark pigeon' waddles awkwardly among a
crowd of 'insufferably loud' seagulls (*PF* 48; ll. 438–42). Hazel, too, is a
solitary being who clashes queerly with the insufferably loud crowd, a culture of the group which is driven by commercialized, standardized conceptions of beauty. It is to this understanding of physical beauty, the negation
of Hazel's mental powers and the source of her torment, that the poem
turns in the following stage of representation. Sybil Shade turns the channel
to a film which embodies the 'artistic' depiction of commercial beauty
which indirectly causes – and definitely echoes – Hazel's doom, in its 'flowing' language of 'swimming' and 'dissolving':

> And we allowed, in all tranquility,
> The famous film to spread its charmed marquee;
> The famous face flowed in, fair and inane:
> The parted lips, the swimming eyes, the grain
> Of beauty on the cheek, odd Gallicism,
> And the soft form dissolving in the prism
> Of corporate desire.   (*PF* 49; ll. 451–7)

The Shades' final act at the television is to switch channels in exclusion of
further intrusions of the vulgar and inane into their lives, including the
previously referred to television murder which foreshadows Shade's death.
Sybil finally turns off the television as Hazel steps from the reedy bank into
water and infinity:

> Oh, switch it off! And as life snapped we saw
> A pinhead of light dwindle and die in black
> Infinity.   (*PF* 50; ll. 472–4)

The simultaneous flow of Hazel's life with that of her parents ends in the
poem's narrative with the word *infinity*, a word which expresses expansion
rather than termination. Sybil and John Shade's life is shown to continue
in a futile bustle of domestic activity which poignantly emphasizes the finality of Hazel's death in understatement. Their time goes on; Hazel's does
not, at least not in a shared dimension. Her life ended in the poem with the
dwindling of the television light. All further representation of Hazel's demise within the poem is composed in the past tense of retrospection.
   Previous to her pitiable attempt as waddling pigeon to join the seagulls
through attempted participation in the ritualized conventions of adolescent
sexuality and her martyrdom to the norms of commercialized beauty, Hazel

foretells the form of her end. Shade describes with the verb 'would,' in the syntax of repeated activity, the occasions when father, mother, and beloved daughter formed scenes of tentative domestic happiness. All at home, each in his separate though connected room, the three were bound together; with Hazel's death, the living link is broken, though thanks to memory the connectedness among the three is fixed in a way that can be recalled with the permanence of a three-part work of art: 'a tryptich or a three-act play / In which portrayed events forever stay' (*PF* 46; ll. 381–2). Consigned to the loving care of his memory, such scenes of quiet, domestic bliss take on the transcendence of timelessness. On one such occasion from the past, Shade describes Hazel's questions concerning 'some phony modern poem,' queries which are subsequently revealed to have been Hazel's inadvertent addition to the 'correlated pattern' of her life:

> 'Mother, what's *grimpen*?' 'What is what?'
>   'Grim Pen.'
> Pause, and your guarded scholium. Then again:
> 'Mother, what's *chtonic*?' That, too, you'd explain,
> Appending: 'Would you like a tangerine?'
> 'No. Yes. And what does *sempiternal* mean?'
> The answer from desk through the closed door.   (*PF* 46; ll. 368–74)

Beginning with Peter Lubin's brilliant 'Kickshaws and Motley,' scholars have identified the 'phony modern poem' as Eliot's *Four Quartets*.[25] John Burt Foster, in his 'Proust over Eliot in *Pale Fire*,' has effectively glossed the contrastive example of Eliot's aesthetics and religious-based metaphysics which derives from the series of parodic allusions to Eliot in *Pale Fire* (Foster 1993b, 221–3). *Grimpen* is a topographical term from 'East Coker' describing a swamp; *chthonic*, mispronounced by Hazel as *chtonic*, is from 'The Dry Salvages' and refers to the underworld, while the word *sempiternal* arises in 'Little Gidding' in the context of a mid-winter thaw and evokes the eternal and transcendent. In 'Pale Fire,' the three words reveal Hazel's participation in the weaving of a pattern which, although inscrutable to her, is revealed in her death. The 'grim pen' of being, life in a plagued body, is surrendered to the underworld in the suicidal step from the 'reedy bank' of waking life into 'a crackling, gulping swamp' during a mid-winter thaw.

Whether Hazel transcends, like Ivanov, the spirit/body impasse into a higher dimension of consciousness is uncertain. Consistent with the first-person format of Shade's poem, the poetic narrative is denied access to the final and most subjective form of another individual's experience. The metaphysical thrust of Shade's poem and Nabokov's novel, however, allows reasonable hope that she will. In her parallels to Shade's life, and in the mysterious molding of her life into art-like pattern – which includes reference to Nabokovian motifs of the otherworld – Hazel seems likely to fulfill one of the hopes expressed by her father before his own death, 'that my darling somewhere is alive' (*PF* 69; l. 978).

Kinbote, in his recognition of Hazel's 'pain' and the seductive example of her suicide, is intrinsically linked to Shade's daughter, if at no other level than as a lover of palindromes or as an object of Shade's pity. As Kinbote admits: '… it is also true that Hazel Shade resembled me in certain respects' (*PF* 193). Within his commentary, Kinbote offers a range of information about Hazel which corroborates her connection to both Aunt Maud and the mysteries of the beyond. Soon after Aunt Maud's death, for instance, strange events take place in the Shade household which seem to emanate from the room so closely associated with her being. The domestic poltergeist, Kinbote observes, 'meant to impregnate the disturbance with the identity of Aunt Maud who had just died' (*PF* 165). Although the source of the spirit is nowhere clearly stated beyond its identification with Maud and Hazel, the trajectory of Kinbote's second- and third-hand account suggests that the Shades attributed the disturbances to Hazel as the rebellious manifestation of her psychic injury at the death of her great-aunt. Kinbote does not refute this rationalization either, and nowhere is the 'illogical' explanation vouchsafed that a poltergeist is in fact present in the house. Nonetheless, in concluding his note to the poltergeist, Kinbote observes the fundamental mystery of both the rational and the irrational in human affairs in a statement which is compatible with the acceptance of the illogical in Nabokov's lyric sensibility in all but the fig leaf of conventional religion appended to its end:

> The phenomena ceased completely and were, if not forgotten, at least never referred to; but how curious it is that we do not perceive a mysterious sign of equation between the Hercules springing forth from a neurotic child's weak frame and the boisterous ghost of Aunt Maud; how curious that our rationality feels satisfied when we plump for the first explanation, though, actually, the scientific and the supernatural, the miracle of the muscle and the miracle of the mind, are *both* inexplicable as are all the ways of Our Lord. (*PF* 167)

'Miracle' is the operative word in this statement – the miracle of the body and of the spirit – and within the world of the poem, the potential for miracles is left open. At the level of Nabokov's metaphysics, although not the sum of Nabokov's poetic identity, his lyric sensibility allows for, to take two convenient examples, the miracle and mystery of poets who dissolve into their verse ('Vasily Shishkov') or florists who climb a tree into heaven ('The Ballad of Longwood Glen'). In repetition of a statement by Nabokov cited elsewhere in this study, the poetic is defined by its amenability to the irrational: '… by poetry I mean the mysteries of the irrational as perceived through rational words' (*NG* 55).

The departure of the poltergeist from the Shade household did not end Hazel's interest in the psychokinetic or sever the apparent link between Aunt Maud and Hazel. Kinbote's commentary to line 347 and the words 'old barn' is the longest piece of text devoted to Hazel, recording her adventures with a spirit in a haunted barn. Alone in the old barn, Hazel is confronted by 'a roundlet of pale light' which, in responding to her recitation of the alphabet, dictates the following occult message to her: 'pada ata lane pad not ogo old wart alan ther tale feur far rant lant tal told' (*PF* 188). Kinbote, who claimed to 'abhor such games,' nonetheless studied the communication 'with a commentator's infinite patience and disgust' (*PF* 189) only to remain flummoxed in his attempt to decipher its possible meaning. More competent exegetes of Shade and Nabokov have been able to produce more promising results. Boyd, with the help of a quotation from Nabokov's private correspondence, suggests that the note is a message of warning from Aunt Maud via Hazel to Shade, which hints 'at the title of his poem to be written many years later. *Padre* should *not go* to the *lane* to be mistaken for *old Goldswart* (worth) after finishing his *tale* (pale) *feur* (fire) [which in Shakespeare is accompanied by] the word "arrant" (*farant*) [and this] with "*lant*" makes up the Atalanta butterfly in Shade's last scene. It is "*told*" by the spirit in the barn' (Boyd 1992, 454). In *Aerial View*, Gennady Barabtarlo has complicated and deepened the potential meaning of the encrypted message by documenting its triple containment of the Red Admirable butterfly (*Vanessa atalanta*) (Barabtarlo 1993, 207–8). Kinbote, as noted, is of considerably less help regarding the message's meaning, although his dismissive reference to it as something composed by someone 'with the empasted difficulty of apoplexy' (*PF* 189) inadvertently suggests Aunt Maud, who lost the faculty of speech shortly before her death. Ultimately, the 'message' is left unregistered or at least ignored by all but Hazel; its fulfillment in Shade's death at the end of the poem not only fills in another detail in the 'correlated pattern' of Shade's life and poem but corroborates Hazel's proximity to the otherworld.

Shade's witnessing of Hazel's adventures with mysterious energies emanating from the beyond is not entirely without issue, however, during his

lifetime. At the conclusion of his note of commentary to Hazel's adventures with the ectoplasmic, Kinbote quotes Shade's poem 'The Nature of
Electricity,' which seems likely to have emerged from consideration of unexplained energies. Whimsical in expression, this poem expresses in lyric
form a real sense of wonder about the undying force of consciousness and
its possible presence among the living:

> The dead, the gentle dead – who knows? –
> In tungsten filaments abide,
> And on my bedside table glows
> Another man's departed bride.
>
> And maybe Shakespeare floods a whole
> Town with innumerable lights,
> And Shelley's incandescent soul
> Lures the pale moths of starless nights.
>
> Streetlamps are numbered, and maybe
> Number nine-hundred-ninety-nine
> (So brightly beaming through a tree
> So green) is an old friend of mine.
>
> And when above the livid plain
> Forked lightning plays, therein may dwell
> The torments of a Tamerlane,
> The roar of tyrants torn in hell.   (PF 192–3)

Composed before his death, though published after it, 'The Nature of
Electricity' not only contains images suggesting its place in the pattern of
Shade's life and autobiographical poem, but obliquely hints at the possibility
of Shade's consciousness assuming a new form after death. Pale Fire's representation of the most immediate experience of the otherworld – Aunt
Maud's ghostly intervention in the barn – thus concludes with a return to
Shade's poetry and a further dimension of the otherworldly pattern uniting
the poet and his art. Ultimately, the theme of the otherworld, as with all of
the Nabokovian poetic themes shared by Shade, culminates in the confluence
of Shade's life and art in 'Pale Fire.' For it is in Shade's understanding of his
art that the strongest claim to the otherworld arises in the poem and novel.

Canto three of 'Pale Fire' begins after the poem's mid-point caesura of
Hazel's suicide. The trauma of Hazel's death and its lyric retelling returns

the poem to Shade's reconsideration of the workings and presence of the 'inadmissible abyss' in waking life. At a still higher level, it also reconfirms the manner in which Shade's poem is also 'about' the transformation of life's pain into sustaining art. 'Pale Fire' demonstrates the achievement of Shade's artistic consciousness in two fundamental ways; the poem is a thing of beauty in itself, but it is also as an illustration of Shade's mastery of life's trauma and his rendering of it into art – a mastery unachieved by, for instance, Waltz and Kinbote. The first lines of canto three immediately evoke death and resurrection in the play of reference to the yew, a tree which symbolizes both. The first reference arises in French as *l'if*; the second is encoded in the name 'Yewshade,' a place non-specifically located 'in another, higher state' (*PF* 52; l. 509), in other words, a location which is geographic but also suggestive of a higher realm of consciousness.[26] The puns and play of otherworldly reference are not restricted to trees; Rabelais's purported last words – *Je m'en vais chercher le grand peut-être* – reappear in Shade's execrable pun from lines 501–2 as 'Your great Maybe, Rabelais: / The grand potato.' The pun's lamentable lack of subtlety is willed. It reflects the lack of subtlety of an institute Shade associated himself with in the earlier stages of his project to plumb the mysteries of the beyond. As an institute, 'I.P.H.' failed Shade's expectations because of its insistent attempt to explain the ineffable, to apprehend in rational language an experience which is not to be rationalized, and, most unacceptably, to encompass the otherworldly in such worldly ideologies as organized religion, communism, and Freudianism. Paradoxically, and in the further elaboration of an intricate theme in his life and poem, Shade's rejection of the 'tasteless venture' concludes in an image which does not so much prove him wrong, as confirm the utter ineffability of the phenomenon he is concerned with:

> That tasteless venture helped me in a way.
> I learnt what to ignore in my survey
> Of death's abyss. And when we lost our child
> I knew there would be nothing: no self-styled
> Spirit would touch a keyboard of dry wood
> To rap out her pet name; no phantom would
> Rise gracefully to welcome you and me
> In the dark garden, near the shagbark tree.   (*PF* 57; ll. 645–52)

Moments before his death, of course, Shade will be met by a phantom in the form of a butterfly which flits to his arm as he crosses his garden 'near the shagbark tree,' in accordance with the message transcribed by Hazel in the old barn.

Discontented with the anthropomorphizing tendencies of 'I.P.H.,' though confirmed in his intuition of an afterlife by his own brush with death, Shade is stymied in his probings of the abyss until the occurrence of the misprint which seemingly corroborated his vision of a *fountain* in the experience of another. What appears to substantiate his experience of the beyond emerges, after further investigation, as corroboration of its incomparable specificity. Shade learns that what Mrs Z saw was not a *fountain* but a *mountain*, thus leaving the veracity of his vision unconfirmed. Rather than despair at the apparent loss of third-person substantiation of his near-death, however, the repeated affirmation of the singularity of his experience becomes the source of its worth. Shade realizes that it is not the text of his vision which validates his presentiment of an otherworld, but the wondrous texture of life's coincidence, the chance event which suggests both the unrepeatable singularity of life and its orchestration by the players of a larger game within a larger pattern:

> But all at once it dawned on me that *this*
> Was the real point, the contrapuntal theme;
> Just this: not text, but texture; not the dream
> But topsy-turvical coincidence,
> Not flimsy nonsense, but a web of sense.
> Yes! It sufficed that I in life could find
> Some kind of link-and-bobolink, some kind
> Of correlated pattern in the game,
> Plexed artistry, and something of the same
> Pleasure in it as they who played it found.   (*PF* 62–3; ll. 806–15)

In contemplating the 'correlated pattern' of life, Shade non-dogmatically postulates the existence of a realm where the 'contrapuntal theme' of being is matched. Shade thus expresses a non-confirmable insight also expressed by Fyodor. Towards the conclusion of *The Gift*, the poet Fyodor is delighted by the visually exquisite scene of five nuns walking through a forest singing a song and pausing to pluck wild flowers. For Fyodor, the unexpected, unadorned simplicity and beauty of the event – its humble, understated perfection – assumed what Shade would term the 'plexed artistry' of experience: '... and it all looked so much like a staged scene – and how much skill there was in everything, what an infinity of grace and art, what a director lurked behind the pines, how well everything was calculated ...' (*Ssoch* IV,

519; *Gift* 344). To both poets, life is a gift the benevolence and beauty of which are manifest in daily trifles of wonder and coincidence. To both as well, the very goodness of being is expressed in the patterned, aesthetic weave of the texture of life – a weave and pattern which intimate some form of artist-like orchestration from another dimension. Shade postulates this non-empirical belief in appropriately non-descriptive terms. It is not the physical description of these 'aloof and mute' otherworldly beings that is of essence, but the signs of their earthly interventions:

> It did not matter who they were. No sound,
> Nor furtive light came from their involute
> Abode, but there they were, aloof and mute,
> Playing a game of worlds, promoting pawns
> To ivory unicorns and ebon fauns;
> ...
>   Coordinating these
> Events and objects with remote events
> And vanished objects. Making ornaments
> Of accidents and possibilities.   (*PF* 63; ll. 816–29)

And it is, in turn, the belief that the 'events and objects' of human existence are subject to otherworldly coordination which consoles Shade with the solace and confidence of some 'faint hope' (*PF* 63; l. 834).

Of the two poets, the elder advances further their shared fundamental insight regarding the inexplicable structural relationship coordinating this world with another. For Fyodor, the experience of the singularity of this world in all its beauty provoked thoughts of an essentially metaphysical nature, albeit with an aesthetic dimension; his metaphoric language of a 'staged scene' and 'director' indicates a poet's propensity to conceptualize the ineffable in the language and imagery of literature. For Shade, the metaphysical quality of his understanding of the 'correlated pattern' of being has clear aesthetic implications for his art, and vice-versa. With his new-found insight, his art assumes metaphysical dimensions in its patterned, aesthetic structuredness. Nabokov seems to be suggesting here a relatedness of form to content which extends beyond the literary text to assume cosmic dimensions. The patterned symmetry of Shade's poem recapitulates the cosmic harmony and order of the otherworldly realm he can only intuit, just as the wonder on permanent display in the enchanted garden of life quietly confirms the fundamental goodness of the cosmos. What's more, in practising his art, Shade does more than bring his textual world into order. He becomes a Promethean figure analogous to the god-like beings who gain pleasure from the game of 'plexed artistry' played from 'their involute / Abode.' Nabokov himself suggested that 'man comes nearest to God through becoming a true creator in his own right' (*LR* 106), and Shade seems to have reached this plateau of consciousness in his art, but also in his insight into the metaphysical relevance of his poetry. In this regard, Shade's apprehension of the correlation between the universe of his art and life and the cosmic universe confirms the legitimacy of his metaphysical intimations. Shade's art bears out his faith in the 'fantastic-ally planned, / Richly rhymed' nature of being:

> Maybe my sensual love for the *consonne*
> *D'appui*, Echo's fey child, is based upon
> A feeling of fantastically planned,
> Richly rhymed life.
>   I feel I understand
> Existence, or at least a minute part
> Of my existence, only through my art,
> In terms of combinational delight;
> And if my private universe scans right,
> So does the verse of galaxies divine
> Which I suspect is an iambic line.   (*PF* 68–9; ll. 967–76)

Shade's love for the *consonne d'appui* – which is formed a final time in the substitution of the poem's first line for its missing last one – is itself expression, not only of his pleasure in 'combinational delight,' but of the correlated pattern uniting his verse and the 'verse of galaxies divine.' Confirmed in the unity of his metaphysical and aesthetic universe, Shade's thoughts and poem turn to the hereafter and the ethics of love which fuels his artistry:

> I'm reasonably sure that we survive
> And that my darling somewhere is alive,
> As I am reasonably sure that I
> Shall wake at six tomorrow, on July
> The twenty-second, nineteen fifty-nine,
> And that the day will probably be fine ...   (*PF* 9; ll. 977–82)

Love, metaphysical belief, and poetic artistry thus merge and coalesce at the end of the poem. Shade, alone in his study, concludes his poem surveying the 'enchanted' garden of his 'private universe' with thoughts of his daughter and wife and the 'dark Vanessa' butterfly which wheels in the setting sun of the evening, a time of transition. Shade subsequently dies, of course, which seems an implied refutation of his 'reasonable' assurances about the time to come, whether the day after or an afterlife. Rather than a refutation of the beliefs that the entire trajectory of the poem has contributed to and developed, this error is, like Shade's mistaken belief about the unlikelihood of being greeted in the garden by the phantom of his daughter, confirmation of the radical inexpressibility of the phenomenon he is attempting to describe.[27] Put in terms close to Shade – and Nabokov – the truth about the otherworld is not to be approached with the rational language of 'text,' but in the acceptance of the irrational 'texture' of an aesthetically expressed belief; not in the declaration of a fact, but in the detection and creative interpretation of a 'web of sense' which unites metaphysical belief, his artistry, and the people he loves.

Here, Shade's deranged commentator plays an irreplaceable role. Final confirmation of Shade's transcendence to another dimension of consciousness cannot be explicitly postulated in a first-person narrative. He is dead, which obviously forecloses further, direct communication. The last entries of Kinbote's commentary, however, narrate the final minutes of Shade's life after the completion of his poem, and they also allow the correlation of the final details of a pattern which suggests Shade's transcendence to a space where he 'lived on, flew on.' Kinbote's last four entries return the commentary from the fantasy of Kinbote's imagined past to the events of Shade's death. Simultaneous with Shade's ending of his poem 'Pale Fire,' Kinbote approaches the poet, whom he sees 'perched' in the enclosure of his arbor-like portico, what Shade – the self-described shadow of a 'waxwing' – appropriately calls his 'Nest.' Textual evidence is thereby mounting that Shade's shadow will soon take flight in fulfillment of the opening lines of the poem. Kinbote's narrative account of their last meeting and the last minutes of the poet's life begins with a description of Shade which, unbeknownst to Kinbote, captures the feeling of completion and beneficence suggested in the final passage of his poem:

> … I openly walked up to his porch or perch. His elbow was on the table, his first supported his temple, his wrinkles were all awry, his eyes moist and misty; he looked like an old tipsy witch. He lifted his free hand in greeting without changing his attitude, which although not unfamiliar to me struck me this time as more forlorn than pensive. (*PF* 287)

Kinbote knows neither love nor true inspiration and thus mistakenly sees in Shade's demeanour a forlorn expression. Shade's emotional discomposure is the result, not of muted despair, but of blissful happiness. The muse has been, as he informs Kinbote, 'exceptionally kind and gentle' (*PF* 288), his poem is finished, and Shade finds himself on what Nabokov referred to in *Speak, Memory* as 'the highest terrace of consciousness' peering beyond the limits of mortality:

> It is ... when one is wide awake, at moments of robust joy and achievement, on the highest terrace of consciousness, that mortality has a chance to peer beyond its own limits, from the mast, from the past and its castle tower. And although nothing can be seen through the mist, there is somehow the blissful feeling that one is looking in the right direction. (*SM* 50)

With the reflections and achievements expressed in the conclusion of his poem, Shade too seems somehow to be 'looking in the right direction.' The ecstatic play of the butterfly which greets Shade in Kinbote's following entry likewise suggests mysterious exit from this world, and transformation and dissolution into another. The 'dark Vanessa' of Maud's encrypted message to Hazel in the barn emerges out of a liminal space marked by the mottled play of light and shade in a garden at evening time. Flashing and vanishing, flashing and vanishing, the butterfly's dissolution into the murk of shaded light seems to portend the dissolving disappearance already presaged for Shade in his two previous experiences of cosmic synchronization:

> One's eyes could not follow the rapid butterfly in the sunbeams as it flashed and vanished, and flashed again, with an almost frightening imitation of conscious play which now culminated in its settling upon my delighted friend's sleeve. It took off, and we saw it next moment sporting in an ecstasy of frivolous haste around a laurel shrub, every now and then perching on a lacquered leaf and sliding down its grooved middle like a boy down the banisters on his birthday. Then the tide of the shade reached the laurels, and *the magnificent, velvet-and-flame creature dissolved in it*. (*PF* 290; emphasis added)

The allusion to cosmic synchronization seems strengthened in Kinbote's following note, a 'tribute,' as Kinbote calls it, to his black gardener, the final figure to be mentioned in Shade's poem after the appearance of the butterfly:

> Some neighbor's gardener, I guess – goes by
> Trundling an empty barrow up the lane.   (*PF* 69; ll. 998–9)

A black gardener of diffuse erotic, Romantic interest to Kinbote, he is also direct reference to the 'clockwork toy – / A tin wheelbarrow pushed by a tin boy' (*PF* 38; ll. 143–4), whose loss under a chair triggered Shade's boyhood fainting spell. Kinbote himself had seen the toy and described it in an earlier note as 'a little Negro of painted tin' (*PF* 137), completing, with the reference to skin pigmentation, a series of details which correlate an early experience of cosmic synchronization with an assumed final one. In his commentary to the missing though assumed thousandth line of 'Pale Fire,' Kinbote fulfills the pattern of Shade's poem and transcendence. 'I was the shadow of the waxwing slain' returns the poem to an image of transition into the azure of a reflected sky. It is thus significant that Kinbote's final representation of his deceased 'friend' describes him with 'open dead eyes directed up at the sunny evening azure' (*PF* 295). Shade's open eyes not only direct attention to the space wherein he will live on, fly on; they also leave the poet with an expression of sight even in death.

Kinbote's commentary concludes the thematic pattern initiated by the poem 'Pale Fire,' the web of sense that is the novel *Pale Fire*. And it is out of Shade's poem that the thematic depth, the poignancy of beauty and pity, emerges. Nabokov's *Pale Fire* is an unusual achievement of formal structure and narrative complexity. The plexed artistry of the novel's structure is not, however, an end in itself, but a portion of the thematic meaning expressed in the poem, though further revealed in its integration in the novel. Nabokov's lyric sensibility and poetic voice, as witnessed in the centrality of cosmic synchronization, inspiration, love, wonder at the pied beauty of this world, and fascination for the mystery and potential of the otherworld, provide the basis for both novel and poem. The above reading of the poem (and novel) was motivated by the urge to illustrate the provenance of Shade's poem in Nabokov's lyric sensibility and poetic practice. The compulsion of this interpretive goal necessarily occluded adequate discussion of the many other issues provoked by the novel; it has, however, emphasized the lyric source of the exceptional thematic and formal achievement of *Pale Fire*.

Conclusion: In Place of an Ending

I should not be surprised if this person or that finds Hodasevich's posthumous fame inexplicable at first blush. Furthermore, he published no poems lately – and readers are forgetful, and our literary critics are too excited and preoccupied by evanescent topical themes to have the time or occasion to remind the public of important matters. Be it as it may, all is finished now: the bequeathed gold shines on a shelf in full view of the future, whilst the gold-miner has left for the region from where, perhaps, a faint something reaches the ears of good poets, penetrating our being with the beyond's fresh breath and conferring upon art that mystery which more than anything characterizes its essence ... Let us turn to the poems.

– Vladimir Nabokov, 'On Hodasevich'

Vladimir Nabokov: Poetry and the Lyric Voice was begun with the two-part intention of descriptively encapsulating Nabokov's lyric voice as expressed in the extended body of his poetic writing and of demonstrating the pervasiveness of that sensibility and voice in the rest of his oeuvre. Given the expansiveness of this goal and the relative limitations of seven chapters of analysis, examination of Nabokov's lyric voice is not here properly concluded, only abruptly ended. As a result, this study is terminated on a note of incompleteness, though a number of important critical gains are to be registered, the first of which is a re-evaluation of the *place* of Nabokov's poetry in his writing. The empirical scope of Nabokov's poetic writing has been located and outlined as a constant presence throughout Nabokov's lengthy, bilingual career. Poetry has *not* been conceptualized as a genre which ought now somehow to be seen to replace prose and the novel at the centre of Nabokov's writing; it has been posited, however, as a form of expression which continually permeates virtually all of Nabokov's work, now more indirectly, now more distinctly. As a portion of the re-evaluation of the place and role of poetry in Nabokov's writing, a review of the past critical reception of Nabokov was also undertaken. Although distinguished by the presence of informative individual studies, the intermittent, historically fragmented tradition of criticism of Nabokov's verse as a whole cannot simply be uncritically accepted as authoritative. The system of overlapping and contradictory appraisals of a single object of study – Nabokov's poetry – suggests that, if not outright disqualified, the critical conclusions derived are to be used with caution. A fresh, comprehensive approach is now required in a context free from polemical assertions regarding the supposed ramifications of Nabokov's writing. As Nabokov said in his tribute to Khodasevich which serves as the epigraph to this conclusion: 'Let us turn to the poems.'

In this study, Nabokov's poetry was explicitly identified as a formative component of the creative consciousness underlying all of Nabokov's writing. Five informing themes were forwarded as representative of a coherent and individual poetic voice – Nabokov's lyric identity. Central to the defining idiosyncrasy, the monographed specificity, of Nabokov's poetry is its dual participation in the wonder and poetic representation of this world and the lyric articulation of the metaphysical mystery of the next. In shifting assessment to Nabokov's accomplishment in other genres, it was suggested that, in a fundamental sense, Nabokov never abandoned poetry. The lyric traits of his artistry, of the creative consciousness orchestrating all of his works, are clearly to be discerned in the other, non-poetic genres Nabokov practised. The claim regarding the lyric-based continuity of Nabokov's writing was made in opposition to, or at least in complication of, the often expressed tenet of Nabokov criticism that, after failed experiments in poetry, Nabokov found his true calling in prose and the novel. This is a legitimate scholarly postulation which seemingly confirms a mid-career caesura in Nabokov's writing separating his conservative Russian poetry from his innovative English prose; it is, however, a conjecture which introduces a deep stylistic chasm into Nabokov's writing. Rather than uncritically accept this bifurcation of an exceptionally integrated oeuvre, this study proposed Nabokov's poetry and the creative consciousness behind all of his writing as the basis for a comprehensive assessment of his artistic achievement. More detailed, though still incomplete, studies of Nabokov's several dramas, his short fiction, and his Russian and English masterpieces *The Gift* and *Pale Fire* illustrated that the formal and thematic interests of Nabokov's poetry are omnipresent in his writing. Although a critical reassessment of Nabokov's poetry has been achieved to the degree suggested above, there are necessarily many things left unsaid. In place of an ending, therefore, this conclusion will briefly review several of the many themes and critical issues still in need of scholarly treatment.

With regard to the thematic scope of Nabokov's poetic voice – what was here identified in terms of five informing themes – legitimate consideration could be made concerning still other themes which merit inclusion. This is not to question the integrity of the argument offered here or to disavow the coherence of the poetic voice identified. For this study, the two themes essential to an identification of the quintessential character of Nabokov's poetic voice are wonder at the trifles of life and the otherworld – dewdrops on honeysuckle and the whispered rustle of a breeze from the beyond. These themes guarantee Nabokov's poetry both its anchoring in this world and its mysterious intimations of the next. Cosmic synchronization, inspiration, and love, if not as central as the first two, are likewise essential to an understanding of the idiosyncrasy and particularity of Nabokov's poetic voice in terms of its aesthetic self-reflectiveness and its ethical motivation. Taken together, all five themes assure the aesthetic, ethical, and metaphysical interconnectedness of Nabokov's lyric sensibility and voice. So much can be, has been, demonstrated.

Nonetheless, other themes likewise invite consideration. A case for the inclusion of another 'informing theme' seems most pressing with regard to the thematic cluster which revolves around the related topics of Russia and memory. Especially memory, though also Russia as the privileged locus of the experience of memory, is – as numerous scholars have shown – an essential theme in Nabokov's writing. However, within Nabokov's poetry, and especially his earliest poetry, the particular relevance of memory was of more restricted importance in terms of a formative role in the emergence of Nabokov's lyric voice. Perhaps the still relatively close historical proximity of Russia to Nabokov's numerous poems of the early 1920s contributed to the preclusion of emphasis on memory as a multi-dimensional theme with ramifications concerning the self-consciously poetic nature of the creative consciousness. Of course, the theme is present in individual early poems and as the epigraph to Nabokov's first volume of poetry, as well as the title of a cluster of poems from *The Cluster*. The pervasiveness of its relevance throughout his oeuvre, however, seems based, in the main, on his prose and later examples of his poetry, where it developed into one of the richest themes in his writing, particularly as it was coupled to the theme of time and the triumph over time by consciousness. Speaking for the integration of the theme of memory into a fuller representation of Nabokov's poetic oeuvre and voice, however, is precisely its presence as theme at the very beginning of his artistic career. Regardless as to how scholarship may evaluate the nature and sophistication of Nabokov's earliest manipulations of the theme, it was, like so many of the themes to distinguish his mature writing, first articulated in his poetry.

Related to the question of the addition of specific themes to a fuller understanding of Nabokov's poetic voice is also the issue of recurrent motifs first found in his poetry. In this study of Nabokov's lyric identity, particular emphasis was placed on motifs expressive of enclosure and transition. Other motifs only lightly touched upon deserve further attention. Introductory reference was made, for instance, to the animal creatures of Nabokov's poetic universe and the transformative potential associated with them. A cluster of motifs such as this merits closer scrutiny, as does Nabokov's programmatic system of lyric reference to the natural world in general. Likewise, the frequent references to eyes and sight, as well as to geometrical shapes, to name but two further clusters of imagery, warrant attention. Lastly, the thematic associations of colours seem an important aspect of Nabokov's poetry. Following the essential division of a two-world cosmology, it was proposed above that blue referred to the beyond and green (and dappled colours) to the phenomenal world of shared reality. This seems verifiable, though further reference could be made to red and the presence of striped or slanting, reflected light. The imagery of colour and light which is so important to Nabokov's prose fictions seems more transparent in meaning in his poetry. This topic within Nabokov's poetry would offer fruitful linkage to the intriguing subject of synesthasia in Nabokov's writing.

Another topic of relevance to Nabokov's poetry concerns its formal qualities. In this study, comment on the form of Nabokov's poetry was primarily descriptive and restricted to the discussion of individual poems. The topic is vast, however, and calls for analysis at various levels. A particularly pressing topic concerns evaluation of the formal quality of Nabokov's verse itself. Nabokov's poetry has often been criticized for its formal conservatism, although, as was noted, the poetry of the widely respected émigré poet Khodasevich was still more traditional in form. A frequently met explanation for this formal conservatism is found in Nabokov's assumed aversion to developments associated with the avant-garde, for Nabokov an ideologically freighted and thus aesthetically disqualified form of art. There is much to this view. For it certainly seems clear that an important portion of Nabokov's project as *homme des lettres* was the preservation of the best of the tradition of Russian literature dormant in a century dominated by Soviet cultural control and the 'method' of socialist realism. His critical writing and especially his translations of Russian poetry suggest the fulfillment of an important critical project;[1] in both endeavours, Nabokov appears to have been salvaging a literary tradition threatened by the ravages of the Soviet literary system at 'home' in Russia and blatant cultural misunderstanding abroad in America. Nabokov might legitimately be read as single-handedly promoting the continuation of a rich tradition – not only in terms of his oeuvre as a whole, but in the very form of his own poetry.

The question of the conservatism of Nabokov's poetry might also be approached from another thematic angle, however – the one suggested in *Pale Fire*. In this reading, the patterned symmetry and constructed perfection of Nabokov's formally 'conservative' poetry might also indicate, as it did for Shade, a portion of the metaphysical quality associated with poetry. Indeed, the normative critical valuation implied in the distinction between the formal conservatism of his poetry, on the one hand, and the formal inventiveness of his prose, on the other, might, as a fruitful critical exercise, be turned on its head. The structuredness of Nabokov's poetry need not be identified as a failing, as captivity to anachronistic structures of artistic expression. From the perspective of the lyric consciousness underlying all of his writing, Nabokov's formal innovations in prose may be seen as the directing of attention away from the interchangeable and malleable conventions of the various generic forms Nabokov parodied to the permanence of the artistic sensibility and voice from which they all so persistently and consistently derive. As in 'An Evening of Russian Poetry,' Nabokov's novels frequently invoke parody, as the conventions of one genre are disguised in the traits of another. Through these and other displays of narrative inventiveness, attention is drawn not just to the creative consciousness directing the fictive construction, but, more precisely, to the unchanging lyric quality of that consciousness. The historical conditions of authorship change, different genres are available for use, conventions may be shuffled and subverted – what remains, always, is the integrity and force of the unique authorial identity. Nabokov's insistence on the worth of established formal conventions is thus perhaps evidence, not of imprisonment in the past, but of a critically motivated desire to emphasize the standards of quality native to his oeuvre and an entire tradition. Another essential aspect of the formal quality of Nabokov's poetry deserving of critical attention is the extent to which the stylistic devices of his poetry influenced his prose. Nabokov's exceptional mastery of prose rests on his total control of the aesthetic function of language first honed to perfection in his writing of poetry. The alliterative and assonant euphony of his prose, the attention to rhythm and cadence, the deployment of brilliant metaphoric and metonymic imagery, all contribute to the shaping of Nabokov's unmistakable authorial voice; the extent to which this stylistic voice in prose emerged from his poetry is a legitimate question which can only be answered after closer consideration of his poetry.

Reflection on the supposed traditionalism of Nabokov's poetry provokes still another, more essential question – perhaps the fundamental issue with regard to an assessment of the place of poetry within Nabokov's oeuvre. It is a consideration derived from the central observation made by various informed commentators on Nabokov's poetry, from Struve to Rabaté, Diment, and Dolinin concerning the conservativism of Nabokov's poetry versus the novelty of his prose. If, as this study has argued, Nabokov's lyric sensibility is the essential element uniting and defining his entire oeuvre, how is it that there seems such a distinction between his traditional poetry and innovative (if not Postmodern) prose? Stated more positively: how can a lyric sensibility be understood to unite traditional poetry with innovative prose? Any reply to this question is by nature speculative, beyond the certainty of a definitive answer. Nonetheless, the outline of a comprehensive – if necessarily interpretive – response is possible. As an initial reaction, it may be observed that although a difference between Nabokov's poetry and prose is to be registered, it is not the qualitative difference it may seem at first blush.[2] The self-reflexiveness characteristic of much of Nabokov's mature prose, for instance, is also a feature of his earliest poetry. Beginning with an early poem such as 'Of the wise and malicious I ask nothing,' as well as the various poems treating encounter with the muse, Nabokov signals sustained, self-reflexive concern for the development of his artistic abilities. And although Nabokov's poetry is less frequently parodic than his prose, there are examples of parody – including self-parody – especially in reference to hackneyed conventions of poetry, as in 'I dreamed of you so often, so long ago...' Poems such as 'On Rulers' and 'What Is the Evil Deed' offer clear parodic reference to contemporary poets. In short, Nabokov's poetry shows self-conscious awareness of the conditions and limitations of artistic creation in ways which are not to be identified as 'traditional' and which mirror 'metaficional' qualities in his prose.[3]

However, an idiosyncratic marker of Nabokov's lyric voice and a source of the ostensible contradiction between his poetry and prose may be understood at still another level. As this study has argued, the nascent qualities of Nabokov's lyric sensibility were established in his poetry already at a young age. Their manner of presentation would gain in sophistication with

the growth of Nabokov's experience as an artist, but the five informing
themes which distinguish Nabokov's lyric identity were present in even his
early poetry. Along with these thematic preferences and preoccupations
of Nabokov's voice, however, a further defining feature of Nabokov's
poetics took shape – Nabokov's championing of a narrative quality in
poetry. By the mid-1920s, Nabokov was articulating a particular understanding of poetry. First formulated in discursive form in reviews of poetry, Nabokov advocated the presence of a 'lyric plot' and the necessity of a
'harmonious dénouement' (*Ssoch* II, 640–1). He further claimed that
'above all, a poem must be interesting,' that a reader 'should begin the
poem with curiosity and conclude it with agitation. It is as necessary to
narrate lyric trepidation or a trifle as arrestingly as a journey to Africa'
(*Ssoch* II, 639–40). Significantly, Nabokov was not simply advocating narrative poetry, but the relevance of a narrative component in *lyric* poetry, a
combination which characterizes his own verse. Throughout his career and
regardless of genre, Nabokov's writing has continually served two impulses:
the need to articulate an intensely individual, idiosyncratic artistic vision
and the necessity to give expression to that vision in a manner which is
communicative and compelling – one is lyric, the other narrative. Poetry,
including more traditional forms of poetry, functioned as a genre congenial to the metaphysical, ethical, and aesthetic specificities of Nabokov's
lyric sensibility. Poetry, including – once again – more traditional forms,
allowed for depiction of the lyric and ineffable in a manner which was at
once compelling and yet distanced from discursively representational forms
of narrative. Poetry – the conventions of both writing and receiving poetry
– granted Nabokov a generic form conducive to Keatsian 'negative capability': 'that is, when man is capable of being in uncertainties, mysteries,
doubts, without any irritable reaching after fact and reason' (Keats 71). In
poetry, Nabokov could express without expounding. The move to prose,
and in particular the novel, was not a turning away from the specificity of
his lyric sensibility but the adopting of a more voluminous form within
which to unfold its maturing, increasingly intricate expressions. Nabokov's
earliest short stories, for instance, seem to confirm this process. Criticized
at times for their excessive lyricism, these stories were literally prose poems,
examples of a lyric sensibility seeking out and exploring a more expansive
form. The complexity and multi-dimensionality of his aesthetic, ethical,
and metaphysical vision was more amply served in prose, though potentially at the expense of betraying its intuited, subjective, lyric quality.
Inherent to prose was the danger of seeming to say the unsayable. The use
of more representational forms of discourse – prose and the novel – thus

necessitated the adoption of strategies with which to mitigate, and compensate for, potential over-extension into discursive depiction of the mysterious and ineffable. Nabokov developed and deployed the 'innovative' narrative strategies of his prose to preserve and underscore the specificity and yet empirical indeterminacy of his subjective lyric sensibility. Nabokov's lyric identity is defined by a love of the wondrous trivia and realia of the phenomenal world as well as intuited cognizance of a mysterious, empirically non-definable beyond. To his prose expressions of this sensibility, Nabokov brought an Acmeist sense of precision and perspicacity of depiction, but also a range of narrative techniques designed resolutely to resist and defer the closure of final pronouncement. Nabokov's prose is detailed, precise, and symmetrically structured; it is also circular, narratively indeterminate, and deceptive. From the identification of the implied author in *The Gift* to detection of the author of the poem 'Pale Fire' through an entire catalogue of narrative conundrums and thematic deceptions, Nabokov is less the Postmodernist juggling literary conventions merely to reveal their levity, to demonstrate the fictionality of literary convention, than the lyric poet forcing renewed care and appreciation of the specificity and wonder of his resolutely individual artistic vision. The prose may seem 'better,' more *zeitgemäß*, because it is unquestionably granted more space within which to develop the aesthetic, ethical, and metaphysical complexity of his artistic sensibility. Read against awareness of this same lyric sensibility, however, his poetry gains in power to become more than simply conservative or traditional verse. Nabokov optimized the potential of both genres to serve his lyric sensibility.

Ultimately, demonstration of the pervasiveness of the lyric consciousness connecting Nabokov's (formally traditional) poetry to his (innovative) prose directs attention away from his poetry to the full generic breadth of his oeuvre. In this study, an indication of this pervasiveness was shown through consideration of Nabokov's drama, limited selections of short fiction, and two novels; Nabokov's other writing must also be considered. In the instance of Nabokov's extensive corpus of novels, this seems readily apparent. From *Mary* to *Look at the Harlequins!* the lyric quality of Nabokov's novels is amply and easily illustrated. Sensitivity to this quality is certain to promote fuller understanding of Nabokov's prose. Indeed, it is even to be suggested that significant portions of the critical resistance to individual works by Nabokov might better be clarified, if not overcome, through exegetical approaches which included consideration of Nabokov's lyric sensibility. The traces of Nabokov's lyric sensibility seem operative not only in his fictional writing, but also in his non-fictional work.

Nabokov's autobiography *Speak, Memory* was read in this study as an account of consciousness; Nabokov's awakening into *artistic* consciousness with the writing of his first poem was posited as an essential event in that account. Nabokov's extensive translations from various languages, too, are distinguished by their emphasis on poetry. Alone, Nabokov's *Notes on Prosody* is worthy of study both as an entry point into Nabokov's understanding and practice of verse and as an introduction to English and Russian prosody (*EO* III, 448–540). Nabokov's discursive, critical studies are frequently concerned with poets and poetry. Even his studies of novelists and literature, in general, reveal the preoccupations native to Nabokov's lyric sensibility. The study of each of these facets of Nabokov's extensive body of work would profit from consideration of the lyric preoccupations of his writing.

Another more diffuse, though still operative, field of relevance derived from awareness of the fundamental lyricism of Nabokov's writing concerns the critical classification of Nabokov's writing. A project that was anathema to Nabokov himself, Nabokov criticism has nonetheless long wrestled with the characterization of his writing in literary historical categories. Romanticism, Realism, Symbolism, Acmeism, and Expressionism are some of the terms which have been advanced at various times, though by far the most prominent are Modernism and Postmodernism, which in itself reflects Nabokov's primary reception as a novelist. In 1995 an entire conference in Nice was devoted to the topic under the title 'Nabokov: At the Crossroads of Modernism and Postmodernism.' In the present study, none of these terms were pressed into service in affirmative description of either Nabokov's poetry or prose. This programmatic resistance to such terms is not motivated by principled rejection of the concepts they represent. On the contrary, as a literary scholar, I openly acknowledge their validity in literary studies. There is such a thing as Modernism and its identification is of use in discussing the specificity of, for example, James Joyce's artistic achievement in *Ulysses*. In the case of Nabokov's poetry and lyric voice, however, the application of such terms seems frequently confused, and, frankly, destined to remain devoid of lasting scholarly value until greater clarity has been achieved concerning their precise context of reference in Nabokov's writing. This, in turn, assumes greater familiarity with Nabokov's poetry, prior to the application of categories of theoretical classification. Nabokov's poetry may, for instance, in individual instances, show the traces of a Symbolist aesthetic, though the explanatory value of Symbolism in relation to 'The Ballad of Longwood Glen' seems less obvious. The identification of Nabokov's poetry *tout court* as 'Symbolist' is thus highly problematic. The same reservations apply to the use of such terms as Expressionism or the more relevant movement of Acmeism. Suspicion regarding the scholarly worth of critical categories of classification mounts further upon consideration that they were not infrequently used in émigré criticism as terms of abuse, as substitutes for dispassionate, exploratory analysis. The situation is rendered still more complicated with, for instance, the term Postmodernism, the classification according to which Nabokov was to a significant degree canonized in Anglo-American criticism. Most commonly deployed in the categorization of prose and in particular the novel, the term's value as a critical instrument seems limited, especially in consideration of the fact that what is being discussed is the novelistic expression of a lyric voice which evolved organically out of poetry from the 1920s. Nabokov's English novels – obviously – are not to be equated with his early poetry, though there is a connection which has to be acknowledged in the interests of critical understanding of *both* his poetry and his prose. Indeed, as the review of the reception of Nabokov's English poetry indicates, the critical expectations established for the *novelist* Nabokov – pre-classified as a Postmodernist – clashed dramatically with the evidence of his poetry. In this instance, critical preconceptions clearly worked to the detriment of a reading of Nabokov's English poetry. To reverse the order of critical approach, it needs to be asked, for instance, to what extent the author of 'Restoration' is a Postmodern author or, more explicitly, how Nabokov's (anachronistic?) views on inspiration may be said to serve an aesthetic deemed Postmodern? Or, alternatively, can an author of consistent metaphysical views write pre-modern poetry and Postmodern prose? Or, finally, what functional purpose does classification serve in terms of a clearer understanding of Nabokov's artistic achievement? None of this is to suggest that the above referred to terms from Symbolism to Postmodernism need be incontrovertibly excluded from the critical discussion of Nabokov. It is to suggest, however, that a critical reading of Nabokov's poetry and the identification of a related lyric sensibility in his writing *will* alter the shape of the assessment and the use of such terms of classification. In short, before the edifice of Nabokov's oeuvre may be granted a label of architectonic classification – for whatever purpose – its foundation in poetry has to be more thoroughly examined.

This, too, points in the direction of further study necessitated by recognition of the formative role of poetry in Nabokov's writing. The present study did not occupy itself with the question of Nabokov's place within a larger poetic tradition or the more thorny issue of potential influences upon Nabokov's poetry. As in the question of Nabokov's potential classification in literary-historical or period terms, this decision was not based on far-reaching considerations of principle, or, more dramatically, out of denial of Nabokov's place in a larger tradition as, somehow, a *sui generis* poet miraculously to have emerged fully formed from the uncharted seas of his own creative consciousness. Rather, this approach was chosen as an attempt to counterbalance a tradition of criticism which, in my opinion, has overstressed the identification of putative influences to the detriment of identification of the unique and specific in his poetry. In the present study, the effort was made to concentrate on the individuality of Nabokov's poetic voice as it is revealed in the particular constellation of thematic interests which he clearly emphasized in his poetry. In a sense, the attempt was made to comprehend Nabokov's poetry and poetic voice in terms of a system of reference internal to his poetic writing. This does not preclude the *subsequent* examination of possible influences and informing forces; it does, however, bar the identification of alleged influences *prior* to a reading of the poetry on its own terms. In my own understanding of Nabokov's poetry, future discussion of the provenance of Nabokov's poetry in terms of a tradition will begin, less with the tightly enclosed systems of aesthetic reference to individual poetic movements, than with the identification of affinity with the general aesthetic and metaphysical thrust of neo-Romantic strains of poetry. Although not a Romantic, Nabokov shares with the Romantics a sensual feeling for nature and unabashed fascination for the mysterious, ineffable sphere of the beyond. As C. M. Bowra has observed, this is an interest shared by the English Romantics: '... five major poets, Blake, Coleridge, Wordsworth, Shelley, and Keats, despite many differences, agreed on one vital point: that the creative imagination is closely connected with a peculiar insight into an unseen order behind visible things.' In a comment eminently applicable to Nabokov, Bowra proceeds to state that 'this belief gave a special character to their work and determined their main contributions to the theory and practice of poetry' (Bowra 271). It is my contention, for instance, that Nabokov's poetic sensibility and identity could very profitably be compared with that of Wordsworth from *The Prelude*. One hastens to add that Nabokov's comparability to the English Romantics represents an elective affinity and does not presuppose direct influence or conscious imitation. The very reference to the English Romantics alludes to the complications of attributing influence; the young Nabokov, while certainly aware of the English poets, was far more intimately familiar with the Russian poetry of Pushkin, Fet, Tiutchev, and others. Furthermore, a demonstrably core element of Nabokov's poetic identity is his self-reflective understanding of himself as a poet of individual expression. As with the novelist Nabokov, this quality of self-awareness as an artist, coupled with fierce independence and the prioritization of individual talent, is not to be underestimated. Nabokov the poet was moved by, and respectful of, past masters of poetic expression, but necessarily unique in the writing of his poetry due to his primary, programmatic reference to the demands of his artistic consciousness. Nabokov's manipulations of the representation of the otherworld or the muse, for instance, illustrate participation in a broader tradition though principal allegiance to the specificity of his own imagination and poetic sensibility. Indeed, the self-reflectiveness of Nabokov's poetry, its constant observation of, and comment upon, the development of his poetic prowess, suggests its modernity, a central feature to be considered in any future assessment of Nabokov's place in broader traditions of poetic writing.

Above reference to the otherworld as a thematic concern of relevance to Nabokov and the Romantics indicates a final realm where awareness of Nabokov's poetry may contribute to a fuller understanding of Nabokov the author. As indicated above, one of the most controversial issues in recent Nabokov criticism has been the identification of a metaphysical dimension in his writing. Despite the thoroughness of Alexandrov's treatment of the topic, there are excellent critics of Nabokov's writing who remain resistant to the identification of this theme. Further discussion of this topic would most certainly profit as well from informed consideration of its presence in Nabokov's poetry and, furthermore, its inclusion in Nabokov's prose as a significant portion of the lyric sensibility which permeated his fiction. Opposition to this theme seems strongest in consideration of Nabokov as a late twentieth-century author of formally inventive novels, a category of writer less frequently associated with representation of the ineffable – except perhaps as parody. In the context of an approach to Nabokov's novels as the product of a lyric sensibility, and after having established the link between his poetry and his prose, the connection between novelist and author of metaphysical fiction seems more palatably formed. Not only is the treatment of such themes as the otherworld unexceptional in (even contemporary) poetry, but the very quality of Nabokov's lyric handling of the topic is of relevance. As a poet, Nabokov's interest in the otherworld was non-dogmatic; his interest in cosmic issues was intense, though non-empiricist or rationalizing. It arose as a subject of poetic, philosophical, and metaphysical reflection insofar as it was associated with the workings of his creative consciousness and artistic gift. Nabokov's concern is steadfastly that of a poet unmoved by, indeed suspicious of, representation of the beyond itself, though passionately taken by its relevance to his sense of self, his consciousness, and his art. Manifestations of the otherworld throughout Nabokov's oeuvre are, I propose, advantageously discussed through the lens of his poetry and lyric sensibility.

The final comment to be made in this unconcluded study of Nabokov's poetry refers to a thus-far unstated consideration which necessarily motivated it, at least in part – assessment of the relative quality of Nabokov's verse. Throughout this study, subjective comment on the quality of Nabokov's verse was kept to a minimum. In a certain obvious sense, my great admiration for Nabokov's poetry and prose is to be assumed; the writing of a lengthy re-evaluation of Nabokov's poetry would be an odd venture indeed, should I dislike his poetry. And here let me state, as a matter of record, that I greatly admire both the intellectual and aesthetic achievement of Nabokov's poetry as a body of creative writing and the exceptional manner in which it was integrated into his entire oeuvre as a defining element of his unmistakable artistry. With regard to specific examples, individual poems by Nabokov may be considered masterpieces of poetic art, in general, and of Nabokov's art, in particular. Poems as diverse as 'The Muse,' 'Soft Sound,' 'Fame,' 'The Swift,' 'The Poem,' 'An Evening of Russian Poetry,' 'Restoration,' but also such enigmatic poems as 'The Ballad of Longwood Glen' or the early, laconic 'To people you will say: it's time! ...' are concentrates of the best of Nabokov's exceptional artistic ability. In his poetry, the features which distinguish his prose – limpidity, the triumph of well chosen imagery, the transformative power of language and metaphor to startle perception and augment consciousness, and the light breeze emanating from an unseen beyond – are presented in a form which emphasizes their compactness. Individual poems by Nabokov share the summit of his artistic achievement. The best of Nabokov's poetry expresses to greatest advantage the best of his artistry, turning the horizon of his writing into 'the jewel of a bluish view' (*PP* 168). This, too, is recommendation for the future study of Nabokov's poetry. It is there in the harbour of world literature. The splendid ship of Nabokov's poetry is not to be unseen.

Notes

1. Introduction: Locating Nabokov's Poetry

1 Vladimir Nabokov, *Stikhi* (Petrograd: privately printed, 1916) and *Stikhi* (Ann Arbor: Ardis, 1979). The exceedingly rare volume of 1916 has been reprinted with a foreword by Vadim Stark, *Stikhi* (St Petersburg: Nabokovskii Fond, 1997). Reference to the poetry-based symmetry uniting Nabokov's oeuvre may be taken further. Nabokov's first poem to be published in a journal – 'Lunnaia greza' ('Lunar Reverie'), in *Vestnik Evropy*, 16 July 1916 – echoes his final poem to be published in a journal fifty years later – 'Lunar Lines,' in the *New York Review of Books*, 26 April 1966.

2 It will be noted that I am not treating a third potential category, that of Russian literature and the post-glasnost literary institution in Russia. The extent to which Nabokov's belated inclusion into this reformulated system is modifying the very understanding of twentieth-century Russian literature is a fascinating question in itself. Since the beginning of the 1990s there has been an explosion of important Russian-language works on Nabokov as both an English- and Russian-language writer. Interestingly, Nabokov's poetry has garnered more interest in this context, as witnessed by various critical appreciations of his poetry and the publication of several collections of his poetry. See, for instance, *Vladimir Nabokov: Stikhotvoreniia*, ed. Vladimir Smirnov (Moskva: Molodaia Gvardiia, 1991); *Vladimir Nabokov: Stikhotvoreniia i poemy*, ed. V. Fedorova (Moskva: Folio, 2001); V.V. Nabokov, *Stikhotvereniia*, ed. M. Malikova (St Petersburg: Novaia Biblioteka Poeta, 2002); and the sole authorized edition of Nabokov's works in Russian, the five-volume *Vladimir Nabokov: Sobranie sochinenii russkogo perioda v piati tomakh* (St Petersburg: Simpozium, 1999).

3 The generic preferences of Nabokov criticism are in themselves a topic of
   interest, reflecting as they do a form of *Rezeptiongeschichte*. Thus far,
   Nabokov's English-language novels have received the most critical attention,
   followed by the Russian novels. While Nabokov's approach to translation has
   been critically discussed in the past, attention now seems to be turning
   towards consideration of Nabokov's achievements in other genres – in
   particular, the short story and Nabokov's scientific writing – and such
   metacritical topics as the metaphysical dimension in Nabokov's writing.

4 See Georgii Adamovich's comments from his review of the fortieth number of
   Sovremennye zapiski: '*The Defense* is something western, European, above all
   French. Were it to be printed in the *Nouvelle Revue française* for example, it
   would seem quite appropriate. I think, however, that printed in a French
   journal it would create significantly less of an impression than in *Sovremennye
   zapiski*' (Adamovich 1929, 16); and Georgii Ivanov's infamous polemic
   against Nabokov in the first number of the Parisian journal *Chisla* (Ivanov
   233–6). See also chapter 15 of Brian Boyd's *The Russian Years*, 'Negative and
   Positive: Berlin, 1929–1930,' for an excellent account of Nabokov's literary
   disputes with Adamovich and Ivanov (Boyd 1990, 341–61).

5 Julian W. Connolly has also described this three-stage history of reception
   (Connolly 1999, 3).

6 As exemplary of this tendency, see, for instance, John O. Stark, *The Literature
   of Exhaustion: Borges, Nabokov, and Barth*.

7 For an account of Nabokov's applicability to the modes of Modernism and
   Postmodernism, see, for instance, Herbert Grabes 'A Prize for the (Post-)
   Modernist Nabokov.'

8 It is as a writer of *postmodern* fiction that Nabokov has been inscribed into
   the canon of post-war American literature as it is represented in influential
   anthologies and literary histories. As representative of this trend, see, for
   instance, the reference to Nabokov in *The Columbia History of the American
   Novel* in the section entitled 'Biographies of American Authors': 'Widely
   considered a literary genius – many consider Nabokov to be the most
   influential postmodern writer – he created difficult, metafictional books,
   characterized by a combination of erudition and humor' (Elliott 797).

9 Robert Alter's '*Invitation to a Beheading*: Nabokov and the Art of Politics' is
   an example of a perceptive, early appreciation of the ethical dimension of
   Nabokov's writing which is based on one of his Russian novels.

10 More recently, Stephen Blackwell in *Zina's Paradox: The Figured Reader in
    Nabokov's Gift* has taken up discussion of the power of love in Nabokov's
    fiction in the example of *The Gift*.

11 The most influential and comprehensive discussion of the 'otherworld' in Nabokov's fiction is to be found in Vladimir Alexandrov's *Nabokov's Otherworld*. See also Boyd's two-volume biography of Nabokov, where the topic is also treated.

12 In the final clause of the following statement, Herbert Grabes, for instance, alludes to the resistance of some critics in following Véra Nabokov's claims regarding the centrality of 'the otherworld' in Nabokov's writing: 'In the last two decades, however – above all through Vladimir Alexandrov's 1991 monograph on *Nabokov's Otherworld* – a growing interest has developed in Nabokov's "metaphysics," even if by no means everybody would take at face value (as Alexandrov does) Véra Nabokov's remark that "potustoronnost" ("the beyond") was the "main theme" of everything her late husband wrote' (Grabes 2002, 336).

13 See, for example, Zoran Kuzmanovich, '"Splendid Insincerity" as "Utmost Truthfulness": Nabokov and the Claims of the Real.'

14 In the Russian version of his autobiography, *Drugie Berega*, Nabokov was as uncompromising in his criticism as in *Speak, Memory*: 'I hasten to add that that first booklet of poetry of mine was exclusively bad and should never have been published. It was immediately and justifiably torn to pieces by the few reviewers who noticed it' (*Ssoch* V, 290–1). Brian Boyd offers an informative account of the writing and reception of this volume of verse (Boyd 1990, 118–19).

15 As early as 1934, Nabokov's interest in 'the burden of memory' enticed critics to draw parallels to Proust (Kantor 125–8).

16 Nabokov made this comment in a letter of 17 December 1945 in response to a letter of 1 October 1945 in which his sister re-established contact from Prague after a hiatus of nine years. In the postscript to her letter, Helene Sikorski had written: 'Just imagine: in the library I found your first book of poems *Poems* V.V. Nabokov. 1916. If you want, I'll copy them all out for you sometime. They are charming' (*Pss* 10).

17 D. Barton Johnson has made this same observation (Johnson 1991, 309); Johnson also comments on similarities to the Ardis summer scenes of *Ada*.

18 Brian Boyd offers a description of this mythical Russian bird (Boyd 1990, 180–1).

19 For an account of the selection of poems for this collection, see Field, *VN: The Life and Art of Vladimir Nabokov* (78–9); Boyd, *Vladimir Nabokov: The Russian Years* (189); and the commentary to *Vladimir Nabokov: Sobranie sochinenii russkogo perioda v piati tomakh* (*Ssoch* I, 779–80).

20 The quotations concerning the title proposals are taken from Nabokov's letter of 1 December 1921 to his parents, cited in M. Malikova's notes to *The Empyrean Path*, in *V.V. Nabokov: Stikhotvoreniia*, 547.

21 The relevance of 1926 and the publication of Nabokov's novel *Mary* to the writing and publication of poetry has been documented by Johnson: 'Although 22 poems were published during the year that *Mashen'ka* was written, the numbers fall off rapidly in following years; 8 – in 1926; 11 each in 1927 and 1928, with substantially smaller figures thereafter' (Johnson 1991, 311).

22 The friend of the poem is very possibly Baron Iuri Rausch von Traubenberg, Nabokov's cousin and best friend, who was killed in 1919 while fighting against the Red Army in northern Crimea. See Nabokov's *Speak, Memory* (*SM* 196–200).

23 The accumulation of volumes of poetry with the modest title *Poems* is potentially confusing, though intriguing in its very repetitiveness. One necessarily unverifiable explanation for this is that Nabokov at some level saw all of his poetry as emerging from an underlying foundational sensibility which was neither susceptible to, nor to be mistaken for, the variations of thematic manifestation suggested by separate titles. It is to be recalled that John Shade of *Pale Fire* also decided simply to name all of his volumes *Poems*: '*Dim Gulf* was my first book (free verse); *Night Rote* / Came next; then *Hebe's Cup*, my final float / In that damp carnival, for now I term / Everything "Poems," and no longer squirm' (*PF* 68; ll. 957–60).

24 V. Nabokov, 'Remembrance,' *The English Review* 144 (1920); 'Home,' *The Trinity Magazine* 5.2 (1920); 'The Russian Song,' *Karussel* (Berlin) 2 (1923). Publication information cited by M. Malikova in *V.V. Nabokov: Stikhotvoreniia*, 562.

25 For an analysis of the formal character of Nabokov's English verse, see B. Scherr, 'Poetry' (Scherr 613–14) and Th. Eekman, 'Vladimir Nabokov's Poetry' (Eekman 97–8).

26 Individual English poems have also been anthologized in *Modern Russian Poetry*, ed. Vladimir Markov and Merrill Sparks; *The New Yorker Book of Poems* (New York: Viking, 1969); and *Songs and Dreams*, ed. James Kirkup.

27 Boyd indicates that *Poems and Problems* was the third of the eleven books Nabokov was contracted to publish with McGraw-Hill (Boyd 1992, 525, 575).

28 For the circumstances around the publication of *Stikhi* (*Poems*), see Boyd 1992, 653, 658; and Johnson 1991, 313.

2. Reading Nabokov's Reception: Nabokov, Poetry, and the Critics

 1 See David M. Bethea's suggestion that had Nabokov used the word 'poet' instead of 'writer' in reporting Gippius's famous evaluation, she would 'have been right' (Bethea 1995a, 381).

2 This poem, along with a fuller reading of peacock imagery, will be more fully analysed in chapter 3.

3 Boyd provides a full account of the background to Ivanov's attack (Boyd 1990, 350).

4 For a concise illustration of this reductivist and oft-repeated narrative of Nabokov's development, see the comments made by the authoritative critic G. Adamovich in the context of his review of the fortieth number of *Sovremennye zapiski*: 'Sirin (Nabokov) made his debut in literature as a poet. In his poems was to be felt undoubted talent in versification, but sometimes there was not one word one would remember, not one line one would want to repeat. The poems were quite ingenious, smooth, clever, albeit watery. Sirin's first novel *Mary* – little noticed here – I personally found charming and, as is often said, "promising." It was immediately apparent that Sirin was much more inclined towards prose than poetry ...' (Adamovich 1929, 16).

5 Of passing interest is Mark Slonim's article 'Molodye pisateli za rubezhom.' This article is indicative of the manner in which Nabokov's poetry was progressively lost to critical memory, even in the émigré community, with the expansion of Nabokov's career as a novelist. The linear narrative outlining Nabokov's development remained, though with a new beginning: 'V. Sirin (Nabokov) is a rather monotonous poet but not at all a bad prose writer. After his novella *Mary*, which was somewhat porous and too lyrical, and after stories in the style of Walter Pater, he completed a very successful novel, *King, Queen, Knave*, in which he attempted to describe the mechanical monotony of the life of a contemporary person, his encirclement by things, and his tragic fate of loneliness and senselessness. A light touch of German expressionism lies on this heavily structured novel, although it would be mistaken to call him an imitator ...' (Slonim 115).

6 Apart from 'Fame,' the poems referred to in this citation were written under the pseudonym Vasily Shishkov in the context of a hoax perpetrated by Nabokov on Adamovich. See chapter 5 below.

7 Interestingly, Andrew Field, Nabokov's one-time biographer, claims that 'there is absolutely no influence upon Nabokov by the artists of the Silver Age except perhaps Aleksandr Blok, and who in St. Petersburg during those years did not know Blok?' (Field 1977, 95).

8 In his above discussed review of *The Return of Chorb* from *Sovremenye zapiski*, Mikhail Tsetlin makes an interesting observation about the pronounced urge of émigré critics to find 'foreign influences' for Nabokov's prose, which has suggestive parallels to the inclination to see 'Russian influences' in his poetry: 'But they [his novels] are so much outside the dominant channel of

Russian literature, so devoid of Russian literary influences, that critics involuntarily search for foreign influences' (Tsetlin 530).

9 This poem is discussed below in chapter 3 in the context of Nabokov's numerous poems about animals, in particular, animals associated with metamorphoses.

10 'I am a little ashamed to confess that the other day I wrote my first English poem and sent it to [Richard] Weeks who called it a "darling" and will print it in the Christmas issue of the *A.M.* I who hate so intensely the way "sincerity" is considered by some critics to be the main *quality* of a writer, must now rely upon "sincerity" in judging that poem!' (*NWL* 57).

11 The charge of 'lightness' was a critical burden Nabokov's prose would also have to bear. In a manner similar to the treatment of his English poetry, the earliest reviews of *Pale Fire* indicate an inability to assimilate the *sui generis* 'difference' of Nabokov's novel. Few commentators would now likely concur with Dwight Macdonald's assessment from 'Virtuosity Rewarded, or Dr. Kinbote's Revenge' that 'Nabokov is a minor writer ...' (Macdonald 437). The explication and reassessment of Nabokov's English prose which has led to the establishment of his esteem as a writer of prose has not, unfortunately, been yet extended to his verse.

12 Dupee's introductory services to American literature and Nabokov preceded his discussion of Nabokov's poetry. Famously, the scholar and former editor of the *Partisan Review* provided the article in *Anchor Review* which accompanied the first publication of excepts from *Lolita* for an American audience.

13 In his excellent study of Nabokov's senior contemporary, *Khodasevich: His Life and Art*, David M. Bethea offers the following response to the charge of formal, especially metrical, conservatism levelled at Khodasevich: 'As recently as 1923 Andrey Bely, by then an avid metrist, made the claim that Khodasevich's use of iambic tetrameter in *The Heavy Lyre* was closest to that of Tyutchev (with Pushkin second). More recently, G.S. Smith has scrutinized the stanza rhythm and stress load of a number of poems in *The Heavy Lyre* and has noted elsewhere that in his mature period Khodasevich used iambic tetrameter more (almost seventy-five percent of the time) than any other major or minor émigré poet ... Khodasevich ... stuck with the leading meter of the nineteenth-century classical tradition; ... But Khodasevich's much discussed traditionalism is always deceptive, and to argue, as the almost breathlessly computing Bely does, that Khodasevich's first cousins are Tyutchev, Pushkin, and Baratynsky is to omit at least half of the problem' (Bethea 1983, 210–11). Likewise, though for different reasons, to argue in the case of Nabokov that his poetry went little further than isolated models from the nineteenth century is to misread both his poetry

and its place in his oeuvre and, to put it mildly, and in Bethea's words, 'to omit at least half of the problem.'

14 Regarding Nabokov's Soviet readership, see Elendea Proffer's brief article 'Nabokov's Russian Readers'; and Slava Paperno and John V. Hagopian, 'Official and Unofficial Responses to Nabokov in the Soviet Union.' See also A.V. Blium, '"Poetic belyi, Sirin ..." (Nabokov o tsenzure i tsenzura o Nabokove).'

15 See Prokhorova's comments in 'Nabokovs Urenkel: Die russische Literatur ist ästhetisches Babylon' ('Nabokov's Great-Grandson: Russian Literature Is an Aesthetic Babylon'): 'Das, was wir im heutigen Russland beobachten, ist nichts anderes, als die vierte ungestüme ästhetische Modernisierung in den letzten zweihundert Jahren der Existenz des Landes im westeur-opäischen Kontext ... de facto sitzt auf dem (trans-)nationalen Thron eines Gründervaters der neuen russischen Literatur am Ende des 20. Jahrhunderts endgültig Nabokov' [That which we are observing in contemporary Russia is nothing other than the fourth tempestuous aesthetic modernization within the last two hundred years of the country's existence in a West European context ... de facto, Nabokov is definitively seated on the (trans-) national throne of a founding father of the new Russian literature at the end of the twentieth-century].

16 In 2005, Scherr published another, equally authoritative, though to my mind more appreciative, overview of Nabokov's history and achievement as a poet. This more recent assessment concludes with a statement which suggests the relatedness of Nabokov's poetry to his prose: 'As many of his earliest reviewers noted, the formal virtuosity of his early poems was often mannered and not matched by an originality in his voice or his ideas. And yet, from the mid-1920s on, particularly as he turned to poetry with a stronger narrative structure, he was able to provide scope for his wit, his inventiveness, and his gift for parody. His poems come to read like miniature versions of his prose works, exploring many of the topics and even employing many of the same techniques' (Scherr 2005, 115–16).

17 See, for instance, the selection of articles published in *Nabokovskii vestnik* (*The Nabokov Bulletin*), especially volume 6 from 2001, devoted to 'Nabokov and the Silver Age.'

18 Critical reference to Nabokov's poetry in the development of interpretive arguments concerning other portions of his writing is still a relatively rare phenomenon in English-language Nabokov criticism, although there are important exceptions, such as D. Barton Johnson's discussion of the naiad motif in Nabokov's writing: '"L'Inconnue de la Seine" and Nabokov's Naiads.'

3. Nabokov's Lyric Voice: The Poetry of This World and Another

1   The poem 'The Rain Has Flown' does not explicitly appear in textual form in *Speak, Memory*, although Nabokov's recreation of his first lyric as his awakening into artistic consciousness clearly refers to this poem. While absent in verse form, the poem is nonetheless present in disguise in the index. At the conclusion of the Foreword to *Speak, Memory*, Nabokov states that the main purpose of the index 'is to list for my convenience some of the people and themes connected with my past years. Its presence will annoy the vulgar but may please the discerning, if only because' – and here Nabokov appends an intriguing little poem: 'Through the window of that index / Climbs a rose / And sometimes a gentle wind *ex / Ponto* blows' (*SM* 15–16). In my parsing of this cryptic reference and poem, the 'rose' climbing through the window of the index is the 'caprifole' or honeysuckle of 'The Rain Has Flown.' 'Honeysuckle' is present as one of the most curiously whimsical items in the index, with four page references. Cross-reference to *Drugie berega* (*Other Shores*) reveals that each of the references to honeysuckle from *Speak, Memory* is absent from the original Russian version of Nabokov's autobiography, as is the chapter 11 restaging of his first poem. The poem appended to the conclusion of the Foreword seems a gentle reference to the honeysuckle climbing through the index into a distant allusion to the poem which inaugurated Nabokov's life as an artist. Boyd has also offered a reading of the relevance of the poem from the Foreword to *Speak, Memory* (Boyd 1992, 445), albeit one integral to an earlier, now modified, reading of *Pale Fire*.

2   The prose rendering of the scene which inspired Nabokov's 'first' poem inevitably recalls Nabokov's return to the scene in other prose works, in particular, the exceptionally 'poetic' novel *The Real Life of Sebastian Knight*. In Nabokov's first novel published in the United States, the imagery from 'The Rain Has Flown' arises in a scene describing the abandonment of husband and son by Knight's mother: '… she left husband and child as suddenly as a rain-drop starts to slide tipwards down a syringe leaf. That upward jerk of the forsaken leaf, which had been heavy with its bright burden, must have caused my father fierce pain' (*RLSK* 7).

3   It is this attachment to the physical world which Struve termed 'realist' in his 'Notes on Nabokov as a Russian Writer': 'He [Nabokov] is a "realist" (I know he himself detests the use of such labels in literature) in the sense that he nearly always uses material with which real life provides him, and in using it displays the astounding keenness of his vision and the uncanny power of his memory' (Struve 1967, 47).

4 The fullest discussion of cosmic synchronization is to be found in Jonathan Borden Sisson's unpublished dissertation 'Cosmic Synchronization and Other Worlds in the Work of Vladimir Nabokov.' I am very much indebted to Sisson's study.

5 Alexander Zholkovsky's article 'Poem, Problem, Prank' provides an intriguing discussion of chapter 11 of *Speak, Memory* and potential references to Russian poetry inserted by the mature Nabokov into the autobiographical account of his 'first poem.' In particular, Zholkovsky notes the possible references to Khodasevich's 'The Monkey.' In contrast to my reading of Nabokov's chapter 11 elucidation of the wonders of inspiration and the creative experience, including cosmic synchronization discussed below, Zholkovsky sees the likelihood of 'an archly fictionalized tall tale.'

6 See, for instance, Ludmila A. Foster, 'Nabokov's Gnostic Turpitude: The Surrealistic Vision of Reality in *Priglašenie na Kazn'.*'

7 '… хочу обратить внимание читателя, на главную тему Набокова. Она, кажется, не была никем отмечена, а между тем сю пропитано все, что он писал; она, как некий водяной знак, символизирует все его творчество. Я говорю о "потусторонности", как он сам ее назвал в своем последнем стихотворении "Влюбленность"' (*Stikhi* 3).

8 Maxim D. Shrayer, in his *The World of Nabokov's Stories*, for instance, argues that 'the otherworld distinguishes Nabokov's short stories from those of his predecessors and contemporaries in Russian literature' (Shrayer 21). The above overview of prominent discussions of the otherworld in Nabokov's writing is by no means complete. Further reference is to be made to, among others, Sergej Davydov, '*Teksty – Metreshki' Vladimira Nabokova.*

9 Nabokov's first novel written in the United States, *Bend Sinister*, contains shades of the obscenity of a Platonic politics in practice.

10 See the conclusion reached in Book X of Plato's *The Republic*: 'And the tragic poet is an imitator, and therefore, like all other imitators, he is thrice removed from the king and from the truth? That appears to be so' (Plato 662).

11 See Nabokov's letter number 190 to Edmund Wilson in *Dear Bunny, Dear Volodya*: 'The decline of Russian literature in 1905–1917 is a soviet invention. Blok, Bely, Bunin and others wrote their best stuff in those days. And never was poetry so popular – not even in Pushkin's days. I am a product of that period, I was bred in that atmosphere' (*NWL* 246). Johnson (1985, 2–3), and especially Alexandrov in his chapter 'Nabokov and the Silver Age of Russian Culture' (Alexandrov 1991, 213–34), discuss the thorny topic of Nabokov's relation to Symbolism. For a review of Nabokov's comments on various Russian modernist poets, see Simon Karlinsky, 'Nabokov and Some Poets of Russian Modernism.'

12 See, for instance, Vladimir Soloviev's formulation in poetic form of the Symbolist understanding of the dual nature of existence: 'Dearest friend, don't you see, / That everything by us seen – / Is but a shadow, but a gleam / Of what eyes cannot perceive? // Dearest friend, don't you hear, That the rasping worldly noise / Is but the disturbed echo / Of exultant harmonies? // Dearest friend, don't you feel, / That one thing only in the world / Counts – what one heart tells / Another heart in mute accord?' (quoted in A. Landman's translation in Victor Terras, *Poetry of the Silver Age: The Various Voices of Russian Modernism* [Terras 9–10]).

13 For a comprehensive discussion of the Symbolists, see, above all, James West, *Russian Symbolism*. See also 'Chapter Four: Symbolism,' in Renato Poggioli, *The Poets of Russia – 1890–1930*; and 'Symbolism,' in Victor Terras, *Poetry of the Silver Age: The Various Voices of Russian Modernism*.

14 See also Nabokov's reference to Brooke as a writer of strong appeal for him between the ages of twenty and forty, but who subsequently lost his interest (*SO* 43).

15 See D. Barton Johnson, 'Vladimir Nabokov and Walter de la Mare's "Otheworld"' and 'Vladimir Nabokov and Rupert Brooke.' For elements of de la Mare in one of Nabokov's short stories, see also Gennady Barabtarlo, 'A Skeleton in Nabokov's Closet: "Mest."'

16 In the explanatory notes to this article, M. Malikova quotes a review contemporary with the publication of Nabokov's article which emphasizes the poetic quality of Nabokov's early criticism: '… the study of the English poet Rupert Brooke, who is still completely unknown beyond the borders of England … is less critical in character than poetic; every line is witness to the fact that it could only have been written by a poet' (*Ssoch* I, 809).

17 One pauses to reflect that just as Nabokov's first reference to the otherworld arose in an early article on Rupert Brooke, so Brooke is granted a brief walk-on reference in the narrative of *Look at the Harlequins!* during discussion of the poem 'Being in Love,' Nabokov's last poem and the one referred to by Véra Nabokov in identification of Nabokov's 'main theme' (*LATH* 28).

18 The sole exception from Nabokov's early career as a poet is his fascination with Andrei Belyi's theories of Russian metrics. See Gerald S. Smith, 'Nabokov and Russian Verse Form' for a discussion of Belyi's appeal to Nabokov as prosodist. While his poetic writing does not bear significant evidence of a sustained attempt to implement Belyi's theories, Nabokov remained complimentary of them throughout his life. In a letter of 1942 to Wilson, Nabokov described Belyi as the author of 'probably the greatest work on verse in any language' (*NWL* 86). Likewise, in his *Notes on Prosody* appended to his *Eugene Onegin*, Nabokov reveals his youthful interest in

Belyi: 'When I was still a boy, I was greatly fascinated by Bely's admirable work, but I have not consulted it since I last read it in 1919' (*EO* III, 459).

19 The importance of sight as a forceful example of the sensual apprehension of the phenomenal world will be discussed in this chapter below in reference to Nabokov's attentiveness to the trifles of life.

20 See, for instance, such poems as 'You will enter and wordlessly sit down ...' (*Ssoch* I, 473), 'O, wondrous agitation of a meeting! ...' (*Ssoch* I, 492), and 'The clock on the tower sang out ...' (*Ssoch* I, 502), among others.

21 Already here in a poem of 1934 are several of the key images which will lend the conclusion of John Shade's 'Pale Fire' its aura of a divine pattern and otherworldly mystery.

22 'Evening on a Vacant Lot' is dedicated to V.D. Nabokov, Nabokov's father, who was tragically murdered on 28 March 1922 by Russian monarchists intent upon assassinating another man, Paul Milyukov, the former Russian minister of foreign affairs. The absurd, literally nonsensical death of Nabokov's father in a case of mistaken identity was the most tragic event in Nabokov's life. See Brian Boyd, *Vladimir Nabokov: The Russian Years* for an account of V.D. Nabokov's death (Boyd 1990, 189–93) and a brief discussion of the poem 'Evening on a Vacant Lot' (Boyd 1990, 380–1).

23 'Гекзаметры' ('Gekzametry' / 'Hexameters') was first published in *Rul'* on 30 March 1923.

24 Compare, for instance, Shelley's rendering in canto 39 of 'Adonais: An Elegy on the Death of John Keats': 'Peace, peace! He is not dead, he doth not sleep – / He hath awakened from the dream of life – / 'Tis we, who lost in stormy visions, keep / With phantoms an unprofitable strife' (Shelley 440).

25 For a related though more closely veiled representation of the mysterious experience of the ineffable while swimming at night, see Nabokov's poem from *The Empyrean Path* 'Вдали от берега, в мерцании морском ...' ('Vdali ot berega, v mertsanii morskom, ...' / 'Far from shore, in the marine shimmering ...') (*Ssoch* I, 479).

26 In chapter 3 of *The Dominion of the Dead*, Harrison also remarks on contrasting modes of enclosure – the house, with its windows and doors, as opposed to coffined or entombed spaces, which have no external apertures. Although tantalizingly brief, these comments further illuminate the complex field of motifs from Nabokov's oeuvre, where life, death, and the otherworld are suggested in imagery ranging from windowed houses and boarding rooms to apertureless graves, wardrobes, and elevators.

27 Nabokov published a translation of Lermontov's poem in the *Russian Review*. This poem is not included in his collection of translated poetry *Three Russian Poets: Selections from Pushkin, Lermontov, Tyutchev*. In a letter to Edmund

Wilson regarding his translation of 'The Angel,' Nabokov criticized its banality (*NWL* 181–2). In his 'Nabokov and Poe,' Dale E. Peterson reads 'In a crystal ball we were enclosed ...' as resonating 'in perfect harmony with the music and standard libretto of much Poe-etry' (Peterson 1995, 467), and thus as evidence of Poe's presence in Nabokov's poetry.

28 The poem 'Лестница' ('Lestnitsa' / 'The Staircase') of *The Empyrean Path* likewise takes up the image of a staircase – here personified as a conscious entity – which is sure to remember the footsteps of the lyric speaker. The concluding lines of the poem likewise derive suggestive, metaphoric force from imagery of spatial enclosure and transition, literally referring to exile but perhaps metaphorically to different realms: 'Your banisters remember, / how I left the splendour of still beckoning rooms / and how for the last times I descended you; / how with the caution of a criminal I closed / one, and the other door and in the half-light of a snowy night / secretly departed – free, without hope ...' (*Ssoch* I, 476).

29 Vladimir Khodasevich also made famous use of the motif of the bare, enclosed room in 'Баллада,' a poem of 1921 subsequently translated by Nabokov as 'Orpheus.' Nabokov considered Khodasevich the greatest Russian poet of the twentieth century and suggested in a review of 1927 that with this poem 'Khodasevich achieved ... the ultimate in poetic technique' (*Ssoch* II, 650).

30 Iu. Aikhenval'd, a literary critic and warm friend of the Nabokovs, died in December 1929 while returning home from a party at the Nabokovs' in Berlin after being struck down by a streetcar (Boyd 1990, 287–8).

31 'The Room' first appeared in the *New Yorker* (13 May 1950) and was later reprinted in both *Poems* and *Poems and Problems*.

32 'O love, you are radiant and winged ...' is the poem referred to by Struve in the context of Nabokov's purported multiple poetic models discussed above in chapter 2.

33 Nabokov's poem of 1923 'Встреча' ('Vstrecha' / 'The Meeting'), which set in verse his meeting with Véra Evseevna Slonim, his future wife and muse, carries an epigraph from Blok's 'Incognita.' This poem will be discussed below in chapter 6 in relation to *The Gift*.

34 Vladimir Nabokov, *Poems: 1929–1951*; the preface is without page number.

35 Interesting, though outside the confines of analysis here, is the extent to which the imagery of an early poem like 'Who will go out in the morning? Who will notice the ripened fruit?' – with its evocation of a peacock in a sun-mottled garden lane – may be transformed for use in the entirely different context of, for instance, *Bend Sinister*: 'The knowledge we may acquire in the

course of such a discussion will necessarily stand in the same relation to the truth as the black peacock spot produced intraoptically by pressure on the palpebra does in regard to a garden path brindled with genuine sunlight' (*BS* 192). However such imagery is to be read, it is many removes from the disparaging identification of Nabokov with a peacock in the first reviews of *The Cluster* discussed in chapter 2.

36 In *Nabokov: His Life in Part*, Field was still more adamant: 'The place of religion in Nabokov's childhood and youth is relevant primarily because of *the large number of Biblical and religious* poems, published and unpublished, which he wrote at the beginning of his career' (Field 1977, 88; emphasis added). Field, of course, was not the only commentator to have struggled vainly with the relevance of supposed religious imagery in Nabokov's early poetry. From the earliest of émigré reviews of Nabokov's poetry discussed in chapter 2 of this study is to be recalled the diametrically opposed interpretations of Alexander Bakhrakh and Vladimir Amfiteatrov-Kadashev. For Bakhrakh, Nabokov's world was 'blasphemous' – hence his attempt to create and recede into a 'soulless' world of 'ultra aestheticism.' For Amfiteatrov-Kadashev, Nabokov was affirming 'a harmonious Unity' understood in a religious sense.

37 Vladimir Nabokov, 'Rupert Bruk': 'He so vividly feels the divine in the surrounding natural environment: of what interest to him that window-dressing eternity, Vrubel-like angels, that lord with the beard of cotton wool?' (*Ssoch* I, 742); *Nikolai Gogol*: 'The appeal to providence, or rather the queer way he had (a propensity which his mother shared) of substituting the hand of God for any whim of his own or any chance occurrence in which none but he (and she) could discern the odor of sanctity, is also most suggestive; and it shows how imaginative, humanly imaginative (and thus metaphysically limited) Gogol's religion was …' (*NG* 22); *Strong Opinions*: '*As a final question, do you believe in God?* To be quite candid – and what I am going to say now is something I never said before, and I hope it provokes a salutary chill – I know more than I can express in words, and the little I can express would not have been expressed, had I not known more' (*SO* 45); *The Gift*: 'Religion has the same relation to man's heavenly condition that mathematics has to his earthly one: both the one and the other are merely rules of the game. Belief in God and belief in numbers: local truth and truth of location' (*Ssoch* IV, 484; *Gift* 309); 'Ultima Thule': '"Falter, allow me to begin like the traditional tourist – with an inspection of an ancient church, familiar to him from pictures. Let me ask you: Does God exist?" "Cold," said Falter … "Forget it," snapped Falter. "I said 'cold,' as they say in the game, when one

must find a hidden object ... How can I answer you whether God exists when the matter under discussion is perhaps sweet peas or a soccer linesman's flag? You are looking in the wrong place and in the wrong way, *cher monsieur*, that is all the answer I can give you'" (*Stories* 517–18).

38 The poem 'На сельском кладбище' ('Na sel'skom kladbishche' / 'In the Village Cemetery') in a similar manner, though to a lesser degree, utilizes the imagery of a cemetery, not in the evocation of religious meaning, but as a platform for depiction of the particularized beauty of the world: 'На кладбище – солнце, сирень и березки, / и капли дождя на блестящих крестах' ('In the cemetery – the sun, lilac and birches / and drops of rain on glistening crosses') (*Ssoch* I, 461).

39 'Нас мало – юных, окрыленных ...' ('Nas malo – iunykh, okrylennykh ...' / 'We are few – the young, the winged ...') bears thematic comparison with Nabokov's famous poem of 1939 'The Poets,' first published in Russian as 'Poety' under the pseudonym Vasilii Shishkov.

40 Nabokov translated and included 'В раю' ('V raiu' / 'In Paradise') of 1927 and 'Вершина' ('Vershina' / 'The Summit') in *Poems and Problems*. In this redaction of 1970, 'Vershina' was printed as 'Люблю я гору' ('Liubliu ia goru' / 'I Like That Mountain') (*PP* 34–5), the Russian title it is also presented under in volume 5 of *Vladimir Nabokov: Sobranie Sochinenii russkogo perioda v piati tomakh*, 433. In Nabokov's collection of 1979, *Poems*, the poem was printed with the title 'Vershina' (*Stikhi* 175).

41 With reference to the verb светишь (*svetish'* / shining) in this poem, Maxim Shrayer, in his study *The World of Nabokov's Stories*, sees encoded reference to Nabokov's first fiancée, Svetlana Siewert (Shrayer 102). If so, Svetlana shone through a lot of Nabokov's verse.

42 Nabokov referred to this poem as 'The Swift' during his reading at Sanders Hall at Harvard University. A tape of this, Nabokov's last, reading is available from the poetry room at Harvard. The poem remains untitled in the English translation of *The Gift*.

43 A.A. Fet, the Russian poet much admired by Nabokov, also entitled a lyric poem of 1884 'Swallows' (Fet 136).

44 Nabokov's narrative description of the poem in *Strong Opinions* emphasizes the importance of attention to particularity in the poem: 'Let me explain it: there are two persons involved, a boy and a girl, standing on a bridge above the reflected sunset, and there are swallows skimming by, and the boy turns to the girl and says to her, "Tell me, will you always remember *that* swallow? – not any kind of swallow, not those swallows, there, but that particular swallow that skimmed by?" And she says, "Of course I will," and they both burst into tears' (*SO* 14).

45 The reference is to Nabokov's poignant and intricate poem 'Softest of Tongues,' *Atlantic Monthly* 168 (December 1941). In this poem, Nabokov converted into art what he in *Strong Opinions* referred to as his 'private tragedy': 'My private tragedy, which cannot, indeed should not, be anybody's concern, is that I had to abandon my natural language, my natural idiom, my rich, infinitely rich and docile Russian tongue, for a second-rate brand of English' (*SO* 15).

46 See the discussions below in chapters 5 and 6 dealing with *The Gift* and *Pale Fire* concerning the composite representations of bad aesthetics in individuals – Yasha Chernyshevski and Gradus – who provide the illumination of contrast to the principles represented by the poets Fyodor Godunov-Cherdyntsev and John Shade.

47 In his 'Strong Opinions and Nerve Points: Nabokov's Life and Art,' Zoran Kuzmanovich has used the poem as a suggestive text in the reading of various motifs from Nabokov's life and works.

48 Brian Boyd records that Nabokov composed 'Restoration' in haste on the occasion of an invitation to offer a poetry reading 'in the Morris Gray poetry series at Harvard's Sever Hall, in a season that had begun with William Carlos Williams and would end with Wallace Stevens' (Boyd 1992, 216).

49 Among the usual and unusual skills and accomplishments of the self-described 'all-round genius' and narrator of *Transparent Things* is the ability to levitate: 'I can levitate one inch high and keep it up for ten seconds ...' (*TT* 28).

50 Andrew Field (*Nabokov: His Life in Art*, 100–1), Brian Boyd (*Vladimir Nabokov: The American Years*, 303–5), and Barry P. Scherr ('Poetry,' 615–16) discuss 'The Ballad of Longwood Glen.'

51 In 'The Ballad of Longwood Glen,' the tree in which Paul's ball is mysteriously lodged is described as a 'grave green pilgrim,' a 'tree that was passing by,' a rendering which offers a curious echo of Nabokov's description of trees in the short story 'Gods' (discussed in chapter 5): 'All the trees in the world are journeying somewhere. Perpetual pilgrimage ... All trees are pilgrims' (*Stories* 45).

52 One of the few discussions of 'The Ballad of Longwood Glen,' and perhaps the longest, is found in Douglas Fowler's *Reading Nabokov*. Fowler is at pains to provide the poem the serious treatment it deserves within a comprehensive reading of the central traits of Nabokov's aesthetic. Fowler's reading of the poem tends to emphasize the element of escape in the poem, suggesting that '... the value that legitimizes Art Longwood's impulse to escape is distinctly Nabokovian. ... Nabokov shows no sign of disapproval or even qualification of this impulse to escape; there is no median way in Nabokov's world: "no conscience and hence no consciousness" can survive the ugly facts' (Fowler

205). This seems to me too pessimistic a reading of a poetics which found beauty in the tragic and comic, indeed, which bundled the two together in forms of artistic expression which revealed a sense of sheer wonder at the unending multiplicity of human experience.

53 Art Longwood's benighted children seem the distant relatives of Cincinnatus C.'s (non-biological) children from *Invitation to a Beheading*, 'lame Diomedon and obese little Pauline' (*IB* 99). Familial resemblances between 'The Ballad of Longwood Glen' and Nabokov's novel of 1938 extend from the shared experience of divestment of the central protagonists to the sorority of insouciant vulgarity joining Cincinnatus's blithely loutish wife, Marthe, to Art's vigorous widow, Mrs Deforest.

4. Staged Lyricism: The Play of Poetry and Dream-Logic in Nabokov's Drama

1 The seemingly smooth trajectory of Nabokov's development through a series of genres until the novel is reached is suggested, for instance, in the preposition *until* from the following comment by Paul Neubauer: 'Having started his career as a writer in the post-romantic mode with a collection of poems, *Stikhi*, privately published in St. Petersburg in 1916, and *not* to be included in his *Collected Poems* [*sic*], Nabokov penned articles, poems, dramulets and stories until his first novel appeared in the Russian emigrant press Slovo ...' (Neubauer 330).

2 Excluded from consideration in this superficial overview of Nabokov's drama is his first, still unpublished, poetic work of 1918 entitled *Весной* (*Vesnoi / In Spring*). Described by Boyd as a 'lyrical something in one act' (Boyd 1990, 141), *In Spring* is a mini-play of sixty-one hexameters about a pair of young lovers, a chess-player, and an unknown figure. Similarly excluded is the 1923 *Агасфер* (*Agasfer / Ahasuerus*), Nabokov's 'dramatic monolog written as the prologue to a staged symphony' composed by Vladimir Sirin in collaboration with Ivan Lukash and V.F. Iakobson. According to the original announcement included in M. Malikova's explanatory notes to the 'dramatic panto-mime in five parts' reprinted in *Sobranie sochinenii*, the authors of *Ahasuerus* 'created a romantic epos about love roaming the earth like the eternal wanderer Ahasuerus ... In terms of contents, *Ahasuerus* or *Love's Apocrypha* is about the eternal clash of man and woman, the eternal search and eternal elusion of love' (*Ssoch* I, 805). Olga Skonechnaia has discussed *Agasfer* as an expression of Nabokov's use of the image of the Wandering Jew in her 'The Wandering Jew as a Metaphor for Memory in Nabokov's Poetry and Prose of the 1920s and 1930s.' Likewise of relevance, though omitted here, is

Nabokov's concluding scene to Pushkin's *Russalka* (*The Water Nymph*), published in the New York *Novyi zhurnal* 2 (1942).

3 Boyd reports that the hoax worked on at least one reader. Nabokov's father cautioned his son not to allow his love of literature to lead him to the translation of works of dubious aesthetic value (Boyd 1990, 187).

4 Silvia's name has Latin overtones of the forest – appropriately enough, given the contents of the speech cited here.

5 The rain and 'golden smoke' recall not only the burning up of rain in 'The Rain Has Flown' but also the wondrous thunderstorm of 'Разбились облака. Алмазы дождевые ...' ('Razbilis' oblaka. Almazy dozhdevye ...' / 'Clouds shattered. Rain-like diamonds ...').

6 Nabokov's staging of an execution in *The Grand-dad* is repeated in the final chapter of *Invitation to a Beheading*, the novel he described in *Strong Opinions* as his 'dreamiest and most poetical novel' (*SO* 76).

7 Vladimir Nabokov, *Трагедия господина Морна* (*Tragediia gospodina Morna* / *The Tragedy of Mister Morn*), *Zvezda* 4 (1997): 9–98. Nabokov presented the play at a reading in Berlin in 1924, excerpts of which were then published in a review of the reading on 5 April 1924 in *Rul'*. In 2008 Andrey Babikov edited a collection of Nabokov's plays and essays on drama for publication under the title *Набоков. Трагедия господина Морна. Пьесы. Лекции о драма.* (*Nabokov. The Tragedy of Mister Morn. Plays. Essays on Drama.*). This collection includes an introductory essay by Babikov and extensive notes and annotations. Unfortunately, at the time of final preparation of this manuscript for publication, I had still been unable to access Babikov's much needed book and to profit from his scholarship.

8 *The Event* was first staged in Paris in March 1938 with Iurii Annenkov acting as both director and set designer. While the premiere was met with incomprehension and critical rejection, the success of the second showing augured well for the subsequent tremendous success of the play in Paris and later in Prague, Warsaw, Belgrade, and New York. Publication followed in the Parisian *Russkie zapiski* (*Russian Annals*) in April 1938.

9 Galya Diment, in her discussion of Nabokov's dramatic works, 'Plays,' suggests that Nabokov's decision to revise and translate *The Waltz Invention* for publication in 1966 derived in part from the consideration that 'rather than his other long plays ...' it had a universal, not strictly émigré, setting' and that 'he saw that the play's pacifist theme might appeal to the anti-Vietnam crowd of the 1960s, but he absolutely did not want to be identified with their movement' (596). With full respect for Diment's reasoning, I cannot concur. Apart from the ethnically Russian characters, *The Event* is no more or less an

émigré play than *The Waltz Invention*, while Nabokov's presentation of the play to Edmund Wilson in 1943 and his return to it for Dmitri Nabokov's translation in 1964 – before the development of anti-war sentiment in the United States – indicate that other than topical considerations were at play. Moulded out of the lyric essence of Nabokov's artistic sensibility, *The Waltz Invention* is the pinnacle of his dramaturgy and, with a proper production, the most appealing and moving of his plays. Nabokov's presentation of the play to Wilson at a time when he was still trying to establish himself in the American literary institution suggests that Nabokov considered it of consider-able artistic value. Though not a thesis to be taken up in this study, Nabokov's mid-1960s return to *The Waltz Invention* could also have been influenced by the success of *Pale Fire*, a novel which also includes in its cast of characters a deluded, pitiable émigré – Botkin/Kinbote – who spins a fantasy of monarchi-cal wonder.

10 D.J. Enright's slighting references to *The Waltz Invention* in an omnibus review for the *New York Review of Books* in 1966 are illustrative of an inability – perhaps unwillingness – to read Nabokov as anything other than a meta-literary writer, an author, in Enright's formulation, with 'a large and fairly comprehensive distaste for the real' (3). Enright's critical response to *The Waltz Invention* is not based on engagement with the play itself, but, seemingly, on his understanding of what Nabokov represents as the author of, above all, *Lolita* and *Pale Fire*. In this, the reception of *The Waltz Invention* resembles that of Nabokov's English poetry, which likewise encountered conceptual obstacles derived from misconceptions concerning the author.

11 To this list could be added Alfred Jarry's *Ubu roi* of 1896, whose tragic-farcical action is supported by a puppet-like cast, including a mad King given over to the basest of appetites and delusions of military grandeur.

12 Reference to the 'actions of our unscrupulous neighbors' provides Nabokov occasion for a bout of clever punning based on the phonetic potential of the Soviet Union and Stalin's name (*Ssoch* V, 521; *WI* 6). Later in act one, Nabokov introduces an untranslatable instance of the self-encodement of his own name in the action of the play (*Ssoch* V, 534).

13 In the English translation, the various generals are provided with names centred on the phonetic potential of 'ump.' As my analysis rests in part on the semantic associations of the Russian names, I have retained them in my discussion.

14 For a seminal discussion of the central features of theatre of the absurd, see Martin Esslin in, among other publications, 'Theatre of the Absurd.' While a by now somewhat hoary concept, theatre of the absurd is useful in character-izing the similarities uniting an otherwise disparate collection of post-war plays.

15 In his 'Illusion, Reality and Parody in Nabokov's Plays,' Karlinsky also makes informed use of Khodasevich's insights.

16 In the stage directions to the Russian version of the play, it is noted that *Son* (Dream) may be played by a woman (*Ssoch* V, 536). In the English version, the strange muse-like qualities of Trance are emphasized in the description of her as 'a reporter and Waltz's factotum; she is a smart woman of 30 in black masculine dress Shakespearean-masquerade style' (*WI* 3).

17 Nabokov's novel of 1957, *Pnin*, provides oblique intertextual evidence of Waltz's suffering through reference to the advertisements for phonographs scanned by the hapless Pnin in the émigré journals he reads; one of the records is entitled 'Broken Life, a Waltz' (75).

18 In Nabokov's short story 'An Affair of Honor,' it is the vulgarian Berg (German for mountain) who threatens Anton Petrovich with destruction, while in 'The Aurelian' it is a mountain which appears to the artist–butterfly collector Pilgram first as the stroke which almost killed him and then as the death which launches him on his long-awaited journey of exploration. John Shade's fellow survivor of life after death, the somewhat philistine Mrs Z, reports having seen a mountain on the other side, as opposed to the fountain seen by Shade.

19 The complex, at times tragic, associations evoked by the toys belonging to (occasionally) dead children function as a recurring motif in Nabokov's writing. Apart from the painting of the boy with the five balls in *The Event* is its reappearance in *Pale Fire*. John Shade's childhood 'wondrous illness,' which foreshadows his eventual death, is provoked during play with 'a clockwork toy,' while Shade loves his wife most in association with a first toy: '… And I love most / When with a pensive nod you greet her ghost / And hold her first toy on your palm …' (*PF* 43; ll. 289–91).

20 Like the characters Vagabundov and Shnap of *The Event*, the puppet-like generals and the deceased Perrault evoke associations not only with Blok's *The Puppet Show* but with the *balagan* folk tradition, Russia's *commedia dell'arte*, including its expression in such elite works as Stravinsky's and Benua's opera *Petrushka*. See Savelii Senderovich and Elena Shvartz, 'Verbnaia shtuchka: Nabokov i populiarnaia kul'tura.' The numerous allusions to folk literature in the play also invite associations with Charles Perrault, the seventeenth-century French collector of folk tales.

21 The possibility that Annabella may have been a previous acquaintance of Waltz's (in a manner similar to Humbert Humbert's acquaintance with a previous Lolita) is suggested by his confused demand that Trance locate her: 'Listen – here's an excellent idea. Not so long ago … or perhaps it was long

ago ... I don't know ... But anyway I did see her ... A very young girl' (*Ssoch* V, 579; *WI* 103).

22 Annabella's death is by no means certain, though the confusion in Berg's and Waltz's argument concerning the topic raises and strengthens, rather than negates, the possibility. The fate of Annabella's and Lolita's avatar in Poe's 'Annabel Lee' likewise suggests death. Like the dead child of *The Event* or such short stories as 'Christmas' and numerous other examples, Annabella of *The Waltz Invention* seems to belong to a group of characters from Nabokov's fiction who comprise what Julian Connolly in *Nabokov's Early Fiction* has discussed as the theme of 'the quest for the other' in Nabokov's writing (Connolly 1992, 10).

23 A scene depicting Waltz's banning of Annabella's music which was introduced into the English translation further suggests a Platonic regime.

24 In *Speak, Memory*, Nabokov discusses the intruding influence of popular songs of this style in his early verse (*SM* 224). See as well Nabokov's short story 'The Admiralty Spire,' which includes reference to '*tzigane* song' as a structural component in the invocation of the past.

5. Nabokov and the Short Story: The Lyric Heights of a Small Alpine Form

1 See Brian Boyd's *The Russian Years*, 509–10, for an account of Nabokov's hoax and the element of homage to the recently deceased Khodasevich contained in it. Maxim D. Shrayer, in *The World of Nabokov's Stories*, 161–89, also discusses the story 'Vasiliy Shishkov' and the short cycle of poems published by Nabokov under this pseudonym.

2 As if in response to the disappearance of the poet Shishkov, in America, on the other side of the Russian-English divide within his career, Nabokov announced his arrival to his American audience with 'Softest of Tongues,' a poem which comments on his rebirth as artist in another language.

3 The 'lost' Russian short story of 1925 'Easter Rain,' for instance, was recently uncovered by Svetlana Polsky in an archive in former East Germany seventy-one years after initial publication in *Russkoe ekho* (*Russian Echo*) in 1925. See Svetlana Polsky, 'Vladimir Nabokov's Short Story "Easter Rain."'

4 See John Burt Foster, Jr, 'An Archeology of "Mademoiselle O"': Narrative between Art and Memory,' for a suggestive discussion of the generic indeterminacy of the story and its relevance to an understanding of Nabokov's conception of writing.

5 See, for instance, the statements by various critics concerning the short story form in Charles E. May's *The New Short Story Theory*.

6 Alex de Jonge, in 'Nabokov's Uses of Pattern,' has discussed the importance of patterning in Nabokov's novels.
7 The forebodings of death and coffin-like associations of certain objects of furniture is also of relevance in Nabokov's play *The Grand-dad*, discussed in chapter 4, wherein de Mérival is inveigled by the grand-dad to peer into the keyhole of an 'enchanted wardrobe' in preparation for his belated execution.
8 In his novel *Dar* (*The Gift*), the focus of the next chapter, Nabokov repeats this conceit in the chapter 2 description of Fyodor's imaginative descent into the very central-Asian environment explored by his father, only to be called back to the setting of his boarding-room: 'All this lingered bewitchingly, full of color and air, with lively movement in the foreground and a convincing backdrop; then, like smoke from a breeze, it shifted and dispersed – and Fyodor saw again the dead and impossible tulips of his wallpaper, the crumbling mound of cigarette butts in the ashtray, and the lamp's reflection in the black windowpane. He threw open the window. The written-up sheets of paper on his desk started; one folded over, another glided onto the floor. The room immediately turned damp and cold' (*Ssoch* IV, 308; *Gift* 125).
9 Boyd recounts the semi-autobiographical background to this early, unpublished (in Russian) story (Boyd 1990, 217–18).
10 A child's ball, the toy which would serve as an important motif in the underlying plot of *The Event*, makes an early appearance in 'Gods': 'In a corner of our bedroom, under the icon, there is a colored rubber ball. Sometimes it hops softly and sadly from the table and rolls gently on the floor' (*Stories* 45). With motifs such as this, Nabokov subtly marks shifts in plot level.
11 Nabokov's 1925 poem 'Тень' ('Ten' / 'Shade'), first published in *The Return of Chorb*, returns to the high-wire act of a travelling circus troupe and the metaphysical associations of the disappearance of an acrobat's shadow from a wall (*Ssoch* I, 568–9).
12 In making his contrastive argument for 'A Guide to Berlin' vis-à-vis poetry, Boyd, in my opinion, overstates both the religiosity of Nabokov's early verse and the discrepancy between the goals and means of his poetry and his prose: 'As a young poet he had tried to show that the world could best be seen by stepping aside, even by stepping right off: hence God and all those angels in his early verse, so meekly responsive to his call. But used too often the angels' wings soon drooped like tatty feather-dusters stirring up the unsought implications of religious belief. Now in "A Guide to Berlin" Nabokov finds his true way, not borrowing the devices of old poets or the panoply of old creeds ...' (Boyd 1990, 251). As was discussed in chapter 3, there are religious

motifs in Nabokov's poetry, though they are extremely rarely used in the demonstration of conventional religious belief. Poems such as 'Through the garden walked Christ with disciples ...' or 'On Golgotha,' for instance, although they deploy religious motifs for poetic ends, are closer in thematic meaning to 'A Guide to Berlin,' with its emphasis on the wonder of detail, than doctrinal religious meaning.

13 In a similar vein, Robert Grossmith, in 'The Future Perfect of the Mind: "Time and Ebb" and "A Guide to Berlin,"' claims that '... "A Guide to Berlin" also provides the earliest and perhaps best summary statement of Nabokov's aesthetic of "details" and "trivia"' (Grossmith 1993a, 153). Both Connolly's and Grossmith's claims, while accurate with reference to Nabokov's prose, ignore the poetic foundation of this aesthetic.

14 Leona Toker's article 'Nabokov's "Torpid Smoke"' offers a comprehensive discussion of the story.

15 Physical infirmity and, in particular, a weak heart beset various characters from Nabokov's prose universe (e.g., Lik, Pnin, and John Shade). Although it does not constitute a motif specific to his poetry, it does suggest the transience of life, the frailty of the vessel containing life before divestment – a thought related to the metaphysical dimension of his poetry.

16 See, for instance, 'I so easily and happily dreamed ...,' 'The Dream,' or 'Forty-three or four years ...'

17 See, for instance, my discussion in chapter 3 of 'In a crystal ball we were enclosed ...'

18 Although undeveloped except as a prelude to the unpleasant confines of a closed sack, the elevator itself is another of the motifs of restricted spaces found throughout Nabokov's writing. *Mary*, Nabokov's first novel of 1926, devotes the first chapter to the unpleasant confinement of the hero, Ganin, in a darkened, stalled elevator and the realization that 'the floor is terribly thin and there's nothing but a black well beneath it' (*Ssoch* II, 46; *Mary* 3).

19 Nabokov's fiction includes various examples of self-portraiture. In his lecture on *Ulysses*, reprinted in *Lectures on Literature*, Nabokov famously described Joyce 'setting his face in a dark corner of the canvas. The Man in the Brown Macintosh who passes through the dream of the book is no other than the author himself' (*LL* 320). Charles Nicol, in an example drawn for Nabokov's short stories, suggests in his '"Ghastly Rich Glass": A Double Essay on "Spring in Fialta"' that the recurring figure of the 'Englishman' in this story is Nabokov.

20 Maxim Shrayer, in his *The World of Nabokov's Stories*, reads the story's opening reference to lines less as a reference to the infinity of the otherworld – the identification of which is elsewhere an important component of

Shrayer's book – than proof of the 'mapping' 'at the heart of the story's poetics' (Shrayer 81).

6. Lyricism and the Novel: Nabokov's Gift for Prose

1 This real-life publication refusal by the editorial board at *Sovremennye zapiski*, all of whose members had belonged to the Social Revolutionary Party before the revolution, mimicked the criticism by Vasiliev, a fictional editor within the novel, and provided Nabokov in the foreword to the English translation with 'a pretty example of life finding itself obliged to imitate the very art it condemns' (*Gift* i).

2 Writing in 1956, the authoritative émigré critic Gleb Struve suggested that '... *The Gift* may emerge, if not the key to his entire oeuvre then at any rate the focus which absorbed into itself his most characteristic traits ...' (Struve 1956, 282n54); Simon Karlinsky, in 'Vladimir Nabokov's Novel *Dar* as a Work of Literary Criticism; A Structural Analysis,' states that '... *Dar* was perhaps the most original, unusual and interesting piece of prose writing in the entire émigré literature between the wars' (Karlinsky 1963, 285); Andrew Field, in *Nabokov: His Life in Art*, claims that '... *The Gift* occupies a singular place in Nabokov's art. It is the greatest novel Russian literature has yet produced in this century' (Field 1967, 149); D. Barton Johnson, in 'The Key to Nabokov's *Gift*,' has reported that 'Nabokov's *Dar* (*The Gift*) is reckoned by its author and by many of his readers as his finest Russian novel' (Johnson 1982, 190); Alexander Dolinin opens his study '*The Gift*' with the claim that it ' ... is the last, the longest and probably the best of Nabokov's Russian novels' (Dolinin 1995, 135); Stephen Blackwell's recent book-length study, *Zina's Paradox: The Figured Reader in Nabokov's 'Gift*,' identifies the novel as one '... many consider the century's greatest Russian novel' (Blackwell 1). Nabokov, too, recorded his respect for *The Gift* in interviews reprinted in *Strong Opinions*: 'It is the longest, I think the best, and the most nostalgic of my Russian novels'; and 'My best Russian novel is a thing called, in English, *The Gift*' (*SO* 13, 52).

3 Karlinsky, for instance observes that 'not since *Eugene Onegin* has a major Russian novel contained such a profusion of literary discussions, allusions and writers' characterizations ... Nabokov presupposes a thorough familiarity with Russian literature (and not only Russian) on the part of the reader of *Dar*' (Karlinsky 1963, 286–7).

4 Marina T. Naumann, in 'The Poetry of Nabokov's Prose: *Mashen'ka* Revisited,' discusses the poetic quality of Nabokov's first novel, stating that '... *Mashen'ka* was literally and figuratively a major thread in Nabokov's artistic career, from its beginning to its conclusion. As such this novel

provides *a short but most valuable model of the poetic facets of Nabokov's prose*' (Naumann 1978, 72; emphasis added).

5 *The Gift* is not, of course, the first example of Nabokov's fictional treatment of a writer. 'Torpid Smoke' of 1935 is, like *The Gift*, also based on the portrait of a young émigré writer in Berlin and, in particular, the mysterious psychology of artistic inspiration. Moving from narrative to lyric forms of expression, there are also Nabokov's various poems treating the subject of 'the poet' and poetic creativity.

6 Much critical energy has been expended on the slippery issue of the identity of the implied author in *The Gift*. Sergej Davydov, Brian Boyd, and, above all, Iurii Levin have argued for an understanding of Fyodor as the novel's implied author. Leona Toker, Pekka Tammi, and, most recently, Alexander Dolinin have argued against the possibility of Fyodor functioning as both character in, and implied author of, *The Gift*. Julian W. Connolly bases his discussion of the novel in *Nabokov's Early Fiction* on a reading of Fyodor fulfilling both *character* and *authorial* functions. Stephen Blackwell has recently added a new twist to the discussion by claiming the involvement of still another character, suggesting that, although Fyodor is the author, the novel is also 'constantly mediated for us by Zina's creative reception' (Blackwell 10). Without wishing to elaborate here my own independent response, I nonetheless indicate my agreement with Tammi's position from *Problems of Nabokov's Poetics*, which is ultimately based on the observation that Fyodor as character is not capable of gaining 'control over a reality *of which his own mind is a part*' (Tammi 1985, 97) and thus cannot be the implied author.

7 Anna Maria Salehar has discussed this passage as an example of 'tonic verse' presented as prose (Salehar 80–1).

8 The depiction of descent into revery while travelling on a tram is also reminiscent of the poems discussed above from the 'Movement' cluster of Nabokov's early volume of poetry *The Cluster*.

9 In referring throughout this chapter to the motif of keys in *The Gift*, I gratefully acknowledge D. Barton Johnson's seminal study of the topic, 'The Key to Nabokov's *Gift*.'

10 Indeed, a variant of the theme of consciousness suddenly and mysteriously releasing memories long 'forgotten' is likewise expressed in Nabokov's verse in the numerous poems of the arrival of former acquaintances in dreams.

11 Nabokov's pairing of a facet of the otherworld and chess seems likewise encoded in his understated reference to the title of the Soviet chess magazine Fyodor reads, *8 X 8*. A clever reference to the real Soviet chess journal *64*, the reformulation of the title as eight times eight suggests the eternity of a lemniscate squared. Nabokov's fiction is studded with related references to lemniscates

and figure eights, from the name Otto in 'A Guide to Berlin' to the imprint left by a bicycle tire. The motif of *8* as an image for eternity is most fully used in *Pale Fire*. In his *Lectures on Literature*, Nabokov described a similar constellation of fatidic eights in Joyce as 'a nice litter of *eights*' (*LL* 365).

12 Alexander Dolinin has noted the dangers of any attempt to read *The Gift* as a *roman à clef*; he also provides a brief characterization of the *angoisse* and solipsism of the Parisian school of poetry (Dolinin 1995, 142). In the introduction to *Poems and Problems*, Nabokov himself refers to 'the dreary drone of the anemic "Paris" school of émigré poetry' (*PP* 14), which he seems in part to have been targeting in the figure of Yasha.

13 Vladimir Alexandrov, in his chapter on *The Gift* in *Nabokov's Otherworld*, also discusses the presence in the novel of chains of motifs which suggest reference to the otherworld (Alexandrov 1991, 108–36).

14 The mystery of Delalande's identity was conclusively lifted by Nabokov in the introduction to the English translation of *Invitation to a Beheading*, where he was identified as both fictional and the only author ever to have influenced Nabokov (*IB* 6).

15 Konstantin Kirillovich's allegiance to detailed observation of the world, or in a formulation taken from Nabokov's in 'The Art of Literature and Commonsense,' his 'capacity to wonder at trifles – no matter the imminent peril,' suggests that he possesses the highest form of consciousness. When Fyodor imagines one of the possible fates met by his father – death to a sordid Bolshevik firing squad – he grants him the same smile of disdain that Nabokov accorded the Russian poet Gumilev when facing his executioners. The expressions of Konstantin Kirillovich's artistic sensibility and consciousness are also effectively contrasted in the figure of Nikolai Gavrilovich Chernyshevskii, the materialist critic of Russian literature and society.

16 Stephen H. Blackwell, in *Zina's Paradox: The Figured Reader in Nabokov's 'Gift,'* provides extensive discussion of Nabokov's poetics of love and *The Gift*.

17 The symbiosis between Fyodor and Nabokov with regard to poetic models and their youthful experience with 'versificatory illness' is demonstrated by the parallel between Nabokov's comments in *Speak, Memory* and Fyodor's apprenticeship in *The Gift*. Vladimir Alexandrov, in *Nabokov's Otherworld*, suggests that Nabokov omitted the eleventh chapter of *Speak, Memory* – the account of his first poem – from the Russian version of his autobiography, *Drugie berega* (*Other Shores*), because of its similarity to *The Gift* (Alexandrov 1991, 108).

18 In Russian, Zina's proximity to poetry is made apparent through Nabokov's clever use of the word *stikhiia* (element), which in its genitive form is almost homophonic with *stikhi* (verses): 'ona kak ten' vnezapno poiavlialas', ot rodstvennoi stikhii otdelias'' ('like a shadow leaving its kindred element').

19 Brian Boyd, in *Vladimir Nabokov: The Russian Years*, discusses this poem as Nabokov's poetic commemoration of his first meeting with his wife at a charity ball. In Nabokov's instance, the 'incognita' was a young woman in a black mask with wolf's profile. The translation of the poem is Boyd's (Boyd 1990, 207).

20 Written in 1923, 'I remember within velvet frames …' remained unpublished until Nabokov's inclusion of it in his 1979 retrospective collection, *Stikhi* (*Stikhi* 115–16). My translation of плюшевой (*pliushevoi*) as 'velvet' is derived from the translation of *The Gift*, from a passage which offers a point of contact between Nabokov's early poem and Fyodor's use of descriptive imagery from the rendering of memories and musings about his father in his love poem to Zina: 'Among the old, tranquil, velvet-framed family photographs in my father's study there hung a copy of the picture: Marco Polo leaving Venice. She was rosy, this Venice, and the water of her lagoon was azure' (*Ssoch* IV, 299; *Gift* 115). In *Pale Fire*, Kinbote will find a photo of the deceased actress Iris Acht (died 1888) in 'a large photograph in a frame of black velvet' (*PF* 121).

21 See the conclusion of chapter 3 for a discussion of this poem.

22 The reference to Fyodor's dead father lends added credence to Dolinin's intriguing reading of 'Evening on a Vacant Lot' (discussed in chapter 3) as a subtext to this lengthy passage within the novel (Dolinin 1995, 156).

7. A Novel Snatched from the Sun: Nabokov's *Pale Fire*

1 Brian Boyd, for instance, has recently suggested that 'whereas *Lolita* sparks moral debate especially among those who have never read it, *Pale Fire* has ignited a critical controversy among those who have read and *re*read it that burns more fiercely every year' (Boyd 2001b, 4).

2 Riemer's article is of interest as more than witness to the challenges to conventional categories of genre once perceived in *Pale Fire*. Riemer's study also testifies to the conflicting, contradictory assessments called forth by the poem 'Pale Fire.' Without any explicit suggestion of justification, Riemer praises the poem before ultimately judging it 'a bad poem': 'But the remarkable feature of the poem "Pale Fire" is that it is, after all, such a good poem … the poem is frequently moving, even beautiful, and throughout Nabokov's verbal virtuosity is little short of staggering. Eventually one must conclude that "Pale Fire" is a bad poem, but it is bad in the way that many people argue Shelley's poetry to be bad, the badness does not proceed from ineptitude or from absolute banality' (Riemer 46).

3 See John Burt Foster's observation in *Nabokov's Art of Memory and European Modernism* that '*Pale Fire* is often viewed as a masterpiece of emerging postmodernism in fiction' (Foster 1993b, 231).

4 Brian Boyd, an early Shadean in his own attribution of authorship (Boyd 1992), offers both an excellent overview of the proponents and arguments behind each position and a new reading which rests on the separateness of Shade and Kinbote (Boyd 2001b, 114–26).

5 For example, Pekka Tammi, in his article '*Pale Fire*' for *The Garland Companion to Vladimir Nabokov*, illustrates the frequency of this approach with the following statement: 'As the most immediate problems that any reader of *Pale Fire* encounters concern narrative structure, the present article will concentrate on structural matters. This means that many fascinating questions must be ignored ...' (Tammi 1995, 572). Following David' Rampton's example from *Vladimir Nabokov: A Critical Study of the Novels*, I too should like to cut 'some critical knots' (Rampton 1984, 149), thereby disentangling my reading from the ties of (important and open) narrative issues. Attention will thus be freed to concentrate on the other 'fascinating questions' referred to by Tammi. I accept what Alter terms the novel's 'basic fictional data,' that Shade is the author of a poem composed before his death and that Kinbote (all but certainly V. Botkin, a Russian émigré) is the author of the commentary. Shade is mistakenly murdered by Jack Grey, an escapee from an insane asylum. This acceptance of the 'basic fictional data' does not deny the intriguing parallels between poem and commentary, but incorporates them into the weave of a larger pattern.

6 In this context, to be lauded is the exceptional analysis proffered by Pekka Tammi in *Problems of Nabokov's Poetics: A Narratological Analysis*. See Tammi 1985, 197–221.

7 The necessity of a critical response appropriate to the challenge of *Pale Fire* seemed far more urgent in the novel's immediate historical context. In the forty-odd years since the appearance of *Pale Fire*, criticism has come to acknowledge *Pale Fire* as a modern classic. Those unpredisposed to this assessment simply do not discuss the novel, and few are now preoccupied with the immanent death of the novel form. It is for perhaps this reason that the enmity of contemporaneous reviews strikes one as so shocking. The vitriol of Chester's review of *Pale Fire*, for instance, eerily recalls the vehemence that Nabokov's art was frequently subjected to in the inter-war émigré community; even in that exceptionally polemicized context, however, Nabokov's fiction was never associated with evil: 'Nabokov hates like Swift, but unlike Swift he is without innocence. His comedy is a lie. It is dead. It is evil, like racial prejudice' (Chester 451).

8 The strengths of Boyd's *Nabokov's 'Pale Fire': The Magic of Artistic Discovery* rest to no small degree in his skilful incorporation of knowledge 'discovered' in the pursuit of such references into an interpretive argument. Although I do not subscribe to Boyd's central thesis that 'Shade composes his poem, dies, and then helps Kinbote orchestrate his Commentary' (Boyd 2001b, 242), I gratefully acknowledge the detail of his reading of the poem and novel for my own understanding of each. For a compact statement of his central argument from *Nabokov's 'Pale Fire*,' see Boyd's earlier article 'Shade and Shape in *Pale Fire.*'

9 The threat of an intentional fallacy looms large here, though it is a calculable risk. While the beliefs and preferences of the fictional character Shade are not to be blithely attributed to the non-fictional author Nabokov – though here, too, significant overlappings may be identified – Shade's poetry and poetic voice may very well be correlated with that of Nabokov on the basis of form and, especially, thematic content. Interestingly, Kernan seems also to make this connection in his alternating reference to Shade's and Nabokov's poetic voice.

10 The establishment or refutation of poetic comparisons to Nabokov (or Shade) is not a project to be pursued in this study. Nonetheless, the linkage with Frost deserves brief comment. Abraham Socher, in a perceptive article entitled 'Shades of Frost: A Hidden Source for Nabokov's *Pale Fire*,' suggests that Frost's short poem 'Of a Winter Evening,' printed in the *Saturday Review of Literature* for 12 April 1958, served as a Frostian source for 'Pale Fire.' With its reference to a bird in flight, a pane of glass, a sunset, and two 'glassed-in' children at a windowsill sharing a brief, vivid experience of nature, 'Of a Winter Evening' must have appealed to Nabokov; it shares a number of the motifs and images which he had been exploring throughout his long poetic career. Despite the Nabokovian cast of this poem, or even Shade's Frostian physique and rural homeliness, the very Nabokovian Shade could *never* say with the speaker of 'Design': 'What but design of darkness to appal? / If design govern in a thing so small.'

11 Philip Sicker, in '*Pale Fire* and *Lyrical Ballads*: The Dynamics of Collaboration,' for instance, sees the formative presence of Wordsworth: 'Despite Shade's critical study of Pope and use of heroic couplets, his personal and poetic kinship with Wordsworth is everywhere apparent' (Sicker 307). John O. Lyons, in '*Pale Fire* and the Fine Art of Annotation,' argues that when *Pale Fire* is 'viewed in the light of the Popean devices of *The Dunciad* Nabokov's intent is clearer' (Lyons 158). In contrast to this critical strategy, Field (1967), Tammi (1985), de Vries (1991), and Alexandrov (1991) all draw isolated reference to parallels between other poetic works by Nabokov and 'Pale Fire.'

12 The implications of the incapacity to critically assimilate Shade's poem and
    thus sufficiently appreciate the thematic depth of the novel are apparent in
    even the early positive reviews of *Pale Fire*. The anonymous author of 'The
    Russian Box Trick' for *Time*, for instance, indicates that both his regard for,
    and confusion about, the novel rests in insecurity regarding the poem: 'A
    more troubling question is this: What did Nabokov have in mind when he
    wrote the book? Everything in it – and particularly the wiry elegance of the
    poem itself – denies the possibility that it is merely aimless entertainment.'
    Emerging from this uncertainty is the reviewer's unsatisfactory final assess-
    ment: 'It may not be significant, but it is done with dazzling skill' (Anon.
    1962b, 61).

13 The reference to a 'magic lantern' seems also a reference – now in the context
    of an English poem – to Afanasii Fet, the Russsian poet so often linked to the
    young poet Sirin. Richard Gustafson discusses Fet's aesthetics in terms which
    indeed suggest congeniality with Nabokov's, although Nabokov created
    something entirely different, as 'An Evening of Russian Poetry' illustrates
    (Gustafson 11–36). Here as well are shades of Nabokov's poetic reworking of
    autobiographic scenes included in the 'Magic Lantern' section from chapter 8
    of *Speak, Memory*.

14 The 'muddy / red road between an orchard and a veil / of tepid rain' recalls,
    of course, Fyodor's extended prose poem from the beginning of chapter 2 in
    The Gift, as well as poems from *Two Paths*.

15 Reference might also be made to Nabokov's translation *The Song of Igor's
    Campaign*, which also contains a foreword, poem, commentary, and index.

16 This approach is, of course, in direct opposition to that of such early readers
    as Dwight Macdonald, who claimed: 'The raison d'être of the book is the
    commentary' (Macdonald 440). It might be suggested that the inversion of
    Macdonald's approach in his negative – though judiciously intended – review
    of *Pale Fire* resulted from his inability to interpretatively normalize
    Nabokov's poetry, as revealed in the following comment: 'The most that can
    be said for the poem is that it is often good pastiche (though more often
    doggerel) ... But the torrent of virtuosity deafens one to whatever meaning
    the poet may have been trying to communicate' (Macdonald 439–40).

17 In terms of length, 'Pale Fire' is followed at a close second by the Russian
    'Universitetskaia poema' ('University Poem') of 1927, which is 882 lines long.

18 The mountain immediately recalls Salvator Waltz's vain attempt to destroy
    the mountain of woe which has so cruelly twisted his life and mind. The
    similarly anguished Kinbote also confronts a mountain before making his
    escape at a seashore, a location equally rich in liminal potential and associa-
    tions. The summit of Kinbote's ascent up the mountain is reached at the

'Bregberg Pass.' The name 'Bregberg' contains within it both points of transition from land – into the heights of the sky and into the depths of the sea – as *breg*, the archaic Russian word for 'shore,' and *berg*, the German word for mountain. Nabokov's repeated play with the otherworldly potential of these words seems anything but random. In his short story 'Torpid Smoke,' for instance, the poet Grisha is left at the conclusion of the narrative in the throes of lyric stimulation associated with the words *breg*, *hlad*, and *vetr* (*Ssoch* IV, 557; *Stories* 400), the archaic Russian words for 'shore,' 'chill,' and 'wind,' which also evoke the cool wind from elsewhere of inspiration. From opposite poles in Nabokov's career, compare the coolness of the poem 'Inspiration' (*Ssoch* I, 509) from 1919 and the breeze of 'Inspiration' from 1972: 'In the meantime, however, a window has opened, an auroral wind has blown, every exposed nerve has tingled. Presently all dissolves …' (*SO* 309).

19 Ellen Pifer has also written of the poem's structural importance as the element binding Shade to Kinbote within the narrative: 'Shade's poem is the bond that links, so tenuously, the disparate lives of its author and its commentator. It serves as a subtle but lucid background for the startling patterns of Kinbote's obsessed mind'.(Pifer 1980, 117).

20 Kinbote's experience with the tunnel and a green door recalls Cinncinnatus's ersatz 'escape' in *Invitation to a Beheading*. In that instance, Cinncinnatus's long crawl through the narrow darkness of a tunnel leads him to M'sieur Pierre's cell, the first sight of the axe that will behead him, and evidence that M'sieur Pierre is his executioner. In a subsequent escape attempt through the tunnel, Cinncinnatus emerges out of the fortress to 'the loud evening cries of the swallows' and the 'glow of sunset' before being returned by a young girl through a 'green door' into a narrow passage leading past dark trunks and a wardrobe. Cinncinnatus is returned to the fortress and captivity, and to the death which will finally free him from the captivity of his unsatisfying life (*Ssoch* IV, 148–9; *IB* 164–5).

21 Line 905 with its 'strawberry-and-cream' imagery of shaving reverberates with the distant echo of death and transition in *Laughter in the Dark*. Chapter 19 of Nabokov's novel of 1938 contains the same image in the description of events surrounding the child Irma's descent into fever and death (*Ssoch* III, 324; *Laugh* 156).

22 Vladimir Nabokov 'Ode to a Model,' (*PP* 173–4). In this poem, Nabokov first used the palindrome 'repaid' and 'diaper,' which was also to figure in *Pale Fire*.

23 Although none of the clues is conclusive, there is much evidence to suggest that the deposed Zemblan king Kinbote is Botkin, a Russian exile and academic at Wordsmith College. Kinbote speaks Russian competently enough

to pun the name Nattochdag into Netochka (*PF* 25) and, more ingeniously, to
contort the Russian word for armpit, *podmyshka*, into 'mousepits' in his
metaphoric description of a naked woman's anatomy (*PF* 110); he is soothed
by his gardener's planting of '*Heliotropium turgenevi*,' flowers 'whose odor
evokes with timeless intensity the dusk, and the garden bench, and a house of
painted wood in a distant northern land,' that is, the Russia of Turgenev
(*PF* 98); he possesses sufficient knowledge of his colleague's inner feelings to
know that 'happily Prof. Botkin … was not subordinated to that grotesque
"perfectionist"' Prof. Pnin of the Russian Department (*PF* 155); he is
anagrammatically termed a 'kingbot' by Sybil Shade, who calls him a
'*king*-sized *bot*fly … the monstrous parasite of a genius' (*PF* 172; emphasis
added); he compulsively emphasizes the combination English and Russian
in his commentary to the words 'two tongues' in line 615 of Shade's poem
(*PF* 235); he claims childhood identification with a Russia similar in character
to the Zembla of his supposed reign, 'a Russia that hated tyrants and
Philistines, injustice and cruelty, the Russia of ladies and gentlemen and
liberal aspirations' (*PF* 245); he is identified by Prof. Pardon as someone 'born
in Russia' with a name that 'was a kind of anagram of Botkin or Botkine'
(*PF* 267); and finally, Botkin is Kinbote's sole fellow academic listed in the
Index (*PF* 306), with all other entries to humans – apart from the Shades –
referring to either Zemblan or literary personages.

24 Gennady Barabtarlo, in *Aerial View*, links the blustering storms from Florida
to Maine' which foretell Shade's near-death with the drowning of his daughter
(Barabtarlo 1993a, 210).

25 Lubin's uncovering of a further possible source of Grimpen is particularly
ingenious. Noting Goethe's presence in 'Pale Fire' via his 'Erlkönig' as well as
the suicide theme of *Die Leiden des jungen Werthers*, Lubin observes that
Goethe 'prefixed an admonitory verse motto' to the second edition of *Die
Leiden* with the line 'Warum quillt aus ihm die grimme Pein?' (Lubin 205).

26 A further reference to the yew (or willow) is found in Aund Maud's 'half-
paralyzed Skye terrier,' a breed known in Zembla as the 'weeping-willow dog.'
The strange movements of the Skye terrier's basket is the first manifestation
of the poltergeist.

27 Shade's 'mistaken' assumptions on topics of metaphysical import recall
Edmond's erroneous belief that he is dead in *Death*, the mysterious fisherman's predictions in 'Perfection,' and Alexander Yakovlevich Chernyshevski's
assertions about life after death on the basis of the falling rain outside his
hospital window. Each mistaken statement affirms nothing more than the
human impossibility of making empirical claims about a realm outside the
realm of the empirical.

Conclusion: In Place of an Ending

1 For a selection of the Russian (and French) poetry translated by Nabokov, see the collection edited by Brian Boyd and Stanislav Shvabrin, *Verses and Versions: Three Centuries of Russian Poetry*. It can only be hoped that Boyd and Shvabrin's edited collection will help prompt further study of the fascinating topic of Nabokov's practice as a translator. It is a topic which promises to yield insights into a range of issues, from Nabokov's 'apprentice-ship' as an author, through his reading of the Russian poetic tradition, to the implications of his changing theories and practice of translation for his artistry.

2 The brief discussion below will, for the sake of argument, leave aside the necessity of a critical clarification of what is meant by traditional. While much of Nabokov's earliest poetry seems to rest within a nineteenth-century tradition of Russian poetry in terms of form, the question can be asked to what extent such poems as 'The Poets,' 'Fame,' 'The Ballad of Longwood Glen,' 'Pale Fire,' and many others are conservative.

3 Indeed, it was due to a portion of this quality that the Anglo-American critics of Nabokov's English poetry (and translated Russian poetry) misidentified it as 'light verse' or a curious *divertissement* on the part of Nabokov the novelist.

References

Primary Sources

Nabokov, Vladimir. *Ada, or Ardor: A Family Chronicle*. New York: Vintage International, 1990.
– 'Aleksandr Saltykov: Ody i rimny.' *Rul'* (1 October 1924). Reprinted in *Vladimir Nabokov: Sobranie sochinenii russkogo perioda v piati tomakh*, 1: 748–9.
  The Annotated Lolita. Ed. with preface, introduction, and notes by Alfred Appel, Jr. New York: Vintage International, 1991.
– 'The Art of Literature and Commonsense.' In *Lectures on Literature*, 371–80.
– *Bend Sinister*. New York: Vintage International, 1990.
– 'Charles Dickens.' In *Lectures on Literature*, 63–124.
– *Dear Bunny, Dear Volodya: The Nabokov-Wilson Letters, 1940–1971*. Edited and annotated, with an introductory essay, by Simon Karlinsky. Berkeley: University of California Press, 2001.
– *The Defense*. Trans. Michael Scammell in collaboration with the author. New York: Vintage International, 1990.
– *Despair*. New York: Vintage International, 1989.
– *The Eye*. Trans. Dmitri Nabokov in collaboration with the author. New York: Vintage International, 1990.
– 'Franz Kafka.' In *Lectures on Literature*, 251–83.
– 'Fyodor Dostoevski.' In *Lectures on Russian Literature*, 97–135.
– *The Gift*. Trans. Michael Scammell in collaboration with the author. New York: Vintage International, 1991.
– *Glory*. Trans. Dmitri Nabokov in collaboration with the author. New York: Vintage International, 1991.
– 'Good Readers and Good Writers.' In *Lectures on Literature*, 1–6.

- *Grozd'*. Berlin: Gamaiun, 1923.
- 'Gustave Flaubert.' In *Lectures on Literature*, 125–77.
- *Invitation to a Beheading*. Trans. Dmitri Nabokov in collaboration with the author. New York: Vintage International, 1989.
- 'James Joyce.' In *Lectures on Literature*, 285–370.
- *King, Queen, Knave*. Trans. Dmitri Nabokov in collaboration with the author. New York: Vintage International, 1989.
- *Laughter in the Dark*. New York: Vintage International, 1989.
- *Lectures on Literature*. Ed. Fredson Bowers. London: Weidenfeld & Nicolson, 1980.
- *Lectures on Russian Literature*. Ed. Fredson Bowers. New York: Harcourt Brace Jovanovich / Bruccoli Clark, 1981.
- 'The Lermontov Mirage.' *Russian Review* 1.1 (November 1941): 31–9.
- *Lolita*. New York: Vintage International, 1989.
- *Look at the Harlequins!* New York: Vintage International, 1990.
- *The Man from the U.S.S.R. and Other Plays*. Translated and introduced by Dmitri Nabokov. San Diego: Harcourt Brace Jovanovich, 1985.
- 'Marcel Proust.' In *Lectures on Literature*, 207–49.
- *Mary*. Trans. Michael Glenny in collaboration with the author. New York: Vintage International, 1989.
- *Nikolai Gogol*. New York: New Directions, 1944.
- 'Novye Poety.' *Rul'* (21 August 1927). Reprinted in *Vladimir Nabokov: Sobranie sochinenii russkogo perioda v piati tomakh*, 2: 640–4.
- 'O khodaseviche.' *Souremennye zapiski* 69 (1939): 262–4. Reprinted in *Vladimir Nabokov: Sobranie sochinenii russkogo perioda v piati tomakh*, 5: 587–90.
- *Pale Fire*. New York: Vintage International, 1989.
- *Perepiska s sestroi*. Ed. Helene Sikorski. Ann Arbor: Ardis, 1985.
- 'Philistines and Philistinism.' In *Lectures on Russian Literature*, 309–14.
- 'Playwriting.' In *The Man from the U.S.S.R. and Other Plays*, 315–22.
- *Pnin*. New York: Vintage International, 1989.
- *Poems*. Garden City: Doubleday, 1959.
- *Poems and Problems*. New York: McGraw-Hill, 1970.
- 'Pouchkine ou le vrai et la vraisemblable' [1937]. Reprinted in *Magazine Littéraire* 233 (September 1986): 49–54.
- 'Pushkin, or the Real and the Plausible.' Translated and introduced by Dmitri Nabokov. *New York Review of Books* 35.5 (31 March 1988): 38–42.
- *The Real Life of Sebastian Knight*. New York: Vintage International, 1992.
- [Review of Dmitrii Kobiakov, *Gorech'* and *Keramika*; and Evgenii Shakh, *Semia na Kamne*]. *Rul'* (11 May 1927). Reprinted in *Vladimir Nabokov: Sobranie sochinenii russkogo perioda v piati tomakh*, 2: 638–40.
- [Review of Iv. Bunin, *Izbrannye Stikhi*]. *Rul'* (22 May 1929). Reprinted in *Vladimir Nabokov: Sobranie sochinenii russkogo perioda v piati tomakh*, 2: 672–6.

- 'Rupert Bruk.' *Grani* 1 (1922): 212–31. Reprinted in *Vladimir Nabokov: Sobranie sochinenii russkogo perioda v piati tomakh*, 1: 728–44.
- *Selected Letters, 1940–1977*. Ed. Dmitri Nabokov and Matthew J. Bruccoli. New York: Harcourt Brace Jovanovich / Bruccoli Clark Layman, 1989.
- *Sobranie sochinenii russkogo perioda v piati tomakh*. 5 vols. St Petersburg: Simpozium, 1999–2000.
- *Speak, Memory: An Autobiography Revisited*. New York: Vintage International, 1989.
- *Stikhi*. Ann Arbor: Ardis, 1979.
- *Stikhotvoreniia: 1929–1951*. Ed. M. Malikova. Paris: Rifma, 1952.
- *The Stories of Vladimir Nabokov*. New York: Vintage International, 1997.
- *Strong Opinions*. 1973. New York: Vintage International, 1990.
- *Tragediia Gospodina Morna*. 1924. Reprinted in *Zvezda* 4 (1997): 9 98.
- 'The Tragedy of Tragedy.' In *The Man from the U.S.S.R. and Other Plays*, 323–42.
- *Transparent Things*. 1972. New York; Vintage International, 1989.
- *Vozrashchenie Chorba: Razkazy i stikhi*. Berlin: Slovo, 1929.
  The Waltz Invention. Trans. Dmitri Nabokov. New York: Phaedra, 1966.
Nabokov, Vladimir, trans. *Eugene Onegin: A Novel in Verse by Aleksandr Pushkin*. With commentary by Vladimir Nabokov. Bollingen Series 72. 4 vols. Princeton: Princeton University Press, 1975.
- *The Song of Igor's Campaign*. New York: McGraw-Hill, 1975.
- *Three Russian Poets: Selections from Pushkin, Lermontov and Tyutchev*. Norfolk: New Directions, 1944.
- *Verses and Versions: Three Centuries of Russian Poetry*. Ed. Brian Boyd and Stanislav Shvabrin. Introd. Brian Boyd. Orlando, FL: Harcourt, 2008.

Secondary Sources

Abrams, M.H. 1971. *Natural Supernaturalism: Tradition and Revolution in Romantic Literature*. London: Oxford University Press.
Adamovich, Georgii. 1929. [Review of *Sovremennye zapiski* 40]. *Illiustrirovannaia Rossiia* 50 (7 December): 16. Reprinted in N.G. Mel'nikov, ed., *Klassik bez retushi*, 57–8.
- 1938. [Review of *Russkie zapiski* 11 (1938)]. *Poslednie novosti* 6351 (24 November): 3. Reprinted in N.G. Mel'nikov, ed., *Klassik bez retushi*, 175–6.
- 1955. 'Vladimir Nabokov.' In *Odinochestvo i svoboda*. New York: Chekhov. Translated and reprinted in *Twentieth-Century Russian Literary Criticism*. Ed. V. Erlich. New Haven: Yale University Press, 1975. 219–31.
Aikhenval'd, Iulii. 1923. [Review of *Grozd'* (*The Cluster*) and *Gornii put'* (*The Empyrean Path*)]. *Rul'* 658 (28 January): 13.
Alexandrov, Vladimir. 1985. *Andrei Bely: The Major Symbolist Fiction*. Cambridge: Harvard University Press.

– 1986. 'The "Otherworld" in Nabokov's *The Gift*.' In Julian W. Connolly and
  Sonia Ketchian, eds, *Studies in Literature in Honor of Vsevolod Setchkarev*,
  15–33.
– 1991. *Nabokov's Otherworld*. Princeton: Princeton University Press.
– ed. 1995. *The Garland Companion to Vladimir Nabokov*. New York: Garland.
Alter, Robert. 1970. '*Invitation to a Beheading*: Nabokov and the Art of Politics.'
  In Alfred Appel, Jr, and Charles Newman, eds, *Nabokov: Criticism,
  Reminiscences, Translations and Tributes*, 41–59.
– 1975. *Partial Magic: The Novel as a Self-Conscious Genre*. Berkeley: University
  of California Press.
– 1979. '*Ada*, or the Perils of Paradise.' In Peter Quennell, eds, *Vladimir Nabokov:
  A Tribute*, 103–18.
Amfiteatrov-Kadashev, Vladimir. 1923. [Review of *Grozd'* (*The Cluster*)].
  Segodnia (25 February): 5. Reprinted in N.G. Mel'nikov, ed., *Klassik bez
  retushi*, 22–3.
Andreev, Nikolai. 1930. 'Sirin.' *Nov'* 3 (October): 6. Reprinted in N.G. Mel'nikov,
  ed., *Klassik bez retushi*, 186–95.
– 1954. 'Zametki chitatelia.' *Vozrozhdenie* 34 (July-August): 157.
Anon. 1962a. 'Multivalence.' *Times Literary Supplement* (16 November): 869.
– 1962b. 'The Russian Box Trick.' *Time Magazine* 79 (1 June): 61.
– 1972. 'Higher Games.' *Times Literary Supplement* 3,678 (25 August): 984.
Appel, Alfred, Jr, and Charles Newman, eds. 1970. *Nabokov: Criticism,
  Reminiscences, Translations and Tributes*. Evanston: Northwestern University
  Press.
Babikov, Andrei. 2002/2003. '*The Event* and the Main Thing in Nabokov's Theory
  of Drama.' *Nabokov Studies* 7: 151–76.
Baer, Joachim T., and Norman W. Ingham, eds. 1974. *Mnemozina: Studia Litteraria
  Russica in Honorem Vsevolod Setchkarev*. München: Wilhelm Fink Verlag.
Bakhrakh Alexander. 1923. [Review of *Grozd'* (*The Cluster*)]. *Dni* 63 (14 January):
  17. Reprinted in N.G. Mel'nikov, ed., *Klassik bez retushi*, 20–1.
Balestrini, Nassim. 2002. 'The Architecture of the Mind: The Depiction of
  Consciousness in Selected Short Works by Vladimir Nabokov and Henry
  James.' *Amerikastudien* 47(3): 345–57.
Barabtarlo, Gennady. 1993a. *Aerial View: Essays on Nabokov's Art and
  Metaphysics*. New York: Peter Lang.
– 1993b. 'A Skeleton in Nabokov's Closet: "Mest."' In Charles Nicol and
  Gennady Barabtarlo, eds, *A Small Alpine Form: Studies in Nabokov's Short
  Fiction*, 15–23.
– 1995. 'English Short Stories.' In Vladimir Alexandrov, ed., *The Garland
  Companion to Vladimir Nabokov*, 101–17.

– 1999. 'Nabokov's Trinity: (On the Movement of Nabokov's Themes).' In Julian
Connolly, ed., *Nabokov and His Fiction: New Perspectives*, 109–38.

Bazarov, Konstantin. 1972. 'Poet's Problems.' *Books & Bookmen* (October): xi–xii.

Ben-Amos, Anna. 1997. 'The Role of Literature in *The Gift*.' *Nabokov Studies* 4:
117–49.

Bethea, David M. 1983. *Khodasevich: His Life and Art*. Princeton: Princeton
University Press.

– 1995a. 'Nabokov and Blok.' In Vladimir Alexandrov, ed., *The Garland
Companion to Vladimir Nabokov*, 374–82.

– 1995b. 'Style.' In Vladimir Alexandrov, ed., *The Garland Companion to Vladimir
Nabokov*, 696–704.

Birnbaum, H., and M.S. Flier, eds. 1995. *The Language and Verse of Russia: In
Honor of Dean S. Worth on His Sixty-Fifth Birthday*. Moscow: Vostochnaya
Literatura.

Blackwell, Stephen H. 2000. *Zina's Paradox: The Figured Reader in Nabokov's
'Gift'*. New York: Peter Lang.

Blium, A.V. 1999. '"Poetic belyi, Sirin ..." (Nabokov o tsenzure i tsenzura o
Nabokove).' *Zvezda* 4: 198–203.

Bloom, Harold, ed. 1987. *Vladimir Nabokov: Modern Critical Views*. New York:
Chelsea House Publishers.

Booth, Philip. 1959. 'Voices That Speak in Verse.' *New York Times Book Review*
(6 September): 6.

Bowra, C.M. 1950. *The Romantic Imagination*. London: Oxford University Press.

Boyd, Brian. 1990. *Vladimir Nabokov: The Russian Years*. London: Chatto &
Windus.

– 1992. *Vladimir Nabokov: The American Years*. London: Chatto & Windus.

– 1997. 'Shade and Shape in *Pale Fire*.' *Nabokov Studies* 4: 173–224.

– 2001a. *Nabokov's 'Ada': The Place of Consciousness* [1985]. Cybereditions:
Christchurch.

– 2001b. *Nabokov's 'Pale Fire': The Magic of Artistic Discovery*. Princeton:
Princeton University Press.

Brodsky, Joseph. 1980. 'New York: Peizazh poeta. Interv'iu Solomona Volkova s
Iosifom Brodskim.' *Chast' rechi* 1: 27–36.

– 1998. *Less than One: Selected Essays*. New York: Farrar Straus Giroux.

Chester, Alfred. 1962. 'Nabokov's Anti-Novel.' *Commentary* 34(5): 449–51.

Clark, Naomi Helen. 1974. 'The Jewel of a Bluish View: An Introduction to the
English Poems of Vladimir Nabokov.' PhD diss., University of California,
Santa Cruz.

Collins, Robert A., and Howard D. Pearce, eds. 1985. *The Scope of the Fantastic:
Theory, Technique, Major Authors*. Westport: Greenwood Press.

Connolly, Julian W. 1991. 'The Otherworldly in Nabokov's Poetry.' *Russian Literature Triquarterly* 24: 329–39.
– 1992. *Nabokov's Early Fiction: Patterns of Self and Other*. Cambridge: Cambridge University Press.
– ed. 1999. *Nabokov and His Fiction: New Perspectives*. Cambridge: Cambridge University Press.
– 2005. *The Cambridge Companion to Nabokov*. Cambridge: Cambridge University Press.
Connolly, Julian W., and Sonia Ketchian, eds. 1986. *Studies in Literature in Honor of Vsevolod Setchkarev*. Columbus: Slavica.
Cosgrove, Ciaran. 1996. 'Nabokov, Heaney: Coping with Parodies of Pale Conglagrations.' *Forum for Modern Language Studies* 32(3) (July): 197–207.
Couturier, Maurice. 1986. 'L'effet *Lolita*.' *Magazine Littéraire* 233 (September): 29–31.
– 1993. 'Nabokov in Postmodernist Land.' *Critique* 34(4) (Summer): 247–60.
Dark, Oleg. 1990. 'Zagadka Sirina: Rannii Nabokov v kritike "pervoi volny" russkoi emigratsii.' *Voprosy literatury* (March): 243–57.
Davydov, Sergej. 1982. *'Teksty – Metreshki' Vladimira Nabokova*. München: Otto Sagner.
de Jonge, Alex. 1979. 'Nabokov's Uses of Pattern.' In Peter Quennell, ed., *Vladimir Nabokov: A Tribute*, 59–72.
Dembo, L.S., ed. 1967. *Nabokov: The Man and His Work*. Madison: University of Wisconsin Press.
de Vries, Gérard. 1991. 'Fanning the Poet's Fire: Some Remarks on Nabokov's Pale Fire.' *Russian Literature Triquarterly* 24: 239–67.
– 1997. 'Nabokov, Pushkin and Scott.' *Revue de Littérature Comparée* 3: 307–22.
Dickins, Anthony. 1972. 'East-West Battle.' *London Magazine* 12: 157–9.
Diment, Galya. 1991. 'Nabokov and Joyce: Portraits of Innovative Writers as Conservative Poets.' *Irish Slavonic Studies* 12: 11–26.
– 1995. 'Plays.' In Vladimir Alexandrov, ed., *The Garland Companion to Vladimir Nabokov*, 586–99.
Dolinin, Alexander. 1995. '*The Gift*.' In V. Alexandrov, ed., *The Garland Companion to Vladimir Nabokov*, 135–69.
– 1999. 'Istinnaia zhizn' pisatelia Sirina.' In *Vladimir Nabokov: Sobranie sochinenii russkogo perioda v piati tomakh*, 1: 9–25.
Dupee, F.W. 1965a. *The King of the Cats and Other Remarks on Writers and Writing*. New York: Farrar, Strauss and Giroux.
– 1965b. 'Nabokov: The Prose and Poetry of It All.' In *The King of the Cats and Other Remarks on Writers and Writing*, 131–41.

Eekman, Th. 1995. 'Vladimir Nabokov's Poetry.' In H. Birnbaum and M.S. Flier, eds, *The Language and Verse of Russia: In Honor of Dean S. Worth on His Sixty-Fifth Birthday*, 88–100.

Elliott, Emory, ed. 1991. *The Columbia History of the American Novel*. New York: Columbia University Press.

Enright, D.J.. 1966. 'Nabokov's Way.' *New York Review of Books* 7(7) (3 November): 3–4.

Esslin, Martin. 1964. 'Theatre of the Absurd.' In M. Freedman, ed., *Essays in the Modern Drama*, 320–34.

Feeley, Margaret Peller. 1985. '"Warp and Weft": Patterns of Artistry in Nabokov's *Pale Fire*.' In Robert A Collins and Howard D. Pearce, eds, *The Scope of the Fantastic: Theory, Technique, Major Authors*, 239–45.

Ferguson, Suzanne C. 1982. 'Defining the Short Story: Impressionism and Form.' *Modern Fiction Studies* 28(1): 13–24.

Fet, A.A. 1965. *Lirika*. Moscow: Khudozhestvennaia Literature.

Field, Andrew. 1967. *Nabokov: His Life in Art*. London: Hodder and Stoughton.

– 1977. *Nabokov: His Life in Part*. New York: Viking Press.

– 1986. *VN: The Life and Art of Vladimir Nabokov*. New York: Crown.

Foster, John Burt, Jr. 1993a. 'An Archeology of "Mademoiselle O": Narrative between Art and Memory.' In Charles Nicol and Gennady Barabtarlo, eds, *A Small Alpine Form: Studies in Nabokov's Short Fiction*, 111–36.

– 1993b. *Nabokov's Art of Memory and European Modernism*. Princeton: Princeton University Press.

Foster, Ludmila A. 1974. 'Nabokov's Gnostic Turpitude: The Surrealistic Vision of Reality in *Priglašenie na Kazn*.' In Joachim T. Baer and Norman W. Ingham, eds, *Mnemozina: Studia Litteraria Russica in Honorem Vsevolod Setchkarev*, 117–29.

Fowler, Douglas. 1974. *Reading Nabokov*. Ithaca: Cornell University Press.

Freedman, M., ed. 1964. *Essays in the Modern Drama*. Boston: D.C. Heath.

Galef, David. 1985. 'The Self-Annihilating Artists of *Pale Fire*.' *Twentieth Century Literature* 31(4) (Winter): 421–37.

Gibian, George, and Stephen Jan Parker, eds. 1984. *The Achievements of Vladimir Nabokov*. Ithaca: Cornell Center for International Studies.

Grabes, Herbert. 1977. *Fictitious Biographies: Vladimir Nabokov's English Novels*. The Hague: Mouton.

– 1995. 'A Prize for the (Post-)Modernist Nabokov.' *Nabokov at the Crossroads of Modernims and Postmodernism*. *Cycnos* 12(2): 117–24.

– 2002. 'Nabokov's Worldmaking: The Marvellous Machinations of McFate.' *Amerikastudien* 47(3): 335–43.

Grayson, Jane, et al., eds. 2002. *Nabokov's World: The Shape of Nabokov's World.* Houndmills: Palgrave.

Gregg, Richard A. 1965. *Fedor Tiutchev: The Evolution of a Poet.* New York: Columbia University Press.

Grossmith, Robert. 1993a. 'The Future Perfect of the Mind: "Time and Ebb" and "A Guide to Berlin."' In Charles Nicol and Gennady Barabtarlo, eds, *A Small Alpine Form: Studies in Nabokov's Short Fiction*, 149–53.

– 1993b. 'Perfection.' In Charles Nicol and Gennady Barabtarlo, eds, *A Small Alpine Form: Studies in Nabokov's Short Fiction*, 73–80.

Gul', Roman. 1923. [Review of *Grozd'* (*The Cluster*)]. *Novaia russkaia kniga* 5-6 (May-June): 23.

Gumilev, Nikolai S. 1990. *Pis'ma o russkoi poezii.* Moskva: Sovremennik.

Gustafson, Richard. 1966. *The Imagination of Spring: The Poetry of Afanasy Fet.* New Haven: Yale University Press.

Harrison, Robert Pogue. 2003. *The Dominion of the Dead.* Chicago: University of Chicago Press.

Hecht, Anthony. 1959. 'The Anguish of the Spirit and the Letter.' *Hudson Review* 12: 593–4.

Hultquist, Marianne K. 1973. 'Views of Nabokov.' *Prairie Schooner* 47: 271.

Iakovlev, Nikolai. 1922. [Review of poetry in *Rul'*]. *Novaia russkaia kniga* 1: 21.

Ivanov, Georgii. 1930. [Review of *Mashen'ka* (*Mary*), *Korol, dama valet* (*King, Queen, Knave*), *Zashchita Luzhina* (*The Defense*), and *Vozvrashchenie Chorba* (*The Return of Chorb*)]. *Chisla* 1 (March): 233–6. Reprinted in N.G. Mel'nikov, ed., *Klassik bez retushi*, 179–81.

James, William. 2004. *The Varieties of Religious Experience.* New York: Barnes & Noble Classics.

Johnson, D. Barton. 1982. 'The Key to Nabokov's *Gift*.' *Canadian-American Slavic Studies* 16(2): 190–206.

– 1985. *Worlds in Regression: Some Novels of Vladimir Nabokov.* Ardis: Ann Arbor.

– 1991. 'Preliminary Notes on Nabokov's Russian Poetry: A Chronological and Thematic Sketch.' *Russian Literature Triquarterly* 24: 307–27.

– 1992. '"L'Inconnue de la Seine" and Nabokov's Naiads.' *Comparative Literature* 44(3) (Summer): 225–48.

– 1999. 'Vladimir Nabokov and Rupert Brooke.' In Julian Connolly, ed., *Nabokov and His Fiction: New Perspectives*, 177–96.

– 2002. 'Vladimir Nabokov and Walter de la Mare's "Otheworld."' In Jane Grayson et al., eds, *Nabokov's World: The Shape of Nabokov's World*, 71–87.

Johnson, D. Barton, and Brian Boyd. 2002. 'Prologue: The Otherworld.' In Jane Grayson et al., eds, *Nabokov's World: The Shape of Nabokov's World*, 19–25.

Johnson, D. Barton, and Ellendea Proffer. 1991. 'Interview with Véra and Dmitri Nabokov.' *Russian Literature Triquarterly* 24: 73–85.

Kantor, Mikhail. 1934. 'Bremia pamiati (o Sirine).' *Vstrechi* 3 (March): 125–8. Reprinted in N.G. Mel'nikov, ed., *Klassik bez retushi*, 199–202.

Karlinsky, Simon. 1963. 'Vladimir Nabokov's Novel *Dar* as a Work of Literary Criticism: A Structural Analysis.' *Slavic and East European Journal* 7(3): 284–90.

- 1967. 'Illusion, Reality and Parody in Nabokov's Plays.' In L.S. Dembo, ed., *Nabokov: The Man and His Work*, 183–94.

- 1995. 'Nabokov and Some Poets of Russian Modernism.' *Nabokov at the Crossroads of Modernism and Postmodernism. Cycnos* 12(2): 63–72

- ed. 2001. *Dear Bunny, Dear Volodya: The Nabokov-Wilson Letters, 1940–1971.* Berkeley: University of California Press.

Keats, John. 1952. *The Letters of John Keats*. Ed. Maurice Buxton Forman. London: Oxford University Press.

Kermode, Frank. 1982. Review of *Pale Fire*. In Norman Page, ed., *Nabokov: The Critical Heritage*, 144–8.

Kernan, Alvin B. 1987. 'Reading Zemblan: The Audience Disappears in Nabokov's *Pale Fire*'. In Harold Bloom, ed., *Vladimir Nabokov: Modern Critical Views*, 101–25.

Khodasevich, Vladislav. 1937. 'O Sirine.' *Vozrozhdenie* 4065 (13 February): 9. Reprinted in N.G. Mel'nikov, ed., *Klassik bez retushi*, 219–24.

Khokhlov, G. 1930. [Review of *Vozvrashchenie Chorba* (*The Return of Chorb*)]. *Volia Rossii* 2–3 (February): 190–1. Reprinted in N.G. Mel'nikov, ed., *Klassik bez retushi*, 47–8.

Kirkup, James, ed. 1970. *Songs and Dreams*. Glasgow: Blackie & Son.

Knapp, Shoshana. 1987. 'Hazel Ablaze: Literary License in Nabokov's *Pale Fire*.' *Essays in Literature* 14(1) (Spring): 105–15.

Kuzmanovich, Zoran. 2002. '"Splendid Insincerity" as "Utmost Truthfulness": Nabokov and the Claims of the Real.' In Jane Grayson et al., eds, *Nabokov's World: The Shape of Nabokov's World*, 26–46.

- 2005. 'Strong Opinions and Nerve Points: Nabokov's Life and Art.' In J.W. Connolly, ed., *The Cambridge Companion to Nabokov*, 11–30.

Lattimore, Richmond. 1971. 'Poetry Chronicle.' *Hudson Review* 24: 506–8.

Levin, Harry. 1972. 'Introducing Vladimir Nabokov.' In *Grounds for Comparison*. Cambridge: Harvard University Press.

Lubin, Peter. 1970. 'Kickshaws and Motley.' In Alfred Appel, Jr, and Charles Newman, eds, *Nabokov: Criticism, Reminiscences, Translations and Tributes*, 187–208.

Lur'e, Vera. 1923. [Review of *Gornii put'* (*The Empyrean Path*)]. *Novaia russkaia kniga* 1 (January): 23. Reprinted in N.G. Mel'nikov, ed., *Klassik bez retushi*, 24–5.

Lyons, John O. 1967. '*Pale Fire* and the Fine Art of Annotation.' In L.S. Dembo, ed., *Nabokov: The Man and His Work*, 157–64.

Macdonald, Dwight. 1962. 'Review of *Pale Fire*.' *Partisan Review* 39(3) (Summer): 437–42.

Malikova, A. 2002. 'Zabytyi Poet.' In *V.V. Nabokov: Stikhotvoreniia*. Ed. A. Malikova. Sankt Peterburg. 5–52.

Maloff, Saul. 1962. 'The World of Rococo.' *The Nation* 194 (16 June): 541–2.

Markov, Vladimir, and Merrill Sparks, eds. 1996. *Modern Russian Poetry*. New York: Bobbs-Merrill.

May, Charles E., ed. 1976. *Short Story Theories*. Athens: Ohio University Press.

– 1994. *The New Short Story Theory*. Athens: Ohio University Press.

McCarthy, Mary. 1970a. 'A Bolt from the Blue.' In *The Writing on the Wall and Other Literary Essays*, 15–34.

– 1970b. *The Writing on the Wall and Other Literary Essays*. London: Weidenfeld and Nicolson.

Mel'nikov, N.G., ed. 2000. *Klassik bez retushi: Literaturnyi mir o tvorchestve Vladimira Nabokova*. Moscow: Novoe Literaturnoe Obozrenie.

Mochul'skii, Konstantin. 1923. [Review of *Grozd'* (*The Cluster*)]. *Zveno* 12 (23 April): 3. Reprinted in N.G. Mel'nikov, ed., *Klassik bez retushi*, 23–4.

Moravia, Alberto. 1976. 'The Short Story and the Novel.' In Charles E. May, ed., *Short Story Theories*, 147–51.

N., A. 1952. 'Stikhi V. Nabokova.' *Grani* 16: 179–80.

Nal'ianch, C. 1930. [Review of *Vozvrashchenie Chorba* (*The Return of Chorb*)]. *Za svobodu* 209 (4 March): 3. Reprinted in N.G. Mel'nikov, ed., *Klassik bez retushi*, 50–1.

Naumann, Marina T. 1978. 'The Poetry of Nabokov's Prose: *Mashen'ka* Revisited.' *Melbourne Slavonic Studies* 13: 71–81.

– 1991. 'Nabokov and Puškin's Tuning Fork.' *Russian Literature* 29: 229–42.

Nemerov, Howard. 1971. Review of *Poems and Problems*. *New York Times Book Review* (25 July): 4–5.

Neubauer, Paul. 2002. 'Introduction.' *Amerikastudien* 47(3): 329–34.

Nicol, Charles. 1991. '"Ghastly Rich Glass": A Double Essay on "Spring in Fialta."' *Russian Literature Triquarterly* 24: 173–84.

Nicol, Charles, and Gennady Barabtarlo, eds. 1993. *A Small Alpine Form: Studies in Nabokov's Short Fiction*. New York: Garland.

Ofrosimov, Iuri. 1922. [Review of Nabokov's translation of *Colas Breugnon*]. *Rul'* 602 (19 November): 9.

Page, Norman, ed. 1982. *Nabokov: The Critical Heritage*. London: Routledge and Kegan Paul.

Paperno, Slava, and John V. Hagopian. 1984. 'Official and Unofficial Responses to Nabokov in the Soviet Union.' In George Gibian and Stephen Jan Parker, eds, *The Achievements of Vladimir Nabokov*, 99–118.

Parker, Stephen Jan. 1991. 'Vladimir Nabokov and the Short Story.' *Russian Literature Triquarterly* 24: 63–72.

Peterson, Dale E. 1989. 'Nabokov and the Poe-etics of Composition.' *Slavic and East European Journal* 33(1): 95–107.

– 1995. 'Nabokov and Poe.' In Vladimir Alexandrov, ed., *The Garland Companion to Vladimir Nabokov*, 463–72.

Pier, John. 1992. 'Between Text and Paratext: Vladimir Nabokov's *Pale Fire*.' *Style: Studies in Fiction* 26(1) (Spring): 12–32.

Pifer, Ellen. 1980. *Nabokov and the Novel*. Cambridge: Harvard University Press.

– 1989. 'Shades of Love: Nabokov's Intimations of Immortality.' *Kenyon Review* 11(2): 75–86.

Plato. 1985. *The Portable Plato*. Ed Scott Buchanan. Harmondsworth: Penquin.

Poe, Edgar Allan. 1986. *Edgar Allan Poe: The Fall of the House of Usher and Other Writings*. Ed. David Galloway. London: Penguin.

Poggioli Renato. 1960. *The Poets of Russia – 1890–1930*. Cambridge: Harvard University Press.

Polsky, Svetlana. 1997. 'Vladimir Nabokov's Short Story "Easter Rain."' *Nabokov Studies* 4: 151–62.

Prokhorova, Irina. 2003. 'Nabokovs Urenkel: Die russische Literatur ist äs thetisches Babylon.' Translated by Christiane Stachau, in *Frandfurter Rundschau online 2003*. 8 October 2003.

Proffer, Carl R., ed. 1974. *A Book of Things about Vladimir Nabokov*. Ann Arbor: Ardis.

Proffer, Elendea. 1970. 'Nabokov's Russian Readers.' In Alfred Appel, Jr, and Charles Newman, eds, *Nabokov: Criticism, Reminiscences, Translations and Tributes*, 253–60.

Quennell, Peter, ed. 1979. *Vladimir Nabokov: A Tribute*. London: Weidenfeld and Nicolson.

Rabaté, Laurent. 1985. 'La poésie de la tradition: Étude du recueil *Stixi* de V. Nabokov.' *Revue des Études Slaves* 57(3): 397–420.

Rampton, David. 1984. *Vladimir Nabokov: A Critical Study of the Novels*. Cambridge: Cambridge University Press.

– 1991. 'The Art of Invocation: The Role of the Apostrophe in Nabokov's Early Poetry.' *Russian Literature Triquarterly* 24: 341–54.

Riemer, Andrew. 1967. 'Dim Glow, Faint Blaze – the "Meaning" of "Pale Fire."' *Balcony* 6: 41–8.

Rodnianskaia, Irina. 1995. *Literaturnoe semiletie*. Moscow: Knizhnyi sad.

Rohrberger, Mary, and Dan E. Burns. 1982. 'Short Fiction and the Numinous Realm: Another Attempt at Definition.' *Modern Fiction Studies* 28(1): 5–12.

Rorty, Richard. 1989. *Contingency, Irony, Solidarity*. Cambridge: Cambridge University Press.

– Introduction to *Pale Fire*. 1992a. New York: Alfred A. Knopf.

– 1992b. Review of *Nabokov's Otherworld* by Vladimir Alexandrov. *Common Knowledge* 1(2): 126.

Salehar, Anna Maria. 1974. 'Nabokov's *Gift*: An Apprenticeship in Creativity.' In Carl R. Proffer, ed., *A Book of Things about Vladimir Nabokov*, 70–83.

Savel'ev, A. (Savelii Grigor'evich Sherman). 1929. [Review of *Vzvrashchenie Chorba* (*The Return of Chorb*)]. Rul' 2765 (31 December): 2–3.

Scherr, Barry. 'Poetry.' 1995. In Vladimir Alexandrov, ed., *The Garland Companion to Vladimir Nabokov*, 608–25.

– 2005. 'Nabokov as Poet.' In J.W. Connolly, ed., *The Cambridge Companion to Nabokov*, 103–18.

Seidel, Michael. 1987. 'Stereoscope: Nabokov's *Ada* and *Pale Fire*.' In Harold Bloom, ed., *Vladimir Nabokov: Modern Critical Views*, 235–57.

Senderovich, Savelii, and Elena Shvartz. 1997. 'Verbnaia shtuchka: Nabokov i populiarnaia kul'tura.' *Novoe literaturnoe obozrenie* 26: 201–21.

Setschkareff, Vsevolod. 1980. 'Zur Thematik der Dichtung Vladimir Nabokovs (aus Anlaß des Erscheinens seiner gesammelten Gedichte).' *Die Welt der Slaven* 25(1): 68–97.

Shakhovskoi, Dmitrii. 1926. [Review of *Mashen'ka* (*Mary*)]. *Blagonamerennyi* 2 (March/April): 173–4. Reprinted in N.G. Mel'nikov, ed., *Klassik bez retushi*, 33.

Shapiro, Harvey, ed. 2003. *Poets of World War II*. American Poets Project / Library of America.

Shelley, Percy Bysshe. 1952. 'Adonais: An Elegy on the Death of John Keats.' In *The Complete Poetical Works of Percy Bysshe Shelley*. Ed. T. Hutchinson. London: Oxford University Press.

Shrayer, Maxim D. 1999. *The World of Nabokov's Stories*. Austin: University of Texas.

Sicker, Philip. 1992. '*Pale Fire* and *Lyrical Ballads*: The Dynamics of Collaboration.' *Papers on Language and Literature* 28(3) (Summer): 305–18.

Sisson, Jonathan Borden. 1979. 'Cosmic Synchronization and Other Worlds in the Work of Vladimir Nabokov.' PhD diss., University of Minnesota. 1979.

– 1995. 'Nabokov and Some Turn-of-the-Century English Writers.' In Vladimir Alexandrov, ed., *The Garland Companion to Vladimir Nabokov*, 528–36.

Skonechnaia, Olga. 2002. 'The Wandering Jew as a Metaphor for Memory in Nabokov's Poetry and Prose of the 1920s and 1930s.' In Jane Grayson et al., eds, *Nabokov's World: The Shape of Nabokov's World*, 186–95.

Skow, John. 1971. 'Drinker of Words.' *Time* (14 June): 66–8.

Slonim, Mark. 1939. 'Literaturnyi dnevnik: Molodye pisateli za rubezhom.' *Volia Rossii* 10-11 (October-November): 100–18.

Smirnov, Vladimir. 1991. 'Stikhi Nabokova.' In *Vladimir Nabokov: Stikhotvoreniia.* Ed. V. Smirnov. Moskva: Molodaia Gvardiia. 5–19.

Smith, Gerald S. 1991. 'Nabokov and Russian Verse Form.' *Russian Literature Triquarterly* 24: 271–305.

Socher, Abraham. 2005. 'Shades of Frost: A Hidden Source for Nabokov's *Pale Fire*.' Zembla. http://www.libraries.psu.edu/nabokov/socher.htm.

Soloukhin, Vladimir. 1989. 'Poet Vladimir Nabokov.' *Moskva* 6: 16.

Stark, John O. 1974. *The Literature of Exhaustion: Borges, Nabokov, and Barth.* Durham: Duke University Press.

Stegner, Page. 1966. *Escape into Aesthetics: The Art of Vladimir Nabokov.* New York: Dial Press.

Struve, Gleb. 1923. 'Pis'ma o russkoi poezii.' *Russkaia mysl'* 1–2 (January–February): 292–9. Reprinted in N.G. Mel'nikov, ed., *Klassik bez retushi*, 21–2.

– 1930a. 'Tvorchestvo Sirina.' *Rossiia i slavianstvo* 77 (17 May): 3. Reprinted in N.G. Mel'nikov, ed., *Klassik bez retushi*, 181–6.

1930b. 'Zametki o stikhakh.' *Rossiia i slavianstvo* 68 (15 March): 3. Reprinted in N.G. Mel'nikov, ed., *Klassik bez retushi*, 49–50.

– 1956. *Russkaia literatura v izgnanii.* New York: Chekhov.

– 1967. 'Notes on Nabokov as a Russian Writer.' In L.S. Dembo, ed., *Nabokov: The Man and His Work*, 45–56.

Tammi, Pekka. 1985. *Problems of Nabokov's Poetics: A Narratological Analysis.* Helsinki: Suomalainen Tiedeakatemia.

– 1995. '*Pale Fire*.' In Vladimir Alexandrov, ed., *The Garland Companion to Vladimir Nabokov*, 571–86.

Tauber, Ekatarina. 1955. 'Stikhotvoreniia V. Nabokova.' *Vozrozhdenie* 37: 139–41.

Terras, Victor. 1998. *Poetry of the Silver Age: The Various Voices of Russian Modernism.* Dresden: Dresden University Press.

Thwaite, Anthony. 1961. 'Several Accomplishments.' *The Spectator* 205 (26 May): 770.

Toker, Leona. 1988. 'Nabokov's "Torpid Smoke."' *Studies in Twentieth Century Literature* 12: 239–48.

– 1989. *Nabokov: The Mystery of Literary Structures.* Ithaca, NY: Cornell University Press.

– 1999. '"The dead are good mixers": Nabokov's Versions of Individualism.' In Julian Connolly, ed., *Nabokov and His Fiction: New Perspectives*, 92–108.

Tolstaia, Nataliia, and Mikhail Meilakh. 1995. 'Russian Short Stories.' In Vladimir Alexandrov, ed., *The Garland Companion to Vladimir Nabokov*, 644–60.

Tomlinson, Charles. 1961. 'Last of Lands.' *New Statesman* 61 (28 April): 674.

Toynbee, Philip. 1962. 'Nabokov's Conundrum' [Review of *Pale Fire*]. *The Observer* (11 November): 24.

Tsetlin, Mikhail. 1930. [Review *Vozvrashchenie Chorba* (*The Return of Chorb*)]. *Sovremennye zapiski* 42: 530–1.

V. 1923. [Review of Nabokov's translation of *Alice in Wonderland*]. *Rul'* 734 (29 April): 11.

Vakar, N.P. 1938. '*Sobytie* – P'esa V. Sirina (beseda s Iu. P. Annenkov).' *Poslednie novosti* 6195 (12 March): 4. Reprinted in N.G. Mel'nikov, ed., *Klassik bez retushi*, 165–6.

Verkheil, Keis [Veerheul, Kees]. 1980. 'Malyi korifei russkoi poezii.' *Ekho: Literaturnyi zhurnal* 4: 138–45.

Walsh, Chad. 1960. 'Nabokov, Poet.' *New York Herald Tribune Book Review* (31 January): 4.

West, James. 1970. *Russian Symbolism: A Study of Vyacheslav Ivanov and the Russian Symbolist Aesthetic*. London: Metheun.

Williams, Carol T. 1975. 'Nabokov's Dozen Short Stories: His World in Microcosm.' *Studies in Short Fiction* 12: 213–22.

Wood, Michael. 1994. *The Magician's Doubts: Nabokov and the Risks of Fiction*. London: Chatto & Windus.

Wordsworth, William. 1953. *The Prelude*. Ed. and introd. by Ernest de Selincourt. London: Oxford University Press.

– 1985. *Wordsworth: Poems*. Selected by W.E. Williams and introduced by Jenni Calder. Harmondsworth: Penguin.

Wright, James. 1959–60. 'A Poetry Chronicle.' *Poetry* 95/96: 373–8.

Wyllie, Barbara. 2003. *Nabokov at the Movies: Film Perspectives in Fiction*. Jefferson: McFarland & Company.

Wyndham, Francis. 1972. 'Ivory-and-Ebony.' *The Listener* 88 (27 July): 116–17.

Zholkovsky, Alexander. 2001. 'Poem, Problem, Prank.' *The Nabokovian* 47 (Fall): 19–28.

Index

Abrams, M.H., 99
Adamovich, Georgii, 47, 52, 53, 55,
58, 226, 241, 296, 390n4, 393nn4, 6;
*Loneliness and Freedom /
Odinochestvo i svoboda*, 52
Aikhenval'd, Iulii, 42, 144, 400n30
Akhmatova, Anna, 84, 86
Alexandrov, Vladimir, 10, 11, 104,
106, 156, 159, 295, 324, 329, 359,
386, 391nn11, 12, 397n11, 413nn13,
17, 416n11; *The Garland Com-
panion to Vladimir Nabokov*
(editor), 82, 415n5; *Nabokov's
Otherworld*, 104, 391nn11, 12,
413nn13, 17
Alter, Robert, 194, 195, 321, 322,
390n9, 415n5
Amfiteatrov-Kadashev, Vladimir, 39,
40, 44, 401n36
Anchor Review, 394n12
Andreev, Nikolai, 7
Annenkov, Iurii, 221, 223, 226, 405n8
Annenskii, I., 87
Appel, Alfredd: *The Annotated Lolita*,
7–8
Arnold, Matthew, 323
Atlantic Monthly, 26, 58, 59, 403n45

Auden, W.H., 111
Augustine, Saint, 100

Babikov, Andrei, 224, 225, 405n7
Bakhrakh, Alexander, 36, 37, 38, 39,
40, 41, 46, 54, 169, 401n36
Bal'mont, Konstantin, 55, 84
Barabtarlo, Gennady, 92, 212, 244,
245, 246, 247, 250, 366, 398n15,
419n24; *A Small Alpine Form:
Studies in Nabokov's Short Fiction*
(editor with Charles Nicol), 244
Barth, John, 8
Barthelme, Donald, 8
Bazarov, Konstantin, 67, 68
Beckett, Samuel, 228
Belyi, Andrei, 55, 106, 113, 303, 394–
5n13, 397n11, 398–9n18
Benediktov, Vladimir, 55
Benua, Alexander, 407n20
Beshentsov, A.I., 240
Bethea, David M., 392n1, 394n13
Blackwell, Stephen, 390n10, 411n2,
412n6, 413n16; *Zina's Paradox: The
Figured Reader in Nabokov's Gift*,
390n10, 411n2, 413n16
Blake, William, 385

Blium, A.V., 395n14

Blok, Aleksandr, 34, 36, 40, 43, 54, 55, 64, 75, 79, 84, 106, 113, 156, 157, 159, 226, 227, 281, 303, 393n7, 397n11, 400n33, 407n20; *Balaganchik / The Puppet Show*, 226, 407n20; 'Incognita,' 400n33; 'Of attainments, of great deeds, of glory …,' 159; *Stikhi o prekrasnoi Dame / Verses about the Wonderful Lady*, 156

Books and Bookmen, 67

Booth, Philip, 60

Bowra, C.M., 385

Boyd, Brian, 10, 11, 12, 91, 95, 104, 212, 227, 252, 257, 259, 323, 366, 390n4, 391nn11, 14, 18, 19, 392nn27, 28, 393n3, 396n1, 399n22, 400n30, 403nn48, 50, 404n2, 405n3, 408n1, 409nn9, 12, 412n6, 414nn19, 1, 415n4, 416n8, 420n1; *Nabokov's 'Ada': The Place of Consciousness*, 104

Brodsky, Joseph, 32

Brooke, Rupert, 16, 56, 110, 111, 112, 113, 170, 175, 216, 355, 398nn14, 15, 16, 17

Browning, Robert, 71, 323, 325

Bunin, Ivan, 19, 20, 34, 38, 42, 43, 44, 55, 79, 84, 86, 397n11

Butler, Samuel, 323

Byron, Lord, 323

Calderón, Pedro, 209, 227; *La vida es sueño*, 209

Carroll, Lewis: *Alice in Wonderland*, 15

Chekhov, Anton, 221

Chernyi, Sasha, 17, 55, 56, 203

Chernyshevskii, N.G., 278, 280, 289, 294, 296, 314, 315, 350, 413n15

Chester, Alfred, 320, 415n7

Chisla (Numbers), 47, 390n4

Clark, Naomi, 69

Coleridge, Samuel Taylor, 88, 303, 385

Commentary, 320

Connolly, Julian W., 76–7, 91, 104, 262, 390n5, 408n22, 410n13, 412n6

Coover, Robert, 8

Couturier, Maurice, 8, 320

Crashaw, Richard, 323

Culler, Jonathan, 78, 305; *The Pursuit of Signs*, 305

Davydov, Sergej, 397n8, 412n6; *'Teksty – Metreshki' Vladimira Nabokova*, 397n8

de Jonge, Alex, 409n6

de la Lafontaine, Jean, 359

de la Mare, Walter, 110, 111, 113, 398n15

de Vries, Gérard, 323, 416n11

DeLillo, Don, 8

Dickens, Charles, 169, 216

Dickins, Anthony, 65

Diment, Galya, 80, 81, 185, 226, 380, 405n9

Dni (Days), 36, 38

Dolinin, Alexander, 87–9, 91, 278, 301, 380, 411n2, 412n6, 413n12, 414n22

Donne, John, 323, 325

Dostoevskii; Fëdor, 42, 44, 177, 178, 214

Dupee, F.W., 62–3, 80, 394n12

Eekman, Th., 83, 84, 392n25

Eliot, T.S., 323, 325, 364; *Four Quartets*, 364

Elkin, Stanley, 8

English Review, 392n24

Enright, D.J., 406n10
Esenin, Sergei, 86, 281
Esquire, 252
Esslin, Martin, 406n14

Fedorova, V., 389n2
Ferguson, Suzanne C., 244, 249, 251
Fet, Afanasii, 34, 40, 43, 48, 49, 55,
    80, 83, 88, 113, 303, 314, 385,
    402n43, 417n13; 'Swallows,' 402n43
Field, Andrew, 12, 62, 63, 64, 175,
    176, 201, 226, 253, 391n19, 393n7,
    401n36, 403n50, 411n2, 416n11
Flatman, Thomas, 323
Foster, John Burt, Jr, 364, 408n4,
    415n3
Foster, Ludmila A., 397n6
Fowler, Douglas, 403n52
Frost, Robert, 323, 324, 325, 362,
    416n10
Frye, Northrop, 320

Gass, William, 8
Gippius, Zinaida, xv, 13, 35, 36, 392n1
Goethe, Johann Wolfgang, 221, 323,
    325, 419n25; 'Erlkönig,' 419n25;
    Die Leiden des jungen Werthers,
    419n25
Gogol, Nikolai, 19, 23, 170, 175, 221,
    226, 230, 280, 284, 314, 401n37;
    Dead Souls, 284; *The Inspector
    General*, 230
Goldsmith, Oliver, 323
Grabes, Herbert, 390n7, 391n12
Grani (*Facets*), 51, 111
Gray, Morris, 403n48
Grossmith, Robert, 267, 410n13
Gul', Roman, 41, 42
Gumilev, Nikolai, 21, 55, 107, 108, 110,
    113, 137, 171, 189, 348, 413n15

Gusev, D., 164
Gustafson, Richard, 417n13

Hagopian, John V., 395n14
Hardy, Thomas, 323
Harrison, Robert Pogue: *The
    Dominion of the Dead*, 139, 399n26
Hawkes, John, 8
Hecht, Anthony, 59, 60, 62
Housman, A.E., 323
Hudson Review, 60, 66
Hultquist, Marianne K., 64

Iakobson, V.F., 404n2
Ibsen, Henrik, 221
Ionesco, Eugène, 228
Ivanov, Georgii, 47, 86, 390n4, 393n3
Ivanov, Viacheslav, 113

James, William, 99, 137; *The Varieties
    of Religious Experience*, 99
Jarry, Alfred: *Ubu roi*, 406n11
Johnson, D. Barton, ix, 10, 26, 76, 77,
    81, 103, 104, 105, 110, 111, 112,
    138, 163, 280, 281, 391n17,
    392nn21, 28, 395n18, 397n11,
    398n15, 411n2, 412n9; *Worlds in
    Regression*, 103
Johnson, Samuel, 323
Joyce, James, 8, 62, 67, 81, 83, 227,
    383, 410n19, 412–13n11; *Ulysses*,
    227, 383, 410n19

Kafka, Franz: *Die Verwandlung*, 329
Kantor, Mikhail, 391n15
Karlinsky, Simon, 227, 397n11,
    407n15, 411nn2, 3
Karussel, 392n24
Keats, John, 71, 114, 323, 381, 385,
    399n24

Kernan, Alvin, 324, 325, 416n9
Khlebnikov, Velimir, 86
Khodasevich, Vladislav, 55, 79, 80, 84,
    85, 86, 87, 88, 213, 214, 224, 231,
    233, 376, 378, 394n13, 397n5,
    400n29, 407n15, 408n1
Khokhlov, G.D., 45, 46
Kipling, Joseph Rudyard, 323
Kirkup, James: *Songs and Dreams* (ed-
    itor), 392n26
Kliuev, N., 86
Kuzmanovich, Zoran, 391n13, 403n47
Kuzmin, M., 87

Landman, A., 398n12
Lattimore, Richmond, 66, 67
Lermontov, Mikhail, 83, 140, 399–
    400n27; 'The Angel,' 140,
    399–400n27
Levin, Iurii, 412n6
Listener, 65
London Magazine, 65
Lowell, Robert, 16
Lubin, Peter, 364, 419n25
Lukash, Ivan, 404n2
Lunts, L'ev, 7
Lur'e, Vera, 42, 43, 44, 78, 295
Lyons, John O., 416n11

MacDiarmid, Hugh, 323
Macdonald, Dwight, 394n11, 417n16
Maiakovskii, Vladimir, 55, 79, 86, 214
Maikov, Apollon, 38, 43, 55
Malikova, M., 86, 87, 389n2, 391n20,
    392n24, 398n16, 404n2
Maloff, Saul, 319, 320, 323
Mandel'shtam, Osip, 32, 55, 56, 83,
    86, 87
Markov, Vladimir: *Modern Russian
    Poetry* (editor with Merrill Sparks),
    392n26

Marvell, Andrew, 323
May, Charles E., 408n5
McCarthy, Mary, 319, 322, 323
Meredith, George, 325
Miliukov, Paul, 399n22
Milton, John, 323
Mochul'skii, Konstantin, 40, 41
Moravia, Alberto, 246
Musset, Alfred de, 246

Nabokov, Dmitri, xxiv, 30, 183, 219,
    226, 405–6n9
Nabokov, V.D., 399n22, 405n3
Nabokov, Véra, 9, 29, 71, 76, 103, 134,
    136, 183, 391n12, 398n17, 400n33
Nabokov, Vladimir
WORKS:
    Criticism:
    'The Art of Literature and
        Commonsense,' 99, 107, 120,
        122, 170, 171, 177, 182, 189, 194,
        197, 199, 233, 348, 351, 413n15
    *Eugene Onegin: A Novel in Verse by
        Aleksandr Pushkin*, 28, 64, 65,
        67, 329, 398–9n18
    'Good Readers and Good Writers,'
        244
    'Inspiration,' 99, 339–40,
        417–18n18
    Lectures on Literature, 410n19,
        412–13n11
    Lectures on Russian Literature, 178
    Nikolai Gogol, 189, 401n37
    Notes on Prosody, 28, 383,
        398–9n18
    'On Hodasevich,' 375
    'Philistines and Philistinism,' 200
    'Playwriting,' 202, 222, 230
    'Rupert Bruk,' 111, 170, 216, 401n37
    The Song of Igor's Campaign,
        417n15

Strong Opinions, 3, 97, 172, 174,
185, 294, 347, 351, 401–2n37,
402n44, 403n45, 405n6, 411n2
*Three Russian Poets: Selections
from Pushkin, Lermontov,
Tyutchev*, 399–400n27
'The Tragedy of Tragedy,' 230
Drama:
Ahasuerus (*Agasfer*), 404–5n2
Death (*Smert'*), 20, 206–9, 215, 218,
299, 346, 419n27
The Event (*Sobytie*), 221–5, 227,
232, 234, 249, 293, 360, 405n8,
405–6n9, 407nn19, 20, 408n22,
409n10
The Grand-dad (*Dedushka*), 20,
209–12, 217, 261, 405n6, 409n7
In Spring (*Vesnoi*), 404–5n2
The Man from the USSR (*Chelovek
iz SSSR*), 218–21, 223, 227
The Pole (*Polius*), 20, 215–18, 269,
293
The Tragedy of Mister Morn
(*Tragediia Gospodina Morna*),
20, 203, 212–15, 218, 405n7
The Waltz Invention (*Izobretenie
Val'sa*), xxiii, 112, 203, 222, 225–
40, 242, 249, 337, 345, 350, 405–
6n9, 406n10, 408n22
The Wanderers (*Skital'tsy*), 20, 203–6,
209, 212, 215, 231, 240, 353
Poetry:
'Allow me to dream. You are my
first torment ...' ('Pozvol' mech-
tat'. Ty pervoe stradan'e ...'),
159–60
Almanac: Two Paths (*Al'manakh:
Dva puti*), 14, 15, 28, 129, 141,
148, 155, 165, 166, 167, 283, 352,
417n14
'Autumnal' ('Osennee'), 13

'The Ballad of Longwood Glen,'
27, 61, 67, 195–201, 215, 353,
366, 383, 387, 403nn50, 51, 52,
404n53, 420n2
'Being in Love,' 103, 134–6, 138,
216, 272, 398n17
'The clock on the tower sang out
...' ('Chasy na bashne raspevali
...'), 160
'Clouds shattered. Rain-like dia-
monds ...' ('Razbilis' oblaka.
Almazy dozhdevye ...'), 122,
405n5
The Cluster (*Grozd'*), 16, 17, 18, 19,
30, 35, 36, 38, 39, 40, 41, 42, 44,
46, 54, 55, 56, 141, 148, 149, 151,
153, 155, 156, 157, 158, 159, 167,
253, 305, 377, 400–1n35, 412n8
'The Cluster' ('Grozd' [section from
The Cluster]), 16
'Dark-blue wallpaper ...' ('Temno-
sinie oboi ...'), 283, 352
'Death' ('Smert'), 179
'Do You Know My Faith?'
('Znaesh' veru moiu?'), 181–3,
185, 197, 317, 343
'The Dream' ('Son'), 152, 213
'The Dream' ('Snoviden'e'), 24, 121,
270, 301, 348, 410n16
'Dreams' ('Sny'), 24
The Empyrean Path (*Gornii put'*),
16, 17, 18, 19, 28, 30, 35, 36, 42,
43, 44, 54, 55, 63, 72, 107, 110,
115, 119, 121, 129, 162, 272, 305,
391n20, 399n25, 400n28
'An Evening of Russian Poetry,' 27,
60, 61, 62, 66, 67, 68, 195, 326–9,
334, 345, 346, 379, 387, 417n13
'Evening on a Vacant Lot' ('Vecher
na pustyre'), 121, 129–32, 139,
248, 258, 301, 399n22, 414n22

'The Execution' ('Rasstrel'), 24

'Fame' ('Slava'), 29, 53, 118, 176, 187–91, 335, 336, 351, 387, 393n6, 420n2

'Far from shore, in the marine shimmering ...' ('Vdali ot berega, v mertsanii morskom, ...'), 272, 399n25

'The fields, the swamp sail by ...' ('Plyvut polia, boloto mimo ...'), 169

'For nocturnal travel I require ...' ('Dlia stranstviia nochnogo mne ne nado ...'), 151–2

'The Forest' ('Les'), 15

'The Formula' ('Formula'), 117, 118, 121, 133

'Forty-three or four years ...' ('Sorok tri ili chetyre goda ...'), 121, 410n16

'From eight until midnight I hide in a small booth...' ('S vos'mi do polnochi taius' ia v budke tesnoi,...'), 160

'Gone' ('Ushedshee' [section from *The Cluster*]), 17

'Hexameters' ('Gekzametry'), 132–3, 248, 399n22

'Himself triangular, two-winged, legless ...' ('Sam treugol'nyi, dvukrylyi, beznogii ...'), 152

'Home,' 26, 392n24

'Hotel Room' ('Nomer v gostinitse'), 142

'How I Love You' ('Kak ia liubliu tebia'), 126–8, 256, 266

'How often, how often I on a fast train ...' ('Kak chasto, kak chasto ia v poezde skorom ...'), 149, 151, 331

'How to explain? There are in memory rays ...' ('Kak ob'iasniu? Est' v pamiati luchi ...'), 140–1, 204

'I dreamed of you so often, so long ago, ...' ('Mechtal o tebe tak chasto, tak davno, ...'), 158–9, 380

'I Like That Mountain' ('Liubliu ia goru'), 179, 402n40 (*see also* 'The Summit' ['Vershina'])

'I love unfamiliar trainstations ...' ('Ia neznakomye liubliu vokzaly ...'), 141

'I remember within velvet frames ...' ('Ia pomniu v pliushevoi oprave ...'), 309, 310, 414n20

'I so easily and happily dreamed ...' ('Mne tak prosto i radostno snilos' ...'), 121, 410n16

'I will be cheerful and fearless' ('Ia budu radosten i besstrashen'), 166

'In a crystal ball we were enclosed ...' ('V khrustal'nyi shar zakliucheny my byli ...'), 139–40, 208, 399–400n27, 410n17

'In Paradise' ('V raiu'), 179, 355, 402n40

'In the Menagerie' ('V zverintse'), 153

'In the Village Cemetery' ('Na sel'skom kladbishche'), 402n38

'Inspiration' ('Vdokhnoven'e'), 417–18n18

'Inspiration – that is voluptuousness ...' ('Vdokhnoven'e – eto sladostrast'e ...'), 119–20, 289

'Lines Written in Oregon,' 27

'Lunar Reverie' ('Lunnaia greza'), 389n1

'The Meeting' ('Vstrecha'), 309, 400n33

'The mist of a nocturnal dream ...'
('Tuman nochnogo sna ...'), 16,
37, 262
'Movement' ('Dvizhen'e [section
from *The Cluster*]), 17, 39, 148,
412n8
'The Muse' ('K muze'), 25, 26, 160–
3, 387
'My blessedness, clouds and sparkling waters ...' ('Blazhenstvo
moe, oblaka i blestiashchie vody
...'), 178
'The Nature of Electricity,' 367
'No, existence is not an unstable
riddle!' ('Net, bytie – ne zybkaia
zagadka!'), 153–4
'Nocturnal Butterflies' ('Nochnye
babochki'), 153
'O, how you strive for the winged
path' ('O, kak ty rvesh'sia v put'
krylatyi'), 179
'O love, you are radiant and
winged' ('O liubov', ty svetla i
krylata ...'), 56, 153, 400n32
'O, muse, teach [me]: / how is spirit
to overflow into understandable
verse?' ('O, muza, nauchi: / v
poniatnyi stikh kak prizrak
perel'etsia?'), 141
'O, wondrous agitation of a meeting! ...' ('O, vstrechi divnoe
volnen'e! ...'), 160
'Oculus' ('Oko'), 180–1, 355
'Ode to a Model,' 67, 340, 418n22
'Of Angels, 1' ('Ob angelakh, 1'), 179
'Of the wise and malicious I ask nothing' ('U mudrykh i zlykh nichego
ne proshu'), 14, 166–7, 380
'On a Train' ('V poezde'), 17, 141–
2, 148–9

'On Golgotha' ('Na Golgofe'), 43,
177, 317, 409–10n12
'On Rulers' ('O praviteliakh'), 380
'On the Death of Blok' ('Na smert'
Bloka'), 54
'On Translating Eugene Onegin,'
61, 67–8
Open Windows (*Raskrytye okna*),
12, 15, 151
'Pale Fire,' xxiv, 185, 322, 324, 325,
326, 329, 330, 331, 332, 333, 340,
342, 347, 348, 349, 352, 354, 355,
357, 358, 359, 360, 364, 367, 368,
372, 374, 382, 399n21, 414n2,
415nn3, 5, 416nn8, 10, 11,
417n17, 419n25, 420n2
'The Paris Poem' ('Parizhskaia
poema'), 335
'The Poem,' 17, 27, 122–4, 132, 136,
195, 340, 341, 343, 387
Poems (*Stikhi*, 1916 [rept. 1997]),
xxi, 4, 12–14, 17, 26, 35, 148,
391n16
Poems (*Stikhi*, 1979), xxi, 4, 9, 29,
30, 35, 57, 62, 70, 76, 95, 103,
392n28, 402n40, 404n1
Poems: 1929–1951 (*Stikhotvoreniia:
1929–1951*), 25, 28, 51, 52
Poems (1959), 26, 27, 28, 58, 59, 60,
61, 64, 193, 196, 400n31
Poems and Problems, 12, 20, 22, 25,
26, 28, 29, 58, 61, 64, 65, 66, 76,
95, 117, 128, 160, 175, 180, 193,
195, 196, 262, 301, 392n27,
400n31, 402n40, 413n12
'Poems 1924–1928' ('Stikhi 1924–
1928' [subtitle of *The Return of
Chorb: Stories and Poems*]), 19
'The Poet' ('Poet,' 1918), 115, 116,
117, 129, 291, 339

'The Poet' ('Poet'), 116, 117

'The Poets' ('Poety'), 53, 241,
402n39, 420n2

'The Rain Has Flown' ('Dozhd'
proletel'), 68, 94–8, 100, 124,
125, 165, 181, 183, 185, 197, 283,
396nn1, 2, 405n5

'The Refrigerator Awakes,' 26

'Remembrance,' 26, 392n24

'Restoration,' 27, 29, 151, 191–5,
198, 201, 208, 269, 307, 384, 387,
403n48

'The Room,' 145–6, 331, 349, 358,
400n31

'The Room' ('Komnata'), 142–4

'The Russian Song,' 26, 392n24

'Sentinel cypresses ...'
('Storozhevye kiparisy ...'), 162

'Shade' ('Ten'), 409n11

'The Snapshot' ('Snimok'), 262

'Soft Sound' ('Tikhii Shum'), 22–3,
151, 251, 387

'Softest of Tongues,' 4, 26, 58, 59,
403n45, 408n2

'The Staircase' ('Lestnitsa'), 400n28

'The storm has melted away. The
sky is clear ...' ('Groza rastaiala.
Nebo iasno ...'), 166, 283

'The Summit' ('Vershina'), 179,
402n40 (see also 'I Like That
Mountain' ['Liubliu ia goru'])

'The Swift' ('Lastochka'), 80, 184–7,
310, 311, 343, 387, 402n42

'Swifts' ('Lastochki'), 42

'There is in solitude freedom ...'
('Est' v odinochestve svoboda
...'), 37

'This life I love with an ecstatic love
...' ('Etu zhizn' ia liubliu isstuplennoi liubov'iu ...'), 112,
179–80

'Thou' ('Ty' [section from The
Cluster]), 16, 155

'Through the garden walked Christ
with disciples ...' ('Sadom shel
Khristos s uchenikami ...'), 177,
197, 316–17, 409–10n12

'To My Soul,' 237, 355

'To people you will say: it's time! ...'
('Liudiam ty skazhesh': nastalo!
...'), 150–1, 387

'To the Poet' ('Poetu'), 18–19, 72

'University Poem' ('Universitetskaia
poema'), 417n17

'We are few – the young, the
winged, ...' ('Nas malo – iunykh,
okrylennnykh, ...'), 178, 402n39

'What Happened Overnight' ('Chto
za-noch''), 193

'What Is the Evil Deed' ('Kadoe
sdelal ia durnoe delo'), 380

'When I on the diamond staircase
...' ('Kogda ia po lestnitse almaznoi ...'), 179

'When, obscure, we saw each other
first ...' ('Kogda, tumannye, my
svidelis' vpervye ...'), 157–8,
253–4, 255

'Who will go out in the morning?
Who will notice the ripened fruit?'
('Kto vyidet poutru? Kto spelyi
plod podmetit?'), 167–8, 400–1n35

'The Wreck' ('Krushenie'), 142

'Yearning, and mystery, and delight
...' ('Toska, i taina, i uslada ...'),
160

'You will enter and wordlessly sit
down ...' ('Ty voidesh' i molcha
siadesh'...'), 160

'You've moved to new lodgings ...'
('Pereshel ty v novoe zhilishche,
...'), 142–3, 144–5, 146

Prose:

Ada, 28, 29, 64, 194, 319, 320, 491n17
'The Admiralty Spire'
  ('Admiralteiskaia igla'), 250, 252,
  408n24
'An Affair of Honor' ('Podlets'),
  247, 407n18
'The Aurelian' ('Pil'gram'), 198,
  407n18
Bend Sinister, 61, 129, 172, 397n9,
  400–1n35
'Beneficence' ('Blagost''), 253–5
'A Busy Man' ('Zaniatoi chelovek'),
  247
'The Circle' ('Krug'), 243
'Cloud, Castle, Lake' ('Oblako, oze-
  ro, bashnia'), 198, 252
Conclusive Evidence, 244
'A Dashing Fellow' ('Khvat'), 247
The Defense (*Zashchita Luzhina*),
  32, 47, 49, 85, 171, 198, 390n4
*Details of a Sunset and Other
  Stories*, 247–8, 259
'Details of a Sunset' ('Katastrofa'),
  247–8, 249, 271, 285
'The Doorbell' ('Zvonok'), 247
'Easter Rain' ('Paskhal'nyi dozhd'),
  408n3
The Eye (*Sogliadatai*), 209
'A Forgotten Poet,' 242, 252
The Gift (*Dar*), xxiii, 30, 62, 75,
  118, 125, 129, 133, 139, 157, 158,
  176, 184, 205, 206, 219, 243, 263,
  275, 276, 277–317, 318, 319, 332,
  333, 338, 339, 343, 348, 350, 360,
  369, 376, 382, 390n10, 400n33,
  401–2n37, 402n42, 403n46,
  409n8, 411n2, 412nn5, 6, 9,
  413nn12, 13, 16, 414n20,
  417n14
Glory (*Podvig*), 198, 215

'Gods' ('Bogi'), 244, 247, 257–9,
  360, 403n51, 409n10
'A Guide to Berlin' ('Putevoditel' po
  Berlinu'), 244, 259–63, 273, 409–
  10n12, 410n13, 412–13n11
Invitation to a Beheading
  (*Priglashenie na kazn'*), 172, 279,
  404n53, 405n6, 413n14, 418n20
King, Queen, Knave (*Korol', dama,
  valet*), 28, 44, 47, 49, 393n5
'Lance,' 243
Laughter in the Dark, 360, 418n21
'A Letter That Never Reached
  Russia' ('Pis'mo v Rossiiu'), 250
'Lik,' 247, 250–1, 269, 410n15
Lolita, xx, 3, 7, 26, 59, 61, 62, 63,
  64, 65, 67, 129, 215, 278, 319,
  320, 360, 394n12, 406n10, 414n1
Look at the Harlequins! 134, 279,
  382, 398n17
'Mademoiselle O,' 243
Mary (*Mashen'ka*), 15, 19, 44, 47,
  49, 202, 215, 279, 382, 392n21,
  393nn4, 5, 410n18
'A Matter of Chance' ('Sluchainost'),
  247
Other Shores (*Drugie berega*), 396n1,
  413n17
Pale Fire, xx, xxiii, xxiv, 3, 27, 62, 64,
  66, 75, 107, 118, 119, 138, 157, 158,
  176, 212, 215, 227, 238, 269, 278,
  288, 314, 318–74, 376, 379, 392n23,
  394n11, 396n1, 403n46, 405–6n9,
  406n10, 407n19, 412–13n11,
  414nn20,1, 2, 415nn3, 5, 7, 416nn8,
  10, 11, 417nn12, 16, 418n22
'The Passenger' ('Passazhir'), 247
'Perfection' ('Sovershenstvo'), xxiii,
  198, 216, 246, 247, 263–76, 277,
  282, 293, 331, 338, 361, 419n27
Pnin, 59, 215, 269, 278, 407n17

The Real Life of Sebastian Knight,
  50, 59, 175, 396n2
'The Return of Chorb'
  ('Vozvrashchenie Chorba'), 215,
  247
*The Return of Chorb: Stories and
  Poems* (*Vozvrashchenie Chorba:
  rasskazy i stikhi*), 19, 20–4, 25,
  28, 30, 32, 44, 45, 46, 47, 48, 49,
  50, 54, 259, 393–4n8, 409n11
'The Reunion' ('Vstrecha'), 247
'Scenes from the Life of a Double
  Monster,' 243
'The Seaport' ('Port'), 247
'Signs and Symbols,' 247
'Solus Rex,' 243
'Sounds' ('Zvuki'), 247, 255–6, 257
Speak, Memory, xv, xxii, 13, 35,
  90, 92, 94, 95, 103, 110, 115, 118,
  124, 125, 133, 134, 151, 158, 159,
  165, 173, 192, 194, 254, 283, 287,
  288, 289, 301, 373, 383, 391n14,
  392n22, 396n1, 397n5, 408n24,
  413n17, 417n13
'Spring in Fialta' ('Vesna v Fial'te'),
  247, 250
'Terra Incognita,' 247, 249
'Terror' ('Uzhas'), 247
'The Thunderstorm' ('Groza'),
  247
'Torpid Smoke' ('Tiazhelyi dym'),
  241, 247, 263, 288–9, 339,
  410n14, 412n5, 417–18n18
Transparent Things, 129, 133, 209,
  403n49
'Tyrants Destroyed' ('Istreblenie
  tiranov'), 252
'Ultima Thule,' 176, 243, 401–2n37
'The Vane Sisters,' 247, 249, 252
'Vasiliy Shishkov,' 241–3, 498n1

'The Visit to the Museum'
  ('Poseshchenie muzeia'), 247
'Wingstroke' ('Udar kryla'), 247
'The Wood-Sprite' ('Nezhit'), 243,
  247
Nabokovskii vestnik (*The Nabokov
  Bulletin*), 395n17
Nal'ianch, C., 48, 49
Naumann, Marina, xix, 411–12n4
Nemerov, Howard, 65
Neubauer, Paul, 404n1
New Statesman, 61
*New York Herald Tribune Book
  Review*, 60
New York Review of Books, 28, 389n1,
  406n10
New York Times Book Review, 60, 65
New Yorker, 26, 27, 61, 65, 84, 195,
  196, 243, 249, 400n31
New Yorker Book of Poems, 392n26
Nicol, Charles, 244, 245, 246, 247,
  250, 410n19; *A Small Alpine Form:
  Studies in Nabokov's Short Fiction*
  (editor with Gennady Barabtarlo),
  244
Nouvelle Revue française, 390n4
Novaia russkaia kniga (*New Russian
  Book*), 41, 42
Novoe literaturnoe obozrenie (*New
  Literary Review*), 82
Novyi zhurnal (*New Journal*), 404–5n2

Paperno, Slava, 395n14
Parisian Poets, 47, 48, 296, 413n12
Parker, Stephen Jan, 244
Partisan Review, 394n12
Pasternak, Boris, 32, 34, 52, 53, 55,
  56, 75, 83, 84, 86, 87
Pater, Walter, 393n5
Perrault, Charles, 407n20

Peterson, Dale E., 108, 399–400n27
Pifer, Ellen, 9, 128, 129, 418n19;
    Nabokov and the Novel, 9
Plato, 105, 106, 238, 397n10; *The
    Republic*, 105, 238, 397n10
Poe, Edgar Allan, 108, 109, 110, 113,
    325, 399–400n 27, 408n22; 'Annabel
    Lee,' 408n22; 'The Fall of the
    House of Usher,' 109; 'The Poetic
    Principle,' 109
Poetry, 60
Poggioli, Renato, 398n13
Polsky, Svetlana, 408n3
Pope, Alexander, 323, 324, 325, 362,
    416n11; 'The Rape of the Lock,' 362
Poplavskii, Boris, 55
Poslednie novosti (The Latest News),
    226, 263
Proffer, Carl, 29
Proffer, Ellendea, 29, 395n14
Prokhorova, Irina, 82, 395n15
Proust, Marcel, 13, 149, 328, 354,
    391n15; *A la Recherche du Temps
    Perdu*, 149
Pushkin, Aleksander, 16, 28, 34, 40,
    43, 55, 63, 64, 80, 83, 88, 164, 191,
    221, 280, 303, 314, 323, 329, 385,
    394n13, 397n11, 404–5n2; *Eugene
    Onegin*, 28, 64, 65, 67, 329, 398n18,
    411n3; 'Exegi Monumentum,' 191;
    Russalka, 404–5n2
Pynchon, Thomas, 8

Rabaté, Laurent, 73, 74, 75, 76, 77, 79,
    80, 81, 380
Rabelais, François, 138, 368
Rampton, David, ix, 9, 76, 78, 305,
    415n5; *Vladimir Nabokov: A
    Critical Study of the Novels*, 9,
    415n5

Ratgauz, Daniil, 55
Rausch von Traubenberg, Baron Iuri,
    392n22
Riemer, Andrew, 320, 414n2
Rolland, Romain: *Colas Breugnon*, 15
Rorty, Richard, 10
*Rossiia i slavianstvo (Russia and
    Slavdom)*, 47, 56
Rul' (The Rudder), 15, 42, 45, 107,
    243, 259, 399n22, 405n7
Russian Literature Triquarterly, 76, 78,
    79, 104
Russian Review, 399n27
Russkaia mysl' (Russian Thought), 38
Russkie zapiski (Russian Annals), 405n8
Russkoe ecko (Russian Echo), 408n3

Salehar, Anna Maria, 280, 281, 412n7
Sandburg, Carl, 323
Savel'ev, A., 45
Scherr, Barry P., 82, 83, 84, 392n25,
    395n16, 403n50
Scott, Robert Falcon, 215, 216
Scott, Walter, 323
Segodnia (Today), 39
Setschkareff, Vsevolod, 71, 72, 73, 76,
    77, 91
Shakespeare, William, 114, 227, 318,
    323, 366, 367, 407n16; *Timon of
    Athens*, 318; *Twelfth Night*, 227, 318
Shakhovskoi, Dmitrii, 44
Shapiro, Harvey: *Poets of World War
    II* (editor), 31
Shcherbina, Nikolai, 55
Shelley, Percy Bysshe, 114, 323, 367,
    385, 399n24, 414n2
Shrayer, Maxim, 34, 397n8, 402n41,
    408n1, 410–11n20; *The World of
    Nabokov's Stories*, 397n8, 402n41,
    408n1, 410–11n 20

Shvabrin, Stanislav, 420n1
Shvartz, Elena, 407n20
Sicker, Philip, 416n11
Sikorski (Nabokov), Helene, 13, 391n16
Sirin, V. (Vladimir Nabokov), 7, 15, 32, 40, 41, 44, 47, 48, 49, 56, 87, 151, 153, 155, 214, 221, 226, 393nn4, 5, 395n14, 404–5n2, 417n13
Sisson, Jonathan Borden, 110, 111, 397n4; 'Cosmic Synchronization and Other Worlds in the Work of Vladimir Nabokov,' 397n4
Skonechnaia, Olga, 404–5n2
Skow, John, 65, 66, 67, 68
Slonim, Marc, 393n5
Smirnov, Vladimir, 32, 85, 86, 389n2
Smith, Gerald S., 76, 79, 80, 81, 82, 83, 394n13, 398n18
Socher, Abraham, 416n10
Sologub, Fedor, 113
Soloukhin, Vladimir, 85
Soloviev, Vladimir, 113, 156, 398n12
Sorrentino, Gilbert, 8
Southey, Robert, 323
Sovremennye zapiski (Contemporary Annals), 46, 184, 241, 278, 390n4, 393n4, 411n1
Sparks, Merrill: Modern Russian Poetry (editor with Vladimir Markov), 392n26
Stalin, Joseph, 227, 406n12
Stark, John O., 390n6
Stark, Vadim, 389n1
Stegner, Page, 28, 63, 64, 322, 323; Escape into Aesthetics: The Art of Vladimir Nabokov, 63; Nabokov's Congeries, 28
Sterne, Laurence, 8

Stevens, Wallace, 100, 325, 403n48
Stravinsky, Igor, 407n20
Strindberg, August, 227
Struve, Gleb, xxi, 7, 32, 35, 38, 39, 40, 44, 47, 48, 50, 52, 53, 54, 55, 56, 57, 73, 78, 83, 87, 88, 89, 169, 202, 278, 325, 380, 396n3, 400n32, 411n2; Russian Literature in Exile / Russkaia literatura v izgnanii, xxi, 32, 35, 50, 53, 56, 202
Swift, Jonathan, 323, 415n7

Tammi, Pekka, xviii, xix, 412n6, 415nn5, 6, 416n11; Problems of Nabokov's Poetics, xviii, 412n6, 415n6
Tauber, Ekatarina, 51, 52
Tennyson, Alfred, 323
Terras, Victor, 398nn12, 13
Thwaite, Anthony, 61, 62
Time, 65, 67, 417n12
Times Literary Supplement, 67
Tiutchev, Fedor, 40, 43, 63, 64, 83, 88, 113, 137, 154, 170, 303, 385; 'Silentium,' 137, 154
Toffler, Alvin, 176
Toker, Leona, ix, 410n14, 412n6
Tolstaia, Nataliia, 242, 243, 252, 254
Tolstoi, Lev, 57
Tomlinson, Charles, 61, 62
Toynbee, Philip, 325
Trinity Magazine, 392n24
Tsetlin, Mikhail, 46, 47, 393–4n8
Tsvetaeva, Marina, 32, 56, 79, 86, 87
Turgenev, Ivan, 44, 418–19n23
Tvardovskii, A., 86
Tynianov, Iurii, 34

Verkheil, Keis [Kees Veerheul], 34, 70, 71

Vestnik Evropy (*The Herald of Europe*), 389n1
Volia Rossii (*Will of Russia*), 45
Voloshin, M., 86
Vozrozhdenie (*Rebirth*), 51

Walsh, Chad, 60, 61
Weeks, Richard, 394n10
West, James, 398n13
White, Katherine, 195, 196, 249
Williams, William Carlos, 403n48
Wilson, Edmund, 59, 110, 226, 397n11, 398–9n18, 399–400n27, 405–6n9
Wordsworth, William, 13, 99, 147, 165, 313, 323, 324, 325, 326, 385;

'Ode: Intimations of Immortality,' 147; *The Prelude*, 99, 165, 313, 385, 416n11
Wright, James, 59, 60, 62
Wyndham, Francis, 65

Yeats, William Butler, 323, 325

Za svobodu (*For Freedom*), 48
Zabolotskii, Nikolai, 86
Zholkovsky, Alexander, 397n5
Zhukovskii, Vasilii, 75, 84
Zveno (*The Link*), 40
Zvezda (*The Star*), 405n7